PREACHING CHRIST FROM DANIEL

PREACHING CHRIST
FROM DANIEL

Foundations for Expository Sermons

SIDNEY GREIDANUS

WILLIAM B. EERDMANS PUBLISHING COMPANY
GRAND RAPIDS, MICHIGAN / CAMBRIDGE, U.K.

Published 2012 by
Wm. B. Eerdmans Publishing Co.
2140 Oak Industrial Drive N.E., Grand Rapids, Michigan 49505 /
P.O. Box 163, Cambridge CB3 9PU U.K.
www.eerdmans.com

Printed in the United States of America

17 16 15 14 13 12   7 6 5 4 3 2 1

Library of Congress Cataloging-in-Publication Data

Greidanus, Sidney, 1935-
Preaching Christ from Daniel: foundations for expository sermons /
Sidney Greidanus.
p.   cm.
Includes bibliographical references and index.
ISBN 978-0-8028-6787-2 (pbk.: alk. paper)
1. Bible. O.T. Daniel — Sermons. 2. Jesus Christ. 3. Expository preaching.
I. Title.

BS1555.54.G74   2012

251 — dc23

2012031284

This book is dedicated
to the Church of Jesus
suffering persecution.

May the comforting messages of Daniel encourage all Christians
to remain faithful to the end.

"I saw one like a son of man
coming with the clouds of heaven."

Daniel 7:13

"I am [the Messiah];
and 'you will see the Son of Man
seated at the right hand of Power,'
and 'coming with the clouds of heaven.'"

Jesus. Mark 14:62

"Look! He is coming with the clouds;
every eye will see him,
even those who pierced him."

John. Revelation 1:7

Contents

Contents

Contents

Preface

I recall how as a young preacher I searched for books with sermon models that would help me prepare relevant biblical sermons. Unfortunately, I found little help. Even my doctorate in biblical hermeneutics and homiletics did not offer much help in preaching a difficult book like Daniel. As a result, in my eight years as a parish pastor, I produced only one sermon on Daniel — a sermon on Daniel 2 (a relatively easy passage) which I preached under the theme, "The Kingdom of God Will Replace All Human Kingdoms" (March 3, 1974). Now, almost forty years later and having retired from seminary teaching, I had time to research the book of Daniel in depth and realize how much good news I missed in my younger years. I am also aware, however, that I could not possibly have preached this controversial book responsibly when I had to produce two new sermons every week.

This book is intended to help busy preachers and Bible teachers proclaim the good news of Daniel. It will enable them to uncover rather quickly the important building blocks for producing sermons and lessons on Daniel: to detect the story line (plot) of each of the six narratives and the four visions; to formulate the heart of the message for Israel in exile (the theme); to discover the author's goal (purpose, intention) for sending this message to Israel and by analogy the preacher's goal for preaching this message to his or her congregation today; to uncover various ways to link each preaching text to Jesus Christ in the New Testament; and to obtain relevant biblical exposition of each passage.

As a companion to my *Preaching Christ from Genesis* and *Preaching Christ from Ecclesiastes,* this book is further intended to demonstrate and reinforce the redemptive-historical Christocentric method — this time demonstrating it with preaching the apocalyptic genre. While Christocentric preaching is always theocentric, it moves beyond the theocentric focus to the fullness of God's self-revelation in Jesus Christ. As the apostle John explains, "No one has ever seen

God. It is God the only Son, who is close to the Father's heart, who has made him known" (John 1:18).

I follow the same basic pattern for each preaching text. This pattern is based on the ten steps from text to sermon I developed for first-year seminary students (see Appendix 1). It gradually draws students from a casual acquaintance with the text to an ever deeper involvement until they are ready to write the sermon. The resulting repetition in each chapter is intended to inculcate a basic hermeneutical-homiletical approach to the biblical text. First we establish the parameters of the preaching text (the literary unit) and check its context. Next we note important literary features, especially the plot line, which is important not only for understanding these passages but also for preaching the sermon in a narrative form. After theocentric interpretation, we seek to formulate the textual theme and goal. With the theme in mind, we can explore various legitimate ways from this particular passage to Jesus Christ in the New Testament. Having seen the Old Testament message in the context of the New, we are ready to extend the textual theme and goal to the sermon theme and goal.

Each chapter concludes with a major section of "Sermon Exposition" which not only explains the meaning of the verses of the preaching text but also provides (often in footnotes) insights of many commentators which preachers may wish to incorporate into their sermons. These sections seek to provide a model for sermons by using oral style as much as possible, giving the verse reference *before* citing it so that the congregation can read along (comprehension is much better when the congregation not only hears but sees the words) and keeping the sermon moving (most quotations, complex arguments, and technical details are relegated to footnotes). In these sections I also show where and how in the sermon I would make the move(s) to Christ. In line with the stated sermon goal, I make brief applications; in actual sermons, these applications will need to be developed with illustrations and concrete suggestions appropriate to the situation of the congregation being addressed. Since these sections seek to explain every verse of the text, for the longer preaching texts preachers will have to select key verses for exposition. Bible teachers can assign the "Sermon Exposition" sections to their students to work their way through Daniel in eleven lessons.

Appendix 2 provides the expository sermon model I developed for first-year seminary students. This model aims for sermons that are biblical, relevant, and well organized. My former seminary student, Ryan Faber, combined the proofreading of this book with the preparation and preaching of a series of eleven sermons on Daniel. With his permission, I have included in Appendices 3 and 4 two of these sermons.

Unless otherwise noted, the Bible version quoted is the NRSV. When the NIV is cited, it is the latest version (2011). Italics in biblical quotations indicate the word(s) I consider important for interpretation and/or would emphasize in reading.

References in the footnotes have been kept to a minimum; full references can be found in the Bibliography. When a book or article is not included in the Select Bibliography, complete information is found in the footnote.

My hope and prayer is that this book will help preachers and teachers to build up the faith, hope, love, and perseverance of God's suffering people with Daniel's messages of the sovereignty of God over human kingdoms and the certainty of God's coming kingdom.

Grand Rapids, Michigan   SIDNEY GREIDANUS

Acknowledgments

First of all, I would like to thank my four proofreaders for their excellent work. In alphabetical order, they were my former seminary student, the Rev. Ryan Faber, of Pella, IA; my brother, the Rev. Morris N. Greidanus, of Grand Rapids, MI; my colleague, the Rev. Dr. Arie C. Leder, of Grand Rapids, MI; and my former seminary student, the Rev. Joel Schreurs, of Denver, CO. Their corrections, questions, and suggestions have made this a much better book than I could have produced without their feedback.

I also express my appreciation to the library of Calvin College and Calvin Theological Seminary for its generous loan policy for faculty and to its staff for their courteous service. I thank the staff of Eerdmans Publishing Company, and especially the copy editor of my last four books, Milton Essenburg, for expertly preparing this book for publication. Again I express my gratitude to my wife, Marie, for taking care of most of the household chores so that I could fully concentrate on the research and writing of this book. Most of all, I am grateful to God for giving me health, strength, insights, and joy in bringing this work to completion.

Since Daniel was written first of all to comfort and encourage Israel suffering in exile, I dedicate this book to the church of Jesus suffering persecution.

Abbreviations

AS	*Aramaic Studies*
AT	*Acta Theologica*
AUSS	*Andrews University Seminary Studies*
AV	Authorized Version
BAR	*Biblical Archaeology Review*
BBR	*Bulletin for Biblical Research*
Bib	*Biblica*
BSac	*Bibliotheca Sacra*
BTB	*Biblical Theology Bulletin*
CBQ	*Catholic Biblical Quarterly*
CBR	*Currents in Biblical Research*
cf.	compare
CTJ	*Calvin Theological Journal*
CovQ	*Covenant Quarterly*
CQ	*The Congregational Quarterly*
ed(s)	editor(s)
ESV	English Standard Version
ET	English Translation
EvQ	*Evangelical Quarterly*
EvRT	*Evangelical Review of Theology*
ExpTim	*Expository Times*
HBT	*Horizons in Biblical Theology*
Heb.	Hebrew
HervTS	*Hervormde Teologiese Studies*
HUCA	*Hebrew Union College Annual*
IB	*Interpreter's Bible*
Int	*Interpretation*

JATS	*Journal of the Adventist Theological Society*
JBL	*Journal of Biblical Literature*
JETS	*Journal of the Evangelical Theological Society*
JHS	*Journal of Hebrew Scriptures*
JQR	*Jewish Quarterly Review*
JSHJ	*Journal for the Study of the Historical Jesus*
JSOT	*Journal for the Study of the Old Testament*
JSS	*Journal of Semitic Studies*
JTS	*Journal of Theological Studies*
LXX	Septuagint
MT	Masoretic Text of the Hebrew Old Testament
n(n).	footnote(s)
NASB	New American Standard Bible
NEB	New English Bible
NIV	New International Version (2011)
NRSV	New Revised Standard Version
NICOT	New International Commentary on the Old Testament
NIDOTTE	*New International Dictionary of Old Testament Theology and Exegesis*
OG	Old Greek
p(p).	page(s)
par(s).	parallel(s)
PRSt	*Perspectives in Religious Studies*
PSBul	*Princeton Seminary Bulletin*
RevExp	*Review and Expositor*
RR	*Reformed Review*
RSV	Revised Standard Version
TDNT	*Theological Dictionary of the New Testament*
TDOT	*Theological Dictionary of the Old Testament*
TJ	*Trinity Journal*
trans.	translated by
TSFBul	*Theological Students Fellowship Bulletin*
TynBul	*Tyndale Bulletin*
v(v)	verse(s)
Vol.	Volume
VT	*Vetus Testamentum*
VTSup	*Vetus Testamentum, Supplements*
W&W	*Word & World*
WTJ	*Westminster Theological Journal*

Issues in Preaching Christ from Daniel

Although the stories of Daniel are favorites for Sunday-school children, Old Testament scholars agree that Daniel is one of the most difficult books for preachers. André Lacocque states that its message "is presented in a form full of traps and snares for the reader."[1] Brent Sandy and Martin Abegg claim that "the apocalyptic genre has been subjected to some of the most fallacious interpretations imaginable, largely because Christians are often not careful to understand it as intended and as originally heard. Any portion of Scripture divorced from its primary culture and the intent of the author is a homeless child wandering the streets, vulnerable to violent abuses."[2]

Thousands, if not tens of thousands, of pages have been written on introductory issues for the book of Daniel. One of the major issues concerns the date of its composition, and related questions concern its author(s) and its original audience. In fact, modern critical scholars, dispensationalists, and others have generated so much controversy about the date of the book, its historicity, and whether Daniel may be used to predict "the end of the world"[3] that many

---

1. Lacocque, *Book of Daniel*, 1. He adds: "The problems the Book of Daniel poses to the critic are incredibly numerous and complex. Not only is apocalyptic language intentionally obscure and its historical allusions deliberately cryptic, but, what is more, the work is pseudepigraphic, antedated, bilingual, and affected by literary and spiritual influences of diverse foreign origins, as well as being represented by Greek versions of greater amplitude and often of a divergent character in relation to the Semitic text, etc."

2. Sandy and Abegg, "Apocalyptic," 187.

3. Many times in church history Daniel has been misused to predict the end of the world. For example, in the 1840s William Miller, leader of the Millerites, understood the 2,300 days of Daniel 8 as 2,300 years and concluded that Christ would return sometime between March 21, 1843, and March 21, 1844. Hal Lindsey's *The Late Great Planet Earth* (Grand Rapids: Zondervan, 1970) became a best-seller in the 1970s. The California radio host Harold Camping declared on billboards, "Save the Date. Return of Christ. May 21, 2011." When that did not happen, he

preachers shy away from even attempting to preach on Daniel. The *Common Lectionary* selects only three passages from Daniel for its three-year cycle: it assigns the reading of Daniel 12:1-3 for all three years on Easter Sunday *evening;* Daniel 7:1-3, 15-18 in Year C for All Saints' Day; and Daniel 7:9-14 in Year B for a Sunday late in the Pentecost season. Sibley Towner puts the issue vividly, "Why should preachers risk taking into their pulpits the time bombs that tick away in the Book of Daniel?"[4]

Since my primary purpose in writing this book is to help pastors preach Daniel's messages, and since discussions of complex introductory matters may detract from that purpose, I refer the reader to other authors for more detailed introductory discussions.[5] Peter Craigie rightly asserts, "We do not grasp the book's relevance by fighting the battles of historical criticism; eventually, the message of this book is revealed to those who would attempt to share its author's vision."[6] Yet we cannot avoid introductory matters entirely. Inasmuch as one's position regarding the date of composition, the author(s), and the original audience will impact the exposition and the goal and application of a passage,[7] we ought at least to indicate our starting point and some of the reasons for it.

---

changed the date to October 21, 2011. Helge Kvanzig, "The Relevance of the Biblical Visions of the End Time," *HBT* 11/1 (1989) 35, observes, "Much of the applications of the Biblical visions of the end time has been a history of disappointment." It seems rather presumptuous for followers of Christ to set the date when Jesus himself said, "About that day and hour no one knows, neither the angels of heaven, nor the Son, but only the Father" (Matt 24:36).

4. Towner, *Daniel,* 1-2.

5. See, e.g., Montgomery, *The Book of Daniel,* 1-109; Young, *Prophecy of Daniel,* 294-306; Baldwin, *Daniel,* 13-74; Goldingay, *Daniel,* xxv-liii, 320-34; Collins, *Daniel,* 1-71; Redditt, *Daniel,* 1-39; Longman, *Daniel,* 19-40; Lucas, *Daniel,* 17-43, 306-25; and Steinmann, *Daniel,* 1-73.

6. Peter C. Craigie, *The Old Testament: Its Background, Growth, and Content* (Nashville: Abingdon, 1986), 248.

7. Commentators are divided on the question whether one's starting point makes a difference for one's interpretation. On the one hand, Miller, *Daniel,* 22-23, states, "One's view concerning authorship and date is significant because it ultimately determines the interpretation of every aspect of this prophecy." On the other hand, Goldingay, *Daniel,* xl, concludes his Introduction: "Whether the stories are history or fiction, the visions actual prophecy or quasi-prophecy, written by Daniel or by someone else, in the sixth century B.C., the second or somewhere in between, makes surprisingly little difference to the book's exegesis." So also Lucas, *Daniel,* 18. We'll have to wait to see if it makes a difference to the exegesis, but certainly the author's goal shifts with the decision whether he is addressing Israel suffering in exile in Babylon or Israel in Palestine being persecuted by Antiochus IV — and with it the modern preacher's goal and application should shift as well. In a sixth-century-B.C. setting, the author's overriding goals would have been to comfort Israel with messages of the sovereignty and faithfulness of their God and to encourage them to be faithful to God. In a second-century-B.C. setting, the author's primary goal would have been "to galvanize the spiritual resistance of the Pious against

The Historical and Geographical Setting of Daniel

The book of Daniel depicts events in the life of Daniel and his friends from 605 B.C. ("the third year of the reign of King Jehoiakim"; 1:1) to 536 B.C. ("the third year of King Cyrus"; 10:1). It also records Daniel's visions pertaining to later times, including the rule of Antiochus IV (8:9-12, 23-25; 11:21-35; 175-163 B.C.) and "the time of the end" (e.g., 11:40; 12:1-3, 13). The following chart provides a quick overview of the major dates, empires, persons, and events together with references to Daniel.

History Covered by Daniel[8]

Dates B.C.

625-539	BABYLONIAN EMPIRE	Dan 2:37-38
605-562	Nebuchadnezzar	Dan 1-4; 7:4
605	Daniel and his friends taken to Babylon	Dan 1:3-4
597	Jerusalem taken; many Jews exiled	2 Kings 24:10-17
587	Jerusalem destroyed; temple burned; remaining Jews exiled	2 Kings 25:8-21
562-560	Amel-Marduk (Evil-Merodach)	2 Kings 25:27-30
560-556	Neriglissar, son-in-law of Nebuchadnezzar	
556	Labashi-Marduk	
556-539	Nabonidus	
550-539	Belshazzar (co-regent with his father Nabonidus)	Dan 5; 7:1; 8:1

---

the persecution of Antiochus IV and the Hellenists" (Lacocque, *Book of Daniel*, 10). Cf. Russell, *Daniel*, 11, "These stories . . . are to be understood against the background of the second century B.C. in the reign of Antiochus Epiphanes, their purpose being to comfort and encourage the Jewish people in a rapidly changing environment and in the midst of an alien culture which, in so many respects, was quite inimical to the teaching and practice of their fathers." Cf. Portier-Young, *Apocalypse against Empire*, 229, "The writers of Daniel outlined for their audiences a program of nonviolent resistance to the edict and persecution of Antiochus and the systems of hegemony and domination that supported his rule."

P.S. After studying all twelve chapters, I have found that the date one assumes for Daniel makes a major difference with the narratives. For example, what comfort do Daniel 3 and 6 provide if the message that God is able to save his people from certain death is a fictional account? But the date makes an even greater difference in discerning and preaching the messages of Daniel's visions (Dan 7–12). On the assumption of a second-century-B.C. date and the fourth kingdom being Greece, the visions concentrate on Antiochus IV and barely reach beyond him, certainly not to the fullness of the kingdom of God. See, e.g., Redditt, *Daniel*, 146, "Daniel 8 was mistaken that the death of Antiochus would usher in the kingdom of God."

8. I compiled this chart with input from Baldwin, *Daniel*, 73; Lucas, *Daniel*, 43; Miller, *Daniel*, 292-304; Steinmann, *Daniel*, 521; Towner, *Daniel*, 16-18; and Young, *Prophecy of Daniel*, 302-3.

539-331	**MEDO-PERSIAN EMPIRE**	Dan 2:39a
550-530	Cyrus/Darius, king of Medo-Persia	Dan 1:21; 5:31; 6:1, 28; 8:3-4, 20; 9:1; 10:1; 11:1
539	Babylon falls to Cyrus	Dan 5:24-30
538	A remnant of Jewish exiles returns	2 Chron 36:22-23; Ezra 1–2
530-522	Cambyses	Dan 11:2
522	Smerdis	Dan 11:2
522-486	Darius I	Dan 11:2
520-516	Temple rebuilt	Ezra 6:15
486-465	Xerxes I/Ahasuerus in Esther	Dan 11:2
465-424	Artaxerxes I	
423	Xerxes II	
423-404	Darius II	
404-358	Artaxerxes II Nothus	
358-338	Artaxerxes III Ochus	
338-336	Arses	
336-331	Darius III Codomannus	
331-63	**GREEK EMPIRE**	Dan 2:39b
336-323	Alexander the Great	Dan 8:5-8, 21; 10:20; 11:3
331	Alexander defeats Darius III	Dan 11:3
301	Greek Empire divided among the four Diadochi	Dan 8:8, 22; 11:4

	EGYPT (Ptolemies)	**SYRIA** (Seleucids)	
323-285	Ptolemy I		Dan 11:5
311-280		Seleucus I	Dan 11:5
285-246	Ptolemy II		Dan 11:6
280-261		Antiochus I Soter	
261-246		Antiochus II Theos	Dan 11:6
252	Berenice, daughter of Ptolemy II, married Antiochus II		Dan 11:6
246-226		Seleucus II Callinicus	Dan 11:7-9
246-221	Ptolemy III Euergetes I		Dan 11:7-9
226-223		Seleucus III Ceraunus	Dan 11:10
223-187		Antiochus III the Great	Dan 11:10-19
221-204	Ptolemy IV Philopator		Dan 11:11-12, 14
204-181	Ptolemy V Epiphanes		Dan 11:13-19
193	Ptolemy V married Cleopatra, daughter of Antiochus III		Dan 11:17
187		Death of Antiochus III	Dan 11:18-19

187-175	Seleucus IV Philopator	Dan 11:20
181-146	Ptolemy VI Philometor (reigned jointly with Ptolemy VII)	Dan 11:25-27
175-164	Antiochus IV Epiphanes	Dan 8:9-12, 23-25; 11:21-35(-39?)
169	Antiochus's first war against Egypt	Dan 11:25-28
168	His second war against Egypt	Dan 11:29
168	Antiochus expelled from Egypt by Roman consul	Dan 11:30
167	Altar to Zeus near Jerusalem temple	Dan 11:31
167-163	Persecution of the Jews	Dan 11:33-35
163	Death of Antiochus IV	Dan 8:25

63 B.C.–A.D. 476 ROMAN EMPIRE	Dan 2:40
"THE TIME OF THE END"	Dan 8:17; 11:35, 40; 12:4, 9, 13
Time of anguish	Dan 7:25; 12:1
God's people delivered	Dan 7:27; 12:1
Resurrection from the dead	Dan 12:2, 13
Kingdom of God on earth	Dan 2:35, 44; 7:14, 27; 9:24; 12:3, 13

As can be seen in this chart, the book of Daniel deals with four major world empires: Babylonia, Medo-Persia, Greece (especially Egypt and Syria), and Rome. The map on page 6 shows the location of these countries, with Israel caught in the middle.

The book of Daniel contains six narratives about Daniel and his friends (chapters 1–6) and four visions of Daniel (chapters 7–12). Traditionally the synagogue as well as the church held that Daniel wrote this book in the sixth century B.C. This view changed in modern times.

A Second-Century-B.C. Composition

In the third century after Christ a pagan critic of Christianity, Porphyry, attacked the traditional position, claiming that prophecy cannot predict events four hundred years in advance. He held that the author of Daniel was a forger who wrote the book in the second century B.C., after these events had taken place *(vaticinium ex eventu)*. The church declared Porphyry's position heretical, and the traditional position was maintained in the church until modern times. "But during the time of the Enlightenment in the eighteenth century, all supernatural elements in Scripture came under suspicion; and Porphyry's the-

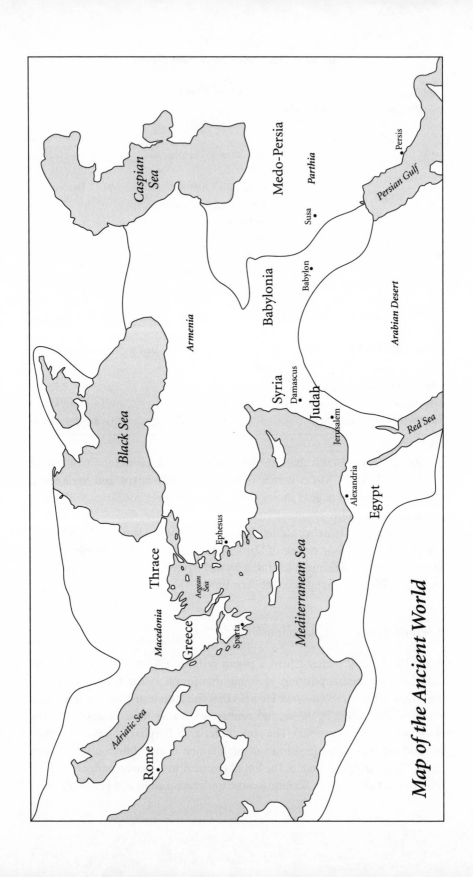

Map of the Ancient World

ory received increasing support."[9] Like Porphyry,[10] these critical scholars presumed that prophecy cannot predict the future in detail.[11] They also claimed that Daniel's account of the sixth-century exile is rather vague, if not "confused,"[12] while his information about the third and second century B.C. in chapter 11 is incredibly accurate (see the chart above). They argued, therefore, that the author(s) must have written this book not in the sixth century B.C. but in the second, after these events had taken place. According to James Montgomery, the author wrote this book in "the first years of the Maccabaean uprising, 168-165 B.C.,"[13] though he probably made use of earlier material in chapters 1–6.[14] His goal was to encourage Israel to join the uprising and throw off the yoke of the cruel Seleucid king Antiochus IV Epiphanes (175-163 B.C.).[15]

These scholars buttressed their position by pointing out apparent historical "errors" about the sixth century B.C. in the first six chapters of Daniel. For example, Daniel 1:1 states, "In the *third* year of the reign of King Jehoiakim of Judah, King Nebuchadnezzar of Babylon came to Jerusalem and besieged it," while Jeremiah assigns this event to "the *fourth* year of King Jehoiakim" (25:1, 9). Norman Porteous claims confidently, "The very first statement in chapter 1 can be shown to be inaccurate."[16] In Daniel 4:30 King Nebuchadnezzar says, "Is this not magnificent Babylon, which I have built as a royal capital by my mighty power and for my glorious majesty?" But Babylon existed long before Nebuchadnezzar, and ancient historians do not refer to Nebuchadnezzar as the

9. Archer, "Daniel," 13, who mentions "J. D. Michaelis (1771), J. G. Eichhorn (1780), L. Berthold (1806), F. Bleek (1812), and many others after them." Cf. John Collins, *Daniel,* 25-26, and Adela Yarbro Collins, "The Rise of Historical Criticism," in ibid., pp. 121-23.

10. Collins, *Daniel,* 25, admits that "Porphyry's line of reasoning is essentially similar to that of modern critics: the correspondence between Daniel's predictions, especially in chap. 11, and the events of the Hellenistic age is most easily explained by the supposition that the prediction was written after the fact."

11. E.g., Towner, *Daniel,* 115, "We need to assume that the vision [Daniel 8] as a whole is a prophecy after the fact. Why? Because human beings are unable accurately to predict future events centuries in advance." Cf. Collins, *Apocalyptic Vision,* 8, "In Dan 11:29-39, Antiochus' second campaign is described with such precision that it is clearly a *vaticinium ex eventu.*"

12. "The references to Hellenistic history in chap. 11 are essentially accurate, whereas those to the Babylonian and Persian periods in the earlier chapters are notoriously confused." Collins, *Daniel,* 26.

13. Montgomery, *Book of Daniel,* 96. Cf. Collins, *Daniel,* 26, "The balance of probability is overwhelmingly in favor of a Maccabean date, at least for the revelations of chaps. 7–12, which clearly have their focus in that period." Collins, ibid., 324, dates Daniel 7 "precisely to late 167 B.C.E. . . . somewhat before the Hebrew revelations of chapters 8–12." Cf. Seow, *Daniel,* 7, "164 B.C.E."

14. Montgomery, *Book of Daniel,* 96, dates chapters 1–6 to the pre-Maccabean period, roughly the third century. So also Collins, *Daniel,* 47-48.

15. See the relevant quotations in n. 7 above.

16. Porteous, *Daniel,* 25. Cf. Collins, *Daniel,* 132, "Dan 1:1 is historically inaccurate."

builder of Babylon. Daniel 5:1 states, "King Belshazzar made a great festival for a thousand of his lords" (cf. 8:1). H. H. Rowley calls this a "grave historical error" because no other text has been found which calls him "King."[17] Daniel 5:11 and 18 speak of Nebuchadnezzar as the "father" of Belshazzar. Rowley asserts that "this is manifestly inaccurate since Belshazzar is known to have been the son of Nabonidus."[18] Daniel 5:31 states that when Belshazzar was killed, "Darius the Mede received the kingdom." Rowley claims, "Daniel is definitely wrong in its ascription of the throne to Darius after the fall of the Neo-Babylonian empire."[19] All these "errors" regarding the sixth century B.C., so the argument goes, point to an author who lived centuries after these events took place. For example, John Collins writes, "That the author is mistaken about the father and rank of Belshazzar . . . suggests that the story as we have it was written at a time when memory of that prince had grown dim."[20]

These scholars further fortified their position for a second-century date with linguistic arguments, noting the author's use of Persian words, Greek loanwords, and supposedly late Hebrew and Aramaic.[21] Their arguments were so extensive that most modern commentators reject a sixth-century date for the book of Daniel. Instead they place the date of composition between 168 and 164 B.C., though some of the stories about Daniel and his friends may date back to the third or fourth century B.C.

Even if these commentators are right, they cannot deny that the "*implied author*" of the book of Daniel is the sixth-century Daniel and that the "*implied reader*" is Israel in exile in Babylon. This means that the "real author" intends his readers to hear and understand these stories and visions in that sixth-century-B.C. setting.

---

17. Rowley, "The Historicity of the Fifth Chapter of Daniel," *JTS* 32 (1930) 12. So also Redditt, *Daniel*, 2.

18. Ibid., 20. Cf. Collins, *Daniel*, 32, "Though 'son' might stand for 'grandson' or even 'descendent,' Nabonidus was not descended from Nebuchadnezzar at all."

19. Ibid., 31. Elsewhere he called the information that Darius the Mede "occupied the throne of Babylon between the death of Belshazzar and the reign of Cyrus . . . , the most serious historical problem in the book. . . . For it is known with certainty that the overthrower of the Neo-Babylonian empire was Cyrus." H. H. Rowley, *Darius the Mede and the Four World Empires in the Book of Daniel: A Historical Study of Contemporary Theories* (Cardiff, 1935; reprint 1964), 9. Cf. Collins, *Daniel*, 30, "No such person as Darius the Mede is known to have existed apart from the narrative of Daniel."

20. Collins, *Daniel*, 33. Cf. Rowley, "The Historicity of the Fifth Chapter of Daniel," *JTS* 32 (1930) 31, "The author of Daniel was not writing authentic history, and most certainly not contemporary history."

21. See, e.g., Montgomery, *Book of Daniel*, 22, "As the evidence stands, these Greek words must incline the scales toward a later dating." Cf. Porteous, *Daniel*, 13, chapters 2:4a–7:28 "[are] in a late (not earlier than third century B.C., perhaps second century) dialect of Aramaic, while the rest of the book is in late Hebrew."

A Sixth-Century-b.c. Composition

The arguments from these modern scholars, however, are not compelling. First, as Collins himself points out, the efforts to show the relevance of chapters 1–6 for the persecution under Antiochus IV are not convincing: "Close consideration of the stories does not support the view that they were composed with that situation [of Antiochus IV] in mind."[22] Even though Nebuchadnezzar had a cruel streak and an awful temper, he did not desecrate God's temple as Antiochus did by installing an altar to Zeus above the altar to Yahweh. On the contrary, in the end he confessed Israel's God to be the sovereign "Most High God" (4:34-35). Belshazzar comes closer to Antiochus as he challenged Israel's God by drinking from the sacred vessels of God's temple at his drunken feast (5:2-4), but that is still not near to profaning the temple itself by consecrating it to Zeus, abolishing "the regular burnt offering" for God and offering swine on the altar — "the abomination that makes desolate" (8:11-14; 11:31). Darius is the very opposite of Antiochus IV: he is "very much distressed" for his friend Daniel; works all day to save him from the lions; wishes, "May your God . . . deliver you!"; decrees "that in all my royal dominion people should tremble and fear before the God of Daniel," and ends with a stirring doxology to Daniel's God as "the living God" (6:14, 16, 25-27).

Second, we need not accept the modern presupposition that prophecy cannot predict the future in detail.[23] It is true that prophets address their messages to their contemporaries, but in doing so, they can certainly predict the future, even in detail (see, e.g., 1 Kings 13:2 and Isa 44:7, 28). God knows the future in detail (e.g., Isa 41:21-23; 46:8-11), and he can reveal that future to a prophet.[24] For example, Isaiah predicts in detail what will happen to God's servant:

22. Collins, *Daniel,* 33. Collins continues, "Rowley's case is weakest with regard to Daniel 6, where the gentile monarch is singularly well disposed to Daniel and the conspiracy against the Jewish hero is inspired by envy at his successful career at court. The Sitz-im-Leben implied by such a story is not religious persecution but the hazards of the Jewish minority who sought to succeed in the gentile world. . . . Despite the arguments of Rowley and others, there is no passage in Daniel 1–6 that is necessarily understood as an allusion to the time of Antiochus Epiphanes or is now generally accepted as such." Cf. Collins, *Apocalyptic Vision,* 9-10; and von Rad, *Old Testament Theology,* II, 309-10.

23. Cf. Baldwin, *Daniel,* 184-85, "With regard to prophecy as foretelling, the church has certainly lost its nerve. An earthbound, rationalistic humanism has so invaded Christian thinking as to tinge with faint ridicule all claims to see in the Bible anything more than the vaguest references to future events. Human thought, enthroned, has judged a chapter such as Daniel 11 to be history written after the event, whereas God enthroned, the one who was present at the beginning of time and will be present when time is no more, may surely claim with justification to 'announce from of old the things to come' (Isa 44:7)."

24. Leupold, *Exposition of Daniel,* 471-72, mentions Jeremiah 50; 51; Zechariah 9:1-8; and Isaiah 13; 14; 21:1-10.

He was despised and rejected by others;
  a man of suffering and acquainted with infirmity. . . .
He was oppressed, and he was afflicted,
  yet he did not open his mouth. . . .
He was cut off from the land of the living,
  stricken for the transgression of my people.
They made his grave with the wicked
  and his tomb with the rich. (Isa 53:3, 7-9)

This prophecy was fulfilled in Jesus' life and death some six hundred years later. Jesus himself, "beginning with Moses and all the prophets, . . . interpreted to them the things about himself in all the scriptures" (Luke 24:27; see also vv. 44-47). Jesus even quoted Daniel to warn about future persecutions: "So when you see the desolating sacrilege standing in the holy place, as was spoken of by the prophet Daniel (let the reader understand), then those in Judea must flee to the mountains . . ." (Matt 24:15-16). Here Jesus not only called Daniel a "prophet" but also assumed that he was predicting a future event: "the desolating sacrilege standing in the holy place" would take place in the future.[25] In fact, according to Deuteronomy 18:21-22, one can tell a true prophet from a false one by checking if the prediction is fulfilled. Prophecy, therefore, can predict the future, and so can its offspring, apocalyptic literature.[26]

Third, the author/editor of Daniel claims that Daniel wrote down the visions he received in the sixth century B.C.: "In the first year of King Belshazzar of Babylon, Daniel had a dream and visions. . . . Then he wrote down the dream: I, Daniel, saw in my vision . . ." (7:1-2). Since the other three visions are written in the first person, Daniel presumably also wrote down these visions: "In the third year of the reign of King Belshazzar a vision appeared to me, Daniel, after the one that had appeared to me at first. In the vision I was looking . . ." (8:1-2); "In the first year of Darius . . . — in the first year of his reign, I, Daniel, perceived . . ." (9:2); "In the third year of King Cyrus of Persia. . . . On the twenty-fourth day of the first month, as I was standing on the bank of the great river (that is, the Tigris), I looked up and saw . . ." (10:1, 4-5). Moreover, Daniel was instructed to "roll up and seal the words of the scroll" (12:4, NIV). The first six chapters describe what happened to Daniel and his friends in the sixth century B.C. Since

---

25. See also Matthew 26:64, where Jesus speaks of himself as Daniel's "Son of Man . . . coming on the clouds of heaven."

26. Regarding Daniel 11, Lucas points out that the "Akkadian Prophecies" have a literary form similar to Daniel 8:23-25 and 11:3-45. This similarity, he writes, "is best explained if they [Dan 8 and 11] originated in the Babylonian Dispersion and if the author was well acquainted with the Babylonian omen literature, someone skilled in the language and letters of the Chaldeans, as the story in Dan 1 indicates." Lucas, *Daniel*, 272.

these chapters are written in the third person, it is possible that someone other than Daniel wrote them. Archer points out, however, that an ancient "author usually writes about himself in the third person, as was the custom among ancient authors of historical memoirs. . . . In general it was apparently considered bad taste for a writer to speak of himself in the first person — a practice that smacked of the boastfulness of the Assyrian and Persian rulers."[27] In any event, since Daniel was taken into exile in the sixth century B.C. (Dan 1:1-6), and since the book is a unity,[28] it is a good working assumption to date the entire book to the sixth century B.C.

A fourth reason for understanding Daniel to be a sixth-century-B.C. document is that the historical errors mentioned by the critical scholars to argue for a late date have subsequently been shown to be mostly the errors of these scholars. It turns out that Daniel 1:1 is not mistaken when it says, "In the *third* year of the reign of King Jehoiakim of Judah, King Nebuchadnezzar of Babylon came to Jerusalem and besieged it." Daniel in Babylon used "the accession-year method" in which the year of accession was not counted, while Jeremiah used the Palestinian-Jewish "nonaccession year method," in which the year of ascension was the first year. Gerhard Hasel's diagram clearly shows that the "third year" and the "fourth year" of Jehoiakim are the same year.[29]

Accession-year method (Dan 1:1)	Nonaccession-year method (Jer 25:1, 9; 46:2)
Accession year	1st year
1st year	2nd year
2nd year	3rd year
3rd year	4th year

The fact that the author of Daniel used the Babylonian accession-year method also confirms that he "wrote from a Babylonian perspective."[30]

---

27. Archer, "Daniel," 4.

28. See below under "The Unity and Rhetorical Structures of Daniel." See Baldwin, *Daniel,* 39, "The problem with composite authorship is that the book bears so little trace of the allegedly differing viewpoints. As a literary work it manifests unity of purpose and design. S. R. Driver assumed that one author was responsible for the whole, and R. H. Pfeiffer saw no reason for questioning the unity of the book, but, like many others, found 'in both its parts the same aim and the same historical background.'" Cf. Young, *Prophecy of Daniel,* 19-20. Rowley, "The Unity of the Book Daniel," 250-60, offers a review of a multitude of theories of the last two centuries about the unity of Daniel or its divisions. Rowley himself argues for the unity of the book (pp. 260-80) but places it in the "Maccabean age."

29. Hasel, "The Book of Daniel: Evidences Relating to Persons and Chronology," *AUSS* 19/1 (1981) 48-49. Cf. Baldwin, *Daniel,* 20-21, and Steinmann, *Daniel,* 260-63.

30. Archer, "Daniel," 14.

As to Nebuchadnezzar's boast, "Is this not magnificent Babylon, which I have built?" archeologists have discovered sixth-century-B.C. records which make the same boast in almost identical words. Hasel remarks, "This historical accuracy is puzzling to those who suggest that Daniel was written in the second century B.C."[31]

Regarding Belshazzar being named "king," "information has been discovered which explains explicitly that his father, King Nabonidus, entrusted Belshazzar with 'kingship' *(sarrutim)*."[32] Since Herodotus (450 B.C.) listed Nabonidus as the final king of Babylonia, "it became startlingly apparent that the writer of Daniel was much more accurately informed about the history of the 540s in Babylonia than Herodotus was in 450 B.C." This discovery is another "powerful argument in favor of a sixth-century date for the writing of the book."[33]

But why would Daniel call Nebuchadnezzar the "father" of Belshazzar (5:18) when Nabonidus was his biological father? The answer is that "the word 'father' in Semitic languages, including Hebrew, also can stand for grandfather, a more remote physical ancestor, or even for a predecessor in office."[34]

Finally, it is true that Darius the Mede is still not known from extrabiblical literature. Joyce Baldwin follows D. J. Wiseman (1957) in identifying Darius with Cyrus the Great.[35] Most recently, Andrew Steinmann made a similar argument: "Daniel knows this king both by his more familiar name Cyrus (1:21; 6:28; 10:1) and as Darius (5:31; 6:1, 6, 9, 25, 28; 9:1; 11:1). Daniel equates the two in 6:28 by means of the epexegetical waw."[36] Thus Daniel 6:28 reads, "during the reign of Darius *and* ["that is," or "namely"] the reign of Cyrus." Steinmann continues, "Daniel's use of the name 'Darius' may be his way of emphasizing the fulfillment of the words of the prophets who spoke of the Medes as the ones who

---

31. Hasel, "Book of Daniel," *AUSS* 19/1 (1981) 38. Even Montgomery, *Book of Daniel,* 243-44, has to admit, "The setting of the scene and the king's self-complaisance in his glorious Babylon are strikingly true to history. Every student of Babylonia recalls these proud words in reading Neb.'s own records of his creation of the new Babylon; for instance (Grotefend Cylinder, *KB* iii, 2, p. 39): 'Then built I the palace the seat of my royalty . . . , the bond of the race of men, the dwelling of joy and rejoicing.'"

32. Hasel, "Book of Daniel," *AUSS* 19/1 (1981) 42-43. Montgomery, *Book of Daniel,* 67, also asserts, "The Bible story is correct as to the rank of kingship given to Belshazzar." Cf. p. 70, "He would have passed in native tradition as the last Babylonian king." Cf. Baldwin, *Daniel,* 21-22. See also Alan Millard, "Daniel and Belshazzar in History," *BAR* 11/3 (1985) 72-78.

33. Archer, "Daniel," 16.

34. Hasel, "Book of Daniel," *AUSS* 19/1 (1981) 44. Cf. Baldwin, *Daniel,* 22-23, and Archer, "Daniel," 16.

35. Baldwin, *Daniel,* 26-28.

36. Steinmann, *Daniel,* 295. An "epexegetical waw" is the word *waw,* "and," followed by words to explain the previous words. The word "and," therefore, "has the force of 'namely,' or 'that is.'" Baldwin, *Daniel,* 132.

would bring about Babylon's fall (Isa 13:17; 21:2; Jer 51:11, 28). Daniel himself speaks about the fall of Babylon to 'the Medes and the Persians' (Dan 5:28)."[37]

Stephen Miller observes that "the author of Daniel exhibited a more extensive knowledge of sixth-century events than would seem possible for a second-century writer. R. H. Pfeiffer (who argued that the work contains errors) acknowledged that Daniel reports some amazing historical details: 'We shall presumably never know how our author learned that the new Babylon was the creation of Nebuchadnezzar (4:30 [Heb. 4:27]), as the excavations have proved . . . and that Belshazzar, mentioned only in Babylonian records, in Daniel, and in Bar 1:11, which is based on Daniel, was functioning as king when Cyrus took Babylon in 538 [539] (chap. 5).'"[38]

A fifth reason for understanding Daniel as a sixth-century-B.C. document is that the linguistic arguments for a late date can be turned on their head for supporting the early date. On the one hand, Miller points out that "the meager number of Greek terms in the book of Daniel is a most convincing argument that the prophecy was not produced in the Maccabean period, the heart of the Greek era. By 170 B.C. Greek-speaking governments had controlled Babylon and Palestine for 150 years, and numerous Greek terms would be expected in a work produced during this time."[39] On the other hand, Andrew Hill observes that "the Persian loanwords for administrative terms and officers suggest a final form for the book when Persian rule in Mesopotamia was firmly established. The apparent misunderstanding of these terms by the later Greek translators of the versions of the LXX further substantiates a pre-Hellenistic date for the book."[40]

---

37. Steinmann, *Daniel*, 295. Cf. Lucas, *Daniel*, 137, "Cyrus, the actual conqueror of Babylon, was partly Median and ruled the Medes as well as the Persians. This is emphasized by giving him the alternative name 'Darius the Mede.'" See also Miller, *Daniel*, 171-77. Others argue that "for most of the first year after the fall of Babylon Cyrus did not claim the title 'King of Babylon,' indicating that someone else was functioning as king under vassalage to Cyrus." Hasel, "Book of Daniel," *AUSS* 19/1 (1981) 48-49. Cf. Baldwin, *Daniel*, 24-25.

38. Miller, *Daniel*, 26. See Baldwin, *Daniel*, 19-29, for more details. Baldwin sums up on p. 29: "In concluding this section on the historical assumptions of the writer of the book of Daniel I strongly assert that there is no reason to question his historical knowledge. The indications are that he had access to information which has not yet become available to the present-day historian, and that where conclusive proof is still lacking he should be given the credit for reliability."

39. Miller, *Daniel*, 30. Cf. ibid, 32, "The linguistic evidence does not necessitate a late date for the composition of the Book of Daniel and in a number of cases rather strongly supports an early date." Cf. Archer, "Daniel," 22, "All this [regarding Greek and Persian loanwords] points unquestionably to composition in the Persian period (c. 530 B.C.). But it renders a later date in the post-Alexandrian period linguistically impossible."

40. Hill, "Daniel," 27. Cf. Steinmann, *Daniel*, 11, "Neither the Persian nor the Greek loanwords offer any proof that Daniel is a late composition."

Daniel's Aramaic also indicates an early date for the book. Hasel concludes, "On the basis of presently available evidence, the Aramaic of Daniel belongs to Official Aramaic and can have been written as early as the latter part of the sixth century B.C.; linguistic evidence is clearly against a date in the second century B.C."[41]

Baldwin sums up the many arguments pro and con as follows: "When all the relevant factors are taken into account, including the arguments for the unity of the book [see below], a late sixth- or early fifth-century date of writing for the whole best suits the evidence."[42] Since the date of the final vision is "the third year of King Cyrus" (Dan 10:1), which is 536 B.C., the memoirs and visions of Daniel must have been compiled shortly after that date,[43] though some later editing/updating is possible.

The Author(s)/Editor(s) and Audiences of Daniel

If the book of Daniel was written in the sixth century B.C., it could have been written by Daniel himself.[44] As we saw above, even the third-person accounts of chapters 1–6 could have been written by Daniel. It is not likely, however, that Daniel would have written, "So *this* Daniel prospered during the reign of Darius and the reign of Cyrus the Persian" (6:28). It may well be, then, that a final editor compiled the book of Daniel, using Daniel's own memoirs and records of his visions.[45] Thus we can still consider Daniel the primary author of the book that bears his name.

Daniel's messages addressed different audiences at different times. Since Daniel's first five narratives deal with the Babylonian kings Nebuchadnezzar

41. Hasel, "The Book of Daniel and Matters of Language," *AUSS* 19/3 (1981) 225; see pp. 216-25 for the reasons for this conclusion. See also Waltke, "The Date of the Book of Daniel," *BSac* 133 (1973) 322-23; Harman, *Study Commentary on Daniel*, 22-25; and Archer, "Daniel," 23-24.

42. Baldwin, *Daniel*, 46. Cf. Longman, *Daniel*, 23, "In view of the evidence and in spite of the difficulties, I interpret the book from the conclusion that the prophecies come from the sixth century B.C. I find the problems amenable to hypothetical solutions and the theological issues of a late date difficult to surmount."

43. "The book itself cannot have existed in its present form before 536 B.C., since that is the date of the final vision. . . . Given the fact that Daniel was probably in his early eighties at this time, it is unlikely that Daniel wrote the book later than about 530 B.C." Steinmann, *Daniel*, 3.

44. For arguments regarding Daniel being a historical figure, see Block, "Preaching Old Testament Apocalyptic to a New Testament Church," *CTJ* 41/1 (2006) 24-27.

45. See Aalders, *Het Boek Daniël*, 33. Cf. Hill, "Daniel," 25, "The book was probably composed in the Babylonian Diaspora by Daniel, or more likely by associates who outlived him, sometime after 536 B.C. (the last date formula in the book; 10:1) and before 515 B.C. (since the composition makes no reference to the rebuilding of the second temple in Jerusalem)."

and Belshazzar and his three visions are carefully dated to the first and third year of King Belshazzar (7:12; 8:1; 550 B.C. and 548 B.C.) and the first year of Darius (9:1; 539 B.C.), we may assume that Daniel originally addressed all his messages (except for his final vision) to Israel in exile before a remnant returned to the Promised Land in 538 B.C.[46] These exiles needed to be encouraged to remain faithful to God and to hear the comforting messages that God was in control of evil empires and that he would bring his people back to the Promised Land and establish his everlasting kingdom.

The second historical horizon is that of the *book* Daniel. Since the date of the final vision is "the third year of King Cyrus" (10:1; 536 B.C.) and the book was completed after that date (between 536 B.C. and 515 B.C.),[47] the book of Daniel addressed Israelites who remained in exile after the remnant had returned to the Promised Land in 538 B.C. as well as the remnant that struggled in Palestine. This book would also be read in later times, of course, such as the second century B.C. when Israel in Palestine would be persecuted by Antiochus IV, the very time of which Daniel wrote in chapters 8 and 11. At that time the book began to throb with new relevance. Four hundred years earlier God had spoken of this time. Their sovereign God was in control then, and he is still in control as they suffer persecution. He will see them through if they remain faithful to him.[48]

The third major historical horizon is that of the New Testament when Jesus especially used Daniel to proclaim, "the kingdom of God has come near" (Mark 1:15; cf. Dan 2:44), to predict "the desolating sacrilege standing in the holy place, as was spoken of by the prophet Daniel" (Matt 24:15; cf. Dan 11:31), and to claim before the high priest, "From now on you will see the Son of Man seated at the right hand of Power and coming on the clouds of heaven" (Matt 26:64; cf. Dan 7:13-14). By way of these three historical horizons, we need to determine God's messages in Daniel for the church in the twenty-first century.

---

46. E.g., Daniel's prayer for the restoration of Jerusalem (9:17-19), dated at 539 B.C. (9:1), obviously took place before 538 B.C., as did God's response, "Know therefore and understand: from the time that the word went out to restore and rebuild Jerusalem until the time of an anointed prince, there shall be seven weeks" (Dan 9:25).

47. See n. 45 above.

48. Baldwin, *Daniel*, 66, "This process [of persecution] came to Antiochus Epiphanes, and the book prepares them ahead of time so th when the test comes." Cf. Lucas, *Daniel*, 308, "By giving the predictio God assures the people of the second century that he is indeed in contr the situation in which they find themselves. One cannot deny that thi plausibility."

Literary Issues of Daniel

Hebrew and Aramaic in Daniel

One peculiarity about the book of Daniel is that it is written in two languages: it begins with Hebrew (1:1–2:4a), which is followed by Aramaic (2:4b–7:28), and concludes with Hebrew (8:1–12:13). Various theories have been advanced to explain the reasons for the switch in languages. Since Aramaic was the international language,[49] Miller suggests that "Aramaic was reserved for the parts of the book that had universal appeal or special relevance to the Gentile nations, and Hebrew was employed for those portions that most concerned the Jews."[50] However that may be, the use of Hebrew indicates that the targeted audience consisted of Hebrew-speaking Jews, for "other peoples of the empire spoke Aramaic; but no other people spoke Hebrew."[51] The additional use of Aramaic indicates that this targeted audience also understood Aramaic, which would be the case for many of the Jews born in Babylonian exile.

Literary Genres and Forms in Daniel

It is difficult to name a single literary genre for the whole book of Daniel. This problem is illustrated by the fact that the Jewish Tanak[52] places this book in the "Writings," between the books of Esther and Ezra-Nehemiah, while English Bibles place Daniel in the "Prophets," between the major and minor prophets. The first six chapters are definitely narrative and thus would fit better in the "Writings" than in the Prophets. The last six chapters, however, seem more like prophecy and thus would fit better in the "Prophets." Yet these chapters with Daniel's four visions are a special kind of prophecy: they are

---

49. "Aramaic was the language of the ancient Aramaeans, first mentioned in the cuneiform texts from the twelfth century B.C. . . . From the eighth century on, Aramaic became the international language, the *lingua franca*, of the Near East, and the Israelites appear to have learned the Aramaic language during the exile. Historically, Aramaic is divided into several major groups: (1) 'Ancient Aramaic' . . . , employed to 700 B.C.; (2) 'Official Aramaic' . . . , used 'from 700 to 300 B.C.E.'; (3) 'Middle Aramaic,' used from '300 B.C.E. to the early centuries C.E.'; and (4) 'Late Aramaic,' employed thereafter." Hasel, "The Book of Daniel and Matters of Language," *AUSS* 19/3 (1981) 216-17, with references to R. Degen and E. Y. Kutscher.

50. Miller, *Daniel*, 48. Cf. Baldwin, *Daniel*, 30, and Archer, "Daniel," 6. For other explanations by many different authors, see Valeta, "The Book of Daniel in Recent Research (Part 1)," *CBR* 6/3 (2008) 340-43.

51. Dorsey, *Literary Structure*, 259.

52. An acronym for the three Jewish divisions of the Old Testament: *Torah* (Law), *Nabhiim* (Prophets), and *Kethubhim* (Writings).

apocalypse.[53] Daniel, therefore, consists of two main literary genres, narrative and apocalypse.[54]

Redemptive-Historical Narrative

Scholars have classified the narratives in many different ways: romance, midrash, legend, myth, folklore, didactic wisdom tale, court tale, or a combination of some of these features.[55] Collins states that "the most widely accepted categorization of these stories is undoubtedly 'court tales.'"[56] If we understand these stories in the context of a popular form of narrative in the ancient Near East, the category of court tale seems quite appropriate. But since these narratives now function in the context of the Bible, a more appropriate category is redemptive-historical narrative. This term indicates that these narratives are part of the literary tradition of narratives that depict the ancient story of God redeeming and saving his people. It also indicates that these narratives should not be read as objective historical reports nor as moral tales or example stories[57] but as God's kerygma, God's good news for his suffering people. The classification of redemptive-historical narrative is confirmed by the fact that "the involvement of God is crucial in the move from the middle to the end of the plot in all six stories."[58]

---

53. "Apocalypses differ from prophetic texts in their combination of heavy use of techniques like vision-reaction-interpretation and heavenly journeys, intense interest in the supernatural world, and eschatology that includes transcendence of death." Murphy, "Introduction to Apocalyptic Literature," *New Interpreter's Bible Old Testament Survey*, 359.

54. This classification is not as easy as it sounds. "Daniel has affinities with earlier prophecy as well as with later apocalyptic." Morris, *Apocalyptic*, 79. Yet apocalypse is unique in being different from earlier prophecy and later extrabiblical apocalypse. Hence James Sims, "Daniel," 326, argues that "on balance, the best generic classification of the book is apocalyptic prophecy." Porteous, *Daniel*, 16, suggests, "Perhaps the wisest course is to take the Book of Daniel as a distinctive piece of literature with a clearly defined witness of its own, and to take note of the various ways in which it borrows from and is coloured by the earlier prophetic literature, the Wisdom literature and the Psalms and has its successors in the apocalypses, though these often exhibit an extravagance and a fantastic imagination which is less prominent in the Book of Daniel." See also n. 59 below.

55. See, e.g., Collins, *Daniel*, 42-47; Lucas, *Daniel*, 22-27; Goldingay, *Daniel*, 6-7, 321; Miller, *Daniel*, 45; Valeta, "The Book of Daniel in Recent Research (Part 1)," *CBR* 6/3 (2008) 333-36; and Redditt, *Daniel*, 11-13, who also mentions structuralist proposals.

56. Collins, *Daniel*, 42.

57. E.g., George M. Schwab, *Hope in the Midst of a Hostile World: The Gospel according to Daniel*, 6, argues for reading these stories as example stories: "Daniel and his friends were examples to follow, models to emulate. Go and do likewise." See also pp. 31-33, "Daniel as Role Model."

58. Lucas, *Daniel*, 28.

As to literary structure, all narratives have a plot line consisting of most of the following components: a setting for the story, some preliminary incidents, an incident that generates the conflict, buildup of the tension till it reaches a climax, the turn in the narrative to the beginning of a resolution, the full resolution, an outcome, and perhaps a conclusion. We can diagram the typical elements in a single plot as follows.[59]

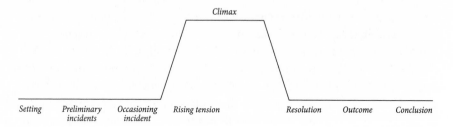

| Setting | Preliminary incidents | Occasioning incident | Rising tension | | Resolution | Outcome | Conclusion |

Most of the narratives have a single plot, relating a single narrative conflict and resolution (Daniel 1, 2, 3, 6, and possibly 5). At least one, however, has a complex plot, relating a conflict and resolution only to usher in a new conflict leading to another resolution (Daniel 4 and possibly 5).

Apocalyptic Literature

The dreams, visions, and their interpretations can be classified as apocalyptic literature. The Apocalypse Group of the SBL's Genres Project (1975-78) defined apocalypse as "a genre of revelatory literature with a narrative framework, in which a revelation is mediated by an otherworldly being to a human recipient, disclosing a transcendent reality which is both temporal, insofar as it envisages eschatological salvation, and spatial insofar as it involves another, supernatural world." Later discussions led to the addition of the function (goal) of apocalypse: "intended to interpret present, earthly circumstances in light of the supernatural world and of the future, and to influence both the understanding and the behavior of the audience by means of divine authority."[60]

59. Adapted from Tremper Longman III, *Literary Approaches to Biblical Interpretation* (Grand Rapids: Zondervan, 1987), 92, who gives credit for the model to V. Poythress and J. Beekman.
60. *Semeia* 14 (1979) 9. Definition reprinted in Adela Yarbro Collins, "Introduction: Early Christian Apocalypticism," *Semeia* 36 (1986) 2, with the addition on p. 7. Also printed in Collins, *Daniel*, 54. Cf. Sandy and Abegg, "Apocalyptic," 188, "The function of an apocalyptic text is the key to understanding it. Though apocalyptic authors do have something important to commu-

Thomas Long notes that "apocalyptic literature draws back the curtains and allows the reader to see the eschatological victory of God, which has already been achieved over whatever forces are, even at the moment, crippling the community of faith." He vividly describes apocalypse as "a '911' genre, for times of emergency — not just the stress of routine problems — times when the ordinary means for addressing life's difficulties are simply not sufficient."[61]

Apocalypses have a literary structure like that of narratives.[62] Collins[63] lists the following structure for the two apocalypses in Daniel 7 and 8 (note how they duplicate the above components of narratives):

An indication of the circumstances [*setting*];
a description of the vision, introduced by a term such as "behold" [*occasioning incident*];
a request for interpretation, often because of fear [*rising tension*];
an interpretation, usually by an angel [*resolution*];
concluding material, which may include the reaction of the seer, instructions, or parenesis [*outcome/conclusion*].

The Unity and Rhetorical Structures of Daniel

Although Daniel consists of two parts, the stories about Daniel and his friends (chapters 1–6) and the four apocalypses (chapters 7–12), the book presents itself as a unit. "The overarching unity of Daniel is shown by the narrative framework, which establishes Daniel's identity in chapters 1–6 and in chapter 12 tells him to seal up the book, as if it were all a single revelation."[64] Moreover, "the

---

nicate, it is more hope for the future than information about the future. Since the meaning of a passage is closely tied to the impact that the passage is designed to have on the readers, apocalyptic is generally not a chronological account of the future but a literary shock treatment of bold and graphic images to take our attention away from the problems we currently face and give us hope that God will win a resounding victory over all evil."

61. Long, "Preaching Apocalyptic Literature," *RevExp* 90/3 (1993) 376-77 and 374.

62. See the definition above, "a genre of revelatory literature with a *narrative* framework." Cf. Murphy, "Introduction to Apocalyptic Literature," 356, "All apocalypses are narratives, stories describing the disclosure of otherwise inaccessible secrets to a human seer by a heavenly being." Cf. Jeffrey Arthurs, *Preaching with Variety*, 187, "Apocalyptic possesses the rudiments of narrative. There is character, plot, setting, and point of view, but those elements are modified."

63. Collins, *Daniel*, 54-55.

64. Collins, *Daniel* (1984), 33. Cf. Murphy, "Introduction to Apocalyptic Literature," 362, "Chapters 1–6 are set in the royal courts of the Babylonian, Median, and Persian empires [Medo-Persian Empire], where Daniel distinguishes himself both as a champion of Jewish piety and as a divinely inspired interpreter of dreams and signs. This portrait of Daniel makes

first part prepares for the second, and the second looks back to the first. Thus, chapter 7 develops more fully what is introduced in chapter 2 as does chapter 8, yet neither 7 nor 8 is understandable without 2. Chapter 2 also prepares the way for the revelations in 9, 10, 11, and 12."[65]

The unity of Daniel is further supported by two chiastic structures. Lenglet was the first to publish the chiastic structure that holds together the Aramaic part of Daniel (chapters 2–7).[66]

    A   Four empires and God's coming kingdom (ch. 2)
        B   Trial by fire and God's deliverance (ch. 3)
            C   A king warned, chastised, and delivered (ch. 4)
            C′ A king warned, defiant, and deposed (ch. 5)
        B′ Trial in the lions' den and God's deliverance (ch. 6)
    A′ Four empires and God's everlasting kingdom (ch. 7)

The three visions in Hebrew may also be designed as a chiastic structure:[67]

    A   Details on the post-Babylonian kingdoms (ch. 8)
        B   Jerusalem restored (ch. 9)
    A′ More details on the post-Babylonian kingdoms (chs. 10–12)

Steinmann argues that these two chiastic structures are interlocked because chapter 7 "serves both as the end of the first chiasm by virtue of its four-kingdom parallel to Nebuchadnezzar's dream and its Aramaic language, and also as the introduction to the visions by virtue of its visionary style and its chronological placement in the first year of Belshazzar."[68]

Paul Tanner agrees that chapter 7 serves as the hinge between the two halves because "it reiterates the succession of ancient Gentile kingdoms [the topic of chapters 2–6] yet it provides more detail about the 'latter days' when the Antichrist ["the 'little horn' that comes out of the fourth beast"] will arrive

---

him an ideal mediator of heavenly secrets. . . . In chapters 7–12, Daniel has his own visions in the night, interpreted for him by an angel." For other references on the unity of Daniel, see n. 28 above.

65. Young, *Prophecy of Daniel,* 19.

66. A. Lenglet, "La Structure Litteraire de Daniel 2–7," *Bib* 53 (1972) 169-90. The wording in the diagram is from Baldwin, "Theology of Daniel," *NIDOTTE,* 4:499. Cf. Dorsey, *Literary Structure,* 260.

67. Steinmann, *Daniel,* 22. The chiastic structure is supported by Hebrew terms used in both chapter 8 and chapters 10–12. See H. J. M. van Deventer, "Struktuur en Boodskap(pe) in die Boek Daniel," *HervTS* 59/1 (2003) 209.

68. Steinmann, ibid., 23.

[the topic of chapters 7–12]."[69] Hence Tanner proposes the following overall structure for Daniel:[70]

							Visions Given to Daniel			
		Concentric Structure Establishing God's Sovereignty over Gentile Empires					Vision 1	Vision 2	Vision 3	Vision 4
Historical Setting	**A** Dream: Four-part Image	**B** Refusal to Worship Image	**C** Humbling of King Neb.	**C′** Humbling of King Bel.	**B′** Refusal to Stop Praying	**A′** Four Beasts	Ram and Goat	Seventy Weeks	Final Vision Antiochus — Antichrist
1	2	3	4	5	6	7	8	9	10–12
Hebrew			Aramaic					Hebrew		

This overall structure will enable us better to understand each chapter in the context of the book of Daniel.

The Message and Goal of Daniel

Since every text must be interpreted in its context, we shall briefly note some of the overarching themes in Daniel before we study the individual narratives and visions.

The Overall Message of Daniel

Throughout his book Daniel emphasizes the sovereignty of God:[71] God is in control and is able to save those faithful to him even from certain death (Daniel's friends from the fire and Daniel from the lions). At a broader level, God is in control of earthly empires, using their actions to further his own plan, judging the evil empires[72] while protecting his suffering people, and in the end

---

69. Tanner, "The Literary Structure of the Book of Daniel," *BSac* 160 (2003) 278, 282. Cf. Block, "Preaching Old Testament Apocalyptic," *CTJ* 41/1 (2006) 29: "Chronologically, the chapter [7] would have fit more naturally before chapter 5, but its location after chapter 6 forces the reader to read it in the light of the preceding and in anticipation of what follows."

70. Tanner, ibid., 277.

71. For explicit statements of God's sovereignty by various characters, Block, "Preaching Old Testament Apocalyptic," *CTJ* 41/1 (2006) 32-35, lists Daniel 2:20-23, 37-38, 44-45, 47; 3:29; 4:2-3, 16-17, 31-32, 34-35, 37; 6:26-27; 7:13-14, 26-27.

72. "The idea of cosmic, eschatological judgment is not a major theme of any of the OT books except Daniel." Beale, "The Influence of Daniel upon the Structure and Theology of John's Apocalypse," *JETS* 27/4 (1984) 414.

bringing his perfect kingdom on earth.[73] Tremper Longman states, "Even though there is a dramatic contrast in genre between the two halves of the book . . . , the overall message of the book is uniform: In spite of present appearances, God is in control."[74]

Daniel Block suggests the following overall theme: "The overruling sovereignty of Yahweh, the one true God, demonstrated in the judgment of rebellious world powers and the vindication of the faithful in fulfillment of his covenant commitments to Israel." "Every chapter of the book," he writes, "makes a significant contribution to this theme."[75] Les Bruce formulates the overall message of Daniel most succinctly: "Only God is truly sovereign, and He will establish His eternal kingdom." This theme, he asserts, "provides coherence for the entire Book of Daniel."[76] This theme is also supported by two explicit statements in Daniel: "The God of heaven will set up a kingdom that shall never be destroyed" (2:44), and "I looked, and there before me was one like a son of man [NRSV n.]. . . . His dominion is an everlasting dominion that shall not pass away, and his kingship is one that shall never be destroyed" (7:13-14).

The Goal of Daniel

Discerning the goal of Daniel depends on the circumstances of the audience being addressed. Since our starting point is that the book was first addressed to Israel in exile in Babylon, the major goal was to comfort and to encourage God's people as they suffered in exile. They suffered as they remembered Jerusalem and the temple where God dwelt. Now the temple was destroyed, the land was devastated, and Israel was in faraway Babylon: "By the rivers of Babylon — there we sat down and there we wept when we remembered Zion" (Ps 137:1). They suffered also "as they were forced to work for the good of the nation that oppressed them." And they suffered "as they found themselves in situations where they were pressed to compromise or else face dire consequences. The

73. "The theme that is central to Daniel as it is to no other book in the OT is the kingdom of God." Goldingay, *Daniel*, 330.

74. Longman, *Daniel*, 19. Cf. Steinmann, *Daniel*, 19, "The reason that Daniel emphasizes God's control over all things is that it serves the four major theological themes of the book: the messianic kingdom of God, God as protector of his people, God's superiority over false gods, and encouragement for God's people to maintain their faith in him with integrity."

75. Block, "Preaching Old Testament Apocalyptic," *CTJ* 41/1 (2006) 37. Cf. Archer, "Daniel," 8, "The theme running through the whole book is that the fortunes of kings and the affairs of men are subject to God's decrees, and that he is able to accomplish his will despite the most determined opposition of the mightiest potentates on earth." Cf. Towner, *Daniel*, 4, "This book glows with the deep conviction that God will not fail to achieve his redemptive purposes."

76. Bruce, "Discourse Theme and the Narratives of Daniel," *BSac* 160 (2003) 175, 186.

message of Daniel that God is all-powerful and in control in spite of present conditions is intended to present a powerful encouragement to these people."[77]

Even Daniel's visions of the future served the purpose of consoling and encouraging God's people in exile. Block observes, "The intention of apocalyptic is not to chart out God's plan for the future so future generations may draw up calendars but to assure the present generation that — perhaps contrary to appearance — God is still on the throne (cf. Dan 7:18, 21-22, 27; 8:25; 12:1-4), and that the future is firmly in his hands."[78]

Issues in Preaching Daniel

A Series of Sermons on Daniel

Daniel is ideally suited for a series of sermons. For example, since the six narratives are in chronological order, one can prepare a series of six sermons on these stories. One can also prepare a series of five sermons on the four visions: one sermon on each of the first three visions and two sermons on the lengthy fourth vision (Dan 10–12). Or one can consider a short series on selected chapters of Daniel, for example, a series of four sermons on Daniel 1, 2, 7, and 9.

Selection of the Preaching Text

The preaching text ought to be a literary unit, not a phrase or a verse. Selecting a proper preaching text is not difficult in Daniel since there are clear breaks between its literary units. The six narratives each have their own chapter in the English Bibles.[79] The first three visions each also have their own chapter (7, 8,

---

77. Longman, *Daniel,* 20. Cf. Block, "Preaching Old Testament Apocalyptic," *CTJ* 41/1 (2006) 36, "If the purpose of the revelations recorded in Daniel was to reassure the generation of exiles that their story was not over, this was also the purpose behind the composition of the book."

78. Block, "Preaching Old Testament Apocalyptic," *CTJ* 41/1 (2006) 52. Cf. ibid., 39: "To a people who have been disillusioned and angered by Yahweh's failure to defend them in the face of the Babylonians, the revelations to and through Daniel offer hope that Yahweh is indeed the living God who remains true to his word." Cf. Tanner, "Discourse Theme and the Narratives of Daniel," *BSac* 160 (2003) 182, "The apocalyptic section is not primarily given to predict the future, to tell people which future kingdoms would emerge. Instead this section was given to encourage God's people to live within terrifying earthly kingdoms by remaining confident that only God's kingdom will last forever, for only He is truly sovereign."

79. The chapter divisions are the same in the Hebrew Bible except for 4:1-3, which is 3:31-33 in Aramaic, and 5:31, which is 6:1.

9). The only problem we will face in text selection is with the fourth vision, which covers three chapters (10–12). Since this vision offers too much material for a single sermon, we will need to decide how to divide it into more manageable literary subunits.

The Theme and Goal of the Text

In order to focus the sermon and guide its development, before writing the sermon we should state the message of the text as a theme, that is, a summary statement of the central thought of the text. The theme should be formulated as a concise sentence, subject and predicate. It makes a single point, *the* point of the text.

The challenge is to keep the sermon focused on this theme of the passage and not stray into moralizing,[80] for such morals can be drawn from almost any story, including that of Little Red Riding Hood. Preachers who desire to preach the Word of God will seek to do so by preaching the message intended by the inspired author as understood in the context of the whole Bible. The best sermons are well focused so that they have the impact of a bullet that penetrates to the heart instead of birdshot that barely scratches the surface.

If a statement of the theme is important for preaching the narratives, it may be even more crucial for Daniel's visions, for frequently preachers have used Daniel's visions to speculate on its details and have misused them for predicting the end of the world.[81] Sandy and Abegg present as one of their guidelines for interpretation, "Seek to understand the main point of an apocalyptic text." They justify that requirement as follows: "Apocalyptic tends to be impressionistic, more like an abstract painting which communicates an overall impression. . . . Sometimes the details in apocalyptic are for dramatic effect; there may be no significance other than how the imagery of the scene is enhanced by the details. The details in apocalyptic must not be seen as allegorical in the sense that each detail has a corresponding reality."[82] A statement of the theme will help keep sermons on Daniel's visions on track.

We must also state the goal or aim/purpose of the author in communicating this message. The goal is the answer to the questions behind the text: Why did the author tell Israel in exile this particular story or vision? What needs did he address? What response(s) did he seek? Did he seek to convince them of God's sov-

---

80. "Moralizing" is to draw one or more morals from the preaching text when the author of the text did not intend such application(s) for his original audience.

81. See n. 3 above.

82. Sandy and Abegg, "Apocalyptic," 189.

ereignty? To assure them of God's faithfulness? To comfort them with his message? To give hope? To encourage faithfulness? The author's goal should guide preachers in applying the message to the church today.[83] The issue of naming the author's goal(s) is ultimately the issue of the relevance of the sermon.

The Relevance of Daniel for the Church Today

Even when we have carefully formulated Daniel's goal, preachers may still face a problem in applying Daniel's messages to the church today. The problem is this: Daniel addressed his messages to Israel suffering in exile while many preachers today will be addressing their messages not to churches suffering state-sponsored persecution but to churches living in relative freedom. How can we bridge this gap? How can we apply the messages aimed at Israel in exile to churches living in relative freedom?

One way to do this is to remind the congregation of the persecuted church today and of the unity of the church. "There is one body and one Spirit, just as you were called to the one hope of your calling, one Lord, one faith, one baptism, one God and Father of all, who is above all and through all and in all" (Eph 4:4-6). "If one member suffers, all suffer together with it" (1 Cor 12:26). Therefore, if even only one church suffers persecution, all churches suffer together with it. It is because of our solidarity with the persecuted church that Daniel's messages can be applied to the church today.[84]

But there is also a more direct way. The church today, even when it lives in relative freedom, is still in exile. Ever since God expelled our ancestors from Paradise, we have been living in exile, east of Eden. This broken, sinful world is not our home. We may call ourselves citizens of a certain country, but really, Paul says, "Our citizenship is in *heaven*, and it is from there that we are expecting a Savior, the Lord Jesus Christ" (Phil 3:20). That is why Peter addresses his first letter "to the exiles of the Dispersion" (1 Pet 1:1), and James "to the twelve tribes in the Dispersion" (Jas 1:1). Jesus also says to his followers, "If you belonged to the

---

83. "The authoritative preaching of the message of apocalyptic texts requires . . . that we draw the applications for the present from the main points — rather than engaging in endless speculation about the spiritual significance of details." Block, "Preaching Old Testament Apocalyptic," *CTJ* 41/1 (2006) 52.

84. Cf. Helge Kvanvig, "The Relevance of the Biblical Visions of the End of Time," *HBT* 11/1 (1989) 52, "Directly, the apocalypses are addressed to those who have lost every possibility to stand up against anything. . . . They are written to those who suffer under the tyranny of oppression and persecution. . . . And when we, who are only indirectly addressed in the apocalypses, read them, we can only do so in solidarity . . . with those directly addressed, because we share their hope."

world, the world would love you as its own. Because you do not belong to the world, but I have chosen you out of the world — therefore the world hates you. . . . If they persecuted me, they will persecute you" (John 15:19-20).

Even if the churches we address do not suffer from overt, state-sponsored persecution, therefore, they still suffer the consequences of living east of Eden. The people we address struggle with thorns and thistles, earthquakes and tornadoes; they suffer from the enmity of Satan, broken relations, pain, death, and murder (Gen 3–4). Hence the comforting messages of Daniel aimed at Israel in exile will also be relevant and life-giving for the church today.

The Form of the Sermon

Since texts communicate with their form as well as their contents, the form of the sermon should respect the form of the text. The six narratives in Daniel can best be preached in a hybrid narrative form, that is, the sermon follows the story line but suspends the story from time to time for explanations of historical details or customs, illustrations, Christocentric moves, or applications. The narrative sermon form not only allows us to follow the plot line of the text but also to engage our hearers holistically, that is, to get them totally involved in the sermon, right brain as well as left brain. The four visions can also be preached in a hybrid narrative form because, as we have seen, their form has similar components as a typical narrative (see above, p. 19).

Some of the narratives and especially the apocalyptic visions paint graphic pictures and symbols: a huge statue is smashed by a rolling stone (Dan 2:34), bizarre beasts come up out of the sea (Dan 7:2-8), a male goat charges a ram and tramples it (Dan 8:5-7), above the river appears a man with a face like lightning, eyes like flaming torches, and a voice like the sound of a multitude (Dan 10:5-6). The sermon form should respect these apocalyptic symbols by engaging the imagination with vivid images. Jeffrey Arthurs suggests, "One way to re-create the panoramic quality of visionary literature is with panoramic illustrations."[85]

Although the sermon form should respect the form of the text, it cannot be exactly the same. Just as a sermon on a prayer (e.g., Ps 142) will not be in the form of a prayer, so a sermon on an apocalypse will not be in the exact form of the apocalypse. This becomes evident especially where the apocalypse speaks in veiled language. For example, the visions of Daniel contain many passive verbs which conceal God as the actor (divine passives). The sermon, by contrast, requires clarity and therefore needs to turn divine passives into the active voice: *God* did it!

85. Arthurs, *Preaching with Variety,* 194.

Preaching Christ from Daniel

This book is not only about preaching the book of Daniel but specifically about preaching *Christ* from Daniel. Some scholars deny that Daniel speaks about a coming royal Messiah.[86] But even if Daniel does not speak of a coming royal Messiah, we can still preach Christ from this book because there are more ways to preach Christ than promise-fulfillment. In *Preaching Christ from the Old Testament,* I defined preaching Christ as "preaching sermons which authentically integrate the message of the text with the climax of God's revelation in the person, work, and/or teaching of Jesus Christ as revealed in the New Testament."[87] I identified seven (sometimes overlapping) ways with which preachers can move legitimately from an Old Testament passage to Jesus Christ in the New Testament, from the periphery to the center. These seven ways are:

1. Redemptive-historical progression — seeing the message of the passage in the context of redemptive history from beginning to end, especially following the progression of redemptive history as it moves forward from the text's historical setting to Jesus' First and/or Second Coming.

2. Promise-fulfillment — showing that the promise of a coming Messiah was fulfilled in Jesus' First Coming or will be fulfilled in his Second Coming.

3. Typology — moving from an Old Testament type prefiguring Jesus to the antitype, Jesus himself.

4. Analogy — noting the similarity between the teaching or goal of the text and the teaching or goal of Jesus.

5. Longitudinal themes — tracing the theme (or subtheme) of the text through the Old Testament to Jesus Christ in the New Testament.

6. New Testament references — moving from the preaching text to Jesus by way of New Testament verses which cite or allude to the preaching text and link it to Christ.[88]

86. E.g., C. Umhau Wolf, "Daniel and the Lord's Prayer," *Int* 15 (1961) 410, "There is no Son of David or royal Messiah in Daniel. There is no truly 'Anointed One.' . . . There is no strong indication of a personal Messiah." Cf. Block's counterarguments, "Preaching Old Testament Apocalyptic," *CTJ* 41/1 (2006) 42-51.

87. Greidanus, *Preaching Christ from the Old Testament,* 10.

88. "The book of Daniel is one of the books of Scripture that is quoted or alluded to in most of the New Testament writings. . . . The index in the Nestle-Aland *Novum Testamentum Graece* (27th ed.), which combines quotations and allusions, lists some 200 references. Proportionately, this puts Daniel in the same category as Isaiah and the Psalms, the books most frequently quoted and alluded to in the New Testament." Evans, "Daniel in the New Testament: Visions of God's Kingdom," in *Book of Daniel,* II, 490. Cf. Stefanovic, *Daniel,* 36, "Daniel was one of Jesus' favorite books, perhaps *the* favorite one."

7. Contrast — noting the contrast between the message of the text and that of the New Testament, a contrast which exists because Christ has come.[89]

In the following chapters we shall check each preaching text for the various ways that can be used to preach Christ and select the most prominent one(s) for the "Sermon Exposition" section.

The Sermon's Oral Style

Many sermons fail to communicate because they are delivered in a complex, written style. In order to communicate well, preachers should write and deliver their sermons in an oral style which the hearers can understand immediately. Typical characteristics of oral style are the following:[90]

1. Short sentences — mostly principal clauses, few relative clauses.
2. Short, familiar words.
3. Vivid, picture words — language that helps us to see the action.
4. Strong nouns and verbs — words that enable us to see the action without complicating adjectives and adverbs.
5. Specific, concrete language instead of general or abstract language.
6. The active voice instead of the passive — the natural order of subject, verb, object.
7. Narration in the present tense instead of the past tense.[91]
8. Verse reference *before* quoting a verse so the hearers can read along.
9. Direct quotation of the dialogue of characters instead of indirect.
10. Use of the indicative mood instead of the imperative.
11. Use of questions to involve people.
12. Use of gender-inclusive language without calling attention to it.
13. Use of the first person plural "we" rather than the second person "you."
14. Verbal punctuation with words like "and," "well," "now," "by the way."
15. Important words at the end or beginning of clauses and sentences.
16. Use of repetition and parallelism.

89. For detailed descriptions of these ways and many examples, see my *Preaching Christ from the Old Testament,* 203-77.

90. For further elucidation on many of these characteristics, see Mark Galli and Craig Brian Larson, *Preaching That Connects: Using the Techniques of Journalists to Add Impact to Your Sermons* (Grand Rapids: Zondervan, 1994).

91. Narration in the present tense is more vivid and immediate than the past tense. Unfortunately, since English translations of the narratives use the past tense, there will be some inconsistency in tense between quoting the text and its retelling.

*   *   *

In the following chapters I will demonstrate how to formulate the theme and goal of each preaching text and how (most of) the seven ways lead to Jesus Christ in the New Testament, formulate the theme and goal of the sermon, and offer sermon expositions for all passages. Especially in the sermon expositions, I will model the oral style as much as is possible in essays.

CHAPTER 1

Daniel and His Friends Taken to Babylon

Daniel 1:1-21

Daniel resolved that he would not defile himself with the royal rations of food and wine; so he asked the palace master to allow him not to defile himself.

Daniel 1:8[1]

About twenty years ago I heard a sermon in which the preacher focused on Daniel's refusing the royal rations of food and wine. He encouraged the young people: "Like Daniel, you should avoid rich food; like Daniel you should avoid alcohol; and like Daniel you should avoid sex."[2] On the bright side, I remember this sermon — even after twenty years! On the down side, the enthusiastic preacher missed the good news God had for us in this passage. Such direct transference applications usually miss the author's intended meaning; they clutter up the sermon; and, in the context of the New Testament, they may be unbiblical.[3] The Israelites in exile were not told this story about Daniel in order to imitate him in avoiding rich food and wine — royal rations of food and wine

1. For all chapters I have selected a verse or two to focus the reader on a central issue. This key verse is not intended to be used as the preaching text; the preaching text is the whole literary unit.

2. I do not recall how he linked "no sex" with Daniel. However, it is likely that the Babylonians had made Daniel and his friends eunuchs. This probability is based partly on Isaiah's prophecy to Hezekiah, "Some of your own sons who are born to you shall be taken away; they shall be eunuchs in the palace of the king of Babylon" (Isa 39:7; 2 Kings 20:18; see Steinmann, *Daniel*, 89-91). If they were indeed made eunuchs, the preacher would be in more trouble than he realized with his direct transference applications.

3. "Surely we cannot pattern our daily conduct on that of Samuel as he hews Agag to pieces, or Samson as he commits suicide, or Jeremiah as he preaches treason." Clowney, *Preaching and Biblical Theology* (Grand Rapids: Eerdmans, 1961), 80.

were not even on their menu. Unfortunately, busy pastors may look for applications before they have taken the time to understand the author's message for Israel and his goal (purpose) in sending this message to them.

The book of Daniel was addressed to God's people suffering in exile. This first narrative is a good preaching text for people who are deeply disturbed about the persecution of Christians around the world. According to the latest estimates, one hundred million Christians are persecuted worldwide.[4] Where is God in all this? Is he powerless to stop the oppression of his people? Many people, especially in Europe, have given up their faith in a sovereign, loving God and have adopted a secular lifestyle. Others are wondering, How will we react when persecution comes our way? Will we give up our Christian faith or stand firm?

Text and Context

In preaching this narrative we must not only avoid moralizing[5] but also cutting up this single narrative into smaller, more manageable preaching texts. For example, a well-known preaching guide on Daniel recommends that "the conquering king's call for qualified Jewish youths to be educated in the Chaldean language and literature (vv. 3-4)" can be developed into two different sermons: "(1) the importance and limits of education and (2) alternative attitudes which religious/Christian communities may take toward secular culture."[6] But surely one cannot base a sermon on "the requirements and cost of a secular education" on the narrative detail that the Jewish youths "were to be taught the literature and language of the Chaldeans" (v. 4). This preaching guide offers other sermon proposals on segments of this narrative,[7] but not one of them comes even close to capturing the point (theme) of Daniel's narrative. Biblical authors communicate their messages not in a few words or phrases but in literary units. In order to do justice to the biblical author and pass on his inspired message, we

---

4. "'Open Doors' 2009 World Watch List." For specific examples and nations, see Paul Marshall, *Their Blood Cries Out: The Worldwide Tragedy of Modern Christians Who Are Dying for Their Faith.* For up-to-date examples, see, e.g., Wikipedia. Googling "Persecution of Christians" provides an abundance of sources.

5. "Moralizing" is to draw one or more morals from the preaching text when the author of the text did not intend such application(s) for his original audience.

6. John G. Gammie, *Daniel,* 11.

7. See ibid., p. 14 for three possible sermons on Daniel 1:5-8 ("So You're Going to College"; "On Being Alone"; and "Beyond the Boundaries"); p. 17 for a "pre-Lenten sermon called 'Diet and Disposition'" on Daniel 1:9-16; and p. 18 for a sermon on "The Kinds of Wisdom" based on Daniel 1:17-21.

need to first determine the literary unit that will function as the preaching text and next the point (theme) he makes with this entire unit. We shall begin, therefore, with establishing the parameters of the literary unit that will function as the preaching text, and next work toward the point this unit seeks to communicate to Israel in exile.

In contrast to the difficulty of discerning the major literary units in a book such as Ecclesiastes, it is easy to spot the textual units in Daniel. Daniel 1:1 begins with a chronological marker, "In the third year of the reign of King Jehoiakim of Judah, King Nebuchadnezzar of Babylon came to Jerusalem and besieged it." Verse 21 concludes the unit with another chronological marker, "And Daniel continued there until the first year of King Cyrus." Daniel 2:1 begins a new literary unit with another chronological marker: "In the second year of Nebuchadnezzar's reign, Nebuchadnezzar dreamed. . . ." The preaching text, therefore, is Daniel 1:1-21.

In its Old Testament context, Daniel 1 links up with 2 Chronicles 36:6-7, "Against him [Jehoiakim] King Nebuchadnezzar of Babylon came up, and bound him with fetters to take him to Babylon. Nebuchadnezzar also carried some of the vessels of the house of the LORD to Babylon and put them in his palace in Babylon." In Daniel 1:2 the narrator relates that the king brought these vessels to "the land of Shinar" — a reminder of the people who, in defiance of God, settled in "the land of Shinar" (Gen 11:2) and built the tower of Babel. This echo of the Babel narrative tips off the reader that Babylon is a place that is opposed to God and God's kingdom.

The description of Daniel as a young man, handsome (v. 4), who was forcibly taken into exile (v. 6), given a foreign name (v. 7), to whom God gave "favor and compassion from the palace master" (v. 9), to whom God gave "insight into all visions and dreams" (v. 17), and who became "ruler" of Babylon (2:48) evokes the story of Joseph, who was also described as a young man, handsome (Gen 39:6b), who was forcibly taken into exile (Egypt; Gen 37:36), given a foreign name (Gen 41:45), "found favor" in the sight of his master (Gen 39:4; 41:37), to whom God gave the ability to interpret dreams (Gen 41:39), and who became ruler of Egypt (Gen 41:41-45). The narrator portrays Daniel as another Joseph, a child of God whom God will use to advance the cause of his kingdom even in a foreign land.[8]

Since this first chapter serves as an introduction to the book of Daniel, it also has many links with the following chapters. Verse 1 introduces Nebuchadnezzar, the king of Babylon, who will play a major role in the first four

---

8. "In the providence of God, Daniel was sent to Babylon [in 604 B.C.] as an advance party to prepare for the coming of the first wave of exiles in 598 B.C." Block, "Preaching Old Testament Apocalyptic," *CTJ* 41 (2006) 26.

chapters. Verse 2 notes that Nebuchadnezzar took "some of the vessels of the house of God . . . and placed the vessels in the treasury of his gods." This information prepares us for chapter 5:3, where we read that Belshazzar desecrated these vessels by drinking from them at his feast. Verse 6 introduces us to Daniel's three friends who join Daniel in his resistance (v. 11). These friends will play a major role in chapter 3 when they refuse to bow down to the king's statue and are thrown into the fiery furnace. Verse 17 states, "To these four young men God gave knowledge and skill in every aspect of literature and wisdom," which qualified Daniel's three friends for high office in Babylon (2:49). Verse 17 continues, "Daniel also had insight into all visions and dreams," which prepares us for chapters 2 and 4 where he interprets the dreams of Nebuchadnezzar, chapter 5 where he interprets the writing on the wall, and the visions of chapters 7–12.

Literary Features

The narrator uses *hyperbole* when he writes that the king found Daniel and his friends "ten times better than all the magicians and enchanters in his whole kingdom" (v. 20). Since "ten" is the number of fullness, they were far superior (cf. the "seven times more" in 3:19). The major literary features we shall explore in order to better understand this narrative and its point are narrative structure, the plot line, character description, and repetition.

Narrative Structure

This narrative consists of three scenes:[9]

Scene 1: Jerusalem, in "the third year of the reign of Jehoiakim" (1:1-2)
    A. The Lord allows Nebuchadnezzar to capture Jerusalem (1:2a)
    B. Nebuchadnezzar brings vessels of the house of God to Babylon (1:2b)
    Characters: Nebuchadnezzar and the Lord

---

9. "Each scene presents the happenings of a particular place and time, concentrating the attention of the audience on the deeds and the words spoken." Jacob Licht, *Storytelling in the Bible* (Jerusalem: Magnes, 1978), 29. Although each scene usually has only two characters (see Robert Alter, *The Art of Biblical Narrative* [New York: Basic Books, 1985], 72), a group, such as Daniel and his friends, can function as a collective character, as we see in scenes 2 and 3. Also, as we see in scene 2, in a single scene one of the two characters can sometimes be replaced by another character.

Scene 2: Babylon: Daniel and his friends reeducated   (1:3-17)
   A. Daniel and his friends are brought to Babylon   (1:3-7)
   B. Daniel resolves not to defile himself with the royal food   (1:8)
   C. Daniel raises the issue with the palace master, who is afraid   (1:9-10)
   D. The guard agrees to withhold royal food for ten days   (1:11-14)
   E. The guard agrees to continue to withhold the royal food   (1:15-16)
   F. God gives the four young men wisdom   (1:17)
   Characters: Daniel/friends and the palace master;
      when the palace master leaves the stage, he is replaced by the guard

Scene 3: Three years later in the king's palace: examination time   (1:18-21)
   A. The king interviews Daniel and his friends   (1:18-19)
   B. The king stations Daniel and his friends at his court   (1:19-21)
   Characters: Daniel/friends and the king

The Plot Line

For understanding the narrative, catching its main point (theme), and retelling the story in the sermon, it is crucial to discern the plot line. The literary setting of this narrative is that the Lord gives Jehoiakim of Judah into the power of Nebuchadnezzar and allows the latter to take some of the vessels of God's temple back to Babylon (vv. 1-2). Preliminary incidents are the king's order to bring some bright young men to Babylon for reeducation and eventual service in the king's palace. The king assigns them daily portions of the royal rations of food and wine. Daniel and his three friends are among the young men. The palace master replaces their Hebrew names with Babylonian names (vv. 3-7).

The occasioning incident is Daniel's resolve to disobey the king's order of eating the royal rations of food and wine in order not to defile himself (v. 8). The pace of the story slows down at this important junction. Also, "the subject of the action words shifts from that of the government to the resolute action of a captive. Now the story becomes shaped by the captive's decision."[10] The tension rises when the palace master, who likes Daniel but fears the king, refuses Daniel's request not to defile himself with the royal food and wine (vv. 9-10). The narrator slows the pace even more in verses 10-13 by using direct discourse instead of indirect, thus adding to the suspense. The tension rises further when Daniel approaches a lower official, the guard of Daniel and his friends, with the proposal that instead of the royal food and wine they be given vegetables and water for ten days (vv. 11-13). The guard agrees to try this test (v. 14).

10. Lederach, *Daniel,* 37.

The tension begins to resolve when after the ten days Daniel and his friends appear "better and fatter" than the other young men and the guard continues to withdraw their royal rations and wine (vv. 15-16). The tension resolves still further when the narrator relates that in addition to their physical well-being God gives these four young men knowledge, skill, and wisdom (v. 17). The tension is fully resolved when at the end of three years the king examines all the young men, concludes that Daniel and his friends are far superior, and places them in his court (vv. 18-19).

The outcome is that the king finds Daniel and his friends "ten times better than all the magicians and enchanters in his whole kingdom" (v. 20). The narrative concludes with the information that Daniel continues in the king's court, outliving all Babylonian kings, until the first year of Cyrus, king of Persia (v. 21).

We can sketch the narrative as a single plot:

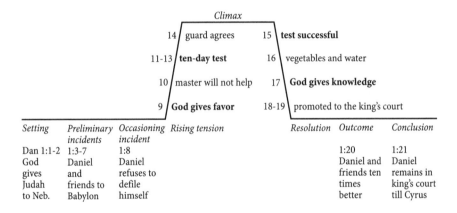

Setting	Preliminary incidents	Occasioning incident	Rising tension		Resolution	Outcome	Conclusion
Dan 1:1-2 God gives Judah to Neb.	1:3-7 Daniel and friends to Babylon	1:8 Daniel refuses to defile himself				1:20 Daniel and friends ten times better	1:21 Daniel remains in king's court till Cyrus

Character Description

The narrator tells this story in the third person. He characterizes Daniel and his friends as "Israelites of the royal family and of the nobility, young men without physical defect and handsome, versed in every branch of wisdom, endowed with knowledge and insight, and competent to serve in the king's palace" (vv. 3-4). All four are "from the tribe of Judah" (v. 6). After the ten-day trial, they appeared "better and fatter" than the other young men (v. 15). Moreover, God gave them "knowledge and skill in every aspect of literature and wisdom; Daniel also had insight into all visions and dreams" (v. 17). "In every matter of wisdom and understanding" the king finds them "ten times better" than his other wise men (v. 20). The character of Daniel is further developed by his actions: he shows his courage and his faithfulness to God's law by resolving "that he would not defile himself with the royal rations of food and wine" (v. 8).

The narrator describes the palace master as giving "favor and compassion" to Daniel (v. 9) and being "afraid" of the king (v. 10). His refusal of Daniel's request for kosher food bears out the palace master's fear of the king (v. 10). The narrator's description of God we will discuss under "Theocentric Interpretation" below.

Repetition

The narrator also uses repetition effectively to emphasize certain ideas. For example, in verse 2 "the repetition of the word 'house' (three times) and 'his god' (twice), evident in the Hebrew text but not in the Greek version followed by the NRSV,[11] underscores the theological crisis that this event created for those who believe in the God of Israel and Judah. The twofold reference to 'his god' stands over against 'the God' of the Jerusalem temple."[12] Daniel and his friends are in a land controlled by foreign gods.

In verse 8 the narrator also underscores with repetition that Daniel was determined not to defile himself: "Daniel resolved that he would *not defile himself* with the royal rations of food and wine; so he asked the palace master to allow him *not to defile himself.*" Further, "in Hebrew, both verse 7 and verse 8 begin with the same verb form, *yāśem,* 'he placed/set,'"[13] which suggests that Daniel's resolve not to defile himself (v. 8) is a direct response to the palace master's replacing Daniel's Hebrew name with the Babylonian name Belteshazzar ("May Bel [the Babylonian head god Marduk] protect his life"; v. 7). Daniel does not want to be a Babylonian "Belteshazzar" but a true Israelite, "Daniel," "God is my judge."

Three times the narrator mentions that the test with vegetables and water was for ten days (vv. 12, 14, 15), highlighting the miraculous nature of Daniel and his friends' looking better than the others after only ten days. Noteworthy especially is that the narrator repeats three times that "the Lord/God gave" (*nātan;* vv. 2, 9, 17; see "Theocentric Interpretation" below).

Repetition also alerts us to more complex literary structures such as inclusio (A-A'), parallelism (A-B; A'-B'), inverted parallelism (A-B; B'-A'), and chiasm (e.g., ABCB'A'). Goldingay suggests that the narrator presents this story as an overall chiastic structure with an inner chiasm (C1,2, C'2,1):

---

11. Cf. NASB, "The house [*bêt*] of God," "the house [*bêt*] of his god," and "the treasury [*bêt*] of his god."

12. Seow, *Daniel,* 22.

13. Lucas, *Daniel,* 49.

A	Babylonians defeat Israel	(vv. 1-2)
B	Young men taken for training	(vv. 3-7)
C 1	Daniel wants to avoid defilement	(v. 8)
2	and takes on a test	(vv. 9-14)
C′ 2	Daniel is triumphant in the test	(v. 15)
1	and avoids defilement	(v. 16)
B′	Young men are triumphant in the training	(vv. 17-20)
A′	Daniel sees out [outlives] the Babylonians	(v. 21)

Since the heart of this chiasm relates how Daniel avoids defilement (CC′), preachers may be tempted to understand and preach this story anthropocentrically, for example, focusing totally on the character of the courageous Daniel with the predictable application: Imitate Daniel![14] Goldingay correctly points out, however, that even though "the story is dominated by the decision making and activity of its human participants, . . . each double panel [AB, CC′, B′A′] refers once to God's activity, each time using the verb *nātan*, "give/make [vv. 2, 9, 17]."[15]

Theocentric Interpretation

In order to do justice to the text and avoid the temptation of horizontal, anthropocentric interpretation and preaching, we ought to ask the question, Where is God in this story? What is God doing? Sometimes God works unobtrusively behind the scenes, as in the book of Esther. But in this story, the narrator accentuates that the sovereign God is actively involved in human history. At three major junctures he highlights God's activity with the words "the Lord/God gave *(nātan)*." In the setting of the narrative he informs us that "the Lord *gave* Jehoiakim king of Judah into his hand" (v. 2, NASB). Though Nebuchadnezzar was strong, it was the Lord *('ădōnāy)*, the owner of all, who gave Judah over into Babylonian hands. In the rising tension of Daniel finding himself in exile, "God [*gave*] allowed Daniel to receive favor and compassion from the palace master" (v. 9). As God, long ago, had given Joseph "favor in the sight of the chief jailer" (Gen 39:21),[16] so God here gives Daniel the favor of the palace mas-

14. See pp. 30-31 above.

15. Goldingay, *Daniel,* 8. Cf. Seow, *Daniel,* 14, "This emphasis on God's giving at the outset should immediately signal that the book is primarily about God's power and activity and only secondarily about any human model of excellence."

16. Seow, *Daniel,* 27, suggests that "the reference to 'grace and mercies' points not so much to the favor of the chief warden (as the NRSV suggests . . .) but to the 'grace and mercies' of God before the prison warden."

ter. This good relationship allows Daniel to make his request for kosher food without fear of punishment. Unfortunately, the fearful palace master refuses his request, but the lower-ranking guard agrees to a test for ten days. What difference can a simple diet make in only ten days? Behind the scenes, God quietly blesses the test so that in only ten days Daniel and his friends look better nourished than the other young men. Finally, in resolving the tension, "to these four young men God *gave* knowledge and skill in every aspect of literature and wisdom" (v. 17), so that they were assigned to the king's court. The story could not have turned out the way it did without the active involvement of Israel's God. Longman correctly asserts, "Though the story focuses on the surface level on the actions of human characters, the chapter primarily intends to teach us about God."[17]

Textual Theme and Goal

Using these insights, we should now be able to formulate the theme of this narrative. The repetition of "God gave" in the setting, rising tension, and resolution of the narrative indicates that God is the subject of the theme. Longman suggests as the theme, "The sovereignty of God far surpasses the power of even the most mighty of human rulers." Although this is a good theme, it is too general, as Longman also realizes when he calls this "a major concern of the *book*."[18] Steinmann suggests a similar theme: "God is in control over all things that happen among humans."[19] This is also a good theme, but again it is too general; it could function as a theme for many biblical passages; it is not *textually specific*.

Another look at the plot line will help us discern the point of this specific story. Because God allows Nebuchadnezzar to overpower Israel (Judah), Daniel and his friends are taken to Babylon for reeducation in order to serve at the king's court. But Daniel refuses to defile himself with the royal food; he obeys his God rather than a human king. God gives Daniel the favor of the palace master so that a way is found for Daniel and his friends not to defile themselves. God also gives them knowledge, skill, and wisdom so that the king selects them for service in his court. A textually specific theme can be formulated as follows:

17. Longman, *Daniel,* 56. Cf. Seow, *Daniel,* 21, "The opening chapter of Daniel is first and foremost about God's sovereignty and freedom and only secondarily about a model of righteous and faithful human conduct."

18. Longman, *Daniel,* 46. My emphasis. His other suggestion focuses more on this particular chapter: "Though in exile, God gives his people the ability to prosper as well as to be faithful." Ibid., 42.

19. Steinmann, *Daniel,* 77.

"The sovereign Lord guides the faithful Daniel and friends to positions of power in Babylon." This is a good summary of the story, but it fails to capture the *message* of Daniel 1. What is the message the exiles were to hear through this story? Imagining ourselves in the predicament of these suffering exiles, we hear the message, *The sovereign Lord, who guided the faithful Daniel and his friends to positions of power in Babylon, will guide his faithful people even in exile.*[20]

The question now is, Why would Daniel communicate this message to God's people? What was his goal or aim? In line with the theme, the primary goal of the narrator is *to comfort God's people with the message that their sovereign Lord will guide his faithful people even in exile.*[21] But the narrator may have a secondary goal in mind as well. He presents Daniel and his friends as true Israelites, faithful to God even when far away from the Promised Land: faithful to God with respect to the food they eat (chapter 1); faithful to God in not falling down and worshiping an idol (chapter 3); faithful to God with respect to daily prayers (chapter 6); in short, even in exile, they remained faithful to God by obeying his law. The narrator intends that the Israelites *identify* with Daniel and his friends — not in the sense of imitating their every action by avoiding royal food and wine,[22] which they did not have anyway, but in the sense of learning that a true Israelite is faithful to God and his law even in exile.[23] Therefore, a secondary goal of the narrator is *to encourage God's people to be faithful to God and his law even in exile.*

Ways to Preach Christ

In this section we look for possible ways to move in the sermon from this Old Testament narrative to Jesus Christ in the New Testament. Usually the best way to do this is to extend the textual theme to Jesus Christ. Since there is no prom-

20. Cf. Seow, *Daniel*, 30, "The story is about the triumph of God not through ordinary manifestations of power but through God's manifold *giving* — even amid suffering, even amid signs of powerless, even amid the threat of death."

21. Cf. Longman, *Daniel*, 56, "God's sovereignty displayed subtly but clearly here and elsewhere in the book has as an intended effect to comfort his people. From their limited human perspective, they think they are simply pawns in the hands of hostile forces. Daniel 1 circumvents that false but understandable perception by pointing them to the reality of divine sovereignty."

22. See, e.g., Collins, *Daniel*, 145, "The story has a specific practical aim: to encourage Jews of the diaspora to avoid defilement in their food while participating actively in the cultural life of their environment."

23. For the difference between superficial character-imitation preaching and identifying with Bible characters, as well as cautions regarding the use of the latter, see my *Modern Preacher*, 175-81.

ise of the coming Messiah in this chapter nor a major contrast with the New Testament, we shall explore in turn the remaining five ways for moving forward to Christ: redemptive-historical progression, typology, analogy, longitudinal themes, and New Testament references.

Redemptive-Historical Progression

Redemptive-historical progression offers a direct way to Jesus in the New Testament. Daniel 1 emphasizes that God "gave": The Lord *gave* Jehoiakim into the hands of Nebuchadnezzar (v. 2). But even when his people are in exile, God continues to be involved with them: God *gave* Daniel favor from the palace master (v. 9), and "God *gave* knowledge and skill" (v. 17). God guides, protects, and saves his people by entering into human history and giving them what they need, even when they are in exile.

In the fullness of time God gave the most precious of all gifts: "God *gave* his only Son, so that everyone who believes in him may not perish but may have everlasting life" (John 3:16). Matthew 1 highlights this progression in redemptive history by depicting fourteen generations from Abraham to David (fourteen is the Hebrew number of the name "David"), fourteen from David to the exile, and fourteen from the exile to Jesus Christ: "So all the generations from Abraham to David are fourteen generations; and from David to the deportations to Babylon, fourteen generations; and from the deportation to Babylon to the Messiah, fourteen generations" (Matt 1:17). Jesus is another King David. He is the Messiah King born to save God's people from their exile in the world and restore them to the Promised Land. In his high-priestly prayer Jesus said to his Father, "I have given them your word, and the world has hated them because they do not belong to the world, just as I do not belong to the world. . . . They do not belong to the world, just as I do not belong to the world" (John 17:14, 16).

Today God's people on earth still live in exile, east of Eden. We may call ourselves citizens of a certain country, but really, Paul says, "Our citizenship is in *heaven,* and it is from there that we are expecting a Savior, the Lord Jesus Christ" (Phil 3:20; cf. 1 Pet 1:1 and Jas 1:1). Jesus will come again and bring us from exile in this sinful, evil world to the Promised Land, that is, the perfect kingdom of God on earth.

Typology

Typology also provides a way of preaching Christ since Daniel prefigures (foreshadows) Jesus Christ. Note the following analogies as well as escalations between Daniel and Jesus: As the sovereign Lord allowed Daniel to be taken from the Promised Land and into exile in sinful Babylon, so God the Father sent his only Son from heaven into this sinful world (John 3:16). As Daniel was a true Israelite, so Jesus was a true Israelite, the very Son of God. Daniel in Babylon was obedient to God with respect to food and drink; Jesus was obedient to God in all things. God gave Daniel wisdom and skill; God gave Jesus wisdom and skill ("All who heard him were amazed at his understanding and his answers" [Luke 2:47]). God guided Daniel to a place of great authority in Babylon; God guided his Son Jesus to a place of even greater authority: "God highly exalted him and gave him the name that is above every name, that at the name of Jesus every knee should bend, . . . and every tongue should confess that Jesus Christ is Lord, to the glory of God the Father" (Phil 2:9-11).

Analogy

Analogy provides another way to Jesus in the New Testament. We can draw an analogy between Daniel's message to Israel in exile and Peter's message to Christians in exile: "To the exiles of the Dispersion . . . , who have been chosen and destined by God the Father and sanctified by the Spirit to be obedient to Jesus Christ and to be sprinkled with his blood" (1 Pet 1:1-2).

We can also draw the analogy from the author's goal: As Daniel 1 comforts God's people with the message that the sovereign Lord will guide his people even in exile, so Jesus comforts his followers: "Do not be afraid, little flock, for it is your Father's good pleasure to give you the kingdom" (Luke 12:32).

Longitudinal Themes

One can also trace the theme of the sovereign God guiding his people from the Old Testament to the New. One can begin with Abraham, whom God led from "Ur of the Chaldeans" (Gen 11:31), the later Babylonia, to the Promised Land; next move to Jacob, whom God led from the Promised Land to Haran (also in the later Babylonia) and back to the Promised Land; then move to Joseph who, like Daniel, was forced into exile but to whom God also gave great wisdom and the power to interpret dreams so that he became second only to Pharaoh and was able to save God's people from starvation. Joseph died in Egypt but instructed the Israelites to bury him in the Promised Land: "When God comes to you, you shall carry up my bones from here" (Gen 50:24). Years later, God did deliver Israel from exile in Egypt, and they did bring Joseph's body with them for burial in the Promised Land (Exod 13:19; Josh 24:32). God guided his people through the time of the judges, the kings, the exile, and the return of a remnant, until the coming of Christ. When Jesus had completed his work on earth and established his church, he promised to guide his church; he said, "I am with you always, to the end of the age" (Matt 28:20).

In sermons one must handle longitudinal themes with care, for tracing a theme in detail can soon become tedious for the congregation. Broad strokes are often more effective than a long-drawn-out journey through the Scriptures.

New Testament References

The appendix of the Greek New Testament lists John 3:35 as an allusion to Daniel 1:2, and Revelation 2:10 as an allusion to the "ten days" in Daniel 1:12, 14. Neither of these references are helpful for preaching Christ. Checking a concordance under God's providence leads us to Jesus' teaching concerning God's guidance of his people. For example, Jesus taught, "Are not five sparrows sold for two pennies? Yet not one of them is forgotten in God's sight. But even the hairs of your head are all counted. Do not be afraid; you are of more value than many sparrows" (Luke 12:6-7). Also, in his high-priestly prayer, Jesus prayed, "Holy Father, protect them [Jesus' followers]. . . . While I was with them, I protected them in your name. . . . I guarded them. . . . But now I am coming to you. . . . I am not asking you to take them out of the world, but I ask you to protect them from the evil one" (John 17:11-15).

Paul also connects his teaching on God's providence with Jesus Christ: "We know that all things work together for good for those who love God. . . . Who will separate us from the love of Christ? Will hardship, or distress, or persecution, or famine, or nakedness, or peril, or sword? . . . No, in all these things we are more than conquerors through him who loved us. For I am convinced that neither death, nor life, nor angels, nor rulers, nor things present, nor things to come, nor powers, nor height, nor depth, nor anything else in all creation, will be able to separate us from the love of God in Christ Jesus our Lord" (Rom 8:28-39).

Sermon Theme, Goal, and Need

Having checked the New Testament especially for connections with the textual theme, we are now ready to formulate the sermon theme and goal. Because of progression in redemptive history and revelation, the sermon theme may sometimes have to be different from the textual theme, though it should always be rooted in it. We formulated the textual theme as, "The sovereign Lord, who guided the faithful Daniel and his friends to positions of power in Babylon, will guide his faithful people even in exile." Since the New Testament does not change this message, we can make the textual theme the sermon theme — except for one phrase. The "even in exile" raises several questions: Is the church today "in exile" the way Israel was? We have seen above that Paul teaches that God's people are in exile because they live in a sinful, evil world: "Our citizenship is in *heaven*" (Phil 3:20). Peter also addresses the New Testament church as "the exiles of the Dispersion" (1 Pet 1:1; cf. Jas 1:1). Therefore, we could keep "in exile" in the sermon theme. But since "exile" may not be clear to people and the theme should be crystal clear, we shall change the "in exile" to "in the world." Another question is, Is it surprising ("even") that God guides the church in the world? Since Jesus promised to be with his church "to the end of the age" (Matt 28:20) and poured out the Holy Spirit upon his church, it is not surprising that God guides his church in the world. Therefore, we can drop the word "even." The sermon theme, then, becomes: *The sovereign Lord, who guided the faithful Daniel and his friends to positions of power in Babylon, will guide his faithful people in the world.*

We concluded that the author may have had two goals for his message: the primary goal, "to comfort God's people with the message that their sovereign Lord will guide his faithful people even in exile," and a secondary goal, "to encourage God's people to be faithful to God even in exile." The sermon can have the same two goals for the church today, though we should again change the "even in exile" to "in the world." The dual goal[24] for preaching this sermon then is: *to comfort God's people with the message that their sovereign Lord will guide his faithful people in the world and to encourage them to be faithful to God.*

With a dual goal it will be more difficult, of course, to keep the sermon focused and unified than with a single goal. But if the biblical author seems to have had a dual goal in mind, we should accept the challenge of preaching a unified sermon with a dual goal. In any event, this dual goal points to a dual congregational need the sermon should address: because of the persecution they experience or observe in this world, God's people tend to question whether God is indeed in control of the evil powers in this world and they are tempted to turn away from God's law.

Sermon Exposition

The sermon introduction can disclose the relevance of this sermon with an illustration of people who were so appalled by the persecution of themselves or other Christians that they began to doubt the existence of a loving God, lost their faith

---

24. For the sake of a unified sermon, the sermon should have a single theme. But a dual goal (application) is certainly possible if the biblical author's goals warrant it.

in God, and began to live a secular lifestyle.[25] For example, many people claim to have lost their faith in God because of the atrocities of Auschwitz. Along with millions of Jews, many Christians died in the Nazi concentration camps. Then raise the question whether we might lose our faith in God when persecution strikes: state-sponsored attacks on the church or even when we are badgered at work because of our Christian beliefs. When we focus on the persecution of God's people, it is easy to lose our faith in a *sovereign* God who *loves* his people.

It certainly was easy for Israel to lose its faith in God when their little country was overrun by Babylonian forces and the people dragged away into exile. They were taken into exile in three waves. First, in 605 B.C., the Babylonians took young men of nobility, including Daniel and his three friends (Dan 1:1-6). Eight years later the Babylonians took a large group of the elite: King Jehoiachin, his officials, the royal family, the warriors, artisans, and smiths (2 Kings 24:10-17). Finally, in 587 B.C., they took all the remaining Jews except for the poorest people. They destroyed the walls of Jerusalem and burned God's holy temple to the ground (2 Kings 25:1-21). Where was God? What kind of God did not have the strength to protect his own city and his own temple? It appeared that the gods of Babylon were far stronger than Israel's God. It was easy for Israel in exile to lose its faith in the Lord their God. Isaiah reports that Israel complained, "The LORD has forsaken me, my Lord has forgotten me" (49:14). Why not serve Marduk, the great god of Babylon? The book of Daniel addresses these hurting, wavering exiles.

Verses 1 and 2, "In the third year of the reign of King Jehoiakim of Judah, King Nebuchadnezzar of Babylon[26] came to Jerusalem and besieged it. The Lord let King Jehoiakim of Judah fall into his power, as well as some of the vessels of the house of God. These[27] he brought to the land of Shinar, and placed the vessels in the treasury of his gods." The author uses the phrase "the land of Shinar" to remind us of Genesis 11, where we read of people settling in "the land of Shinar" and in defiance of God building the tower of Babel. Right from the beginning, then, we are reminded that Babylonia is an evil place, the kingdom of darkness. Its people are proud and defiant, enemies of God and his people.[28]

---

25. For another option of a relevant introduction, see Ryan Faber's sermon in Appendix 3.

26. "Nebuchadnezzar King of Babylon (the Hebrew has, literally, 'king of Babel') is trying to show God up. Nebuchadnezzar comes from Babel to Jerusalem and seizes the sacred vessels from God's house. Military power dares to defy the power of God." Seow, *Daniel*, 23.

27. "These" seems to refer to Jehoiakim and the vessels (cf. 2 Chron 36:6-7). Although Jehoiakim may have been taken to Babylon, perhaps to swear loyalty to Nebuchadnezzar, he soon returned to Jerusalem to serve as a Babylonian vassal king (cf. 2 Kings 24:1). See Steinmann, *Daniel*, 84.

28. "*Shinar* as a term for Babylonia, the southeastern part of modern Iraq, is an archaism in the OT. . . . The name especially suggests a place of false religion, self-will, and self-

Note further that verse 2 claims that "*the Lord* let King Jehoiakim of Judah fall into" Nebuchadnezzar's power. A modern historian would say that Judah fell because it was over-powered by the most powerful nation on earth. A Babylonian priest would have said that the powerful gods of Babylon simply over-powered the God of Israel. But our text gives us a totally different perspective on Judah's tragedy: "The Lord let King Jehoiakim of Judah fall into" Nebuchadnezzar's power. Literally it says, "The Lord *gave* King Jehoiakim of Judah to Nebuchadnezzar." The Hebrew word for "Lord" here is *'ădōnāy,* which "emphasizes God's ownership, his control."[29] So from the outset Daniel informs us that Israel's Lord is the sovereign God who owns and controls all things. The gods of Babylon do not even come close.[30]

Why, then, did the sovereign Lord allow this disaster to take place to his very own people? We find the answer in Daniel 9. Daniel confesses in his prayer, "All Israel has transgressed your law and turned aside, refusing to obey your voice. So the curse and the oath written in the law of Moses, the servant of God, have been poured out upon us, because we have sinned against you" (Dan 9:11).[31] Israel's continual disobedience was the reason why God allowed Judah to fall into the power of Babylon.

The Lord even allowed Nebuchadnezzar to take "some of the vessels[32] of the house of God" — his own sacred house. We read in verse 2, "These he brought to the land of Shinar and placed the vessels in the treasury of *his* gods."[33] Removing these gold and silver vessels was "a sign of the victory of Nebuchadnezzar and his god over the Israelite king and his god. Wars were fought in god's name and plunder thus belonged to him."[34]

---

aggrandizement (Gen 11:1-9; Zech 5:11)." Goldingay, *Daniel,* 15. Cf. Porteous, *Daniel,* 27: "From the very outset . . . it is hinted that the environment of the Jewish exiles, whose adventures are to be told, contains an element hostile to faith."

29. Longman, *Daniel,* 46.

30. "The divine names 'Lord' and 'God' may serve as foils emphasizing the supremacy of the one Hebrew God over the many 'non-gods' of the Babylonian pantheon." Hill, "Daniel," 48.

31. For the covenant curses for disobedience, see Deuteronomy 28:15-68. Cf. Jeremiah 21:1-7; 25:8-14.

32. Some of these vessels were gold and silver cups which King Belshazzar would later desecrate by using them at his pagan feast (Dan 5:2-4).

33. "This act reflects a common ancient Near Eastern practice. A victorious army plundered the temple of the vanquished nation and placed the symbols of the defeated god in their own temple." Longman, *Daniel,* 47.

34. Goldingay, *Daniel,* 15. He notes further, "Many were made of precious metals . . . and would be worthwhile plunder. . . . They are also of religious significance, being the Jerusalem temple's nearest thing to images." Ibid. Cf. Smith-Christopher, "Book of Daniel," 38: "The Babylonians were highly aware of the propaganda value of placing captured religious symbols 'under' the Babylonian gods in the Babylonian imperial shrines, thus symbolizing the captivity of conquered gods as well as people."

In verses 3 and 4 we read, "Then the king commanded his palace master Ashpenaz to bring some of the Israelites of the royal family and of the nobility, young men without physical defect and handsome, versed in every branch of wisdom, endowed with knowledge and insight,[35] and competent to serve in the king's palace; they were to be taught the literature and language of the Chaldeans."[36] These young men were the cream of the crop. They were from the upper class, teenagers who could easily be retrained, in top physical condition, well educated, and "endowed with knowledge and insight," that is, with a high IQ. They were the kind of boys who aced every class and lettered every varsity sport. They were to be taken to Babylon and there "to be taught the literature and language of the Chaldeans." In other words, they were to be reeducated in the Babylonian ways and language.[37] They were to be "reprogrammed." Nebuchadnezzar would brainwash these Israelite teenagers and turn them into Babylonian wise men.

The king had several reasons for bringing intelligent Israelites to Babylon. It would bring the best minds in Israel to the king's court in Babylon. It would drive home to Israel that they were now subject to Babylon. And it would discourage rebellion in Judah.[38]

Verse 5 adds that "the king assigned them a daily portion of the royal rations of food and wine." It's not that the king wanted to pamper these Jewish boys. Rather, he wished to wean them from their God-given diet. They had to become Babylonians even in their eating and drinking.[39] They had to be Babylonians in every moment of their existence. Verses 5 and 6 continue, "They were to be educated for three years,[40] so that at the end of that time they could be stationed in the king's court. Among them were Daniel, Hananiah, Mishael,

35. "The three expressions referring to intellectual capabilities . . . should probably be regarded as synonyms for 'gifted learners' rather than signifying distinctive aspects of the human intelligence (cf. Miller, [*Daniel*], 61). The cumulative effect of the triad simply stresses the emphasis King Nebuchadnezzar placed on inherent intellectual ability." Hill, "Daniel," 50.

36. "The Kaldu were a people from southern Babylonia to whom Nebuchadnezzar's father Nabopolasser belonged; they were thus the ruling caste in Babylonia during the exile. In the OT, however, *Chaldeans* is the regular word for the people of Babylonia in general." Goldingay, *Daniel*, 16.

37. "Probably the sacred Sumerian language along with the highly complicated cuneiform script and the sacred myths and rituals and omen texts characteristic of Babylonian religion." Porteous, *Daniel*, 27.

38. See Baldwin, *Daniel*, 79, and Goldingay, *Daniel*, 15.

39. "Those old-fashioned Jewish regulations about food would be cast aside — together with all the other customs and habits of their fathers. The last threads tying them to their own people would have to be cut — hence the prescribed menu." Veldkamp, *Dreams and Dictators*, 12.

40. "According to some ancient Persian and Greek sources [three years] was the standard period for higher education that typically began when the boys were fourteen years old and lasted until they were sixteen or seventeen." Seow, *Daniel*, 24.

and Azariah, from the tribe of Judah." We don't know how many young men were captured for this retraining program, but among them were these four, all from the tribe of Judah.

They had beautiful Hebrew names that godly parents might meaningfully give their children. All four names testify to Israel's God, Yahweh. Daniel means, "*El* (God) is my judge." Hananiah means, "*Yah* (Yahweh) has been gracious." Mishael means, "Who is what *El* (God) is?" and Azariah means, "*Yah* (Yahweh) has helped."[41]

Unfortunately, the first thing the palace master does is to replace these beautiful names. These young men need to be cut off from their past and cut off from their God.[42] Their identity needs to change from Israelite youths to Babylonian wise men. So the palace master replaces the beautiful Hebrew names with Babylonian names with references to Babylonian gods. Verse 7, "The palace master gave them other names: Daniel he called Belteshazzar," which probably means "May Bel protect his life" — *Bel* means "lord," referring to the Babylonian head god, Marduk. "Hananiah he called Shadrach," which means "The command of Aku," the moon god, or "The command of Marduk," the head god. "Mishael he called Meshach," which may mean, "Who is what Aku is?" And, finally, "Azariah he called Abednego," which means "Servant of Nebo," the Babylonian god of wisdom and agriculture.[43] Instead of serving Yahweh, the God of Israel, from now on these young men are in the service of Babylon and its gods.

names

Verse 8, "But Daniel resolved that he would not defile himself with the royal rations of food and wine; so he asked the palace master to allow him not to defile himself." Resistance among the captives! Daniel could not help being taken to Babylon. He also could not help having his name changed, though he must have realized that this was a first step in becoming a good Babylonian. But when it comes to consuming the royal rations of food and wine, Daniel resists.[44] He re-

41. See Leupold, *Exposition of Daniel*, 64; Goldingay, *Daniel*, 17; and Steinmann, *Daniel*, 88.

42. Cf. Calvin, *Commentaries on Daniel*, I, 96, "The names were changed to abolish the remembrance of the kingdom of Judah from their hearts."

43. Steinmann, *Daniel*, 88-89. See also Collins, *Daniel*, 141, and Miller, *Daniel*, 65-66. Steinmann, ibid., 92, notes that "The new names they were assigned are probably all corrupted forms of Babylonian theophoric names honoring gods of the Babylonian pantheon. . . . The theophoric element in each name contains a corruption involving an addition, deletion, or change of one or more consonants." He surmises that Daniel may have corrupted the names on purpose to indicate that "they did not personally approve of having names associated with pagan gods instead of their God."

44. The renaming of Daniel and his friends "is meant to symbolize their becoming good Babylonians. At this point Daniel decides to make a stand, as the opening verbs of vv. 7 and 8 indicate. The head courtier 'put' (*wayyāśem*) the names on the Judeans, and in response Daniel 'put' (*wayyāśem*) it on his heart' not to eat the king's food and wine." Lucas, *Daniel*, 57-58.

solves not to defile himself. To indicate that Daniel is dead serious about this, the narrator repeats twice in verse 8 that he would "not defile himself."

Why would the royal rations of food and wine defile Daniel?[45] The word "defile" *(gā'al)* is a cultic, a religious term. People who defile themselves become "unclean," that is, unholy. They are no longer allowed in God's holy presence. So the first thing that comes to mind is that these royal rations were not kosher. They might include pork and other forbidden meat. Even with meat that God allowed to be eaten, the animals were not slaughtered properly because they did not have their blood drained.[46] According to God's law,[47] eating such meat would make an Israelite unclean. But that would not account for Daniel's refusal to drink the king's wine, which was kosher for all Israelites except for Nazirites (Num 6:3).

There is a second reason why Daniel may have refused the royal rations of food and wine. Usually a portion of the meat and the wine on the king's table would first have been offered to the Babylonian gods. "Partaking of this food would have been an indirect act of worshiping the Babylonian deities."[48] When Daniel takes his stand not to eat the royal food and drink the royal wine, he takes his stand against the Babylonian gods and for the God of Israel.[49] This is a dangerous position to take. Daniel can be executed for taking this stand. Four hundred years later, under Antiochus IV, many Jews were killed for refusing to eat unclean food. A book from that time, 1 Maccabees, informs us, "Yet there were many in Israel who stood firm and found the courage to refuse unclean food. They chose death rather than contamination by such fare or profanation of the holy covenant, and they were executed."[50]

Daniel takes a dangerous stand. Yet he courageously asks "the palace master to allow him not to defile himself." If the palace master reports this resistance to the king, it can cost Daniel his life. But we read in verse 9, "Now God

45. For a consideration of several possibilities, see Goldingay, *Daniel*, 18-19, and Steinmann, *Daniel*, 99.

46. "In Babylon, the blood was not drained when an animal was slaughtered for consumption, so defilement by blood was virtually unavoidable." Stefanovic, *Daniel*, 62.

47. See Leviticus 11; 17:10-14; Deuteronomy 12:23-25; 14:3-21.

48. Miller, *Daniel*, 67, with a reference to L. Wood, *A Commentary to Daniel* (Grand Rapids: Zondervan, 1973), 37. Cf. Archer, "Daniel," 33-34, "Probably most of the meat items on the menu were taken from animals sacrificed to the patron gods of Babylon (Marduk, Nebo, and Ishtar, for example), and no doubt the wine from the king's table (v. 5) had first been part of the libation to these deities. Therefore, even those portions of food and drink not inherently unclean had been tainted by contact with pagan cultic usage."

49. See Lucas, *Daniel*, 54-55.

50. 1 Maccabees 1:62-63, *The Jerusalem Bible*. Cf. 2 Maccabees 7 about seven brothers and their mother being tortured and killed, one after the other, for refusing to eat "pig's flesh, which the Law forbids."

allowed Daniel to receive favor and compassion from the palace master." As God earlier "gave" Judah into the hands of Nebuchadnezzar (v. 2), so now God "gave" Daniel the favor and compassion of the palace master.[51] Israel's God controls human history. Israel's God can work also in far-off Babylon. He allows Daniel "to receive favor and compassion from the palace master." It sounds very much like the story of Joseph when he was in exile in Egypt. We read in Genesis, "But the LORD was with Joseph and showed him steadfast love; *he gave him favor* in the sight of the chief jailer" (Gen 39:21). Israel's God is the sovereign God. He was there for his people in Egypt, and he is there now for his people in Babylon. God gives Daniel the favor and compassion of the palace master.

But even though the palace master has taken a liking to Daniel, he is not about to disobey the king's orders. Verse 10, "The palace master said to Daniel, 'I am afraid of my lord the king; he has appointed your food and your drink. If he should see you in poorer condition than the other young men of your own age, you would endanger my head with the king.'" The palace master is afraid of the king. Withholding the royal food can cost him his head. Nebuchadnezzar can fly into one of his violent rages and have the palace master killed. The king was known for his violent rages. In Daniel 2:12 we read of the king's rage and ordering that "all the wise men of Babylon be destroyed." In Daniel 3 we read again of his rage and ordering that Daniel's friends be thrown into the fiery furnace. The palace master knows the king well and is not about to risk his own head for Daniel.

What is Daniel to do? The palace master is afraid that a restricted diet will cause Daniel to lose weight and that the king will notice this. Daniel hatches a plan, bypassing the fearful palace master this time. He goes to a lower official. Verses 11 to 13, "Then Daniel asked the guard whom the palace master had appointed over Daniel, Hananiah, Mishael, and Azariah: 'Please test your servants for ten days. Let us be given vegetables to eat and water to drink. You can then compare our appearance with the appearance of the young men who eat the royal rations, and deal with your servants according to what you observe.'" Daniel suggests that the guard give him and his friends only vegetables to eat and water to drink for a period of ten days.[52] Surely a test period of ten days

---

51. "Behind this English translation we see the same verb that we encountered in v. 2, 'God gave.' While the Babylonians thought they were in control of the world and local scene, the Hebrew narrative makes it clear again that the true God is the One who orchestrates events for the good of his people." Longman, *Daniel*, 53-54.

52. "Since the food defiled by idol sacrifices was meat and wine, a part of the former of which was laid on the altar, and a part of the latter poured out as a libation, 'vegetables,' *zērō'îm*, 'things sowed,' would be outside the pale of the defiled things." Leupold, *Exposition of Daniel*, 70.

cannot do any harm. They will be there for three years. At the end of ten days the guard can compare their appearance with that of the other young men.

Daniel sits on pins and needles as he waits for the guard's response. But he does not have to wait long. We read in verse 14, "So he [the guard] agreed to this proposal and tested them for ten days." Ten days is hardly enough time to make a major difference. The narrator emphasizes this brief time by repeating the phrase "ten days" three times. But you never know, they may lose some weight.

Strangely, exactly the opposite happens. Verse 15, "At the end of ten days it was observed that they appeared better and fatter than all the young men who had been eating the royal rations." They appear "better and fatter," that is, healthier, better nourished.[53] How is it possible that they look better nourished on vegetables and water than the young men who had the rich food and wine? The author does not have to tell us how that is possible. By now we know that God works in human history. "The Lord *gave*" the king of Judah into the hand of the king of Babylon (v. 2). "God *gave*" Daniel the favor of the palace master (v. 9). Of course, God gave Daniel and his friends a miracle so that they, in only ten days, looked better nourished than the other young men.[54]

This positive result convinces the guard. Verse 16, "So the guard continued to withdraw their royal rations and the wine they were to drink, and gave them vegetables." Daniel and his friends do not have to defile themselves. For three years they continue on their diet of vegetables and water. They will always know that their good physical appearance is not due to the rich Babylonian food but due to the blessing of their God.

And there is more. Verse 17, "To these four young men *God gave* knowledge and skill in every aspect of literature and wisdom; Daniel also had insight into all visions and dreams." Here for the third time the narrator writes, "God *gave*": God gave Judah into the hand of Babylon (v. 2); God gave Daniel the favor and compassion of the palace master (v. 9); and now, "God gave knowledge and skill in every aspect of literature and wisdom" to these four young men. Three special gifts are for these young men, and these alone: knowledge, understanding of all kinds of literature, and wisdom. The terms "denote supernaturally revealed knowledge."[55] But to Daniel God gives an additional special gift: "Daniel also had insight into all visions and dreams." This special gift will become im-

---

53. "Fatter" is literally "fatter of flesh." "This phrase does not necessarily mean that the youths became fat but is an idiom for healthy, the idea being that a well-fed person would not appear gaunt." Miller, *Daniel,* 70, n. 71.

54. "Their robust appearance, usually attained by a rich fare of meats and wine, is miraculously achieved through a diet of vegetables. Only God could have done it." Longman, *Daniel,* 53. Cf. Portier-Young, *Apocalypse against Empire,* 211, "Like the memory of manna in the wilderness, this detail emphasizes the miracle of divine provision."

55. Goldingay, *Daniel,* 20.

portant in the following chapters when Daniel interprets dreams and receives visions.

Verses 18 and 19, "At the end of the time that the king had set for them to be brought in, the palace master brought them into the presence of Nebuchadnezzar, and the king spoke with them. And among them all, no one was found to compare with Daniel, Hananiah, Mishael, and Azariah; therefore they were stationed in the king's court." Notice that the narrator identifies the four young men by their Hebrew names. "This may be the storyteller's way of attributing the competence of the four to the God to whom their Hebrew names bore witness."[56] The king himself examines them and finds Daniel and his friends far superior to the other young men. So the king stations these four Judeans in his court to be his advisors.

The king of Babylon is extremely pleased with the work of Daniel and his friends. In fact, verse 20 tells us, "In every matter of wisdom and understanding concerning which the king inquired of them, he found them *ten times better* than all the magicians and enchanters in his whole kingdom." They are far superior even to all the experienced wise men in his kingdom. The king may have thought that this success was due to his excellent educational system. But we, the readers of this story, know better. *God* gave them knowledge, skill, and wisdom.[57]

The narrative concludes with verse 21, "And Daniel continued there until the first year of King Cyrus." King Cyrus was the king of Persia, modern-day Iran. He conquered Babylon (modern-day Iraq) and in his first year allowed the Israelites to return to the Promised Land. Daniel's story began in 605 B.C. when the first Judeans were taken into exile, and now he is still living when a remnant of exiles returns in 539 B.C., nearly seventy years later.[58] Daniel is in his eighties now. God blesses him with such a long life that he outlasts even the great Babylonian empire and all six of its kings.[59] Daniel experiences God's faithfulness, even in exile.

Daniel in the Old Testament prefigures Jesus Christ in the New. Note the analogies. As the sovereign Lord allowed his child Daniel to be taken from the

56. Lederach, *Daniel,* 41. Cf. Woodard, "Literary Strategies and Authorship in the Book of Daniel," *JETS* 37/1 (1994) 46, "They are identified by their Hebrew, not Babylonian, names. So much for Nebuchadnezzar's decrees!"

57. "At this point in the story, the stage is set for the God of the Hebrews to triumph over the Babylonian pantheon. The young men triumphed thanks to God's providence and not to the king's." Stefanovic, *Daniel,* 65.

58. Jeremiah foretold the Babylonian captivity and added, "Then after seventy years are completed, I will punish the king of Babylon and that nation, the land of the Chaldeans, for their iniquity, says the LORD" (Jer 25:12).

59. "The presence of the Israelite named Daniel in the royal court of seven [six?] Babylonian monarchs and the first king of Persia was a tangible reminder that God is the one who sets up kings and deposes them (Dan 2:21)." Hill, "Daniel," 56.

Promised Land into sinful Babylon, so God the Father sent his only Son from heaven into this sinful world: "God so loved the world that he *gave* his only Son, so that everyone who believes in him may not perish but may have everlasting life" (John 3:16). As Daniel in Babylon was obedient to God's laws, so Jesus was obedient to God's will in all things. Even when it became clear that God's will for Jesus was to offer up his own life, Jesus prayed, "My Father, if this cannot pass unless I drink it, *your will* be done" (Matt 26:42). As God guided Daniel to a place of great authority in Babylon, so God guided his Son Jesus to a place of even greater authority: "God highly exalted him and gave him the name that is above every name, that at the name of Jesus every knee should bend, . . . and every tongue should confess that Jesus Christ is Lord, to the glory of God the Father" (Phil 2:9-11).

The Israelites in exile who heard this story about Daniel and his friends must have been encouraged to remain faithful to their faithful God. They did not have to deal with the issues of *royal* food which was not kosher. Their issues were somewhat different, but the principle was the same: Be faithful to God by obeying his laws.

As Christians, we also are called to be faithful to God, even in dangerous circumstances. For us it is not a matter of eating kosher food: Jesus "declared all foods clean" (Mark 7:19). And so did God in giving Peter a dream about unclean animals which God had made clean (Acts 10:9-16). But Jesus also declared that as Christians we live *in* the world but are not *of* the world. In his high-priestly prayer Jesus said to his Father, "I have made your name known to those whom you gave me from the world. They were yours, and you gave them to me, and they have *kept your word*. . . . I have given them your word, and the world has hated them because they do *not belong to the world,* just as I do not belong to the world. I am not asking you to take them out of the world, but I ask you to protect them from the evil one. They do *not belong to the world,* just as I do not belong to the world. Sanctify them in the truth; your word is truth. As you have sent me into the world, so I have sent them into the world" (John 17:6, 14-18).

What makes Christians distinctive in this world is that they do not conform to the world and its standards but remain faithful to God. They seek to honor God in all they do and say. Jesus said to his followers, "You are the light of the world. A city built on a hill cannot be hid. . . . Let your light shine before others, so that they may see your good works and give glory to your Father in heaven" (Matt 5:14, 16; cf. 1 Pet 2:12). In the book of Revelation the risen Lord encourages his suffering, persecuted church, "Be faithful until death, and I will give you the crown of life" (Rev. 2:10).

Daniel's story comforted the Israelites suffering in exile. In spite of appearances, it gave them hope that their God had not been conquered by the Babylonian gods. Israel's God was still in control and was guiding his people even in exile. Jesus also comforted his followers who would face persecution and martyrdom. Jesus taught us to trust our heavenly Father. He said, "Are not five sparrows sold for two pennies? Yet not one of them is forgotten in God's sight. But even the hairs of your head are all counted. Do not be afraid; you are of more value than many sparrows" (Luke 12:6-7). Jesus encouraged us when he said, "Do not be afraid, little flock, for it is your Father's good pleasure to give you the kingdom" (Luke 12:32).

How will we react when persecution comes our way? When we lose our jobs because of our Christian beliefs? When our family disowns us because we have become Christians? When our father and mother are taken away because they are Christians? How will we react when Christian public worship is banned? When our earthly possessions are taken away? Jesus says, "Do not be afraid, little flock, for it is your Father's good pleasure to give you the kingdom." God the Father is sovereign. He is in control. He is faithful and will see us through. And he will give us "the kingdom"!

In Romans 8 Paul asks, "Who will separate us from the love of Christ? Will hardship, or distress, or persecution, or famine, or nakedness, or peril, or sword? . . . No, *in* all these things we are more than conquerors through him who loved us." Paul does not say that in spite of hardships we are still more than conquerors. No, "*in* all these things we are more than conquerors through him who loved us. For I am convinced that neither death, nor life, nor angels, nor rulers, nor things present, nor things to come, nor powers, nor height, nor depth, nor anything else in all creation, will be able to separate us from the love of God in Christ Jesus our Lord" (Rom 8:35-39). As Christians we can count on it that nothing on earth can separate us from the love of Christ. God will be faithful to us. Let us be faithful to him no matter what happens.[60]

---

60. A sermon on Daniel 1 is included in Appendix 3, pp. 415-20.

CHAPTER 2

Nebuchadnezzar's Dream of a Great Statue

Daniel 2:1-49

And in the days of those kings the God of heaven will set up a kingdom that shall never be destroyed, nor shall this kingdom be left to another people. It shall crush all these kingdoms and bring them to an end, and it shall stand forever.

Daniel 2:44

Daniel 2 is an excellent preaching text for addressing people who tend to get so wrapped up in their own problems that they lose sight of the big picture of human history. This passage will focus their attention on the sovereignty of God and God's promise that his perfect kingdom, which will replace all earthly kingdoms, is indeed coming.

In preparing a sermon on this chapter, however, we must avoid especially two pitfalls. First, we should avoid getting sidetracked by including in the sermon part of the endless discussions about the identity of the kingdoms of gold, silver, bronze, and iron, and especially about the feet and toes of iron and clay.[1]

1. See pp. 5-14. Until the nineteenth century there was general agreement that the kingdoms of gold, silver, bronze, and iron represented Babylon, Persia, Greece, and Rome. Miller, *Daniel*, 96, states that "Josephus and 2 Esd 12:10-51 identified the fourth empire as Rome. Childs acknowledges that the writers of the New Testament Gospels considered the Roman Empire to be the fourth kingdom, and Walton comments, 'The evidence in the writings of the Church fathers is massive and in unison in favor of the Roman view.'"

But this all changed in modern times. Those who deny prophetic prediction of the future and hold that Daniel was compiled during the second century B.C. identify the fourth kingdom as Greece. Towner, *Daniel*, 36, states, "Most modern interpreters agree that the historical epochs symbolized by the four parts of the statue are the Babylonian empire (the head of gold), the 'Median empire' (although it hardly ever existed in actual historical fact but here equals the upper torso of silver), the Persian Empire (the lower torso of bronze) and the Hellenistic king-

Second, we should again avoid moralizing. With the encouragement of several commentators it will be tempting to leave the track laid out by the theme of the narrative and to follow little rabbit trails that seem more practical. For example, as Daniel called his friends together for prayer when faced with catastrophe, so should we.[2] And as Daniel took time to thank God for hearing their prayer, so should we.[3] Of course, we should. But that's not the point of this narrative. Nor is it the point that, like Daniel (2:27-28), we should not brag about ourselves but give praise to God;[4] or that if we wish to be as successful as Daniel was (2:48), we should be as pious and wise as he was.[5] The antidote to such moralizing is to

---

doms of the Ptolemies of Egypt and the Seleucids of Antioch in Syria (the legs of iron and the feet of clay)." Towner admits that there really was not a separate Median Empire, but claims that this "does not invalidate the list given above." He argues, "If one begins with the equation 'the head of gold equals Babylon,' as the text itself demands, and if one identifies the divided kingdoms contemporary with the writer with the Hellenistic regimes of the Seleucids and the Ptolemies after 323 B.C., no other list of four world empires is really possible."

Obviously, his whole argument is based on his second assumption that the fourth kingdom is the Greek kingdom of Alexander the Great and its sequel. But why could the fourth kingdom not be that of the Romans? Miller, *Daniel*, 95, counters that "the author of Daniel demonstrates throughout the book that he was well aware that Media and Persia were not two separate world kingdoms but a unified empire. For example, in 8:20 the two-horned ram (symbolizing one kingdom) represents 'the kings of Media and Persia,' and in chapter 6 the author referred to the 'laws of the Medes and Persians' (cf. vv. 8, 15), indicating that Darius ruled by the laws of the Medo-Persian Empire, not a separate Median kingdom." See also 5:28 and pp. 213-18 below. On "The Identity of the Fourth Empire," see also Young, *Prophecy of Daniel*, 275-94, and Archer, "Daniel," 24-26. For arguments pro (the Roman view) and con (the Greek view), see Steinmann, *Daniel*, 144-57. For a listing of "The Successive Empires in Daniel's Prophecies [Dan 2, 7, and 8] according to Modern Interpretive Systems," see Block, "Preaching Old Testament Apocalyptic," *CTJ* 41/1 (2006) 41.

2. E.g., Miller, *Daniel*, 88: "Daniel also illustrated the necessity of collective prayer as he summoned his friends to join him"; and Harman, *Study Commentary on Daniel*, 62, "Whenever believing children of God are faced with danger they must turn in prayer to God like Daniel."

3. "Should we not, like Daniel, thank and praise God for the richness of his gift to us, treasure this source of heavenly wisdom, and share it with our puzzled neighbors?" Duguid, *Daniel*, 26. Cf. p. 24. Cf. Miller, *Daniel*, 88: "Daniel did not forget to thank God for answered prayer, which is another lesson for us."

4. "There is a model here for all of us in our relationships with those who do not know our God." Duguid, *Daniel*, 33. On p. 43 Duguid even uses the cruel King Nebuchadnezzar as a model for imitation: Nebuchadnezzar "acknowledged, 'Surely your God is the God of gods and the Lord of kings and a revealer of mysteries, for you were able to reveal this mystery' (Dan 2:46-47). This same response should be ours as well." One wonders on what basis one would isolate this element for imitation and ignore the king's anger, his decree to execute all the wise men, including Daniel and his friends (v. 13), and his worshiping Daniel and offering a grain offering and incense to him (2:46).

5. Towner, *Daniel*, 42, rightly objects to this "wistful and simplistic" idea: "After all, the latter half of the book is very much aware that even the saints 'shall fall by sword and flame, by captivity and plunder' (Dan 11:33-35)."

distinguish between holding up Daniel as a model for imitation of his every action (which he is not)[6] and Daniel as a model for identification (which he was for Israel) and to keep the sermon focused on the theme and goal of this passage.

Text and Context

The textual unit is easy to detect. It begins with the chronological marker, "In the second year of Nebuchadnezzar's reign, Nebuchadnezzar dreamed such dreams that his spirit was troubled and his sleep left him" (2:1). The unit ends in 2:49, "Daniel made a request of the king, and he appointed Shadrach, Meshach, and Abednego over the affairs of the province of Babylon. But Daniel remained at the king's court." This conclusion is similar to the conclusion of Daniel 1, "And Daniel continued there until the first year of King Cyrus" (1:21). Daniel 3:1 begins a new unit as indicated by the new topic: "King Nebuchadnezzar made a golden statue. . . ." Our preaching text, therefore, is Daniel 2:1-49.

As to the context, chapter 2 continues the story of Daniel and his three friends of chapter 1, using both their Hebrew and Babylonian names (2:17, 49; cf. 1:7). Chapter 2 also has many links with the following chapters. The information about Daniel and his friends being promoted to high office in Babylon (2:48-49) prepares us for chapter 3 where jealous astrologers report to Nebuchadnezzar that Daniel's friends do not bow down to the king's statue and he orders them thrown into the fiery furnace. Many of the expressions and ideas found in chapter 2 return in chapter 4, where Daniel interprets another dream of Nebuchadnezzar.[7] The four kingdoms of Daniel 2 reappear in chapter 7 as four beasts rising out of the sea.[8] And Daniel's statement in his prayer that God "reveals deep and hidden things" (2:22), while directly related to Nebuchadnezzar's dream, prepares the way for God's revealing hidden things in Daniel's own four visions in chapters 7 to 12.

Daniel 2 also displays many parallels with other Old Testament passages. The similarities with Joseph interpreting Pharaoh's dream (Gen 41) are obvious: both Joseph and Daniel acknowledge that only God can interpret dreams (Gen 40:8; 41:16; Dan 2:28), assure the king that their interpretation will happen (Gen 41:25, 28; Dan 2:28), and rise to prominence because of their ability to in-

---

6. See chapter 1 above, pp. 30-31.

7. E.g., Nebuchadnezzar's first calling his wise men (4:6), the listing of the wise men and their failure at interpretation (4:7), finally Daniel coming in (4:8), being the "chief of the magicians" (4:9), and giving the correct interpretation (4:10-27). See further, Goldingay, *Daniel,* 38.

8. Daniel 2 and 7 are the first and the last narratives in the Aramaic section of Daniel, thus forming the bookends of a chiastic structure ABCC'B'A'. See Introduction above, pp. 20, 21.

terpret dreams (Gen 41:40; Dan 2:48).[9] Daniel 2 also contains many echoes of Isaiah 40–66. In the words of Goldingay: "Those chapters, too, suggest that silver and gold, bronze and iron, end up useless as clay (40:19; 45:2; 41:25), crushed and blown away like chaff (41:15-16; also 41:12; cf. Dan 2:35). They, too, see Israel's God as Lord even of things hidden in darkness, the Lord of light and darkness (45:3, 7; cf. Dan 2:22). They, too, picture the nations and their kings doing obeisance before the exiles and their God (45:3, 14; 49:23; 60:6-7, 14) . . . [cf. Dan 2:46-47]. They, too, promise an ultimate realization of the Lord's kingship (44:6; 52:7 [cf. Dan 2:44-45])."[10]

Literary Features

In Daniel 2:4, "The Chaldeans said to the king (in Aramaic)," the language switches from Hebrew to Aramaic and will remain in Aramaic until it switches back to Hebrew in chapter 8:1.[11] The narrative, as expected, is written in prose but switches to poetry for the prayer of Daniel (2:20-23). We shall analyze in more detail the structure of this narrative, its plot line, character description, and repetition.

Narrative Structure

Scenes can usually be identified by a change in location, time, and at least one of the characters. Each scene usually has two characters.[12] This narrative con-

---

9. For further details, see Collins, *Daniel*, 39-40, and Segal, "From Joseph to Daniel: The Literary Developments of the Narrative in Daniel 2," *VT* 59/1 (2009) 142. Collins, *Daniel*, 39, writes, "Though some of these similarities derive from the common setting in a Near Eastern court and the common concern for dream interpretation, the verbal correspondences make it highly likely that the author of Daniel knew and was influenced by the story of Joseph."

10. Goldingay, *Daniel*, 37-38.

11. For more information on the Aramaic language and the possible reasons for it in Daniel, see the Introduction above, p. 16.

12. Commentators disagree on what constitutes a scene and therefore arrive at different numbers of scenes. For example, Towner, *Daniel*, 31, comes up with five scenes (2:1-12, 13-23, 24-30, 31-45, 46-49), which is followed by Goldingay, *Daniel*, 41-42, and Redditt, *Daniel*, 51 (different from my five scenes focusing on changes in location), while Lucas, *Daniel*, 67, sees six "acts," and Venter, "The Function of Poetic Speech in the Narrative in Daniel 2," *HervTS* 49/4 (1993) 1015, comes up with "three episodes and eight scenes." I will follow the definition of Jacob Licht, *Storytelling in the Bible* (Jerusalem: Magnes, 1978), 29: "Each scene presents the happenings of a particular place and time, concentrating the attention of the audience on the deeds and the words spoken." Another marker for detecting scenes is that usually each scene has only two characters (see Robert Alter, *The Art of Biblical Narrative* [New York: Basic Books, 1985], 72).

sists of five scenes arranged as a chiastic structure, ABCB′A′, centering on God's revealing "the mystery" to Daniel and Daniel blessing God.[13]

Scene 1: The king's throne room: the failure of Babylon's wise men   (2:1-13)
    A. The king is troubled by his dreams   (2:1)
    B. He commands his wise men to tell him his dream; they fail   (2:2-11)
    C. The king decrees to kill all wise men   (2:12-13)
    Characters: King Nebuchadnezzar and his wise men

Scene 2: The king's palace: Daniel requests more time   (2:14-16)
    A. Daniel asks Arioch why the decree is so urgent   (2:14-15)
    B. Daniel asks for more time   (2:16)
    Characters: Daniel and Arioch

Scene 3: Daniel's home: God reveals the king's dream   (2:17-23)
    A. Daniel and his friends plead with God   (2:17-18)
    B. God reveals the mystery in a vision   (2:19)
    C. Daniel blesses God   (2:20-23)
    Characters: Daniel/friends and God

Scene 4: The king's palace: Daniel requests to see the king   (2:24-25)
    A. Daniel asks Arioch to be brought before the king   (2:24)
    B. Arioch tells the king about Daniel   (2:25)
    Characters: Daniel and Arioch

Scene 5: The king's throne room: Daniel tells the dream and
its interpretation   (2:26-49)
    A. Daniel witnesses to the king about "the God of heaven"   (2:26-30)
    B. Daniel recounts the dream for the king   (2:31-35)
    C. Daniel gives the king the interpretation of the dream   (2:36-45)
    D. The king responds by honoring Daniel, his God, and friends   (2:46-49)
    Characters: Daniel and the king

This chiastic arrangement focusing on scene 3 will help us in discerning the theme of this narrative. The narrator further highlights these verses by switching from prose to poetry when he comes to Daniel's prayer blessing God (2:20-23).

---

13. I am indebted to my proofreader, Ryan Faber, for detecting that Daniel 2:24-25 is a separate, fourth, scene so that the scenes form a chiastic structure.

The Plot Line

Tracing the plot line will not only help us in discerning the theme of this narrative but also in designing a narrative sermon form. Daniel 2:1a gives the setting: "In the second year of Nebuchadnezzar's reign." There are no preliminary incidents; the narrator begins immediately with the occasioning incident: "Nebuchadnezzar dreamed such dreams that his spirit was troubled and his sleep left him." The king calls for his wise men to tell him his dream (2:1b-3). The narrative time taken for the dialogue between the king and his wise men (2:3-11) is pace retardation, which gradually increases the tension.

The conflict begins when the wise men ask the king to tell them his dream so that they can interpret it, but the king refuses, threatening severe punishment if they fail to tell him his dream but offering rewards if they do so (2:4-6). The tension rises when the wise men again ask that the king tell them his dream and the king accuses them of conspiring to lie to him. This time the king offers no rewards, just severe punishment for failure (2:7-9). The tension rises still further when the astrologers say that the king is asking the impossible. The king flies into a rage and decrees the death penalty for all the wise men in Babylon (2:10-12).[14] The tension rises still higher when the narrator informs us that Daniel and his friends are also to be executed (2:13). Daniel asks the chief executioner why the king is in such a hurry to have his wise men killed. Hearing the explanation, Daniel asks for more time and says that he will tell the king the interpretation (2:14-16). Then Daniel goes home and invites his friends to pray with him for God's mercy (2:17-18).

The turn to the resolution comes in God's answer to their prayers: "Then the mystery was revealed [divine passive][15] to Daniel in a vision of the night" (2:19). Before Daniel tells the king, he blesses "the God of heaven," who "deposes kings and sets up kings. . . . He reveals deep and hidden things" (2:20-23). Next he asks Arioch, the chief executioner, to bring him before the king (2:24-25). The king asks Daniel to tell him the dream and its interpretation, but before Daniel does so, he credits God for revealing the mystery (2:26-30). Then Daniel relates the dream and gives its interpretation: "In the days of those kings the God of heaven will set up a kingdom that shall never be destroyed" (2:31-45). There is still some tension: Will the king accept Daniel's interpretation? The tension is fully resolved when the king falls on his face before Daniel and

14. For this escalation from punishment and reward to punishment to the death penalty, see Michael Segal, "From Joseph to Daniel: The Literary Developments of the Narrative in Daniel 2," *VT* 59/1 (2009) 125.

15. Narrators will use a "divine passive" when they wish to indicate God's activity in a veiled way. The implication here is that *God* revealed the mystery to Daniel. On the divine passive, see further below, p. 155, n. 27, and p. 276, n. 79.

praises Daniel's God (2:46-47). The outcome is that the king promotes Daniel and his friends (2:48-49).

We can sketch the plot line as a single plot:

			Climax		
	17-18	Daniel/friends pray	19	God reveals mystery to Daniel
			20-23	Daniel blesses God
14-16	Daniel asks for time	24-25	Daniel asks to see the king
13	Kill Daniel and friends	26-30	Daniel credits God
10-12	Kill the wise men!	31-35	Daniel tells king the dream
7-9	punishment	36-41	Daniel gives its interpretation
4-6	punishment and reward	46-47	the king praises God

Setting	*Occasioning incident*	*Rising tension*		*Resolution*	*Outcome*
Dan 2:1a	2:1b-3				2:48-49
Second	Neb. dreams				King promotes
year	Demand:				Daniel and
Neb.	**Tell the dream!**				friends

Character Description

The characters are sketched partly by character description, which is unusual and therefore significant in Hebrew narrative, but mostly by dialogue. The narrator begins by describing the king as being "troubled" (2:1; cf. 2:3), noting also his "violent rage" (2:12). The character of the king is further developed by his speeches, which show him to be suspicious, unreasonable, stubborn, short-tempered, angry, and cruel. The king's wise men, by contrast, appear to be patient but helpless. After Daniel tells the king his dream and its interpretation, the king's closing speech honoring Daniel's God reveals that he is deeply religious, while his action in promoting Daniel and his friends shows that he can also be generous.

The narrator describes the character of Daniel with the words "prudence and discretion" (2:14). His question to Arioch (2:15) confirms Daniel's prudence and discretion, while his statement, even before God revealed the dream, that "he would tell the king the interpretation" (2:16) shows his boldness and confidence in God. Daniel's prayer further reveals his piety, while his long speech to the king reveals both his faith in God's revelation (2:28) and his humility (2:30).

Repetition

We should also note some of the repetitions since they frequently indicate what the author wishes to highlight. The narrative begins with Nebuchadnezzar dreaming dreams. The narrator uses the word "dream" fifteen times (*ḥălôm* in 2:1, 2, 3 [2x], and *ḥĕlem* in 2:4, 5, 6 [2x], 7, 9 [2x], 26, 28, 36, and 45). Along with the word "dream," he repeats the word "interpretation" thirteen times (*pešar* in 2:4, 5, 6 [2x], 7, 9, 16, 24, 25, 26, 30, 36, and 45). He lists four categories of wise men: "the magicians, the enchanters, the sorcerers, and the Chaldeans" (2:2) and repeats a similar listing in 2:10 and 27.[16] The narrator uses the word "mystery" eight times (*rāz* in 2:18, 19, 27, 28, 29, 30, and 47 [2x]) and the word "reveal" six times (*gelah* in 2:19, 22, 28, 29, 30, and 47). Three times Daniel states that God reveals mysteries (2:22-23, 28, 29) — a thought later echoed by Nebuchadnezzar himself (2:47). Twice Daniel repeats "what would/shall be hereafter" (2:29, 45). He also mentions twice that the stone was cut out "not by human hands" (2:34, 45). Four times he names God "the God of heaven" (2:18, 19, 37 and 44) — "the name speaks to God's transcendence and supremacy over all that is temporal and earthbound."[17] And perhaps most importantly for discerning the theme, in the interpretation of the dream he repeats the word "kingdom" nine times (2:37, 39 [2x], 40, 41, 42, 44 ([3x]).

Theocentric Interpretation

In this narrative God provides the solution to the problem. The king demands that the wise men tell him his dream, but they rightly respond: "No one can reveal it to the king except the gods, whose dwelling is not with mortals" (2:11). In response to the prayer of Daniel and his friends, the God of heaven reveals (divine passive in the original) the mystery to Daniel. Daniel blesses "the God of heaven" — the God who is far superior to the Babylonian gods of sun, moon, and stars. Daniel prays, "Blessed be the name of God from age to age, for wisdom and power are his. He . . . deposes kings and sets up kings. . . . He reveals deep and hidden things. . . . To you, O God of my ancestors, I give thanks and praise, for you have given me wisdom and power . . ." (2:20-23).

When Daniel comes before the king, the first thing he tells him is, "No wise men, enchanters, magicians, or diviners can show to the king the mystery that the king is asking, but there is a God in heaven who reveals mysteries" (2:27-28). And in interpreting the dream he tells the great king clearly that "the God of heaven has given [you] the kingdom, the power, the might, and the glory" (2:37). But it will not last. God will give Nebuchadnezzar's kingdom to another,

---

16. "They are all variant synonyms for the Babylonian diviners whose role was central to Babylonian religious and political life, though the author uses a number of the terms in combination to convey the impression of the various guilds." Goldingay, *Daniel*, 46.

17. Hill, "Daniel," 64.

to another, and to another until finally "the God of heaven will set up a king-dom that shall never be destroyed. . . . It shall crush all these kingdoms and bring them to an end, and it shall stand forever" (2:44). Finally, the pagan king himself confesses (2:47), "Truly, your God is God of gods and Lord of kings and a revealer of mysteries, for you have been able to reveal this mystery!"

Textual Theme and Goal

Commentators do not agree on what constitutes the heart and thrust of this nar-rative. Some focus on the confession of King Nebuchadnezzar: "The theological message of the story is summed up in verse 47, when Nebuchadnezzar confesses that the God Daniel serves is 'God of gods and Lord of kings, and reveals myster-ies.'"[18] Others zero in on the prayer of Daniel: "The theological center of the chapter is not the dream and its interpretation, but Daniel's prayer (2:20-23). This prayer fuses the two major theological themes in the chapter: God governs all human history, and God alone grants knowledge and wisdom."[19]

But, one may ask, why look for the theme of the narrative in the confession of a pagan king or in the prayer of a faithful Israelite? After all, the whole narra-tive (see the plot line above) turns on the question of God's revelation to Nebuchadnezzar in a dream about what will be "hereafter" (2:29). In answer to prayer, God reveals this "mystery" to Daniel (2:19), who reports it to the king (2:27-45): "The great God has informed the king what shall be hereafter. The dream is certain, and its interpretation trustworthy" (2:45). Venter notes that "sixty-six percent of the total discourse time is spent in . . . [vv. 29-45], telling

18. Lucas, *Daniel*, 78. Cf. p. 77, "The terms used of 'your' (Daniel's) God in Nebuchad-nezzar's confession (47) really sum up the message of this story." So also Anderson, *Signs and Wonders*, 26, "Nebuchadnezzar's confession that the God of Daniel is truly 'God of gods and Lord of kings, and a revealer of mysteries . . .' (v. 47) is the climactic point of the chapter." Cf. Collins, *Apocalyptic Vision*, 13, "The effect of . . . chapter [2] is not primarily to present an escha-tological vision but to demonstrate the superiority of Daniel over the pagan wise men. The king reacts by praising Daniel's god for his power to reveal secrets — not for his power to control his-tory." Cf. Smith-Christopher, "Book of Daniel," 51, "The theme, as many scholars have pointed out, is that the wisdom of the world will prove impotent before knowledge of the true God." Longman, *Daniel*, 73, formulates the theme of this narrative as, "Only God's wisdom can reveal the mysteries of life." He adds, "It is not the content of the revelation of the future that is pri-mary; what is most important here is the fact that it is only Daniel's God that knows that fu-ture." See also ibid., p. 84.

19. Steinmann, *Daniel*, 109. Cf. p. 124. Goldingay, *Daniel*, 41, sees two facets, "a theme within a theme": "Both facets (and the whole chapter) reflect the unique sovereign power of the God of Israel, simultaneously unveiled to and concealed from Nebuchadnezzar, relied on by Daniel, revealed through and in the dream/vision, and recognized by Nebuchadnezzar. Only God controls history, and only he reveals what it holds."

what the contents of the dream and its future meaning are." He concludes, therefore, that "the basic theme of the narrative is the dream and its meaning. This is the object searched for and found in the plot. God gives that revelation and the king's problem is solved. The poem [prayer] refers to that theme and makes it explicit to the reader."[20]

Focusing on the dream and its interpretation, the textual theme could be formulated as, "God's heavenly, everlasting kingdom is coming to replace all human kingdoms."[21] But because the narrator highlighted Daniel's prayer in poetry and made it part of the center of a chiastic structure, we should also consider incorporating its ideas into the theme. In the prayer Daniel says, the God of heaven "deposes kings and sets up kings" (2:21) — as we see in the interpretation of the dream, kingdoms going and coming. He says further, the God of heaven "reveals deep and hidden things" (2:22) — as he does when he reveals "the mystery" of the dream to Daniel (2:19) as well as its interpretation (2:28). Taking these ideas also into account, the textual theme can be formulated as follows, *The God of heaven, who deposes and sets up kings, reveals that in the end he will replace all human kingdoms with his everlasting kingdom.*

The author's goal for presenting this message to Israel depends on the historical circumstances in which the first readers found themselves. Goldingay observes, "Like chapter 1, Daniel 2 presupposes a setting in a dispersion community where Jews are a religious and ethnic minority."[22] Chapter 1 reminded Israel that Babylon was a sinful kingdom ("the land of Shinar"; 1:2)[23] which rejected the God of heaven and oppressed God's people. The author's goal in chapter 2, then, was *to give hope to the Israelites in exile that their bondage would not last forever because their God could depose kings and in the end would replace all human kingdoms with his everlasting kingdom.*[24]

---

20. Venter, "The Function of Poetic Speech in the Narrative in Daniel 2," *HervTS* 49/4 (1993) 1,016 and 1,019.

21. Porteous, *Daniel*, 37, speaks of "the revelation regarding the course and climax of world history which the chapter is to record and which forms its kernel."

22. Goldingay, *Daniel*, 44. See also p. 51, "The implied readers of Daniel in the Persian period, perhaps disillusioned and depressed like those to whom prophecies in Haggai, Zechariah, and Isaiah 56–66 were addressed, are invited to hold onto the conviction that the Chaldean colossus will not stand forever. It has feet of clay." Cf. Towner, *Daniel*, 31.

23. "*Shinar* as a term for Babylonia, the southeastern part of modern Iraq, is an archaism in the OT. . . . The name especially suggests a place of false religion, self-will, and self-aggrandizement (Gen 11:1-9; Zech 5:11)." Goldingay, *Daniel*, 15.

24. Cf. Ferguson, *Daniel*, 66: "The people of God have the assurance from God's word of the ultimate triumph of the kingdom of God. In both the dream and the interpretation, this is the central fact."

Ways to Preach Christ

In this section we seek to list all legitimate ways to Jesus Christ in the New Testament. When we write the sermon, we can select one or more of the clearest roads to Christ. Since there is no promise of Christ in this narrative nor a contrast of its message with that of the New Testament,[25] we shall explore the remaining five ways: redemptive-historical progression, typology, analogy, longitudinal themes, and New Testament references.

Redemptive-Historical Progression

The textual theme is, "The God of heaven, who deposes and sets up kings, reveals that in the end he will replace all human kingdoms with his everlasting kingdom." In the beginning God established his kingdom on earth (Gen 1–2). Regrettably, because of the human fall into sin (Gen 3), people began to build their own autonomous kingdoms on earth: Cain built a city (Gen 4:17); later in defiance of God people settled in the land of Shinar[26] and built Babel (Gen 11:1-4). But God determined to restore his kingdom on earth. He called Abram to leave his country (Babylonia), kindred, and father's house to form a separate nation in the Promised Land. But Abraham's descendants, Israel, failed in their calling to be a holy nation. At last God cast Israel out of the Promised Land and sent them back to the land of Shinar (Babylonia). While Israel suffered in exile under various pagan kings, God had a message of hope for them. He gave King Nebuchadnezzar a dream, and revealed the dream and its meaning to Daniel. In the dream the series of human kingdoms were depicted as a huge statue of precious metals but standing on feet of iron mixed with clay. A stone was cut out, not with human hands, and smashed into the feet of the statue, whereupon all these human kingdoms broke in pieces and disappeared from the earth. But the stone "became a great mountain and filled the whole earth" (Dan 2:35). The kingdom of God will replace the human kingdoms and "shall stand *forever*" (2:44).

In New Testament times, the angel Gabriel announced to Mary that she would bear a son and that "he will reign over the house of Jacob *forever*, and of

---

25. Evans, "Daniel in the New Testament: Visions of God's Kingdom," 513, sees some contrast between Daniel's prayer that God "gives wisdom to the wise and knowledge to those who have understanding" (2:21b) and Jesus thanking his Father "because you have hidden these things from the wise and the intelligent and have revealed them to infants" (Matt 11:25). But Jesus' use of "the wise" is quite different from Daniel's use of "the wise" who receive this supernatural wisdom by revelation.

26. See n. 23 above.

his kingdom there will be no end" (Luke 1:33). When Jesus began his ministry, he came "proclaiming the good news of God, and saying, 'The time is fulfilled, and *the kingdom of God* has come near'" (Mark 1:14-15). Jesus clearly stated, "My kingdom is not from this world" (John 18:36). With Jesus' preaching and miracles he brought God's kingdom into this world. Jesus said, "If it is by the Spirit of God that I cast out demons, then the kingdom of God has come to you" (Matt 12:28).

But the Roman kingdom was still in charge. In fact, when Roman soldiers crucified Jesus, it looked as if the kingdom of God had failed. The sovereign God, however, turned defeat into victory. He raised Jesus from death. When the disciples met the risen Lord, they asked him, "Lord, is this the time when you will restore the kingdom to Israel?" They did not realize at that time that the kingdom of God is coming in two stages: the "already" with Jesus' first coming and the "not yet" with his second coming. Jesus replied, "It is not for you to know the times or periods that the Father has set by his own authority" (Acts 1:6-7). Then Jesus ascended into heaven, where he reigns at the right hand of God (Acts 2:32-36). But he promised to return at the time determined by his Father (John 14:3; cf. Matt 26:64). Then the "not yet" of the kingdom of God will also become the "already." John bears this out when he heard loud voices in heaven proclaiming, "The kingdom of the world has become the kingdom of our Lord and of his Messiah, and he will reign forever and ever" (Rev. 11:15).

Typology

The stone that "was cut out, not by human hands" (2:34) is a type of Christ.[27] Jerome thought that this phrase referred to Jesus' virgin birth. Other interpreters think that this phrase refers to the heavenly origin of the kingdom Jesus inaugurated. Jesus said, "My kingdom is not from this world. If my kingdom were from this world, my followers would be fighting to keep me from being handed over to the Jews. But as it is, my kingdom is not from here" (John 18:36). I think both interpretations are right. According to the New Testament, Jesus' conception was "not by human hands" but by the Holy Spirit (Matt 1:20). Jesus also saw *himself* as the stone. He asked the people, "Have you never read in the scriptures: 'The stone that the builders rejected [i.e., Jesus] has become the cornerstone . . .'? [Ps 118:22]. Therefore I tell you, the kingdom of God will be taken

---

27. "The stone, mentioned in verses 34-35 and interpreted in verse 44 as the Kingdom of God, belongs to the Messianic sphere. This follows from Genesis 28:10-22, and above all from one text so abundantly reused by Daniel, Genesis 49:24. God, as 'the rock of Israel,' supports Joseph." Lacocque, *Book of Daniel*, 52.

away from you and given to a people that produces the fruits of the kingdom. The one who falls on this stone will be broken to pieces; and it will crush anyone on whom it falls" (Matt 21:42-45). In the last sentence, Jesus clearly alludes to Daniel 2, for the stone struck the feet of the statue and crushed them; then the whole statue toppled and fell on the stone and was broken to pieces. However, when that stone becomes a great mountain that fills "the whole earth" (2:35), it can only refer to the kingdom of God which Jesus brings. The stone, therefore, is a type of both Jesus and his kingdom.

It is also possible to present Daniel again as a type of Christ, although the analogies are not as many as in the first chapter. In this narrative Daniel risked his life to save the lives of "the wise men of Babylon" (2:24); Jesus not only risked his life but willingly gave it up to save Jews and Gentiles who believe in him. Moreover, Daniel was a man of prayer who sought mercy from "the God of heaven"; Jesus also was a man of prayer who taught us, "Pray then in this way: Our Father in heaven" (Matt 6:9). Further, Daniel was able to reveal the mystery of the coming kingdom of God; Jesus, especially in his parables (e.g., Mark 4:26-32), revealed the mystery of the coming kingdom of God. And as God guided Daniel to a place of great authority in Babylon, so God guided Jesus to a place of much greater authority. Jesus said to the high priest, "I tell you, from now on you will see the Son of Man seated at the right hand of Power and coming on the clouds of heaven" (Matt 26:64). After his resurrection, he said to his disciples, "All authority in heaven and on earth has been given to me" (Matt 28:18).

Since one should not present two different types of Christ in a sermon, however, I would select the one that is most closely related to the theme. In this case, that would be the stone that "was cut out, not by human hands" (2:34).

Analogy

In the sermon we can also make our way to Christ in the New Testament by analogy. As Daniel 2 teaches that the kingdom of God will grow and fill "the whole earth" (2:35), so Jesus teaches that "the kingdom of heaven is like a mustard seed that someone took and sowed in his field; it is the smallest of all the seeds, but when it has grown it is the greatest of shrubs and becomes a tree, so that the birds of the air come and make nests in its branches" (Matt 13:31-32). To accomplish this growth, Jesus instructs his disciples, "You will be my witnesses in Jerusalem, in all Judea and Samaria, and to the ends of the earth" (Acts 1:8).

Another analogy can be drawn from the author's goal: as Daniel gave hope to the exiles with the message that the kingdom of God would replace all human kingdoms, so Jesus gives hope to his disciples and church: "Fear not, little flock, for it is your Father's good pleasure to give you the kingdom" (Luke 12:32). Moreover, when Jesus sends his disciples out into a hostile world, he comforts them, "Remember, I am with you always, to the end of the age" (Matt 28:20).

Longitudinal Themes

We can also use the way of longitudinal themes to move to Jesus Christ. Under redemptive-historical progression above we already traced the history of the coming kingdom of God through successive epochs of redemptive history.[28] We can also trace the theme of God's kingdom coming on earth from God's original intent in Genesis 1 and 2 to God's intent after the fall into sin to restore his kingdom on earth by calling out from the world a holy people (Abram/Israel) to represent his kingdom. Through his prophets God promised,

> I am about to create new heavens
>   and a new earth;
> the former things shall not be remembered
>   or come to mind.
> But be glad and rejoice forever in what I am creating;
>   for I am about to create Jerusalem as a joy,
>   and its people as a delight.
> I will rejoice in Jerusalem,
>   and delight in my people;
> no more shall the sound of weeping be heard in it,
>   or the cry of distress. . . .
> They shall build houses and inhabit them;
>   they shall plant vineyards and eat their fruit. . . .
> The wolf and the lamb shall feed together,
>   the lion shall eat straw like the ox;
>   but the serpent — its food shall be dust!
> They shall not hurt or destroy on all my holy mountain,
>   says the LORD.   (Isa 65:17-25; cf. Isa 11:6-9; Mic 4:1-5)

Other passages add that, in contrast to human kingdoms, the kingdom of God will last forever. The Psalmist proclaims,

> Your kingdom is an everlasting kingdom,
>   and your dominion endures throughout all generations.
>   (Ps 145:13; cf. Pss 10:16; 29:10; 146:10)

---

28. The ways of redemptive-historical progression and longitudinal themes are closely related and often intertwined.

In the New Testament Gabriel announces to Mary that her son "will reign over the house of Jacob *forever,* and of his kingdom there will be no end" (Luke 1:33). Peter also promises his readers that "you will receive a rich welcome into the *eternal* kingdom of our Lord and Savior Jesus Christ" (2 Pet 1:11). The letter to the Hebrews proclaims, "But of the Son he says, 'Your throne, O God, is forever and ever'" (Heb 1:8). The book of Revelation declares, "To him who loves us and freed us from our sins by his blood, and made us to be a kingdom, priests serving his God and Father, to him be glory and dominion forever and ever. Amen" (Rev. 1:6).[29] John adds his vision of the perfect kingdom of God coming on earth:

> Then I saw a new heaven and a new earth; for the first heaven and the first earth had passed away, and the sea was no more. And I saw the holy city, the new Jerusalem, coming down out of heaven from God, prepared as a bride adorned for her husband. And I heard a loud voice from the throne saying,

> "See, the home of God is among mortals.
> He will dwell with them as their God;
> they will be his peoples,
> and God himself will be with them;
> he will wipe every tear from their eyes.
> Death will be no more;
> mourning and crying and pain will be no more,
> for the first things have passed away." (Rev. 21:1-4)

New Testament References

The appendix to the Greek New Testament lists some thirty-four New Testament references or allusions to Daniel 2. Several of these we have already used above to support the various ways to Christ. Some of the other references are parallel Gospel passages or do not refer to Christ but to the use of Daniel 2 by other New Testament writers. Still other references, however, do refer to Jesus or his teachings.

For Daniel 2:28, "what will happen at the end of days," the appendix lists Jesus' statement in Matthew 24:6 (and par.), "You will hear of wars and rumors of wars; see that you are not alarmed; for this must take place, but the end is not yet."

For Daniel 2:47, "God of gods and Lord of kings and a revealer of myster-

---

29. Cf. Revelation 11:15, "Then the seventh angel blew his trumpet, and there were loud voices in heaven, saying, 'The kingdom of the world has become the kingdom of our Lord and of his Messiah, and he will reign forever and ever.'"

ies," it lists Jesus' words in Mark 4:11, "To you has been given the secret [*mystērion*] of the kingdom of God," and the phrase of Revelation 17:14, "The Lamb will conquer them, for he is Lord of lords and King of kings." (See also Rev. 19:16, "On his robe and on his thigh he has a name inscribed, 'King of kings and Lord of lords.'")

Sermon Theme, Goal, and Need

We formulated the textual theme as, "The God of heaven, who deposes and sets up kings, reveals that in the end he will replace all human kingdoms with his everlasting kingdom." Although Jesus came to usher in God's kingdom, he did not with his first coming replace all human kingdoms. Since this replacement still lies in the future (the "already" and the "not yet" of God's coming kingdom), we can keep the textual theme as the sermon theme: *The God of heaven, who deposes and sets up kings, reveals that in the end he will replace all human kingdoms with his everlasting kingdom.*

We formulated the author's goal as, "to give hope to the Israelites in exile that their bondage would not last forever because their God could depose kings and in the end would replace all human kingdoms with his everlasting kingdom." With a slight change, we can make the author's goal the goal for this sermon: *to give hope to God's people today with the message that our God can depose kings and in the end will replace all human kingdoms with his everlasting kingdom.*

This goal discloses the need to be addressed in this sermon: God's people today lack hope because of all the persecution and pain they see and experience in this world.

Scripture Reading and Sermon Introduction

Because of the length of this narrative, some have suggested preaching sermons on shorter "episodes" of the narrative.[30] But this is not a good idea since the narrator seeks to make his point with the whole narrative, not with individual "episodes." Because this narrative is fairly long, one may decide to omit its reading before the sermon and inform the congregation that the Scripture reading will be integrated into the sermon. Of course, in the sermon one need not touch on every verse, as I do in the "Sermon Exposition" below. Therefore, it

---

30. E.g., John G. Gammie, *Daniel,* 21-34, proposes a separate sermon on each of "five episodes": vv. 1-11, "That Unsettling Dream"; vv. 12-23, "The Urge to Destroy"; vv. 24-35, "The Purpose of Counsel"; vv. 36-45, "For Thine Is the Kingdom"; and vv. 46-49, "Athens Turns to Jerusalem."

may be possible to read the whole narrative before the sermon. For the sake of interest I suggest that the parts of the narrator and the various characters be divided among several good readers.

One must also give some thought to whether to include a formal introduction in the sermon. For example, one can begin the sermon with an illustration of Christians suffering persecution today, and then relate it to the Israelites suffering in exile ("By the rivers of Babylon — there we sat down and there we wept" [Ps 137:1]). In that setting hear the good news as it spoke to Israel then and to the suffering church today. But since the text is a narrative, and since story has the inherent power to draw people in, one can also omit a formal sermon introduction and begin immediately with the narrative. In the following exposition, I will omit a formal introduction and begin immediately with the narrative "setting."

Sermon Exposition

The great King Nebuchadnezzar wakes up in a sweat. He has had that frightening dream again — a nightmare! He is getting more and more upset. He had been a successful general. He had conquered many nations. Here he is king of the mightiest nation on earth, and he cannot get back to sleep. What is the meaning of these awful dreams? In the dreams he saw a huge statue of a man. The man had a head of gold, chest and arms of silver, middle and thighs of bronze, legs of iron, and feet partly of iron and partly of clay. Suddenly a stone is cut out of the mountain. It rolls down the hill and smashes the statue into powder. The wind blows the powder away. There is no trace of that big statue left. But, strangely, the stone begins to grow. It becomes a huge mountain, so huge that it fills the whole earth.[31]

The dream comes back night after night.[32] It fills the king with dread. In Babylonia people believed that the gods often spoke through dreams. It must be

31. Although the narrator does not divulge the dream until the fifth and last scene (2:31-35), since most people will know this story, I think it advantageous to describe it briefly at this stage. I also assume, contrary to some commentators (e.g., Calvin, *Commentaries on Daniel*, I, 119-20, and Baldwin, *Daniel*, 87-88), that the king remembered his dream; why else would he become so agitated that he could not sleep? Moreover, Young, *Prophecy of Daniel*, 58, notes that "this seems to be established by his desire to test the wise men (v. 9)." Miller, *Daniel*, 81, adds that this was "the understanding of the wise men, who continued to plead with him [the king] to reveal it." See also n. 37 below.

32. "Dreams" in 2:1 is plural, while the following narrative records only one dream. Collins, *Daniel*, 155, takes this usage to be "idiomatic" for the singular. Miller, *Daniel*, 77, understands the plural to mean that "the king was in a state of dreaming." Leupold, *Exposition of Daniel*, 82, writes that "the king dreamed several dreams, one of which finally roused and disturbed him." I rather like the suggestion of Wallace, *The Lord Is King*, 49, that it was a recurrent dream: "Yet night after night it happened — this dream!" So also Redditt, *Daniel*, 51.

an important message if the dream comes back night after night. But the king does not know what the dream means. This is only his second year as king of Babylon.[33] He probably wonders if the gods are trying to tell him that *he* is that huge statue of a man. Is there an enemy out there who will grind his great empire into the dust?[34] Is there an assassin out there waiting to do him in?[35] We read in verse 1 that "Nebuchadnezzar dreamed such dreams that his spirit was troubled and his sleep left him." "His spirit was troubled." He is so agitated that he cannot sleep anymore. If only he can find out the meaning of the dream — what the gods are trying to tell him. Well, that should be no problem for the king.

Verses 2 to 4, "So the king commanded that the magicians, the enchanters, the sorcerers, and the Chaldeans [astrologers][36] be summoned to tell the king his dreams. When they came in and stood before the king, he said to them, 'I have had such a dream that my spirit is troubled by the desire to understand[37] it.' The Chaldeans [astrologers] said to the king (in Aramaic), 'O king, live forever! Tell your servants the dream, and we will reveal the interpretation.'"

The king's wise men are gathered in the throne room, except for Daniel and his friends. Perhaps they were not invited because of some jealousy of these

---

33. The question has been raised how Daniel and his friends could be trained for three years (1:5) while this is Nebuchadnezzar's second year (2:1). Various answers have been suggested: (1) Since they counted a part of a year as a year, Daniel's training could have been less than two years (Miller, *Daniel*, 77). (2) Nebuchadnezzar first reigned with his father and then alone; this is the second year of his sole rule (Calvin, *Commentaries on Daniel*, I, 116). (3) Miller, *Daniel*, 76, writes: "Driver explains the three years on the basis of the accession year reckoning employed in Babylon . . . [see Introduction above, p. 11]. By this method the time until the first Nisan (March-April) is considered the accession year of the king, not his first year (see chart)."

Years of Training	Year of King's Reign	Date
First	Accession year	From Sept. 605 (Neb. assumed throne) to Nisan (March-April) 604 B.C.
Second	First year	Nisan 604-603 B.C.
Third	Second year	Nisan 603-602 B.C.

34. "We know from other historical sources that his expansionist policy met with some fierce resistance during the early years of his reign." Ferguson, *Daniel*, 50.

35. "Two out of the next three Babylonian kings were assassinated." Miller, *Daniel*, 82.

36. "The term may be understood in two ways in Daniel: either to refer to the Babylonian people generally in an ethnic sense (see . . . 1:4) or (in a more restricted sense) to delineate a special class of Babylonian priest-scholar. . . . No doubt their expertise includes but is not restricted to astrology, as evidenced by the use of the term elsewhere in Daniel (e.g., 2:5, 10; 4:7; 5:7, 11)." Hill, "Daniel," 62.

37. "The king says (lit.), 'my spirit is troubled to know the dream.' Does this mean that he has forgotten it, as Josephus infers (*Ant.* 10.10.3)? . . . It seems reasonable to take 'know' here in the sense of 'perceiving the meaning of, understand.'" Lucas, *Daniel*, 70. Hence the NRSV translates, "to understand," and the NIV, "to know what it means."

bright, young Judeans. Anyway, they have just graduated from their reeducation program, so the wise men of Babylonia can do without these novices. With so many experts present — magicians, enchanters, sorcerers, and astrologers — they cover every field and will surely be able to help the king.[38]

But first the king must tell them the dream. They cannot interpret a dream without knowing its contents. Long ago the Pharaoh of Egypt also told his wise men his dreams about the cows and the ears of grain (Gen 41:17-24).[39] So here the astrologers say to the king, "Tell your servants the dream, and we will reveal the interpretation." Once they know the dream, they can check their dream manuals[40] to see what the dream means.

But the king refuses to tell them his dream. Verses 5 and 6, "The king answered the Chaldeans, 'This is a public decree: if you do not tell me *both the dream and its interpretation,* you shall be torn limb from limb, and your houses shall be laid in ruins. But if you do tell me *the dream and its interpretation,* you shall receive from me gifts and rewards and great honor. Therefore tell me *the dream and its interpretation.*'" Three times the king insists that they tell him the dream and its interpretation. He has received an important message from the gods. He wants to make sure that the wise men interpret it correctly. If he tells them his dream, they can come up with *any* interpretation. How is the king to know that it is the correct one? But if they can first tell the dream, the king will know that they are indeed in contact with the gods. Then the king will know that their interpretation is trustworthy.

The king uses the stick and carrot approach. If they do not do not tell him both the dream and its interpretation, they will be torn limb from limb. That's quite a stick. They will be dismembered either by being pulled apart or hacked to pieces. This kind of cruel punishment was widespread in the ancient Orient.[41] Nebuchadnezzar is not bluffing. In the next chapter he has Daniel's friends thrown into a fiery furnace. Later he will slaughter the sons of King Zedekiah before Zedekiah's eyes and then gash out his eyes (2 Kings 25:7). Nebuchadnezzar is not bluffing. But besides this big stick, he also offers a carrot. If they tell him the dream and its interpretation, they will receive gifts and rewards and great honor from the king.

---

38. "The variation of the terms in the different lists shows that the writer is not using them with any great exactness, but is simply piling up a number of terms to give a picture of an impressive group of experts whose failure offsets Daniel's success." Lucas, *Daniel,* 70.

39. For the similarities and differences between Genesis 41 and Daniel 2, see Goldingay, *Daniel,* 37 and 42-43. Cf. Michael Segal, "From Joseph to Daniel: The Literary Developments of the Narrative in Daniel 2," *VT* 59/1 (2009) 142-43.

40. "A number of extant dream-books were found in Mesopotamia, veritable reference works that the ancient diviners consulted on every conceivable dream scenario." Seow, *Daniel,* 39.

41. See Montgomery, *Book of Daniel,* 146.

What a predicament for the wise men! They cannot give an interpretation without knowing the dream. Verses 7 to 9, "They answered a second time, 'Let the king first tell his servants the dream, then we can give its interpretation.' The king answered, 'I know with certainty that you are trying to gain time, because you see I have firmly decreed: *if you do not tell me the dream, there is but one verdict for you*. You have agreed to speak lying and misleading words to me until things take a turn. Therefore, tell me the dream, and I shall know that you can give me its interpretation.'"

The king raises the stakes. In this second round he takes back the carrot and mentions only the stick: "if you do not tell me the dream, there is but one verdict for you," that is, being torn limb from limb. The king accuses his wise men of "trying to gain time" because they know that he will carry out his decree. He also accuses them of having "agreed to speak lying and misleading words to him until things take a turn" for the better. The king is getting angry now. The wise men had better come up with the dream, and do so quickly.

For a third and last time the wise men dare to speak to the king. Verses 10 and 11, "The Chaldeans answered the king, 'There is no one on earth who can reveal what the king demands! In fact no king, however great and powerful, has ever asked such a thing of any magician or enchanter or Chaldean. The thing that the king is asking is too difficult, and no one can reveal it to the king except the gods, whose dwelling is not with mortals.'" The wise men give up. What the king is asking is impossible. No king has ever asked this of his wise men. Here they are, all the wise men of Babylon — magicians, enchanters, sorcerers, and astrologers. They give up. They say, "The thing that the king is asking is too difficult, and no one can reveal it to the king except the gods," who do not live with human beings. The wise men admit that they have no contact with the gods.

Verse 12, "Because of this the king flew into a violent rage and commanded that all the wise men of Babylon be destroyed." After the first dialogue the king offered a stick and a carrot; after the second he threatened only with the stick of being torn limb from limb; now he commands that the stick be used and the wise men of Babylon be torn limb from limb.

Verse 13, "The decree was issued, and the wise men were about to be executed; and they looked for Daniel and his companions, to execute them." Even though Daniel and his friends are not in the throne room, they are not off the hook. They had graduated from their reeducation program and now belong to the class of wise men. So they are about to be executed along with the other wise men of Babylon. Daniel and his friends are about to be slaughtered. What are they to do?

Daniel has a plan that may yet save them and all the wise men in Babylon. He seeks out the chief *executioner*, of all people. Verses 14 and 15, "Then Daniel responded with prudence and discretion to Arioch, the king's chief executioner, who had gone out to execute the wise men of Babylon; he asked Arioch, the royal official, 'Why is the decree of the king so urgent?' [Why is the king in such a hurry to execute all his wise men?] Arioch then explained the matter to Daniel." When Arioch fills Daniel in, Daniel responds that he will be able to tell the dream and its interpretation, but he needs time. Arioch agrees. We read in verse 16, "So Daniel went in and requested that the king give him time and he would tell the king the interpretation."[42]

Verses 17 and 18, "Then Daniel went to his home and informed his companions, Hananiah, Mishael, and Azariah,[43] and told them to seek mercy from the God of heaven concerning this mystery, so that Daniel and his companions with the rest of the wise men of Babylon might not perish." The mystery here is the contents of the king's dream and its interpretation.[44] At stake are the lives of Daniel, his companions, and the other wise men of Babylon. You can imagine that Daniel and his friends pray fervently to the God of heaven — the transcendent God, the God who created and controls the sun, moon, and stars, the gods of the Babylonians — the God of heaven who controls all of history.

That very night, verse 19, "The mystery was revealed to Daniel in a vision of the night,[45] and Daniel blessed the God of heaven." Daniel responds to God's miraculous revelation with a prayer of thanksgiving.[46] He says, verse 20,

> "Blessed be the name of God from age to age,
>   for wisdom and power are his."

Daniel prays that the name of God, that is, God himself, may be praised from age to age because "wisdom and power are his."

---

42. "The account is quite evidently condensed at this point by the omission of certain obvious details of court etiquette. For everyone still knows, and more assuredly knew in Daniel's day, that it was quite unthinkable that any man should venture into the king's presence unannounced or unsummoned, cf. Esther 4:11." Leupold, *Exposition of Daniel,* 96.

43. In requesting his companions to join him in praying to the God of heaven, the author uses their Hebrew names which testify to the God of Israel, respectively to Yahweh, El, and Yahweh. See Chapter 1 above, p. 47.

44. "Initially, here, the connotation [of the word *rāz*, 'mystery'] seems to be simply the puzzle of the dream, but the dream itself is found to disclose an eschatological mystery. The word *rāz* may imply the expectation that the dream contains some such significant revelation." Collins, *Daniel,* 159. Cf. Lucas, *Daniel,* 72, "In the Dead Sea Scrolls it [the word *rāz*] seems to be almost a technical term for that which can be understood only by means of divine revelation, especially God's hidden purpose in history."

45. Note the divine passive. Anderson, *Signs and Wonders,* 15, observes, "There, in that brief statement, is contained one of the essential elements of the book. The God of heaven rules the course of history and reveals this to his faithful servant."

46. For a detailed analysis of this prayer, see Venter, "The Function of Poetic Speech in the Narrative of Daniel 2," *HervTS* 49/4 (1993) 1,009-14.

Daniel next elucidates God's wisdom and power. He begins in verse 21 by illustrating God's power:

"He changes times and seasons,
 deposes kings and sets up kings [as Daniel has seen in the night vision]."

In short, God is to be praised from age to age because he controls the seasons of nature as well as the history of this world. Next he explains God's wisdom,

"He gives wisdom[47] to the wise
 and knowledge to those who have understanding.
He reveals deep and hidden things [as Daniel has just experienced];
 he knows what is in the darkness, and light dwells with him."

What a comfort for Israel in exile to hear that God knows what is in the darkness. And God not only knows but also has the power to do something about it. That gives Israel hope for a better future.

God also "knows what is in the darkness" today. We are appalled to read that today "100 million Christians are persecuted worldwide"[48] — 100 million! But we also can take comfort from the fact that "God knows what is in the darkness." We are shocked to hear of calamities striking our friends and families. But we also can take comfort from the fact that "God knows what is in the darkness." And our God has the power to do something about it. He controls human history!

Daniel concludes his thanksgiving in verse 23,

"To you, O God of my ancestors, I give thanks and praise,
 for you have given me wisdom and power,
  and have now revealed to me what we asked of you,
  for you have revealed to us what the king ordered."

After giving thanks to God for revealing the king's dream to him, we read in verses 24 and 25, "Therefore Daniel went to Arioch, whom the king had appointed to destroy the wise men of Babylon, and said to him, 'Do not destroy the wise men of Babylon; bring me in before the king, and I will give the king the interpretation.' Then Arioch quickly brought Daniel before the king and said to him: 'I have found among the exiles from Judah a man who can tell the king the interpretation.'" Arioch, of course, had not found anyone; Daniel had

---

47. "The 'wisdom' of vv. 20-23 is again supernatural insight rather than empirical, rational knowledge. It is not something human beings achieve but something they receive from God by revelation, equivalent to the knowledge of God's purposes that prophets receive from being admitted to Yahweh's council." Goldingay, *Daniel*, 48.

48. "Open Doors' 2009 World Watch List."

sought him out. But Arioch wants to take some credit for resolving the national crisis: "*I have found* . . . a man who can tell the king the interpretation." The *interpretation!* But the king wants to hear the *dream* so as to know that the interpretation is trustworthy.

Not surprisingly, verse 26, "The king said to Daniel, whose name was Belteshazzar,[49] 'Are you able to tell me the *dream* that I have seen and its interpretation?'" Daniel does not respond with a quick, "Yes, I can." Instead of taking credit for himself the way Arioch had done, Daniel gives his God the credit. He answers the king in verses 27 to 30, "No wise men, enchanters, magicians, or diviners can show to the king the mystery that the king is asking, but there is a *God in heaven who reveals mysteries,*[50] and he has disclosed to King Nebuchadnezzar what will happen at the end of days [i.e., "the closing days of history . . . when God will bring in this kingdom"].[51] Your dream and the visions of your head as you lay in bed were these: To you, O king, as you lay in bed, came thoughts of what would be *hereafter*, and the revealer of mysteries disclosed to you *what is to be*. But as for me, this mystery has not been revealed to me because of any wisdom that I have more than any other living being, but in order that the interpretation may be known to the king and that you may understand the thoughts of your mind." Daniel again refuses to take any credit. It's not his wisdom, nor the education he received in Babylon. All the credit belongs to the God of heaven who reveals mysteries.[52]

By this time, we can imagine, the king is getting a little impatient. Is Daniel stalling for time like the wise men were? But finally Daniel is ready to relate the king's dream. Verses 31 to 33: "You were looking,[53] O king, and lo! there was a

---

49. Ironically, Daniel, who was renamed Belteshazzar after the king's god Bel, "comes to the king as a Jewish exile (v. 25) who had received his revelation from his father's God (v. 23)." Goldingay, *Daniel*, 57.

50. Note the parallel and contrast to the wise men's statement in verses 10-11.

51. Porteous, *Daniel*, 44. Some commentators take the phrase "at the end of days" in Daniel (2:28 and 10:14) to refer to "a definite change in the future but not to an end of history" (e.g., Collins, *Daniel*, 161, and Seow, *Daniel*, 43), while others understand it as referring to "the time of fulfillment," in this context with an "eschatological perspective" (e.g., Goldingay, *Daniel*, 48, 56; cf. Miller, *Daniel*, 90), and still others understand it more specifically as "the messianic era" (Steinmann, *Daniel*, 26, 133), "the coming of the messianic age which God will bring in as the climax of history" (Russell, *Daniel*, 47). The context in Daniel 2 makes clear that "at the end of days" refers to the end of human history when human kingdoms will be replaced by the kingdom of God (v. 44). Cf. the same phrase in Hebrew in 10:14 in the context of the final vision with its double resurrection (12:2, 13) and the fullness of God's kingdom (12:3).

52. "Daniel's success is owing neither to his personal gifts nor to his Chaldean education, but to the wisdom and the power of God alone." Seow, *Daniel*, 37.

53. "The verb 'to be' with the participle (*ḥāzēh*) is a distinctively Aramaic way of expressing continued action which is found frequently in this book. It pictures how the king was entranced by the sight, unable to take his eye off what he saw." Leupold, *Exposition of Daniel*, 107.

great statue. This statue was huge, its brilliance extraordinary; it was standing before you, and its appearance was frightening. [No wonder the king's spirit was troubled.] The head of that statue was of fine gold, its chest and arms of silver, its middle and thighs of bronze, its legs of iron,[54] its feet partly of iron and partly of clay." Notice that the statue is of human design and making, just like the tower of Babel (Gen 11). Only here, instead of brick and bitumen, this monument is made of precious metals: gold, silver, bronze, iron, and iron and clay.[55] It is a statue of a human made by human hands.

Verses 34 and 35 contrast the statue with the stone: "As you looked on, a stone [an insignificant, valueless stone][56] was cut out, *not by human hands,*[57] and it struck the statue on its feet of iron and clay and broke them in pieces. Then the iron, the clay, the bronze, the silver, and the gold, were all broken in pieces [the statue collapsed and its various parts smashed on the stone] and became like the chaff of the summer threshing floors; and the wind carried them away, so that not a trace of them could be found.[58] But the stone that struck the statue became a great mountain[59] and filled the whole earth."[60]

54. "In his *Works and Days,* 109-201, he [the Greek poet Hesiod (eighth century b.c.)] divides history into five eras. Four are characterized by metals, in the sequence of gold, silver, bronze and iron. Between the bronze era and the iron he inserts the era of the Greek heroes, without linking it to any metal. This sequence of metals . . . seems to rest on the historical memory of the transition from the Bronze Age to the Iron Age. In describing the era of bronze, the poet comments, 'of bronze were their implements: there was no black iron' (line 151)." Lucas, *Daniel,* 73. Cf. Collins, *Daniel,* 162-65.

55. "As one moves down the sequence of metals in the statue, its splendor dissipates (from gold to iron and clay) but its hardness increases (from gold to iron)." Hill, "Daniel," 67. Cf. Baldwin, *Daniel,* 92, "From its head of gold to its fragile feet of glazed china mixed with iron it represented a top-heavy figure, liable to topple to its ruin."

56. "The valuable and precious statue contrasts directly with the unimpressive, dull, valueless stone. The difference between the stone and the statue is that no man's hand has touched the stone." Nel, "A Literary-Historical Analysis of Daniel 2," *Acta Theologica* 22/1 (2002) 88.

57. "A stone cut 'not by human hands,' an expression that occurs also in 8:25 and meaning probably that it originates by divine will and power (see also Job 34:20). . . ." Seow, *Daniel,* 44. Cf. Anderson, *Signs and Wonders,* 20, "The complete independence of the destructive stone is asserted. It has required no human aid to exist nor any human aid to act. Yet the result is eminently effective and the telling of it is as brief as it is dramatic."

58. "The wind sweeping away the remnants of the statue (2:35) points to this being a dream whose meaning is about history and eschatology. The image of chaff being swept away by the wind is a familiar one in the OT [see Isa 41:15-16]. This metaphor combines the concepts of transience and impermanence with the ease with which God can sweep away humans and their achievements." Steinmann, *Daniel,* 135-36.

59. Cf. Isaiah 2:2 (par. Mic 4:1), "In days to come the mountain of the Lord's house shall be established as the highest of the mountains."

60. Cf. Isaiah 11:9, "They will not hurt or destroy on all my holy mountain; for the earth will be full of the knowledge of the Lord as the waters cover the sea."

Now suppose the new king, only in his second year, thought that this statue represented him. In his dream he sees a stone cut out and striking the statue, reducing him to dust. And then that stone becomes a great mountain filling the whole earth. There must be an enemy lurking out there, ready to destroy him.[61] No wonder his spirit was troubled. No wonder he insisted on getting a trustworthy interpretation.

But Daniel is able to reassure the king. Verses 36 to 38, "This was the dream; now we[62] will tell the king its interpretation. You, O king, the king of kings — to whom the God of heaven has given the kingdom, the power, the might, and the glory, into whose hand he has given human beings, wherever they live, the wild animals of the field, and the birds of the air, and whom he has established as ruler over them all — you are the head of gold." That makes the king feel a lot better. He is the head of *gold* — precious. He is calling the shots. He has power over human beings and even over "the wild animals of the field." As a symbol of his power over wild animals,[63] he even keeps ferocious lions in a lions' den. Nebuchadnezzar[64] is the head of gold.

But notice that Daniel insists that this "king of kings" did not become that head of gold by his own power and ingenuity. The God of heaven has given him "the kingdom, the power, the might, and the glory." No matter how great the king, in the final analysis all that he has is given to him by the God of heaven. The God of heaven is the sovereign God. He is "the Lord of kings" (v. 47). He controls history and the destiny of kings and peoples.

Daniel continues in verses 39 to 43, "After you shall arise another kingdom inferior to yours [still a splendid kingdom, silver, but not as glorious as that of Babylon], and yet a third kingdom of bronze, which shall rule over the whole earth.[65] And there shall be a fourth kingdom, strong as iron; just as iron crushes

---

61. See Baldwin, *Daniel*, 92.

62. "While the pl might denote deference/meekness (cf. v. 30), less plausible reference to the divine council or use of the 'royal we,' the incidental but deliberate emphasis on including the friends in vv. 17-18, 23, 49 suggests that this is also the point here." Goldingay, *Daniel*, 35.

63. "The Babylonian kings generally pretended that they ruled over the savage beasts and the wild birds. They kept animals captured while hunting in menageries, probably as symbols of their universal domination." Lacocque, *Book of Daniel*, 50. Cf. Jeremiah 27:6; 28:14.

64. "Frequently in Scripture the terms 'king' and 'kingdom' are employed interchangeably since the king was considered to be the embodiment of the kingdom. . . . Nebuchadnezzar *was* the Neo-Babylonian Empire, for after his forty-three-year reign the kingdom endured only about twenty-three years." Miller, *Daniel*, 93. Cf. Young, *Prophecy of Daniel*, 73-74.

65. "There can be no doubt that such a description ["rule over the whole earth"] applies far more accurately to the reign of Alexander the Great than it does to Persia. . . . Greece was universal in her sway." Young, *Messianic Prophecies*, 21. Cf. Ferguson, *Daniel*, 62-63, "Here we instinctively think of the remarkable rise to power of Alexander the Great, who is said to have wept while still in his twenties because there were no more lands for him to conquer."

and smashes everything, it shall crush and shatter all these.[66] As you saw the feet and toes partly of potter's clay and partly of iron, it shall be a divided kingdom; but some of the strength of iron shall be in it, as you saw the iron mixed with the clay. As the toes of the feet were part iron and part clay, so the kingdom shall be partly strong and partly brittle.[67] As you saw the iron mixed with clay, so will they mix with one another in marriage,[68] but they will not hold together, just as iron does not mix with clay."[69]

These four kingdoms have traditionally been identified as Babylon, Medo-Persia, Greece (Alexander the Great), and Rome.[70] But more important than identifying these kingdoms is detecting the message of this narrative.[71] This

---

66. "Five terms are utilized in this verse ('breaks,' 'smashes,' 'breaks to pieces,' 'crush,' 'break') to emphasize the tremendous power this fourth empire would exert. Rome ruled the nations with an iron hand and like a huge iron club shattered all who resisted its will." Miller, *Daniel*, 95.

67. "This lack of cohesion signifies the eventual dissolution of the Roman Empire, but the continuing influence of its institutions. Thus much of the heritage of Rome lasts even to this day, especially in the West (Europe and the Americas), but all attempts in subsequent history to revive a semblance of the Roman Empire with its power have failed." Steinmann, *Daniel*, 137.

68. Leupold, *Exposition of Daniel*, 120, suggests that this refers to "Roman stock and Germanic and other stock intermarried — a melting-pot experiment — but the resultant stock was not the material that enduring empires are made of." In contrast, Collins, *Daniel*, 170, sees this verse as "a reference to one or the other of the interdynastic marriages of the Ptolemies and Seleucids, the first being that of Antiochus II to Bernice in 252 B.C.E., the second that of Ptolemy Epiphanes to Cleopatra, daughter of Antiochus III, in 193-192. These marriages are mentioned in Dan 11:6, 17."

69. "The quality of the respective empires deteriorates as one's gaze moves downward from the head of gold (Babylon) to the chest of silver, the belly and thighs of bronze, the legs of iron, and finally the feet of a mixture of iron and clay, but the picture as a whole is as impressive as the tower of Babel in Genesis 11. This is a glorious monument to human political achievement. However, the feet of iron and clay imply a fundamental instability to the colossus." Block, "Preaching Old Testament Apocalyptic," *CTJ* 41/1 (2006) 40.

70. See the note on Daniel 2:32-43 in the *NIV Study Bible*. Many modern commentators argue for Babylon, Media, Persia, and Greece. See p. 54, n. 1 above.

71. Longman, *Daniel*, 82, cautions, "Though it [the dream] starts in the concrete present, it is a wrong strategy to proceed through history and associate the different stages of the statue with particular empires. The vision intends to communicate something more general, but also more grand: God is sovereign; he is in control despite present conditions." Cf. Lucas, *Daniel*, 79, "The 'mystery' it [the dream] reveals is not the details of the course of events in history, but the fact that history is under the control of God and that it has a purpose, which will be achieved." Cf. Duguid, *Daniel*, 37, "The passage itself gives us virtually no data about the specifics of these kingdoms, because it intends to give a philosophy of history rather than a precise analysis of history ahead of time." These authors obviously wish to avoid the endless and fruitless debates about the identity of these kingdoms. But the solution does not lie in toning down the specificity of this revelation and turning it into a generalized philosophy of history (Dan 2:37-38 clearly identifies the kingdom of Babylon, while Dan 8:20-21 speaks specifically of the Medo-Persian kingdom and the kingdom of Greece) but in focusing on the specific message of this narrative.

message becomes crystal clear in verse 44, "And in the days of those kings[72] the God of heaven will set up a *kingdom* that shall never be destroyed, nor shall this kingdom be left to another people. It shall crush all these kingdoms and bring them to an end, and it shall stand *forever*."

After all these human kingdoms "the God of heaven will set up a kingdom that shall never be destroyed." The human kingdoms crumble, one after the other. They have "feet of clay." But God's kingdom is eternal. It "shall never be destroyed." "Nor shall this kingdom be left to another people." When the kingdom of Babylon fell, it was left to the Medo-Persian people, and when that kingdom collapsed, it was left to the Greek people, and when that kingdom caved in, it was left to the Roman people. Not so with the kingdom of God. It is eternal. It will not disintegrate, nor will it be left to another people.

On the contrary, Daniel says in verses 44-45 that the kingdom of God "shall crush all these kingdoms and bring them to an end . . . ; just as you saw that a stone was cut from the mountain not by hands, and that it crushed the iron, the bronze, the clay, the silver, and the gold." When God's kingdom comes in its fullness, it will not exist side by side with human kingdoms; it will destroy these evil kingdoms.[73] And then God's kingdom, like the stone in the dream, will grow and fill the whole earth. Daniel concludes in verse 45, "The great God has informed the king what shall be hereafter. The dream is certain, and its interpretation trustworthy."

In verses 46 and 47, the king responds to this message, "Then King Nebuchadnezzar fell on his face, worshiped Daniel, and commanded that a grain offering and incense be offered to him. The king said to Daniel, 'Truly, your God is God of gods and Lord of kings and a revealer of mysteries, for you have been able to reveal this mystery!'" We wonder why the humble Daniel now allows the king to worship him and even bring offerings to him. Could Daniel have been thinking of the prophecies of Isaiah where God promised, "Kings . . . shall bow down to you. . . . Then you will know that I am the LORD; those who wait for me shall not be put to shame" (Isa 49:23; cf. 60:14)?

The king had ordered Daniel's death. But Daniel and his friends pleaded with God. And they were not put to shame. The king who ordered Daniel's execution

---

72. "The toes, generally speaking, represent the kingdoms into which the Roman Empire broke up when the disintegration set in. . . . The number ten is definitely a symbolic number as are numbers generally in visions or dreams of this type. . . . Ten represents the totality of whatever number there is." Leupold, *Exposition of Daniel*, 122. The number "ten" is often read back into this chapter from the "ten horns" in Daniel 7:7 and the assumption that the statue must have had ten toes since normal people have ten toes. But since the number "ten" is not mentioned in this chapter, we should not complicate the sermon by making it an issue here.

73. "When God's time comes, his kingdom requires the destruction of earthly kingdoms rather than his working through them." Goldingay, *Daniel*, 59.

now bows down to him, for Daniel represents this God of heaven.[74] The king calls Daniel's God "a revealer of mysteries." Where Babylon's wise men had failed, Daniel came through. Where Babylon's gods were blind and inept, Daniel's God revealed the mystery. Therefore the king calls Daniel's God, "God of gods." He is greater than the Babylonian gods. And he calls him, "Lord of kings." For Daniel's God had given the king his kingdom and will give this kingdom to other kings until he makes an end of all human kingdoms and ushers in his own perfect kingdom. Daniel's God is sovereign over all: "God of gods and Lord of kings."

The story concludes in verses 48 and 49, "Then the king promoted Daniel, gave him many great gifts, and made him ruler over the whole province of Babylon and chief prefect over all the wise men of Babylon. Daniel made a request of the king, and he appointed Shadrach, Meshach, and Abednego over the affairs of the province of Babylon. But Daniel remained at the king's court."

The message God gives to Nebuchadnezzar is that the Babylonian kingdom will be replaced by another kingdom and another and another until finally the kingdom of God will replace all human kingdoms. This message is later recorded for God's people suffering in exile. Imagine the hope it brought to them: we may be far from the Promised Land, we may weep here in exile, but our God can depose kings and set up kings (2:21). The Babylonian kingdom will not last; it will be replaced by another kingdom and another until God's kingdom comes. God's kingdom is on the way; it will replace all human kingdoms; it will fill the whole earth; it will last forever.

Some five hundred years later, Jesus comes to earth. The kingdoms of Babylon, Medo-Persia, and Greece are long gone. Rome now rules the world. The angel Gabriel announces Jesus' birth to Mary: "He [Jesus] will reign over the house of Jacob *forever*, and of his *kingdom there will be no end*" (Luke 1:33). Some thirty years later, Jesus begins his ministry. He proclaims "the good news of God, and say[s], 'The time is fulfilled, and the *kingdom of God* has come near'" (Mark 1:14-15).[75] With Jesus' preaching and miracles he brings the kingdom of God into the world. Jesus says, "If it is by the Spirit of God that I cast out demons, then the *kingdom of God has come to you*" (Matt 12:28). But the kingdom of God does not come fully during Jesus' lifetime. The Roman kingdom is still in charge. In fact, when Roman soldiers crucify Jesus, it looks like the kingdom of God has failed.

---

74. "Daniel is honored because of what his God has done, not because of what he has done." Longman, *Daniel*, 82.

75. For arguments that "the book of Daniel may be the primary background to the Gospels' teaching about the Kingdom," see David Wenham, "The Kingdom of God and Daniel," *ExpTim* 98/5 (1987) 132-34; see also Craig Evans, "Daniel in the New Testament: Visions of God's Kingdom," 490-527. For the more general influence of Daniel on the New Testament, see Adela Yarbro Collins, "The Influence of Daniel on the New Testament," 90-123.

The sovereign God, however, can turn defeat into victory. He raises Jesus from death. When the disciples meet the risen Lord, they ask him, "Lord, is this the time when you will restore the kingdom to Israel?" They do not realize that God's kingdom will come in two stages: first, the "already" of the kingdom with Jesus' First Coming and, second, the "not yet" of the fullness of God's kingdom at Jesus' Second Coming. Jesus replies, "It is not for you to know the times or periods that the Father has set by his own authority" (Acts 1:6-7). Instead of satisfying their curiosity, Jesus sends his disciples on a mission: "You will be my witnesses in Jerusalem, in all Judea and Samaria, and to *the ends of the earth*" (Acts 1:8). The kingdom of God begins to spread to the ends of the earth.

It sounds just like the stone in the dream, doesn't it? "The stone that struck the statue became a great mountain and *filled the whole earth*" (Dan 2:35). As a matter of fact, Jesus also sees himself as the stone. At one point Jesus asks the people, "Have you never read in the scriptures: 'The stone that the builders rejected has become the cornerstone . . .'? The one who falls on this stone will be broken to pieces; and it will crush anyone on whom it falls" (Matt 21:42-45). In the dream, the stone struck the feet of the statue and crushed them; then the whole statue toppled and fell on the stone and was broken to pieces. The stone is Jesus. But when it begins to grow and fill the whole earth, it is also his kingdom.[76] The kingdom of God, the kingdom of Jesus Christ, is coming. It will replace all human kingdoms.

Many Christians today suffer at the hands of various states. Since 1990 an average of 160,000 Christians have been martyred every year.[77] 160,000 every year! It's hard to imagine the pain in these Christian communities. Of course, there are other forms of persecution than execution. Christians are arrested, imprisoned, tortured, and blacklisted so they cannot find work. As mentioned earlier, according to the latest estimates 100 million Christians are persecuted worldwide in countries like North Korea, Saudi Arabia, and Iran.[78] But even in countries where there is relative freedom, people suffer because of corruption in government, unjust wars, fraud, bribery, pork barrel bills, bad decisions leading to injustice. Human kingdoms are not getting any better. They can be cruel and evil.

But here is the good news: the kingdom of God has come with Jesus' First Coming and will come in perfection with his Second Coming. Just before Jesus

---

76. See p. 78, n. 64 above.

77. David Barrett and Todd M. Johnson, *World Christian Encyclopedia* (2d ed.; New York: Oxford University Press, 2001), I, 11. They estimate that the number of Christian martyrs in the twentieth century was 45 million people.

78. "Open Doors' 2009 World Watch List." For persecution in specific countries, see Paul Marshall, *Their Blood Cries Out: The Worldwide Tragedy of Modern Christians Who Are Dying for Their Faith.*

was crucified he told the high priest, "*From now on* you will see the Son of Man seated at the right hand of Power and coming on the clouds of heaven" (Matt 26:64). Even now Jesus is seated in heaven at the right hand of God the Father (Mark 16:19), ruling his church from his heavenly throne (Acts 2:32-36). When Jesus comes again, his kingdom will replace all earthly kingdoms and fill the whole earth. Then, as we read in Revelation (11:15), "The kingdom of the world has become the kingdom of our Lord and of his Messiah, and he will reign forever and ever."

So take heart! Whatever our circumstances, God's kingdom of peace and justice is on the way. Jesus himself offers us good hope. He encourages us, "Fear not, little flock, for it is your Father's good pleasure to *give you the kingdom*" (Luke 12:31-32).

> Jesus shall reign where'er the sun
> does its successive journeys run;
> his kingdom stretch from shore to shore,
> till moons shall wax and wane no more.
>
> Blessings abound where'er he reigns:
> the prisoners leap to lose their chains,
> the weary find eternal rest,
> and all who suffer want are blest.[79]

79. Isaac Watts, 1719, "Jesus Shall Reign," alt.

CHAPTER 3

Daniel's Friends in the Fiery Furnace

Daniel 3:1-30

"Who is the god that will deliver you out of my hands?"
"There is no other god [than Israel's God] who is able to deliver in this way."

Daniel 3:15, 29

Daniel 3 relates a fascinating story about God's ability to deliver his people even from certain death. This story offers comfort to God's suffering people today even as it comforted Israel suffering in exile. It will also encourage God's people to remain faithful to God no matter what threats they face.

Unfortunately, some commentators nudge preachers toward anthropocentric moralizing. One asserts, "It is worth noticing that there were only three men in the whole vast crowd who refused to bow down to Nebuchadnezzar's statue [3:12]. This highlights the fact that standing up for God will often be a lonely activity. There are times in every life when to do what is right we cannot simply hide in the crowd; we have to stand more or less alone."[1] This may be true enough, but it is not the point of this passage. Another commentator even uses the king's rage (3:19) as a warning example: "Do you respond with inordinate anger like Nebuchadnezzar? . . . The antidote to inordinate anger, or any other idolatrous response to not getting one's own way, is to give up the idol for the sake of God."[2] The only way to avoid this piecemeal moralizing is to focus the application on the goal the author intended for Israel in exile. Again, a ser-

1. Duguid, *Daniel*, 50. Miller, *Daniel*, 120, gets sidetracked on a questionable translation of verse 17: "Here is a pertinent lesson for believers today. Does God have all power? Yes. Is God able to deliver believers from all problems and trials? Yes. But does God deliver believers from all trials? No. . . ."

2. Schwab, *Daniel*, 53.

84

mon is more effective when it is shaped like a bullet that penetrates to the heart rather than birdshot that barely scratches the surface.

Text and Context

The textual unit, again, is quite obvious. Daniel 3:1 sets the stage for the new narrative: "King Nebuchadnezzar made a golden statue . . . in the province of Babylon." After the refusal of Shadrach, Meshach, and Abednego to bow to the statue, their punishment of being thrown into the fiery furnace, and their miraculous salvation, the story concludes, just like chapter 2:49, with the king promoting them in "the province of Babylon" (3:30).[3] The preaching text, therefore, is Daniel 3:1-30.

Although not as long as chapter 2, Daniel 3 is also a fairly long chapter.[4] Leupold rightly states, "It will hardly do to break up the chapter into several texts for separate sermons. It is too much of one piece for that." Instead of several preaching texts, he suggests reading the entire chapter before the sermon "and then, perhaps, choose verses 24-27 as a text, drawing upon the entire chapter in the course of the sermon whenever necessary."[5] I agree that the entire narrative should be read before the sermon, especially so that people hear the whole story at once and not miss the obvious satire in the back-to-back repetition of the long lists of "all the officials of the provinces" (vv. 2 and 3) and of the "entire musical ensemble" (vv. 5 and 7; see "Literary Features" below). But I suggest that the whole narrative serve as the preaching text because selecting only verses 24-27 neglects the powerful tension in the story: "If our God . . . is able to deliver us from the furnace of blazing fire. . . . But if not . . ." (vv. 17-18). Moreover, selecting only a part of the narrative might lead to a wrong theme.[6]

Within the book of Daniel this narrative about Daniel's three friends follows naturally upon 2:49, which informs us that the king "appointed Shadrach, Meshach, and Abednego over the affairs of the province of Babylon. But Daniel remained at the king's court." This explains the presence of the three friends in

---

3. The only question is whether 4:1-3, which is 3:31-33 in the Aramaic, concludes this narrative or belongs to the next narrative. It seems clear that these three verses belong to the next narrative (see pp. 115-16 below).

4. Roman Catholic preachers will have to deal with a much longer narrative since the Septuagint and Vulgate versions insert after 3:23 verses 24-90 consisting of "The Song of Azariah in the Furnace" and "The Song of the Three Young Men" so that the whole narrative consists of 97 verses (see, e.g., the Jerusalem Bible).

5. Leupold, *Exposition of Daniel*, 165.

6. E.g., Gammie, *Daniel*, 42-44, suggests a sermon on Dan 3:24-30 entitled "The Holocaust: Past and Present."

this narrative and possibly the absence of Daniel on the plain of Dura. The story of God saving Daniel's friends from the fiery furnace has its counterpart in chapter 6, where God saves Daniel from the lions.[7] The phrase "all the peoples, nations, and languages" (3:4) is repeated not only in 3:7 and 3:29 (singular) but also in 4:1; 5:19; 6:25; and 7:14. This underscores the universal perspective of these Aramaic narratives.

In the broader biblical context, a phrase similar to "all the peoples, nations, and languages" is repeated many times in the book of Revelation.[8] This narrative also has some parallels to the stories of Joseph and Esther. "The movement [in all three stories] is from scurrilous accusation to unjust punishment, and from imminent death to miraculous rescue."[9] More significantly, the language of Daniel 3:5, "You are to fall down and worship the golden statue," echoes the words of the Decalogue, "You shall not bow down to them or worship them" (Exod 20:5). Israel's unfaithfulness to Yahweh, bowing down and worshiping other gods, led to their exile (e.g., Deut 4:25-27; 29:25-28; Ezek 22:3-4, 15; Amos 5:26-27). The fact that Daniel's friends refused to bow down to the king's statue and worship his gods marks them as true Israelites.

Moreover, the story of God's people being saved from the fiery furnace has some interesting metaphorical parallels in the Old Testament. Deuteronomy 4:20 speaks of Egypt as "the iron furnace": "The LORD has taken you and brought you out of the iron-smelter, out of Egypt, to become a people of his very own possession."[10] Later Isaiah (48:10) speaks of the Babylonian exile as a "furnace of adversity": the LORD says, "See, I have refined you, but not like silver; I have tested you in the furnace of adversity."[11]

Literary Features

Before exploring major literary features that will help us understand the point of this narrative, we shall first identify a few minor rhetorical devices. The king's question in verse 15, "Who is the god that will deliver you out of my

---

7. "The God of the Jews can *deliver;* this thematic word resonates to its first use in the king's sarcastic question (v. 15), and to the tentative but faithful use of it in the testimony of the Jews (v. 17). It will resonate again in Daniel's own trial by lions in chapter 6 and finally at the moment of universal divine deliverance (12:1)." Towner, *Daniel,* 56.

8. Collins, *Daniel,* 183, mentions Revelation 5:9; 7:9; 10:11; 13:7; 14:6; and 17:15.

9. Anderson, *Signs and Wonders,* 27.

10. "The conjunction of Daniel 3 with this text was certainly recognized by the Author and his Israelite readers." Lacocque, *Book of Daniel,* 60. See also 1 Kings 8:51 and Jeremiah 11:4, NASB.

11. Cf. Malachi, who speaks of the final judgment as a "refiner's fire" (3:2) and the day "burning like an oven" (4:1).

hands?" is a rhetorical question which expects the answer, "There is no such god." Heating up the furnace "seven times more than was customary" (v. 19) is hyperbole. Since the number "seven" is the number of perfection, it means in this context stoking the furnace as hot as possible. The report that the very officials who "fell down and worshiped the golden statue" (v. 7) become the first witnesses to God's miracle in preserving his own (v. 27) is dramatic irony.[12] We shall now analyze the major literary features of narrative structure, plot line, character description, and repetition.

Narrative Structure

The narrative consists of four scenes:[13]

Scene 1: On the plain of Dura   (3:1-7)
  A. King Nebuchadnezzar sets up a golden statue and sends for
    his officials   (3:1-3)
  B. The herald proclaims: At the music worship the statue!   (3:4-6)
  C. All the peoples fall down and worship the golden statue   (3:7)
  Characters: King Nebuchadnezzar/herald and all his officials

Scene 2: In the king's presence   (3:8-20)
  A. Certain Chaldeans accuse Daniel's friends   (3:8-12)
  B. The king threatens Daniel's friends   (3:13-15)
  C. Daniel's friends refuse to worship the golden statue   (3:16-18)
  D. The king commands that Daniel's friends be thrown
    into the fire   (3:19-20)
  Characters: Chaldeans/the king and Daniel's friends

Scene 3: At the fiery furnace   (3:21-25)
  A. Soldiers bind the three friends and throw them into the fire   (3:21-23)
  B. The king sees four men, unbound, walking in the fire   (3:24-25)
  Characters: soldiers/king/counselors and Daniel's friends

Scene 4: Next to the furnace   (3:26-30)
  A. The king calls Daniel's friends to come out   (3:26)

---

12. Hill, "Daniel," 86.

13. The Aramaic marks new sections with "Then Nebuchadnezzar" and "Then King Nebuchadnezzar" at 3:13, 19, 24, and 26. See Collins, *Daniel,* 179. This phrase marks new acts of the king but not necessarily the beginning of a new scene.

B. The king's officials witness the miracle (3:27)

C. The king blesses God, decrees freedom to worship this God,
   and promotes Daniel's friends (3:28-30)

Characters: the king/officials and Daniel's friends

The Plot Line

The narrator gives the setting in 3:1: King Nebuchadnezzar made a giant golden statue and "set it up on the plain of Dura in the province of Babylon." Next he relates the preliminary incidents: the king invites all the officials of the provinces to come for the dedication of the statue (v. 2); they come (v. 3); the herald commands them at the sound of the music to fall down and worship the statue or else they will "immediately" be thrown into the fiery furnace (vv. 4-6); they hear the music and all fall down and worship the statue (v. 7).

The occasioning incident begins at verse 8 with Scene 2. Certain Chaldeans accuse Daniel's friends of disobeying the king by not worshiping the golden statue (vv. 8-12). The tension rises as the king "in furious rage" has the three men brought in. Will he "immediately" (v. 6) throw them into the furnace? But the king does not really trust the Chaldeans. He can hardly believe that anyone would dare to disobey him. The tension is drawn out as the king asks the three friends in disbelief, "Is it true?" (v. 14). He will give them a chance to demonstrate that it is not true. The orchestra will play one more time, and if they fall down and worship the statue, all will be well. If not, they will "immediately be thrown into a furnace of blazing fire, and who is the god that will deliver you out of my hands?" (vv. 13-15).

What will they do? They respond boldly that they see no need to give "an answer concerning this matter" (v. 16, NASB). Whether or not their God will deliver them from the furnace, they will not serve the king's gods nor worship the golden statue (vv. 16-18).

The tension mounts: What will the king do now? He is so angry at this insolence that his face is distorted and he orders the furnace to be stoked to maximum heat. Then he orders his strongest soldiers to bind the three men and throw them into the fire (vv. 19-20). The soldiers bind the three men and throw them down into the fire, losing their own lives in the process (vv. 21-22). The narrative reaches its climax at verse 23: Shadrach, Meshach, and Abednego falling down,[14] bound, into the furnace of blazing fire. No chance of escape is possible.

The narrator keeps the tension at the climax by not informing us immedi-

---

14. Instead of falling down (*nepal* in vv. 5, 6, 7, 10, 11, 15) to worship the golden statue, they fall down (v. 23) into the fire.

ately about the resolution to this conflict. He lets us see what is happening through the king's eyes. The king is astonished and rises up quickly. What did he see? The narrator uses dialogue to slow the pace (pace retardation). The king asks his counselors, "Was it not three men that we threw bound into the fire?" They answer, "True, O king." He replies, "But I see four men unbound, walking in the middle of the fire, and they are not hurt; and the fourth has the appearance of a god" (vv. 24-25). The king then rushes up to the lower opening of the furnace and calls for Shadrach, Meshach, and Abednego to come out of the fire, which they do (v. 26). But are they hurt? The king's officials check them out and determine that "the hair of their heads was not singed, their tunics were not harmed, and not even the smell of fire came from them" (v. 27). The conflict is fully resolved.

The outcome is that the king blesses God, decrees that any people who blaspheme this God will be executed, and declares that "there is no other god who is able to deliver in this way" (vv. 28-29). In the conclusion the king promotes Daniel's friends (v. 30).

We can sketch the plot line as a single plot.

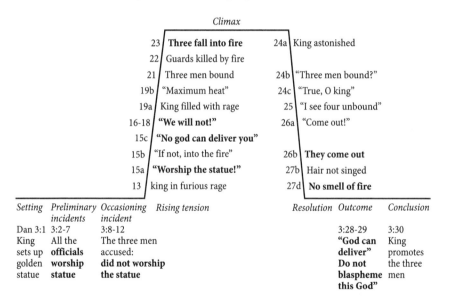

	Climax		
23	**Three fall into fire**	24a	King astonished
22	Guards killed by fire		
21	Three men bound	24b	"Three men bound?"
19b	"Maximum heat"	24c	"True, O king"
19a	King filled with rage	25	"I see four unbound"
16-18	**"We will not!"**	26a	"Come out!"
15c	"No god can deliver you"		
15b	"If not, into the fire"	26b	**They come out**
15a	**"Worship the statue!"**	27b	Hair not singed
13	king in furious rage	27d	**No smell of fire**

Setting	Preliminary incidents	Occasioning incident	Rising tension		Resolution	Outcome	Conclusion
Dan 3:1	3:2-7	3:8-12				3:28-29	3:30
King sets up golden statue	All the **officials worship statue**	The three men accused: **did not worship the statue**				**"God can deliver" Do not blaspheme this God"**	King promotes the three men

Character Description

Nebuchadnezzar is the antagonist. "He is the only 'full fledged' character in the story. He speaks, acts and shows emotions."[15] Twice the narrator describes the king's rage: "in furious rage" and "filled with rage," the second time adding the

15. Lucas, *Daniel*, 87.

vivid "that his face was distorted" (vv. 13, 19). When he saw four men in the fire instead of three, he "was astonished" (v. 24). His character is further developed by his words and actions: he shows his pride when he sets up the golden statue that all peoples must worship; he reveals his arrogance when he asks, "And who is the god that will deliver you out of my hands?" (v. 15); he confirms his furious rage and hostility when he orders that the furnace be heated up seven times more than normal (v. 19). But when he sees the miraculous deliverance, he is quick to bless the God of Israel, to decree that those who blaspheme this God will be executed, to make the astonishing statement for a polytheist, "there is no other god who is able to deliver in this way," and to promote Daniel's friends (vv. 28-30).

The narrator portrays the Babylonian officials as cold, mechanical creatures. He uses satire[16] in the back-to-back repetition of the list of officials. Reading this list aloud, one cannot help but smile: "Then King Nebuchadnezzar sent for the satraps, the prefects, and the governors, the counselors, the treasurers, the justices, the magistrates, and all the officials of the provinces, to assemble and come to the dedication of the statue that King Nebuchadnezzar had set up. So the satraps, the prefects, and the governors, the counselors, the treasurers, the justices, the magistrates, and all the officials of the provinces, assembled for the dedication of the statue that King Nebuchadnezzar had set up" (vv. 2-3). It all sounds very stilted and mechanical.[17] The Babylonian officials come across as puppets on a string. Soon the band will play, and they will all fall down. The narrator repeats the list of officials three times (vv. 2, 3, and a shorter version in v. 27) and the list of musical instruments four times (vv. 5, 7, 10, 15).[18]

Daniel's friends are the protagonists. The narrator depicts them as true Israelites who refuse to bow down and worship other gods and bravely suffer the consequences. He describes them as being "bound, still wearing their tunics, their trousers, their hats, and their other garments" (v. 21) — which would quickly ignite. Also, when they were examined afterward, "the hair of their heads was not singed, their tunics were not harmed, and not even the smell of fire came from them" (v. 27). In the end the king describes them as trusting in

---

16. "The main source of satire stems from the contrast between the mechanistic and automatic behavior of the pagans and the assertive and pious behavior of Shadrach, Meshach, and Abednego." Avalos, "The Comedic Function of the Enumerations of Officials and Instruments in Daniel 3," *CBQ* 53 (1991) 584. Cf. Baldwin, *Daniel*, 102.

17. "The immediate and mechanical reproduction of the enumeration of v. 2 in v. 3 is an effective reflection of the immediate and mechanistic acceptance of the king's request by the entire pagan bureaucracy." Avalos, ibid., 585.

18. "The six specific instruments, plus the general formula ('and every kind of music'), could have been mentioned once. Their iteration is consistent with the description of mechanistic actions in comedy by Bergson. . . . In effect, the iteration of enumerations helps to portray those pagans as a version of Pavlov's dogs." Ibid.

their God, disobeying the king's command, and yielding up "their bodies rather than serve and worship any god except their own God" (v. 28).[19] Their only speech in the narrative (vv. 16-18) shows them to be courageous, faithful Israelites who chose the possibility of death rather than serve the king's gods and worship his golden statue.

Repetition

Repetition may also help us discern where the narrator wishes to place the emphasis. Nine times he repeats that *Nebuchadnezzar* "set up" the golden statue (vv. 1, 2, 3 [2x], 5, 7, 12, 14, 18). Three times the narrator repeats the phrase "peoples, nations, and languages" (vv. 4, 7, and v. 29 in the singular): Nebuchadnezzar requires universal submission. The narrator repeats the phrase "fall down and worship" five times (vv. 5, 6, 10, 11, 15). He clarifies the meaning of falling down before the statue by linking four times worshiping the golden statue with serving *(pelā')* the king's gods (vv. 12, 14, 18, 28). He uses the same word *pelā'* for serving Israel's God (v. 17).

He mentions "the furnace of blazing fire" nine times (vv. 6, 11, 15, 17, 20, 21, 22, 23, 26). Thirteen times he names "Shadrach, Meshach and Abednego" (vv. 12, 13, 14, 16, 19, 20, 22, 23, 26 [2x], 28, 29, 30). Three times the narrator informs us that they were "bound" (vv. 21, 23, 24), leading to its marvelous reversal in the fire: "unbound" (v. 25). Most important for detecting the theme of this narrative is the repetition of the word "deliver": the king asks the rhetorical question, "Who is the god that will deliver *(shêzāb)* you out of my hands?" (v. 15); Daniel's friends twice repeat this word "deliver": "If our God whom we serve is able to deliver us from the furnace . . . , let him deliver us" (v. 17). Finally, the king acknowledges with a different Aramaic word, "There is no other god who is able to deliver *(neṣal)* in this way" (v. 29).

Lucas proposes a chiastic structure for this narrative:

A   Nebuchadnezzar's decree to worship the golden image (1-7)
    B   The Jews accused (8-12)
        C   The Jews threatened (13-15)
            D   The Jews confess their faith (16-18)
        C'   The Jews punished (19-23)
    B'   The Jews vindicated (24-27)
A'   Nebuchadnezzar's decree honoring the Jews and their God (28-30)

---

19. "The rejection of idolatry and trust in Yahweh [are] basic to Israel's covenantal relationship with God (Ps 31:6, 14; Isa 26:3-4; Jer 17:5, 7)." Hill, "Daniel," 85.

Lucas observes, "This shows a chiastic structure that highlights the words spoken by Shadrach, Meshach and Abednego in verses 16-18, which are the only words they speak in the whole story. This is clearly a key point in the story."[20]

Theocentric Interpretation

Since God is mentioned five times in the last half of the narrative (vv. 17, 26, 28 [2x], 29), it seems that the theocentric emphasis is concentrated in that last half. But rightly understood, the theocentric focus is evident from the beginning. In the foregoing narrative King Nebuchadnezzar said to Daniel, "Truly, your God is God of gods and Lord of kings" (2:47). Perhaps due to the passage of time (see p. 99, n. 37 below), the king has forgotten this wonderful confession, for in Daniel 3 he directly challenges "the God of gods and Lord of kings." In any event, the king's pride gets the better of him. He sets up a golden statue and commands all "peoples, nations, and languages" to fall down and worship the statue — which entails serving not "the God of gods" but the king's gods (see 3:12, 14, 18, 28). All the officials from the various Babylonian provinces comply, except for Daniel's three friends, who refuse to serve the king's gods (3:12, 14). The king asks arrogantly, "Who is the god that will deliver you out of my hands?" (3:15). The king, who defeated Israel and its God (1:2), thinks that he (and his gods) are more powerful than Israel's God. Daniel's friends respond, "If our God whom we serve is able to deliver us from the furnace of blazing fire and out of your hand, O king, let him deliver us.[21] But if not, be it known to you, O king, that we will not serve your gods and we will not worship the golden statue that you have set up" (3:17-18). They have made their choice for "the God of gods."

But the king still clings to the notion that he, with his gods, is more powerful than the God of Israel. So he has God's servants thrown into the blazing fire. Much to the king's astonishment, they are not incinerated. Instead, the king reports seeing "four men unbound, walking in the middle of the fire, and they are not hurt; and the fourth has the appearance of a god" (3:25). Later the king will identify this fourth person as an angel sent by God (3:28). This miracle of salvation convinces the king again that the God of the three men is indeed "the God of gods." He calls out, "Shadrach, Meshach, and Abednego, servants of *the Most High God*, come out!" (3:26). And he blesses their God, "who has sent his angel and delivered his servants who trusted in him" (3:28). The king then makes a decree that "any people, nation, or language that utters blasphemy against the

---

20. Lucas, *Daniel*, 86.
21. For various translations of this verse, see p. 105, n. 64 below.

God of Shadrach, Meshach, and Abednego shall be torn limb from limb, and their houses laid in ruins; for there is no other god who is able to deliver in this way" (3:29). Although the king is still a polytheist, he confesses that "there is no other god who *is able to deliver in this way*." Israel's God is "the God of gods," the only one who can deliver his people from a fiery furnace.

Textual Theme and Goal

The plot line, the repetitions, and the theocentric interpretation seem to make it rather easy to discern the message of this narrative. We might formulate the theme as follows: "Through an angel, God delivers his faithful children from certain death in Nebuchadnezzar's[22] fiery furnace." This is a good summary of the narrative, but it is not the *message* Israel was to hear. It also fails to capture the tension in the story: "*If our God . . . is able* to deliver us from the furnace of blazing fire . . . , let him deliver us. *But if not, . . .* we will not serve your gods . . ." (3:17-18). The friends raise the question about God's ability to save them from the fiery furnace. Then they boldly declare that even if their God is not able to deliver them, they will not serve Babylon's gods. The issue is about their refusal to serve other gods.[23] Significantly, this message is addressed to Israelites who suffer in exile because they worshiped other gods.[24] The more textually specific message, therefore, is, *Our sovereign God is able to deliver his oppressed children who refuse to serve other gods — even from a fiery furnace.*

To determine the author's goal in proclaiming this message, we must again consider the circumstances of the original audience. The Israelites in exile were suffering through what God called "the furnace of adversity" (Isa 48:10; cf. Deut 4:20).[25] These people had heard about King Nebuchadnezzar taking the vessels of God's house in Jerusalem and placing them "in the treasury of *his* gods" (1:2; 605 B.C.). They had also heard about the king returning in 587 B.C. and razing the walls of Jerusalem, burning God's holy temple, and taking most of the in-

---

22. "The specific purpose of the chapter within the book should not be lost sight of. This purpose is not merely to set forth God's power in being able to protect His own but specifically the fact that 'the world power cannot imperil the safety of God's saints.'" Leupold, *Exposition of Daniel,* 165.

23. "A central theme of the story about the golden image is worship (3:5-6, 10-12, 14-15, 18, 28)." Lederach, *Daniel,* 76. Cf. p. 83, "The issue is faithfulness, whether believers will reject idolatry and refuse to divide their loyalties even when their lives are at stake."

24. See, e.g., Deuteronomy 4:25-27; 29:25-28; Ezekiel 22:3-4, 15; and Amos 5:26-27.

25. "The exile itself is a white-hot crucible that tests by threatening to consume (see Ps 66:10-12). For many Jews who are not threatened with a literal furnace, the latter gives concrete form to the image of walking through fire." Goldingay, *Daniel,* 74.

habitants into exile. To all appearances, the Babylonian gods had defeated Israel's God; they seemed to be far more powerful than Yahweh. Therefore the author's first goal with this narrative was *to reassure God's oppressed people in exile that their God is sovereign and able to deliver them from the furnace of exile.*

But the author probably had a second goal in mind as well. He has sketched Daniel's friends as true Israelites. Even though they were not certain that God could save them from the fiery furnace, they courageously told the king, "Be it known to you, O king, that we will not serve your gods" (3:18). They were faithful to their God and obedient to his law, "You shall not bow down to them [idols] or worship them" (Exod 20:5). Even with death staring them in the face, they remained faithful to their covenant God. In the king's words, "They disobeyed the king's command and yielded up their bodies rather than serve and worship any god except their own God" (3:28). The Israelites who heard this story in exile would have identified with these true Israelites. A second goal for this narrative, therefore, was *to encourage God's people in exile not to serve other gods, even if such refusal might result in death.*[26]

Ways to Preach Christ

At first glance, preaching Christ from Daniel 3 seems rather simple. Preachers, past and present, have often identified the fourth person in the fiery furnace as an appearance of the preincarnate Christ.[27] Even if this interpretation were linguistically possible — many commentators think it is not[28] — such identification by itself does not make a sermon Christocentric. Rather, to preach a Christocentric sermon is to integrate the message of the Old Testament text

26. "The object of this chapter is to encourage the Jews to maintain a steadfast loyalty to their own faith and to reject all the trappings of heathen worship. They are to welcome death rather than turn aside from the faith (see verses 17-18)." Hammer, *Daniel*, 38.

27. See, e.g., Boice, *Daniel*, "It is not difficult to know who that fourth person was. He was Jesus Christ in a preincarnate form." So also Anderson, *Unfolding Daniel's Prophecies*, 65, "That was a theophany, a preincarnate appearance of our Lord who later was born in Bethlehem." Cf. Miller, *Daniel*, 123-24, "Most likely the fourth man in the fire was the angel of the Lord, God himself in the person of his Son Jesus Christ." So also Steinmann, *Daniel*, 193-95, "It is quite possible that the fourth man he observed was the preincarnate Christ, since the second person of the Trinity existed from eternity . . . and could manifest himself in OT times" (p. 193).

28. Starting with Jerome, who argued theologically, "I do not know how an ungodly king could have merited a vision of the Son of God" (quoted by Steinmann, *Daniel*, 194). But others consider this identification impossible on linguistic grounds. E.g., Porteous, *Daniel*, 61, "The idea that the fourth figure in the furnace is Christ is impossible and, indeed, contrary to the plain meaning of the author. The *bar 'ĕlāhîn* here is one of a class of beings who are called in Hebrew the *bĕnê 'elōhîm* and are to be thought of as attendants upon the deity." Cf. Lucas, *Daniel*, 92.

with the climax of God's self-revelation in his Son Jesus in the New Testament.[29] How, then, shall we move forward with this message to the person, work, and/or teaching of Jesus Christ in the New Testament? Since there is no promise of the coming Messiah in this narrative, nor a contrast with the message of the New Testament, we shall check the remaining five ways.

Redemptive-Historical Progression

Redemptive-historical progression offers a good option. Early in redemptive history God sent his angel to deliver his people Israel from enslavement in Egypt (Exod 14:19). Moses called Egypt "the iron furnace" (Deut 4:20, NASB; cf. 1 Kings 8:51 and Jer 11:4). Later God promised to deliver his people from the Babylonian exile (Isa 43:1-7), which he called the "furnace of adversity" (Isa 48:10, 20). While Israel was in exile, God sent his angel to deliver Shadrach, Meshach, and Abednego from Nebuchadnezzar's fiery furnace. In the fullness of time, God sent his only Son to save his people from the furnace of hell. Jesus said that at the end of time, "the Son of Man will send his angels, and they will collect out of his kingdom all causes of sin and evildoers, and they will throw them into the *furnace of fire*[30] where there will be weeping and gnashing of teeth. Then the righteous will shine like the sun in the kingdom of their Father" (Matt 13:42-43).

Typology

Typology offers another option for moving to Jesus Christ. In the history of Christian interpretation and preaching, the fourth person who joined the three friends in the fiery furnace has often been identified as the preincarnate Christ.[31] But this identification rests on a weak basis, for the text speaks not of the Angel of Yahweh but of "the appearance of a god" and of God's "angel" (3:25, 28). A better case can be made for seeing the angel as a type of Christ.[32] Jerome already considered the angel to be "a typological prefiguration of Christ."[33] Note the analogies and escalations: as the angel represents God's presence with his people, so Jesus represents God's presence with his people —

---

29. See my *Preaching Christ from the Old Testament,* 10 and 197.

30. "The furnace of fire" (*kaminon tou pyros;* Matt 13:42, 50) seems to be a reference to Daniel 3:6, *kaminon tou pyros."* See Evans, "Daniel in the New Testament," *Book of Daniel,* II, 522.

31. See n. 27 above.

32. See Towner, *Daniel,* 56, and Longman, *Daniel,* 112.

33. Collins, *Daniel,* 190.

only in a more direct way: the very Son of God with us, Emmanuel, "God is with us" (Matt 1:23). As the angel saved the three friends from burning in "the furnace of fire," so Jesus saves God's people from burning in the *eternal* "furnace of fire" (Matt 13:42-43; cf. John 3:16). Perhaps thinking of this story of the fiery furnace,[34] Jesus calls hell "the furnace of fire where there will be weeping and gnashing of teeth" (Matt 13:42). Further, although the angel saved the three friends from death, they would still die at a later time. But Jesus saves God's people from death, and they will never die again. Jesus says, "Those who believe in me, even though they die, will live" (John 11:26). Moreover, although the angel joined the friends in the furnace, he did not give his life to save them. Jesus joined humanity and gave his own life to save God's people.

Analogy

One can also use analogy as a way to Christ in the New Testament. As Nebuchadnezzar tempted Daniel's friends "to fall down and worship the golden statue," so the devil tempted Jesus: "'All these [kingdoms of the world and their splendor] I will give you, if you will fall down and worship me.'"[35] Daniel's friends said to the king, "We will not worship your gods" (Dan 3:18). Jesus said to the devil, "Away with you, Satan! for it is written, 'Worship the Lord your God, and serve only him'" (Matt 4:9-10).

One can also draw an analogy from the goal of the author. As the author's goal was to encourage God's people in exile not to serve other gods, even if such refusal might result in death, so Jesus exhorted his followers to be faithful unto death. One can support this analogy with Jesus' teachings: "See, I am sending you out like sheep into the midst of wolves. . . . You will be dragged before governors and kings because of me, as a testimony to them and to the Gentiles. . . . You will be hated by all because of my name. But the one who endures to the end will be saved" (Matt 10:16-22). And again, "I tell you, everyone who acknowledges me before others, the Son of Man also will acknowledge before the angels of God; but whoever denies me before others will be denied before the angels of God" (Luke 12:8-9). Jesus also said, "Those who love their life lose it, and those who hate their life in this world will keep it for eternal life. Whoever serves me must follow me, and where I am, there will my servant be also. Whoever serves me, the Father will honor" (John 12:25-26).

34. See n. 30 above.

35. Evans, "Daniel in the New Testament," *Book of Daniel*, II, 521, suggests an echo between the "to fall down and worship" (*pesōn proskynēsē*) of Daniel 3:6, 10, and 15, and the "will fall down and worship" (*pesōn proskynēsēs*) of Matthew 4:9.

Longitudinal Themes

One can also trace from the Old Testament to the New the theme of God's presence with his people in order to deliver them. God was with Joseph when he first arrived as a slave in Egypt, delivered him from prison, and raised him to high office (Gen 39:2, 23; 41:38-40). God was also with Moses as he sent him back to Egypt to deliver his people (Exod 3:12). God made his presence known in Egypt with mighty signs and wonders and delivered Israel (Exod 7–12, 15). God, in the form of his angel, was with Shadrach, Meshach, and Abednego in the fiery furnace and delivered them (Dan 3:25). Later, in the lions' den, Daniel said, "My God sent his angel and shut the lions' mouths so that they would not hurt me" (Dan 6:22). Through Zephaniah God promised, "The LORD, your God, is in your midst, a warrior who gives victory. . . . I will deal with all your oppressors at that time. . . . At that time I will bring you home" (Zeph 3:17-20). Finally, God showed his presence among us by coming to earth in his Son, Emmanuel, "God with us" (Matt 1:23). An angel told Joseph to name this child, "Jesus, for he will save his people from their sins" (Matt 1:22). Paul writes that God "has rescued us from the power of darkness and transferred us into the kingdom of his beloved Son, in whom we have redemption, the forgiveness of sins" (Col 1:13-14).

New Testament References

The appendix to the Greek New Testament lists some seventeen references or allusions to verses or phrases in Daniel 3, but only a few of them, such as Matthew 13:42, 50 (used above), are helpful for moving from Daniel 3 to Jesus Christ in the New Testament. A topical concordance, however, will lead to other New Testament quotations that could possibly be used in the sermon.

Speaking about the coming persecution, Jesus said to his disciples, "I tell you, my friends, do not fear those who kill the body, and after that can do nothing more. But I will warn you whom to fear: fear him who, after he has killed, has authority to cast into hell. Yes, I tell you, fear him! Are not five sparrows sold for two pennies? Yet not one of them is forgotten in God's sight. But even *the hairs of your head* ['the hair of their heads was not singed'; Dan 3:27] are all counted. Do not be afraid; you are of more value than many sparrows" (Luke 12:4-7).

Paul suffered persecution yet desired to remain faithful to Christ. He wrote to the Christians in Philippi: "It is my eager expectation and hope that I will not be put to shame in any way, but that by my speaking with all boldness, Christ will be exalted now as always in my body, whether by life or by death. For to me, living is Christ and dying is gain" (Phil 1:20-21).

Peter encouraged Christians suffering from persecution: "In your hearts sanctify Christ as Lord. *Always* be ready to make your defense to anyone who demands from you an accounting for the hope that is in you; yet do it with gentleness and reverence" (1 Pet 3:15-16). Peter may have had the fiery furnace in mind when he wrote, "Beloved, do not be surprised at the fiery ordeal that is taking place among you to test you, as though something strange were happening to you. But rejoice insofar as you are sharing Christ's sufferings, so that you may also be glad and shout for joy when his glory is revealed. If you are reviled for the name of Christ, you are blessed, because the spirit of glory, which is the Spirit of God, is resting on you" (1 Pet 4:12-14; cf. 1 Pet 1:6-7).

The risen Lord himself encouraged the persecuted church in Smyrna: "Do not fear what you are about to suffer. Beware, the devil is about to throw some of you into prison so that you may be tested, and for ten days you will have affliction. Be faithful until death, and I will give you the crown of life. Let anyone who has an ear listen to what the Spirit is saying to the churches. Whoever conquers will not be harmed by the second death" (Rev. 2:10-11).

Sermon Theme, Goal, and Need

We formulated the textual theme as, "Our sovereign God is able to deliver his oppressed children who refuse to serve other gods — even from a fiery furnace." Since the New Testament confirms God's power to save, we can keep the same theme for the sermon, taking the fiery furnace in both a literal and metaphorical sense: *Our sovereign God is able to deliver his oppressed children who refuse to serve other gods — even from a fiery furnace.*

We concluded that the author probably had a dual goal in mind: "to reassure God's oppressed people in exile that Israel's God is sovereign and able to deliver them from the furnace of exile," and "to encourage God's people in exile not to serve other gods, even if such refusal might result in death." In a very real sense, the church of Christ today is also in exile, for the kingdoms of this world are not our home but the kingdom of God is. Jesus stated clearly, "My kingdom is not from this world" (John 18:36), and "They [my disciples] do not belong to the world, just as I do not belong to the world" (John 17:16). Paul writes, "Our citizenship is in heaven, and it is from there that we are expecting a Savior, the Lord Jesus Christ" (Phil 3:20; cf. Rom 12:2 and 2 Cor 5:1-9). Jesus promised, "In my Father's house there are many dwelling places. . . . If I go and prepare a place for you, I will come again and will take you to myself, so that where I am, there you may be also" (John 14:1-3). Since God's people in this world are still in "exile," only a slight change will make the dual textual goal the dual goal of the sermon: *to reassure God's people today that our God is sovereign and able to deliver us from the furnace of "exile" today, and to encourage God's people not to serve other gods, even if such refusal might result in death.*[36]

This dual goal points to a dual need being addressed. On the one hand, the people's God may be too small: they may doubt that God is "mighty to save," even from certain death. On the other hand, people may be serving modern gods such as materialism, consumerism, and/or hedonism. One can begin the sermon introduction by illustrating this dual need in contemporary society with a story of a person who has no hope in God for the future and therefore lives totally for pleasure in the here and now. Then ask if this contemporary attitude has also infiltrated the church. Next relate how Israel in exile tended to think that the Babylonian gods had defeated Israel's God (their God was too small) and that they were tempted to worship these Babylonian gods. Then retell the story of Daniel's friends, suspending it here and there for explanation, moves to Christ, and application. In a sermon series, however, one can also dispense with a formal sermon introduction and begin immediately with the narrative after a short paragraph linking it to the last narrative. In the sermon exposition below, I will demonstrate the latter.

Sermon Exposition

The last time we heard of King Nebuchadnezzar, he was really impressed by the ability of Daniel's God to tell him his dream about the huge statue with the golden head. He was even more impressed by the interpretation: "You [Nebuchadnezzar] are the head of gold" (2:38). The king had said to Daniel, "Truly, your God is *God* of gods and *Lord* of kings" (2:47). Then the king had promoted Daniel to be ruler over the whole province of Babylon, the head office being in the king's court in the city of Babylon. And Daniel's friends, Shadrach, Meshach, and Abednego, became administrators over the province of Babylon (2:48-49).

That is where this story about Daniel's friends picks up. It is many years later.[37] The king has apparently forgotten his wonderful confession, "Truly,

---

36. With a dual goal it will be more of a challenge to produce a unified, well-focused sermon, but our primary responsibility is to do justice to the biblical text as it addressed Israel.

37. The Greek versions add the date, "In the eighteenth year," in 3:1, which would be 586 B.C. Cf. Jeremiah 52:12, 29 and 2 Kings 25:8. This date would mean that this story takes place after Nebuchadnezzar had sacked Jerusalem, burned the temple, and taken most of the people into exile. "The dating makes the point that Nebuchadnezzar is substituting his god for the God of Israel." Hammer, *Daniel*, 39. Steinmann, *Daniel*, 167, comparing Jeremiah and the surviving chronicles of Nebuchadnezzar's reign, suggests a date of "late December 594 or January 593 B.C." If he is correct, it would place this narrative nine years after that of Daniel 2.

your God is God of gods and Lord of kings" (2:47). We don't know if it was old age or just plain forgetfulness, but the king's memory was short. He had been very successful in expanding his empire. But not everything went smoothly. In the year 594 B.C. he had to suppress a rebellion in Babylon. He also had to make "a trip to his western provinces to collect tribute from his vassals" and keep things calm.[38] He does not want his empire to break up. The fact that he is the head of gold has gone to his head. He wants to be more than just a head of gold. He wants to be a whole statue of gold.[39] He wants his empire to last forever.

We read in chapter 3:1, "King Nebuchadnezzar made a golden statue whose height was sixty cubits and whose width was six cubits; he set it up on the plain of Dura[40] in the province of Babylon." A cubit is about a foot and a half, so sixty cubits would make it ninety feet (30 meters) tall — the height of a nine-story building. That probably included the base on which it stood. But the statue was only six cubits wide, nine feet. This makes scholars think that the statue was a tall pillar that was partly sculptured, perhaps with the bust of a human being.[41] We can think of a nine-story tall column with a figure carved in the top part. The whole statue was plated with gold.

The statue represented the great King Nebuchadnezzar[42] as well as his gods.[43] So much for just being the head of gold. Nine times[44] this chapter repeats that *Nebuchadnezzar* "set up" this golden statue. In chapter 2, Daniel told the king that the God of heaven had given him the kingdom (2:37) but that it would be replaced by a kingdom of silver, then a kingdom of bronze, and finally one of iron, with feet of iron and clay. Well, the king will not wait for his dynasty to be toppled. He challenges the God of heaven. He sets up his own statue, entirely of gold, and certainly no feet of clay.

38. See Steinmann, *Daniel*, 167.

39. Schwab, *Hope*, 47, suggests that Nebuchadnezzar "created an image entirely of gold in rebellion against the vision of Babylon limited to a head of gold in world history. Nebuchadnezzar erected a golden 'image' [statue], Aramaic *ṣelem*, the same word as used in his dream of Daniel 2:31, highlighting the equation between them."

40. The site has not been positively identified. Some think it was a plain just outside the walls of Babylon (the Akkadian word *duru* referring to a "walled place"), while others think it must have been farther out. Miller, *Daniel*, 111, suggests that the site is "about sixteen miles south of Babylon called *Tulul Dura* (tells of Dura), where Oppert thought he had discovered the base of the statue."

41. Montgomery, *Book of Daniel*, 196.

42. Redditt, *Daniel*, 70, notes with respect to verse 19a, "The MT includes before the word 'face' the Aramaic word *ṣelem*. It is the word for 'image' or 'statue' used in 3:1, 2, 3, 5, 7, 10, 12, 14, 15 and 18. The narrator was reminding the reader once more that the king resembled his statue." See also Young, *Prophecy of Daniel*, 84.

43. Verses 12, 14, 18, and 28 link worshiping the golden statue with serving the king's gods.

44. Daniel 3:1, 2, 3 (2x), 5, 7, 12, 14, and 18.

Interestingly, the king sets up his statue "in the province of Babylon." That is the place (Shinar) where people long ago built the tower of Babel. They had said, "Come, let us build ourselves a city, and a tower with its top in the heavens, and let us *make a name for ourselves;* otherwise we shall be scattered abroad upon the face of the whole earth" (Gen 11:4). The same pride drives King Nebuchadnezzar: he will make a *name* for himself. The same motivation also drives him: he will not have his empire fall apart. The golden statue will serve to unify his kingdom.

Verse 2, "Then King Nebuchadnezzar sent for the satraps, the prefects, and the governors, the counselors, the treasurers, the justices, the magistrates, and *all the officials of the provinces* to assemble and come to the dedication of the statue that King Nebuchadnezzar had set up." The officials are listed in order of importance. They are to come from *all* the provinces of Babylonia. By this time Nebuchadnezzar had conquered many nations, each with its own culture and language. The danger is very real that revolutions may break out and his empire disintegrate. So the king needs something that will solidify the unity of his empire. He needs a concrete demonstration of the loyalty of all these diverse peoples to him, the great King Nebuchadnezzar.[45] So he orders all these officials to come to the dedication of his giant, golden statue. And come they do.

Verses 3 to 6, "So the satraps, the prefects, and the governors, the counselors, the treasurers, the justices, the magistrates, and all the officials of the provinces, assembled for the dedication of the statue that King Nebuchadnezzar had set up. When they were standing before the statue that Nebuchadnezzar had set up, the herald proclaimed aloud, 'You are commanded, O *peoples,*[46] *nations, and languages,* that when you hear the sound of the horn, pipe, lyre, trigon, harp, drum, and entire musical ensemble,[47] you are to fall down and worship the golden statue that King Nebuchadnezzar has set up. Whoever does not fall down and worship shall *immediately* be thrown into a furnace of blazing fire.'"

45. "The various categories of people in the list are political officials from around the empire, which may signal that this was Nebuchadnezzar's attempt to solidify control over the diverse elements of his vast empire." Longman, *Daniel,* 98. Cf. Steinmann, *Daniel,* 168, "Since twice in the first three verses we are told that 'all the rulers of the provinces' . . . came for the dedication, we should infer that it was a carefully designed ceremony to ensure the loyalty of officials outside of Babylon, as suggested by comparison to events recorded in the Babylonian Chronicle."

46. The peoples of the whole known world "were represented by the assembled officials." Collins, *Daniel,* 183.

47. "The sound of such a heterogeneous assortment of musical instruments shrieking, blowing, and thrumming simultaneously would seem truly barbarous to us. But it must be remembered that they furnished only a signal and were designed to impress the hearers by their variety and their volume of sound." Leupold, *Exposition of Daniel,* 144.

They are all to fall down with their face to the ground and worship the statue. The statue represents both the king and his gods. Worshiping the golden statue is the same as worshiping the gods of Babylon. Anyone who refuses to do so will immediately be thrown into the fiery furnace. The officials know that this is no idle threat. The punishment of burning by fire was quite common in the ancient world.[48] Jeremiah names two people "whom the king of Babylon roasted in the fire."[49]

Not far from the statue the officials can see the furnace of blazing fire, belching smoke into the clear, blue sky. The furnace had probably been used for firing the bricks[50] needed for building the base and the frame for the statue. The furnace must have been cone-shaped like nuclear power plants today.[51] A large opening at the top created a strong draft and allowed for adding fuel to the fire, while a smaller opening at the bottom allowed for extracting the fired bricks. The furnace was probably set up near a hillside so that fuel could be added through the top opening. This had the further advantage that anyone refusing to fall down and worship the statue could immediately be thrown down through the top of the furnace.[52]

Verse 7, "Therefore, as soon as all the peoples heard the sound of the horn, pipe, lyre, trigon, harp, drum, and entire musical ensemble, all the *peoples, nations, and languages* fell down and worshiped the golden statue that King Nebuchadnezzar had set up." "The original reads literally, 'As soon as they were hearing they were falling down.' There was total and immediate response."[53] Like mindless robots, all these officials fall down and worship the golden statue and the Babylonian gods it represents. As the king looks over the plain of Dura, all he can see is this mass of people lying facedown before the golden statue he had set up. The king is pleased: mission accomplished.

But his pleasure is short-lived. Verse 8, "Accordingly, at this time certain

48. On Babylonian, Persian, and Greek punishment by fire, see Goldingay, *Daniel*, 70. See also Genesis 38:24; Leviticus 20:14; 21:9; Joshua 7:15; 1 Chronicles 14:12.

49. Jeremiah 29:21-22.

50. "Furnaces in Babylon were connected with the firing of bricks (cf. Gen 11:3), which were widely used in the absence of stone. The fuel was charcoal which, given the needed draught, produced the high temperature required at the brick-kiln." "It is estimated that the temperature would have been 900-1000 degrees C. [about 1800 degrees Fahrenheit]." Baldwin, *Daniel*, 99, 103, n. 3.

51. Montgomery, *Book of Daniel*, 202, suggests that it "must have been similar to our common lime-kiln, with a perpendicular shaft from the top and an opening at the bottom for extracting the fused lime."

52. Daniel 3:23 reads, the three men "fell *down*, bound, into the furnace of blazing fire." Miller, *Daniel*, 122, observes that they "'fell into' (*nĕpalû lĕgô*', lit., 'fell down to the middle of') the furnace, language that suggests they were thrown in through an opening at the top."

53. Baldwin, *Daniel*, 103.

Chaldeans [astrologers[54]] came forward and denounced the Jews." Literally it says that these astrologers "ate pieces of the Jews." We might say, "They made mincemeat" of these Jews.[55] They are envious of the three Jews. They hate these foreigners the king had placed over them. They want to devour them. They finally have the evidence that will destroy these Jews. The three Jews will surely be tossed into the fiery furnace and burn alive.

Verses 9 to 12, "They [the astrologers] said to King Nebuchadnezzar, 'O king, live forever! You, O king, have made a decree, that everyone who hears the sound of the horn, pipe, lyre, trigon, harp, drum, and entire musical ensemble, shall fall down and worship the golden statue, and whoever does not fall down and worship shall be thrown into a furnace of blazing fire. There are certain Jews whom you have appointed over the affairs of the province of Babylon: Shadrach, Meshach, and Abednego. These pay no heed to you, O King. They do not serve your gods and they do not worship the golden statue that you have set up.'"

These are serious charges. These friends of Daniel[56] "pay no heed to you," the great king; they ignore your command. For "they do not serve your gods and they do not worship the golden statue that you have set up." Clearly worshiping the golden statue is equivalent to serving the king's gods.[57] Literally they say, "Your gods they do not serve and the statue of gold that you have set up they do not worship." "The emphatic placement of 'your gods' in the accusation . . . highlights that what is at stake is not simply civil authority (the king's royal power), but religious loyalty and theological belief."[58]

This is a dangerous rebellion in the highest ranks. Daniel's friends have not only disobeyed the command of the great king but also rejected his gods. Ac-

---

54. Because of the contrasting phrases "Chaldean men" and "Judean men" several commentators understand Chaldeans here as an ethnic identification. Others understand the Chaldeans as "astrologers" (so the NIV). For a listing of commentators on either side, see Steinmann, *Daniel*, 182, n. 5. I favor understanding the "Chaldeans" as "astrologers" for three reasons: first, the continuity with 2:2, 4, 5, 10 and 4:7 argues for this. Second, they seem to act out of professional jealousy (see 3:12 and 6:3-4). And third, it is not likely that ordinary Chaldeans would have been allowed in the king's presence to accuse his high officials.

55. Russell, *Daniel*, 65.

56. If the question should come up, Where is Daniel? the answer is probably given in 2:49, "Daniel remained at the king's court." As such he was not required to attend this dedication for "officials from the provinces." See Steinmann, *Daniel*, 183-84. Archer, "Daniel," 55-56, offers several other possibilities such as, Daniel was absent from Babylon at this time; he may have been ill (cf. 8:27); as the king's vizier his loyalty to the king was assumed.

57. See also verses 14, 18, and 28.

58. Steinmann, *Daniel*, 182-83. Cf. Redditt, *Daniel*, 69, "In effect, the narrator had the Chaldeans themselves link the worship of the statue with the worship of Babylonian gods." Cf. Hill, "Daniel," 79, "The behavior of Shadrach, Meshach, and Abednego is both an act of treason (since they do not serve the king's gods, v. 12) and insubordination (since they refuse to obey the king's edict and bow to the golden image, v. 12)."

cording to his edict, they should immediately be thrown into the roaring fire. The astrologers have their rivals right where they want them. They even quote the king's threatened punishment: "whoever does not fall down and worship shall be thrown into a furnace of blazing fire." They have an iron-clad case.

Verses 13 and 14, "Then Nebuchadnezzar in furious rage commanded that Shadrach, Meshach, and Abednego be brought in; so they brought those men before the king. Nebuchadnezzar said to them, 'Is it true, O Shadrach, Meshach, and Abednego, that you do not serve my gods and you do not worship the golden statue that I have set up?'"[59] "Is it true?" The king seems not to trust the accusers. He knows about professional jealousies. He is not going to throw these wise Jews immediately into the raging fire. He will give them another chance. He will have his orchestra play the music again, just for the three of them.

Verse 15, "Now if you are ready when you hear the sound of the horn, pipe, lyre, trigon, harp, drum, and entire musical ensemble to fall down and worship the statue that I have made, well and good. But if you do not worship, you shall immediately be thrown into a furnace of blazing fire, and who is the god that will deliver you out of my hands?"

If you were an Israelite in exile, at this point in the story you would be biting your nails. What are Daniel's friends going to do? It would be so easy just to fall down before the statue — with reservations, of course. They don't have to mean it as real worship. The statue is not a real god anyway. If they can bow before it and save their life, why not? It won't hurt anyone. . . .

But then there is God's commandment, "You shall *not* bow down to them [idols] or worship them" (Exod 20:5; cf. Deut 6:13). What are they going to do? If they obey God's commandment, the king will throw them immediately into the furnace of blazing fire. The king's question echoes in their minds, "Who is the god that will deliver you out of my hands?" The king believes the answer is obvious. No god! No god can — no god will — deliver them out of his hands. Because no god is greater than King Nebuchadnezzar.[60] No god can save them in the blazing fire.

Verse 16, "Shadrach, Meshach, and Abednego answered the king, 'O

---

59. Literally, "'Is it true . . . that *my gods* you do not serve and *the statue of gold that I set up* you do not worship?' Since 'my gods' is in the emphatic position in both 3:12 and 3:14 . . . the focus of the intense pressure now brought to bear on the three Judeans is religious and theological — a matter of faith and worship." Steinmann, ibid., 184.

60. "He now makes the arrogant and blasphemous claim . . . to the possession of a human power so great that there is no divine power to which the victims can turn for help. We see here the worldly power absolutely confident that there is no limit to its authority." Porteous, *Daniel*, 59. Cf. Collins, *Daniel*, 187, "The question recalls the taunt of the king of Assyria in Isa 36:19-20; 37:11-12 (2 Kings 18:33-35; 19:12-13)."

Nebuchadnezzar, *we*[61] have no need to present a defense to you in this matter.'"
More literally they say, "O Nebuchadnezzar, we do not need to give you an answer concerning this matter" (NASB). The "matter" is the king's declaration
that no god can deliver them out of his hands.[62] Daniel's friends need not answer that assertion; only the God they serve can answer it.

They continue in verses 17 to 18, "*If* our God whom we serve *is able* to deliver us from the furnace of blazing fire and out of your hand, O king, let him
deliver us. *But if not,*[63] be it known to you, O king, that we will not serve your
gods and we will not worship the golden statue that you have set up."

Apparently Daniel's friends are not sure their God is able to deliver them
from the inferno they see before them.[64] That's not surprising, seeing that in the

---

61. "The Aramaic word order of v. 16 places an emphasis on the pronoun 'we,' implying
that it is the Lord himself who will deal with this king who thinks he is sovereign on earth." Archer, "Daniel," 54.

62. "The Aramaic text says simply that there is no need 'to give back' or 'to return' to the
king on the matter. The point is that these men feel no compunction to give a comeback, as it
were, regarding 'this matter,' namely, the theological challenge raised by Nebuchadnezzar: 'who
is the god who will deliver you out of my hand?'" Seow, *Daniel*, 56.

63. Coxon, "Daniel III 17: A Linguistic and Theological Problem," *VT* 26 (1976) 408, points
out that the answer of Daniel's friends, "If our God is . . . able to save us, he will save. . . . But if
not, let it be known to you . . ." is modeled on the foregoing (v. 15) conditional sentence of the
king, "Now if you are ready . . . to fall down and worship the statue. . . . But if you do not worship. . . ." Seow, *Daniel*, 56-57, adds that "the three men shift the question from their being ('you
are') to God's being ('God is') — from their being ready to fall down and worship
Nebuchadnezzar's edifice to God's being able to deliver them. The issue is not whether or not
they are, but whether or not God is! . . . By structuring the dialogue on this point-counterpoint
fashion, the narrator indicates that the decisive issue at hand is really not the courage of the
Jews, although that aspect is part of the story. Rather, the critical question is the presence and
power of God: inasmuch as a God exists who is able, it is entirely up to God to deliver, if that be
the divine will."

64. Bible versions and commentators are divided on the translation and interpretation of
this verse. The issue is, Does the author depict Daniel's friends as not being certain about God's
ability to save them from the fire? Do they doubt God's omnipotence? The older Bible versions
(KJV, RV, RSV) and some newer ones (such as the NASB and NIV) sought to avoid this impression. For example, the older NIV as well as the 2011 version translates verse 17, "If we are thrown
into the blazing furnace, *the God we serve is able to save us* from it, and he will rescue us from
your hand, O king." The 2005 TNIV translates, "*If the God we serve is able to deliver us,* then he
will deliver us from the blazing furnace and from Your Majesty's hand." The latter translation is
similar to that of the NRSV. Some recently discovered examples of a similar construction in
nonbiblical Hebrew may well be the reason for the switch. In any event, it seems rather elementary to observe that the doctrine of God's omnipotence should not influence the translation or
interpretation of this verse. For the history of translating this verse and arguments pro and con,
see Lucas, *Daniel*, 84-85, 90-91. See also Montgomery, *Book of Daniel*, 206-7; Coxon, "Daniel III
17: A Linguistic and Theological Problem," *VT* 26 (1976) 400-409; Towner, *Daniel*, 51-53, and
Miller, *Daniel*, 119, n. 57.

past God had never delivered people from a literal blazing fire. God had done many miracles in delivering his people from Egypt, but delivering them from a red-hot fire was not one of them. Neither had God delivered them from the furnace of Babylonian exile. So they are not sure. *If he is able,* let God deliver them. *"But if not,"* they bravely tell the king, "we will not serve your gods and we will not worship the golden statue that you have set up." Their uncertainty about God's ability to deliver them from the fire makes their loyalty to God even more impressive. They obey God's law not because they know that God *will* deliver them. They obey God's law not because it will pay off, because God will reward them for their loyalty.[65] They obey God simply because of their faithfulness to God. Their God had delivered their ancestors from enslavement in Egypt, made a covenant with them, and had given them his sacred law: "You shall not make for yourself an idol. . . . You shall not bow down to them or worship them" (Exod 20:4-5). They will be loyal and faithful to their covenant God, no matter what happens. They will not worship the gods of Babylon.

Upon hearing their bold testimony, we read in verses 19 and 20, "Then Nebuchadnezzar was so filled with rage against Shadrach, Meshach, and Abednego that his face was distorted. He ordered the furnace heated up seven times more than was customary, and ordered some of the strongest guards in his army to bind Shadrach, Meshach, and Abednego and to throw them into the furnace of blazing fire."

The king is so angry that he orders the furnace to be heated up "seven times more than was customary," that is, as hot as possible.[66] Then he orders some of his strongest soldiers to tie up the three friends and throw them into the open top of the blazing furnace.

Verse 21, "So the men were bound, still wearing their tunics, their trousers, their hats, and their other garments, and they were thrown into the furnace of blazing fire." The king is in such a hurry to punish these three rebels that there isn't even time to strip them of their clothes. Fully clothed, they are bound and thrown into the red-hot furnace. Their clothes will catch fire immediately. And being bound, they cannot flee through the lower door. There is absolutely no way of escape.

Verse 22 underscores that there is no escape possible for the three friends: "Because the king's command was urgent and the furnace was so overheated, the raging flames killed the men who lifted Shadrach, Meshach, and Abednego."

65. "The negation of verse 18 certainly has to do with the power of God. It may be that God will be unable to save them, but this is not sufficient to undermine the three martyrs' fidelity. Their attachment to God is wholly without expectation of a reward (see Job 1:9; 13:15. . . . Cf. Gen 22)." Lacocque, *Book of Daniel,* 63.

66. "According to an ancient tradition, the king had his men throw naphtha and pitch into the furnace to make the fire burn hotter." Jeske, *Daniel,* 61.

The flames apparently shoot out of the top of the furnace. They kill the strong soldiers who throw the three friends down into the furnace.[67]

And then it happens, verse 23, "But the three men, Shadrach, Meshach, and Abednego, *fell down, bound, into the furnace of blazing fire.*" What a tragedy! The only people who are faithful to God fall into the red-hot fire. And they are bound. God promised in Isaiah (43:2), "When you pass through the waters, I will be with you; . . . when you walk through *fire* you shall not be burned, and the *flame* shall not consume you." But this was figurative language. Will the three friends not be burned? Will the flame not consume them even as it consumed the superstrong soldiers?

As we ponder this question, the narrator turns our eyes to the king who is peering through the opening at the bottom of the furnace. The king wants to see these rebels roast. Verse 24, "Then King Nebuchadnezzar was *astonished* and rose up quickly. He said to his counselors, 'Was it not three men that we threw *bound*[68] into the fire?' They answered the king, 'True, O king.' He replied, 'But I see four men *un*bound, walking in the middle of the fire, and they are not hurt; and the fourth has the appearance of a god.'"

What is going on? Three men thrown into the fire. Now there are four. The three were bound. Now they are "unbound, walking in the middle of the fire." Moreover, "they are not hurt" *in* the furnace while his strongest soldiers were incinerated outside the furnace. "And the fourth has the appearance of a god."[69] Who is that fourth person? In verse 28 the king will explain that God sent his angel to deliver his servants.[70] Does God make use of angels to protect his people? And can this God deliver his servants even from a scorching fire?

Note that the king sees "four men unbound, walking *in the middle* of the fire." "The text gives no indication that the three men are rescued *from* the fire. Rather, the story is that they are with a divine being *in the midst* of the fire. They encounter divine presence in the middle of the fire."[71]

The king rushes up to the door in the furnace. Verse 26, "Nebuchadnezzar

67. "The idea is that a flame leaps up and kills those standing at the opening on the top." Collins, *Daniel*, 189.

68. "Note the emphatic position of 'bound' . . . at the end of the question in Aramaic." Steinmann, *Daniel*, 193.

69. "The fourth figure seen by the king is like 'a son of the gods.' This is a Semitic idiom for a member of the class of 'gods.' For a polytheist like Nebuchadnezzar, this would mean a member of the pantheon." Lucas, *Daniel*, 92.

70. "Angels were thought to be attendants upon God, or members of his court, who could be sent out with messages or who could be agents through whom the divine will was accomplished. . . . The presence of the angel symbolizes the presence of God himself with his faithful servants." Hammer, *Daniel*, 42.

71. Seow, *Daniel*, 59. Cf. p. 18. Cf. Romans 8:37, "*In* all these things [hardship, persecution, etc.] we are more than conquerors through him who loved us."

then approached the door of the furnace of blazing fire and said, 'Shadrach, Meshach, and Abednego, servants of the Most High God, come out! Come here!'" Notice that the king calls God "the Most High God" again. "So Shadrach, Meshach, and Abednego came out from the fire." They really walk out of this hellish fire. But are they hurt? The king, peering through the opening into the fire, thought that they were not hurt, but one cannot be sure with such a blistering fire. So he calls some of his officials together again to examine the three men. These are the very officials who at the sound of the music had automatically fallen down and worshiped the image. Ironically, these mindless idolaters now become the first witnesses to an incredible miracle worked by "the Most High God."

Verse 27, "And the satraps, the prefects, the governors, and the king's counselors gathered together and saw that the fire had not had any power over the bodies of those men; the hair of their heads was not singed, their tunics were not harmed, and not even the smell of fire came from them." It's simply amazing. The officials determine that the red-hot fire had no power "over the bodies of those men." No third-degree burns. No burns at all. And their clothes not harmed. "Not even the smell of fire came from them." When you sit by a campfire at night, you can still smell the smoke in your clothes the next morning. Here not even the smell of fire.[72] It's as if they had never been near the fire. And "the hair of their heads was not singed." God had taken care even of the hair of their heads.

In the New Testament, Jesus warns his followers of the coming persecution but assures them, "Not a hair of your head will perish" (Luke 21:18). That is because God is able to protect his people down to the smallest details. On another occasion Jesus says, "Even the hairs of your head are all counted. Do not be afraid" (Luke 12:7). Daniel's friends can testify to the fact that God is true to his promise in Isaiah: "When you walk through fire you shall not be burned, and the flame shall not consume you" (Isa 43:2). God saved his faithful children even from the blazing fire.

God has shown King Nebuchadnezzar who is really in charge. The king had boasted, "Who is the god that will deliver you out of *my* hands?" The God of Israel delivered the three friends out of the king's hands. God could also have snuffed out the fire, of course. But he was with them *in* the fire. Calvin writes that God wanted the fire "to burn in the sight of all, to render the power of this deliverance the more conspicuous."[73] The message is clear: Israel's sovereign

---

72. "Even the most subtle test of all, the smoke test, could be met, for ordinarily the mere nearness of a fire is sufficient to have the smell of smoke pass upon the garments. Here no smoke smell could be detected." Leupold, *Exposition of Daniel*, 160.

73. "God could extinguish the fire of the furnace, but he wished it to burn in the sight of all, to render the power of this deliverance the more conspicuous." Calvin, *Commentaries on Daniel*, I, 234.

God is able to deliver his oppressed children who refuse to serve other gods. He is able to deliver them even from a fiery furnace.

Israel's sovereign God delivered his faithful children throughout its history.[74] Even before Israel became a nation, God sent his angel (Exod 14:19) to deliver his people from enslavement in Egypt. Moses called Egypt "the iron *furnace*" (Deut 4:20, NASB). When Israel was unfaithful to God by serving other gods, God sent them into exile in Babylon. God called Babylon "the *furnace* of adversity" (Isa 48:10). But God promised to deliver his people from this "furnace" as well (Isa 40:1-31; 48:20). In Daniel 3 God demonstrated his ability to deliver his people even from a literal fiery furnace. God's angel delivered Daniel's friends from the king's fiery furnace.

This story of God's ability to save even from a fiery furnace gave his exiled people hope: their God is able to deliver them also from the furnace of their exile. They knew their Psalms: "The angel of the LORD encamps around those who fear him and *delivers* them" (Ps 34:7). And, "No evil shall befall you, no scourge come near your tent. For he will command his angels concerning you to *guard you* in all your ways" (Ps 91:11). God's deliverance of Daniel's three friends was but a small token of the deliverance God would bring about a few years later when Israel could return to the Promised Land.

In the fullness of time, God sent his only Son to save his people from another fiery furnace. The church of Christ today is also in exile. The kingdoms of this world are not our home, but the kingdom of God is. Jesus stated clearly, "My kingdom is not from this world" (John 18:36). He also said, "They [my followers] do not belong to the world, just as I do not belong to the world" (John 17:16). Paul writes, "Our citizenship is in heaven, and it is from there that we are expecting a Savior, the Lord Jesus Christ" (Phil 3:20). Jesus promised, "In my Father's house there are many dwelling places. . . . If I go and prepare a place for you, I will come again and will take you to myself, so that where I am, there you may be also" (John 14:1-3). Thus Jesus will save us from our exile in this sinful world.

But Jesus will save us from a "fiery furnace" in an even deeper sense. He said that at the end of time, "the Son of Man will send his angels, and they will collect out of his kingdom all causes of sin and evildoers, and they will throw them into the *furnace of fire*[75] where there will be weeping and gnashing of

---

74. At first, I was going to use typology here to move to Christ. But I found that demonstrating the analogies and escalations between the angel and Christ was rather theoretical and might stall the sermon. Redemptive-historical progression and New Testament references provide a more interesting way.

75. "Jesus warns his contemporaries that at the end of the age the 'son of man will send forth his angels' who will cast sinners into 'the furnace of fire [*kaminon tou pyros*]' (Matt 13:42, 50). This graphic image may derive from Nebuchadnezzar's threat to cast those who refuse to

teeth. Then the righteous will shine like the sun in *the kingdom of their Father*" (Matt 13:42-43). Jesus came to save his people from the fire of hell and bring them into the kingdom of his Father. The risen Lord proclaims in the book of Revelation, "I was dead, and see, I am alive forever and ever; and I have the keys of death and of Hades [hell]" (Rev. 1:18). Our risen Savior can save us from the fire of hell and bring us into the kingdom of his Father.

When King Nebuchadnezzar hears that the three friends are in excellent shape, as if they had never been in the fire at all, he finally acknowledges God again as "the God of gods." He says in verses 28 and 29, "Blessed be the God of Shadrach, Meshach, and Abednego, who has sent his angel and *delivered* his servants who trusted in him. They disobeyed the king's command and yielded up their bodies rather than serve and worship any god *except their own God*. Therefore I make a decree: Any people, nation, or language that utters blasphemy against the God of Shadrach, Meshach, and Abednego shall be torn limb from limb, and their houses laid in ruins;[76] for there is no other god who *is able to deliver* in this way*."

Earlier, in verse 15, the king had said arrogantly, "Who is the god that will *deliver* you out of my hands?" Daniel's friends responded with the conditional, "*If* our God . . . *is able to deliver* us from the furnace of blazing fire and out of your hand, O king, let him deliver us." *If he is able*. After witnessing God's miraculous deliverance, the king declares, "There is no other god who *is able*[77] *to deliver* in this way." Israel's God is able to deliver his people even when they are in a fiery furnace.

Verse 30, "Then the king promoted Shadrach, Meshach, and Abednego in the province of Babylon." The story turns out well for Daniel's friends. They obeyed their God rather than the Babylonian king. Even though they were not at all certain that God was able to save them in the fiery furnace, they courageously told the king, "Be it known to you, O king, that we will not serve your gods and we will not worship the golden statue that you have set up" (3:18). They were faithful to their covenant God and his law: "You shall *not* bow down to them [idols] or worship them" (Exod 20:5). Even facing death, they refused to bow down to the Babylonian idol gods. In the king's words in verse 28, "They disobeyed the king's command and *yielded up their bodies*[78] rather than serve and worship any god *except their own God*." Daniel's friends were true Israelites:

---

worship his image 'into a burning furnace of fire' [*kaminon tou pyros*]" (Dan 3:6). Evans, "Daniel in the New Testament," *Book of Daniel*, II, 522.

76. For the Jews in exile this means freedom of religion. They can worship their God without fear of persecution, without fear of being thrown into a fiery furnace. See Goldingay, *Daniel*, 75.

77. "*Is able*" (*'itai . . . ykl*) in both v. 17 and v. 29.

78. See Revelation 12:11, "They [our brothers] did not cling to life even in the face of death."

faithful to God and his law through thick and thin. Their faithfulness would have encouraged the Israelites in exile to refuse to bow down to idols and remain faithful to their sovereign God, even unto death.

This story also encourages us to "flee from idolatry"[79] and remain faithful to God, even unto death. The modern gods are different from the Babylonian gods, but they have the same alluring but devastating attraction. In North America we are bombarded with messages to pursue wealth and pleasure, to live it up, to live for ourselves.[80] But to give in to those messages is to be unfaithful to God and his law. Jesus said that the essence of Christian living is to "love the Lord your God with *all* your heart, and with *all* your soul, and with *all* your mind. . . . [And] you shall love your neighbor as yourself" (Matt 22:37-40).

Some nations in the world, like ancient Babylon, are police states where absolute loyalty to the state is demanded. To love God with all your heart will result in persecution and even death (see Rev. 13:11-18). Peter may have had the story of the fiery furnace in mind when he wrote to the early Christians, "Beloved, do not be surprised at the *fiery ordeal* that is taking place among you to test you, as though something strange were happening to you. But rejoice insofar as you are sharing Christ's sufferings, so that you may also be glad and shout for joy when his glory is revealed. If you are reviled for the name of Christ, you are blessed, because the spirit of glory, which is the Spirit of God, is resting on you" (1 Pet 4:12-14). The Spirit of God is with us *in the midst* of our suffering (cf. Rom 8:35-39).

God may not take persecution and pain away from us, but God will surely be with us in our suffering. The risen Lord himself encouraged the persecuted church in Smyrna: "Do not fear what you are about to suffer. Beware, the devil is about to throw some of you into prison so that you may be tested, and for ten days you will have affliction. Be faithful until death, and I will give you the crown of life" (Rev. 2:10).

---

79. Paul urges the Corinthian Christians, "Flee from idolatry" (1 Cor 10:14). Significantly, John concludes his first letter, "Little children, keep yourselves from idols" (1 John 5:21). Cf. Revelation 14:9-12, "Those who worship the beast and its image, and receive a mark on their foreheads or on their hands, they will also drink the wine of God's wrath . . . , and they will be tormented with fire and sulfur. . . . And the smoke of their torment goes up forever and ever. . . . Here is a call for the endurance of the saints, those who keep the commandments of God and hold fast to the faith of Jesus."

80. Paul writes, "Be sure of this, that no fornicator or impure person, or one who is greedy (that is, an idolater), has any inheritance in the kingdom of Christ and of God" (Eph 5:5). Lederach, *Daniel,* 88-89, applies the message of this story to the modern idol of "God and Country": "Today this takes the form of civil religion, or religious nationalism in which the nation is the object of glorification and adoration, in which national values are religionized, national heroes are divinized, and the actions of the nation are equated with God's redemptive work."

Peter writes about the last day, the day of the Lord, when "the heavens will pass away with a loud noise, and the elements will be dissolved with *fire*" (2 Pet 3:10). The whole world will be a fiery furnace which no one can escape. What will happen to people who have remained faithful to God? Those who refused to serve other gods? God is able to save them also from that fire; he *will* save them. Peter writes, "In accordance with his promise, we wait for new heavens and a new earth, where righteousness is at home" (2 Pet 3:13).

The book of Revelation echoes this good news. It explains that the people robed in white "are they who have come out of the great ordeal; they have washed their robes and made them white in the blood of the Lamb."

"For this reason they are before the throne of God,
    and worship him day and night within his temple,
    and the one who is seated on the throne will shelter them.
They will hunger no more, and thirst no more;
    the sun will not strike them,
    nor any scorching heat;
for the Lamb at the center of the throne will be their shepherd,
    and he will guide them to springs of the water of life,
and God will wipe away every tear from their eyes." (Rev. 7:14-17)

CHAPTER 4

Nebuchadnezzar's Dream of a Great Tree

Daniel 4:1-37[1]

The sentence is rendered . . .
in order that all who live may know
   that the Most High is sovereign over the kingdom of mortals;
he gives it to whom he will
   and sets over it the lowliest of human beings.

Daniel 4:17

Daniel 4 is the last narrative on King Nebuchadnezzar. It relates how God humbles the proud king of all the earth (4:22) and restores him again when the king acknowledges that Israel's God is "the Most High," "the King of heaven" (4:34, 37). It is a powerful message for those who are fearful of or intimidated by the might of human kings and kingdoms.

In preaching this narrative, the major pitfall to avoid is moralizing. One commentator states forthrightly, "Nebuchadnezzar is an example — a warning of how not to be led astray by power and achievement, a model of how to respond to chastisement and humiliation."[2] It is indeed tempting for preachers to

---

1. Aramaic 3:31–4:34.

2. Goldingay, *Daniel*, 97, quoted approvingly by Lucas, *Daniel*, 118. Lucas himself sketches Nebuchadnezzar first as a positive role model: In contrast to 3:29 where the king relied on the power of physical force to prevent blasphemy against God, here he relies "on the power of personal testimony. Sadly, Christian churches have sometimes given way to the temptation to act more like the Nebuchadnezzar of 3:29 than of 4:1-3." Ibid., 114. Next he uses Nebuchadnezzar as a warning example: "There is a message here not only to national rulers: parents, teachers, business managers, politicians and many others have in some measure the role of being the 'tree of life' to others. If that role is not carried out with due humility, the result can be disastrous for all concerned (4:14)." Ibid., 115-16. Goldingay, *Daniel*, 87 and 91, is much more on target when he

hold up Nebuchadnezzar as a warning example of pride leading to a fall, especially since the narrative ends with the king's statement that God "is able to bring low those who walk in pride" (4:37). Longman writes, "The lesson is learned and the moral of the story is the last word: 'Those who walk in pride he is able to humble.'"[3]

However, God's ability to humble those who walk in pride is not the main theme of this narrative (see "Textual Theme" below). If we wish to preach against the sin of human pride, we should select a text that addresses that issue directly — a text such as Proverbs 16:18, "Pride goes before destruction, and a haughty spirit before a fall."[4] In that case we can certainly use the pride and fall of Nebuchadnezzar to illustrate the theme of Proverbs 16:18. But if the preaching text is Daniel 4, we need to focus the sermon on the theme and goal intended by its author.

Another commentator also wants us to identify with Nebuchadnezzar: "We can become so like Nebuchadnezzar — especially if our hard work has brought us some apparently solid achievement."[5] This commentator next moves from the king lifting his eyes to heaven (v. 34) to the need for pastors to help their parishioners "to look away from themselves, their emotions and moods, their difficulties and mental problems, and 'fix both eyes' . . . on the mercy of God alone."[6] It is not very likely, however, that the biblical author would have the exiles identify with and imitate the very person who brought them into captivity and destroyed Jerusalem and God's holy temple.

Still another commentator finds an application in Nebuchadnezzar's words in verse 2, "I am pleased to recount": "'It is my pleasure' [NIV] shows that it was a true joy for the king to share what God had done in his life — delivered him from madness. This should be the attitude of any believer. If God has done something wonderful, an individual should be delighted to share that experience with others."[7] Again, the pagan king is a rather unlikely character for Israel's identification and imitation.

Daniel is a more likely character for Israel's identification. But here, too, we must be careful not to isolate textual fragments for imitation. For example, the king says that Daniel "is endowed with a spirit of the holy gods" (v. 8). This information leads one commentator to claim, "There was something special about Daniel. . . . Daniel's qualification for interpreting dreams was that God

---

writes, "Nebuchadnezzar does not stand for ordinary humanity being judged for ordinary human pride"; and "The chapter concerns the question, who is king?"

3. Longman, *Daniel,* 122.

4. Cf. Proverbs 29:23, "A person's pride will bring humiliation."

5. Wallace, *The Lord Is King,* 73.

6. Ibid., 81.

7. Miller, *Daniel,* 129.

dwelt within him, and this is the prerequisite for spiritual understanding today."[8] Another commentator uses Daniel's coming before the king to interpret the dream (the same v. 8) to make the point that we all need a good friend: "The fact that Daniel was there with this man at this time is a reminder to us about our own need for each other at times when things, in a similar way, are hard for us, and difficult to understand."[9] The same commentator uses Daniel's direct, "It is you, O king!" (v. 22), to remind preachers that they should be direct in their application: "Those of us who are pastors, when we preach our sermons, slide far too often into an application of the Word so general and vague that no one can possibly take offence and no life can possibly be changed."[10]

Notice that these applications are attached to mere elements in the text and transferred directly to the hearers today. Although these applications are not necessarily unbiblical, they fail to respect the specific *genre* of the redemptive-historical narrative, the *unity* of the narrative and its message, and go beyond the *goal* (intention) of the inspired biblical author. If we wish to do justice to the biblical author, we must first ask the important hermeneutical questions, How did the author intend his original audience to understand this narrative? What is the theme of this narrative, and what is the author's goal? Before we can answer these questions, however, we first need to inquire about the text, its context, and its literary features.

Text and Context

Since the Aramaic text ends chapter 3 at our English 4:3, the question is whether 4:1-3 should be included with chapter 3 or 4. Although there were some reasons to include 4:1-3 with chapter 3,[11] there are even better reasons for including

---

8. Miller, ibid., 131. Cf. Lucas, *Daniel*, 115, "Although Daniel's experience depicted in this story is far removed from that of the ordinary believer, the intuitive spiritual insight he shows is something that all believers need. . . . Just as Daniel's insight grew out of his close relationship with God (Dan 4:8), so the Christian cannot expect to 'have the mind of Christ' without developing a Christlike way of life."

9. Wallace, *The Lord Is King*, 79.

10. Ibid., 82. Cf. W. G. Heslop, *Diamonds from Daniel* (n.p.: Nazarene, 1937), 71, "The prophet speaks plainly and pointedly. . . . While we may not rant, rage, or fume against sinners under the pretext of being hot or zealous, we must not on the other hand use flattering words and compromise with sin under the pretext of winning sinners to the church, or keep the young people."

11. When the chapter divisions were introduced in the thirteenth century, the Vulgate included 4:1-3 with chapter 3 (3:31-33). The reason for this division was probably that these verses include praise of God, which usually comes at the end of the Daniel narratives, as in 4:34-37. Later, the Vulgate chapter divisions were added to the Hebrew/Aramaic text, but both Luther

these verses with the present narrative. Verse 1 marks this narrative as being in the form of an epistle, a proclamation of the king to all peoples. Hence verse 4 continues in the first person, "I, Nebuchadnezzar, was living at ease in my home." Moreover, in verse 2 the king writes about "the signs and wonders that the Most High God has worked *for me*," which applies more to God's restoring the king from his insanity in chapter 4 than to God's saving Daniel's friends from the fiery furnace in chapter 3.[12] And, finally, the king's praise of God in verse 3,

> His kingdom is an everlasting kingdom,
>   and his sovereignty is from generation to generation,

is matched (inverted parallelism) by his praise in verse 34,

> For his sovereignty is an everlasting sovereignty,
>   and his kingdom endures from generation to generation.

This inclusio marks the boundaries of this literary unit at 4:1-37. Chapter 5:1 begins a new narrative about a new character, King Belshazzar. Our preaching text, therefore, is Daniel 4:1-37.[13]

As to the context, this final narrative about King Nebuchadnezzar forms a pair with chapter 5 — another narrative about God punishing a Babylonian king, this time with disastrous results. In fact, the author briefly retells the story of chapter 4 in 5:18-21. The dream narrative of chapter 4 is also related, of course, to the first dream narrative (chapter 2), where King Nebuchadnezzar is troubled by a dream and his wise men are not able to relate the dream or its interpretation, but Daniel succeeds on both counts.[14] The difference in Daniel 4 is that the king *tells* his dream, and still his wise men cannot tell him the interpretation while Daniel can.

The "peoples, nations, and languages" (v. 1) that are invited to hear the king's witness to the greatness of the Most High God are the same "peoples, nations, and languages" that were earlier commanded to fall down and worship the golden statue (3:4; cf. 3:29). Moreover, Nebuchadnezzar's confession that God's "kingdom is an everlasting kingdom" (see vv. 3 and 34 above) is echoed

---

and Calvin moved these three verses to chapter 4. See, e.g., Collins, *Daniel*, 221-22; Lucas, *Daniel*, 107-8; and Steinmann, *Daniel*, 209.

12. See Leupold, *Exposition of Daniel*, 167.

13. One could ask three good readers to read the parts of Nebuchadnezzar (4:1-18, 30, 34-37), Daniel (4:19-27), and the narrator (including the voice from heaven; 4:28-29, 31-33). But if time is a major consideration, one might also consider informing the congregation that the Scripture reading will be incorporated into the sermon itself.

14. For eleven points of similarity between Daniel 2 and 4, see Stefanovic, *Daniel*, 158.

by the similar confession of King Darius (6:26-27) and the vision of the coming kingdom (7:14, 27; cf. Dan 2:44 and Ps 145:13).

This narrative also has many links to passages beyond Daniel. As in chapter 2, the narrator sketches Daniel as another Joseph whom God uses in exile to interpret dreams for a foreign king. Pharaoh described Joseph as "one in whom is the spirit of God" (plural *'ĕlōhîm;* Gen 41:38). In this narrative the king three times describes Daniel as being "endowed with a spirit of the holy gods" (4:8, 9, 18; cf. 5:11, 14). Joseph told Pharaoh that God would give seven years of plenty followed by seven years of famine (Gen 41:28-31). In this narrative Daniel tells the king that he will be living as an animal for "seven times" (4:25).

The king dreams of a great tree with its top reaching to heaven, animals finding shade under it, and birds nesting in it. The interpretation is that King Nebuchadnezzar is that great tree. Ezekiel 31:1-14 presents a similar description of Pharaoh, king of Egypt, being a great tree with birds nesting in its branches and animals giving birth to their young under its branches. In both cases the proud trees fall under the judgment of God and are cut down (cf. Ezek 17:1-10).[15]

The subtheme of God punishing the proud can be traced back to God driving the first human pair from the Garden for desiring to be "like God" (Gen 3:5-6) and God scattering the builders of the Tower of Babel who wished to build "a tower with its top in the heavens," and "make a name" for themselves (Gen 11:4). The more specific theme of God punishing proud kings who think they are gods is also found in Isaiah 10:5-12; 14:12-15 and Ezekiel 28:1-10.[16]

The repeated statement that "the Most High is sovereign over the kingdom of mortals; he gives it to whom he will" (4:17, 25, 32) is similar to God's word in Jeremiah, "I give it to whomever I please. Now I have given all these lands into the hand of King Nebuchadnezzar of Babylon" (27:5-6). The addition of "and sets over it the lowliest of human beings" (4:17) refers to God exalting the lowly — a common theme in the Old as well as the New Testament (the song of Hannah in 1 Sam 2:7-8; Job 5:11; Ps 113:7-8; Ezek 17:24; the song of Mary in Luke 1:52; 1 Cor 1:26-29; and Phil 2:6-11). Finally, Daniel's advice that the king practice "righteousness" and show "mercy to the oppressed" is similar to God's commands through his prophets; for example, "Seek justice, rescue the oppressed" (Isa 1:17).[17]

---

15. For the above parallels, see Steinmann, *Daniel,* 233-34, and Lucas, *Daniel,* 109-10.

16. Porteous, *Daniel,* 65.

17. For some of the references above, see Collins, *Daniel,* 228, 230. For a king's obligation to practice righteousness, see also Jeremiah 22:15-16 and Psalm 72:2, 4.

Literary Features

This chapter consists of a variety of literary genres. As already noted, it is in the form of an epistle written "to all peoples, nations, and languages that live throughout the earth" (4:1). "This 'royal letter' form gives the content of the story special authority."[18] While written mostly in prose, it also contains sections of poetry, as can be seen from the parallelisms in 4:3, 10-12, 14-17, 34b-35, and 37b.[19] The epistle begins with a doxology (4:2-3), continues with a narrative (4:4-36), and concludes with another doxology (4:37). The narrative itself contains the literary forms of a symbolic vision (4:10-17), an oracle (4:14-17), and an admonition (4:27).[20]

Since the overall genre is epistle, most of it is written in the first-person singular, "I, Nebuchadnezzar," except for 4:19-33, which is third-person narrative. The best explanation for the switch to the third person is that in the section 4:19-27 the king is no longer in control but completely dependent on Daniel's interpretation and even admonition, and in 4:28-33 he loses his mind and thus cannot report his experiences. But when his reason returns, "when that period was over, I, Nebuchadnezzar" returns (4:34-37).[21]

Narrative Structure

The narrative proper has three scenes which are marked by change of place and time.

Scene 1: In the king's palace   4:4-27
    A. The king's dream (first person)   4:4-18
    B. Daniel's interpretation and advice (third person)   4:19-27
    Characters: King Nebuchadnezzar and Daniel

Scene 2: Twelve months later, on the roof of the palace   4:28-33
    A. The king's pride (third person)   4:29-30
    B. God's punishment (third person)   4:31-33
    Characters: King Nebuchadnezzar and God ("voice from heaven")

18. Lucas, *Daniel*, 103. "The way it begins, with identification of the writer and of the addressees, and a greeting, is a regular feature of Aramaic letters." Ibid. This kind of introduction is also found in most New Testament epistles (see, e.g., Rom 1:1-7; 1 Cor 1:1-3; 2 Cor 1:1-2; Gal 1:1-5; Eph 1:1-2).

19. These are the sections the NRSV has printed as poetry. Since the line between prose and poetry is somewhat fluid, translators do not always agree where to draw the line. The NIV prints as poetry only 4:3 and 34b-35.

20. See Collins, *Daniel* (1984), 61-64.

21. See Lacocque, *Book of Daniel*, 83, and Lucas, *Daniel*, 104.

Scene 3: Seven times later, in the field   4:34-37
     A. The king acknowledges the Most High (first person)   4:34-35
     B. The king is restored to his kingdom (first person)   4:36-37
     Characters: King Nebuchadnezzar and God ("the King of heaven")

The Plot Line

The opening verses (vv. 1-3) are not part of the narrative proper. Verse 2, "the signs and wonders the Most High God has worked for me," declares the good outcome before the story even begins. After this opening the narrator will have to work hard to create suspense.

He gives the setting in verse 4, "I, Nebuchadnezzar, was living *at ease* in my home and *prospering* in my palace." All is well with the king and his kingdom. Suddenly the mood changes: verse 5, "I saw a dream that *frightened me;* my fantasies in bed and the visions of my head *terrified me.*" The king's dream is the occasioning incident. What was that awful dream? The narrator keeps us in suspense.[22] He first tells us about the king's decree that his wise men be brought in to tell the interpretation of the dream (v. 6). The wise men come but fail (v. 7). "*At last* Daniel came in before me" (v. 8), but we have to wait until verse 10 before the king relates his dream about the beautiful great tree. Even then there is nothing in the dream that should have frightened the king. We have to wait until verse 14 before we are informed what frightened him: a holy watcher crying out, "Cut down the tree," and predicting how things will get progressively worse: "chop off its branches, strip off its foliage and scatter its fruit. Let the animals flee from beneath it and the birds from its branches. But leave its stump and roots in the ground. . . . Let him [the king] be bathed with the dew of heaven, and let his lot be with the animals of the field in the grass of the earth. Let his mind be changed from that of a human, and let the mind of an animal be given to him. And let seven times pass over him" (vv. 14-16). It's a nightmare! What does it mean?

The king asks Daniel to give the interpretation. But before Daniel does so, the narrator first sketches Daniel's reaction: "Daniel . . . was *severely distressed* for a while. His thoughts *terrified him*" (v. 19). Just as the king had been terrified by the dream, so Daniel is now terrified by its meaning. What is so terrifying about the meaning of the dream? Again the narrator keeps us in suspense. We have to wait until verse 22 before he informs us that the tree represents the king and that the cutting down means that the king will be brought low: he will be "driven away from human society," dwell with the animals, and eat grass like

---

22. See Goldingay, *Daniel,* 84, and Lucas, *Daniel,* 102.

oxen and sleep outdoors until seven times have passed by, until the king has learned "that the Most High has sovereignty over the kingdom of mortals, and gives it to whom he will" (v. 25). God's punishment of the king will be severe. But there is hope for restoration if the king will finally acknowledge that God is the King of kings (v. 26). Daniel advises the king to break with his sins by promoting "righteousness" and showing "mercy to the oppressed, so that your prosperity may be prolonged" (v. 27). Will the king mend his ways?

Twelve months later, while looking out over his many edifices in Babylon, the king brags about his "mighty power" and "his glorious majesty" (v. 30). He speaks about himself as if he were God. God's punishment follows immediately: the king loses his mind, is driven from human society, lives outdoors with the animals, and eats grass like oxen. He even begins to look like an animal with long hair like eagles' feathers and nails like birds' claws (v. 33). How far the mighty king has fallen! The king who, like a tree, had sheltered animals has himself become nothing but an animal.

The turn to a resolution takes place in verse 34: "When that period was over, I, Nebuchadnezzar, lifted my eyes to heaven, and my reason returned to me. I blessed the Most High, and praised and honored the one who lives forever. For his sovereignty is an everlasting sovereignty, and his kingdom endures from generation to generation." The king finally acknowledges God as the Most High, the King of kings. The outcome is that the king is re-established over his kingdom (v. 36). The conclusion follows, "Now I, Nebuchadnezzar, praise and extol and honor the King of heaven" (v. 37).

We can sketch the plot line of this narrative as complex.[23]

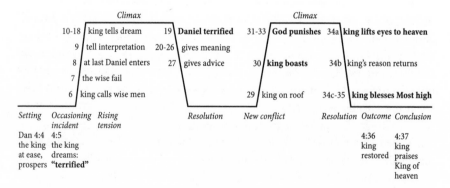

23. A single plot line is also possible with the climax at God punishing the king (vv. 31-33) and the turn to resolution with the king lifting his eyes to heaven (v. 34). But a complex plot line can do better justice to the scenes with the question in Scene 1, Will Daniel be able to interpret the dream when the wise men failed? And the questions in Scenes 2 and 3, Will the king mend his ways or will the dream be fulfilled? Will the king honor God and be restored?

This plot line is helpful in discerning the movement in the story, its climaxes and resolutions, and the most appropriate form for the sermon — a hybrid narrative form, even though the overall genre is that of epistle.

Character Description

The main character in this narrative is Nebuchadnezzar. He describes himself as "living at ease in my home and prospering in my palace" (v. 4). By sharp contrast the dream frightens and terrifies him (v. 5). But when Daniel is terrified by the meaning of the dream, the king shows his compassion for him: "Belteshazzar, do not let the dream or the interpretation terrify you" (v. 19). Daniel describes the king as follows: "You have grown great and strong. Your greatness has increased and reaches to heaven, and your sovereignty to the ends of the earth" (v. 22). The king reveals his pride when he says to himself, "Is this not magnificent Babylon, which *I* have built as a royal capital *by my mighty power* and *for my glorious majesty?*" (v. 30).[24] He is immediately punished with the loss of his mind/reason, dwelling outside with the animals and eating grass like oxen (v. 33). When the seven times are up, the king lifts his eyes to heaven and his reason returns (v. 34). Then the king gives God the glory: "Now I, Nebuchadnezzar, praise and extol and honor the King of heaven, for all his works are truth, and his ways are justice; and he is able to bring low those who walk in pride" (v. 37).

Daniel is a minor character in this narrative. The king describes Daniel three times as being "endowed with a spirit of the holy gods" (vv. 8, 9, 18). When Daniel hears the dream, he is "severely distressed for a while" and "terrified" (v. 19a). His character is further developed by his speech, which shows his concern for the king: "May the dream be for those who hate you" (v. 19c). He also shows his courage by passing on to the king the bad news and even offering him the prophetic advice to "atone for your sins with righteousness, and your iniquities with mercy to the oppressed, so that your prosperity may be prolonged" (vv. 25-27).

Actually, Daniel functions as a spokesperson for God, for God is the other main character in this story.[25] God is described as "the Most High God" (v. 2; cf.

---

24. As translated this is a rhetorical question, but the argument has been made that "*hălā'* (traditionally understood as 'isn't?') does not introduce a rhetorical question but marks an exclamation." See Steinmann, *Daniel*, 250.

25. "The real focus and center of this story is Nebuchadnezzar himself; here even Daniel lacks personality and character and functions merely as a conduit for the message of the Most High. In this sense, it can be said that the real protagonists of this narrative are two sovereigns, one in heaven and one in Babylon." Towner, *Daniel*, 59.

3:26), "the Most High" (vv. 17, 24, 25, 32, 34), "Heaven" (metonymy in v. 26), "a voice from heaven" (v. 31), and, as a climax, "King of heaven" (v. 37). God's kingdom is described as "an everlasting kingdom," and his sovereignty as being "from generation to generation" (vv. 3, 34). God's character is further developed by his actions: his patience with the king in warning him with a dream and giving him time to repent, and his sovereignty over all by humbling the mighty king of Babylon and later restoring him to his throne.

Repetition

The author again uses repetition to show his emphases. We already noted some repetitions above: the king describing Daniel three times as being "endowed with a spirit of the holy gods" and the various names used for God ("the Most High God," "the Most High," "Heaven," "a voice from heaven," and "King of heaven"). "Most High occurs in this chapter more often than in any other chapter" (vv. 2, 17, 24, 25, 32, 34).[26] In this chapter, and only here, the author uses the term "watcher" three times (vv. 13, 17, 23). The author uses the word "earth" ten times,[27] "four of which concern the impression of Nebuchadnezzar's power on earth (vv. 10, 11, 20, 22)," and the word "heaven" sixteen times,[28] "most of which appear in connection with the domain and power of God."[29] Seow concludes, "Clearly at issue in the chapter is the relationship of earthly power and heavenly power — the power of Nebuchadnezzar versus the power of God."[30] Significantly, the final time the narrator uses the word "heaven," he speaks of God as "the King of heaven," an expression found only here in the Old Testament.[31]

This phrase, "King of heaven," links the concepts of domain and power with kingship. The author uses the words "king" and "kingdom" so often that Goldingday concludes, "Chapter 4 is centrally concerned with the kingship of Nebuchadnezzar and the kingship or rule of the Most High (God) or of (the King/Lord of) Heaven (cf. 4:17, 18, 22, 24, 25, 26, 30, 31, 32, 34, 36, 37)."[32] Of particular importance for discerning the point of this narrative is the threefold repetition by three different characters:

The holy watcher warns,

26. Lederach, *Daniel*, 92.
27. 4:1, 10, 11, 15 (2x), 20, 22, 23, 35 (2x).
28. 4:11, 12, 13, 15, 20, 21, 22, 23 (2x), 25, 26, 31, 33, 34, 35, and 37.
29. Seow, *Daniel*, 65.
30. Ibid.
31. Collins, *Daniel*, 232, who notes that "Daniel uses the phrase 'Lord of heaven' in 5:23."
32. Goldingay, *Daniel*, 87. Cf. n. 25 above.

". . . in order that all who live may know
that the Most High is sovereign over the kingdom of mortals;
he gives it to whom he will." (v. 17)

Daniel says,

". . . until you have learned
that the Most High has sovereignty over the kingdom of mortals,
and gives it to whom he will." (v. 25; cf.v. 26)

And the voice from heaven declares,

". . . until you have learned
that the Most High has sovereignty over the kingdom of mortals
and gives it to whom he will." (v. 32)

The various repetitions may also be evidence for more complex literary structures. Baldwin suggests an A B B′ A′ structure: "The king begins and ends with an ascription of praise to the Most High (vv. 1-3; 34-37), while the main story divides into two parts: 1. Nebuchadnezzar's narration of his dream (vv. 4-18) and 2. Its interpretation and fulfillment (vv. 19-33)."[33] More recently Shea suggested the following chiastic structure:[34]

Prologue: Post-fulfillment Proclamation — Poem I		vv. 1-3
A Dream Reception		vv. 4-7
X Dialogue I. King to Daniel		vv. 8-9
B Dream Recital		vv. 10-17
Y Dialogue II. King to Daniel; Daniel to king		vv. 18-19
B′ Dream Interpretation		vv. 20-26
Z Dialogue III. Daniel to king		v. 27
A′ Dream Fulfillment		vv. 28-33
Epilogue: Post-fulfillment Restoration — Poem II		vv. 34-37

Although this chiasm is not helpful for discerning the theme because verses 18-19 are not the focal point of this epistle, it does show that the passage has been carefully crafted.

---

33. Baldwin, *Daniel*, 107.

34. Shea, "Further Literary Structures in Daniel 2-7: An Analysis of Daniel 4," *AUSS* 23/2 (1985) 202.

Theocentric Interpretation

Since God is one of the main characters in this narrative, we can almost skip this step of theocentric interpretation. But because of our inclination to draw application(s) primarily from the human characters (see pp. 113-15 above), it will be well to highlight how the author presents God. We noted above that God is called "the Most High God" (v. 2) and the Most High" (vv. 17, 24, 25, 32, 34).[35] Evidently, the author wishes to focus in this chapter particularly on the sovereignty of God. In addition to highlighting these names for God, the narrative itself also focuses on God's sovereignty: God changed the king's mind from that of a human to that of an animal (v. 16; divine passives). God drove him away from human society and made him dwell with the wild animals (v. 25; divine passives).[36] And God shows his sovereignty again by "returning" the king's reason and "restoring" his majesty and splendor (v. 36, divine passives). Within the narrative the author repeats three times that "the Most High is sovereign over the kingdom of mortals" (vv. 17, 25, 32; cf.v. 26). He further underscores the sovereignty of God by ending the narrative with the mighty king of Babylon praising, extolling, and honoring "the King of heaven" (v. 37). Moreover, the author has framed the narrative with a magnificent description of God's kingdom: in contrast to human kingdoms, God's "kingdom is an everlasting kingdom, and his sovereignty is from generation to generation" (vv. 3, 34).

Textual Theme and Goal

Some commentators hold that "the main theme of the story is the humiliation and restoration of Nebuchadnezzar."[37] The goal that would match this theme would be to warn against human pride (see pp. 113-14 above). But we noted earlier that this is a subtheme and that Israel, humbled as it was in exile, hardly needed a warning against pride.

Towner rightly states, "Chapter 4 is a story about two sovereignties"[38] (see

35. Goldingay, *Daniel*, 85-86, notes that no other chapter of the Old Testament uses the title "Most High" as often as this chapter.

36. Redditt, *Daniel*, 82.

37. E.g., Collins, *Daniel* (1984), 62. But see also ibid., 65, "The intention of Daniel 4 is made quite explicit in v. 22 [25]: Nebuchadnezzar is told that his humiliation will last 'till you know that the Most High rules the kingdom of men, and gives it to whom he will." Lederach, *Daniel*, 92, states, "The strong motif of human or especially royal pride is secondary to the primary emphasis on divine sovereignty, as shown in the reason for the decree . . . (4:17)."

38. Towner, *Daniel*, 59, "Chapter 4 is a story about two sovereignties. It comes to juxtapose

pp. 122-23 above). Seow calls attention to Nebuchadnezzar's confessional praise of God both at the beginning (4:2-3) and end of this chapter (4:34-37). He concludes, "Indeed, by this framing, the key theological issue in this chapter is identified as the sovereignty of God over against human kingship, and for this reason the terms for sovereignty and kingship . . . are reiterated throughout the chapter (vv. 3, 17, 18, 22, 25, 26, 31, 32, 34, 36)."[39] We might, therefore, formulate the theme as, "The Most High God is sovereign over earthly kingdoms." This theme, however, is too general, for many other biblical passages could be preached with this theme. We need to formulate a theme that is more textually specific.

Note that the narrator clearly states the goal of this narrative in the words of the holy watcher, "The sentence is rendered by decree of the watchers . . . , *in order that* all who live may know that the Most High is sovereign over the kingdom of mortals; he gives it to whom he will" (v. 17). This idea is repeated two more times (vv. 25, 32; cf. v. 26). Because theme and goal are related, we can often back into the theme from the stated goal. We can, therefore, formulate the theme as follows, *The Most High God, being sovereign over earthly kingdoms, gives them to whom he will.*[40]

As indicated, the "holy watcher" states the goal as, "in order that all who live may know that the Most High is sovereign over the kingdom of mortals" (v. 17). With his emphasis on "may know" (v. 17), we may be tempted to formulate the author's goal as, "*to teach* people that the Most High God is sovereign over earthly kingdoms and gives them to whom he will." But we may be able to formulate the goal more existentially by taking into account the circumstances of the original audience addressed by this book. Israel is suffering in exile in Babylon. It looks like the Babylonian gods have conquered Israel's God. By means of this letter from the mightiest king on earth, however, the author informs the exiles of their God bringing down the mighty Babylonian king until even he confesses that their God is the Most High and gives the kingdom to whom he will. The author's goal, therefore, is more than simply to teach; he seeks *to assure the suffering, bewildered Israelites that, despite appearances, their God is sovereign over earthly kingdoms and gives them to whom he will.*[41]

---

the strength or power of the greatest of all human sovereigns (making the Aramaic term *t-q-f,* 'grow strong, mighty,' a kind of pivot — cf. vv. 11, 20, 22, 30 as applied to Nebuchadnezzar, and v. 3 as applied to the Most High God) with the strength and power of the Most High."

39. Seow, *Daniel,* 64.

40. Cf. Porteous, *Daniel,* 65, "The theme of this chapter is summed up in verse 25 in what is to be Nebuchadnezzar's discovery after he has been disciplined by God, that is, that 'the Most High is sovereign over the kingdom of men, giving it to the man of his choice.'" So also Parry, "Desolation of the Temple and Messianic Enthronement in Daniel 11:36–12:3," *JETS* 54/3 (2011) 487.

41. Cf. Longman, *Daniel,* 122, "The purpose of the story is to encourage their (Israel's) con-

Ways to Preach Christ

Since there is no promise of the coming Messiah in this chapter,[42] nor a type of Christ,[43] nor a contrast of its message with that of Jesus in the New Testament, we shall explore the remaining four ways to Christ.

Redemptive-Historical Progression

Redemptive-historical progression offers a good way to move in the sermon from Daniel 4 to Jesus Christ in the New Testament. Daniel 4 proclaims that the Most High God, being sovereign over earthly kingdoms, gives them to whom he will. Nebuchadnezzar's earlier dream of the statue of gold, silver, bronze, and iron vividly portrayed this theme as God gave the Babylonian kingdom first to Medo-Persia, then to Greece, next to Rome (Dan 2).

In the time of the Roman Empire the sovereign God sent his Son Jesus into this world to do battle with the most powerful ruler on earth, Satan. Jesus called Satan "the ruler of the world" (John 12:31; 14:30; 16:11). As soon as Jesus began his mission, Satan attacked him: "The devil took him to a very high mountain and showed him all the kingdoms of the world and their splendor; and he said to him, 'All these I will give you, if you will fall down and worship me.' Jesus said to him, 'Away with you Satan! For it is written, "Worship the Lord your God, and serve only him"'" (Matt 4:8-10). Jesus withstood the temptation of Satan and began to win this fierce battle. Jesus healed people and cast out demons. His disciples reported, "Lord, in your name even the *demons* submit to us!" Jesus responded, "I watched Satan fall from heaven like a flash of lightning" (Luke 10:17-18).

---

fidence in the light of their helplessness before a seemingly all-powerful ruler." Cf. p. 126, "God's people are called to take comfort in this truth." Cf. Collins, *Daniel* (1984), 65, "The significance of this message for Jews in the service of a pagan king was that it assured them that their God was in control, despite appearance to the contrary."

42. Towner, *Daniel*, 67, suggests that "God's absolute sovereignty appears to be a promise. To Jews languishing in Babylonian exile it is a long-term basis for hope." But there is no promise of the coming Messiah in this passage.

43. Gregory Beale argues quite convincingly that the title "Lord of lords and King of kings" in Revelation 17:14 has its origin in Daniel 4:37 (LXX). He concludes, "By the application of this title to Christ, the author [of Revelation] may view God's sovereign humbling of the king of Babylon in Daniel 4 as a typological prophecy of Christ's sovereign defeat of the end-time foe who is closely associated with eschatological Babylon." Although the author of Revelation may well have seen God defeating the mighty king of Babylon as a type of Christ defeating Satan, we cannot use this line of reasoning in the sermon, since Daniel 4:37 (LXX) is "an interpretative expansion of Daniel 4:32 of the Masoretic Text," and therefore not in our English versions.

But Satan managed to have Jesus killed and thought he had won the battle. His victory was his defeat, however, for Jesus rose victoriously from the dead, thus conquering sin and death. After his resurrection Jesus declared, "*All authority* in heaven and on earth has been given to me" (Matt 28:18). From that time forward the power of Satan was severely limited. The book of Revelation describes Satan as a ferocious dragon who is now bound with a great chain (Rev. 20:1-2). It also predicts that at the end of this period of time Satan will be released and will seek to destroy the church worldwide (Rev. 20:7-9). Revelation describes it as a war: Satan and his hosts "will make war on the Lamb, and the Lamb will conquer them, for he is Lord of lords and King of kings" (Rev. 17:14). The Lamb, Jesus, will be completely victorious over Satan. An angel cries out, "Fallen, fallen is Babylon the Great!" (Rev. 14:8). Thus "the kingdom of the *world* has become the kingdom of our *Lord* and of his *Messiah*, and he will reign forever and ever" (Rev. 11:15). In the end, the Most High God gives the kingdom to his Son Jesus Christ.

Analogy

The way of analogy also offers several possibilities to move from our text to Christ in the New Testament. For example, as Daniel 4:17 teaches that "the Most High is sovereign over the kingdom of mortals; he gives it to whom he will," so Jesus says to Pilate, "You would have no power over me unless it had been given you from above" (John 19:11).

Another analogy would be, as the sovereign God brought low the mighty Babylonian king, so Jesus defeated an even mightier "ruler of the world," Satan.[44] Jesus said, "Now is the judgment of this world; now the ruler of this world will be driven out" (John 12:31).

We can also draw an analogy from the author's goal "to encourage the suffering, bewildered Israelites with the message that, despite appearances, their God is sovereign over earthly kingdoms and gives them to whom he will." Jesus similarly encouraged his followers. He said, "See, I am sending you out like sheep into the midst of wolves. . . . When they hand you over, do not worry about how you are to speak or what you are to say; for what you are to say will be given to you at that time; for it is not you who speak, but the Spirit of your Father speaking through you" (Matt 10:16, 19; cf. Matt 28:19-20). Again, Jesus said, "Do not be afraid, little flock, for it is your Father's good pleasure to give you the kingdom" (Luke 12:34; cf. Matt 25:34).

---

44. "The book of Revelation, often likening the powers of evil to Babylon of old, shows God's ultimate victory on behalf of his faithful people." Longman, *Daniel,* 128.

Longitudinal Themes

Longitudinal themes offers another way to preaching Christ. Although one can trace the subtheme that God will humble the proud (as he humbled Nebuchadnezzar) and lift up the humble (4:17) from the song of Hannah (1 Sam 2:7-8) to the song of Mary (Luke 1:52) to 1 Corinthians 1:26-29 and finally to Philippians 2:6-11, this is bound to detract listeners from the theme of the text, "the Most High God, being sovereign over earthly kingdoms, gives them to whom he will."

For a well-focused sermon, it is much better to trace longitudinal themes that are part of the textual theme. In this case, we can trace the theme of God being sovereign from Daniel 4 to Daniel 7 where the Ancient of Days gives the one like a son of man "dominion and glory and kingship. . . . His dominion is an everlasting dominion that shall not pass away, and his kingship is one that shall never be destroyed" (7:14). From there we can move to the New Testament where Jesus identifies himself as "the Son of Man," and after his resurrection claims, "All authority in heaven and on earth has been given to me."

Another possibility is to trace that part of the textual theme that speaks of God giving the kingdom "to whom he will," perhaps focusing on, he "sets over it the lowliest of human beings" (4:17). In Israel's history God set over his kingdom the young David, bypassing his older brothers; he chose the younger Solomon over Adonijah. Isaiah prophesied about God's chosen Servant, "He was despised and rejected by others" (53:3), but God allotted him "a portion with the great" (53:12). From there we can move to the New Testament to Jesus born in a stable, poor, despised, crucified, but claiming after his resurrection that God had given to him "all authority in heaven and on earth" (Matt 28:18). This claim was echoed in the early Christian hymn,

> Therefore God also highly exalted him
> and gave him the name that is above every name,
> so that at the name of Jesus every knee should bend,
> in heaven and on earth and under the earth,
> and every tongue should confess that Jesus Christ is Lord,
> to the glory of God the Father. (Phil 2:9-11)

New Testament References

The appendix of the Greek New Testament lists Matthew 13:32 (and par. Mark 4:32; Luke 13:19) as an allusion to Daniel 4:9 (12) and 18 (21). The king dreamed about a tree so great that "the animals of the field found shade under it, [and] the birds of the air nested in its branches" (4:12, 21). Jesus said, "With what can we compare the kingdom of God, or what parable will we use for it? It is like a mustard seed, which, when sown upon the ground, is the smallest of all the seeds on earth; yet when it is sown it grows up and becomes the greatest of all shrubs, and puts forth large branches, so that the birds of the air can make nests in its shade" (Mark 4:30-32). Collins surmises that the change from a great world tree to a mustard shrub "was probably deliberate in the teaching of Jesus: the kingdom will be manifested in the social order but not in the way that his audience expected. It will not be a mighty international empire, but nevertheless it will provide a home for its members."[45] Note, however, that in Matthew 13:32, "the greatest of shrubs . . . becomes a tree."[46]

A concordance may offer some other suitable references. For example, Jesus taught us to pray, "Our Father in heaven ["King of heaven," Dan 4:37], your kingdom come" (Matt 6:9-10). Paul writes concerning the resurrection, "But each in his own order: Christ the first fruits, then at his coming those who belong to Christ. Then comes the end, when he hands over the kingdom to God the Father, after he has destroyed every ruler and every authority and power" (1 Cor 15:23-24). Paul also writes concerning Jesus Christ, "In him all things in heaven and on earth were created, things visible and invisible, whether thrones or dominions or rulers or powers — all things have been created through him and for him" (Col 1:16). Peter urges Christians, "Therefore, brothers and sisters, be all the more eager to confirm your call and election. . . . For in this way, entry into the eternal kingdom of our Lord and Savior Jesus Christ will be richly provided for you" (2 Pet 1:10-11).

Sermon Theme, Goal, and Need

The sermon theme and goal should be based on the textual theme and goal. Since there is no contrast between this textual theme and the New Testament, we can use it as our sermon theme, *The Most High God, being sovereign over earthly kingdoms, gives them to whom he will.*

We formulated the author's goal as "to assure the suffering, bewildered Is-

---

45. Collins, *Daniel*, 107.

46. In addition, the appendix sees allusions to Daniel 4:27 [30], "Is this not magnificent [great] Babylon, which I have built as a royal capital by my mighty power and for my glorious majesty?" in Ephesians 1:19, "what is the immeasurable greatness of his power," and in Revelation 14:8, "Fallen, fallen is Babylon the great!" For Daniel 4:31 [34], "I blessed the Most High, and praised and honored the one who lives forever," it lists Revelation 4:9, the living creatures giving "glory and honor and thanks to the one who is seated on the throne, who lives forever and ever." None of these allusions make for strong bridges to Jesus Christ.

raelites that, despite appearances, their God is sovereign over earthly kingdoms and gives them to whom he will." We can have a similar goal for the sermon: *to assure God's suffering, bewildered people today that, despite appearances, our God is sovereign over earthly kingdoms and gives them to whom he will.*

This goal points to the need that should be addressed in this sermon: because of worldwide, state-sponsored persecution, God's people begin to question whether God is indeed sovereign over earthly kingdoms. The sermon introduction could illustrate this questioning of God's sovereignty (Why doesn't God stop the terrible persecution of his people around the world?), link it to our questions today, move to Israel's questions about God's sovereignty as it suffered in exile, and then begin the exposition. But in a sermon series, and since this is the last narrative on King Nebuchadnezzar, one can also quickly review the earlier stories about the king[47] and then move into exposition. I will demonstrate the latter below.

Sermon Exposition

Daniel 4 is the final story about King Nebuchadnezzar. The king has arrived at the height of his power. We first met him in Daniel 1 when he besieged Jerusalem, took some of the gold and silver vessels from the house of God, and placed these items in the house of his gods. He also captured young men whom he took into his palace for a thorough reeducation. Among them were Daniel and his three friends. Daniel refused to eat the king's non-kosher food and requested vegetables and water for himself and his friends. God blessed their faithfulness and gave them superior wisdom. The king therefore stationed them in his palace.

In Daniel 2 we read that Nebuchadnezzar had this strange dream about a huge statue with a head of gold, chest and arms of silver, middle and thighs of bronze, legs of iron, and feet of iron and clay. Then a stone was cut out and struck the statue on its feet of iron and clay, annihilating the statue. But the stone "became a great mountain and filled the whole earth" (2:35). When his wise men could not tell him what the dream was, the king threatened to butcher them all. But God revealed the mystery of the dream as well as its interpretation to Daniel. God had given the great Babylonian kingdom to Nebuchadnezzar, the head of gold, but after him would give it to Medo-Persia, then to the Greeks, and finally to the Romans. But in the end God would replace all these human kingdoms with his own kingdom — a kingdom "that shall never be destroyed" (2:44).

In Daniel 3 we read that King Nebuchadnezzar wanted to be more than the

---

47. See, e.g., Boice, *Daniel,* 52-53.

head of gold. He made a huge statue for himself and overlaid the whole image with gold. Then he forced all "peoples, nations, and languages . . . to fall down and worship" this idol (3:4-5). All fell down except Daniel's three friends. The king gave them another chance, but they refused to worship the king's gods. Then the king had them thrown into the fiery furnace. But God was with them in the middle of the fire and saved them. In response the king decreed that no one might utter blasphemy against the God of the three friends, "for there is no other god who is able to deliver in this way" (3:29).

The events of Daniel 4 take place about twenty years later.[48] We are now at the peak of the king's reign. The king had finished his battles to expand his kingdom. He had plundered Egypt, Tyre, Israel, and other nations and brought their treasures to Babylon. He used them to beautify existing temples and to build new ones (4:30). For his wife he built the famous Hanging Gardens, which became one of the seven wonders of the ancient world. There is peace in his kingdom (4:4). The king has arrived.

Then the king writes a letter. Chapter 4:1, "King Nebuchadnezzar to all peoples, nations, and languages that live throughout the earth: May you have abundant prosperity!" The king addresses "all peoples, nations, and languages that live *throughout the earth*." Like the Assyrian kings before him, King Nebuchadnezzar considers himself the king of all the earth.[49] And indeed, he rules much of the then-known world. His kingdom stretches from the Persian Gulf in the east to the Mediterranean Sea in the west and from Egypt in the south to Iran in the north. King of all the earth!

But in verses 2 and 3 this king of all the earth makes a surprising statement: "The signs and wonders[50] that the Most High God has worked for me[51] I am

---

48. Miller, *Daniel*, 127-28, calculates that "this incident must have taken place no later than the thirty-fourth year (571 B.C.) of his forty-three-year reign (605-562 B.C.)." Steinmann, *Daniel*, 208, comes to a similar conclusion: "It is most likely that Daniel 4 is set sometime during 573-569."

49. "The Assyrian and Babylonian kings regarded themselves as kings of all the earth, and in their inscriptions were accustomed thus to speak of themselves. This practice was also in vogue among the Persian rulers. . . . [cf.] 6:25." Young, *Prophecy of Daniel*, 97.

50. "These signs were events of an extraordinary or miraculous nature, and the word 'wonders' serves to designate the effect which they produced." Ibid. Seow, *Daniel*, 65, points out that "the reference to divine performance of 'signs and wonders' recalls the manifestation of God's power in the liberation of Israel from bondage (Exod 7:3; Deut 6:22; 7:19; Ps 135:9). Moreover, the deity is called 'the Most High God,' an epithet of God as the supreme ruler of heaven and earth (see, for example, Gen 14:19-20; Num 24:16)." Hill, "Daniel," 90, adds, "The report of divine 'signs and wonders' makes the point that God is still in the business of performing miracles for his people — the Hebrew community in exile needed this assurance."

51. "The king is still deeply impressed by what has just befallen him. . . . It was a rare deliverance that the king had experienced." Leupold, *Exposition of Daniel*, 171.

pleased to recount. How great are his signs, how mighty his wonders! His kingdom is an everlasting kingdom, and his sovereignty is from generation to generation." He declares forthrightly that there is a greater king and a greater kingdom than his: the kingdom of the Most High God is "an everlasting kingdom, and his sovereignty is from generation to generation." How did Nebuchadnezzar learn that there is a greater king and a greater kingdom than his?

Verse 4, "I, Nebuchadnezzar, was living at ease in my home and prospering in my palace." Times were good. There was peace in his kingdom. The king could live at ease in his home and prosper in his palace. He was content.[52]

But suddenly his mood changed abruptly.[53] He shifted from being content to being terrified. What happened? The king writes in verse 5, "I saw a *dream* that frightened me; my fantasies in bed and the visions of my head *terrified* me." Years earlier, the king had had a strange dream that troubled him (2:1, 3). But this was such a nightmare that it frightened him. He woke up drenched in sweat. And when he reflected further on the dream, he was absolutely terrified.[54]

What does the king of all the earth do when he is terrified by a nightmare? He makes a decree, of course. He writes in verses 6 and 7, "So I made a decree that all the wise men of Babylon should be brought before me, in order that they might tell me the interpretation of the dream. Then the magicians, the enchanters, the Chaldeans, and the diviners came in, and I told them the dream, but they could not tell me its interpretation." These wise men had failed him before. We don't know why the king still relied on them. Perhaps he assumed that Daniel would be with them, but Daniel may have been out of town.[55] In any event, he was not with the wise men. And these wise men could not give him an interpretation of the dream. So the king of all the earth remained terrified.

Verses 8 and 9, "*At last* Daniel came in before me — he who was named Belteshazzar after the name of my god,[56] and who is endowed with a spirit of

---

52. "'Contented' is a translation of the Aramaic word *šĕlēh*, which means properly 'at ease' or 'at rest,' conveying both contentment and security." Miller, *Daniel*, 130.

53. "The abruptness with which this verse is introduced is a literary device to indicate how utterly unexpectedly the dream came." Leupold, *Exposition of Daniel*, 172-73. Cf. Anderson, *Signs and Wonders*, 41, "The contrast between his state of mind in v. 4 and in v. 5 is dramatic. The storyteller has effected it in just two short sentences."

54. "Apparently awakened by the dream, though he is still lying down, he is alarmed also by his 'thoughts' upon his bed, the reflections occasioned by the dream. Furthermore, certain fancies or blurred images reminiscent of the dream, here called 'visions of my head,' contributed to the same result." Leupold, *Exposition of Daniel*, 173.

55. "A simple explanation is that Daniel was not at the palace with the other wise men when the call came forth, and this may be the truth of the matter." Miller, *Daniel*, 131.

56. "From the point of view of a Jewish reader, there is irony in Nebuchadnezzar's use of

the holy gods[57] — and I told him the dream: 'O Belteshazzar, chief of the magicians, I know that you are endowed with a spirit of the holy gods and that no mystery[58] is too difficult for you. Hear the dream that I saw; tell me its interpretation.'"

At last we get to hear the dream that so frightened the king. Verses 10 to 12, "Upon my bed this is what I saw; there was a tree at the center of the earth, and its height was great. The tree grew great and strong, its top reached to heaven, and it was visible to the ends of the whole earth." The phrase "its top reached to heaven" reminds us of the defiance against God when people decided to build the Tower of Babel "with its top in the heavens" (Gen 11:4). The king continues, "Its foliage was beautiful, its fruit abundant, and it provided food for all. The animals of the field found shade under it, the birds of the air nested in its branches, and from it all living beings were fed." So far so good. Except for "its top reached to heaven,"[59] it is a beautiful, peaceful picture. Nothing that should frighten the king. I can imagine that this dream reminded the king of himself. Was not his kingdom "visible to the ends of the whole earth"? Did he not provide "food for all"? Did not many nations find shelter in his great kingdom? Yes, the dream is about King Nebuchadnezzar! But why then was he so frightened, even terrified?

Finally the king gets to that point. Verse 13, "I continued looking, in the visions of my head as I lay in bed, and there was a holy[60] watcher, coming down from heaven." The phrase "coming down from heaven" again reminds us of the Tower of Babel: "the LORD *came down* to see the city and the tower, which mor-

---

popular etymology ('Bel' being taken as a title of Marduk) to link Daniel (and presumably his prowess) with Marduk, the god of Babylon." Lucas, *Daniel,* 109.

57. "The only other person so characterized in Scripture is Joseph, whom Pharaoh says is 'a man in whom is a spirit of gods . . . (Gen 41:38). That Daniel preserves this comment signals that he is drawing a parallel between Joseph and himself. . . . He wants to emphasize that the God of Israel — who protected Joseph, enabled him to prosper in Pharaoh's court, and eventually led his own people out from bondage in Egypt — was still with his people exiled in Babylon, and eventually would deliver them from bondage there." Steinmann, *Daniel,* 233.

58. "A mystery of this sort is one which has been created and therefore can only be solved by God. However, he does use human intermediaries to do so, those in whom God's spirit does in fact dwell, those to whom he chooses to give the power of interpretation." Towner, *Daniel,* 62.

59. "To Daniel's original audience of Judean exiles, this [the tree's top reaching to heaven] would have signaled that the tree represented Babylon and its hubris, since this is parallel to the description of the plan for the Tower of Babel (Gen 11:4). Moreover, since the tree 'was visible to the end of the entire earth' (Dan 4:11), it represented the prominence of Babylon as a world power. The various nationalities that came under Babylonian dominance are symbolized by the creatures for which it provides food and shelter." Steinmann, *Daniel,* 234.

60. "The use of the epithet *holy* does not point to moral excellence, but indicates the celestial origin of the watcher." Hammer, *Daniel,* 51.

tals had built" (Gen 11:5). Holy watchers watch the earth for God.[61] They are messengers from God. We can think of angels.

In verse 14 we read the message of the holy watcher: "He cried aloud and said: 'Cut down the tree and chop off its branches, strip off its foliage and scatter its fruit.[62] Let the animals flee from beneath it and the birds from its branches.'" It's a disaster! No wonder the king is frightened. He had identified himself with that great tree, and now he hears the orders to cut down that beautiful tree. It is to be destroyed. Its large branches are to be chopped off; its foliage stripped off; its fruit scattered. And the animals and birds it had sheltered are to flee. There will be nothing left. Except a stump.

Verse 15, "But leave its stump and roots in the ground, with a band of iron and bronze, in the tender grass of the field." This is a note of hope. We remember the familiar words of Isaiah, "A shoot shall come out from the *stump* of Jesse, and a branch shall grow out of his roots" (11:1).[63] Even though the royal tree of King David was cut down, a shoot would later come out of that stump, the great son of David, Jesus Christ. So here in Nebuchadnezzar's dream, the tree is cut down but the stump remains in the ground "with a band of iron and bronze" around it. The band of iron and bronze is probably added to protect the stump.[64] In any event, though the stump is evidence of the disaster that has taken place, it offers a note of hope for the future.

---

61. "The class of heavenly beings known as 'Watchers' may have been conceived as those whose activities reflected this particular divine concern to look after and protect humans." Lucas, *Daniel*, 110. Cf. Psalm 121:3-4, "He who keeps you will not slumber. He who keeps Israel will neither slumber nor sleep."

62. "The imperative forms are all plural: 'You (plural) cut down . . . chop off . . . strip off . . . scatter' (v. 13). . . . Poignantly . . . , the plural forms recall the Tower of Babel story: 'Come, let *us* go down.'" Seow, *Daniel*, 68.

63. Cf. Isaiah 6:13 and Job 14:7, "For there is hope for a tree, if it is cut down, that it will sprout again."

64. Commentators are not agreed on the meaning of the band of iron and bronze around the stump. See Young, *Prophecy of Daniel*, 104, for five different interpretations. There are two main positions. Some think "that it is part of the shift of imagery, and refers to the demented king's being restrained in fetters" (Lucas, *Daniel*, 112; so also Goldingay, *Daniel*, 89, and Steinmann, *Daniel*, 245). Others think it is placed around the stump to keep it from splitting or "to protect it from destruction" (Miller, *Daniel*, 133; so also Baldwin, *Daniel*, 112). Others retort that no evidence of that practice has been found in "ancient arboriculture" (Montgomery, *Book of Daniel*, 233). However, Collins, *Daniel*, 226, reports that "there is some evidence of a Mesopotamian custom of putting metal bands on trees. . . . Bands of metal are shown around the trunk of a tree on cylinder seals and slabs from the palace of Ashurnasirpal at Nimrud." Cf. Buchanan, *Book of Daniel*, 117. But more important than the evidence of this ancient practice or the lack thereof is the fact that the "band of iron and bronze" is mentioned in connection with the *stump*, not with "the shift of imagery" to "him" which takes place in the following sentence. In any case, since Daniel does not give an interpretation of the band of iron and bronze, I would not elaborate on it in the sermon.

In the middle of verse 15 the image suddenly switches from the tree that would be cut down to a person who will be brought down. We read, "Let *him* be bathed with the dew of heaven, and let his lot be with the animals of the field in the grass of the earth. Let his mind be changed from that of a human, and let the mind of an animal be given to him. And let seven times pass over him." The beautiful, great, strong tree represents a powerful person. He will be cut down — just a stump left. A poor reflection of his former self. This person who sheltered animals will himself turn into an animal. He will be out in the field with the animals. He will be "bathed with the dew of heaven." "In the Near East there is a heavy dew almost every night, because the days are hot and the nights are cold. The night temperature condenses the moisture from the air."[65] He will be exposed to the elements, storms and rain. And his human mind, his reason, will be changed to the mind of an animal. This punishment will last for seven times. Since seven is the Hebrew number of completeness, "seven times" means a complete period of time.[66]

No wonder the king was frightened by the dream and terrified by his reflections on its meaning. Who is the most powerful person on earth? The king, of course. He is king of all the earth. Could the dream mean that he will be cut down? That he will be deposed? Just a stump left in the ground? It sounds ominous. The king is terrified. Is there no way out?

The holy watcher concludes his message in verse 17, "The sentence is rendered by decree of the watchers, the decision is given by order of the holy ones, in order that all who live may know that the Most High is sovereign over the kingdom of mortals; he gives it to whom he will and sets over it the lowliest of human beings." The "decree of the watchers" is the decree of God himself, as Daniel explains in verse 24: "it is a decree of the Most High."[67] God gives this

---

65. Buchanan, *Book of Daniel*, 117.

66. Many commentators understand the "seven times" as seven years (for a number of these commentators see Miller, *Daniel*, 134, n. 27). Steinmann, *Daniel*, 236-37, however, offers seven reasons why it should be taken as "an indeterminate, but clearly delimited period of time that was sufficient for God to accomplish his purpose." The five top reasons are: 1. "Daniel has already used 'seven' as a number representing completeness or thoroughness (3:19)." 2. "The duration of the seven times is defined later in this chapter not in terms of years, but in terms of the time it will take for Nebuchadnezzar to acknowledge that God is sovereign over the affairs of humans (4:26)." 5. "The Aramaic word 'time' used in 4:16 is used elsewhere by Daniel in an undetermined (but finite) sense (2:8-9, 21; 7:12)." 6. "When Daniel interprets Nebuchadnezzar's dream, he continues to use the phrase 'seven times' (4:25, 32) from 4:16, and not 'seven years,' which we would have expected if the 'times' in 4:16 really represented years." 7. In 4:34 the king does not say "at the end of seven years" but "uses the vague phrase (literally) 'at the end of the days.'"

67. "The Watchers do not act on their own. They are agents of the Most High, probably to be understood as members of the Divine Council (e.g., Ps 82:1; 1 Kgs 22:19-23). . . . Their activity

decree, says verse 17, "in order that *all who live* may know that the *Most High is sovereign over the kingdom of mortals; he gives it to whom he will* and sets over it the lowliest of human beings."[68] This is the key sentence in this chapter. All who live should know that the Most High God is sovereign over earthly kingdoms and gives these kingdoms to whom he will.

The king continues his letter in verse 18, "This is the dream that I, King Nebuchadnezzar, saw. Now you, Belteshazzar, declare the interpretation, since all the wise men of my kingdom are unable to tell me the interpretation. You are able, however, for you are endowed with a spirit of the holy gods."

Verse 19, "Then Daniel, who was called Belteshazzar, was severely distressed for a while. His thoughts terrified him." Earlier the dream had frightened the king, and his thoughts about it terrified him. Now it is Daniel's turn to be terrified. He knows the meaning of the dream, and it is terrible news for the king — but it can also be terrible news for Daniel. He knows that the king has a violent temper. The king has a reputation for shooting the messenger. When the king's wise men could not interpret the earlier dream, he "flew into a violent rage and commanded that all the wise men of Babylon be destroyed" (Dan 2:12). When Daniel's friends refused to worship the king's statue, he was filled with rage; he ordered the fire to be stoked seven times as hot and Daniel's friends thrown into the fire (3:19-20). What will the king do to the messenger who tells him that he will lose not only his kingdom but also his mind? With good reason Daniel hesitates for a while.

The king notices that Daniel is terrified. He says to Daniel, "Belteshazzar, do not let the dream or the interpretation terrify you." And diplomatically Daniel answers, "My lord, may the dream be for those who hate you, and its interpretation for your enemies!" But Daniel knows that the bad news is not for the king's enemies but for the king himself. Then, reluctantly, he begins to talk. He does not want to give the bad news immediately. So he begins with the positive features, repeating the king's report of the dream almost word for word.

Verses 20 to 22, "The tree that you saw, which grew great and strong, so that its top reached to heaven and was visible to the end of the whole earth, whose foliage was beautiful and its fruit abundant, and which provided food for all, under which animals of the field lived, and in whose branches the birds of the air had nests — it is you, O king! You have grown great and strong. Your greatness has increased and reaches to heaven, and your sovereignty to the ends of

---

on earth expresses God's concern to protect people. This will involve combating evil, and sometimes punishing the evildoer." Lucas, *Daniel*, 117.

68. "The Most High demonstrates divine power by making the lowliest people sovereign, a statement probably meaning that God has the power to elevate the exiles over the Babylonians and Nebuchadnezzar." Redditt, *Daniel*, 81.

the earth."[69] It's as the king thought. He is the great, strong tree:[70] the king of all the earth.

But when Daniel gets to the bad news, he tries to soften the blow. He tries to spare the king from embarrassment by abbreviating the lengthy description of the tree's destruction. He also diplomatically skips over the parts that the king will lose his mind and that God sets over the kingdom "the *lowliest* of human beings."[71] Verses 23 to 25, "And whereas the king saw a holy watcher coming down from heaven and saying, 'Cut down the tree and destroy it, but leave its stump and roots in the ground, with a band of iron and bronze, in the grass of the field; and let him be bathed with the dew of heaven, and let his lot be with the animals of the field, until seven times pass over him' — this is the interpretation, O king, and it is a decree of the Most High that has come upon my lord the king: You shall be driven away from human society, and your dwelling shall be with the wild animals. You shall be made to eat grass like oxen,[72] you shall be bathed with the dew of heaven, and seven times shall pass over you, until you have learned that the Most High has sovereignty over the kingdom of mortals, and gives it to whom he will.'"

The king will be deposed and driven away from people; he will live with the animals, eating grass[73] like oxen. But the duration of this punishment will be limited. It will last "seven times," that is, the king's punishment will last an indefinite but complete period of time.[74] This period of time will be over, Daniel explains, when "*you have learned* that the Most High has sovereignty over the

69. "By repeating the favourable details of the dream (20, 21) and coming to the point, *it is you, O king* (22), while he could speak of greatness, strength and dominion, Daniel tempered the fearful impact of his message." Baldwin, *Daniel*, 113.

70. In the light of the Assyrian Tree of Life, "Nebuchadnezzar's dream shows that he identifies himself with the cosmic tree; he is the keeper of the cosmos, the true image of God, the Perfect Man." Longman, *Daniel*, 119.

71. "Daniel mentions that the king will live with the animals, but he omits a direct reference to his insanity (the loss of his human mind). Finally, by not repeating that God gives the kingdom to the lowliest of humans, Daniel avoids the equation of Nebuchadnezzar with a lowly person, thereby preserving Nebuchadnezzar's royal honor." Steinmann, *Daniel*, 244.

72. There may be an allusion here to God's judgment upon Adam and Eve, driven from the garden and its fruit trees onto the cursed ground where "you shall eat the plants of the field" (Gen 3:18). For details, see Lucas, *Daniel*, 116.

73. "The king's diet . . . may not have consisted solely of 'grass,' for the Aramaic word *'ăśab* also includes vegetables and other herbs." Miller, *Daniel*, 137.

74. "The word *'iddānîn* is not specifically 'years' but can signify 'seasons.' It is the word 'time' in 2:8 and 3:5. Its duration is uncertain, and this is intentional." Baldwin, *Daniel*, 112. Cf. Hill, "Daniel," 96, "The cryptic 'seven times' (vv. 16, 25; cf. v. 34) refers to 'seven periods of time' (NASB) of unknown length (whether days, weeks, months, change of seasons, or years). . . . The seven periods of time may simply be a symbolic cipher rather than an indicator of any specific length of time" (with a reference to Longman, *Daniel*, 120, n. 13). See also n. 66 above.

kingdom of mortals." There is that important sentence again. In verse 17 it was "that *all who live* may know that the Most High is sovereign over the kingdom of mortals." Here it is specifically King Nebuchadnezzar who has to learn "that the Most High has sovereignty over the kingdom of mortals." He may be king of all the earth, but *God* is King of the *universe*. He is "the Most High." And he has sovereignty over all earthly kingdoms. The king is king only by permission of the Most High. The king is king under God, "the Lord of kings" (Dan 2:47).

Daniel continues in verses 26 and 27, "As it was commanded to leave the stump and roots of the tree, your kingdom shall be reestablished for you *from the time that you learn that Heaven* [i.e., the God of heaven][75] *is sovereign.*[76] Therefore, O king, may my counsel be acceptable to you: atone for your sins with righteousness, and your iniquities with mercy to the oppressed, so that your prosperity may be prolonged."

Daniel dares to offer the king some advice. The translation "atone for your sins" is confusing, for we cannot *atone* for our sins — only Christ can. As the footnote indicates, Daniel says literally, "break off your sins" — like breaking off a conversation.[77] Break off, discontinue, your sins and do what is right. The NIV translates: "*Renounce* your sins by doing what is right." Daniel knows the king's volatile temper. Yet he has the courage to name the king's sins specifically. He follows up, "Break off your sins by doing what is right" with "and your iniquities with mercy to the oppressed." He concentrates on one of the king's major sins: mercilessly oppressing the poor and helpless.[78] We know from history that King Nebuchadnezzar oppressed many peoples, destroyed their cities, exiled them to different regions in his empire, skimmed off the brightest to serve him, and used slave labor to build his beautiful Babylon. Break off "your iniquities with mercy to the oppressed!"[79]

---

75. "This is the only place in the Old Testament where 'Heaven' is used as a synonym for 'God,' though it is so used in the Apocryphal books (see 1 Macc 3:18; 2 Macc 9:21)." Harman, *Study Commentary on Daniel*, 102.

76. "Nebuchadnezzar is promised that he can be king from the point he acknowledges that actually he is not, because God is." Goldingay, *Daniel*, 94.

77. NRSV note: "Aram *break off.*" Cf. Baldwin, *Daniel*, 114, "The root meaning of the verb is clearly seen in such contexts as Genesis 27:40, 'You shall break his yoke from your neck' and Exodus 32:2, 'Break off the golden rings' (RV). Accordingly the meaning is 'break with the old habits' and 'do what is right.'" Cf. Young, *Prophecy of Daniel*, 108-9, and Miller, *Daniel*, 138, n. 38.

78. Synonymous parallelism:

"break off your sins with righteousness,
    and your iniquities with mercy to the oppressed."

Cf. Seow, *Daniel*, 71, "Daniel's counsel . . . is simply a call for Nebuchadnezzar to submit to the will of heaven for earthly governance (see Ps 72:1-2; Isa 11:3-4; Jer 22:15-16)."

79. Leupold, *Exposition of Daniel*, 194, "Nebuchadnezzar, too, must have been guilty of ty-

The result, Daniel suggests, could be "that your prosperity may be prolonged." Perhaps God's judgment will be postponed if he breaks off his proud, arrogant iniquities by showing "*mercy* to the oppressed." In the New Testament Jesus teaches, "Blessed are the merciful, for they will receive mercy" (Matt 5:7). Perhaps the king will receive mercy from God if he is merciful to the oppressed.

Apparently, the king did not bother to follow Daniel's advice. He did not begin to show mercy to the oppressed. For we read in verse 28, "All this came upon King Nebuchadnezzar." Everything Daniel had predicted happened to the king. This is how it came about.

Verse 29, "At the end of twelve months he was walking on the roof of the royal palace of Babylon." The palace had a flat roof so that the king could relax and walk there in the cool breeze. From the roof he looked down on the processional avenue which he had "paved with limestone and decorated with lion figures."[80] He could also see the famous Hanging Gardens he had built for his wife. A little farther down he saw the temple he had built for his god Marduk. And next to it the ziggurat tower consisting of seven levels, the top being 288 feet high — a thirty-story tower. He could also see many of the fifty-three temples he had built or beautified. Then there was the double inner wall with its large defensive towers. And beyond the inner wall he could see the huge double outer wall he had built and some of the eight massive gates that gave access to the city. "Babylon was one of the preeminent cities of history and during Nebuchadnezzar's reign . . . the most magnificent (and probably the largest) city on earth."[81]

Only twelve months after his awful dream, the king seems to have forgotten it. For as he struts on the roof of his palace and drinks in all the beauty and strength of his capital, he says, verse 30, "Is this not magnificent Babylon,[82] which *I* have built as a royal capital by *my* mighty power and for *my glorious majesty?*"[83] The king of all the earth prides himself in his accomplishments. Instead of giving God the glory, he boasts of his own "glorious majesty."

---

rannical behavior, of violence, of highhanded dealings. All these and similar faults are to be renounced, and the primary virtue of monarchs is to be cultivated — plain, straightforward righteousness." Cf. Smith-Christopher, "Book of Daniel," 75, "The Babylonian emperor must no longer behave like a [proud] Babylonian emperor; he must no longer act like the destroyer of Jerusalem and tyrannical mover of whole populations like pieces on a chess board. The branches of this oppressive tree must be torn away."

80. Goldingay, *Daniel,* 90.

81. Miller, *Daniel,* 140, where the above information and sources are found.

82. "Babylon the great." NASB. "The boastful title is used as a negative symbol in Rev. 14:8; 16:19; 18:2, with reference to Rome." Collins, *Daniel,* 230.

83. "Three times the king uses the first-person pronoun in his boastful musings over his architectural achievements in Babylon. . . . Beyond this, Nebuchadnezzar applies the words 'mighty power . . . glory . . . majesty' to his own rule (v. 30). Typically these terms are reserved

Verse 31, "While the words were still in the king's mouth, a voice came from heaven" — this is the voice of God.[84] God says, "O King Nebuchadnezzar, to you it is declared: The kingdom has departed from you! You shall be driven away from human society, and your dwelling shall be with the animals of the field. You shall be made to eat grass like oxen, and seven times shall pass over you, until you have learned that the Most High has sovereignty over the kingdom of mortals and gives it to whom he will."[85] There is that important sentence again: "until you have learned that *the Most High has sovereignty over the kingdom of mortals and gives it to whom he will.*"

Verse 33, "Immediately the sentence was fulfilled against Nebuchadnezzar. He was driven away from human society, ate grass like oxen, and his body was bathed with the dew of heaven, until his hair grew as long as eagles' feathers and his nails became like birds' claws."

The dream is being fulfilled. The instant the king brags about his accomplishments and gives himself the glory, he loses his mind. The king becomes insane and loses his kingdom. In an age when there were no mental hospitals or psychiatric wards, the king is simply driven away from human society. He lives outdoors with the animals. There, like cattle, he eats grass. He thinks he is an animal. He probably has what psychologists call "lycanthropy"[86] — the delusion of believing oneself to be an animal. This sickness, though rare, still occurs today.[87] Apparently King George III of England (1738-1820) also suffered from

---

for the God of Israel — the Most High — and he bestows them on human rulers as he wills (2:37; cf. Exod 15:6-7; Isa 35:2; 48:11)." Hill, "Daniel," 97. Montgomery, *Book of Daniel*, 243-44, notes, "The setting of the scene and the king's self-complaisance in his glorious Babylon are strikingly true to history. Every student of Babylonia recalls these proud words in reading Neb.'s own records of his creation of the new Babylon; for instance (Grotefend Cylinder, *KB* iii, 2, p. 39): 'Then built I the palace the seat of my royalty . . . , the bond of the race of men, the dwelling of joy and rejoicing.'"

84. See Daniel 4:26, "Heaven is sovereign," and 4:37, "King of heaven." See also Matthew 3:17, "A voice from heaven said, 'This is my Son, the Beloved, with whom I am well pleased,'" and John 12:28, "'Father, glorify your name.' Then a voice came from heaven, 'I have glorified it, and I will glorify it again.'"

85. "The emphasis here is not on Nebuchadnezzar's being for a time the one chosen, but on the tenuous nature of being God's chosen leader. As the kings of Israel and Judah were to learn . . . , God's sovereignty is partially guaranteed by the fact that someone else can be chosen at any time." Smith-Christopher, "Book of Daniel," 75.

86. Also called "zoanthropy" or "therianthropy." Anderson, *Unfolding Daniel's Prophecies*, 72, quotes the *Dictionary of Psychological Medicine*, which describes lycanthropy as "the complete loss of personal identity and the conviction of being changed into one of the lower animals."

87. For details, see Young, *Prophecy of Daniel*, 112, and Miller, *Daniel*, 134. Miller mentions R. K. Harrison (*Introduction to the Old Testament*, 116-17), who, in 1946, observed a patient in a British mental hospital "who wandered about the grounds of the institution eating grass as if he were a cow. His drink consisted of water."

this illness.[88] Nebuchadnezzar thinks he is an ox. He stays outdoors day and night, his body being exposed to the elements, the burning sun during the day and the cold mist at night. After a while he even begins to look like an animal. Verse 33 tells us that "his hair grew as long as eagles' feathers" — long and matted like eagles' feathers. And "his nails [growing long started to curl and] became like birds' claws." How far the mighty king has fallen! The king of all the earth, who had been given dominion also over the animal world (Dan 2:37-38; cf. Jer 27:5-6), has himself become an animal.

"Seven times shall pass over you," the text says. The king will be in that animal state a complete period of time, until he has learned "that the Most High has sovereignty over the kingdom of mortals." The king has to learn that God is the King of kings. Nebuchadnezzar is king under God and should give the glory not to himself but to God.

The king reports in verse 34, "When that period was over, I, Nebuchadnezzar, lifted my eyes to heaven." To lift one's eyes to heaven is to seek out God for help. The Psalmist says, "To you I lift up my eyes, O you who are enthroned in the heavens!"[89] So the king lifts his eyes to heaven.[90] In doing so he acknowledges the sovereignty of God. He thereby fulfills God's condition for lifting the curse, "until you have learned that the Most High has sovereignty over the kingdom of mortals" (v. 32). And immediately God heals him of his disease. The king reports, "my reason returned to me."

Immediately he is able to proclaim the sovereignty of God.[91] The king's report continues in verse 34, "I blessed[92] the *Most High,* and praised and honored the one who lives *forever.* For his sovereignty is an *everlasting sovereignty,* and *his kingdom* endures from generation to generation. All the inhabitants of the earth are accounted as nothing,[93] and he does what he wills with the host of heaven and the inhabitants of the earth. There is no one who can stay his hand[94] or say to him, 'What are you doing?'" Not even the king of all the earth

88. Lacocque, *Book of Daniel,* 80.

89. Psalm 123:1. Cf. Psalms 25:15 and 141:8.

90. "It is almost a touching detail to notice that the outward evidence of the return to reason is the upward look, the most noticeable feature that differentiates man from beast." Leupold, *Exposition of Daniel,* 202.

91. His closing words are parallel to but inverted from the way he began his letter in verse 3 (see p. 116 above).

92. "To bless God is to acknowledge that all blessing comes from him (cf. Ps 103:2, 'Bless the LORD, my soul, and forget none of his benefits')." Hammer, *Daniel,* 56.

93. Cf. Isaiah 40:17.

94. Literally, "to strike his hand." "To strike [*meḥa'*] on the hand, to hinder, derived from the custom of striking children on the hand in chastising [or restraining] them." Keil, *Book of Daniel,* 161. Cf. Young, *Prophecy of Daniel,* 113, "In later language it comes to have the meaning 'to reprove' or 'to interfere with.' Here it means that none can oppose God's action."

can oppose God's actions or raise objections to what he is doing.[95] Nebuchadnezzar speaks from painful experience.

What a powerful assurance the words of the king must have had for Israel in exile. Their God is the sovereign God. He is in control even of their captors. He can deliver them from their exile whenever he desires.

In verse 36 the king reports the happy ending, "At that time my reason returned to me; and my majesty and splendor were restored to me for the glory of my kingdom. My counselors and my lords sought me out, I was reestablished over my kingdom, and still more greatness was added to me." As promised, God restored the king to his throne; he reestablished him over his kingdom. For the king now acknowledged that "the Most High is sovereign over the kingdom of mortals; he gives it to whom he will" (vv. 17, 25, 32).

The king concludes his letter with more praise of God. "Now I, Nebuchadnezzar, praise and extol and honor the King of heaven, for all his works are truth, and his ways are justice; and he is able to bring low those who walk in pride." This is the only place in the Old Testament where God is called "the King of heaven."[96] The king of all the earth acknowledges one more time that there is a greater King, a King who has dominion over all — the King of heaven. And he confesses that *"all his works are truth,* and *his ways are justice;*[97] and he is able to bring low those who walk in pride" — that is, those who pit their power against that of the King of Heaven.[98]

The message of Daniel 4 is that God is sovereign over human kings and earthly kingdoms. He can give earthly kingdoms to whom he will. Even while I am reworking this chapter, long-term dictators are being toppled in Tunisia and Egypt while other dictators are tottering. Who could have predicted these abdications even a few months ago? God is sovereign over earthly kingdoms and can give them to whom he will.

What an encouragement this message must have been for the Israelites suffering in exile in Babylon.[99] The Babylonian kings might seem great, but Israel's God is greater. The Babylonian kings might seem mighty, but Israel's God is *almighty.* He can take down the mightiest human king just by confusing his

---

95. Cf. Isaiah 14:27.

96. Collins, *Daniel,* 232. Collins adds, "The expression is equivalent to 'the God of heaven' [2:18] but has the advantage of emphasizing the theme of kingship in this context."

97. "Nebuchadnezzar experienced God as truthful in that God acted as promised, and Nebuchadnezzar also experienced God as just in punishing the haughty king for his pride." Redditt, *Daniel,* 85.

98. Towner, *Daniel,* 64.

99. "The captive Jews needed to know that even the apparently limitless power of Nebuchadnezzar was under the control of the Lord God Almighty, who still cared for them and had a great future for them in their land." Archer, "Daniel," 68.

mind. Israel's God is King of kings. Israel may not understand why they are still suffering in exile. But the message that their God is sovereign over human kings gives them hope for deliverance. Surely this God can set them free and bring them back to the Promised Land.

God reveals his sovereignty not only in the Old Testament, but especially in the New. God sent his Son, Jesus, to this world to do battle with the most powerful being on earth, Satan. Jesus called Satan "the ruler of the world" (John 12:31; 14:30; 16:11). As soon as Jesus began his mission, Satan attacked him: "The devil took him to a very high mountain and showed him all the kingdoms of the world and their splendor; and he said to him, 'All these I will give you, if you will fall down and worship me.' Jesus said to him, 'Away with you, Satan!' For it is written, 'Worship the Lord your God, and serve only him'" (Matt 4:8-10). Jesus withstood the temptation of Satan and began to win this fierce battle. Jesus healed people and cast out demons. He sent seventy followers out on a mission trip. When they returned they reported, "Lord, in your name even the *demons* submit to us!" Jesus responded, "I watched Satan fall from heaven like a flash of lightning" (Luke 10:17-18; cf. Col 2:15).

But Satan managed to have Jesus killed, and it looked as if he had won the battle. His victory was his defeat, however, for Jesus rose victoriously from the dead. He conquered sin and death. From that time forward the power of Satan was severely limited. The Bible describes Satan as a ferocious dragon who is now bound with a great chain, locked in a pit, "so that he would deceive the nations no more" (Rev. 20:1-3). He can still do harm, but is not free to do his worst. The Bible also says that at the end of "the thousand years," this full period of time,[100] Satan will be released and will seek to destroy the church worldwide (Rev. 20:7-9). The book of Revelation describes it as a war: Satan and his hosts "will make war on the Lamb, and the *Lamb* will conquer them, for he is Lord of lords and King of kings" (Rev. 17:14).[101] The Lamb, Jesus, will be victorious. Then, in the familiar words of Revelation, "The kingdom of the *world* has become the kingdom of our *Lord* and of his *Messiah,* and he will reign forever and ever" (Rev. 11:15).

Today we live in the time between Jesus' First Coming and his Second Coming. Even though Satan is bound, we are bewildered by all the persecution we see in the world. The church is still at war. Some nations seek to wipe out the Christian church. Thousands of Christians are killed every day. Others are imprisoned, tortured, or blacklisted. According to the latest estimates, 100 million

---

100. The "thousand years" in this New Testament apocalyptic book is also a symbolic number. Ten is the biblical number of fullness (cf. the Ten Commandments). A thousand years is 10 x 10 x 10, that is, a full period of time.

101. Cf. Revelation 14:8, "Then another angel, a second, followed, saying, 'Fallen, fallen is Babylon the Great!'"

Christians are persecuted worldwide in countries like North Korea, Saudi Arabia, and Iran.[102] Even where there is no danger of overt persecution, fear hangs in the air that a rogue nation may launch a nuclear missile or terrorists may strike in any number of ways.

When we think of the millions of Christians suffering persecution today, we may begin to question God's sovereignty. If God is a sovereign and loving God, why do his people suffer so much in this world? If God is sovereign, why does he not rescue his people from their distress? There are no easy answers to these questions. But the message of Daniel 4 is beyond doubt: God is sovereign over earthly kingdoms. He can replace rulers at will. Nebuchadnezzar is long gone. Nero is long dead. Hitler, Stalin, Chairman Mao (Zedong), Kim Jong Il — they are all gone. But God is still here. And his kingdom has come with Jesus' coming and will come in perfection when Jesus comes again.[103] This kingdom will replace all earthly kingdoms. Then the new earth will overflow with justice and peace. Then all will praise the King of kings and Lord of lords. Thanks be to God.

---

102. "Open Doors' 2009 World Watch List." Marshall, *Their Blood Cries Out*, 4, estimates that "over two hundred million" Christians suffer from "massacre, rape, torture, slavery, beatings, mutilations, and imprisonment. . . . [as well as from] extortion, harassment, family division, and crippling discrimination in employment and education."

103. Jesus may have had Nebuchadnezzar's dream of that gorgeous tree in mind when he said, "The kingdom of heaven is like a mustard seed that someone took and sowed in his field; it is the smallest of all the seeds, but when it has grown it is the greatest of shrubs and becomes a tree, so that the birds of the air come and make nests in its branches" (Matt 13:31-32). The kingdom of God is like a great tree that spreads its branches around the globe. But unlike Nebuchadnezzar's tree, this tree will not be cut down. This kingdom "is an everlasting kingdom"; this kingdom "endures from generation to generation" (Dan 4:3, 34).

CHAPTER 5

The Writing on the Wall

Daniel 5:1-31[1]

"This is the writing that was inscribed: MENE, MENE, TEKEL, and
PARSIN.
This is the interpretation of the matter:
MENE, God has numbered the days of your kingdom and
brought it to an end;
TEKEL, you have been weighed on the scales and found wanting;
PERES, your kingdom is divided and given to the Medes and
Persians."

Daniel 5:25-28

People all over the world fear evil human kingdoms. In the Second World War it was Nazi Germany. After the war it was the Soviet Union. Then it became China, and recently "rogue nations." For those who live in fear of evil human kingdoms, the story of Daniel 5 has a tremendous message of comfort.

But in preaching this narrative we again need to avoid the pitfall of focusing on the human characters in order to draw morals from their behavior for the congregation. Some commentators even recommend presenting the evil king as a warning example: "This man too is here so that we can learn from him. His story stands out like a sign on the top of a dangerous rock, warning us to keep away and directing us to the safe navigation channel. It warns us that we can all drift easily into the habit of trifling with God."[2] But that is not the point of Daniel 5. Neither is it the point that "all human beings might have such a

1. Aramaic 5:1–6:1.
2. Wallace, *The Lord Is King*, 94.

145

warning written on their own walls — weighed and found wanting, numbered days, kingdom lost."[3]

Daniel, on the other hand, is sometimes preached as a positive role model. For example, one commentator focuses on Daniel's speech to the king and concludes, "Daniel 5 is a call to modern Christians to involve themselves in prophetic delivery of God's judgment on the gluttony of the hundreds of 'Belshazzar's feasts' that have victimized so many people over the centuries."[4] Another uses Daniel's rebuke of the king as a positive example for pastors who in rare cases and circumstances have "little else to do but warn."[5] Still another notes that Daniel at first refuses to accept the king's gifts "to make it plain that spiritual gifts cannot be bought. . . . We need to recover something of that spirit in the Western church today."[6] Concentrating on the theme and goal will enable us to avoid these pitfalls and produce a relevant sermon in line with the author's intention.

Text and Context

After four narratives about King Nebuchadnezzar, chapter 5:1 clearly begins a new literary unit with the statement, "King Belshazzar made a great festival. . . ." The only question is where this unit ends since "the Masoretic division concludes the story dramatically with 5:30,"[7] the death of Belshazzar, so that 5:31 would begin the next unit. But our English versions rightly include 5:31 with chapter 5. Goldingay observes, "The reference to Darius in 6:1 [5:31] looks more like part of the closure of chapter 5 (so EVV), denoting how power passes from the Chaldeans to a Median, than the introduction to chapter 6, which relates a specific incident in Darius' reign."[8]

Echoes of the previous narratives can be heard throughout this chapter. In dealing with chapter 4 we noted that chapters 4 and 5 form a pair — both narratives relating God's punishment of a Babylonian king for pride and insolence. This close connection is confirmed when this chapter (5:18-21) briefly retells the story of chapter 4. Both kings are frightened and terrified (4:5; 5:6, 10). In both

---

3. Kim Monroe, *Daniel 5*, cassette WBS 6/26, New Life Cassettes, 2003, quoted approvingly by Schwab, *Hope*, 75. Neither is this narrative about the doctrine of election such as, "Belshazzar was rejected while Nebuchadnezzar was elected." Wallace, *The Lord Is King*, 92. See pp. 90-94.

4. Smith-Christopher, "Book of Daniel," 85.

5. Wallace, *The Lord Is King*, 101.

6. Ferguson, *Daniel*, 120-21.

7. Montgomery, *Book of Daniel*, 266, who continues that 6:1 Aramaic "belongs as a postscript to chapter 5."

8. Goldingay, *Daniel*, 105.

narratives the wise men of Babylon fail to come up with an interpretation while Daniel is successful. The queen's words describing Daniel as being "endowed with a spirit of the holy gods" (5:11) are the same as Nebuchadnezzar's earlier description of Daniel (4:8, 9, 18). In both narratives the king provokes God: "Is this not the magnificent Babylon, which I have built . . . by my mighty power and for my glorious majesty?" (4:30); and "They drank the wine [from the vessels of God's temple] and praised the gods of gold and silver, bronze, iron, wood, and stone" (5:4). In both cases God instantly declares his sentence (4:31; 5:5), and it is "immediately fulfilled" (4:33; 5:30). The theme of Daniel 4, "that the Most High has sovereignty over the kingdom of mortals, and gives it to whom he will" (4:17, 25, 32), is repeated in 5:21. Finally, Nebuchadnezzar's closing statement in chapter 4:37, "the King of heaven . . . is able to bring low those who walk in pride" forms a fitting introduction to God bringing low King Belshazzar.

Chapter 5 is also linked to chapter 2 where "the magicians, the enchanters, the sorcerers, and the Chaldeans" were offered "rewards and great honor" (2:6) but could not tell the king his dream and therefore not its interpretation. Here "the enchanters, the Chaldeans, and the diviners" are offered rewards and great honor (5:7), but they cannot even read the writing on the wall, let alone give its interpretation. In both cases Daniel appears after their failure, is successful, and receives the promised rewards and honor. Also, the fall of Babylon and its replacement by another kingdom (5:30-31) fulfills the dream of chapter 2: "After you shall arise another kingdom" (2:39). The mention of "the vessels of gold and silver that his father Nebuchadnezzar had taken out of the temple in Jerusalem" (5:2) refers back to information provided in chapter 1:2.

Daniel's interpretation, "your kingdom is divided and given to the Medes and Persians" (5:28), as well as the introduction of Darius the Mede (5:31), points forward to the narrative about Darius and Daniel in chapter 6.

Daniel 5 also has several connections with other Old Testament passages.[9] Daniel again evokes Joseph. This time the narrator highlights that "Daniel was clothed in purple, a chain of gold was put around his neck, and a proclamation was made concerning him that he should rank third in the kingdom" (5:29), which is similar to the rewards Joseph received: Pharaoh "arrayed him in garments of fine linen, and put a gold chain around his neck. He had him ride in the chariot of his second-in-command" (Gen 41:42-43).

9. Michael Hilton, "Babel Reversed — Daniel Chapter 5," *JSOT* 66 (1995) 107, sees another connection between Babel (Gen 11:8-9) and Babylon: "As Babylon was born in misunderstanding and confusion of languages, so it ends in the same way. As God intervened directly at the start of Babylon's history, so he intervenes again at its end. For he is the God of all history. Both stories are stories of hubris, of the arrogance of people who are under the illusion that they have power."

Daniel 5 also links up with the messages of the prophets who foretold the fall of Babylon. For example, Jeremiah predicted: "These nations shall serve the king of Babylon for seventy years [7 x 10]. Then after seventy years are completed, I will punish the king of Babylon and that nation, the land of the Chaldeans, for their iniquity, says the LORD" (Jer 25:11-12; cf. 50:1-3; 51:64; Isa 13:1-22; 14:3-22; 21:1-10).

Literary Features

The genre of this chapter is narrative, but it is dominated by the speeches of the queen (vv. 10-12), Belshazzar (vv. 13-16), and Daniel (vv. 17-28). Daniel's speech is an indictment speech (vv. 18-23) and includes God's sentence (vv. 24-28). "The pattern of the argument resembles the so-called *rîb* or covenant lawsuit in the prophetic books (e.g., Mic 6:1-8). First, Daniel recalls the antecedent history, in this case the experience of Nebuchadnezzar; then he brings the accusation ('you have not humbled your heart'); and finally, the interpretation of the writing announces the sentence."[10] We shall analyze in turn the narrative structure, the plot line, character description, and repetition.

Narrative Structure

Since all acts in Daniel 5 take place in the king's palace, it is not entirely clear how many scenes make up this narrative. But the different characters and the passing of time suggest four scenes:

Scene 1: The king's drunken feast[11] in his palace   5:1-6
    A. King Belshazzar at his feast mocks the God of Israel   5:1-4
    B. A hand from God writes on the wall and the king is terrified   5:5-6
    Characters: the king and God

Scene 2: The king seeks an interpretation of the writing   5:7-12
    A. The king calls for his wise men to interpret, but they fail   5:7-9
    B. The queen tells the king to call Daniel for the interpretation   5:10-12
    Characters: The king and his wise men;
        when the wise men leave the stage, the queen takes their place

---

10. Collins, *Daniel*, 254.

11. The narrative "begins with a scene that can be read as one of ostentation, decadence, carousing, coarseness, wantonness, and self-indulgence." Goldingay, *Daniel*, 113.

Scene 3: Later: Daniel before the king   5:13-29
    A. The king will reward Daniel if he can read and interpret
       the writing   5:13-16
    B. Daniel rebukes the king   5:17-23
    C. Daniel reads the writing on the wall and interprets the words   5:24-28
    D. The king rewards Daniel   5:29
    Characters: the king and Daniel

Scene 4: Later that night: God fulfills the writing on the wall   5:30-31
    A. God has the Chaldean king killed (divine passive)   5:30
    B. God gives the kingdom to Darius the Mede   5:31
    Characters: God and Belshazzar;
       when Belshazzar leaves the stage, Darius takes his place

The Plot Line

The narrator gives the setting in verse 1: Belshazzar makes a great feast for his
many lords. The occasioning incident is given in verse 2: under the influence of
the wine, Belshazzar commands that the sacred vessels from the temple in Jerusalem be brought to the party so that they may drink wine from them. Will they
really go through with this sacrilege? The tension mounts as the vessels from
"the house of God" are brought and they all drink wine from them (v. 3). The
tension mounts further when they add insult to injury by drinking the wine
from God's vessels while praising their idol gods (v. 4). Will they get away with
this sacrilege?

"Immediately the fingers of a human hand appeared and began writing on
the plaster of the wall" (v. 5). The narrator keeps us in suspense as to what the
hand wrote on the wall. Instead he vividly describes the king's reaction to the
writing (v. 6). It must be a bad omen. In great fear the king cries loudly for his
wise men to read the writing and give its interpretation (v. 7). Will they be able
to satisfy the king? They cannot even read the writing (v. 8). The king now becomes even more terrified (v. 9). What does the writing say? At this point the
queen enters, gives a lengthy recommendation for Daniel (pace retardation
adding to the suspense), and tells the king to call Daniel to give the interpretation (vv. 10-12).

Daniel is brought before the king (v. 13). The king now gives a lengthy
speech (more pace retardation; vv. 13-16) in which he promises to rank Daniel
"third in the kingdom" if he is "able to read the writing and tell me [the king]
its interpretation" (v. 16). Daniel responds with a lengthy speech, first recalling
God's humbling of Nebuchadnezzar for his pride and then charging Belshazzar,

who knew all this, with exalting himself against the Lord of heaven (more pace retardation; vv. 17-23).

Finally, Daniel is ready to read and interpret the writing. This is the climax: it's a message from the Most High God himself (v. 24). The writing consists of four words: "MENE, MENE, TEKEL, and PARSIN" (v. 25). But what do these words mean? Daniel provides the interpretation as well: "MENE, God has numbered the days of your kingdom and brought it to an end; TEKEL, you have been weighed on the scales and found wanting; PERES, your kingdom is divided and given to the Medes and Persians" (vv. 26-28). The tension is almost resolved. One more question remains: After receiving such bad news, will the king be true to his word? Yes, he clothes Daniel in purple, puts a chain of gold around his neck, and declares him "third in the kingdom" (29).[12]

The outcome follows in verses 30-31: Belshazzar, the Chaldean king, is killed; and Darius the Mede receives the kingdom.

We can best sketch the plot line as a single plot:[13]

Climax

17-23	**Daniel's speech**	24	**the hand from God**
13b-16	"third in kingdom"		
13a	Daniel brought		
10-12	queen's advice	25	**MENE, MENE, TEKEL, PARSIN**
9	king terrified		
8	**wise men fail**		
7b	**read writing!**	26	MENE: numbered
7a	calls wise men		
6	king terrified	27	TEKEL: weighed
5	**hand writes on wall**		
4	**praise their gods**	28	PERES: divided
3b	**drink wine from them**		
3a	vessels brought	29	Daniel "third in kingdom"

Setting	*Occasioning incident*	*Rising tension*	*Resolution*	*Outcome*
Dan 5:1	5:2			5:30-31
King's drunken feast	**"Bring the sacred vessels!"**			**Belshazzar killed; Darius the Mede king**

12. In the light of the scenic structure (above), I have made verse 29 the final item in the resolution. One could also argue that verse 29 is part of the outcome because the question of the meaning of the writing is fully resolved in verse 28.

13. One can also sketch it as a complex plot: the first question (Scene 1) is: Will the king get away with this sacrilege? (vv. 1-4 resolved in vv. 5-6); the second question is, What does the writing say? (vv. 7-23 resolved in vv. 24-28).

Character Description

The main character in this narrative is King Belshazzar. The narrator describes him vividly: drinking wine (v. 1), under the influence of the wine (v. 2), his face turning pale, terrified, limbs giving way, knees knocking together (v. 6), crying aloud (v. 7), greatly terrified, face turning pale (v. 9), being killed (v. 30). His character is further developed with his condescending speech to Daniel: "So you are Daniel, one of the *exiles of Judah*" (v. 13), and his grudging acknowledgment, "I have heard of you that a spirit of the gods is in you" (v. 14), when the queen had said, "a spirit of the *holy* gods" (v. 11). Note also the contrast with Nebuchadnezzar's enthusiastic endorsement of Daniel, "I know that you are endowed with a spirit of the holy gods and that no mystery is too difficult for you" (4:9). Belshazzar with his, "Now if you are able" (v. 16), questions Daniel's ability.

The queen mother is a minor character; her role is simply to introduce Daniel. She is not described directly, but her action and lengthy speech show that she has great authority. She enters the king's presence without being invited (v. 10; cf. Esth 4:16) and tells him what to do: "Now let Daniel be called" (v. 12).

Daniel is described by the queen as a man "who is endowed with a spirit of the holy gods. . . . He was found to have enlightenment, understanding, and wisdom like the wisdom of the gods. Your father, King Nebuchadnezzar, made him chief of the magicians . . . because an excellent spirit, knowledge, and understanding to interpret dreams, explain riddles, and solve problems were found in this Daniel" (vv. 11-12). His character is further filled out by his actions and speech. He is courageous and even shows anger. He does not politely greet the king as the queen had done with her, "O king, live forever!" (v. 10). Instead he brusquely turns down the king's offer of gifts: "Let your gifts be for yourself, or give your rewards to someone else!" (v. 17). Then he tells the story of God deposing Nebuchadnezzar from his throne "until he learned that the Most High God has sovereignty over the kingdom of mortals, and sets over it whomever he will" (v. 21). Next he forcefully confronts the king with his sins: "And you, Belshazzar his son, have not humbled your heart, even though you knew all this! You have exalted yourself against the Lord of heaven! The vessels of his temple have been brought in before you, and you . . . have been drinking wine from them. You have praised the gods of silver and gold, . . . which do not see or hear or know; but the God in whose power is your very breath, and to whom belong all your ways, you have not honored" (vv. 22-23).

Repetition

The narrator again uses repetition to highlight central issues in this story. In verse 1 he uses twice the word "thousand" to underscore the enormous size of this party. Three times he repeats the list of those attending the feast and drinking wine from the sacred vessels: "the king and his lords, his wives, and his concubines" (vv. 2, 3, 23). The whole Babylonian aristocracy follows the evil king in challenging the God of Israel.

Six times the narrator calls Nebuchadnezzar Belshazzar's "father" (vv. 2, 11 [3x], 13, 18), in this context, his predecessor,[14] to indicate the close relationship between Nebuchadnezzar's position, pride, and punishment and those of Belshazzar (the pairing of Daniel 4 and 5).[15] In verse 2 the king commands "that they bring the vessels of gold and silver that his father Nebuchadnezzar had taken out of the temple in Jerusalem." In verse 3 the narrator repeats, "So they brought in the vessels of gold and silver that had been taken out of the temple, the house of God in Jerusalem." This repetition underscores the king's shocking insolence. But verse 3 makes a significant addition: "*the house of God in Jerusalem.*" "The author did not feel there was ambiguity in verse 2. It is inconceivable that his readers could have confused 'the Temple in Jerusalem' with some other sacred building. Instead, this is the phrase which gives us the narrator's point of view and emphasizes his concerns. This ravenous act of Belshazzar was more than drunken recklessness. It was blasphemy against the God of Israel, whose Temple is in Jerusalem."[16]

Twice the narrator repeats the list of gods Belshazzar praised: "the gods of gold and silver,[17] bronze, iron, wood, and stone" (vv. 4, 23), thus "making the faceless, nameless, artificial, anonymous, stone-cold-dead, impotent gods appear absurd."[18] Four times he refers to the "hand" of God (anthropomorphism), contrasting the living God with the dead idols (v. 5 [2x] and vv. 23, 24: "You did not honor the God who holds in his *hand* your life and all your ways. Therefore he sent the *hand* that wrote the inscription" [NIV]). Twice he repeats that the writing "was inscribed" (vv. 24, 25), thereby stressing that the writing was not a figment of the king's imagination; the words were inscribed for all to see. Twice he also points out that the king's wise men could not interpret the inscription (vv. 8, 15).

---

14. The biological father of Belshazzar was not Nebuchadnezzar but Nabonidus. The reason why the author names Nebuchadnezzar as his "father" is that in Semitic languages "'father' may refer to one's immediate father, grandfather, ancestor, or, as in the case of kings, a predecessor." Miller, *Daniel*, 149.

15. "The father-son language serves to link the two kings: the one who took the vessels from the temple in Jerusalem with the one who desacralized them; the one who ruled at the beginning of Judah's exile under the Chaldeans with the one who ruled at the end of that period." Seow, *Daniel*, 77.

16. Arnold, "Wordplay and Narrative Techniques in Daniel 5 and 6," *JBL* 112/3 (1993) 481.

17. Verse 23 reverses the "gold and silver" to "silver and gold." See p. 167, n. 62 below.

18. Schwab, *Hope*, 75.

The narrator also uses wordplay (paronomasia) several times. Three times he uses the word *nĕpaq:* "bring *(nĕpaq)* in the vessels" (v. 2), "they brought *(nĕpaq)* in the vessels" (v. 3), and "Immediately appeared *(nĕpaq)* the fingers of a human hand" (v. 5). "The purpose of the wordplay is clear. The two occurrences of the *hapel* (vv. 2 and 3) emphasize the arrogant blasphemy of Belshazzar. Then the paronym in verse 5 subtly, and without mentioning God directly, introduces the divine reaction to human insolence."[19] Another play on words is found in the writing on the wall. "Peres" *(prs)* can mean both "divided" and "Persia."[20]

The narrator also uses the word "knots" *(qiṭrîn)* three times: the king's "limbs gave way" (literally, "the knots of his loins were loosened," *qiṭrê harṣēh;* v. 6); the queen says that Daniel can "solve problems" (literally, "untie knots," *mĕšārē' qiṭrîn;* v. 12); and the king says to Daniel, "I have heard that you can give interpretations and solve problems" (literally, "untie knots"; v. 16). Al Wolters makes a good case for understanding this repetition as a wordplay in which the first use, in the context of describing the king's physical appearance (v. 6), pictures the king as being so terrified that "the knots of his loins were loosened," that is, he became incontinent. Next, the queen says unwittingly to the king that Daniel can "untie knots"— "an example of dramatic irony involving *double entendre.*" Finally, the king himself says to Daniel, "I have heard that you can . . . untie knots." Wolters writes, "We see how the story uses burlesque humor to underscore the sovereignty of the Israelite God, before whom the great kings of the earth can at a moment's notice be reduced to figures of fun, preparatory to being brought to justice."[21]

Repetition may also alert us to discovering more intricate rhetorical structures. "The reference to drinking wine [in vv. 1 and 4] clearly forms an inclusion . . . , marking these verses as a literary unit."[22] Another inclusio marking off a literary unit may be verses 13 to 29 (see Scene 3 above), with the king promising Daniel, "you shall be clothed in purple, have a chain of gold around

19. Arnold, "Wordplay and Narrative Techniques in Daniel 5 and 6," *JBL* 112/3 (1993) 482.

20. "*Pĕrēs* [divided] is also understood as referring punningly to the Aramaic word for 'Persian,' and so hinting at the victory of Persia over Babylon." Porteous, *Daniel,* 81. Cf. Steinmann, *Daniel,* 287. Wolters, "The Riddle of the Scales in Daniel 5," *HUCA* 62 (1991) 170-76, argues that this play on words also occurs with the other two words: "*whšlmh (mĕnē)* and paid it out" and "*whštkḥt ḥsyr (tĕqēl)* and found too light." He further argues (pp. 168-70) "that the verb *pĕrās* in Dan 5:28 should be taken to mean not 'divide' but 'assess.'" Ibid., 170.

21. Wolters, "Untying the King's Knots: Physiology and Wordplay in Daniel 5," *JBL* 110/1 (1991) 121. Cf. p. 118, "My proposal is that v. 6 refers to the king's panic-stricken loss of sphincter control and that vv. 12 and 16 are a mocking and ironic allusion to this ignominious incontinence on the king's part."

22. Arnold, "Wordplay and Narrative Techniques in Daniel 5 and 6," *JBL* 112/3 (1993) 481. Cf. Lucas, *Daniel,* 123.

your neck, and rank third in the kingdom" (v. 16), and Daniel actually being "clothed in purple, a chain of gold . . . around his neck, and . . . third in the kingdom" (v. 29).

In suggesting a chiastic structure, Shea has detected some interesting synthetic parallelisms at the beginning and end of his proposed chiasm:[23]

| A | (1) The Banquet (1-4)

(2) Handwriting on the Wall (5)
(3) Offer of Honors for Interpretation (6-8a) | A′ | (1) Interpretation of the Banquet (22-23)
(2) Interpretation of the Handwriting (vv. 24-28)
(3) Bestowal of Honors for Interpretation (v. 29) |

Several commentators suggest different chiastic structures for this narrative.[24] The most compelling, I think, is that of Hilton,[25] whose prose I will format as a chiasm and present partly in my own words:

A The king's feast: God's sacred vessels desecrated (1-4)
  B A hand writes on the wall (5)
    C The king's speech and fear (6-9)
      D The queen's speech about Daniel (10-12)
        E Daniel is brought in (13a)
      D′ The king's corresponding speech to Daniel (13b-16)
    C′ Daniel's speech showing the king has reason to fear (17-23)
  B′ Daniel reads the writing on the wall (24-25)
A′ God's punishment: he gives the kingdom to another (26-31)

Hilton writes, "The significance of the structure in our story is that it highlights the key elements: the writing on the wall at the beginning and end of the chapter, and Daniel at the centre."[26]

---

23. Shea, "Further Literary Structures in Daniel 2–7," *AUSS* 23/3 (1985) 290. On p. 279 Shea calls it "synonymous parallelism."

24. Lucas, Shea, Dorsey, and Hilton. See Lucas, *Daniel*, 124. The weaknesses of Lucas's proposal are that "A Introduction (1-4)" is not balanced by an "A′," and C D′ makes a better pair than C C′ does. Shea, "Further Literary Structures in Daniel 2–7," *AUSS* 23/3 (1985) 290, proposes another chiasm. Weaknesses in his proposal are that his "Epilogue (30-31)" is not balanced by a Prologue and that it centers on "C. Belshazzar's Speech." Dorsey, *Literary Structure*, 261, proposes still another chiasm. His chiasm is actually quite close to Hilton's.

25. See Hilton, "Babel Reversed," *JSOT* 66 (1995) 104-5.

26. Ibid., 105.

Theocentric Interpretation

The author first makes mention of God when he notes that the vessels that were brought to the feast originally came from "the temple, the house of God in Jerusalem" (v. 3). It is clear that King Belshazzar seeks to subordinate the God of Israel to the local gods (vv. 4, 23). How will God respond to this defiant challenge? "Immediately the fingers of a human hand appeared and began writing on . . . the wall." At this point neither the king nor his lords know whether these are the fingers of *God*. But those who know their Bibles would suspect that these are God's fingers, since earlier in redemptive history the magicians in Egypt described God's judgment of plagues as "the finger of God" (Exod 8:19). Later "the two tablets of the covenant, tablets of stone, [were] written with the finger of God" (Exod 31:18; Deut 9:10; cf. Ps 8:3). Therefore one would suspect that these fingers also refer to God, as the author will make clear a little later (v. 24).

In his speech, Daniel constantly refers to God. Daniel reminds the king that "the Most High God gave your father Nebuchadnezzar kingship" (v. 18). But when "he acted proudly, he was deposed from his kingly throne" (v. 20), that is, God deposed him (divine passive).[27] The king's reason left him, "until he learned that the Most High God has sovereignty over the kingdom of mortals, and sets over it whomever he will" (v. 21). Daniel then accuses Belshazzar, "You have exalted yourself against the Lord of heaven! . . . You have praised the gods of silver and gold . . . ; but the God in whose power [hand] is your very breath . . . you have not honored" (v. 23).

Finally, Daniel identifies the hand: "So from his [God's] presence the hand was sent" (v. 24), and it spells divine judgment: "MENE, God has numbered the days of your kingdom" (v. 26). "TEKEL, you have been weighed on the scales [by God] and found wanting" (v. 27). "PERES, your kingdom is divided [by God] and given [by God] to the Medes and Persians" (v. 28; divine passives). "That very night Belshazzar, the Chaldean king, was killed" (v. 30), that is, God had him killed (divine passive).[28] "And Darius the Mede received the kingdom [from God]" (v. 31). As Daniel had said earlier, "wisdom and power are his [God's]. He changes times and seasons, deposes kings and sets up kings" (2:20-21).

---

27. Narrators will use a "divine passive" when they wish to indicate God's activity in a veiled way. On the so-called *passivum divinum*, see Wolters, "The Riddle of the Scales in Daniel 5," *HUCA* 62 (1991) 167. See also the Introduction above, p. 26.

28. "Who God's agent might have been, if anyone, was of no interest; the point was that God punished Belshazzar's blasphemy." Redditt, *Daniel*, 99.

Textual Theme and Goal

Longman is undoubtedly correct when he writes that "the theme of Daniel 5 fits into the theme of the whole book: In spite of present appearances, God is in control!"[29] The challenge for us at this stage is to formulate a theme that captures the specific point of this particular narrative. Unique in this narrative is Daniel's indictment speech, that is to say, God's judgment stands out in this chapter. In response to Belshazzar's defiant sacrilege, God pronounces his judgment on the king and has him killed. But the narrator is even more concerned to point out that in judging the king, God judges the Babylonian kingdom. It is not just the king who commits this sacrilege. With his repetition of "the king and his lords, his wives, and his concubines," the narrator underscores that the ruling class was involved in this sacrilege: "Belshazzar commanded that they bring in the vessels of gold and silver . . . so that the king and his lords, his wives, and his concubines might drink from them. So they brought in the vessels of gold and silver, . . . and the king and his lords, his wives, and his concubines drank from them. *They* drank the wine and praised the gods of gold and silver, bronze, iron, wood, and stone" (vv. 2-4; cf. v. 23).[30]

This broader concern about the Babylonian kingdom is also brought out in God's judgment. Notice, "God has numbered the days of your *kingdom* and brought it to an end. . . . Your *kingdom* is divided and given to the Medes and Persians" (vv. 26, 28). In distinction from chapter 4 where God judged and deposed King Nebuchadnezzar while the Babylonian kingdom continued, God's judgment on the king here results in the collapse of the Babylonian Empire and God's giving the kingdom to the Medes and Persians. Therefore a good summary of this narrative is: "Israel's sovereign God judges the last Babylonian king for his sacrilege, giving his kingdom to the Medes and Persians." The message Israel would have heard would be, *Our sovereign God judges the last Babylonian king for his sacrilege, giving his kingdom to the Medes and Persians.*

What would be the author's goal in sending this message to the Israelites in exile? God's judgment of the king's sacrilege is "immediate" (vv. 5, 30), and it brings down the great Babylonian Empire. The author's goal must have been *to comfort the fearful Israelites in exile with the message that their sovereign God can bring down even the mightiest kingdom on earth.*[31]

---

29. Longman, *Daniel,* 134.

30. "As the mindless Babylonian court gathered at Dura to worship the golden image, here a similar unthinking group drinks from the sacred vessels, either oblivious or hostile to Yahweh." Woodard, "Literary Strategies and Authorship in the Book of Daniel," *JETS* 37/1 (1994) 51.

31. "Belshazzar's downfall in particular offered [the exiled Jewish reader] a needed reminder that God's judgment on the defiant remained swift, sudden and sure." Ibid., 50. Cf. Lederach,

Ways to Preach Christ

Since there is no promise of the coming Messiah in this narrative, nor a type of Christ, nor a major contrast with the message of Jesus in the New Testament, we shall explore the four remaining ways to Christ: redemptive-historical progression, analogy, longitudinal themes, and New Testament references.

Redemptive-Historical Progression

In redemptive history God frequently judges people in order to advance the cause of his kingdom. Early on God judged the disobedient, arrogant builders of the Tower of Babel and scattered them. This scattering created room for God to call Abraham and Sarah from Babylonia to the Promised Land to be the forebears of God's holy nation Israel. When Israel was unfaithful to God, God sent them into exile, back to Babylonia. In Daniel 5 God judges the last Babylonian king for his sacrilege and gives his kingdom to the Medes and Persians. This change from the golden kingdom in Nebuchadnezzar's dream to the silver one (Dan 2:32, 39) sets the stage for the return of a remnant of Israel from exile. King Cyrus of Persia had a different policy than the kings of Babylon. He made a written edict: "Thus says King Cyrus of Persia: The LORD, the God of heaven, has given me all the kingdoms of the earth, and he has charged me to build him a house at Jerusalem, which is in Judah. Whoever is among you of all his people, may the LORD his God be with him! Let him go up" (2 Chron 36:23; see also Ezra 1:1-11). A remnant of the exiles returned to the land of Judah and in due time rebuilt the city of Jerusalem and the temple of the Lord.

In the fullness of time, Jesus was born in Bethlehem in Judah. The stone cut out "not by human hands" (Dan 2:34, 45) started to roll down the mountainside on its way to smashing all human kingdoms. Jesus began his ministry, "proclaiming the good news of God, and saying, 'The time is fulfilled, and *the kingdom of God* has come near; repent, and believe in the good news'" (Mark 1:14-15). Jesus fulfilled his mission by dying on the cross for "the sin of the *world*" (John 1:29; cf. 6:51; 12:47; Col 1:20), rising from the dead, and sending out his followers to "make disciples of *all* nations" (Matt 28:19). At his trial the evening before he died, Jesus said to the high priest, "From now on you will see the Son of Man seated at the right hand of Power and coming on the clouds of heaven" (Matt 26:64; cf. Mark 16:19). Paul calls Christ "the first fruits" of the resurrection, "then at his coming those who belong to Christ. Then comes the end,

---

Daniel, 110, "The story speaks eloquently to the Jewish community, calling for faithfulness and hope even when the sacred is profaned."

when he hands over the *kingdom* to God the Father, after he has *destroyed every ruler and every authority and power.* For he must reign until he has put all his *enemies* under his feet" (1 Cor 15:23-25). Then "the kingdom of the world . . . [will] become the kingdom of our Lord and of his Messiah" (Rev. 11:15).

Analogy

Analogy provides additional possibilities for moving to Christ. For example, as Daniel 5 teaches that the sovereign God has the power to remove mighty kings from office and give their kingdom to others, so does Jesus. When Pilate said to him, "Do you refuse to speak to me? Do you not know that I have power to release you, and power to crucify you?" Jesus answered him, "You would have no power over me unless it had been given you from above" (John 19:10-11).

Another possibility is to move from "the fingers of a human hand" sent from God's "presence" (5:5, 24) — fingers that pronounce God's judgment on the evil Babylonian king — to Jesus' pronouncement in Luke 11:20, "If it is by the finger of God that I cast out *demons,* then the kingdom of God has come to you."

We can also draw an analogy from the author's goal. As the author of Daniel 5 sought to comfort the fearful Israelites in exile with the message that their sovereign God can bring down even the mightiest kingdom on earth, so Jesus comforted God's fearful people suffering under Roman occupation. Jesus said, "Do not be afraid, little flock, for it is your Father's good pleasure to give you the kingdom" (Luke 12:34). Again, Jesus said, "When the Son of Man comes in his glory, . . . he will sit on the throne of his glory. . . . Then the king will say to those at his right hand, 'Come, you that are blessed by my Father, inherit the kingdom prepared for you from the foundation of the world'" (Matt 25:31, 34; cf. John 10:27-29).

Longitudinal Themes

One can also trace from the Old Testament to Christ the theme of God destroying evil human kingdoms. It begins in Genesis 6–8 when "the earth was corrupt in God's sight, and the earth was filled with violence" (Gen 6:11). God sent a great flood and started over with the righteous Noah. In Genesis 11 we read of disobedient humankind seeking to defy God by building their own autonomous kingdom. God confused their language and scattered them from there "over the face of all the earth" (Gen 11:9). Later God freed his people Israel from enslavement in Egypt by sending plagues upon the Egyptians ("the finger of God"; Exod 8:19) and drowning Pharaoh's army in the sea (Exod 14:24-31). In

Daniel 5 God's "fingers" (5:5) pronounce his judgment on the wicked Babylonian king and his evil kingdom. God has him killed and gives his kingdom to the king of Medo-Persia.

Through Isaiah (21:9) the Lord prophesied, "Fallen, fallen is Babylon; and all the images of her gods lie scattered on the ground." The prophets speak of the fall of Babylon as "the day of the LORD" (e.g., Isa 13:9, 13). Jesus speaks of this day as "the coming of the Son of Man": "Immediately after the suffering of those days the sun will be darkened, and the moon will not give its light; the stars will fall from heaven, and the powers of heaven will be shaken. Then the sign of the Son of Man will appear in heaven, and then all the tribes of the earth will mourn, and they will see 'the Son of Man coming on the clouds of heaven' with power and great glory" (Matt 24:29-30). The book of Revelation also connects the fall of Babylon with the Day of the Lord with several allusions to Daniel 5: "After this I saw another angel. . . . He called out with a mighty voice, '*Fallen, fallen is Babylon the great!* It has become a dwelling place of demons. . . . For all the nations have *drunk of the wine* of the wrath of her fornication. . . . Her plagues will come in a *single day* . . . and she will be burned with fire; for *mighty is the Lord God who judges her*'" (Rev. 18:2-4, 8).

New Testament References

Although the appendix to the Greek New Testament lists two New Testament references (Rom 9:28 and Rev. 9:20), neither refers to Christ. A passage that we may be able to use is Paul's sermon on the Areopagus in Athens: "Since we are God's offspring, we ought not to think that the deity is like *gold, or silver, or stone,* an image formed by the art and imagination of mortals. While God has overlooked the times of human ignorance, now he commands all people everywhere to repent, because he has fixed a day on which he will have *the world judged* in righteousness by a man whom he has appointed, and of this he has given assurance to all by raising him from the dead" (Acts 17:29-31).

Sermon Theme, Goal, and Need

We formulated the textual theme as follows, "Our sovereign God judges the last Babylonian king for his sacrilege, giving his kingdom to the Medes and Persians." Since there is no contrast between this Old Testament message and that of the New, we can turn the textual theme into the sermon theme by broadening the principle to cover our day and age. The sermon theme then becomes, *Our sovereign God can bring down the mightiest evil king, giving his kingdom to another.*

We formulated the author's goal as, "to comfort the fearful Israelites in exile with the message that their sovereign God can bring down even the mightiest kingdom on earth." With a slight change we can make the textual goal the goal for the sermon: *to comfort God's fearful people today with the message that our sovereign God can bring down even the mightiest evil kingdom on earth and give it to another.*

This goal suggests that the need being addressed in this sermon is God's people's fear of the power of evil human kingdoms. In the sermon introduction, one can illustrate this fear, for example, with the fear of state-sponsored persecution of Christians, or the fear of terrorist attacks by al-Qaeda. Then move to Israel's fear of Babylon as it suffered in exile. Against that background retell the story of our sovereign God bringing down a wicked king and his evil empire. In a series of sermons on Daniel, of course, one can also begin with a brief review of one or more of the earlier narratives and show how this narrative fits its literary context. I will demonstrate the latter below.[32]

Sermon Exposition

In Daniel 4 God humbled the Babylonian king Nebuchadnezzar for his pride. God took away his reason so that he lived like an animal. Nebuchadnezzar had to learn "that the Most High has sovereignty over the kingdom of mortals and gives it to whom he will" (4:32). Three times the narrator repeats that "the King of heaven" is sovereign over earthly kingdoms and can give "it to whom he will." Nebuchadnezzar concludes his praise of "the King of heaven" with the words, "He is able to bring low those who walk in pride" (4:37).

Daniel 5 begins about thirty years after God humbled Nebuchadnezzar.[33] Once again God needs to remind a proud king that he can bring low those who walk in pride and give the kingdom to whom he will. Chapter 5:1 begins, "King Belshazzar[34] made a great festival for a thousand of his lords, and he was drinking

---

32. It is difficult to model sermon introductions in a book since such introductions should be up-to-date and connect with the local congregation.

33. In 562 B.C. Nebuchadnezzar died. He was succeeded by his son, who ruled only three years before being assassinated. In quick succession four more Babylonian kings (including Belshazzar, who was co-regent with his father, Nabonidus) followed until the year 539 B.C., when Cyrus captured Babylon. For details, see Longman, *Daniel*, 134-35. Since Cyrus captured Babylon on October 12, 539, the events related in Daniel 5 must have taken place "on the evening of October 11, 539." Steinmann, *Daniel*, 258.

34. In the past there was no extrabiblical evidence for a "King Belshazzar." Some scholars in the nineteenth century were quick to seize on this lack of evidence to claim that this story was fiction. But in 1854 small clay cylinders were discovered with the inscription Bel-sarra-usur, the Belshazzar of Daniel. His father, Nabonidus, was king, but when he left for Arabia for some ten

wine in the presence of the thousand." Oriental kings were known for throwing enormous parties.[35] The narrator underscores that this is such a party by repeating the word "thousand." What is unusual here is that the king "was drinking wine in the *presence* of the thousand." Oriental kings would usually dine in a separate room with a few invited guests. But Belshazzar sits "in full view of his subjects" and takes "the lead in this drinking bout."[36] He is "showing off."[37]

Soon the king is sufficiently intoxicated to give an order he may not have given had he been sober. Verse 2, "Under the influence of the wine, Belshazzar commanded that they bring in the vessels of gold and silver that his father [i.e., his predecessor][38] Nebuchadnezzar had taken out of the temple in Jerusalem, so that the king and his lords, his wives, and his concubines[39] might drink from them." This might seem tame compared to the drunken exploits of others, but make no mistake, this was an extremely foolhardy plan.[40] These vessels from the temple in Jerusalem are holy to God and his people. King Belshazzar wants to mock the God of Israel.

Some seventy years earlier, King Nebuchadnezzar had brought these vessels as war trophies from God's temple in Jerusalem. According to Ezra (1:11) there were "five thousand four hundred" of these vessels in Babylon. Nebuchadnezzar had placed them "in the treasury of his gods" (Dan 1:2), thus exhibiting that his Babylonian gods had defeated Israel's God. King Belshazzar goes Nebuchadnezzar one better. He wants to demonstrate to his lords that Israel's God is insignificant and worthless. They will drink from his holy vessels. At this party they will trample the honor of Israel's God. They will spit in God's face and get away with it. The Babylonian ruling class en masse will disgrace Israel's God.

---

years, according to the *Verse Account of Nabonidus* 2.20, he "entrusted the kingship" to Belshazzar. See Collins, *Daniel*, 32-33, 243; Young, *Prophecy of Daniel*, 116-17; Lucas, *Daniel*, 126; and Millard, "Daniel and Belshazzar in History," *BAR* 11/3 (1985) 74-78.

35. See Young, *Prophecy of Daniel*, 118. Young calls "a thousand" a round number "to indicate the enormity of the feast."

36. Miller, *Daniel*, 151.

37. Seow, *Daniel*, 78.

38. Although the author six times calls Nebuchadnezzar Belshazzar's "father" (vv. 2, 11 [3x], 13, 18), we know that his biological father was Nabonidus. "'Father' may refer to one's immediate father, grandfather, ancestor, or, as in the case of kings, a predecessor." Miller, *Daniel*, 149. The terms "father" and "son" (5:22) "make the point that both Nebuchadnezzar and Belshazzar held the same office and responsibility before God, but ironically Belshazzar the pagan 'son' resembled and repeated the hubris and idolatry of his pagan 'father,' Nebuchadnezzar." Steinmann, *Daniel*, 262.

39. "The first term [his wives] is an honorable one . . . ; the other [his concubines] denotes the inferior class of harem women." Montgomery, *Book of Daniel*, 251.

40. "The king must have lost his sense of decency to commit what is to the Oriental view a sacrilege even with holy things of another religion." Ibid.

Hopefully, someone is sober enough to realize that the intoxicated king is playing with fire. Hopefully, someone will stop his foolish plan. But no, the Babylonians obey his commands to the letter. Verse 3, "So they brought in the vessels of gold and silver that had been taken out of the temple, *the house of God* in Jerusalem, and the king and his lords, his wives, and his concubines drank from them." To underscore the gravity of this act the narrator adds in this verse that these vessels had been taken out of "the house of *God*." These vessels were used in the house of God to honor the God of Israel. They belong to the Most High God. By drinking from these holy vessels at their drunken party, the Babylonian king and aristocracy challenge Israel's God and treat him with contempt.

Then they add insult to injury: they raise the sacred vessels of Israel's God and drink to the Babylonian gods. Verse 4, "They drank the wine and praised the gods of gold and silver, bronze, iron, wood, and stone." Significantly, the author does not name the Babylonian gods. Instead he notes twice what they were made of: "gods of gold and silver, bronze, iron, wood, and stone" (vv. 4 and 23). In other words, these gods are *dead;* there is no life in them.[41] While mocking the living God, the Babylonians praise their lifeless gods.[42] Thus they insult and taunt Israel's God. They commit "an act of arrogant defiance against the Most High" and challenge him "to avenge his honor."[43]

How will this challenge turn out? Will God respond? Remember the story of King David bringing the ark of the covenant to Jerusalem? They carefully placed the ark of God on a new cart. But on the way something spooked the oxen. When the ark began to shake, a man by the name of Uzzah "reached out his hand to the ark of God and took hold of it." Then, we read, "The anger of the LORD was kindled against Uzzah; and God struck him there because he reached out his hand to the ark; and he died there beside the ark of God" (2 Sam 6:6-7). If God so punished an Israelite who touched his holy ark, how will God respond to Gentiles who touch his holy vessels and insult him by drinking wine from them while praising their dead gods?

The answer is not long in coming. Verse 5, "*Immediately* the fingers of a human hand appeared and began writing on the plaster[44] of the wall of the royal

41. "The redundant list of building materials underscores the lifeless and artificial quality of the so-called gods they worshiped." Schwab, *Hope*, 75.

42. "The praising of these pagan gods is a direct affront to Israel's God by implying that he is subordinate to gods of gold, silver, bronze, iron, wood, and stone." Steinmann, *Daniel*, 273.

43. Leupold, *Exposition of Daniel*, 215. Cf. Seow, *Daniel*, 78, "The sovereignty and power of the God of the exiles are, thus, blatantly called into question."

44. "Koldewey, who led a number of excavations at Babylon beginning in March 1899, commented that the walls of the throne room 'were washed over with white gypsum.'" Miller, *Daniel*, 155, quoting from R. Koldewey, *The Excavations at Babylon* (London: Macmillan, 1914), 104.

palace, next to the lampstand. The king was watching the hand as it wrote." God writes his response to this challenge "next to the lampstand" where it can easily be seen. The king is watching the hand as it writes. He knows it must be a bad omen. He is deeply affected.

Verse 6, "Then the king's face turned pale, and his thoughts terrified him. His limbs gave way, and his knees knocked together." The blood drains from his face; he is terrified. His limbs give way and his knees knock together. "His limbs gave way" is literally "the knots of his loins were loosened." Some scholars think that this means that the king is so terrified that he soiled his pants.[45] He is emotionally and physically shaken. What a humiliation for the show-off king![46] He is utterly humiliated — and that in front of "his lords, his wives, and his concubines."

The king cannot read the words, but he knows instinctively that they must be bad news. Israel's God must be responding to his defiant challenge. Verse 7, "The king cried aloud to bring in the enchanters, the Chaldeans, and the diviners; and the king said to the wise men of Babylon, 'Whoever can read this writing and tell me its interpretation shall be clothed in purple, have a chain of gold around his neck, and rank third in the kingdom.'" The wise men of Babylon were supposed to be experts in solving ominous signs. They had encyclopedias which listed various signs together with their meaning.[47]

The king offers rich rewards to the one who can read and interpret the writing. He will be clothed in royal purple, receive a gold chain around his neck — another sign of royalty — and be "third in the kingdom." Since Belshazzar was co-regent with his biological father, Nabonidus, he offers the next highest royal position, "third in the kingdom."[48]

Verse 8, "Then all the king's wise men came in, but they could not read the writing or tell the king the interpretation." Jewish tradition has it that they could not read the writing because instead of being written horizontally, the words were written vertically in columns. Rembrandt knew this tradition from his Jewish friends, so in his famous painting of this scene you will see the words

---

45. See p. 153, n. 21 above.

46. "What a pitiful spectacle of a king who had a few moments before ventured to defy the Almighty!" Leupold, *Exposition of Daniel*, 221.

47. "Some signs were specific to an individual; others referred to the king; still others to the nation or its enemies." Millard, "Daniel and Belshazzar in History," *BAR* 11/3 (1985) 77.

48. See Longman, *Daniel*, 139, and Steinmann, *Daniel*, 268-69. Several commentators, e.g., Collins, *Daniel*, 247, follow Montgomery's proposal that "third" merely is "a high official title" (*Book of Daniel*, 254, 256-57). Miller, *Daniel*, 157-58, counters: "First, the wise men already were of high rank, and elevation merely to the position of a high official would not seem significant. Second, the other rewards offered indicated more than the status of high official, the purple robe even suggesting that the interpreter would be promoted to royalty."

written vertically.[49] But there is a more natural explanation. Ancient Aramaic (like ancient Hebrew) used only consonants (the vowels were added by Masoretic scribes six hundred years after Christ). Moreover, the words were probably run together without spaces: *mn'tqlprs*. This string of consonants could be divided into different words depending on where one put the spaces. Adding different vowels to the consonants added still other possibilities.[50]

To give an example of the difficulty of this riddle in English, imagine that a string of eight consonants appears on the wall: PNDNCHLF.[51] In order to read this riddle we would first have to decide where to place the spaces to identify the words. There are many possibilities. After weighing the various options, suppose we put a space after the third letter. This results in the letters PND. Now we have to supply the proper vowels. Again there are a host of options. PND can be read as PEND, PINED, PAINED, POND, POUND, PANDA, and other English words. And that's only the first word. We have two or three more to go. And then we have to interpret what these words mean. An extremely difficult riddle.

Small wonder the Babylonian wise men are stumped. They cannot even read the writing, let alone give its interpretation. Verse 9, "Then King Belshazzar became greatly terrified and his face turned pale, and his lords were perplexed." Things are going from bad to worse. The king suspects that something bad will happen, but he has no idea what it is. His wise men have failed him. He discusses with his lords what he can do next, but his lords are equally perplexed.

Enter the queen. In a nearby room, the queen has overheard this discussion. Since the king's wives are already in the banqueting hall (vv. 2-3), this queen must be the queen mother.[52] In the ancient world a queen mother had a great deal of authority. She demonstrates this authority by entering the hall un-

---

49. Steinmann, *Daniel*, 274.

50. "Word-divisions . . . were not infrequently omitted, especially in shorter texts. . . . Since a riddle by its nature exploits ambiguity, it is likely that the nine letters on the wall were written without such word-dividers." Wolters, "The Riddle of the Scales in Daniel 5," *HUCA* 62 (1991) 158, n. 19. On pp. 159-60, Wolters offers several possibilities for different readings. Cf. Steinmann, *Daniel*, 274-76.

51. One would have to use PowerPoint for this illustration or print the letters on the bulletin cover.

52. Most commentators think that the queen was Belshazzar's mother, the wife of Nabonidus. Towner, *Daniel*, 69-70, gives five reasons why the queen should be understood as the queen mother: "(a) she talks to Belshazzar about 'your father'; (b) she has intimate knowledge of events of the previous generation; (c) Herodotus . . . thinks [the powerful queen Nitocris] was the *wife* of Nebuchadnezzar and the *mother* of Nabonidus; (d) the term *malkĕtā'* given as her title (v. 10) differs from the term used for Belshazzar's wives (v. 2) . . . ; (e) unlike Esther, . . . this queen bursts right in on the revelry in the 'banqueting hall.'" Cf. Young, *Prophecy of Daniel*, 122; Goldingay, *Daniel*, 109; Miller, *Daniel*, 159-60, and Lucas, *Daniel*, 130.

invited and speaking directly to the king (cf. Esth 4:11). Verses 10 to 12, "The queen, when she heard the discussion of the king and his lords, came into the banqueting hall.[53] The queen said, 'O king, live forever! Do not let your thoughts terrify you or your face grow pale. There is a man in your kingdom who is endowed with a spirit of the holy gods. In the days of your father he was found to have enlightenment, understanding, and wisdom like the wisdom of the gods. Your father, King Nebuchadnezzar, made him chief of the magicians, enchanters, Chaldeans, and diviners, because an excellent spirit, knowledge, and understanding to interpret dreams, explain riddles, and solve problems were found in this Daniel, whom the king named Belteshazzar. Now let Daniel be called, and he will give the interpretation.'"

Daniel is in his eighties now and may have retired. It's been twenty-three years since Nebuchadnezzar died. Or Daniel may have been fired by one of the five kings after King Nebuchadnezzar.[54] But the queen mother remembers Daniel. She lists all his many skills: "endowed with a spirit of the holy gods"; having "enlightenment, understanding, and wisdom," "an excellent spirit, knowledge, and understanding to interpret dreams, explain riddles, and solve problems."[55] It's quite a resume. She concludes confidently, "Now let Daniel be called, and he will give the interpretation."

The king listens to the queen mother. But, after mocking the God of the Jews, he is none too happy about calling a Jew to solve his predicament. You can tell by the way he interrogates Daniel. Verse 13, "Then Daniel was brought in before the king. The king said to Daniel, 'So you are Daniel, one of the *exiles of Judah,* whom my father the king brought *from Judah?*'" The king immediately puts Daniel in his place: "one of the exiles of Judah." John Calvin writes, "He interrogates Daniel . . . as a captive."[56]

Next the king shows his lack of confidence in Daniel's skills by repeating twice, "I have heard." Verses 14 to 16, "*I have heard* of you that a spirit of the gods[57] is in you, and that enlightenment, understanding, and excellent wisdom are found in you. Now the wise men, the enchanters, have been brought in before me to read this writing and tell me its interpretation, but they were not able to give the interpretation of the matter. But *I have heard* that you can give interpretations and solve problems. Now *if you are able* to read the writing and tell me its interpretation, you shall be clothed in purple, have a chain of gold

---

53. "Banqueting hall" is, literally, "house of drinking." Towner, *Daniel,* 70.

54. "With the coming of a new king, especially when usurpers arose, wholesale dismissal of the men in office was the rule." Leupold, *Exposition of Daniel,* 226.

55. For an explanation of the skills the queen mother attributes to Daniel, see Goldingay, *Daniel,* 109-10.

56. Calvin, *Commentaries on Daniel,* I, 328.

57. He tones down the queen mother's description, "spirit of the *holy* gods."

around your neck, and rank third in the kingdom." The king doubts that Daniel will be able to read the writing. His wise men "were not able"; surely this old Jew will not be able to read the writing. But the king is desperate, so he is willing to give Daniel a shot. "If you are able . . . you shall be clothed in purple, have a chain of gold around your neck, and rank third in the kingdom."

Daniel is obviously angry. He is angry at the king's sacrilege and at the treatment he receives. He responds brusquely in verse 17. "Then Daniel answered in the presence of the king, 'Let your gifts be for yourself, or give your rewards to someone else!'" Daniel does not want to be beholden to the king. God's word cannot be bought. Nor can a reward change a bad omen into a good one.[58]

"Nevertheless," Daniel continues, "I will read the writing to the king and let him know the interpretation. O king, the Most High God *gave* your father Nebuchadnezzar kingship, greatness, glory, and majesty. [Whatever greatness Nebuchadnezzar had, it was all a gift from the Most High God.] And because of the greatness that he *gave* him, all peoples, nations, and languages trembled and feared before him. He killed those he wanted to kill, kept alive those he wanted to keep alive, honored those he wanted to honor, and degraded those he wanted to degrade." He could do whatever he wanted; he could do as he pleased; he had absolute, unrestrained power.[59] But remember, it was all a gift from the Most High God. Unfortunately, Daniel reminds the king, Nebuchadnezzar forgot this elementary fact.

Verses 20 and 21, "But when his heart was lifted up and his spirit was hardened[60] so that he acted proudly, he was deposed from his kingly throne, and his glory was stripped from him. He was driven from human society, and his mind was made like that of an animal. His dwelling was with the wild asses, he was fed grass like oxen, and his body was bathed with the dew of heaven, until he learned that the Most High God has sovereignty over the kingdom of mortals, and sets over it whomever he will."

After recalling Nebuchadnezzar's pride and God's punishment, Daniel turns directly to Belshazzar. Verse 22, "And you, Belshazzar his son,[61] have not

---

58. "Daniel begins by dissociating himself from any thought of reward. This was in line with prophetic consciousness that the needed word of wisdom came from the Lord, and could not be bought at any price (Num 22:18; Mic 3:5)." Baldwin, *Daniel,* 122. Goldingay, *Daniel,* 110, thinks "he is sidestepping any pressure to modify the portent's message."

59. "There was no power behind the throne: the king did exactly as he pleased without regard to men. . . . These words [of v. 19b] are not designed to convey the idea of arbitrariness but rather the idea of unhampered, unrestrained power. Every day men were moved up or down, consigned to death or to pardon, as the king might be minded to decree." Leupold, *Exposition of Daniel,* 231.

60. "Probably the phrase means that 'because' his heart was hardened toward God, he acted proudly." Miller, *Daniel,* 162-63.

61. See p. 161, n. 38 above.

humbled your heart, even though you knew all this!" Knowing how the Most High God humbled his proud predecessor, Belshazzar should have realized that he could not defiantly challenge God. He should have humbled himself. But he had done just the opposite. He challenged the Most High God!

Verse 23, "You have *exalted* yourself against the Lord of heaven!" How? First, "The vessels of his temple have been brought in before you, and you and your lords, your wives and your concubines have been drinking wine from them." Second, "You have praised the gods of silver and gold,[62] of bronze, iron, wood, and stone, which do not see or hear or know" (cf. Ps 115:4-7). And third, "but the God in whose power [literally, in whose hand] is your very breath, and to whom belong all your ways, you have not honored." Daniel contrasts the gods "which do not see or hear or know" with "the God in whose hand is your very breath, and to whom belong all your ways." The living God has only to close his hand and the king will die on the spot (cf. Job 12:10; 34:14-15; Ps 104:28-29). But the king had praised these lifeless gods and failed to honor the living God. It's quite an indictment of the king. "To the sin of pride he had added that of sacrilege. To sacrilege he had added the sin of idolatry."[63] "In these two verses [22-23] the words 'you' and 'your' are used fourteen times in a machine-gun-like application of Belshazzar's foolishness."[64]

After this indictment of the king, Daniel proceeds to God's judgment of the king. Verses 24 and 25, "So from his [God's] presence the hand was sent[65] and this writing was inscribed. And this is the writing that was inscribed: MENE, MENE, TEKEL, and PARSIN." Daniel reads the string of consonants the wise men could not decipher. He comes up with three different words, each standing for a different weight used on a balance scale for weighing precious metal.[66] The

---

62. This verse reverses the "gold and silver" of 5:4 to "silver and gold." Shea, "Further Literary Structures in Daniel 2–7," 283-84, suggests an intentional reversal: "The naming of metals carries us back to Nebuchadnezzar's dream in Dan 2, where gold and silver occur in descending order at the top of the metal image. . . . This was the very night when the silver kingdom subjugated and supplanted the golden kingdom of Babylon — a fact altogether appropriate to note in this list of metals in Dan 5."

63. Porteous, *Daniel*, 81. Porteous adds: "Commentators point out that the language here echoes that of Deut. 4:28; Pss 115:4-8; 135:16-17."

64. Ferguson, *Daniel*, 122.

65. "The parallel with Ezra [7:14, "you are sent by the king"] suggests that the hand functions as God's own scribe, an ambassador going out from before him, rendering his commands in written form at the court of another monarch, Belshazzar." Polaski, "Mene, Mene, Tekel, Parsin," *JBL* 123/4 (2004) 659.

66. "Many Babylonian weight-stones with a value of a mina, a shekel or a half-mina are now housed in archeological museums, some of them inscribed in Aramaic with the very words of our passage: *měnē', těqēl*, or *pěrēs*." Wolters, "The Riddle of the Scales in Daniel 5," *HUCA* 62 (1991) 163.

first is "mene," that is a mina. The mina is the heaviest weight; it weighs 500 grams. Daniel repeats "mene" for emphasis. The second word is "tekel," that is, a shekel: 10 grams. The third word is "parsin," that is, a half-mina, 250 grams.[67] Picking up on our earlier example, in English terms the string of consonants PNDNCHLF might have been read like, "pound, ounce, half-pound."[68]

Obviously, this is not a meaningful message. What do these different weights mean? In his interpretation Daniel understands these nouns as verbs: "numbered," "weighed," and "divided."[69] Verse 26, "This is the interpretation of the matter: MENE, God has *numbered* the days of your kingdom and brought it to an end." We still use the expression "your days are numbered." But Daniel does not just say that God has numbered the king's days but the days of his *kingdom*. The days of the Babylonian kingdom are numbered. This very night it will be brought to an end.

Daniel continues in verse 27, "TEKEL, you have been *weighed* on the scales and found wanting." God has weighed King Belshazzar on his balance scale and found him "too light."[70] Belshazzar did not measure up to God's demand for righteousness and justice. In fact, he dishonored and challenged the sovereign God.

Verse 28, "PERES,[71] your kingdom is *divided*[72] and given to the Medes and

67. Millard, "Daniel and Belshazzar in History," *BAR* 11/3 (1985) 77, and others, take "parsin" to be a half-shekel, while other commentators, e.g., Towner, *Daniel*, 75, take it to be "a half-mina." Wolters, "The Riddle of the Scales in Daniel 5," *HUCA* 62 (1991) 160, n. 32 writes, "Whenever *prs* refers to a unit of *weight*, it clearly means a half-mina. Besides, the regular Aramaic word for 'half-shekel' is *zûz*."

68. Towner, *Daniel*, 75, suggests that "In modern terms [the inscription] might read, '(A half dollar), a half dollar, a penny, and two bits.'" But since these are weights for a balance scale and not coins, we might better think of the writing as, "five-hundred grams, ten grams, and two-hundred and fifty grams." "Quite apart from the fact that coinage had not yet been introduced into Mesopotamia in Belshazzar's day, there were in fact never coins in either Babylonia or Palestine that weighed as much as a mina or half-mina." Wolters, "The Riddle of the Scales in Daniel 5," *HUCA* 62 (1991) 162.

69. "The three nouns listed in verse 25 are treated as passive verbs by Daniel in verses 26-28: Mene is related to the verb *m-n-h*, 'numbered'; Tekel is related to the verb *t-q-l*, 'weighed'; and Peres is construed as the verb *p-r-s*, 'divided.'" Towner, *Daniel*, 76. Cf. Lucas, *Daniel*, 133-34, and Steinmann, *Daniel*, 286-87. Hill, "Daniel," 112, adds, "The perfect form of the verbs (i.e., 'has numbered,' 'have been weighed') indicates that the matter has been decided — the outcome is certain." For more details on Daniel's interpretation, see Wolters, "The Riddle of the Scales in Daniel 5," *HUCA* 62 (1991) 155-77.

70. "We can be quite confident that the meaning 'you are too light' was indeed intended by the author." Wolters, "The Riddle of the Scales in Daniel 5," *HUCA* 62 (1991) 174.

71. "Peres" is the singular form of "parsin" in verse 25.

72. Wolters, "The Riddle of the Scales in Daniel 5," *HUCA* 62 (1991), 168-70, shows that the lexical evidence is stronger for translating the verb *pĕrēs* not as "divide" but as "assess," which would also be more in line with the idea of God weighing the king on his balance scale and be

Persians." Again the focus is on the kingdom. "God destroys Babylon's power by breaking it in two and then delivers it to the rising empire of the Medes and the Persians."[73] It's a devastating message. The writing is on the wall. God weighed King Belshazzar on his scale of justice and found him too light. The days of his kingdom are numbered. God will take away the kingdom from Babylon and give it to the next kingdom, that of Medo-Persia.

Verses 29 to 30, "Then Belshazzar gave the command, and Daniel was clothed in purple, a chain of gold was put around his neck, and a proclamation was made concerning him that he should rank third in the kingdom.[74] That very night Belshazzar, the Chaldean king, was killed." Throughout the chapter Belshazzar is called "king." Here the author stresses that he was "the Chaldean king," the Babylonian king. The author does not say who killed the Chaldean king, but it is understood that God had him killed.[75]

Ancient sources relate that "the Medo-Persian army diverted water from the Euphrates River (which ran under the walls into Babylon) into a marsh."[76] Thus the soldiers were able to wade through shallow water down the riverbed under the walls and into the city. They entered the palace, found King Belshazzar, and killed him. The name "Belshazzar" means "O Bel [another name for the highest Babylonian god, Marduk], protect the king."[77] But the highest Babylonian god could not protect the king from the anger of Israel's God.[78] As Nebuchadnezzar had said, "The King of heaven . . . is able to bring low those who walk in pride" (4:37). Belshazzar was the last Babylonian king.

Verse 31, "And Darius the Mede received the kingdom, being about sixty-two years old." Darius seems to be another name for King Cyrus.[79] Again, the

---

closer in meaning to the other two words, "reckoned/numbered" and "weighed." But since this is a technical detail that does not change the message, it is better in the sermon to use the wording given in the pew Bibles.

73. Steinmann, *Daniel*, 287.

74. If the question is raised why the evil king did not kill the messenger but fulfilled his promise, we could simply say that we do not know. Calvin, *Commentaries on Daniel*, I, 345-46, suggests the following reasons, "To shew himself unmoved, he commands Daniel to be clothed in these robes, as if his threat had been perfectly harmless. . . . He wished to persuade his nobles and all his guests of his perfect indifference to God's threats. . . . To continue, therefore, his reverence among his subjects, he is desirous of appearing exceedingly careless and undisturbed."

75. Divine passive; see p. 155, n. 27 above.

76. Miller, *Daniel*, 167, with references to Herodotus's *Histories* and Xenophon's *Cyropaedia*.

77. Collins, *Daniel*, 243.

78. Cf. Isaiah 46:1-13.

79. Darius the Mede is not known from extrabiblical literature. Baldwin, *Daniel*, 26-28, follows D. J. Wiseman (1957) in identifying Darius with Cyrus the Great. More recently, Steinmann, *Daniel*, 290-96, made a similar argument: "Daniel knows this king both by his more familiar name Cyrus (1:21; 6:28; 10:1) and as Darius (5:31; 6:1, 6, 9, 25, 28; 9:1; 11:1). Daniel equates

author does not say who gave Darius the kingdom, but it is clear from the book of Daniel that it was *God* who gave Darius the kingdom (cf. Dan 1:2). As Nebuchadnezzar had learned, "the Most High God has sovereignty over the kingdom of mortals, and *sets over it whomever he will*" (4:17, 25, 32; cf. 5:21). The author contrasts Darius the *Mede* with the *Chaldean* king. With Darius the Mede God ushers in a new dynasty and a new world power.

What a message of comfort for fearful Israel suffering in exile in Babylon. Their God is not helpless over against the Babylonian gods. On the contrary, their God is the Most High God while the Babylonian gods are as dead as the metals from which they are constructed. Israel's God has demonstrated his sovereignty by judging the Babylonian king for his sacrilege and giving his kingdom to the Medes and Persians. Israel's God is sovereign over all. Their future is in God's almighty hand.

The change from the golden kingdom in Nebuchadnezzar's dream to the silver one (2:32, 39) sets the stage for the return of a remnant of Israel from exile. We read in 2 Chronicles that King Cyrus of Persia made a written edict: "Thus says King Cyrus of Persia: The Lord, the God of heaven, has given me all the kingdoms of the earth, and he has charged me to build him a house at Jerusalem, which is in Judah. Whoever is among you of all his people, may the Lord his God be with him! Let him go up" (2 Chron 36:23; cf. Ezra 1:1-11). A remnant of the exiles returned to the land of Judah and in due time rebuilt the city of Jerusalem and the temple of the Lord.

In the fullness of time, Jesus was born in Bethlehem in Judah. The stone in Nebuchadnezzar's dream which was cut out "not by human hands" (Dan 2:34, 45) started rolling down the mountainside on its way to smashing all human

---

the two in 6:28 by means of the epexegetical *waw*. Daniel's use of the name 'Darius' may be his way of emphasizing the fulfillment of the words of the prophets who spoke of the Medes as the ones who would bring about Babylon's fall (Isa 13:17; 21:2; Jer 51:11, 28). Daniel himself speaks about the fall of Babylon to 'the Medes and the Persians' (Dan 5:28)." Ibid., 295. Cf. Lucas, *Daniel*, 137, "Cyrus, the actual conqueror of Babylon, was partly Median and ruled the Medes as well as the Persians. This is emphasized by giving him the alternative name 'Darius the Mede.'" See also Bulman, "The Identification of Darius the Mede," *WTJ* 35 (1972-73) 247-67; Baker, "Further Examples of the *Waw Explicativum*," *VT* 30 (1980) 129-36; Colless, "Cyrus the Persian as Darius the Mede in the Book of Daniel," *JSOT* 56 (1992) 113-26; Miller, *Daniel*, 171-77; Harman, *Study Commentary on Daniel*, 126; and Stefanovic, *Daniel*, 200. The latter gives four examples of other kings who had two names: "Tiglath-pileser III was also called Pul (2 Kings 15:19, 29 [cf. 1 Chron 5:26]); Azariah was also known as Uzziah (2 Kings 15:1; 2 Chron 26:1); Solomon was given the name Jedidiah at his birth (2 Sam 12:25); and Jeremiah called King Jehoiachin 'Coniah' in Jeremiah 22:24 and 'Jeconiah' in 24:1." Stefanovic adds (p. 203), "Most of the indicators from the Bible . . . point to Cyrus the Great, who may have been known by two titles due to his dual (Medo-Persian) parentage (Dan 6:28)." Moreover, in this very chapter, the queen mother uses the two names for Daniel, "Daniel" and "Belteshazzar" (Dan 5:12).

kingdoms. Jesus began his ministry "proclaiming the good news of God, and saying, 'The time is fulfilled, and *the kingdom of God* has come near; repent, and believe in the good news'" (Mark 1:14-15). Jesus healed people and cast out demons. He said, "If it is by *the finger of God* that I cast out demons, then *the kingdom of God* has come to you" (Luke 11:20). Jesus comforted God's people fearful of the Roman occupation forces. He said, "Do not be afraid, little flock, for it is your Father's good pleasure to give you *the kingdom*" (Luke 12:34). Jesus earned the kingdom of God for us by dying on the cross for "the sin of the *world*" (John 1:29), rising from the dead, and sending out his followers to "make disciples of *all* nations" (Matt 28:19). At his trial the evening before his death, Jesus said to the high priest: "From now on you will see the Son of Man seated at the right hand of Power and coming on the clouds of heaven" (Matt 26:64). Jesus is now seated at the right hand of God the Father. From there he rules his kingdom until the last day, when he comes on the clouds of heaven.

Paul reflects on that last day. He writes, "Christ the first fruits [of the resurrection], then *at his coming* those who belong to Christ. Then comes the end, when he hands over the *kingdom* to God the Father, after he has destroyed *every ruler* and *every authority and power.* For he must reign until he has put all his enemies under his feet" (1 Cor 15:23-25). When that end comes, we read in Revelation, "the kingdom of the *world* has become the kingdom of our *Lord* and of his *Messiah*" (Rev. 11:15).

Our sovereign God is in control of world history from beginning to end. What a message of comfort for us when we live in fear of what may happen in the future. What calamities will we have to face? What persecution will our children face? Jesus predicted that "nation will rise against nation, and kingdom against kingdom; there will be great earthquakes, and in various places famines and plagues; and there will be dreadful portents and great signs from heaven" (Luke 21:10-11).

"Nation will rise against nation." Today there are thousands of nuclear weapons able to incinerate this world many times over. During the Cold War people looked for comfort to the U.S. nuclear arsenal. They thought that the Soviet Union would not dare start a nuclear war because they themselves would be destroyed as well. They called it MAD — Mutually Assured Destruction. It was mad indeed. What an awful basis for comfort! The incineration of the whole world.

Even that little comfort no longer obtains in this age of suicide bombers. Terrorists don't mind blowing themselves up — as long as they take the enemy with them. What will happen when North Korea or Iran develops nuclear weapons? What will happen when Pakistani or American nuclear weapons fall into the wrong hands? We fear for the future, and rightly so.

But our comfort is that our sovereign God is in control of human history.

He can bring down the most wicked king. He can destroy the mightiest evil empire. He can bring down the most vicious terrorist. Our sovereign God is in control of human history. And one day, he will destroy all human kingdoms and replace them with his perfect kingdom. He will restore Paradise on earth as he intended this world to be from the beginning. Our sovereign God is in control. Our destiny and that of our children, grandchildren, and all God's people is in his almighty hand. That is solid comfort!

CHAPTER 6

Daniel in the Lions' Den

Daniel 6:1-28[1]

Then King Darius wrote to all peoples and nations.... "I make a decree,
that in all my royal dominion people should tremble and fear before the
God of Daniel:

> *For he is the living God,*
> *enduring forever.*
> *His kingdom shall never be destroyed,*
> *and his dominion has no end.*
> *He delivers and rescues,*
> *he works signs and wonders in heaven and on earth;*
> *for he has saved Daniel from the power of the lions."*
>
> Daniel 6:25-27

This most familiar story from the book of Daniel is not just for children. It is
extremely relevant for God's people today, but probably not in the way they expect. This story's message is aimed first of all at Israelites in exile who were
tempted to ignore God's law and no longer trust God for deliverance from exile.
Do we have people in our congregations who are tempted to ignore God's law
by living just for themselves? Do we have people who feel quite at home in this
broken world and/or don't trust God to make all things new? Well, exactly for
such people this story of God delivering Daniel from the lions' den provides an
appropriate message.[2]

Though this narrative presents a relevant message for today, for preachers

---

1. Aramaic 6:2-29.

2. Lucas, *Daniel*, 150, argues that the English translation of "lions' den" elicits the wrong
picture. "The Aramaic word that is traditionally translated 'den' (of lions), *gōb*, really refers to a
'pit.'" Although I agree with him, in a sermon I would follow the common English translation
of "den" found in the pew Bibles, explaining that it really means a "pit."

it is not without its challenges. Since most hearers will already know the outcome of this story, one of the challenges will be to create some sense of suspense. Another challenge is to formulate a theme that is textually specific for this narrative and does not merely duplicate the theme of its parallel narrative, God delivering Daniel's friends from the fiery furnace (Dan 3).

Still another challenge, again, will be to avoid the piecemeal superficial moralizing which simply holds up Daniel and his actions as a model for imitation for Christians today. For example, one commentator, citing Mahatma Gandhi, promotes Daniel as a model of passive resistance: "Two issues seem of particular importance when reflecting on Daniel 6: (1) the meaning of nonviolent resistance and (2) the violence of reactions to injustice."[3] Other commentators urge imitation of some aspects of Daniel's prayer life. One states, "A healthy prayer life follows Daniel's example of regular seasons of prayer."[4] Another commends Daniel's practicing his faith openly: "Some people . . . privatize their convictions. Daniel did not do that, and in this he showed true greatness. Instead of hiding his convictions, he knelt before his window in the sight of Babylon and prayed as he had always done. We need more Daniels. We need more people . . . who are willing to open their windows and honor him [God] before a watching world."[5] Still another looks for application in Daniel's "giving thanks to his God" (6:10, NIV): "As he faced imminent death . . . Daniel was on his knees, giving thanks to God. How amazing is his faith! Here is a good test of the depth of your prayer life: how much of your time and energy in prayer is spent complaining about the circumstances of your life and asking for things to be different, and how much is spent in giving thanks for God's overwhelming goodness?"[6]

Although these applications are not necessarily unbiblical, they miss the point of this narrative (see theme and goal below). Biblical preachers will seek to do justice to the inspired author's intention and transfer that message to God's people today. To be sure, the author does portray Daniel as a true Israelite — a person with whom the Israelites in exile should identify. But this does not mean that we should necessarily imitate Daniel in his passive resistance, his praying three times a day, his posture of kneeling and facing Jerusalem, and his

---

3. Smith-Christopher, "Book of Daniel," 94.

4. Ferguson, *Daniel*, 137.

5. Boice, *Daniel*, 76. On p. 70 Boice offers the following application on verse 5, "The men said, 'We shall not find any ground for complaint against this Daniel unless we find it in connection with the law of his God'": "Is not that wonderful? Would it not be wonderful if that could be said of every Christian, especially of us?" Boice entitles this chapter, "A Busy Man's Devotional Life." Wallace, *The Lord Is King*, 109, also comments on verse 5, "The point brought out . . . seems to be that when men bear witness clearly and faithfully to the God of Israel — in their life as well as in their words — the truth of what they are pointing to is unassailable in face of any honest criticism."

6. Duguid, *Daniel*, 96.

praying before open windows (Didn't Jesus say, "Whenever you pray, go into your room and *shut* the door and pray to your Father who is in secret; and your Father who sees in secret will reward you" [Matt 6:6]?). Only a clear statement of the author's theme and goal can chart the direction for our message and its application to the church today.

Text and Context

Again the textual unit is easy to detect. Chapter 5:30-31 concluded with the news that "Belshazzar, the Chaldean king, was killed. And Darius the Mede received the kingdom, being about sixty-two years old." Chapter 6:1 (English versions) begins a new narrative about a particular event that happened during the reign of King Darius. Verse 28 signals the end of this unit by concluding, "So this Daniel prospered during the reign of Darius and the reign of Cyrus the Persian" (cf. 1:21). Chapter 7:1 begins a new literary unit about visions Daniel received "in the first year of King Belshazzar." The preaching text, therefore, is Daniel 6:1-28.

As to its literary context, Daniel 6 brings to a climax the six narratives in the first half of Daniel. In this narrative, Daniel himself is threatened with capital punishment, receives the death sentence for obeying God's law, and is miraculously saved by God. Also, Darius's concluding decree that all people in his royal dominion "should tremble and fear before the God of Daniel" (6:26) goes beyond the earlier decree of Nebuchadnezzar that none of the people should blaspheme the God of Daniel's friends (3:29).

This narrative also repeats elements of the earlier narratives. Darius's confession that God is "the living God" is similar to Nebuchadnezzar's confession in 2:47, and Darius's confession concerning God's kingdom (it "shall never be destroyed"; 6:26) also mirrors that of Nebuchadnezzar (4:3, 34). Darius's testimony that God "works signs and wonders" (6:27) repeats Nebuchadnezzar's earlier testimony about God's "signs and wonders" (4:2-3) and echoes the foundational "signs and wonders" by which God delivered Israel from enslavement in Egypt (e.g., Deut 6:22).

Daniel 6 parallels Daniel 3 in many ways. Darius signs a law that people pray only to him (6:7-9), which is similar to Nebuchadnezzar's command that people worship his golden statue (3:5). Daniel refuses to obey the king's law (6:10), as his friends had done earlier (3:18). The narrator describes the conspirators as "those who had accused [ate pieces of] Daniel" (6:24), which is the same as his earlier description of the enemies of Daniel's friends who "denounced [ate pieces of] the Jews" (3:8). Daniel is "thrown into [*remô'*] the den of lions" (6:16), just as Daniel's friends were "thrown into [*remô'*] the furnace of blazing fire" (3:20). Daniel is saved by God's angel (6:22), just as Daniel's friends were saved by God's angel (3:28). "No kind of harm" is found on Daniel (6:23), just as Daniel's friends were found to be totally unharmed (3:27). King Darius makes "a decree, that . . . people should tremble and fear before the God of Daniel" (6:26), which is similar to but, as noted above, goes beyond Nebuchadnezzar's decree against uttering "blasphemy against the God of Shadrach, Meshach, and Abednego" (3:29). King Darius confesses that Daniel's God "delivers and rescues" (6:27), just as King Nebuchadnezzar confessed that "there is no other god who is able to deliver in this way" (3:29).[7] Lucas concludes, "These correspondences may indicate that these stories, in the form in which we have them, were deliberately composed as a pair."[8]

The story of Daniel being thrown into the lions' "pit" and subsequently prospering (6:28) again evokes the story of Joseph being thrown into a pit and subsequently prospering (Gen 37:24; 39:23; 41:40). Daniel's being rescued from the lions' den while his accusers are killed by these lions is also similar to the story of Haman being "hanged on the gallows that he had prepared for Mordecai" (Esth 7:10). This theme of poetic justice is also reflected in the law (see Deut 19:10) and in wisdom literature. For example, Ecclesiastes 10:8 states, "Whoever digs a pit will fall into it." Proverbs 14:32 declares, "The wicked are overthrown by their evil-doing, but the righteous find a refuge in their integrity" (cf. Prov. 6:12-19). The Psalms also speak about God rescuing from the lions and the wicked falling into their own pit. For example, Psalm 57:4-6 states, "I lie down among lions that greedily devour human prey; their teeth are spears and arrows, their tongues sharp swords. . . . They set a net for my steps; my soul was bowed down. They dug a pit in my path, but they have fallen into it themselves."[9]

Literary Features

Since the overall genre of Daniel 6 is narrative,[10] most of this chapter is written in prose. The king's confession of faith in the God of Daniel (vv. 26-27), however, blossoms into poetry, as can be seen in the parallel constructions. The narrative also includes several other forms of literature.[11]

---

7. For some other parallel details and Aramaic words, see Goldingay, *Daniel*, 126.

8. Lucas, *Daniel*, 145.

9. See also Psalm 91:9-11, "Because you have made the LORD your refuge, the Most High your dwelling place, no evil shall befall you, no scourge come near your tent. For he will command his angels concerning you to guard you in all your ways." Cf. Psalm 22:13, 19-21.

10. Goldingay, *Daniel*, 122, calls it "a tale of court conflict and intrigue."

11. Collins, *Daniel* (1984), 72, lists these forms as: "(1) *Petition* by the conspirators to the king (vv. 6-8), consisting of a salutation, a statement of what is desired, and a request for an edict. . . . (2) *Accusation* (vv. 12-13), consisting of a question to the king, his self-committing an-

There is irony in the fact that the conspirators think they have found Daniel's weakness when they find him praying to God, while prayer is his greatest strength. "Indeed, it is his devotion to God that delivers him from the lions."[12] There is also irony in the king's signing a law that seems to elevate him to semidivine status while in fact "it forces him to do what he does not want to do. His attempt to claim absolute power makes him a puppet of his officials and a dupe of his own law."[13] The conspirators' statement to the king that "*All the presidents* of the kingdom, the prefects and the satraps, the counselors and the governors are agreed that the king should establish an ordinance and enforce an interdict" is at best a form of hyperbole.[14] At worst this is an outright lie, for President Daniel was not among them. We shall analyze in more detail the narrative structure, the plot line, character description, and repetition.

Narrative Structure

This narrative contains less reported speech than the four previous narratives (Dan 2–5). The conspirators briefly speak five times (6:5, 6-8, 12, 13, 15); the king speaks four times (6:12, 16, 20, 25-27), while Daniel speaks only once (6:21-22). The narrative is "carried along by repeated use of the conjunction *bĕ'dayin*, or, without the prefix, *'ĕdayin*, 'then.' This occurs fifteen times."[15]

The narrative consists of six scenes:

Scene 1: In the palace: the conspirators plot against Daniel   6:1-9
    A. King Darius plans to appoint Daniel over the whole kingdom   6:1-3
    B. The conspirators, finding no corruption in him, shift to his
       obedience to the law of his God   6:4-5
    C. The conspirators propose a law that prayer be made only to
       the king   6:6-8
    D. King Darius signs the document   6:9
    Characters: King Darius and the conspirators

---

swer, and the accusation proper. . . . (3) *Prayer of petition* (v. 16) on the lips of the king for the deliverance of Daniel. (4) *Epistle* of Darius (vv. 25-26), marked by the epistolary greeting and containing two other forms: (5) *Decree* or proclamation, which is simply stated in verse 26, and (6) *Doxology*, which is a descriptive hymn of praise, giving the rationale for the decree."

12. Arnold, "Wordplay and Narrative Techniques in Daniel 5 and 6," *JBL* 112/3 (1993) 485.

13. Lucas, *Daniel*, 154-55.

14. Leupold, *Exposition of Daniel*, 254.

15. Lucas, *Daniel*, 146 (English versions, vv. 3, 4, 5, 6, 11, 12, 13, 14, 15, 16, 18, 19, 21, 23, 25; for MT add 1 to each verse reference).

Scene 2: In Daniel's house: Daniel caught praying to God   6:10-11
     A. Daniel continues to pray to his God   6:10
     B. The conspirators find him praying to his God   6:11
     Characters: Daniel and the conspirators

Scene 3: Back in the palace: the conspirators accuse Daniel
before the king   6:12-15
     A. The conspirators accuse Daniel of breaking the law   6:12-13
     B. The king seeks to save Daniel until sundown   6:14
     C. The conspirators remind the king of the irrevocable law   6:15
     Characters: the conspirators and King Darius

Scene 4: That evening near the lions' den: Daniel thrown to the lions   6:16-18
     A. The king orders that Daniel be thrown into the lions' den   6:16
     B. A stone is laid on the den's mouth and sealed   6:17
     C. The king spends a sleepless night in his palace   6:18
     Characters: Daniel and the king

Scene 5: Early the next morning by the lions' den:
God works a miracle   6:19-24
     A. The king hurries to the lions' den: "Daniel, has your God
        been able to deliver you?"   6:19-20
     B. Daniel responds that God's angel shut the lions' mouths   6:21-22
     C. The king orders that Daniel be taken up out of the den   6:23
     D. The king orders that Daniel's accusers be thrown into the den   6:24
     Characters: the king and Daniel
        when Daniel leaves the stage (den), his accusers take his place

Scene 6: Back at the palace: the king writes a decree   6:25-28
     A. The king writes that all people fear the God of Daniel   6:25-27
     B. Daniel prospers during the reign of Darius   6:28
     Characters: the king and Daniel

The Plot Line

The setting for this narrative is given in verses 1-2: Darius organizes his government with one hundred twenty satraps under three presidents. The occasioning incident is the king's plan to appoint Daniel over the whole kingdom (v. 3).[16]

16. One can also consider assigning the actions in the remainder of Scene 1 (vv. 3 to 9) as

Inspired by jealousy, the other two presidents and the satraps seek to find grounds for complaint against Daniel (v. 4). When they cannot find any negligence or corruption in Daniel, they conspire to trap him with "the law of his God" (vv. 4-5). They go to the king and propose that he "establish an ordinance and enforce an interdict, that whoever prays to anyone, divine or human, for thirty days, except to you, O king, shall be thrown into a den of lions" (v. 7). The unsuspecting king signs the document into law (v. 9), and the trap for Daniel is set. Will he obey the law of the Medes and Persians or the law of his God?[17]

Although Daniel knows that the document has been signed, he continues "to go to his house . . . to pray to his God and praise him, just as he had done previously" (v. 10). The tension mounts. What will happen to Daniel now that he has chosen to disobey the king's law? The conspirators find him praying to his God (v. 11) and triumphantly rush off to the king to accuse Daniel of paying no attention to the king or his law (vv. 12-13). The king is distressed and tries all day to find ways to rescue Daniel (v. 14). But the conspirators come back again to remind the king that the law of the Medes and Persians cannot be broken (v. 15). Daniel's fate is sealed. The king gives the command and Daniel is thrown into the lions' den (v. 16). A stone is placed on the mouth of the den and sealed by the king and his lords (v. 17). The king spends a sleepless night in his palace (v. 18). What is happening to Daniel? Have the lions ripped him apart and eaten him? Have the conspirators triumphed?

Very early the next morning the king rushes to the lions' den. He cries out anxiously, "O Daniel, servant of the living God, has your God whom you faithfully serve been able to deliver you from the lions?" (v. 20). The king listens intently for any response from the lions' den. Suddenly he hears Daniel's voice: "O king, live forever! My God sent his angel and shut the lions' mouths so that they would not hurt me" (vv. 21-22). Daniel is alive! The king is "exceedingly glad" and orders that Daniel be taken up out of the den (v. 23). Then he orders that Daniel's accusers be thrown into the den. Before they even reach the bottom,

---

"preliminary incidents" and label verse 10 (Daniel defying the decree and praying to his God) as the occasioning incident. Boogaart, "Daniel 6: A Tale of Two Empires," *RR* 39/2 (1986) 109, defends this analysis on the ground that "the suspense begins to rise in dramatic literature when a challenge, threat, or danger to the aspirations of the protagonist is first glimpsed." One can also argue, however, that the king's plan to appoint Daniel over the whole kingdom and the reaction of the other two presidents "to find ground for complaint against Daniel" (vv. 3-4) is our *first* glimpse of the danger facing Daniel.

17. According to Longman, *Daniel*, 166, "The basic tension in Daniel 6 is the conflict between God's law and the law of the Medes and Persians. Daniel must choose between the two laws." Cf. Towner, *Daniel*, 78-79. Although this is true for the first part of the story, the overall conflict is between Daniel and the conspirators: Will the conspirators be successful in eliminating Daniel? Cf. Hill, "Daniel," 118, "The king's intention stirs up professional (or ethnic?) jealousy among Daniel's colleagues, and this becomes the point of conflict in the story."

the lions overpower them and break all their bones in pieces (v. 24). The conflict is resolved.

The outcome is that Darius issues a decree that all people fear the God of Daniel, "for he is the living God" (v. 26). In conclusion the narrator informs us that "Daniel prospered during the reign of Darius" (v. 28).

We can sketch the plot line as a single plot:[18]

Climax

20	**"Did God save?"**	22	**"My God sent his angel"**	
19	king hurries to den			
18	king sleepless	23a	king exceedingly glad	
17	den sealed with stone			
16	**Daniel into lions' den**	23b	"Take Daniel out!"	
15	conspirators force king			
14	king tries to save Daniel	23c	no kind of harm	
12-13	accuse him to king			
11	conspirators see him	23d	**"he trusted in his God"**	
10	**Daniel prays to God**			
8-9	**law of Medes and Persians**	24a	conspirators into the lions' den	
6-7	prayer only to the king			
5	**law of his God**	24b	all bones broken	
4	conspirators plot against Daniel			

Setting	*Occasioning incident*	*Rising tension*		*Resolution*	*Outcome*	*Conclusion*
Dan 6:1-2	6:3				6:25-27	6:28
Daniel one	King plans				Decree:	Daniel
of three	to promote				**"Fear the**	prospers
presidents	Daniel				**God of**	
					Daniel!"	

Character Description

The narrator vividly describes three characters: Daniel, the conspirators, and King Darius.[19] He describes Daniel, the protagonist, as having "an excellent spirit" (v. 3; cf. "endowed with a spirit of the holy gods," 4:8, 18; 5:11), being "faithful" and without "negligence or corruption" (v. 4), and being so faithful to God's law that he continues to pray to his God when he knows that this act transgresses the law of the Medes and the Persians (v. 10). The king twice de-

---

18. Because of the two conflicts (see n. 17 above), one can also sketch the plot line as a complex plot which resolves two questions: (1) Will Daniel obey God's law or the law of the Medes and Persians? (vv. 4-10), and (2) Will the conspirators be successful in eliminating Daniel? (vv. 11-24).

19. For the description of God, see "Theocentric Interpretation" below.

scribes Daniel as "faithfully" serving his God (vv. 16, 20). Daniel himself says that he is "blameless" before God and the king (v. 22). Finally, the narrator reports that Daniel was not harmed "because he had trusted in his God" (v. 23) and that he prospered during the reign of Darius (v. 28).

The narrator does not describe Daniel's accusers, the antagonists,[20] except for mentioning their functions, "presidents and satraps" (v. 4), and that they "conspired" (v. 6). However, their words and actions make clear that they are sly, despicable creatures. They try to find "grounds for complaint" against Daniel, but they cannot find any (v. 4). So they look for grounds for complaint "in connection with the law of his God" (v. 5). No problems there either, unless they can get the king to enact a law contrary to the law of God. They politely approach the king, "O King Darius, live forever!" (v. 6). They persuade the king to sign a law that "whoever prays to anyone, divine or human, for thirty days, except to you, O king, shall be thrown into a den of lions" (v. 7). Then they spy on Daniel and find him praying to his God. Immediately they go to the king, skip the polite greeting, and slyly ask him: "Did you not sign an interdict . . . ?" The king acknowledges that he had indeed signed this interdict (v. 12). Now they are ready to spring the trap: "Daniel, one of the exiles from Judah, pays no attention to you, O king, or to the interdict you have signed" (v. 13). When the king does not execute Daniel immediately, they brazenly come back a third time and practically threaten the king by telling him, "Know, O king, that it is a law of the Medes and Persians that no interdict . . . that the king establishes can be changed" (v. 15). They will have Daniel dead before nightfall. They almost get their wish, but when Daniel survives the night with the lions, he is lifted out of the den and these accusers are thrown to the lions and receive their just desert (v. 24).

The narrator describes King Darius as being on an emotional roller coaster: "very much distressed" (v. 14), crying out "anxiously" (v. 20), and being "exceedingly glad" (v. 23). He further develops the king's character by his speeches and actions: naively signing the interdict (v. 9), trying the whole day "to save Daniel" (v. 14), expressing hope that Daniel's God may yet save him (v. 16), being so concerned about Daniel that he spends "the night fasting" and sleepless (v. 18), hurrying to the lions' den at daybreak (v. 19), resolutely commanding "that Daniel be taken up out of the den" (v. 23), commanding that Daniel's accusers be thrown into the den (v. 24), making a decree that all people should fear the God of Daniel (v. 26), and offering a powerful confession concerning "the living God" and his everlasting kingdom (vv. 26-27). King Darius is clearly on the side of Daniel but not in control of his fate.

---

20. Hill, "Daniel," 116, vs. Towner, *Daniel*, 80, who calls the conspirators "the protagonists" and Daniel "the other chief protagonist."

Repetition

Repetition of key words may again disclose the author's emphases. After the conspirators decide to find a ground for complaint against Daniel in connection with "the law of his God" (v. 5), the word "law" is repeated three more times as "the law of the Medes and Persians, which cannot be revoked" (vv. 8, 12, 15). This contrast sets the early tension in this narrative: Which law is supreme? When the law of God and the law of the Medes and Persians conflict, which law must be obeyed? Another key word is "save/deliver," which is repeated four times (vv. 14, 16, 20, 27). This repetition sets the tension later in the narrative: Will God save Daniel from the hungry lions?

Other words are repeated many times to form wordplays. For example, the word "find" *(šěkāḥ)* is used seven times (vv. 4 [2x], 5 [2x], 11, 22, and 23) and a form of the word *bě'ā'*, "seek, ask, pray, petition," four times (vv. 4, 7, 11, 13). Verses 4-5 set the tone: "So the presidents and the satraps tried [*sought*] to *find* grounds for complaint against Daniel in connection with the kingdom. But they could *find* no grounds for complaint or any corruption, because he was faithful, and no negligence or corruption could be *found* in him. The men said, 'We shall not *find* any ground for complaint against this Daniel unless we *find* it in connection with the law of his God.'" Then "the conspirators came and *found* Daniel praying [*seeking* his God]" (v. 11). Arnold observes, "Daniel's enemies are *seeking* to *find* a fault in him (v. 4), but instead they *find* him *seeking* God (v. 11). The recurrences here throw into bold contrast the differences between Daniel's character and conduct and that of his enemies."[21] In addition, Daniel tells King Darius that the lions did not hurt him "because I was *found* blameless before" God (v. 22). "So while the enemies of Daniel tried to find fault, God found innocence in Daniel. The narrator goes on to state that when Daniel was lifted out of the den, no harm was *found (hištěkah)* in him, because he had trusted in his God (v. 23)."[22]

Repetition sometimes leads to the discovery of more complex rhetorical structures. For this narrative Goldingay suggests the following chiastic structure:[23]

---

21. Arnold, "Wordplay and Narrative Techniques in Daniel 5 and 6," *JBL* 112/3 (1993) 484.

22. Ibid., 485. In Daniel's speech we find more wordplays: "Just as Darius closed . . . the mouth . . . of the den, so God closed the mouth . . . of the lions. And Daniel first addressed the king with the request that he live forever . . . , echoing the king's claim that Daniel's God is the Living God. . . . Daniel semantically links his survival in the lions' den ('they did not harm me . . .') to his attitude toward the king ('I have done no harm')." Polaski, "Mene, Mene, Tekel, Parsin: Writing and Resistance in Daniel 5 and 6," *JBL* 123/4 (2004) 664. For other wordplays, see Goldingay, *Daniel,* 125.

23. Goldingay, *Daniel,* 124.

A Introduction: Daniel's success (1-3)
  B Darius signs an injunction but Daniel takes his stand (4-10)
    C Daniel's colleagues plan his death (11-15)
      D Darius hopes for Daniel's deliverance (16-18)
      D′ Darius witnesses Daniel's deliverance (19-23)
    C′ Daniel's colleagues meet with their death (24)
  B′ Darius signs a decree and takes his stand (25-27)
A′ Conclusion: Daniel's success (28)

Though not entirely convincing,[24] this chiasm reinforces the climax of the plot line (see above) centering on Daniel's deliverance and thus is helpful for reinforcing the theme of this narrative.

Theocentric Interpretation

Will God save Daniel from the lions? That is the central question in this narrative.[25] Even though Daniel knew that disobedience to the king's law would result in the death penalty, he still chose to obey "the law of his God" (v. 5): "He continued to go to his house . . . to pray to his God and praise him" (v. 10). When the king had no choice but to throw Daniel to the lions, the king uttered the prayer, "May your God, whom you faithfully serve, deliver you!" (v. 16).[26] At daybreak, the king rushes to the lions' den and asks anxiously, "O Daniel, servant of the *living* God, has your God whom you faithfully serve been able to deliver you from the lions?" Daniel responds, "O king, live forever! My God sent his angel and shut the lions' mouths so that they would not hurt me, because I was found blameless before him; and also before you, O king, I have done no wrong" (vv. 21-22). They lift Daniel up out of the den, and no kind of harm is found on him, "because he had trusted in his God" (v. 23). The king makes a decree, that in all his dominion "people should tremble and fear before the God of

---

24. Hill, "Daniel," 116, rightly considers this "outline somewhat artificial in that the report of Darius's publishing of his decree (v. 9) more naturally concludes the unit containing the conspiracy against Daniel" (see Scene 1 above). Hill adds, "Finally, Darius's edict and doxology (B/B′) are loosely related at best."

25. "The traditional plot is given a specifically religious twist by making Daniel's deliverance depend on divine intervention rather than on human initiative. This point is underlined by the inability of the king to save Daniel and his prayer that God do so (v. 16)." Collins, *Daniel* (1984), 71.

26. "It is this prayer above all that makes this chapter different from all that has gone before, because an 'outsider,' a king of the nations, is exercising faith, however dimly." Baldwin, *Daniel*, 130.

Daniel," which is followed by his powerful confession, "For he is the *living* God, *enduring forever*. His kingdom shall never be destroyed, and his dominion has no end. He delivers and rescues, he works signs and wonders in heaven and on earth; for he has saved Daniel from the power of the lions" (vv. 26-27). In conclusion the narrator states that God "prospered" Daniel (divine passive) "during the reign of Darius" (v. 28).

Textual Theme and Goal

At this point we should be ready to formulate the textual theme and goal. However, since this story is so similar to its parallel story of God saving Daniel's friends from the fiery furnace (see "Context" above), we may end up with a theme similar to that of Daniel 3: "Our sovereign God is able to deliver his oppressed children who refuse to serve other gods — even from a fiery furnace." It's all the more important, therefore, to seek to discern the textually specific theme of this particular narrative. We can do this by inquiring how this narrative about God saving Daniel from the lions is different from that of God saving his friends from the fire. Three items in particular stand out: first, whereas Nebuchadnezzar in a furious rage had Daniel's friends thrown into the furnace, Darius befriends Daniel, spends the whole day trying to save him, and then only reluctantly has him thrown into the lions' den. Second, and more important, while Nebuchadnezzar had questioned God's *ability* to save ("Who is the god that will deliver you out of my hands?" 3:15), Darius prays that God will save Daniel: "May your God, whom you faithfully serve, deliver you" (6:16). Third, and most important, although Daniel's friends obeyed God by not worshiping Nebuchadnezzar's statue, they were not sure that God would *be able* to save them from the fire ("*If* our God is able to deliver us from the furnace of blazing fire . . . ," 3:17). Daniel does not question God's ability to save as his friends had done, and neither does Darius, who calls God "the living God" (6:20, 26). Moreover, the narrator sums up that no harm was found on Daniel "because he had *trusted in his God*" (6:23).[27] The point in this narrative seems to be that God saved his faithful servant because "he had trusted" that his God was able to save him. So we could formulate the author's theme as, "The living God saves his faithful servant from the lions because he trusted that God was able to save him." But this is a one-sentence summary of the story rather than the message Israel heard in exile. Imagining ourselves to be Israel, we hear the message, *Our living God can save even from certain death his faithful servants who trust his ability to save them.*

As to the author's goal, he has sketched Daniel as a true Israelite who obeys

---

27. For other differences between Daniel 3 and 6, see Goldingay, *Daniel*, 126-27.

God's law even when he knows it will result in the death penalty and who entrusts his life completely to God. The Israelites in exile can identify with Daniel. As Daniel finds himself in the "pit," so they are in the "pit" of exile.[28] Like Daniel, therefore, they should continue to be faithful to God and trust that God is able to deliver them.[29] Hence the author's has a dual goal: *to encourage Israel in exile to remain faithful to God and to trust that their God is able to deliver them from their "pit" of exile.*[30]

Ways to Preach Christ

As with Daniel 3, with this narrative, too, there is the temptation simply to identify God's angel (6:22) with the angel of the Lord, the preincarnate Word.[31] This move to Christ, however, is not only speculative, but it stops with the angel of the Lord in the Old Testament and fails to move forward to the climax of God's revelation in the Word incarnate in the New Testament. Since there is no promise of the coming Messiah in this passage and there is no major contrast with the message of the New Testament,[32] we shall explore the remaining five ways to Jesus Christ in the New Testament. In order to avoid overlap, however, we shall combine the ways of redemptive-historical progression and longitudinal themes.

---

28. On the use of the "pit" literally for the lions' pit and figuratively for the exile, see Mason, "The Treatment of Earlier Biblical Themes in the Book of Daniel," *PRSt* 15/4 (1988) 85-86: "Just as God delivered the Psalmist from the 'Pit' (Pss 40:3/2; 57:5, 7/4, 6), so God will deliver his people in Exile. . . . Such language of the 'Pit' could apparently be used in a general figurative sense of God's judgement (see . . . Ezek 26:20). It seems to have furnished also a salvation theme of God's deliverance, embodied in specific instances such as those of Joseph being delivered from the 'Pit' (Gen 37:24ff.) and Jeremiah (Jer 38:6ff.)."

29. "If it was obedience to God's law that landed him [Daniel] in the pit . . . , it was trust in God that delivered him. . . . The lesson was not subtle: Judeans living in a foreign court had better trust God, even if keeping the law got them into trouble." Redditt, *Daniel,* 111.

30. "Daniel's emerging from the lions' den unharmed was a source of hope for surviving the exile itself." Smith-Christopher, "Book of Daniel," 90. Cf. Hill, "Daniel," 127: King Darius's confession "acknowledging the living, eternal, saving, and active power of Daniel's God [was] an affirmation desperately needed by the Hebrews enduring the dark days of Babylonian exile."

31. E.g., Miller, *Daniel,* 187, The angel "may have been a member of the angelic host, but it is more likely that this heavenly being was the divine angelic messenger, the angel of the Lord."

32. Some see a contrast between Darius's command that Daniel's accusers as well as their children and their wives be thrown into the lions' den (6:24) and Jesus' command, "Love your enemies" (Matt 5:44). But Darius's command is not the message of this passage. Moreover, punishing the children and the wives for the deeds of the fathers/husbands is also contrary God's Old Testament law: "Parents shall not be put to death for their children, nor shall children be put to death for their parents; only for their own crimes may persons be put to death" (Deut 24:16). Hence there is no contrast between the message of this narrative and that of the New Testament.

Redemptive-Historical Progression / Longitudinal Themes

We can trace throughout redemptive history the theme that "God can save even from certain death his faithful servants who trust his ability to save them." Early in redemptive history, when God saw that "the wickedness of humankind was great in the earth" (Gen 6:5), he sent a flood to blot out human beings but saved the family of the "blameless" Noah (Gen 6:9; cf. Dan 6:21) who trusted in God's ability to save him and his family (Gen 6:22). Later, when Jacob's sons threw their brother Joseph into a "pit" (Gen 37:24) and then sold him into the "pit" of slavery, the Lord was present with him (Gen 39:2, 20, 23), saved him, and made him "prosper" (Gen 39:3, 23; 41:40; cf. Dan 6:16, 28). Still later, when Israel was in the "pit" of slavery in Egypt, Pharaoh commanded all Israelites to drown their baby boys in the river Nile. But Moses' parents trusted God's ability to save their baby, and placed him in a basket in the river (Exod 2:2-4); then God saved Moses (Exod 2:5-10) and later used him to deliver Israel from Egypt with "awesome signs and wonders" (Deut 6:22). The same God later used "signs and wonders" to deliver Daniel from the lions' "pit" (Dan 6:27). After that, through King Cyrus, God delivered Israel from the "pit" of exile (2 Chron 36:22-23).

In the fullness of time, God's saving power took on deeper dimensions. God sent his Son Jesus to "save his people from their *sins*" (Matt 1:21) and to give them "*eternal* life" (John 3:16). Jesus said, "I am the resurrection and the life. Those who *believe in* [trust] me, even though they die, will live" (John 11:25). When Jesus comes again, he will deliver us from the brokenness we still experience in this life: "Death will be no more; mourning and crying and pain will be no more"; and God himself will dwell with his people (Rev. 21:3-4). Consequently, Paul looks forward to the day when death will be "swallowed up in victory. . . . Thanks be to God, who gives us the victory through our Lord Jesus Christ" (1 Cor 15:54-57).

Typology

The strongest bridge to Jesus Christ in the New Testament may be typology, for there are many analogies and escalations between Daniel and Jesus.[33] We shall first note the major analogies and then show the escalations.

As the presidents and satraps "conspired" against Daniel (6:6), so "the chief

---

33. I tracked down most of these analogies by working my way through Daniel 6 in *The Treasury of Scripture Knowledge,* available on *PC Study Bible,* Version 5, and on *Logos 2.1 Bible Software.* Many of these analogies are also noted in commentaries such as Towner, *Daniel,* 81, 84-85, and Goldingay, *Daniel,* 136.

priests and the elders of the people gathered in the palace of the high priest . . . and they conspired to arrest Jesus by stealth and kill him" (Matt 26:3-4). The conspirators could find no corruption in Daniel (6:4); "the chief priests and the whole council were looking for testimony against Jesus to put him to death; but they found none" (Mark 14:55; cf. John 19:4). As Daniel was convicted by trickery (6:7), so was Jesus: "The high priest tore his clothes and said, 'He has blasphemed! Why do we still need witnesses?'" (Matt 26:65). Daniel was found guilty of transgressing the law of the Medes and Persians; Jesus was found guilty of transgressing the law of the Jews: "We have a law, and according to that law he ought to die because he has claimed to be the Son of God" (John 19:7). Darius unsuccessfully tried to save Daniel (6:14); Pilate unsuccessfully tried to save Jesus (Matt 27:24). Daniel "trusted in his God" (6:23); Jesus trusted his Father (Matt 26:39, 42; cf. 27:43; 1 Pet 2:23). Daniel descended into "the pit" (6:16), his "grave" (cf., e.g., Pss 30:3; 143:7; Ezek 32:23); Jesus' body was laid in a tomb (Matt 27:60). Daniel's "grave" was covered with a stone (6:17); Jesus' tomb was covered with a great stone (Matt 27:60). The king sealed the stone on Daniel's "grave"; Jesus' tomb was made "secure by sealing the stone" (Matt 27:66). The king found Daniel alive early the next morning and had him lifted out of his "grave" (6:19, 23); "very early on the first day of the week, when the sun had risen, they [the three women] went to the tomb" where an angel told them, Jesus "has been raised" (Mark 16:2, 6). And Daniel prospered after God saved him from certain death (6:28); Jesus prospered after God saved him from death: after his resurrection, Jesus said, "All authority in heaven and on earth has been given to me" (Matt 28:18).

But Jesus was far greater than Daniel. Although Daniel claimed to be "blameless" before God (6:22), he was still a sinner.[34] Jesus, by contrast, was the sinless Son of God (Heb 4:15; 1 John 3:5). Daniel faced the possibility of death while Jesus actually died (John 19:34-35). Daniel rose from his "grave" only to die at a later date; Jesus rose from his grave and lives forever. God "prospered" Daniel during the reign of Darius (6:28), but God "highly exalted . . . [Christ Jesus] and gave him the name that is above every name, so that at the name of Jesus every knee should bend, . . . and every tongue should confess that Jesus Christ is Lord, to the glory of God the Father" (Phil 2:9-11; cf. the "*all* authority" in Matt 28:18 above).

Analogy

We can use the way of analogy as follows: As Daniel 6 teaches that God is able to save his faithful servants even from certain death, so Hebrews 7:25 declares con-

---

34. "The writer is not claiming that Daniel was sinless, but only that he was law-abiding, and that his first allegiance was to his God." Baldwin, *Daniel,* 128.

cerning Jesus that "he is able for all time to save those who approach God through him, since he always lives to make intercession for them."[35]

We can also draw analogies from the author's dual goal to Jesus in the New Testament: As the author sought to encourage Israel in exile to remain faithful to God's law, so Jesus encouraged his followers to remain faithful to God's law (e.g., the Sermon on the Mount; Matt 5–7). Jesus said, "Whoever does them [God's commandments] and teaches them will be called great in the kingdom of heaven" (Matt 5:19; cf. 22:37-40). And as the author sought to encourage Israel to trust that their living God was able to deliver them from the pit of exile, so Jesus encourages us to trust that Jesus, the living One, will be able to deliver us. Jesus said, "Believe in God, believe also in me. In my Father's house there are many dwelling places. . . . I will come again and will take you to myself, so that where I am, there you may be also" (John 14:1-3).[36]

New Testament References

The appendix to the Greek New Testament lists six New Testament references or allusions to Daniel 6.

For Daniel 6:17,[37] the king sealing the stone, it lists Matthew 27:66, the chief priests sealing the stone on Jesus' tomb.

For both Daniel 6:20 and 27, about deliverance "from the lions," it refers to 2 Timothy 4:17, Paul's speech, "But the Lord stood by me and gave me strength. . . . So I was rescued from the lion's mouth."

For Daniel 6:22, Daniel's speech about God sending his angel, it lists Acts 12:11, Peter saying, "Now I am sure that the Lord has sent his angel and rescued me from the hands of Herod."

For Daniel 6:25, "May you have abundant prosperity," it refers to 1 Peter 1:2, "May grace and peace be yours in abundance."

Finally, for Daniel 6:26, "He is the living God, enduring forever," it lists 1 Peter 1:23, "the living and enduring word of God," and Revelation 4:9, "the one who is seated on the throne, who lives forever and ever."

Except for the first one, Matthew 27:66, which we used to support "typology" above, none of these references makes a direct connection with

35. "The salvation of good and trusting Daniel from the lions' den is an anticipation of the rescue from destruction by God's own transcendent power of God's people." Towner, *Daniel*, 86.

36. Also, when the Philippian jailor asked, "What must I do to be saved?" Paul answered, "Believe on the Lord Jesus, and you will be saved, you and your household" (Acts 16:30-31). Cf. 1 Timothy 4:10, "We have our hope set on the living God, who is the Savior of all people, especially of those who believe."

37. I am using the verse references of the English Bibles.

Christ. This is also the case with Hebrews 11:33 about those "who through faith
. . . shut the mouths of lions," a reference missing in the appendix.

Sermon Theme, Goal, and Need

We formulated the author's theme as, "Our living God can save even from certain death his faithful servants who trust his ability to save them." Since the
New Testament also teaches this, the textual theme can function as the theme of
the sermon: *Our living God can save even from certain death his faithful servants
who trust his ability to save them.* We concluded that the author had a dual goal
in mind: "to encourage Israel in exile to remain faithful to God and to trust that
their God is able to deliver them from their 'pit' of exile." With slight changes
these two goals can also become the goals for the sermon: *to encourage God's
people today to remain faithful to God and to trust that their God is able to deliver
them from their exile in this fallen world.* These two goals point to a dual need:
God's people today are tempted to ignore God's law and fail to trust God for
their deliverance from this fallen world.

Sermon Exposition

One can introduce the sermon with an illustration of some well-known persons
who ignore God's law and do not trust God for their salvation. Instead they live
for themselves and feel quite at home in this fallen world. They do not need
God's law nor God. Then raise the question, Is it possible that this attitude is also
creeping into the church? Are we sometimes tempted to live just for ourselves?
That would be to ignore God's law that we ought to live for God and our neighbor. Are we sometimes quite satisfied with the world as it is and do not long for
Christ's Second Coming? That would be to deny that we live in a *broken* world. It
also implies a failure to *trust* that God will deliver us from this fallen world.

Daniel 6 was written first of all for Israel when it was in exile in Babylon. At
that time Israel was also tempted to ignore God's law. When in Babylon, do as
the Babylonians do! Try to fit in. Why not disregard the law of God and obey
the law of the Medes and Persians? This would avoid discrimination and offer a
safer future. Also, after almost seventy years in exile, they were getting used to
living in Babylon. They had pretty well given up hope that God would deliver
them from their exile and bring them back to the Promised Land. By this time
the Babylonian armies had even destroyed God's city, Jerusalem, as well as
God's holy temple. It looked like the gods of Babylon had defeated Israel's God.
The Israelites were about ready to give up on their God.

Then they receive another message from Daniel. The mighty kingdom of Babylon, which captured Israel, is no more. A new age has dawned. As God predicted in Nebuchadnezzar's dream, the kingdom of gold (Dan 2:37-38) went bankrupt and has been replaced by the kingdom of silver (Dan 2:39). Daniel 6 highlights the first king of the Medo-Persian empire, King Darius, also known as Cyrus.[38]

Darius begins his reign by reorganizing the government of his huge empire. Chapter 6:1 and 2, "It pleased Darius to set over the kingdom one hundred twenty satraps [literally "protectors of the kingdom"], stationed throughout the whole kingdom, and over them three presidents, including Daniel; to these the satraps gave account, so that the king might suffer no loss." Satraps were government officials "responsible for security and for the collecting of tribute."[39] These satraps were to report to the three presidents "so that the king might suffer no loss." Being accountable to the three presidents prevented them from withholding collected taxes from the king.

Verse 3, "Soon Daniel distinguished himself above all the other presidents and satraps because an excellent spirit was in him, and the king planned to appoint him over the whole kingdom." This plan does not sit well with the other presidents and satraps. Promotion for Daniel means demotion for the other two presidents. Moreover, Daniel is a foreigner, an exile from Judah.[40] They do not want a foreigner to rule over them. Driven by jealousy, the two presidents and some[41] of the satraps begin to look for ways to get rid of Daniel.

Verses 4 and 5, "So the presidents and the satraps tried to find grounds for complaint against Daniel in connection with the kingdom. But they could find no grounds for complaint or any corruption, because he was faithful, and no negligence or corruption could be found in him. The men said, 'We shall not find any ground for complaint against this Daniel unless we find it in connec-

---

38. See p. 197, n. 73 below.

39. Goldingay, *Daniel*, 127.

40. "The exiled Jews did not erase the shame of their deportation in the days of Nebuchadnezzar. Though they were the objects of Cyrus's charity . . . — they were nevertheless considered an inferior race, especially by their conquerors." Archer, "Daniel," 78.

41. It is not likely that all 120 satraps were involved in the plot. Since they were spread throughout the empire, it would have been difficult to get all of them together for the plot. Also, so many accusers and their wives and children would not have fit into the lions' den (6:24). Keil, *Book of Daniel*, 218, suggests, "only a small number of the special enemies of Daniel." Cf. Young, *Prophecy of Daniel*, 138. Hill, "Daniel," 126, observes, "Nowhere does the text explicitly cite 'all' these officials as coconspirators." As noted above under "Literary Features," the claim of "all the presidents," etc. in verse 7 at best is hyperbole, at worst an outright lie. Interestingly, "the Old Greek actually says only that the other two presidents plotted to eliminate Daniel. On the surface that makes more sense than a conspiracy involving 127 [120?] additional people, whose status would not be affected anyway." Redditt, *Daniel*, 105.

tion with the law of his God.'" They fail to find anything against Daniel in his work as president. They find him faithful in carrying out his duties; they can find no negligence or corruption in him. They cannot accuse Daniel of any wrongdoing in his work for the Medo-Persian kingdom.[42]

But they are not ready to give up. They may be able to find something "in connection with the law of his God."[43] They know that this exile from Judah observes the law of the God of Israel. If they can only find a way to force Daniel to choose between the law of his God and the law of the land. . . .

They have it! They will propose to the king that he sign a law that will bring Daniel into conflict with the law of his God. Verses 6 and 7, "So the presidents and satraps conspired and came to the king and said to him, 'O King Darius, live forever! All the presidents of the kingdom, the prefects and the satraps, the counselors and the governors are agreed that the king should establish an ordinance and enforce an interdict, that whoever prays to anyone, divine or human,[44] for thirty days, except to you, O king, shall be thrown into a den of lions.'"

They come to the king and begin with a lie. They pretend to speak for "all the presidents" — but certainly Daniel is not one of them. They also pretend to speak for "the prefects and the satraps, the counselors and the governors" — but it is highly unlikely that they had been in touch with all these officials throughout the empire. They exaggerate to impress the king. If all these officials are for this law, it must be a good one.

The conspirators conclude their speech by urging the king to sign their proposal into law. Verse 8, "Now, O king, establish the interdict and sign the document, so that it cannot be changed, according to the law of the Medes and the Persians, which cannot be revoked." The signature of the king will guaran-

---

42. "Specifically we are told that Daniel is honest, trustworthy, and reliable (v. 4). In short, his impeccable record as a civil servant places him beyond indictment." Hill, "Daniel," 118.

43. "The Persian word *dāt* used here represents the Hebrew word *tôrâ* (see Ezra 7:10, 12, 14). . . . These words virtually mean religion thought of as the observance of a rule of life imposed by God." Porteous, *Daniel*, 89. Cf. Russell, *Daniel*, 100, "Having failed to trap him in respect to his civic responsibilities which were impeccable in their execution, they tried to catch him out in respect of private religious observances which, if performed without proper state authority, were indictable offences and punishable by the law of the land."

44. Their proposal does not make Darius a god for thirty days. The proposed law states, "whoever prays to anyone, divine or *human,* for thirty days, except to you, O king, shall be thrown into a den of lions" (v. 7). The humans to whom people would pray were the priests "through whom petitions were mediated to the gods. Thus Darius was to be the only priestly mediator. In his role as mediator, prayers to the gods were to be offered through him rather than through the priests." Miller, *Daniel*, 180. For more arguments that the decree does not deify the king but designates "him as the only legitimate representative of deity for the stated time," see Walton, "The Decree of Darius the Mede in Daniel 6," *JETS* 31/3 (1988) 280-86.

tee that this law "cannot be changed." Not even the king himself can revoke this law once it is signed.[45]

The king considers their proposal. It seems like a good law. It will unify the empire under the new king. It will also be a good test of the people's loyalty to the new king. And, of course, it's flattering to have everyone pray to you. It's a win-win situation. He fails to see the trap for his friend Daniel.

Verse 9, "Therefore King Darius signed the document and interdict." It's official now. Anyone caught praying to a god or priest other than King Darius will be thrown into the lions' den for an excruciating death.

Daniel soon hears about this new law and its penalty of death. He knows about the lions' den. The original speaks of "the lions' *pit*." It was an underground cistern which had an opening at the top that could be closed off with a large stone. Such cisterns could be used "for water storage or as a prison."[46] In this case the king kept lions in this underground cave. Thus he could use it for capital punishment. It was a cruel but effective deterrent to anyone who even thought about disobeying a law of the Medes and Persians.

Now Daniel had made it a habit to pray to God three times a day in the upper room of his house. The upper room was built on a corner of the flat roof of his house. "It had latticed windows to allow free circulation of the air."[47] The new law need not be a hardship for Daniel. It's only for thirty days. Moreover, he can close his windows when he kneels down to pray. Better yet, he can wait till nightfall and then pray in the privacy of his bedroom.

But Daniel sees it differently. He sees this law as a direct attack on the law of his God. "Daniel has to choose between loyalty to his Lord and obedience to a sinful government commanding him to perform idolatry."[48] As a teenager he had "resolved that he would not defile himself with the royal rations of food" (Dan 1:8) because they were not kosher according to the law of God. Now, in his old age, he is not about to depart from God's law when it comes to praying to God, even if it means being thrown to the lions. God's people "must be prepared to live dangerously."[49] Jesus himself said, "Those who want to save their life will lose it, and those who lose their life for my sake will find it" (Matt 16:25).

Verse 10, "Although Daniel knew that the document had been signed [he knew the risks], he continued to go to his house, which had windows in its up-

---

45. The book of Esther (1:19; 8:8) also states that a law of the Medes and Persians cannot be revoked. See Montgomery, *Book of Daniel*, 270, for extrabiblical evidence that "it was not possible to undo what was done by royal authority."

46. Goldingay, *Daniel*, 128.

47. Collins, *Daniel*, 268.

48. Archer, "Daniel," 80.

49. Hammer, *Daniel*, 68.

per room open toward Jerusalem, and to get down on his knees three times a day to pray to his God and praise him, just as he had done previously." Daniel's kneeling down is a sign of reverence for and submission to God.[50] He faces Jerusalem because God promised Solomon, "I have consecrated this house that you have built, and put my name there forever; my eyes and my heart will be there for all time" (1 Kings 9:3).[51] God's temple in Jerusalem was God's earthly throne. Even though Nebuchadnezzar had destroyed the temple, Daniel still faces Jerusalem. It is a sign of Daniel's hope while in exile that Jerusalem and the temple will be rebuilt.[52] In spite of the new law, Daniel continues to pray to his God three times a day: "evening and morning and at noon" (Ps 55:17).

Verse 11, "The conspirators came and found Daniel praying and seeking mercy before his God." They now have the evidence they need.[53] They are overjoyed. Their trap worked. Soon they will be rid of Daniel. They rush off to the palace.

But they do not accuse Daniel immediately. Cunningly they first ask the king whether he had signed a new law. Verses 12 and 13, "Then they approached the king and said concerning the interdict, 'O king! Did you not sign an interdict, that anyone who prays to anyone, divine or human, within thirty days except to you, O king, shall be thrown into a den of lions?' The king answered, 'The thing stands fast, according to the law of the Medes and Persians, which cannot be revoked.'" They have the king trapped by his own words. The law cannot be revoked!

Now they are ready to charge Daniel. Verse 13, "Then they responded to the king, 'Daniel, one of the exiles from Judah, pays no attention to you, O king, or to the interdict you have signed, but he is saying his prayers three times a day.'" When they say, "Daniel, one of the *exiles from Judah*," you can hear the hatred drip from their lips. "One of the exiles from Judah" — that's all Daniel is to them. Not a president but a dirty, foreign slave. These foreigners cannot really be trusted.[54] Then they add that this exile from Judah pays no attention to the king. He is not a friend of the king; he ignores the king. After picturing Daniel

---

50. "Kneeling is the posture in which a person is the most 'defenseless,' and in prayer it is a symbol of dependence, humility, and contrition before God." Hill, "Daniel," 122.

51. On praying "toward this house," see 1 Kings 8:27-53 and 2 Chronicles 6:36-39.

52. "Jerusalem is the summation of all the redemption that is to come. Jerusalem is the *future*." Towner, *Daniel*, 83.

53. Duguid, *Daniel*, 97, raises the question why God did not close the eyes of the conspirators as he later closed the mouths of the lions. "Certainly, he [God] could have done that, but his purpose was not to save Daniel *from* trials but to save Daniel *through* trials."

54. Goldingay, *Daniel*, 132, adds that Daniel's accusers may imply "that as an exile, his maintaining his alien religious practices is a political act, an act of rebellion." Cf. Keil, *Book of Daniel*, 214.

in as bad a light as possible, they are ready to bring the charge: this exile "pays no attention . . . to the interdict you have signed." Instead of praying only to King Darius, "he is saying his prayers [to God] three times a day." Three times a day! His prayers are not a simple lapse. He repeatedly violates the king's law. His "disobedience is not accidental, but willful rebellion."[55]

Verse 14, "When the king heard the charge, he was very much distressed." Suddenly he sees through the plot. How naive he has been! These presidents never had the interest of the king or his empire at heart. They only wanted to get rid of Daniel because the king planned to "appoint him over the whole kingdom." They had first trapped the king into signing an irrevocable law and now they had trapped Daniel. The king is "very much distressed."

We read in verse 14 that he "was determined to *save* Daniel, and until the sun went down he made every effort[56] to *rescue* him." He consults with experts to see if there is a way around the law. Can they find a loophole somewhere that will save Daniel? They have to work fast because, "according to Oriental custom," the sentence has to be carried out "on the evening of the day in which the accusation" is made.[57] The king makes every effort to rescue Daniel but fails to find a way. His hands are tied.

As the sun is about to set, the conspirators brazenly put pressure on the king. Verse 15, "Then the conspirators came to the king and said to him, 'Know, O king, that it is a law of the Medes and Persians that no interdict or ordinance that the king establishes can be changed.'" They rub it in. No law "that the king establishes can be changed." Ironically, the king who is supposed to be in control is trapped in his own law. He is powerless, and he knows it.

Reluctantly the king gives orders that the sentence be carried out. Verse 16, "Then the king gave the command, and Daniel was brought and thrown into the den of lions. The king said to Daniel, 'May your God, whom you faithfully serve, deliver you!'" The king cannot save Daniel. He hopes Daniel's God can.

Verses 17 and 18, "A stone was brought and laid on the mouth of the den, and the king sealed it with his own signet and with the signet of his lords, so that nothing might be changed concerning Daniel [no one can now interfere with Daniel's punishment, either to rescue or kill him].[58] Then the king went to his palace and spent the night fasting; no food[59] was brought to him, and sleep

---

55. Steinmann, *Daniel*, 318.

56. "'Striving' is the picture of the animal caught in the toils." Montgomery, *Book of Daniel*, 275.

57. Keil, *Book of Daniel*, 215.

58. "In terms of its rhetorical function . . . this notice of the sealing of the pit preempts alternative explanations for Daniel's liberation as anything but an act of God, a possibility that Darius himself has already broached." Seow, *Daniel*, 93.

59. Commentators are not agreed on the meaning of the Aramaic word. Some take it as

fled from him." The king spends a restless night in the palace, tossing and turning. He can think only of Daniel in the lions' den. Has he already been ripped limb from limb and eaten by the lions? Or is he still alive? Can his God possibly save him from the lions? Anxiously the king waits for sunrise. He sees a small glimmer of hope: there is an ancient Babylonian custom that a victim of torture will be pardoned if he has "not died by the following day."[60]

Verses 19 and 20, "Then, at break of day, the king got up and hurried to the den of lions. When he came near the den where Daniel was, he cried out anxiously to Daniel, 'O Daniel, servant of the living God, has your God whom you faithfully serve been able to deliver you from the lions?'" Darius calls Daniel by his Hebrew name, "God is my judge." Will God judge favorably and save him? Darius also calls Daniel, "servant of the *living God*."[61] Dead gods made of gold and silver cannot save. But might the *living* God be able to save Daniel from the lions? Anxiously the king waits for a response. He is hoping against hope. The seconds seem like hours to him.

Verses 21 and 22, "Daniel then said to the king, 'O king, live forever![62] My God sent his angel and shut the lions' mouths so that they would not hurt me, because I was found blameless before him; and also before you, O king, I have done no wrong.'" As God's angel kept Daniel's friends alive in the fiery furnace, so God sent his angel[63] to protect Daniel from the hungry lions. Daniel says, "They would not hurt me, because I was found blameless[64] before him [God]; and also before you, O king, I have done no wrong."

Daniel had undergone what is now known as "a trial by ordeal." The best-

---

"table" and therefore "food," others as "musical instruments" or "musicians," still others as "concubines" or "dancing girls." See Collins, *Daniel*, 270, who favors Montgomery's neutral suggestion of "diversions."

60. Lacocque, *Book of Daniel*, 118.

61. "The God of the Jews is referred to in various ways in these stories, but the epithet 'the living God' is unique to this chapter (20 [21], 26 [27]). . . . To speak of God as 'the living God' is to imply that he is powerful and active. The epithet is used of God as the one who spoke out of the fire and cloud on the mountain when the law was given (Deut 5:26)." Lucas, *Daniel*, 157. Cf. Goldingay, *Daniel*, 133, and Seow, *Daniel*, 93.

62. This is "the only time in the book that the phrase 'live forever' is spoken by a Jew in reference to the king. Coming immediately after the designation of the deity as 'the living God,' the phrase serves to link and to subsume the life of the king to the will of the God from whom life derives and on whom life depends." Seow, *Daniel*, 93.

63. Cf. Psalm 34:7, "The angel of the LORD encamps around those who fear him, and delivers them." Cf. Psalm 91:9-11 and Hebrews 1:14.

64. "Not that Daniel was sinless, but he was innocent of the charge of which he had been accused, namely, disloyalty to the king." Young, *Prophecy of Daniel*, 138. Cf. Lederach, *Daniel*, 137, "When the laws of the empire conflict with the law of God, the faithful will break the laws of the empire with a clear conscience. Consequently, Daniel sees himself as *blameless* before God and King Darius."

known trial by ordeal in the ancient Near East was "the water ordeal." Individuals suspected of a crime were thrown into a lake or river. If they died, they were guilty. But if they survived, they were innocent and set free.[65] So Daniel was thrown into the lions' den. When he was still alive the next morning, he was judged to be innocent of the charges against him and the ordeal could end.

Verse 23, "Then the king was exceedingly glad and commanded that Daniel be taken out of the den. So Daniel was taken up out of the den, and no kind of harm was found on him, because he had trusted in his God." God had earlier protected Daniel's friends in the fiery furnace so that "the hair of their heads was not singed" (3:27). Here God protects Daniel completely: "No kind of harm was found on him, because he had trusted in his God." By working this miracle for Daniel, God shows himself to be "the living God." God may not always protect his people from trouble (e.g., Dan 7:25; 8:24),[66] but as the *living* God he is always with them and *able* to save them from harm.

Verse 24, "The king gave a command, and those who had accused[67] Daniel were brought and thrown into the den of lions — they, their children, and their wives [as was customary in ancient Persia].[68] Before they reached the bottom of the den, the lions overpowered them and broke all their bones in pieces." Guilty! The lions are so hungry that they overpower the bodies thrown at them even before they hit the bottom. This comment makes clear that Daniel did not escape the lions because they were not hungry. On the contrary, the living God had performed a great miracle for Daniel in saving him from these ferocious, hungry lions.

Next God works another miracle.[69] The pagan king of the mightiest nation on earth makes a powerful confession of faith concerning Israel's God. Verses 25 to 27, "Then King Darius wrote to all peoples and nations of every language

---

65. See Longman, *Daniel*, 163. Cf. Numbers 5:11-31.

66. "These stories in the book of Daniel [3 and 6] are not about what God will inevitably do whenever the faithful are threatened, but about what God can do whenever God so wills." Seow, *Daniel*, 87.

67. See p. 190, n. 41 above.

68. It seems unjust to us that not only the accusers but also their wives and children are thrown into the lions' den. In fact, God's law in Deuteronomy 24:16 forbade this. God had said, "Parents shall not be put to death for their children, nor shall children be put to death for their parents; only for their own crimes may persons be put to death" (cf. Jer 31:29-30; Ezek 18). But Persia did not live by God's law. "The condemning to death of the wives and children along with the men was in accordance with Persian custom." Keil, *Book of Daniel*, 218. Cf. Lacocque, *Book of Daniel*, 118, "It is . . . historically correct that the Persians inflicted upon the wives and children of condemned men the same penalty given them."

69. "Surely it is nothing short of miraculous that the king of the mightiest empire of the day and a follower of a god other than Yahweh should be presented as singing a hymn of faith and praise to the God who saved Daniel from the power of the lions." Towner, *Daniel*, 90.

throughout the whole world: 'May you have abundant prosperity! I make a decree, that in all my royal dominion people should tremble and fear before the God of Daniel:[70]

> For he is the *living God*,
>   enduring forever.
> His kingdom shall never be destroyed,
>   and his dominion has no end.
> He delivers and rescues,
>   he works signs and wonders in heaven and on earth;
> for he has saved Daniel from the power of the lions.'"

Darius again calls Daniel's God "the living God." He adds that this living God endures "forever" and that "his kingdom shall never be destroyed." Moreover, this God demonstrates that he is the living God by his saving acts: "He delivers and rescues, he works signs and wonders[71] in heaven[72] and on earth; for he has saved Daniel from the power of the lions."

The story concludes in verse 28, "So this Daniel prospered during the reign of Darius and[73] the reign of Cyrus the Persian." Daniel prospers after God saved him from certain death in the lions' den.

Christians have long noted the similarities between this story about Daniel and the New Testament story about Jesus Christ. We read in Daniel 6:6 that "the presidents and satraps conspired" against Daniel. In the New Testament we read that "the chief priests and the elders . . . conspired to arrest Jesus by stealth and kill him" (Matt 26:3-4). The conspirators could find no corruption

---

70. "Through his entire empire, Daniel's God is not merely to be tolerated but to be worshiped with reverence and awe." Goldingay, *Daniel*, 135. Cf. Boogaart, "Daniel 6: A Tale of Two Empires," *RR* 39/2 (1986) 111, "At the beginning of the story, Darius issues a decree that establishes his sovereignty throughout his empire. At the end of the story, he issues a decree declaring the sovereignty of Daniel's God and the stability of God's kingdom."

71. "Perhaps for the Hebrews in Babylonian captivity the testimony by a pagan king to God's power to perform signs and wonders and deliver his people stirred thoughts of the 'signs and wonders' associated with the exodus from Egypt and the possibility of a 'second exodus.'" Hill, "Daniel," 127.

72. "It is not clear if particular miracles or merely the wonders of the universe in general are in view. The miracle the Lord had performed on earth was the rescue of Daniel 'from the power [lit., "hand"] of the lions.'" Miller, *Daniel*, 189.

73. Several commentators argue that this is an epexegetical or conjunctive *waw* so that it translates, "So this Daniel prospered during the reign of Darius, *that is* (or *even* or *namely*), the reign of Cyrus the Persian." See Steinmann, *Daniel*, 293. For other commentators, see p. 169, n. 79 above. Hill, "Daniel," 127, adds that this "approach has merit in that it unifies the court-stories section of the book by forming an envelope construction with the reference to Cyrus in 1:21."

in Daniel (6:4). Similarly, "the chief priests and the whole council were look-ing for testimony against Jesus to put him to death; but they found none" (Mark 14:55). Daniel was found guilty of transgressing the law of the Medes and Persians; Jesus was found guilty of transgressing the law of the Jews; they said, "We have a law, and according to that law he ought to die because he has claimed to be the Son of God" (John 19:7). Darius unsuccessfully tried to save Daniel (6:14). Similarly, Pilate unsuccessfully tried to save Jesus (Matt 27:24). In Daniel 6:23 we read that Daniel "trusted in his God." In the New Testament we read that Jesus trusted his Father completely: the night before he was cruci-fied, Jesus prayed, "My Father, if this [cup of suffering] cannot pass unless I drink it, your will be done" (Matt 26:42; cf. 26:39; 27:43; 1 Pet 2:23). Daniel de-scended into "the pit" (6:16), his "grave" (cf., e.g., Pss 30:3; 143:7; Ezek 32:23). Similarly, Jesus' body was laid in a tomb (Matt 27:60). Daniel's "grave" was covered with a stone and sealed (6:17). Jesus' tomb was also covered with a stone and sealed (Matt 27:60, 66). The king found Daniel alive early the next morning and had him lifted out of his "grave" (6:19, 23). In the New Testament we read, "Very early on the first day of the week, when the sun had risen, they [the three women] went to the tomb" where an angel told them, "Jesus . . . has been raised" (Mark 16:2, 6). After God saved Daniel from certain death, we read that "Daniel prospered" (6:28). After God raised Jesus from death, Jesus prospered. Jesus said, "*All authority* in heaven and on earth has been given to me" (Matt 28:18).

Daniel clearly prefigures Jesus Christ. But Jesus is much greater than Dan-iel. God saved Daniel from certain death, but God raised Jesus after he actually died (John 19:34-35). Moreover, Daniel rose from his "grave" only to die at a later date. Jesus, by contrast, rose from his grave and lives forever. In addition, whereas God "prospered" Daniel during the reign of Darius (6:28), God "highly exalted . . . [Christ Jesus] and gave him the name that is above every name, so that at the name of Jesus every knee should bend, . . . and every tongue should confess that Jesus Christ is Lord, to the glory of God the Father" (Phil 2:9-11). And finally, God's delivering Daniel from the lions' pit gave Israel hope that God would deliver them from their "pit" of exile. But God's raising his Son Je-sus from the dead gives us hope that God will raise us also from the dead. As Paul put it, "Christ has been raised from the dead, the first fruits of those who have died. . . . Christ the first fruits, then at his coming those who belong to Christ" (1 Cor 15:20, 23). The point is that our God is the *living* God who is able to deliver even from death those who put their trust in him.

In telling Israel this story of God's saving Daniel from the lions, the author had primarily two purposes in mind. First, he wanted to encourage Israel in ex-ile to remain faithful to God's law even as Daniel in exile had remained faithful to God's law. The same application holds for us today. When there is a conflict between the law of the land and the law of God, we are to remain faithful to the law of God.

What this principle means concretely depends on the situation. Like Daniel, Jesus' disciples were faced with such a predicament. When the Jewish council gave them "strict orders not to teach in this [Jesus'] name" (Acts 5:28; cf. 4:18), they continued to do so. Brought before the council to explain this act of disobedience, "Peter and the apostles answered, 'We must obey God rather than any human authority'" (Acts 5:29).

When there is a conflict between the law of the land and the law of God, Christians ought to obey the law of God. The law of the land forbade Daniel to pray to his God; Daniel continued to pray to his God. The Jewish council forbade Jesus' disciples to teach in Jesus' name; they continued to teach in Jesus' name. When the Roman government allowed for the killing of infants, the early Christians opposed such laws and rescued discarded babies from the garbage dumps in Roman cities. When the Nazis adopted laws to exterminate Jews, Gypsies, and the mentally ill, genuine Christians opposed such laws because they are contrary to the law of the living God. When the law of the land forbids prayer in public places, Christians ought to obey God's law and continue to pray to God. When a government seeks to legitimize a preemptive strike, Christians ought to oppose such action because it results in an unjust war — just imagine the chaos that results if every nation claimed the right to a preemptive strike. When government officials demand a kickback before letting out a contract, Christians ought to object because bribery is contrary the law of God. Christians ought to "obey God rather than any human authority" (Acts 5:29).

Jesus says, "Whoever does . . . [God's commandments] and teaches them will be called *great* in the kingdom of heaven" (Matt 5:19). What are God's commandments? Jesus summarizes God's law for us: "'You shall love the Lord your God with all your heart, and with all your soul, and with all your mind.' This is the greatest and first commandment. And a second is like it: 'You shall love your neighbor as yourself'" (Matt 22:37-39). If the law of the land hinders us from loving the Lord our God above all else and our neighbor as ourselves, we ought to obey the law of God. Jesus declares, "Not everyone who says to me, 'Lord, Lord,' will enter the kingdom of heaven, but only the one who *does the will of my Father in heaven*" (Matt 7:21; cf. 25:31-40).

In addition to encouraging Israel and us to remain faithful to the law of God, the author had a second purpose in mind: he wanted to encourage Israel to *trust* God. We read in Daniel 6:23 that "Daniel was taken up out of the den, and no kind of harm was found on him, because he had *trusted in his God*." The author portrays Daniel as a true Israelite who trusts his God. And God delivered him from the lions' pit. So Israel must trust their God to deliver them from their "pit" of exile.[74] Israel did not trust God in vain. The last name in Daniel 6 is that of King Cyrus of Persia. We read in 2 Chronicles 36:23 that this Cyrus wrote an edict: "Thus says King Cyrus of Persia: The LORD, the God of heaven, has given me all the kingdoms of the earth, and he has charged me to build him a house at Jerusalem, which is in Judah. Whoever is among you of all his people, may the LORD his God be with him! Let him go up." It was the year 538 B.C. when the first of the exiles returned to Jerusalem. The living God delivered his people from exile and brought them home.

In a sense, we Christians are also exiles in this world. Paul said, "Our citizenship is in heaven" (Phil 3:20; cf. 1 Pet 1:1; Jas 1:1). The kingdoms of this world are not our home, but the kingdom of God is. That's why Jesus taught us to pray, "Our Father in heaven, . . . *Your* kingdom come" (Matt 6:9-10). We know that our life in this world will end in death. But we ought to trust that the *living* God is able to deliver us even from certain death. Jesus said, "I am the resurrection and the *life*. Those who *believe in* [trust] me, even though they die, will *live*" (John 11:25). Before his own death and resurrection, Jesus also said, "Do not let your hearts be troubled. Believe in God; *believe also in me*. In my Father's house there are many dwelling places. . . . If I go and prepare a place for you, I will come again and will take you to myself, so that where I am, there you may be also" (John 14:1-3).

We do not trust our living God in vain for our deliverance. On Easter Sunday God raised Jesus from the dead. Jesus rose as "the first fruits of those who have died" (1 Cor 15:20). When Jesus comes again, he will also raise our mortal bodies from death. We can trust our *living* God to deliver us from that final enemy, death. He raised Daniel from the lions' pit; he raised Jesus from the dead; he will also raise us and bring us home into his glorious kingdom. Then, according to the book of Revelation, "Death will be no more; mourning and crying and pain will be no more"; and God himself will dwell with his people (Rev. 21:3-4). "Thanks be to God, who gives us the victory through our Lord Jesus Christ" (1 Cor 15:57).

74. See p. 185, n. 28 above.

CHAPTER 7

Daniel's Vision of Four Beasts
and God's Kingdom

Daniel 7:1-28

*"As for these four great beasts, four kings shall arise out of the earth. But
the holy ones of the Most High shall receive the kingdom and possess the
kingdom forever — forever and ever."*

Daniel 7:17-18

What a marvelous chapter Daniel 7 is! It provides a grand vision of world history from the time of the Babylonian Empire until the full arrival of the kingdom of God. Towner calls Daniel 7 "the single most important chapter of the Book of Daniel. Its position is pivotal, both in terms of the architecture of the book as a whole and in terms of the brilliance of the vision which it contains."[1] Baldwin asserts, "Once convinced of the truth this chapter is proclaiming, the reader is in possession of the key to history."[2]

Yet, as a young pastor, I never preached a sermon on this great chapter. I thought it was just too controversial and too difficult to tackle when I had to prepare two sermons per week. Now that I have more time for research and writing, I hope that this presentation will encourage pastors, young and old, to preach this magnificent chapter.

The main reason why this key chapter in Daniel is so controversial and

---

1. Towner, *Daniel*, 91. Cf. Lacocque, *Book of Daniel*, 122, "The vision reported in chapter 7 is the most important one; it constitutes the veritable centre of the book. With it, Holy Scripture reaches one of its highest summits." Cf. Steinmann, *Daniel*, 332, "Daniel 7 . . . simultaneously closes out the Aramaic chiasm while introducing the visions that continue in subsequent chapters in Hebrew. This careful arrangement of the divinely inspired book points to this chapter as the book's most important section."

2. Baldwin, *Daniel*, 137. Cf. von Rad, *Old Testament Theology*, II, 304, "The very conception from which apocalyptic literature gains its splendour [is] that of the unity of world history."

difficult to understand is its genre: apocalyptic literature. One of the primary characteristics of apocalyptic literature is that it employs symbolic language. Baldwin explains, "The reader is confronted by mysterious symbols, allusions, enigmatic phrases and numbers, which have baffled interpreters through the ages and have given rise to many different schemes of interpretation."[3] In this chapter we read about bizarre beasts coming up "out of the sea" (v. 3), one of them with "ten horns" (v. 7), another horn with "a mouth speaking arrogantly" (v. 8), "an Ancient One" who takes his throne (v. 9), "a season and a time" (v. 12), "one like a human being coming with the clouds of heaven" (v. 13), "the holy ones of the Most High" (v. 22), and "a time, two times, and half a time" (v. 25).

How does one understand these perplexing images? Longman cautions, "The key to the interpretation of images is to find the point of connection [between the images and their intended meaning] and not push the peripheral elements of the comparison. This means we will be left with a gray area in our interpretation. Some of the points of comparison will be obvious, but others will not be. At such points we need to hold back and not insist on our interpretation."[4]

Unfortunately, many commentaries send us off in the wrong direction because they either "push the peripheral elements of the comparison," which results in speculation,[5] or they proceed from the wrong starting point, which skews the resulting interpretation.[6] With good reason Block warns against "domesticating" this profound literature: "This illicit domestication occurs in three dimensions, each of which is expressed in polar opposite forms: (1) through overly symbolic or overly spiritual readings; (2) through overly futuristic or overly historicized readings; and (3) through overly credulous or overly suspicious readings. . . . [In classical dispensationalism] excessively symbolic, futuristic, and credulous interpretations tended to drown out the message of the book as the original audience might have heard it. The critical scholarly world tends to be plagued by excessive historicism and suspicion, as if specific prediction of distant events is impossible."[7]

---

3. Baldwin, *Daniel*, 136.

4. Longman, *Daniel*, 193. Cf. Block, "Preaching Old Testament Apocalyptic," *CTJ* 41 (2006) 50, "Authoritative preaching of the message of apocalyptic literature demands that we major on the major themes and be less concerned about the meaning and significance of fine details."

5. E.g., the dispensational interpretation of the "ten horns" as the recent European Union.

6. The fourth beast *must* be Greece. E.g., Towner, *Daniel*, 36 (see quotation on p. 54, n. 1 above). So also Redditt, *Daniel*, 119, "Since Rome appears as the Kittim in 11:30 and is named nowhere else in the book, the 'Roman interpretation' appears to be unjustified."

7. Block, "Preaching Old Testament Apocalyptic," *CTJ* 41 (2006) 21-22.

An additional challenge we face in preparing a sermon on Daniel 7 is to formulate a textual theme that is specific for the message of this chapter and does not just duplicate the theme of its twin chapter (Daniel 2, the statue of precious metals representing four kingdoms). And most challenging of all, we will have to gain some clarity on the identities of several of the symbols: the four beasts (kingdoms), the "one like a human being coming with the clouds," "the holy ones," and the "little horn."

Text and Context

Determining the parameters of the preaching text is the easiest part in preaching this passage. Chapter 7:1 opens the literary unit with a chronological marker giving the setting: "In the first year of King Belshazzar of Babylon, Daniel had a dream and visions of his head as he lay in bed." Chapter 7:28 clearly closes the literary unit with, "Here the account ends," and a brief description of Daniel's reaction to the vision, "As for me, Daniel, my thoughts greatly terrified me, and my face turned pale; but I kept the matter in my mind." Chapter 8:1 begins a new literary unit with another chronological marker. The preaching text, therefore, is Daniel 7:1-28.

However, because it will be difficult to do justice to all the elements in this important chapter in a twenty-five-minute sermon, one may wish to consider a series of two sermons on Daniel 7. This can be done because the chapter quite naturally falls into two parts: (1) Daniel's vision and the angel's brief interpretation (7:1-18), and (2) Daniel's request for the "truth" about the fourth beast and especially the little horn and the angel's lengthy interpretation (7:19-28). The first sermon would then focus on the full sweep of the history of human kingdoms from the Babylonian kingdom to the coming of the kingdom of God, while the second sermon would concentrate especially on the last days, the final tribulation, God's judgment, and the kingdom of God.[8]

As to the context, formally the four visions of Daniel 7–12 are linked chronologically to the kings introduced in Daniel 5–6: Daniel's first vision takes place in the first year of Belshazzar (7:1), his second vision in the third year of Belshazzar (8:1), his third vision in the first year of Darius (9:1), and his fourth vision in the third year of Cyrus (10:1). More substantively, Daniel 7 is the last Aramaic chapter in Daniel. Chapters 1–6 proclaimed in various ways the sovereignty of God, his power to depose kings and set up kings (2:21), and his power to save his faithful people even from certain death (the fiery furnace, the lions' den). This final Aramaic chapter "constitutes the climax, and it is the high point

8. See the plot line below. See p. 232, n. 91 below for a suggested theme for each sermon.

in relation to the whole book; subsequent chapters treat only part of the picture and concentrate on some particular aspect of it."[9]

The clearest link of Daniel 7 to the foregoing chapters is its twin,[10] that is, chapter 2, Nebuchadnezzar's dream of a great statue. As the statue consisted of four metals representing four kingdoms, so Daniel's vision has four beasts representing four kingdoms. These are the same four kingdoms, both beginning with the kingdom of Babylon and the fourth[11] presented as the last kingdom before the kingdom of God replaces all human kingdoms. In both passages God's kingdom is said to last "forever" (2:44; 7:14, 27). The main difference between these two presentations of history is the perspective. Daniel 2 describes the four kingdoms from the human perspective: they are precious metals, "humane, majestic, but plagued with weakness and incoherence" and gradually deteriorating. Daniel 7 describes the four kingdoms from God's perspective: "basically amoral, self-seeking, cruelly destructive, animal-like power-blocks."[12] Moreover, Daniel 7 goes into much more detail on the fourth kingdom (ten horns and a little horn) and on those who receive the kingdom of God ("one like a human being" and "the holy ones").

Daniel 7 describes the first beast as being like a lion with eagles' wings. "Then, as I watched, its wings were *plucked off*, and it was lifted up from the ground and made to stand on two feet like a human being; and a human 'mind' [*lĕbab*] was given to it" (7:4). This punishment and restoration reminds us of Daniel 4, where God punishes Nebuchadnezzar by taking away his human "mind" (*lĕbab*; 4:16) and later restoring his "reason" (4:34).

In Daniel 7 we also read of "one like a human being" receiving a kingdom "that shall never be destroyed" (v. 14) and of "the holy ones" possessing "the kingdom forever" (v. 18). This idea links up with Nebuchadnezzar's confession that God's "kingdom is an everlasting kingdom" (4:3) and Darius's confession that "God's kingdom shall never be destroyed" (6:26).

"The books" that are opened (7:10) will be mentioned again in Daniel 12:1. Also "the holy ones" who suffer persecution "for a time, two times, and half a

---

9. Baldwin, *Daniel*, 137.

10. See the Introduction, p. 20 above, for the chiastic structure of Daniel 2–7, which twins chapters 2 and 7, 3 and 6, and 4 and 5.

11. Daniel 7:7 describes the fourth beast as "exceedingly strong." "The same adjective for 'strong' . . . describes the fourth kingdom represented by the statue . . . (2:40, 42). The fourth beast's 'iron' teeth (7:7) are reminiscent of the fourth metal, 'iron,' in the shins and feet of the statue (2:33-35, 40-45). This beast also 'crushed' . . . and 'trampled with its feet' (7:7), just as the fourth kingdom represented by Nebuchadnezzar's statue had the ability to 'crush' . . . and 'shatter' (2:40)." Steinmann, *Daniel*, 347.

12. Gooding, "The Literary Structure of the Book of Daniel and Its Implications," *TynBul* 32 (1981) 60-61.

time" (7:25) will return in 12:7 as "the holy people" whose power will be shattered "for a time, two times, and half a time." By way of these connections, the author encourages us to interpret each vision not in isolation but in the light of the earlier reported dreams and the later visions.

Literary Features

Although most of Daniel 7 is written in vivid prose, some sections blossom into poetry. The fluid line between prose and poetry is again apparent. While the NIV prints only verses 9-10 as poetry, the NRSV discerns poetry not only in verses 9-10 but also in verses 13-14 and 23-27. Steinmann argues that the shift from prose in verses 1-8 to poetry in verses 9-10 and again from prose in verses 11-12 to poetry in verses 13-14 highlights Daniel's shift from describing events among human kingdoms to divine actions.[13] Even though the telltale parallelism of poetry is lacking in verses 23-27, Baldwin suggests that the alliterations and repetitions in these verses "build up an emphatic assurance of divine control over events, from the most dreaded suffering history can bring to the triumph of right in a world-wide kingdom."[14]

The overall form of Daniel 7 is a dream-vision report which includes the setting (v. 1), an animal allegory on history (vv. 2-8), a judgment scene (vv. 9-12), the epiphany of a heavenly figure (vv. 13-14), Daniel's fear and request for interpretation (vv. 15-16), the angel's interpretation (vv. 17-18), Daniel's request concerning the fourth beast and the little horn (vv. 19-20), a vision report about the little horn (vv. 20-22), the angel's further interpretation (vv. 23-27), and a concluding formula concerning Daniel's fear (v. 28).[15]

We should also note a few literary differences between the earlier narratives and this chapter. The previous narratives were all related by a narrator, that is, they are written in the third person. In chapter 7:2 Daniel switches to the first person: "I, Daniel, saw." Except for chapter 10:1, he will maintain this first-person reporting to the end of his book. Moreover, although Daniel continues to use the Aramaic language in chapter 7, he switches the genre in this chapter from narrative to apocalyptic and will maintain apocalyptic to the end of his book.

13. Steinmann, *Daniel*, 355. Cf. Seow, *Daniel*, 106, to the effect that the shift from prose to poetry reflects "a shift from the prosaic realities of earthly experience to the sublime encounter of the heavenly court."

14. Baldwin, *Daniel*, 145-46.

15. For more details, see Towner, *Daniel*, 91-92; Collins, *Daniel* (1984), 78-79; and Goldingay, *Daniel*, 146-47. Block and his Ph.D. student Jenny M. Lowery argue that this chapter should "be classified as a dream rather than vision account." See Block, "Preaching Old Testament Apocalyptic," *CTJ* 41 (2006) 28.

Since we will be interpreting apocalyptic literature in the next six chapters, we will first briefly discuss some of the features of apocalyptic literature[16] and then move on to analyze the structure of Daniel 7, its plot line, character description, and repetition.

Apocalyptic Literature

As mentioned, one of the main characteristics of apocalyptic literature is its symbolic language.[17] Andrew Hill provides a good description of apocalyptic literature and its goals: it "is 'crisis' literature, typically conveying specific messages to particular groups of people caught up in dire situations. . . . Visionary literature announces an end to the way things are and opens up alternative possibilities to the audience as a result of God's impending intervention in human affairs. Three types of messages are usually associated with the visionary literature of the Bible: (1) a message of encouragement to the oppressed; (2) a warning to the oppressor; and (3) a call to faith for those wavering between God's truth and human 'wisdom.'"[18]

Block rightly cautions that "the intention of apocalyptic is not to chart out God's plan for the future so future generations may draw up calendars but to assure the present generation that — perhaps contrary to appearance — God is still on the throne (cf. Dan 7:18, 21-22, 27; 8:25; 12:1-4), and that the future is firmly in his hands."[19] Block helpfully lists eight common features of apocalyptic texts:[20]

1. Temporal dualism: the distinction of the present age from the age to come.
2. Pessimism regarding the present and optimism concerning the future [God's coming kingdom]. . . .
3. The periodization of history. . . .
4. The imminent arrival of the reign of God, . . . [which] will spell the doom of existing earthly powers.
5. A cosmic perspective. . . .

---

16. See also the Introduction, pp. 18-19 above.

17. Consequently, Ferguson, *Daniel,* 146-47, asserts that "we are meant to see, hear, and smell the strange beasts that appear throughout this chapter. . . . This section of God's word is not meant to be an amusement for armchair theological sleuths. It is intended to give an overwhelming impression of the mysteries of God's purposes and the awful conflict that lies behind and beneath history."

18. Hill, "Daniel," 131.

19. Block, "Preaching Old Testament Apocalyptic," *CTJ* 41 (2006) 52.

20. Ibid., 20-21, with credit to D. E. Aune, "Apocalypticism," in *Dictionary of Paul and His Letters,* eds. G. F. Hawthorne and R. P. Martin (Downers Grove: InterVarsity Press, 1993), 27.

6. The vindication of the righteous. . . .
7. The involvement of supernatural beings. . . .
8. A messianic element. God designates a royal figure as a symbol and executor of his rule.

Structure

This dream-vision is carried along by Daniel's "I saw"/"I watched"/"I looked" (*ḥāzēh hăwêt:* vv. 2, 4, 6, 7, 9, 11 [2x], 13, 21). Although the scenes are not as clearly delineated in Daniel 7 as in the foregoing narratives, we can discern four scenes in the vision and its interpretation:

Scene 1. Four beasts come up out of the sea (2-8)
    A. A lion with eagles' wings (4)
    B. A bear raised up on one side (5)
    C. A leopard with four wings and four heads (6)
    D. A monster with ten horns and a little horn (7-8)
    Characters: God (divine passives) and in quick succession a lion, a bear,
        a leopard, and a monster with a little horn

Scene 2. The heavenly court convenes (9-14)
    A. The Ancient One takes his seat (9-10b)
    B. The books are opened (10c)
    C. The fourth beast is burned with fire (11)
    D. Dominion is taken away from the first three beasts (12)
    E. The Ancient One gives dominion to one like a human being (13-14)
    Characters: The Ancient One and the fourth beast; when the fourth beast
        leaves the stage, he is replaced by "one like a human being"

Scene 3. Daniel requests an interpretation of his vision (15-18)
    A. Daniel's fear and request (15-16)
    B. The angel's interpretation (17-18)
    Characters: Daniel and an angel

Scene 4. Daniel asks for the truth about the fourth beast (19-27)
    A. Daniel inquires about the fourth beast and the little horn (19-20)
    B. Daniel's flashback to a detail of his vision (21-22)
        1. The little horn makes war with the holy ones and prevails (21)
        2. The Ancient One comes, judges for the holy ones, and gives them
           the kingdom (22)
    C. The angel's interpretation of the fourth beast and the little horn (23-27)
    Characters: Daniel and an angel

The Plot Line

In the Introduction (p. 19 above) we noted that Daniel's apocalyptic visions have a literary structure like that of the narratives.[21] Though the plot line of this vision is not as clear as that of the earlier narratives, we can certainly detect its contours in this chapter. The setting is given in verse 1, "the first year of King Belshazzar," with the occasioning incident in verses 2-6, the vision of the three beasts. The tension gradually rises with the description of the fourth beast, its ten horns, and a little horn with human eyes and an arrogant mouth (vv. 7-8). What will happen to this arrogant monster? The tension quickly resolves with the judgment scene: the Ancient One being seated on his fiery throne, books being opened, the monster being burned with fire, the rest of the beasts having their dominion taken away, and everlasting dominion being given to the "one like a human being" (vv. 9-14). The outcome is that Daniel is terrified, asks for an explanation, and is assured that the four beasts are "four kings [that] shall arise out of the earth. But the holy ones of the Most High shall receive the kingdom and possess the kingdom forever — forever and ever" (vv. 15-18).[22]

Another conflict begins when Daniel wants to know more about the fourth beast and the little horn (vv. 19-20). The tension rises when Daniel sees this little horn making war with the holy ones and prevailing over them (v. 21). The tension is briefly broken when Daniel sees the judgment scene again and the Ancient One giving possession of the kingdom to "the holy ones" (v. 22). But the tension picks up again when the angel explains that the fourth kingdom will "devour the whole earth," and that the little horn "shall speak words against the Most High [and] shall wear out the holy ones," and that "they shall be given into his power" for a time (vv. 23-25). The tension is finally resolved with the angel's interpretation of the judgment scene: the little horn will be consumed and totally destroyed and the everlasting kingdom given to the holy ones (vv. 26-27). The outcome is that Daniel is still terrified but keeps the matter in mind (v. 28).

We can sketch the plot line of this dream-vision and its interpretations as a complex plot (see p. 210). Note the parallels between Daniel's vision and the angel's interpretation of the vision, both finally resolving the conflict with God giving his everlasting kingdom to a son of man and to the holy ones. This resolution, surely, is a good clue to the theme of this passage.

---

21. Cf. Block, "Preaching Old Testament Apocalyptic," *CTJ* 41 (2006) 23, "These chapters should be classified as autobiographical narrative."

22. One could sketch verses 15-18 as a little subplot with its own tension and resolution, but in order to simplify the sketch I will keep them together under "Outcome."

Character Description

Because apocalyptic literature is picture language, it is rich in description. Daniel relates that "the four great beasts came up out of the sea" (v. 3). In the Old Testament the sea frequently stands for the chaos God had to control in the beginning (Gen 1:2-10).[23] "The sea is a negative entity, a hostile element tamed by God, a chaotic world in opposition to the civilized world."[24] Thus these beasts coming up out of the chaotic sea depict disorder and hostility to God. Another indication that these beasts represent disorder is that they are described as hybrid creatures: a lion with eagles' wings, a bear with three tusks like a boar, a leopard with four wings, and a monster with ten horns. These hybrids stand in striking contrast to God's good creation where God created creatures "according to their kinds."[25] "In the light of the laws on clean and unclean animals in Leviticus 11 and Deuteronomy 14, Jews would regard hybrid creatures as unclean."[26] The fourth beast, apparently, is so awful that it cannot even be pictured as an animal. Instead Daniel describes it as "terrifying, dreadful, exceedingly strong," with "great iron teeth," "ten horns" (v. 7), and "claws of bronze" (v. 19).[27]

Daniel describes God as "an Ancient One," literally, "an Ancient of days" — the One who has existed from eternity. He continues the description in anthropomorphic terms: a person sitting on a throne, wearing clothing "white as snow" and having hair "like pure wool" (v. 9). The synonymous parallelism between the clothing and hair suggests that the hair like pure wool is also white as snow (cf. Rev. 1:14). The color white signifies that God is holy (cf. Isa 1:18; "cleansed" in Dan 11:35; 12:10 is literally "made white"). Daniel portrays God's throne as "fiery flames" with "wheels" of "burning fire" (v. 9c; cf. Ezek 1:13-21, 27). The fire also signifies the holiness of God, "especially as he reveals himself in theophany [e.g., Exod 3:2; Dan 7:10]. By fire he can mete out judgment upon sinners (Dan 7:11). Yet by fire he can also refine and purify his people (Zech 13:9; Mal 3:2-3; cf. 1 Cor 3:11-15)."[28] The "wheels" indicate that God's throne is not bound to a certain place but can be present anywhere.

23. "This 'sea' appears as a power hostile to God and to the world, confronting God at the beginning of the world. At Yahweh's rebuke, the deep *(tĕhom)* or the waters *(mayim)* covering the earth fled (Ps 104:6f.). Thus he set a bound *(gĕbûl)* for the sea, which it can no longer pass; cf. Jer 5:22, where a bound or *ḥōq* is set for the sea *(yām)*, and Job 38:8-10, where Yahweh sets the sea doors and *ḥōq*." Helmer Ringgren, *"yām,"* TDOT, VI, 92.

24. Ibid., 97.

25. Longman, *Daniel*, 183, with references to Genesis 1:11-12, 21, 24, 25.

26. Lucas, *Daniel*, 171. Also, according to Deuteronomy 22:9-11, God did not allow Israel to sow their vineyards "with a second kind of seed," to plow their fields "with an ox and a donkey yoked together," and to wear clothes "made of wool and linen woven together."

27. For more details on the four beasts, see pp. 213-18 below, "The Four Beasts."

28. Steinmann, *Daniel*, 353.

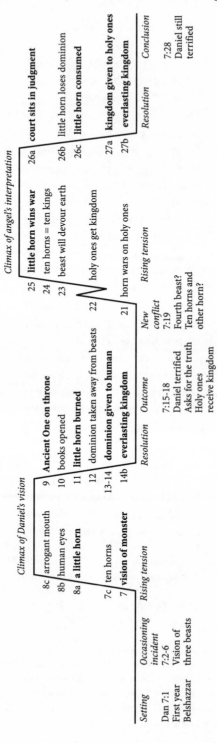

Daniel describes another important character as "one like a human being" and "coming with the clouds of heaven" (v. 13). Since the Old Testament depicts God as "riding on the clouds" (e.g., Pss 68:4; 104:3; Isa 19:1), this figure "like a human being" must be divine. This divine human-like figure receives everlasting "dominion, glory, and kingship" (v. 14).[29]

Daniel portrays "the other horn" as "little," having "eyes like human eyes," "a mouth speaking arrogantly" (v. 8), making "war with the holy ones and prevailing over them" (v. 21), and "wearing out the holy ones" (v. 25). Small wonder that Daniel describes himself as being "troubled," "terrified" (v. 15), "greatly terrified," and his face as turning pale (v. 28). He has seen the terrifying threat of disorder engulfing and wearing out God's people.

Repetition

The overall structure reveals repetition in the following parallelisms:

A   The main vision report (vv. 2-14)
B   A brief interpretation (vv. 17-18)
A′ A supplementary vision report (vv. 19-22)
B′ A lengthy interpretation (vv. 23-27).

Because of this parallel structure, there is considerable repetition of elements connecting vision reports and interpretations: "fourth beast" (vv. 7, 19, 23), "ten horns" (vv. 7, 20, 24), "little horn" (vv. 8, 11, 20, 21, 24, 25), "divine judgment" (vv. 10, 22, 26), "the holy ones" (vv. 18, 22, 25, 27), and the final "kingdom" (vv. 14, 18, 22b, 27). Goldingay comments, "The repetition and the elaboration show what the chapter regards as important, namely the suffering and triumph of the holy ones."[30]

An even more important repetition for discerning the theme of this passage is the seven-fold repetition of "dominion" (*šolṭān:* vv. 6, 12, 14 [2x], 26, 27 [2x]). The earlier narratives related that everlasting "dominion" belongs to God (4:3, 34; 6:26) but that he gives "dominion" to human kings/kingdoms (4:22). In Daniel 7, Daniel repeats that God gives "dominion" to the third king/kingdom (divine passive; 7:6) but then adds that God will take away the "dominion" of these human kingdoms (7:12, 26) and give "everlasting dominion"

---

29. See further pp. 219-22 below, "One like a Human Being."

30. Goldingay, *Daniel,* 156. On pp. 155-56 he presents these and more repetitions in the form of a chart.

to the "one like a human being" (7:14) and to "the holy ones" (7:27).[31] As a matter of fact, this passage repeats three times that God's kingdom will be given to "the holy ones" (7:18, 22, 27), climaxing the third time with, "The kingship and dominion and the greatness of the kingdoms under the whole heaven shall be given to the people of the holy ones of the Most High; their kingdom shall be an everlasting kingdom, and all dominions shall serve and obey them."

Repetition may further alert us to more complex rhetorical structures, which are based on repetition. The original vision report (vv. 2-14) seems to be designed as a chiastic structure centering on the throne scene:[32]

    A   Four beasts appear (2b-3)
        B   The first three beasts (4-6)
            C   The fourth beast appears (7)
                D   A small horn makes great claims (8)
                    E   A throne scene (9-10)
                D' The small horn makes great claims (11a)
            C' The fourth beast is destroyed (11b)
        B' The fate of the first three beasts (12)
    A' A human-like figure appears (13-14)

This chiasm focusing on the throne scene coincides with the turn to resolution in the plot line above.

Interpretation of Specific Images

Because of the controversies surrounding the identification of specific symbols in Daniel 7, we need to spend some time here to come to clarity on the identity of several of these images. We have this discussion at this point so that in the "Sermon Exposition" below we will not be side-tracked into controversial issues but can concentrate on the message of Daniel 7.

In identifying several figures, the identity of the fourth beast is most important: Is it the kingdom of Greece or that of Rome? Our decision on this issue will influence the interpretation of other figures. We shall first discuss the identity of "the four beasts," therefore, and then follow up with the identity of "the little horn," the "one like a human being," and "the holy ones."

---

31. See Steinmann, *Daniel*, 331.

32. The wording is from Lucas, *Daniel*, 164, with credit for discovering this chiasm to Goldingay, *Daniel*, 153.

The Four Beasts

The angel interprets for Daniel that the four beasts are "four *kings* [that] shall arise out of the earth. But the holy ones . . . shall receive the *kingdom*" (7:17-18). There is general agreement that Daniel uses "kings" and "kingdoms" almost interchangeably.[33] In fact, in verse 23 the angel explains that the four beasts (kings) are four kingdoms.[34] Therefore the key question is, What is the identity of these four kingdoms?[35] Scholars who believe that Daniel 7 was written in 167 B.C.,[36] the time of Antiochus IV, argue that the fourth kingdom is Greece (the Greek view). Since the first kingdom is Babylon, the four kingdoms must be Babylonia, Media, Persia, and Greece.[37]

There are several problems with the Greek view, however. First, the assumption that Daniel 7 was written in 167 B.C. has its weaknesses (see Introduction above, pp. 9-14). Second, historically Media never replaced Babylonia but was swallowed up by Persia eleven years *before* the Medo-Persian Empire replaced Babylonia.[38] Thus the proponents of the Greek view are left with only three historical kingdoms instead of the four required.[39]

33. See p. 78, n. 64 above.

34. The Greek and Latin versions translate the "four kings" of verse 17 as "four kingdoms." See Collins, *Daniel*, 311-12; Lucas, *Daniel*, 187; and Steinmann, *Daniel*, 365.

35. Note that Longman, *Daniel*, 185, seeks to dodge this issue. He argues that, "though the vision begins with the Babylonian empire, its multivalent imagery intends to prohibit definite historical identifications with the remaining three beasts." But this is not a valid way of escaping between the "horns" of the dilemma of the Greek or Roman view. If Daniel intended us to identify the first beast with the Babylonian Empire, it would seem to follow that the next three beasts also represent historical empires. In fact, in the next vision the angel Gabriel specifically identifies the kings of Media and Persia and the king of Greece (8:20-21). Duguid, *Daniel*, 111, follows Longman and opts "to take the number of the beasts as representing a symbol of completeness rather than a particular number of world empires. On such a view, the message of Daniel 7 is that life in this present age will *always* be this way until the end of this age." See also p. 79, n. 71 above.

36. "The most specific clue to the date of this chapter is found in 7:25: 'He will think to change times and law.' The reference is to the decree of Antiochus Epiphanes suppressing the traditional cult and imposing pagan worship. There is no reference, however, to the desecration of the temple, which looms large in the subsequent chapters. Because only a few months elapsed between the decree and the profanation of the temple, we can date Daniel 7 rather precisely to late 167 B.C.E." Collins, *Daniel*, 323-24. The question, of course, is whether 7:25 speaks of Antiochus IV or of some future Antichrist figure (see below).

37. See Chapter 2, p. 54, n. 1.

38. "The Medes had been subsumed under the Persians eleven years before Babylon was conquered by Cyrus the Great." Steinmann, *Daniel*, 148.

39. "If, then, it can be shown that the second kingdom is Medo-Persia, the Grecian hypothesis is lost." Young, *Prophecy of Daniel*, 280. See his arguments on pp. 281-86 that the second kingdom cannot be Media by itself but must be Medo-Persia.

A third weakness in the Greek view is that Daniel 7:5 describes the second beast as one that "looked like a bear. It was raised up on one side." This picture fits the Medo-Persian Empire with the Persian side being dominant (see below). This identification is also supported by Daniel 8:3, where Daniel sees a ram with two horns, one "longer than the other." The angel Gabriel identifies the ram with two horns as "the kings of Media and Persia" (8:20), that is, the Medo-Persian kingdom, with Persia being the longer horn. Proponents of the Greek view argue that the ram with two horns must represent two separate kingdoms, Media and Persia. But in Daniel each beast represents a single kingdom, never two separate kingdoms. Moreover, the identification of the ram with two separate kingdoms "violates the clear statements in 8:6-7 (see also 8:20-21) that picture the goat representing Greece as breaking off *both* horns of the ram. This action can only be understood if the ram represents the combined kingdom of the Medes and the Persians, commonly called the Persian empire."[40]

Fourth, in Daniel 7:6 the third kingdom, the swift leopard, ends up with "*four* heads." Similarly the swift goat of Daniel 8:5 ends up with "*four* prominent horns" (8:8). And in Daniel 11:3-4, the warrior king's "kingdom shall be broken to the *four* winds of heaven." Steinmann states, "There is agreement among all scholars that the male goat of Daniel 8 and the kingdoms mentioned in 11:3-4 represent the Greeks, beginning with Alexander the Great (the single horn and the mighty king). Therefore, the third kingdom of Daniel 7 represented by the leopard must also be the Greeks."[41] For the Persian kingdom never split into "*four* heads,"[42] while the Greek kingdom did exactly that (see below).[43]

Fifth, proponents of the Greek view tend to ignore the fifth kingdom, the kingdom of God, which is the culmination of Daniel's vision (vv. 13-14) and of its interpretation (v. 27). Those who do pay attention to this fifth kingdom have to conclude that this prophecy failed because the kingdom of God did not

40. Steinmann, *Daniel*, 150.

41. Ibid., 151.

42. "There is no way in which a quadripartite character can be made out for the Persian Empire either under Cyrus or under any of his successors. That empire remained unified till its end, when it suddenly collapsed under the onslaught of Alexander the Great in 334-331." Archer, "Daniel," 86.

43. See also Young, *Prophecy of Daniel*, 287-88, for arguments that the description of the male goat of Daniel 8:5-8, 21, 22, which Gabriel identifies as "the king of Greece" (8:21), is not at all like the fourth beast in Daniel 7. Cf. Young's *Messianic Prophecies*, 34, "It is surely clear that the nondescript beast of chapter seven and the he-goat of chapter eight are described in such a way that they differ both in their origin, purpose and destiny. The writer of Daniel did not intend them to be regarded as one and the same in their representation." Moreover, the Greek kingdom does not fit the description of the kingdom of iron in Daniel 2:40.

come right after the kingdom of Greece. Thus the Greek view tends to rob Daniel 7 of its gospel.[44]

A better approach than the Greek view is to pay attention to Daniel's whole vision concerning the course of human history: four successive human kingdoms which will in the end be replaced by the kingdom of God. Both sides agree that the first kingdom was Babylonia (605-539 B.C.). It was replaced by the kingdom of Medo-Persia (539-331 B.C.), which in turn was replaced by the kingdom of Greece, including the Ptolemies and Seleucids (331-63 B.C.). Historically there is only one worldwide kingdom left that can be the fourth kingdom, and that is Rome (the Roman view). During the time of the Roman Empire and its aftermath the kingdom of God has come and will come.

This scenario matches our interpretation of the four metals/kingdoms of Daniel 2. It also fits Gabriel's identification of Medo-Persia and Greece in Daniel 8:20-21. And it fits with the New Testament, for during the time of the Roman Empire Jesus was born and began proclaiming, "The time is fulfilled, and the kingdom of God has come near" (Mark 1:15). Information from Daniel 2, 7, and 8 about these kingdoms is consolidated in the table on page 216.

This scenario of the Roman view also fits better with the descriptions of the beasts than does the Greek view. The first beast "was like a lion and had eagles' wings" (7:4). The lion is the king of land animals and the eagle king of birds. The Old Testament prophets compare King Nebuchadnezzar to a lion (e.g., Jer 4:7; 50:17, 44) and to an eagle (e.g., Jer 48:40; Ezek 17:3). There is general agreement, therefore, that the first beast represents Babylon, the head of gold in Nebuchadnezzar's dream (Dan 2:38).

The second beast "looked like a bear[45] . . . raised up on one side" (7:5). In the Old Testament, bears were known as ferocious animals who mauled people (see 2 Kings 2:24) and could weigh "up to 250 kilos."[46] "It was raised up one side" so that this side was higher than the other.[47] "One side of the bear being

---

44. See Steinmann, *Daniel*, 379, "The Critical View Nullifies the Gospel." For example, Collins, *Daniel*, 123, claims, "Several major themes in the traditional understanding of Daniel are now recognized as invalid. The prophecies of Daniel can no longer serve as christological proofs; nor can the chronological schemata serve to structure universal history." Note that though Lucas, *Daniel*, 190-91, argues for Macedonia [Greece] as the fourth kingdom, he still seeks to rescue "a theology of history" (p. 199).

45. "Hosea 13:7-8 ["I will become like a lion to them, like a leopard I will lurk . . . , I will fall upon them like a bear robbed of her cubs"] is likely to have been the primary impetus behind the choice of the 'bear' to represent the Medes and Persians who were established as one empire." Gardner, "Decoding Daniel: The Case of Daniel 7:5," *Bib* 88/2 (2007) 232-33.

46. Baldwin, *Daniel*, 139.

47. See Steinmann, *Daniel*, 343-44.

Daniel 2	Daniel 7	Daniel 8	Kingdom	Dates
Head of gold	Lion with eagles' wings		Babylon	605-539 B.C.
Chest and arms of silver	Bear with one side higher than the other	Ram with two horns, one longer	Medo-Persia	539-331 B.C.
Belly and thighs of bronze	Leopard with four wings, four heads	Fast goat with four horns	Greece Ptolemies and Seleucids	331-323 B.C. 323-63 B.C.
Legs of iron Feet and toes of iron and clay	Monster with iron teeth, ten horns		Rome and ten kings	63 B.C.– A.D. 476 Present period
Stone, not by human hands, smashes statue	God burns the monster	Little horn destroyed, not by human hands		Last day
Mountain fills whole earth	Kingdom given to son of man and God's people		Kingdom of God	Everlasting

higher or larger could indicate that the empire symbolized by the bear consisted of two parts, one being greater than the other. If so, the two divisions would be Media and Persia, and the higher side would symbolize Persia, which rose to a position of dominance in the alliance."[48] This interpretation is confirmed in Daniel 8, where Daniel sees a ram with two horns: "Both horns were long, but one was longer than the other, and the longer one came up second" (8:3). Again, an empire made up of two parts. The angel Gabriel identifies this empire for Daniel: "As for the ram that you saw with the two horns, these are the kings of Media and Persia" (8:20). Not Media alone but this united empire of Medo-Persia would "arise, and devour many bodies" (7:5).

The third beast looked "like a leopard. The beast had four wings . . . and four heads" (7:6). The leopard is one of the fastest animals in the animal kingdom. But with the addition of four wings, this animal was incredibly fast. This speedy animal is an apt representation of Alexander the Great of Macedonia

48. Miller, *Daniel*, 198. Leupold, *Exposition of Daniel*, 291, suggests that "the Median half of these two sections was the more passive, the part inclined to lie down. The more aggressive Persian part of the empire will then be signified by the side that is raised up."

and the amazing speed with which he conquered the then-known world. Alexander "invaded Asia Minor in 334 B.C. and within ten short years (by the age of thirty-two) had conquered the entire Medo-Persian Empire to the borders of India."[49] This third beast, then, is the kingdom of Greece.

This interpretation is confirmed by the fact that when Alexander died at a young age, the Greek Empire did indeed split into "*four* heads" (7:6), four sections, each governed by one of Alexander's generals: Ptolemy, Seleucus, Lysimachus, and Cassander. The identification of Greece as the third beast is further confirmed in Daniel 8, where Daniel describes his next vision: "A male goat appeared from the west, coming across the face of the whole earth without touching the ground [lightning speed!]. The goat had a horn between its eyes. . . . The male goat grew exceedingly great; but at the height of its power, the great horn was broken, and in its place came up *four* prominent horns toward the four winds of heaven" (8:5, 8). The angel Gabriel identifies this kingdom for Daniel: "The male goat is the king of Greece, and the great horn between its eyes is the first king" (8:21).

The fourth beast is like nothing in the animal kingdom. It was "terrifying and dreadful and exceedingly strong [*taqqîpâ*]. It had great iron [*parzel*] teeth and was devouring, breaking in pieces [*dĕqaq*], and stamping what was left with its feet" (7:7). This is the kingdom of iron of Nebuchadnezzar's dream, as Daniel explained to the king, "And there shall be a fourth kingdom, strong [*taqqîpâ*] as iron [*parzel*]; just as iron [*parzel*] crushes [*dĕqaq*] and smashes everything, it shall crush [*dĕqaq*] and shatter all these" (2:40).

We see the Roman legions marching across the world, breaking in pieces what was left of the Greek Empire, forcing regions in Asia, Africa, and Europe to submit to the Caesar in Rome. This monster "was different from all the beasts that preceded it" (7:7b). "Rome showed itself to be the first truly universal empire of antiquity. Rome was characterized by its conquering and crushing power and by its ability to consolidate the territories which it seized."[50]

Daniel describes this fourth beast as having "ten horns" (v. 7). Evidently,

---

49. Miller, *Daniel*, 199. Montgomery, *Book of Daniel*, 289, identifies the leopard as Cyrus the Persian. Miller, *Daniel*, 200, n. 27, retorts, "The description of this empire undoubtedly suits Alexander's swift conquest and lust for new territories far better than the activities of Cyrus."

50. Young, *Prophecy of Daniel*, 288. Cf. Steinmann, *Daniel*, 347, "Only the fourth beast was so destructive that 'it devoured and crushed, and what was left it trampled with its feet' (7:7). This is an apt description of cruel Roman power and Rome's willingness to use that power ruthlessly to subdue conquered peoples." Cf. Miller, *Daniel*, 201, "Rome possessed a power and longevity unlike anything the world had ever known. Nations were crushed under the iron boot of the Roman legions, its power was virtually irresistible, and the extent of its influence surpassed the other three kingdoms." Cf. Leupold, *Exposition of Daniel*, 297-98.

these ten horns arrive after the glory days of Rome, for the angel says: "As for the ten horns, out of this kingdom ten kings shall arise" (v. 24). As Greece was split up into four heads after reaching its pinnacle, so Rome will break up into "ten kings" or kingdoms after its peak. Since apocalyptic literature frequently uses numbers as symbols, we should probably understand the number "ten" symbolically as the number of fullness (cf. the "ten times better" in 1:20). Thus the kingdom of Rome will continue after its glory days with a full number of partly brittle kingdoms. After that, according to 7:24, "another shall arise. This one shall be different from the former ones" — the little horn.

The Little Horn

Proponents of the Greek view claim that the "little horn" of Daniel 7 is to be identified with the Seleucid king Antiochus IV Epiphanes (175-163 B.C.). On the Roman view this is impossible because the little horn arises *after* the glory days of the Roman Empire.

But there are other reasons why this "little horn," in distinction from the "little horn" in Daniel 8, cannot be identified with Antiochus IV. Whereas the little horn in Daniel 8 came out of one of the *four* horns (8:9) that remained from the kingdom of Greece (8:21), the little horn in Daniel 7 came up among the *ten* horns that remained from the fourth beast and uprooted three of them (7:7-8).[51]

In contrast to the four *beasts*, the little horn is described as a *human* being with "eyes like human eyes . . . , and a mouth speaking arrogantly" (7:8, 20). Young suggests that "these features seem to point to an intelligence which is directed toward the overthrow of the kingdom of God."[52] But God's judgment will strike down the little horn. The angel explains that "the court shall sit in judgment, and his dominion shall be taken away, to be consumed and totally destroyed. The kingship and dominion and the greatness of the kingdoms under the whole heaven shall be given to the people of the holy ones of the Most High; their kingdom shall be an everlasting kingdom . . ." (7:26-27; cf. 7:11).

The angel's interpretation places the little horn in the last days, just before

---

51. For more differences, see Chapter 8 below, pp. 257-58. See also Young, *Prophecy of Daniel*, 276-79, and Steinmann, *Daniel*, 151-54. See pp. 151-53 and 376-79 for Steinmann's critique of higher-critical interpretations of the little horn and pp. 380-84 for his critique of dispensational premillennial interpretations.

52. Young, *Prophecy of Daniel*, 278.

the final judgment and the arrival of the everlasting kingdom of God. Therefore the little horn may be identified as the person Paul calls "the Man of Lawlessness" (2 Thess 2:3) and John calls "the Antichrist" (1 John 2:18, 22; 4:3; 2 John 7). John writes that "the spirit of the antichrist . . . is already in the world" (1 John 4:3) because "it is the last hour!" (1 John 2:18). Paul agrees that "the mystery of lawlessness is already at work, but only until the one who now restrains it is removed. And then the lawless one will be revealed, whom the Lord Jesus will destroy with the breath of his mouth, annihilating him by the manifestation of his coming" (2 Thess 2:7-8).[53]

In the light of the New Testament, therefore, we can identify the little horn with the Antichrist whose spirit is already at work in this world through its forerunners but whose full attack on God's people still lies in the future.[54] This final tribulation will be followed by "the Lord Jesus . . . annihilating him by the manifestation of his coming" (2 Thess 2:8) and establishing his perfect kingdom on earth (cf. Matt 24:29-31; 25:31-34; Rev. 7:14-17). This understanding of the little horn and his end is in harmony with Nebuchadnezzar's dream: "A stone was cut out, *not by human hands,* and it struck the statue on its feet of iron and clay and broke them in pieces. . . . *In the days of those kings* the God of heaven will set up a kingdom that shall *never be destroyed*" (2:34, 44).

One Like a Human Being

The phrase "one like a human being" has probably elicited more scholarly debate than any other phrase in Daniel.[55] Daniel 7:13-14 describes the one like a human being as follows:

> I saw one like a human being
>> coming with the clouds of heaven.
> And he came to the Ancient One
>> and was presented before him.
> To him was given dominion and glory and kingship,
>> that all peoples, nations, and languages should serve him.
> His dominion is an everlasting dominion
>> that shall not pass away,

---

53. On John's use of "the Antichrist" and Paul's use of "the Man of Lawlessness," see Hoekema, *The Bible and the Future,* 157-63. On Paul's "Man of Lawlessness," see also Herman Ridderbos, *Paul: An Outline of His Theology,* 514-21.

54. See further under "Longitudinal Themes," pp. 229-31 below.

55. See the lengthy "short list" of works on the identity of this figure compiled by Steinmann, *Daniel,* 355, n. 53.

and his kingship is one
    that shall never be destroyed.

The NRSV notes that the Aramaic for "one like a human being" is literally "one like a son of man." The NIV translates, "one like a son of man," with a note, "The Aramaic phrase *bar 'ĕnāš* means *human being*. The phrase *son of man* is retained here [in the NIV] because of its use in the New Testament as a title of Jesus, probably based largely on this verse."

Collins states, "There is nearly universal consensus that the phrase 'one like a son of man' means simply 'one like a human being'. . . . the general sense of 'someone, anyone.'"[56] In other words, in Daniel it is not a title for a special person, though later[57] it will become precisely that. Still, it is significant that this figure in Daniel is "*like* a son of man," "*like* a human being," in contrast to the first three characters who were like animals: "like a lion," "resembling a bear" and "like a leopard" (vv. 4-6).

The description of this figure "like a human being *coming with the clouds of heaven*" sets up a further contrast with the "four great beasts [who] came up out of the *sea*" (7:3) — the biblical symbol for chaos and disorder. This human-like figure comes "with[58] the clouds of *heaven*." The prophets and psalmists picture God as riding on the clouds: "See, the LORD is riding on a swift cloud and comes to Egypt" (Isa 19:1); "Sing to God, sing praises to his name; lift up a song to him who rides upon the clouds" (Ps 68:4); "You [LORD] make the clouds your chariot" (Ps 104:3; cf. Ps 18:9-12).[59] The clouds, therefore, signal that this human-like figure is divine.

Daniel reveals still more about the "one like a son of man": "To him was given dominion and glory and kingship, that all peoples, nations, and languages should serve him. His dominion is an everlasting dominion that shall not pass away, and his kingship is one that shall never be destroyed" (7:14). As the beasts represent kings ruling over human kingdoms (7:17), so the "one like a son of man" will be a king ruling over a kingdom. He will receive his dominion after the human kings and kingdoms have been judged (7:11-12). But in contrast

---

56. Collins, *Daniel,* 304, 305.

57. Lucas, *Daniel,* 184, mentions "*1 Enoch* 37-71, the NT and 2 Esdras/4 Ezra 13."

58. Collins, *Daniel,* 311, n. 297, acknowledges that "clouds are associated with the Deity in a wide variety of ways in the Hebrew Bible, and the association is not dependent on the use of a preposition 'on' (Yahweh appears *in* a cloud in Exod 19:9; 34:5; Num 11:25)." Cf. Lucas, *Daniel,* 184.

59. See also God guiding Israel through the desert "in a pillar of cloud by day, to lead them along the way" (Exod 13:21; 14:19, 24). Later "Mount Sinai was wrapped in smoke because the LORD had descended upon it in fire" (Exod 19:18). Still later the cloud covered "the tent of meeting, and the glory of the LORD filled the tabernacle" (Exod 40:34).

to the human kings, "his dominion is an everlasting dominion" and his kingdom "shall never be destroyed" (7:14).

Proponents of the Greek view have identified this "one like a son of man" with a variety of figures. Some argue for Judas Maccabee, others for a collective symbol for the holy ones, and still others for a heavenly being, either the archangel Michael or Gabriel.[60] In the context of the New Testament, however, it is not so difficult to establish the identity of the "one like a son of man" since Jesus clearly identifies himself as the son of man of Daniel 7. James Dunn concludes that "Jesus himself used *bar 'ĕnāš* with reference to himself and was the first to combine it with allusion to Daniel 7:13."[61]

But some object, "Since the figure in Daniel 7 is not called a messiah (unlike his counterpart in the *Similitudes of Enoch*) and there is no identifiable reference in the book to the restoration of the Davidic line, the messianic interpretation must be regarded as unwarranted."[62] However, the first rule of biblical hermeneutics is that a text must be understood in its historical and canonical contexts. Therefore, even if Daniel did not clearly envision the coming Messiah from David's line, in the New Testament Jesus identifies himself with the Son of Man Daniel had described: like a son of man (a human being), yet, like God (divine), coming with the clouds of heaven and receiving a kingdom that "shall never be destroyed."[63]

As a matter of fact, Jesus himself clearly connected the messianic promise of Psalm 110:1, "The LORD says to my lord, 'Sit at my right hand . . . ,'" with the "son of man" of Daniel 7. When the high priest asked Jesus, "Are you the Messiah, the Son of the Blessed One?" Jesus responded, "I am; and you will see the

---

60. See Collins, *Daniel*, 308-10. Redditt, *Daniel*, 127, offers a "sampling" of many authors and their identifications of the "one like a human being": the Davidic king, a priestly figure, the high priest, a faithful subgroup in Israel, Israel, the divine kingdom, the Messiah, angels or glorified Israelites, the angel Michael, the angel Gabriel.

61. Dunn, "The Danielic Son of Man in the New Testament," 546. See also Shepherd, "Daniel 7:13 and the New Testament Son of Man," *WTJ* 68 (2006) 99-111.

62. Collins, *Daniel*, 309. Cf. von Rad, *Old Testament Theology*, II, 312, "Apocalyptic ideas are far removed from the tradition of the Davidic Messiah — the anointed one of the prophets comes from the line of David and from Bethlehem (Mic 5:2), and not down from heaven; but at the same time there can be no doubt that the son of man described in Dan 7:13 is initially presented as a Messianic figure in the wider sense of the term."

63. This does not mean that we are reading Jesus back into Daniel 7. For example, when an Old Testament passage has a messianic promise such as Isaiah 9:6 ("For a child has been born for us, a son given to us; authority rests upon his shoulders. . . ."), we do not read the later fulfillment back into the earlier promise; rather, we move forward in the Bible/redemptive history from the promise to its later fulfillment with the birth of Jesus. Just so, we do not read Jesus, the Son of Man, back into Daniel's "son of man"; rather, we move forward in the Bible/redemptive history to Jesus, who identifies himself as the "Son of Man." See, e.g., Luke 1:33; Matthew 28:18; John 3:13; Ephesians 1:20-23; 1 Peter 3:21-22; Revelation 1:5; 3:21; 5:9-13.

Son of Man [Dan 7] seated at the right hand of power [Ps 110] and 'coming with the clouds of heaven' [Dan 7]" (Mark 14:61-62).[64]

Jesus also linked his Second Coming to the suffering of the last days. Jesus said, "But in those days, after that suffering, the sun will be darkened, and the moon will not give its light. . . . Then they will see 'the Son of Man coming in clouds' with great power and glory. Then he will send out the angels, and gather his elect from the four winds, from the ends of the earth to the ends of heaven" (Mark 13:24-27). The book of Revelation takes over this theme from Daniel and Jesus: "Look! He is coming with the clouds; every eye will see him, even those who pierced him" (Rev. 1:7).[65]

The Holy Ones

The referent of the phrase "the holy ones," or "the holy ones of the Most High," is also widely disputed.[66] The phrase occurs in Daniel 7:18, 22, 25, and 27. The traditional interpretation was that "the holy ones" referred to "the saints," God's holy people. But many critical scholars think that "the holy ones" should be identified as angels. The main reason for this opinion is that elsewhere in Daniel (in Aramaic in 4:13, 17, 23; and in Hebrew in 8:13) this phrase refers to heavenly beings[67] (but see Dan 12:7 on p. 224). Collins argues, "In view of the clear use of 'holy ones' to refer to angels in the Book of Daniel itself, we must expect that it carries that reference in chapter 7."[68] But if this chapter was written to encourage the Jews in their battle against Antiochus IV, as these scholars claim, there would be little comfort in a message that angels will receive the kingdom (7:18, 22, 27).

More importantly, although the Old Testament frequently uses the adjective "holy" as a substantive noun, "holy ones," to refer to angels, it can also refer

---

64. Block, "When Nightmares Cease," *CTJ* 41 (2006) 113, observes that "the image of the Ancient of Days handing over authority to the Son of Man is reminiscent of Psalm 2, where Yahweh answers the rebellion of the nations by handing authority over them to his adopted Son, the Davidic king. This interpretation is reinforced by the use of singular pronouns in Daniel 7:27 (contra NRSV, ESV), and confirmed by the New Testament, particularly the 'little apocalypses' of the Gospels . . . (Matt 24:29-31; cf. Mark 13:26; Luke 21:27)." See also p. 248, n. 159 below.

65. Cf. Acts 1:11, "This Jesus, who has been taken up from you into heaven, will come in the same way as you saw him go into heaven."

66. "The phrase 'the holy ones of the Most High' has produced almost as much debate as the phrase 'one like a human being.'" Lucas, *Daniel,* 191.

67. For other reasons and counterarguments, see Hasel, "The Identity of 'The Saints of the Most High' in Daniel 7," *Bib* 56 (1975) 173-92; Steinmann, *Daniel,* 366-70; and Lucas, *Daniel,* 191-92.

68. Collins, *Daniel,* 317.

to God's people.[69] For example, Psalm 16:3 clearly refers to God's people: "As for the holy ones in the land, they are the noble, in whom is all my delight."[70] Psalm 34:9 also uses "holy ones" to refer to God's people: "O fear the LORD, you his holy ones, for those who fear him have no want." If, then, "holy ones" can mean either angels or God's people, there is no reason to insist that in Daniel 7 the "holy ones" must be angels. The context will have to decide.

In Daniel 7:21 and 25 we read, "This horn made war with the holy ones and was *prevailing* over them. . . . He shall speak words against the Most High, shall *wear out* the holy ones of the Most High . . . , and they shall be *given into his power* for a time, two times, and half a time." It is incongruous to think that angels should be worn out by the little horn and that they should be in his power for a short time.[71] It makes much more sense to identify "the holy ones" of Daniel 7 with the holy people of God.

In fact, the expanded phrase in 7:27 makes clear that the "holy ones" are God's people: "The greatness of the kingdoms under the whole heaven shall be given to the *people* of the holy ones of the Most High." "'People' (*'am*) must refer to human beings, not angels (so uniformly in the OT)."[72] According to Steinmann, the phrase "to the people of the holy ones of the Most High" means that the greatness of the kingdoms shall be given "to (the) people [comma], the saints of the Most High": "'The people' consist of 'the saints of the Most High.'"[73]

Moreover, as Hasel points out, "There is a direct connection between 'the holy ones' (saints) of the apocalyptic vision of chapter 7 and the *'am-qōdeš*,

69. Goldingay, *Daniel*, 178, writes that "Daniel 7 is too allusive to enable us to decide with certainty whether the holy ones are celestial beings, earthly beings, or both." Cf. Longman, *Daniel*, 188-89, "In the Aramaic *(qaddîsê 'elyônîn)* and in the context of its use in the Dead Sea scrolls and elsewhere in Daniel (4:13; 8:13), the phrase refers to angelic beings. . . . Nonetheless, the phrase can refer to human beings as well, and perhaps is best understood to imply both God's human and angelic creatures."

70. A note in the *NIV Study Bible* refers to Psalm 101 as a confession of such a holy one.

71. Especially if that "little horn" is identified with Antiochus IV. Cf. Redditt, *Daniel*, 128, "Hartman and Di Lella (*The Book of Daniel*, 95) are correct that it seems implausible that Daniel 7 portrayed an attack on angels by Antiochus, who controlled them for three and a half years and changed their laws, though Collins (*Daniel*, 320) argues that is precisely what v. 25 means. It seems better to understand the 'holy ones' in vv. 25 and 27 as Israel, or perhaps a righteous subgroup within Israel."

72. Poythress, "The Holy Ones of the Most High in Daniel VII," *VT* 26/2 (1976) 209. Cf. Lederach, *Daniel*, 164, "When the writer refers to *people of the holy ones* (7:27; 8:24) or *holy people* (12:7), the word *people ('am)* is added to a form of the word *holy*. . . . Early in Israel's history, the concept of a holy people was applied to the Israelites . . . (Exod 19:5-6; cf. Dan 12:7)."

73. Steinmann, *Daniel*, 369, 364. Cf. Redditt, *Daniel*, 128, "The phrase 'the people of the holy ones of the Most High' should be taken, not as a genitive of possession, but as an appositional construct phrase, to be translated 'the people, i.e. the holy ones of the Most High' (Hartman and Di Lella, *The Book of Daniel*, 95)."

'the holy people,' in 12:7." In both 7:25 and 12:7 they are persecuted for "a time, two times, and half a time."[74] There is good evidence within Daniel, therefore, that the phrase "the holy ones" refers not to angels but to God's people. Thus the NASB translates this phrase as "saints," while the NIV translates it as "holy people."

If there should be any ambiguity left as to the identity of "the holy ones" — this is, after all, apocalyptic literature — subsequent revelation may offer greater clarity or confirmation of correct interpretation. Three times Daniel 7 reiterates that the holy ones will receive the kingdom: "The holy ones of the Most High shall receive the kingdom and possess the kingdom forever"; "The holy ones gained possession of the kingdom"; and "The kingship and domin-ion and the greatness of the kingdoms under the whole heaven shall be given to the people of the holy ones of the Most High" (7:18, 22, 27). In the New Testa-ment, Jesus declares, "Blessed are the poor in spirit, for theirs is the *kingdom of heaven*. . . . Blessed are the meek, for they will inherit *the earth*" (Matt 5:3, 5). Je-sus also says, "When the Son of Man comes in his glory, . . . he will sit on the throne of his glory. . . . Then the king will say to those at his right hand, 'Come, you that are blessed by my Father, inherit the *kingdom* prepared for you from the foundation of the world'" (Matt 25:31, 34). Another time Jesus tells his disci-ples, "You are those who have stood by me in my trials; and I confer on you, just as my Father has conferred on me, a *kingdom*, so that you may eat and drink at my table in my kingdom, and you will sit on thrones [cf. Dan 7:9] judging the twelve tribes of Israel" (Luke 22:29-30). And Paul writes that God the Father "has rescued us from the power of darkness and transferred us into the *king-dom* of his beloved Son . . ." (Col 1:13; cf. Rev. 1:6). Thus the New Testament con-firms that "the holy ones" who will receive the kingdom are not angels but God's people.

Theocentric Interpretation

Although the focus in this vision initially seems to be on human kingdoms and activities, God is active not only behind the scenes but especially at the final judgment and the consummation of history. We see God at work behind the scenes especially in the "divine passives." The lion's "wings were plucked off, and it was lifted up from the ground . . . , and a human mind was given to it" (7:4). God plucked off the wings of Nebuchadnezzar by turning him into an an-imal and later restored him, lifting him up and giving him a human mind again (see Dan 4:31-36). The bear "was raised up on one side," and it "was told, 'Arise,

---

74. Hasel, "The Identity of 'The Saints of the Most High' in Daniel 7," *Bib* 56 (1975) 191.

devour many bodies'" (7:5). God raised up Persia and authorized the Medo-Persian Empire to conquer many nations.[75]

It puzzles us that God would authorize war — and it was no less puzzling for Israel. How could God allow their king and the kingdom of Judah to fall into the power of Nebuchadnezzar (Dan 1:2-3)? Why would God "rouse the Chaldeans" to "gather captives like sand" (Hab 1:6, 9)? Habakkuk cried out, "Why do you look on the treacherous, and are silent when the wicked swallow those more righteous than they?" (Hab 1:13; cf. Isa 28:21 about God's "alien work"). There are no easy answers, but if God is indeed sovereign, he must somehow control and allow even evil to take place (cf. Dan 2:21). Daniel 7:8 states that God plucked up three of the earlier horns to make room for the little horn (they "were plucked up").[76] But God is also involved in the judgment of the little horn ("an Ancient One" takes his throne), and "the beast was put to death, and its body [was] destroyed and [was] given over to be burned with fire" (7:11). "Who kills the creature is . . . unstated; the passive verb again implies it is God or his agent."[77]

Next Daniel reports that the dominion of the rest of the beasts "was taken away" and that "dominion and glory and kingship" "was given" to the one like a son of man (7:12-14). Again, the passives imply that it was God who took away the dominion of the human, earthly kingdoms and gave it and more to the one who came with the clouds of heaven. When the little horn makes war with the holy ones and prevails over them, the Ancient One interferes: "then judgment was given *for* the holy ones of the Most High" (v. 22); God judges in their favor and gives them the kingdom. In his interpretation of the vision, the angel reports that the little horn "shall speak words against the Most High" (v. 25), but when the court sits in judgment, "his dominion shall be taken away" and "the kingship and dominion . . . shall be given to the people of the holy ones of the Most High" (vv. 26-27). In other words, God shall take the kingdom away from the Antichrist and give his "everlasting kingdom" to his people, "the holy ones of the Most High."

Textual Theme and Goal

The theme of this chapter will be very similar to the theme of its twin chapter, Daniel 2, the dream of the great statue of metals that is brought down by a

---

75. "The command is given by God, thus showing that Divine Providence overruled in the affairs of the mighty human kingdom." Young, *Prophecy of Daniel,* 145.

76. "The passive [in v. 8] suggests the action of God (as in vv. 4, 5, 6), who clears the way for the small horn by removing three others." Goldingay, *Daniel,* 164.

77. Ibid., 189.

stone. We formulated the theme of that chapter as, "The God of heaven, who deposes and sets up kings, reveals that in the end he will replace all human kingdoms with his everlasting kingdom." In order to formulate a textually specific theme for this passage, we need to concentrate on how Daniel 7 differs from Daniel 2. We have noted that the human kingdoms in Daniel 7 are much more sinister and evil: they are not precious metals but hideous beasts coming up out of the sea. Moreover, the fourth kingdom is described in much more detail: the terrifying monster has ten horns, and then there appears a little horn with "eyes like human eyes . . . , and a mouth speaking arrogantly" (7:8). Instead of the stone crushing the statue of human kingdoms, here the vision is very specific that the holy God seats himself on the judgment throne, opens the books, and has this evil beast destroyed by fire (7:9-12). Then, instead of the stone becoming a great mountain that fills the whole earth (2:35), one like a son of man comes with the clouds of heaven and receives the everlasting kingdom (7:13-14).[78] Thus the focus in this chapter is much more on this divine humanlike person receiving the everlasting kingdom of God.[79]

In the sequel of the vision and its interpretation, Daniel reveals still more details of the last days. The little horn defies God himself and makes war on God's people. He seems to win this battle, but God intervenes, sits in judgment, and totally destroys this evil ruler (7:21-22, 25-26). Then God gives his everlasting kingdom to his people (7:18, 22, 27).[80] We can, therefore, formulate the theme of Daniel 7 as follows: *After the final judgment in which God will destroy the last defiant ruler, God will give his everlasting kingdom to the divine son of man and to God's people.*

The author's goal with this message was not to satisfy people's curiosity in the twenty-first century about the end times. God's people were suffering in exile, far away from the Promised Land. They felt abandoned by God and were losing all hope. Daniel's goal with this message was *to reassure God's people in exile that their sovereign God is in control of evil empires and will in the end give his people his everlasting kingdom through a divine son of man.*[81]

78. "The poetic form of vv. 13-14 then serves to emphasize the establishing of the everlasting kingship as the climax of the vision." Lucas, *Daniel*, 165.

79. "The structure of this chapter makes clear what it is that the author wants to emphasize. Both the central place it holds in the palinstrophic structure of the main vision report, and its poetic form, highlight the importance of the throne scene." Ibid.

80. "The judgment of the small horn and the establishing of the everlasting kingship also form the climax of the interpretation of the vision given in the second half of the chapter." Ibid. Cf. Hill, "Daniel," 129, "The repetition of the judgment of the 'little horn' and the establishment of the everlasting kingdom in the interpretation of the dream (vv. 26-27) reiterate the climax of Daniel's symbolic vision."

81. "The chaos that results from the kingdoms of this world exercising their power is not the last word. The court of heaven sits in judgment on the beasts of history. They are destroyed,

Ways to Preach Christ

Although the "son of man" connection seems to be the most obvious way to Christ in the New Testament, we shall again demonstrate this Christocentric method by checking all legitimate ways to Christ. Since this passage has no type of Christ and there is no contrast with the message of the New Testament, we can concentrate on the remaining five ways.

Redemptive-Historical Progression

For Daniel and Israel in exile the message that God will give his everlasting kingdom to a divine son of man and God's people was still in the distant future. More evil empires will come and go before God will destroy the last defiant ruler and bring in his everlasting kingdom. But since Judah's exile in the sixth century B.C., redemptive history has moved forward. During the reign of the terrifying fourth beast, God sent his Son Jesus to this earth. The angel Gabriel announced his birth: "He will be great, and will be called the Son of the Most High, and *the Lord God will give to him the throne* of his ancestor David. He will reign over the house of Jacob *forever,* and *of his kingdom there will be no end*" (Luke 1:32-33).

Jesus' arrival on earth was the beginning of the fulfillment of Daniel's vision about the distant future. Jesus' disciples at first thought it was the complete fulfillment. After his resurrection they asked Jesus, "Lord, is this the time when you will restore the kingdom?" Jesus replied, "It is not for you to know the times or periods that the Father has set by his own authority. But you will receive power when the Holy Spirit has come upon you; and you will be my witnesses in Jerusalem, in all Judea and Samaria, and to the ends of the earth" (Acts 1:6-8). Jesus sent his disciples on a mission to the ends of the earth. We see the stone of Nebuchadnezzar's dream becoming a great mountain that will fill "the whole earth" (Dan 2:35). Having given his disciples their assignment, Jesus ascended to his throne in heaven,[82] "and a *cloud* took him out of their sight" (Acts 1:9). Two angels explained to the disciples that Jesus would return: "This Jesus, who has been taken up from you into heaven, will come *in the same way* as you saw him go into heaven" (Acts 1:11). The disciples learned that Jesus "will restore the kingdom" fully only at his Second Coming.

---

while the faithful saints receive the rule and dominion that only the Most High can give. No greater message of hope could be given to a people in exile, to a people enduring bitter persecution, or to the faithful today living in the midst of violence, bloodshed, and corruption!" Lederach, *Daniel,* 150.

82. Cf. Stephen's testimony: "Look, I see the heavens opened and the Son of Man standing at the right hand of God!" (Acts 7:56).

Peter later writes, "The Lord is not slow about his promise, as some think of slowness, but is patient with you, not wanting any to perish, but all to come to repentance. But the day of the Lord will come like a thief, and then the heavens will pass away with a loud noise, and the elements will be dissolved *with fire,* and the earth and everything that is done on it will be disclosed" (2 Pet 3:9-10). John writes about that time, "Look! He [Jesus Christ] is coming with the clouds; every eye will see him, even those who pierced him" (Rev. 1:7). And when the seventh angel blows his trumpet, John hears voices in heaven saying, "The kingdom of the world has become the kingdom of our Lord and of his Messiah, and he will reign *forever and ever*" (Rev. 11:15).

Promise-Fulfillment

Daniel 7 contains the vision and implied promise of "one like a son of man coming with the clouds of heaven" and receiving from God, "dominion and glory and kingship, that all peoples, nations, and languages should serve him. His dominion is an everlasting dominion . . ." (v. 14). In other words, God promised that he will give all authority to this person "like a son of man."

In the New Testament, Jesus claimed that he was the fulfillment of God's promise: Jesus identified himself as "the son of man" of Daniel 7 who had received all authority.[83] When some scribes questioned Jesus' authority to forgive sins, Jesus said, "the *Son of Man* has *authority* on earth to forgive sins" (Mark 2:10). After his resurrection Jesus declared, "*All authority* in heaven and on earth has been given to me" (Matt 28:18).[84]

Jesus, of course, frequently spoke of himself as "the Son of Man." As we noted earlier, Jesus himself connected the messianic promise of Psalm 110:1, "The LORD says to my lord, 'Sit at my right hand . . . ,'" with the son of man of Daniel 7. When the high priest asked Jesus, "Are you the Messiah, the Son of the Blessed One?" Jesus responded, "I am; and you will see *the Son of Man* [Dan 7] seated at the right hand of power [Ps 110] and 'coming with the clouds of

---

83. On the basis of "the fact that the Jesus tradition in effect confines the son of man/Son of Man motif exclusively to Jesus' own words," James Dunn concludes that "Jesus himself used *bar 'ĕnāš* with reference to himself and was the first to combine it with allusion to Dan 7:13." "The Danielic Son of Man in the New Testament," 546. See Miller, *Daniel,* 209-10, for further arguments for this identification from the New Testament itself and from the history of interpretation.

84. "Jesus' proclamation of the 'kingdom,' his frequent self-designation as 'the son of man,' and his claims of 'authority' (which are recognized by an astonished public and questioned by an increasingly worried opposition) constitute a collocation adumbrated by Dan 7:13-14, where the one 'like a son of man' receives 'kingdom' and 'authority.'" Evans, "Defeating Satan and Liberating Israel," *JSHJ* 1/2 (2003) 163.

heaven' [Dan 7]" (Mark 14:61-62). Jesus was speaking of his Second Coming. Jesus spoke further of the last days: "In those days, after that suffering, the sun will be darkened, and the moon will not give its light. . . . Then they will see *'the Son of Man coming in clouds'* with great power and glory. Then he will send out the angels, and gather his elect from the four winds, from *the ends of the earth* to the ends of heaven" (Mark 13:24-27).[85]

Analogy

As God in Daniel 7 promised his people the everlasting kingdom, so Jesus said, "Let the little children come to me; do not stop them; for it is to such as these that the *kingdom of God* belongs" (Mark 10:13). Jesus also said, "In my Father's house there are many dwelling places. . . . And if I go to prepare a place for you, I will come again and will take you to myself, so that where I am, there you may be also" (John 14:2-3). Paul also speaks of God the Father giving us his everlasting kingdom through Jesus: "He has rescued us from the power of darkness and transferred us into the *kingdom of his beloved Son,* in whom we have redemption, the forgiveness of sins" (Col 1:13-14). In addition, Peter encourages his readers to confirm their call and election, "for in this way, entry into the *eternal kingdom of our Lord and Savior Jesus Christ* will be richly provided for you" (2 Pet 1:11). Finally, the book of Revelation describes the new Jerusalem and promises that God's servants "will see his face" and "they will *reign forever and ever*" (Rev. 22:4-5).

We can also draw an analogy from Daniel's goal to reassure God's people that their sovereign God is in control of evil empires and will in the end give his people his everlasting kingdom. Jesus also reassures God's people suffering under Roman domination, "Do not be afraid, little flock, for it is your Father's good pleasure to give you the *kingdom*" (Luke 12:32).

Longitudinal Themes

We can also trace several subthemes (parts of the main theme) to Jesus Christ in the New Testament. We can trace the subtheme of God's coming kingdom from Daniel 7 to Jesus' announcement of the nearness of the kingdom (Mark 1:14-15), to his declaration that by casting out demons, "the kingdom of God has

---

85. See also Matthew 25:31-32 and Revelation 14:14, "Then I looked, and there was a white cloud, and seated on the cloud was one like the Son of Man, with a golden crown on his head, and a sharp sickle in his hand!"

come to you" (Matt 12:28). Yet Jesus also stated clearly that the fullness of God's kingdom still lies in the future. For example, when Jesus' disciples asked him to explain his parable of the weeds, he said, "The one who sows the good seed is the Son of Man; the field is the world, and the good seed are the children of the kingdom; the weeds are the children of the evil one, and the enemy who sowed them is the devil; the harvest is at *the end of the age . . .*" (Matt 13:37-43).[86] John reveals the final outcome: "Then I saw a new heaven and a new *earth;* for the first heaven and the first earth had passed away, and *the sea* was no more. . . . And I heard a loud voice from the throne saying, 'See, the home of God is among mortals'" (Rev. 21:1, 3). Then, as John put it earlier, "the kingdom of the world has become the kingdom of our Lord and of his Messiah, and he will reign forever and ever" (Rev. 11:15).

We can also trace the subtheme of God's final judgment from the Ancient One taking his throne and judging the fourth beast (Dan 7:9-11) to Jesus' declaration: "Just as the Father has life in himself, so he has granted the Son also to have life in himself; and he has given him authority to execute *judgment,* because he is the *Son of Man*" (John 5:26-27).[87] Jesus saw himself as the judge in the final judgment. He said, "When the *Son of Man* comes in his glory, and all the angels with him, then he will sit on the *throne* of his glory. All the nations will be gathered before him, and he will separate people one from another as a shepherd separates the sheep from the goats . . ." (Matt 25:31-32).[88] In fact, Jesus promised his disciples, "At the renewal of all things, when the *Son of Man* is seated on the *throne* of his glory, you who have followed me will also sit on twelve thrones, judging the twelve tribes of Israel" (Matt 19:28).[89]

It is also possible to trace the subtheme of the little horn who "shall speak words against the Most High, and shall wear out the holy ones of the Most High" from Daniel 7 to the New Testament figure of the Antichrist and from there to its counterpart, Jesus Christ. John speaks of the "Antichrist" in terms of realized eschatology when he writes, "Children, it is the last hour! As you have heard that antichrist is coming, so now many antichrists have come. . . . Who is

---

86. See further, e.g., Matthew 6:10; 19:28; 26:29; 28:18-20; Acts 1:6-11.

87. Cf. John 5:22, "The Father judges no one but has given all judgment to the Son." Cf. 2 Timothy 4:1.

88. Jesus explained his parable of the weeds as follows: "Just as the weeds are collected and burned up with fire, so will it be at the end of the age. The Son of Man will send his angels, and they will collect out of his kingdom all causes of sin and all evildoers, and they will throw them into the furnace of fire, where there will be weeping and gnashing of teeth. Then the righteous will shine like the sun in the kingdom of their Father" (Matt 13:40-43). Cf. 2 Corinthians 5:10, "All of us must appear before the judgment seat of Christ."

89. For the connections with Daniel 7:9-10, see Evans, "Daniel in the New Testament," 516-19.

the liar but the one who denies that Jesus is the Christ? This is the antichrist, the one who denies the Father and the Son" (1 John 2:18, 22; cf. 4:3; 2 John 7). Jesus, similarly, warns his disciples, "Beware that you are not led astray; for many will come in my name and say, 'I am he!' and 'The time is near!' Do not go after them" (Luke 21:8; cf. Matt 24:23-27).

Paul sees the "Antichrist" at work not only in the present time but especially at the end of time. Paul writes, "That day [of the Lord] will not come unless the rebellion comes first and the *lawless one* is revealed, the one destined for destruction. He opposes and exalts himself above every so-called god . . . , so that he takes his seat in the temple of God, *declaring himself to be God. . . .* The mystery of lawlessness is already at work, but only until the one who now restrains it is removed. And *then the lawless one will be revealed, whom the Lord Jesus will destroy* with the breath of his mouth, annihilating him by the manifestation of his coming" (2 Thess 2:3-8).

One can trace this subtheme further into the book of Revelation where John sees "a beast rising out of the sea, having ten horns. . . . The beast was given a *mouth uttering haughty and blasphemous words*, and it was allowed to exercise authority for forty-two months. . . . Also it was allowed to *make war on the saints and to conquer them*" (Rev. 13:1, 5, 7; cf. 11:7). John sees further that the ten horns, which are ten kings, "will make war on the Lamb, and the Lamb will conquer them, for he is Lord of lords and King of kings" (17:14). Then the beast will be thrown into "the lake of fire" (19:20). In tracing this theme of the little horn/"Antichrist" in the sermon, one must be careful not to lose sight of the main theme of this passage, which is that God will give his everlasting kingdom to the divine son of man and to God's people.

New Testament References

The appendix in the Greek New Testament lists some fifty-eight New Testament verses that cite or allude to Daniel 7, many of them in the book of Revelation.[90]

---

90. See Evans, "Daniel in the New Testament," 525-26. Dunn, "The Danielic Son of Man in the New Testament," 536, provides the following chart (continued on p. 232):

Daniel		Revelation
7:2	four winds	7:1
7:3	beasts from sea	13:1
7:4-6	lion, bear, leopard	13:2
7:6	given authority	13:2, 5, 7
7:7, 20	beast with 10 horns	12:3; 13:1
7:7, 21	destructive power	11:7; 13:7
7:8, 20	arrogant mouth	13:5

Several of these verses we have already used above to support the other ways to Christ in the New Testament. In addition, for Daniel 7:9 the appendix lists the description of the Son of Man in Revelation 1:14: "His head and his hair were white as white wool, white as snow." Other verses are connected to Daniel but do not link up with Christ.

Sermon Theme, Goal, and Need

We formulated the textual theme of Daniel 7 as, "After the final judgment in which God will destroy the last defiant ruler, God will give his everlasting kingdom to the divine son of man and to God's people." Since the New Testament does not contradict this message, we could make the textual theme the sermon theme. But in the light of the New Testament, we can now clarify a few terms for the sermon theme. As we saw above, the New Testament calls that last defiant ruler "the Antichrist" (1 John 2:18, 22; 4:3; 2 John 7) and the "Man of Lawlessness" (2 Thess 2:3). Therefore, we can substitute "the Antichrist" for "the last defiant ruler." Also, as we saw above, Jesus claims that he is Daniel's "son of man" who comes "with the clouds of heaven" and who will receive from God "dominion and glory and kingship, that all peoples, nations, and languages should serve him" (Dan 7:13-14). Therefore, we can substitute "Jesus, the divine Son of Man," for "a divine son of man." The sermon theme then becomes, *After the final judgment in which God will destroy the Antichrist, God will give his everlasting kingdom to Jesus, the divine Son of Man, and to God's people.*[91]

The author's goal we formulated as, "to reassure God's people in exile that their sovereign God is in control of evil empires and will in the end give his

Daniel		Revelation
7:9	white hair	1:14
7:9-10	throne, books opened	20:11-12
7:10	myriads before throne	5:11
7:13	son of man, clouds	1:13; 14:14
7:14, 18	kingdom, forever and ever	11:15
7:22	judgment of saints	20:4
7:24	10 horns interpreted	17:12
7:25	42 months	12:14; 13:5
7:27	saints reigning	20:4; 22:5

91. If one opts for a series of two sermons on Daniel 7, the first one on Daniel 7:1-18 could be prepared under the theme, "The succession of violent human kingdoms will end when God, after destroying the last human kingdom, gives his everlasting kingdom to Jesus, the divine Son of Man, and to God's people." The second sermon on Daniel 7:19-28 could be prepared under the theme, "Although the Antichrist will severely persecute God's people in the last days, God, after destroying the Antichrist, will give God's everlasting kingdom to his people."

people his everlasting kingdom through a divine son of man." With a few slight changes we can make this the goal for the sermon: *to reassure God's people today that their sovereign God is in control of evil kingdoms and will in the end give his everlasting kingdom to his people through his Son, Jesus Christ.*

This goal discloses the need that should be addressed in this sermon. Earthly kingdoms such as North Korea, Iran, Saudi Arabia, and Pakistan[92] still overtly persecute God's people today. In other nations the persecution may be more subtle, but all genuine Christians long for God's perfect kingdom on earth. Jesus promised to come again to establish this kingdom, but where is it? Christians have been waiting generation after generation for a long two-thousand years. Some are beginning to wonder if God is indeed in control and if his kingdom will ever come.

Sermon Exposition

As I was writing this chapter, the radio reported that some two hundred un-armed Christians were slaughtered near Jos, Nigeria. Many of them were women and children. Even a four-day-old baby. Ruthlessly cut down with ma-chetes. They are only a small number of the many Christians who are massa-cred around the world. It has been estimated that since 1990 an average of 160,000 Christians have been killed every year.[93] Thousands of others are im-prisoned, tortured, exiled, blacklisted, deprived of their property, or abused in more subtle ways.

When Jesus ascended into heaven, he promised to come again to establish his perfect kingdom on earth. But when persecution erupted, people began to ask, "Where is the promise of his coming?" (2 Pet 3:3). Especially in times of per-secution and after waiting some two thousand years, people still ask, "Where is the promise of his coming?" We long to see God's perfect kingdom on earth.

Israel experienced this same longing. God had punished them for their sins by sending them into exile in Babylon. "By the rivers of Babylon — there we sat down and there we wept when we remembered Zion" (Ps 137:1). How they longed to go back to the Promised Land. But they remained in captivity. A gen-eration came and a generation went, but they were still in captivity.

When their suffering reached a climax under the evil King Belshazzar, God gave Daniel a dream-vision of what was to come. It was a grand overview of hu-

---

92. For a fuller listing from 1997, see Marshall, *Their Blood Cries Out.*

93. The number of Christian martyrs in the twentieth century has been estimated at 45 million. See David Barrett and Todd M. Johnson, *World Christian Encyclopedia* (2d ed.; New York: Oxford University Press, 2001), I, 11.

man history. In the vision Daniel saw four human kingdoms, one coming after the other, and then finally the arrival of the perfect kingdom of God. Daniel had mentioned these four kingdoms before. Daniel 2 reports that King Nebuchadnezzar had a dream of a giant statue made up of four different metals: gold, silver, bronze, and iron. "A stone was cut out, not by human hands, and it struck the statue on its feet of iron and clay and broke them in pieces." Then the stone "became a great mountain and filled the whole earth" (2:34-35). Daniel explained to the king that Babylon was the head of gold. But Babylon would be replaced by another kingdom, the Medo-Persian Empire. And this kingdom in turn would be replaced by another, the Greek Empire. And finally the Roman Empire. "In the days of those kings," Daniel had said, "the God of heaven will set up a kingdom that shall never be destroyed" (2:44).

Some fifty years after God gave King Nebuchadnezzar his dream, God gave Daniel this dream-vision. Nebuchadnezzar had died and was succeeded by several other kings. The last king of Babylon was the evil King Belshazzar, who challenged God by drinking wine from the sacred temple vessels at his drunken party. We read in Daniel 7:1-3, "In the first year of King Belshazzar of Babylon, Daniel had a dream and visions of his head as he lay in bed. Then he wrote down[94] the dream: I, Daniel, saw in my vision by night the four winds of heaven stirring up the great sea, and four great beasts came up out of the sea, different from one another." The "four winds of heaven" cover the entire compass: north, south, east, and west. These winds from every direction of the compass are stirring up the great sea. "The turbulent, chaotic waters [are] moving in all directions."[95]

Then, as Daniel was watching, "four great beasts came up *out of the sea*, different from one another." In the Bible the sea is a symbol for chaos, disorder, and hostility to God. The turbulent great sea stands for the sea of sinful humanity which is in "a constant state of unrest, chaos, and turmoil."[96] The fact that these beasts come up out of the *sea* is the first clue that these beasts are evil: they stand for disorder and hostility to God.

Daniel also writes that these beasts are "different from one another." They

---

94. Writing down the vision "made a prophecy more solid, concrete, and certain of fulfillment; indeed, putting something into writing initiated its fulfillment. It also made prophecy, prophet, and God open to vindication." Goldingay, *Daniel*, 160. Hill, "Daniel," 132, adds, "The documentation of prophetic dreams, visions, and oracles made the prophecies more concrete and facilitated their dissemination to the intended audience."

95. Longman, *Daniel*, 180.

96. Miller, *Daniel*, 195. Cf. Isaiah 17:12-13; 57:20; and Jeremiah 6:23. Cf. Kvanzig, "The Relevance of the Biblical Visions of the End Time," *HBT* 11/1 (1989) 45, "The beasts are described in the same way as the Babylonians described and depicted their demons. These demons also came from the sea, which in the Babylonian imagination was a designation for the underworld."

are represented by different animals; they stand for four different kingdoms. Even today nations are represented by animals: the American eagle, the British lion, the Russian bear, and many others. But what Daniel sees are not ordinary animals. They are hybrids, mutants. This is the second clue that these beasts are evil. For, according to Genesis 1, God created creatures not as hybrids but "according to their kinds."[97] These hybrid beasts, these mutants, depict disorder. They represent "evil, malignant human kingdoms."[98]

Verse 4, "The first was like a lion and had eagles' wings." This is Babylon. The lion is the king of land animals and the eagle king of the birds. The Old Testament prophets compare King Nebuchadnezzar to a lion (e.g., Jer 4:7; 50:17, 44) and to an eagle (e.g., Jer 48:40; Ezek 17:3). Moreover, the major processional street in Babylon was lined with statues of lions with eagles' wings.[99] Winged lions also "guarded the gates of royal palaces among the Babylonians. Daniel had seen these figures ever since his deportation to Babylon. They were practically emblems of the Babylonian power."[100] The first beast, therefore, represents Babylon, the head of gold in Nebuchadnezzar's dream (Dan 2:38).

"Then," Daniel continues, "as I watched, its wings were plucked off, and it was lifted up from the ground and made to stand on two feet like a human being; and a human mind was given to it." We are reminded of the story in Daniel 4 that God punished the proud King Nebuchadnezzar by giving him "the mind of an animal" (4:16). His wings were plucked off.[101] He was stripped of his kingdom. He was no longer able to lead his conquering armies into battle. But when he "lifted his eyes to heaven" acknowledging God, God gave him back his human reason (4:34-36). He could again "stand on two feet like a human being; and a human mind was given" to him. But eventually King Nebuchadnezzar would die. Only twenty-three years after his death the Babylonian kingdom would fall to the kingdom of Medo-Persia.

Verse 5, "Another beast appeared, a second one, that looked like a bear. It was raised up on one side, had three tusks[102] in its mouth among its teeth and

97. Longman, *Daniel,* 183, with references to Genesis 1:11-12, 21, 24, 25. Because God created creatures "according to their kinds," Israel was forbidden to sow their vineyard "with a second kind of seed," to plow their fields "with an ox and a donkey yoked together," and to wear clothes "made of wool and linen woven together" (Deut 22:9-11).

98. Hill, "Daniel," 136.

99. See Young, *Messianic Prophecies,* 29. Archer, "Daniel," 86, adds, "The Ishtar Gate entrance was adorned on either side with a long procession of yellow lions on blue-glazed brick, fashioned in high relief."

100. Leupold, *Exposition of Daniel,* 288-89.

101. "This obviously connotes a loss of power, but it also prepares for the following transformation of the lion into human form." Collins, *Daniel,* 297.

102. The NIV translates, "It had three ribs in its mouth between its teeth." If they are ribs, they might denote conquered kings or kingdoms. "This corresponds perfectly to the three ma-

was told, 'Arise, devour many bodies!'" "The brown Syrian bear may weigh up to 250 kilos [550 pounds] and has a voracious appetite."[103] A bear is a powerful, frightening animal. But there is something odd about that bear. God[104] had raised up one side of the bear so that this side was higher than the other; it was a lopsided bear. This description of two sides matches the Medo-Persian kingdom, which consisted of Media, the lower side, and Persia, the higher, more dominant, side. So the lopsided bear is the same as the "chest and arms of silver" in Nebuchadnezzar's dream (2:32). God tells this beast: "Arise, devour many bodies!" God gives this kingdom permission to conquer many nations. God is in control, even of evil empires. As God earlier allowed the Babylonian kingdom to punish his disobedient people Israel by taking them into exile (1:2-4), so now God allows the Medo-Persian kingdom to conquer the kingdom of Babylon (see Jer 51:11-14, 28-33) and beyond. The Persian Empire stretched from Egypt and the Aegean Sea in the west to the Indus River in the east. "More territory was controlled by this empire than any other up until that time."[105]

Verse 6, "After this, as I watched, another appeared, like a leopard. The beast had four wings of a bird on its back and four heads; and dominion was given to it." A leopard is one of the fastest animals in the animal kingdom. But with the addition of four wings, this animal would be incredibly fast. This speedy leopard represents the kingdom of Greece, "the middle and thighs of bronze" in Nebuchadnezzar's dream (2:32). Alexander the Great of Macedonia conquered the then-known world at an amazing speed. He "invaded Asia Minor in 334 B.C. and within ten short years (by the age of thirty-two) had conquered the entire Medo-Persian Empire to the borders of India. According to legend, he then wept because there were no more lands to conquer."[106]

At the end of verse 6 Daniel states that "dominion was given" to this third

---

jor conquests the Medes and Persians made under the leadership of King Cyrus and his son Cambyses: viz., the Lydian kingdom in Asia Minor (which fell to Cyrus in 546), the Chaldean Empire (which he annexed in 539), and the kingdom of Egypt (which Cambyses acquired in 525)." Archer, "Daniel," 86. If they are three "tusks," they might denote prominent Persian kings. Commentators offer widely divergent identifications. Calvin wisely counsels, "Those who understand three definite kingdoms by the three ribs seem to refine far too minutely." *Commentaries on Daniel*, II, 16. Certainly in sermons one should avoid such details since it will detract from the main message.

103. Baldwin, *Daniel*, 139.

104. Divine passives here and throughout this passage. See "Theocentric Interpretation" on pp. 224-25 above. See also p. 155, n. 27 above and n. 110 below.

105. Miller, *Daniel*, 199.

106. Ibid. Montgomery, *Book of Daniel*, 289, identifies this rapid conquest as "the velocity of [the Persian] Cyrus' conquests." Miller, *Daniel*, 200, n. 27, responds: "The description of this empire undoubtedly suits Alexander's swift conquest and lust for new territories far better than the activities of Cyrus."

kingdom. Who gave dominion to Alexander the Great? No one else but God. God controls the nations. And God gave dominion to Alexander the Great. "No other explanation can account for the fact that Alexander's thirty-thousand man army was able to conquer Persian armies of several hundreds of thousands."[107]

Verse 6 also mentions that this beast had four heads. "In Scripture 'heads' may represent rulers or governments."[108] When Alexander died at a young age, the Greek Empire did indeed split into "four heads," four rulers who each ruled over a part of Alexander's empire: Ptolemy, Seleucus, Lysimachus, and Cassander.

But a fourth world empire is yet to come. It is so ruthless and evil that there is no voracious beast to which it can be likened. Daniel can only describe how evil it looks and acts. Verse 7, "After this I saw in the visions by night a fourth beast, *terrifying* and *dreadful* and *exceedingly strong*. It had *great iron teeth* and was devouring, breaking in pieces [*crushing*], and *stamping* what was left with its feet." This monster uses its great iron teeth to break in pieces everything in its path. What is left it stamps and crushes with its feet. Total destruction!

This is the kingdom of iron of Nebuchadnezzar's dream. In chapter 2 Daniel had said of this kingdom: "There shall be a fourth kingdom, *strong* as *iron;* just as iron *crushes* and smashes everything, it shall *crush and shatter* all these" (2:40).[109] We see the Roman legions marching across the world, breaking in pieces what was left of the Greek Empire, forcing regions in Asia, Africa, and Europe to submit to the Caesar in Rome.

This monster, Daniel says, "was different from all the beasts that preceded it."[110] "Rome possessed a power and longevity unlike anything the world had ever known. Nations were crushed under the iron boot of the Roman legions, its power was virtually irresistible, and the extent of its influence surpassed the other three kingdoms."[111]

At the end of verse 7 Daniel notes that this monster "had ten horns." The leopard, we have seen, had four heads. After the death of Alexander the Great, the Greek Empire did indeed break into four sections, each ruled by one of Alexander's generals. This fourth beast, Daniel says, has *ten horns*. As the Greek

---

107. Feinberg, *Daniel,* 88.

108. Miller, *Daniel,* 200, with references to Daniel 2:38; Isaiah 7:8-9; and Revelation 13:3, 12.

109. See p. 204, n. 11 above.

110. Daniel repeats the fact that it was *different* in 7:19, 23, and 24. Whereas he describes the other beasts by means of passive verbs, "so that the emphasis has been on what God does to them, says to them, and gives them," this fourth beast "is characterized by means of active verbs, so that the emphasis is on its own deeds. The way is thus prepared for the action of God that directly confronts the self-initiated action of the fourth creature." Goldingay, *Daniel,* 163. Seow, *Daniel,* 105, adds, "These pernicious creatures seem to have become increasingly bold in their activity and in asserting their independence from the source of all dominion and power."

111. Miller, *Daniel,* 201.

Empire broke into four sections, so the Roman Empire will eventually split into ten kingdoms.[112] This will be a *second* phase of the Roman empire, ten kings or kingdoms. Horns symbolize strength, so they will still be strong kingdoms. Ten is the number of fullness, so we should probably think of this second phase as consisting of a full number of kingdoms coming out of the Roman Empire.

Then there will be a short, final phase.[113] Verse 8, "I was considering the horns, when another horn appeared, a little one coming up among them; to make room for it, three of the earlier horns were plucked up by the roots. There were eyes like human eyes in this horn, and a mouth speaking arrogantly." In contrast to the large beasts and the ten horns, this horn is described as being "little." But don't let that fool you. This little horn is extremely smart and persuasive. In contrast to the four *beasts,* this little horn is described as a *human* being: "eyes like human eyes." In the Bible, eyes "function as instruments of observation and learning and are therefore appropriately symbolic of intelligence, insight, and wisdom. . . . This individual will be extremely intelligent and clever."[114] He also has "a mouth speaking arrogantly [literally, "great things"]." The little horn is evil personified. He is so dangerous precisely because he is intelligent and speaks persuasively. We'll hear more about this little horn later.

From the succession of evil human kingdoms, verse 9 takes us to the next scene: God's judgment.[115] "The balanced poetry conveys the order and beauty which surround the divine judge as opposed to the chaos of the sea and its beasts."[116]

> As I watched,
> thrones[117] were set in place,
> > and an Ancient One took his throne,

112. See also the explanation of the angel in verse 24: "As for the ten horns, out of this kingdom ten kings shall arise."

113. For these three phases, see Young, *Messianic Prophecies,* 31-32, 35-36.

114. Miller, *Daniel,* 202, with references to Zechariah 3:9; 4:10; and Revelation 4:6; 5:6.

115. "The opening phrase of v. 9 implies a continuity of perspective: Daniel continues to look in the direction he had been looking. That the scene takes place on earth is presupposed by v. 22 (the one advanced in years *came*)." Goldingay, *Daniel,* 164-65.

116. Baldwin, *Daniel,* 141.

117. For the various interpretations of the plural "thrones," see Lucas, *Daniel,* 181-82. Steinmann, *Daniel,* 350-51, gives it a messianic interpretation in that "the Son of Man (7:13) will occupy a throne beside God the Father," and "in light of the fuller revelation to come in the NT," he suggests "thrones set up that are for the Ancient of Days (7:9), the Son of Man (7:13), and the saints of the Most High (7:18)." In the sermon I would not make too much of the plural "thrones." Daniel sees only the Ancient One taking his throne. I agree with Leupold, *Exposition of Daniel,* 303: "For whom were the remaining thrones intended? As far as Daniel's account of the proceeding is concerned, he does not venture to place anyone on these thrones. It seems best to let it go at that."

his clothing was white as snow,
  and the hair of his head like pure wool;
his throne was fiery flames,
  and its wheels were burning fire.

Up to this point God had been working behind the scenes, but now we see God actively in control of his creation.[118] "An Ancient One," that is, the eternal God,[119] takes his throne. It is the throne of judgment. God will judge the nations. God is described as having clothing "white as snow." The color white is a symbol for purity and holiness. The hair of his head is also white,[120] "like pure wool." So in contrast to the evil human kingdoms, God is depicted as absolutely pure and holy.

"His throne," we read, "was fiery flames, and its wheels were burning fire." Fire, too, is a symbol for God's holiness. Think of Moses at the burning bush: "Moses, Moses! . . . Remove the sandals from your feet, for the place on which you are standing is *holy* ground" (Exod 3:4-5). "Fire is a symbol for the numinous, awe-inspiring divine presence."[121] But fire is also a symbol for God's judgment. Moses told Israel, "The LORD your God is a devouring fire, a jealous God" (Deut 4:24; cf. Heb 12:29).[122] Malachi (3:2-3) said of Israel's God, "He is like a refiner's fire . . . ; he will . . . refine them like gold and silver, until they present offerings to the LORD in righteousness." When Daniel writes about an Ancient One taking his throne and that his throne is fiery flames, therefore, he is writing about the great day of judgment.

Interestingly, God's throne is also described as having wheels. This means that God's judgment is not confined to only one place. As God is present everywhere, so his judgment is present everywhere.[123] There is no place to hide from God, no place to escape his judgment.

---

118. See Calvin, *Commentaries on Daniel*, II, 33.

119. "There is perhaps an allusion to the notion of God's existing from eternity (Isa 41:4; Ps 90:2; 93:2; 102:25-28 [24-27]; Job 36:26)." Goldingay, *Daniel*, 165. Cf. Harman, *Study Commentary on Daniel*, 168, "Probably in this context the use of 'ancient' is intended to contrast the ephemeral nature of the earthly kingdoms with the enduring nature of God and his kingdom."

120. Synonymous parallelism between the clothing and the hair would argue for both being white as snow. Cf. Revelation 1:13-14, "In the midst of the lampstands I saw one like the Son of Man. . . . His head and his hair were white as white wool, white as snow; his eyes were like a flame of fire."

121. Collins, *Daniel*, 302. Cf. Goldingay, *Daniel*, 165, Fire "suggests something transcendent and absolute, awesome and dangerous, mysterious and destructive."

122. Cf. Psalm 97:1-4, "The LORD is king! . . . Righteousness and justice are the foundation of his throne. Fire goes before him, and consumes his adversaries on every side. His lightnings light up the world; the earth sees and trembles." Cf. Isaiah 66:15-16, "For the LORD will come in fire. . . . For by fire will the LORD execute judgment. . . ." Cf. Jeremiah 21:12 and Ezekiel 21:31.

123. "God's judgment, as is he himself, is omnipresent." Leupold, *Exposition of Daniel*, 302.

Verse 10, "A stream of fire issued and flowed out from his presence." This river of fire is a river of judgment. It's like the fiery lava flowing down a volcano. It will incinerate all that is opposed to God. Verse 10 continues to describe the scene: "A thousand thousands served him, and ten thousand times ten thousand stood attending him. The court sat in judgment, and the books were opened." The scene is cosmic. The number of angels serving God is staggering. In the ancient world, the highest number for which they had a word was "ten thousand." So "ten thousand times ten thousand" is absolutely the highest number they could imagine.[124] There are so many angels serving the God of the universe, they simply cannot be counted. "The court sat in judgment, and the books were opened."[125]

In this vision Daniel receives a glimpse of the final judgment, but it is focused particularly on the little horn. Daniel must have been outraged by the arrogant words of the little horn, for he mentions the little horn again in verse 11: "I watched then because of the noise of the arrogant words that the horn was speaking. And as I watched, the beast was put to death, and its body destroyed and given over to be burned with fire." Apparently the little horn's arrogant words are so vicious and wicked that they call forth God's immediate judgment upon the fourth beast. As Daniel watched, the fourth beast was put to death and its body destroyed and burned with fire.[126] "By mention of the *body,* the *utter* destruction of the beast is intended. It will exercise no further power in any sense, since it is to be completely done away. . . . With the destruction of the little horn, the power of the fourth beast disappears *entirely.*"[127]

In contrast to the utter annihilation of the fourth beast, verse 12 states, "As for the rest of the beasts, their dominion was taken away, but their lives were prolonged for a season and a time." The first three beasts were not annihilated, but their dominion, that is, their sovereignty, was taken away. "Their lives were prolonged for a season and a time," that is, for "a predetermined time."[128] When

---

124. "The phrase 'ten thousand times ten thousand' was 'the square of the highest number for which ancient peoples had a word.'" Miller, *Daniel,* 205, quoting G. A. F. Knight, "The Book of Daniel," *The Interpreter's One-Volume Commentary on the Bible* (Nashville: Abingdon, 1971), 445. Cf. Psalm 91:7, "A thousand may fall at your side, ten thousand at your right hand." Cf. Micah 6:7, "Will the Lord be pleased with thousands of rams, with ten thousands of rivers of oil?" Cf. 1 Samuel 18:7.

125. "In Scripture 'the books' are symbolic of God's memory of the deeds, words, and thoughts of every person who has ever lived (cf. Exod 32:32; Dan 12:1; Luke 10:20; and Rev. 20:12)." Miller, *Daniel,* 205. See also Psalm 69:28; Malachi 3:16; Revelation 3:5; 13:8; 17:8; and 20:15.

126. "The burning of a corpse in the Old Testament was a punishment reserved for those guilty of particularly heinous crimes (Lev. 20:14; 21:9; Josh 7:25)." Hill, "Daniel," 138.

127. Young, *Prophecy of Daniel,* 153 (his emphases). Young adds, "This, it seems to me, is a serious objection to finding the primary reference of the little horn to Antiochus, for after Antiochus' time, there were other Syrian kings who afflicted the Jews."

128. Ibid., 154.

the Babylonian kingdom was overthrown by the Medo-Persian Empire, it lost its sovereignty but continued to exist under the Persian kingdom. And when the Persian kingdom next was overthrown by Alexander the Great, it lost its dominion but continued to exist as part of the Greek kingdom. And when the Greek kingdom was overthrown by Rome, it lost its sovereignty but continued to exist as part of the Roman Empire.

The Roman Empire, however, is different (v. 7). Its depraved, evil nature will come to expression especially in the little horn, a ruler who will appear at the end of time. When God judges the little horn, the last remnant of the Roman Empire will be annihilated.[129] And with its demise the earlier human kingdoms will also come to an end. It's the same picture as in the dream of Nebuchadnezzar in chapter 2: the stone smashed into the brittle feet of the statue, but then all the earlier nations — gold, silver, bronze, and iron — collapsed and were destroyed at once. After that the stone "became a great mountain and filled the whole earth" (2:34-35). The message is that a new world order will replace the sinful human kingdoms.

> Verse 13, As I watched in the night visions,
> I saw one like a human being
>   coming with the clouds of heaven.
> And he came to the Ancient One
>   and was presented before him.

The NRSV note says that the Aramaic for "one like a human being" is literally "one like a son of man." Notice the contrast between this "son of man" and the earlier kingdoms. The human kingdoms were described in verses 4-7 as being like animals: "like a lion," "resembling a bear," "like a leopard," and finally "a fourth beast, terrifying and dreadful and exceedingly strong," with great iron teeth and ten horns. But this fifth king is described as being "*like* a son of man," "*like* a human being." Moreover, the "four great beasts came up out of the *sea* — the biblical symbol for chaos and evil. But the one like a son of man comes "with the clouds of *heaven*."

In the Old Testament it is God who comes with the clouds of heaven. For example, Isaiah writes: "See, the LORD is riding on a swift cloud and comes to Egypt" (19:1). Psalm 68 enjoins us, "Sing to God, sing praises to his name; lift up a song to him who rides upon the clouds" (68:4). Psalm 104 states, "You [LORD] make the clouds your chariot" (104:3). Daniel's "son of man" who comes with "the clouds of heaven" is a divine being like God.

---

129. "The powers that can be said to have anything like world dominion are segments of the old Roman empire, and so the fourth beast is still in a sense alive though Rome was overthrown." Leupold, *Exposition of Daniel*, 314.

We read at the end of verse 13, "And he came to the Ancient One and was presented before him." "The Judge had found the beasts guilty and sentenced them." God took away their dominion and kingdom. The one like a son of man now stood before the Judge "as their replacement."[130] Verse 14,

> To him was given dominion and glory and kingship,
>> that all peoples, nations, and languages should serve him.
> His dominion is an everlasting dominion
>> that shall not pass away,
> and his kingship is one
>> that shall never be destroyed.

Earlier Daniel had confessed that God is so great that he "deposes kings and sets up kings" (2:21). And to Nebuchadnezzar he had said that "the Most High has sovereignty over the kingdom of mortals and gives it to whom he will" (4:25). Now Daniel sees that at the end of time God will take away the dominion from human kings and give the "dominion, glory and kingship"[131] to the one "like a son of man." Then this "son of man" will be served by "all peoples, nations, and languages."

Verse 14 continues, "His dominion is an everlasting dominion that shall not pass away and his kingship is one that shall never be destroyed." In contrast to the human kings and kingdoms who lose their dominion and whose kingship will be destroyed, the dominion of this son of man "shall not pass away, and his kingship is one that shall never be destroyed."[132]

In the New Testament Jesus identified himself as "the son of man" of Daniel 7.[133] In line with Daniel's statement, "to him was given *dominion* and glory and *kingship*," Jesus said to the scribes, "the Son of Man has *authority* on earth to forgive sins" (Mark 2:10). He also said, "The Son of Man is *lord* even of the sabbath" (Mark 2:28). After his resurrection Jesus claimed, "*All authority* in heaven and on earth has been given to me" (Matt 28:18).[134]

Jesus also spoke of his Second Coming as "the Son of Man coming with *the*

---

130. Redditt, *Daniel*, 129.

131. "The three terms together emphasize that he would replace the beasts as the dominant empire on earth." Ibid.

132. Cf. Daniel 4:3, 34; and 6:26.

133. James Dunn, "The Danielic Son of Man in the New Testament," 546, concludes that "Jesus himself used *bar 'ĕnāš* with reference to himself and was the first to combine it with allusion to Dan 7:13." See also Shepherd, "Daniel 7:13 and the New Testament Son of Man," *WTJ* 68 (2006) 99-111, and Harman, *Study Commentary on Daniel*, 172-74.

134. Cf. John 17:1-2, "After Jesus had spoken these words, he looked up to heaven and said, 'Father, the hour has come; glorify your Son so that the Son may glorify you, since you have given him *authority* over all people, to give eternal life to all whom you have given him.'"

clouds of heaven." In speaking of the last days, Jesus said, "In those days, after that suffering, the sun will be darkened, and the moon will not give its light.... Then they will see *'the Son of Man coming in clouds'* with great power and glory" (Mark 13:24-26). Similarly, when the high priest asked Jesus, "Are you the Messiah, the Son of the Blessed One?" Jesus responded, "I am; and you will see *the Son of Man* seated at the right hand of power and *'coming with the clouds of heaven'*" (Mark 14:61-62).[135]

Daniel continues in verse 15, "As for me, Daniel, my spirit was troubled within me, and the visions of my head terrified me." Daniel was understandably "terrified." Such evil beasts, especially the last monster. What awful pain and suffering would God's people have to undergo before God's final victory?[136] Daniel was also "troubled." What did it all mean? When would this take place? He needed help.

Verses 16-18, "I approached one of the attendants [an angel] to ask him the truth concerning all this. So he said that he would disclose to me the interpretation of the matter: 'As for these four great beasts, four kings shall arise out of the earth.[137] But the holy ones of the Most High shall receive the kingdom and possess the kingdom forever — forever and ever.'" In verse 14 we heard that God gave his everlasting kingdom to the one "like a son of man." Verse 18 adds that God will also give this everlasting kingdom to "the holy ones of the Most High," that is, to God's holy people.[138] And they will "possess the kingdom forever — forever and ever."[139]

But Daniel is not satisfied with this brief answer. He has a lot of questions. He wants to know more about that monstrous fourth beast and especially the little horn. In verses 19-22 Daniel not only asks for a more detailed interpretation, but he also provides more details of his earlier dream-vision. Verse 19, "Then I desired to know the truth concerning the fourth beast, which was different from all the rest, exceedingly terrifying, with its teeth of iron and claws

135. Cf. Revelation 1:7, "Look! He is coming with the *clouds,*" and Revelation 14:14, 16, "Then I looked, and there was a white cloud, and seated *on the cloud was one like the Son of Man,* with a golden crown on his head, and a sharp sickle in his hand!... And the earth was reaped."

136. "Despite the victorious conclusion of his dream, Daniel was distressed (v. 15) about the suffering the future might hold for his people." Archer, "Daniel," 92.

137. In verse 3 the beasts come out of the sea to express their evil nature. "The expression was figurative because it occurred in a vision that portrayed the truth symbolically. The same thought is here expressed in a more literal form and conveys the idea that these kings are of the earth, earthy." Leupold, *Exposition of Daniel,* 317. Moreover, these kingdoms arising out of the earth stand in contrast to the kingdom which comes with the son of man from heaven.

138. See above, pp. 222-24, "The Holy Ones."

139. "The Aramaic word *'ālam,* like the Hebrew word *'ôlām,* refers to the indefinite past or future. Repetition of the word was an attempt to emphasize extreme duration. Hence the clause probably means that God's kingdom on earth would last and last and last." Redditt, *Daniel,* 130.

of bronze,[140] and which devoured and broke in pieces, and stamped what was left with its feet; and concerning the ten horns that were on its head, and concerning the other horn, which came up and to make room for which three of them fell out — the horn that had eyes and a mouth that spoke arrogantly, and that seemed greater than the others." The little horn may have seemed greater than the other horns because of its intelligence, its big mouth, and its belligerent attitude.[141]

Daniel continues in verses 21-22, "As I looked, this horn made war with the holy ones and was *prevailing* over them, *until* the Ancient One came; then judgment was given *for* the holy ones of the Most High, and the time arrived when the holy ones gained possession of the kingdom." It's the same judgment scene Daniel sketched in verses 9 to 11. But in his earlier report Daniel stressed that in response to the little horn's arrogant words, the Ancient One came, took his throne, and judged *against* the little horn. The beast was put to death and burned with fire. In verse 22 he emphasizes the other side of that judgment, the Ancient One gave judgment "*for* the holy ones of the Most High." God rules in favor of his people. And then he will give them possession of the kingdom (cf. 7:18).[142]

Daniel had asked for further interpretation of his vision regarding the fourth beast, the ten horns, and the little horn. With verse 23 the angel begins his interpretation: "This is what he said: 'As for the fourth beast, there shall be a fourth kingdom on earth that shall be *different* from all the other kingdoms; it shall devour the *whole earth*, and trample it down, and break it to pieces."[143] The Roman Empire would be different from the other kingdoms in that it would devour "all the surrounding nations bite by bite"[144] until it encompassed the whole earth.

Verse 24, "As for the ten horns, out of this kingdom ten kings shall arise,

---

140. Daniel had not mentioned the "claws of bronze" in his earlier description. "Metal claws could tear a victim to shreds and further signifies the tremendous destructive power of the empire symbolized by this beast." Miller, *Daniel,* 212.

141. Daniel may be "referring to the haughty, swaggering appearance of the little horn." Young, *Prophecy of Daniel,* 158. Redditt, *Daniel,* 130, thinks that "the point seems to be that it was stronger than the other horns."

142. "The reason for emphasizing the participation of God's people in the final kingdom seems to be that it is a literal, earthly kingdom, replacing the previous empires of men, rather than a spiritual domain, a sort of ideal kingdom of God consisting only of the Lord himself." Archer, "Daniel," 93. See, e.g., Revelation 21:1-4.

143. "'Trample down, break to pieces': both verbs imply wanton destruction." Baldwin, *Daniel,* 146.

144. "The Roman state is seen here as devouring all the surrounding nations bite by bite (i.e., by the picturesque term *'ĕkal,* 'to eat,' 'devour') and thus acquiring an entire complex of subject kingdoms and nations." Archer, "Daniel," 93.

and another shall arise after them." This verse speaks of the demise of the Roman Empire in several phases. As the Greek Empire of Alexander the Great at its fall had split into four "heads"/kingdoms, so the fall of the Roman Empire will result in ten kings or kingdoms arising from the ashes of Rome. Since ten is the number of fullness, it is probably best to interpret it symbolically: a *full number* of kings or kingdoms shall arise from the fallen Roman Empire. And then, verse 24 continues, "another [king] shall arise after them. This one shall be different from the former ones, and shall put down three kings."[145] This little horn is different from the other kings in that he will challenge God himself and will seek to annihilate God's people.

Verse 25 details his appalling actions: "He shall speak words *against* the Most High, shall *wear out* the holy ones of the Most High, and shall attempt to *change the sacred seasons and the law;* and they shall be given into his power for a time, two times, and half a time."[146] "He shall speak words against the Most High" means that he will blaspheme God himself. "He shall *wear out* the holy ones of the Most High" means that he will oppress and persecute God's people until they are worn out like a worn-out sandal.[147] He also "shall attempt to change the sacred seasons and the law." In other words, the little horn will try to dethrone God and himself take the place of God:[148] he will try to dictate when people worship, whom they worship,[149] and the laws by which they order their lives.[150]

---

145. "The variation in the verbs used to describe what happens to the three horns, which are 'uprooted' (7:8), 'fell' (7:20), and now are humbled [put down] (7:24), cautions against pressing the meaning of any one of them. Instead the thrust seems to be that some significant portion of the power and influence of the beast will eventually pass to the little horn." Steinmann, *Daniel,* 373.

146. Cf. a similar vision in Revelation 13:5-7, "The beast was given a mouth uttering haughty and blasphemous words, and it was allowed to exercise authority for forty-two months. It opened its mouth to utter blasphemies against God, blaspheming his name and his dwelling, that is, those who dwell in heaven. Also it was allowed to make war on the saints and to conquer them."

147. "By cruel and systematic pressure, he will 'oppress' (*yĕ ballē'*, from *bĕla'*, which in the Pael means 'wear away' or 'wear out' as friction wears out clothes or sandals)." Archer, "Daniel," 94. Cf. Baldwin, *Daniel,* 146.

148. "The little horn will seek the prerogatives of God. The horn's words and teaching will usurp God's authority by seeking to change the worship and piety of God's people." Steinmann, *Daniel,* 374.

149. "Believers will daily be harassed until their lives become miserable. Religious freedom will be abolished." Miller, *Daniel,* 214.

150. Leupold, *Exposition of Daniel,* 324-25, holds that "the 'times and law' mentioned cannot be restricted to 'festival times' and 'the law of God.'" He refers to attempts made "in the days of the French revolution to abolish the seven-day week in favor of the ten-day week. . . . Russia has added such revolutionary efforts at overthrowing government, property, and marriage laws."

At the end of verse 25, the angel says that "they [God's people] shall be given into his power for a time, two times, and half a time." The little horn will be allowed to harass and persecute God's people, but only for a limited time. The length of time is given as "a time, two times, and half a time." Since three and a half is one half of the perfect number "seven," it probably denotes a short period of persecution.[151] But the important thing to note is the three-fold repetition of the word *"time"* in contrast to "the *everlasting* kingdom" in verse 27. No matter how long the persecution lasts, it will only be temporary. "As such, it is subject to the eternal God, the One who 'changes times and seasons' (2:21)."[152]

In the New Testament, Jesus reiterates that God is also in control of the length of the end time persecution. Jesus says, "At that time there will be great suffering, such as has not been from the beginning of the world until now, no, and never will be. And if those days had not been cut short, no one would be saved; but for the sake of the elect those days *will be cut short*" (Matt 24:21-22).

The little horn's persecution of God's people will be for only a limited time. At the end of that time, we read in verses 26-28, "'Then the court shall sit in judgment, and his dominion shall be taken away, to be consumed and totally destroyed. The kingship and dominion and the greatness of the kingdoms under the whole heaven shall be given to the people of the holy ones of the Most High; their kingdom shall be an *everlasting* kingdom, and all dominions shall serve and obey them.' Here the account ends. As for me, Daniel, my thoughts greatly terrified me, and my face turned pale; but I kept the matter in my mind."[153]

Daniel is still terrified. His face even turns pale. He had seen some awful things happening on earth. And the angel's words that the evil little horn would harass and persecute God's people were not reassuring. Even though God promised his people the "everlasting kingdom," they would still have to go through devastating trials. And when would it end? Daniel did not know.

From our perspective after the first coming of Jesus Christ, we know more than Daniel did. We know that the fall of the fourth beast, the Roman Empire, lies in our past. After its fall, the influence of the Roman Empire continued in separate, independent kingdoms — the ten (complete number of) horns. Then comes the "little horn." The New Testament identifies this little horn as the "Man of Lawlessness," also called "the Antichrist." In Daniel 7:25 we read that

---

151. See, e.g., Lucas, *Daniel,* 194, and Lederach, *Daniel,* 167. Since it reads literally, "a time, and times, and a portion of time," others suggest that this sequence may indicate that the little horn will have modest success for a time, then great success for times, but just when it looks like the little horn will be victorious, there will be only a portion of time. Then Judgment Day. See Leupold, *Exposition of Daniel,* 326; Keil, *Book of Daniel,* 244; and Longman, *Daniel,* 190-91.

152. Seow, *Daniel,* 112.

153. "The expression of Daniel's perplexity in v. 28b encourages the reader to expect more to come, to clarify things further." Lucas, *Daniel,* 194.

the little horn "shall speak words against the Most High, shall wear out the holy ones of the Most High." In other words, he will attack both God and his people. Paul writes about the Man of Lawlessness, "He opposes and exalts himself above every so-called god or object of worship, so that he takes his seat in the temple of God, *declaring himself to be God*" (2 Thess 2:4). That's his attack on God. Then Paul writes that the coming of the Man of Lawlessness "is apparent in the working of Satan, who uses all power, signs, lying wonders, and every kind of wicked deception for those who are perishing" (2 Thess 2:9-10). That's his attack on people. But, according to Paul, that time still lies in the future. He urges his readers "not to be quickly shaken in mind or alarmed . . . that the day of the Lord is already here. . . . That day will not come unless the *rebellion comes first* and the lawless one is revealed, the one destined for destruction" (2 Thess 2:1-3). Although "the mystery of lawlessness is already at work," right now the Man of Lawlessness is being *restrained*.[154] But when "the one who now restrains it is removed, . . . the lawless one will be revealed, whom the Lord Jesus will destroy with the breath of his mouth, annihilating him by the manifestation of his coming" (2 Thess 2:7-8).

In his letters, John calls this enemy of God and his people the "Antichrist." "The original meaning of the Greek prefix *anti* is 'instead of' or 'in place of.' . . . The antichrist is both a *rival* Christ and an *opponent* of Christ."[155] John claims that the Antichrist is already present in his day.[156] He writes, "Children, it is *the last hour*! As you have heard that antichrist is coming, so now many antichrists have come. From this we know that it is the last hour" (1 John 2:18; cf. 2:22; 4:3; 2 John 7). John was very much aware that with the death, resurrection, and ascension of Jesus, we have entered upon "the last days." Jesus came to reestablish God's kingdom on earth, but it will come in two stages. With his First Coming Jesus inaugurated God's kingdom on earth; with his Second Coming he will bring it to completion. So now we live in the in-between times, in "the last days," awaiting the coming of the Son of Man with the clouds to receive God's everlasting kingdom (Dan 7:13-14). In this time before the end, many Antichrists are at work in the world defying Christ and opposing God's people.

---

154. The one doing the restraining has been variously identified as the Roman emperor, the church's proclamation of the gospel, the Holy Spirit, and a supernatural power ordained by God. For the pros and cons, see Ridderbos, *Paul: An Outline of His Theology*, 521-26, and Hoekema, *The Bible and the Future*, 160-61. In the light of Paul's reference to Satan in 2 Thessalonians 2:9 and John's reference to the *binding* of Satan for a complete period of time (1,000 years; Rev. 20:3), I favor identifying the restrainer with a supernatural power ordained by God (see "an angel from heaven," Rev. 20:1). See also p. 267, n. 44 below and p. 283, n. 108.

155. Hoekema, *The Bible and the Future*, 157, with a reference to Arndt-Gingrich, *Greek-English Lexicon of the New Testament*, 72.

156. Cf. Paul, 2 Thessalonians 2:7, "The mystery of lawlessness is *already* at work."

But they are only precursors, forerunners, of the final personal Antichrist.[157] They point forward to that horrendous figure who will come at the end of time.[158]

According to John's vision in the book of Revelation, an angel from heaven "seized the dragon, that ancient serpent, who is the Devil and Satan, and bound him for a thousand years. . . . After that he must be let out for a little while" (Rev. 20:2-3). The thousand years (10 x 10 x 10) is a symbolic number for a full period of time that began with Jesus' defeat of Satan by rising from the dead and ascending to his throne in heaven. Right now the dragon is bound. He cannot do his worst. He is like a chained lion, limited in the damage he can cause. But at the end of this full period of time he will be set loose for a little while (Rev. 20:3, 7). That will be the time of the little horn. In John's words, "Satan will be released from his prison and will come out to deceive the nations." The nations will then unite to turn upon the church of Christ. They will surround "the camp of the saints [the holy ones] and the beloved city." In those dark days it will look like the church will be annihilated. But then, as in Daniel 7, God intervenes: "*Fire* came down from heaven and consumed them. And the devil who had deceived them was thrown into the lake of *fire*" (Rev. 20:7-10).

But news about the little horn, "the Antichrist," is not the main message of Daniel 7. Three times Daniel 7 reiterates that *God's people will receive the kingdom:* verse 18, "The holy ones of the Most High shall receive the kingdom and possess the kingdom forever"; verse 22, "The holy ones gained possession of the kingdom"; and verse 27, "The kingship and dominion and the greatness of the kingdoms under the whole heaven shall be given to the people of the holy ones of the Most High; their [his][159] kingdom shall be an everlasting kingdom, and all dominions shall serve and obey them [him]." God's people will inherit a universal, everlasting kingdom — the kingdom of God.

In the New Testament, Jesus declares, "When the Son of Man comes in his glory, and all the angels with him, then he will sit on the throne of his glory. All the nations will be gathered before him, and he will separate people one from

---

157. Cf. Hoekema, *The Bible and the Future,* 158, "Since John sees these 'many antichrists' in the world already, he concludes that we are now, in this present era, in 'the last hour.' We can thus expect to continue to find antichristian powers and persons in every era of the church of Jesus Christ until his Second Coming."

158. "The words 'as you have heard that antichrist is coming' indicate that John did indeed, along with the early Christian church, expect a personal antichrist at the end of the age." Ibid.

159. The NIV has the better translation when it translates the last part of verse 27, ". . . the holy people of the Most High. *His* kingdom will be an everlasting kingdom, and all rulers will worship and obey *him*." The pronominal suffixes refer not to the antecedent of "holy people" but to "the Most High." Leupold, *Exposition of Daniel,* 328, notes, "In every other instance where this verb ["serve," *pĕlaḥ*] occurs in biblical Aramaic — that is to say, nine times — this verb is used with reference to the deity." Cf. Miller, *Daniel,* 217.

another as a shepherd separates the sheep from the goats. . . . Then the king will say to those at his right hand, 'Come, you that are blessed by my Father, inherit the *kingdom* prepared for you from the foundation of the world'" (Matt 25:31-34). Later Jesus tells his disciples, "You are those who have stood by me in my trials; and I confer on you, just as my Father has conferred on me, a *kingdom*, so that you may eat and drink at my table in my kingdom" (Luke 22:29-30).[160]

Daniel 7 reassures us that our sovereign God is in control even of mighty human empires. We may get disheartened when we hear of the awful persecution of our brothers and sisters in North Korea, Saudi Arabia, Iran, Iraq, and many other nations.[161] We may fear for our lives and that of our loved ones when we hear about the horrible weapons of mass destruction that could fall into the hands of terrorists. We may get discouraged when we ourselves are persecuted. But in giving to Daniel this overview of human history, God seeks to encourage us: Take heart; things are not what they seem. God is still sovereign. He is still in control. True, he still allows evil human kingdoms to exist and even to harass and persecute God's people. At the end of time, he will even allow the Antichrist to decimate his church. But don't give up hope. Deliverance is near. When the persecution reaches its climax, God will step in and judge the nations. He will totally destroy the wicked human rulers and kingdoms. And then he will establish his perfect kingdom on earth. He will give this perfect kingdom to his Son, Jesus Christ, and to those who follow him. A wonderful future awaits God's people.

> Crowns and thrones may perish,
>   kingdoms rise and wane,
> but the church of Jesus
>   constant will remain;
> gates of hell can never
>   'gainst that church prevail.
> We have Christ's own promise,
>   and that cannot fail.[162]

---

160. See also Matthew 5:3 and 5, "Blessed are the poor in spirit, for theirs is the *kingdom of heaven*. . . . Blessed are the meek, for they will inherit the *earth*."

161. See Marshall, *Their Blood Cries Out: The Worldwide Tragedy of Modern Christians Who Are Dying for Their Faith.*

162. Sabine Baring-Gould, 1865, "Onward, Christian Soldiers," alt.

Daniel's Vision of a Ram, a Goat, and a Little Horn

Daniel 8:1-27

A king of bold countenance shall arise, skilled in intrigue. . . .
By his cunning he shall make deceit prosper under his hand,
*   and in his own mind he shall be great.*
Without warning he shall destroy many
*   and shall even rise up against the Prince of princes.*
But he shall be broken, and not by human hands.

Daniel 8:23-25

In contrast to Daniel 7, which provides a grand overview of the history of human kingdoms from the Babylonian kingdom to the consummation of God's kingdom, chapter 8 zooms in on the second and third kingdoms, a time frame of roughly two hundred years (350 B.C. to 164 B.C.). Also in contrast to Daniel 7, in chapter 8 the angel specifically identifies the ram as the Medo-Persian kingdom and the goat as the Greek kingdom (8:20-21). Although this information simplifies the interpretation of this chapter, there are other figures that still need to be identified: "the little horn" (v. 9), "the host of heaven" (v. 10), "the prince of hosts" (v. 11), and especially the "two thousand three hundred evenings and mornings" (v. 14).[1] Moreover, preachers will also ask, What is the relevance for us today of a prophecy that was apparently fulfilled long ago? In addition, we will have to make decisions about the translation of obscure Hebrew words in verse 12[2] and elsewhere. We have our work cut out for us.

---

1. Leupold, *Exposition of Daniel*, 354, calls this expression "one of the major cruxes of the whole book."

2. "The sequence of the verbs, as the text now stands, is extremely difficult." Young, *Prophecy of Daniel*, 172. For both verses 12 and 13 the NRSV notes, "Meaning of Heb uncertain."

Text and Context

Determining the parameters of the preaching text again is the easiest part in preaching this passage. Daniel 8:1 begins with the chronological marker, "In the third year of the reign of King Belshazzar a vision appeared to me, Daniel, after the one that had appeared to me at first." He retells the vision and Gabriel's interpretation. In chapter 8:27 he concludes, "But I was dismayed by the vision and did not understand it." The next literary unit begins with another chronological marker, "In the first year of Darius . . ." (9:1). Our preaching text, therefore, is Daniel 8:1-27.

As to its context, Daniel 8 is most closely linked to Daniel 7. While Daniel received the vision of Daniel 7 "in the first year of King Belshazzar" (7:1), he received this vision "in the third year of the reign of King Belshazzar" (8:1). The mention of King Belshazzar brings to mind the sacrilege Belshazzar committed by drinking from the sacred temple vessels, which led to God's having him killed "that very night" (Dan 5:30). The vision of chapter 8 focuses on the even greater sacrilege that will be committed by the "king of bold countenance" who will take away from God "the regular burnt offering" and overthrow the place of God's sanctuary (8:11), which will lead to God's having this king killed ("He shall be broken, and not by human hands"; 8:25).

Also, in this vision the second and third kingdoms of Daniel 7 are again portrayed as animals. Instead of the bear with one side higher than the other, Daniel 8:3 describes a ram with one horn longer than the other; and instead of a leopard with four heads, Daniel 8:8 pictures a goat whose single horn is broken and replaced by four horns.

This chapter also has connections with the following chapters. Daniel 8:9 speaks of "the beautiful land" — a phrase that will return in Daniel 11:16, 41 (cf. Ezek 20:6, 15). Daniel 8:13 mentions "the transgression that makes desolate," which corresponds to "the abomination that makes desolate" in 11:31 and a similar phrase in 9:27 and 12:11. Jesus will refer to this phrase in the New Testament ("the desolating sacrilege," Mark 13:14 par. Matt 24:15; "desolation," Luke 21:20; cf. 2 Thess 2:3-4). Daniel 8:19 speaks of "the period of wrath" — a phrase that will be used again in 11:36. Finally, Gabriel's assurance that the vision is "true" (8:26) will be repeated in Daniel 10:1 and 11:2; be repeated in different words in 12:7; and later be used in Revelation 19:9; 21:5; and 22:6.

Literary Features

Starting at 8:1, Daniel switches back to the Hebrew language. The most likely reason for this switch is that the Aramaic chapters 2–7 stressed God's universal rule over the nations (see, e.g., 4:1-3; 6:25-27; 7:13-14), which could best be communicated to Israel and the nations in Aramaic, the international language. Chapters 8–12, by contrast, focus more on Israel, Jerusalem, and the temple (e.g., 8:13; 9:2, 24; 11:31), which could best be communicated to Israel in the Hebrew language.[3] Although most of chapter 8 is written in prose, at the height of its description of the little horn (vv. 23-25) it switches to poetry (see the NRSV) or what has been called "rhythmic prose with some parallelism."[4]

The genre of this chapter, like that of Daniel 7, is apocalyptic literature. The form is a vision report. According to Collins, "it conforms to the pattern of the symbolic dream vision. . . . The chapter exhibits the full pattern of the . . . [form]: indication of circumstances, description of the vision introduced by 'behold,' request (or desire) for interpretation, interpretation, and concluding material."[5] The vision report also contains an epiphany of the angel Gabriel. We shall explore in more detail the structure of Daniel 8, its plot line, character description, and repetition.

Structure

This chapter can be divided into four scenes:

Scene 1. Daniel sees himself in Susa and receives a vision (1-12)
    A. The vision of the ram with two horns (3-4)
        1. The second horn longer than the first (3)
        2. The ram charges westward, northward, and southward (4)
    B. The vision of the goat (5-12)
        1. The goat from the west with one central horn (5)
        2. The goat breaks the two horns of the ram (6-7)
        3. The goat's horn is broken and replaced by four horns (8)
        4. Out of one of the four horns comes a little horn (9)
        5. The little horn's arrogant, violent acts (10-12)
            a. Against the host of heaven (10)
            b. Against the Prince of the host (11)
            c. Against the sanctuary (12)
Characters: Daniel and, in quick succession, the ram, the goat, four horns, and the little horn

---

3. See Goldingay, *Daniel,* 207; Lederach, *Daniel,* 17-22; and Lucas, *Daniel,* 212.
4. Lucas, *Daniel,* 210.
5. Collins, *Daniel* (1984), 86.

Scene 2. Daniel overhears the dialogue between two holy ones (13-14)

    A. "How long will this punishment last?" (13)

    B. "2,300 evenings and mornings" (14a)

    C. "Then the sanctuary shall be restored" (14b)

    Characters: two "holy ones"

Scene 3. The appearance of Gabriel and Daniel's trance (15-18)

    A. Gabriel appears before Daniel (15)

    B. God tells Gabriel to explain the vision to Daniel (16)

    C. "The vision is for the time of the end" (17)

    D. Daniel falls into a trance; Gabriel sets him on his feet (18)

    Characters: Gabriel and Daniel

Scene 4. Gabriel's interpretation (19-26)

    A. These things will take place "later in the period of wrath" (19)

    B. The ram with two horns is the kings of Media and Persia (20)

    C. The goat is the king of Greece and the horn its first king (21)

    D. When the horn is broken, the kingdom splits into four kingdoms (22)

    E. A king of bold countenance will arise (23-25)

        1. His rise (23)

        2. His success (24)

        3. His attack against the Prince of princes and his fall (25)

    F. The vision is true; seal it up, "for it refers to many days from now" (26)

    Characters: Gabriel and, in quick succession, kings of Medo-Persia, the king of Greece, four kings, the king of bold countenance

This scenic structure shows in the climaxes of its key scenes, I and IV, that this vision focuses on "the little horn"/"king of bold countenance" and his arrogant acts (see I.B.5.a.b.c, and IV.E.1.2.3).

The Plot Line

Though not as clear as in the narratives, we can still detect the contours of a plot line in Daniel 8. The setting is given in verses 1-2, "the third year of the reign of King Belshazzar," and Daniel seeing himself in Susa, the capital, by the river Ulai. The occasioning incident is when Daniel sees a ram charging westward, northward, and southward; "it did as it pleased and became strong" (vv. 3-4). The tension rises when Daniel sees a male goat coming from the west, "coming across the face of the whole earth without touching the ground" (v. 5). The goat heads for the ram, runs at it with savage force, strikes the ram, throws it to the ground, and tramples it (vv. 6-7). The goat grows "exceedingly great," but at the height of its power, its great horn is broken and replaced by four horns (v. 8). Which of the four horns will succeed as the world empire?

Suddenly Daniel sees a little horn coming out of one of the four horns. This little horn grows "exceedingly great toward the south, toward the east, and toward the beautiful land" (v. 9). It grows as high "as the host of heaven," throwing "down to the earth some of the host and some of the stars" and trampling on them (v. 10). He even takes on "the Prince of the host" by taking away from him the regular burnt offering and overthrowing the place of his sanctuary (v. 11). The host is given over to the little horn together with the burnt offering; the little horn casts truth to the ground and keeps prospering in his destructive acts (v. 12). At this climax, Daniel hears an angel ask, "How long?" (v. 13). The answer resolves the tension somewhat: the persecution won't last forever; it will last for "2,300 evenings and mornings; then the sanctuary shall be restored to its rightful state" (v. 14).[6]

A new conflict begins when Daniel tries to understand the vision and "a human voice" tells Gabriel to explain the vision (v. 16). Gabriel explains "that the vision is for the time of the end" (v. 17). But Daniel falls into a trance and has to be brought back to his feet by Gabriel (v. 18). Then Gabriel explains that these events will not take place while Israel is in exile in Babylon (the first kingdom of Daniel 2 and 7) but "later in the period of wrath" (v. 19). The ram with two horns "is the kings of Media and Persia," and the "goat is the king of Greece." When its horn (the first king) is broken, four kingdoms will arise from this nation (vv. 20-22). "At the end of their rule," a fierce-looking king will arise, "skilled in intrigue" (v. 23). He will grow strong, cause fearful destruction, and succeed in what he does. He will destroy the powerful and the people of God (v. 24). Without warning he will destroy many and "even rise up against the Prince of princes" (v. 25). This is the second climax.

The tension is resolved when Gabriel predicts that this fierce king "shall be broken, and not by human hands" (v. 25c). Gabriel, referring back to the length of the persecution ("2,300 evenings and mornings"; v. 14), says, "The vision of the evenings and the mornings . . . is true." He tells Daniel to "seal up the vision, for it refers to many days from now" (v. 26; cf. v. 19, "what will take place later in the period of wrath"). The outcome is that Daniel is "overcome," lays "sick for some days," goes back to work, but is dismayed by the vision and does "not understand it" (v. 27).

We can sketch this vision report as a complex plot:

---

6. "The . . . conversation indicates that the small horn is under control, though it does not reveal what will actually happen to it. That is left for the climactic line of the vision in v. 25." Goldingay, *Daniel*, 204.

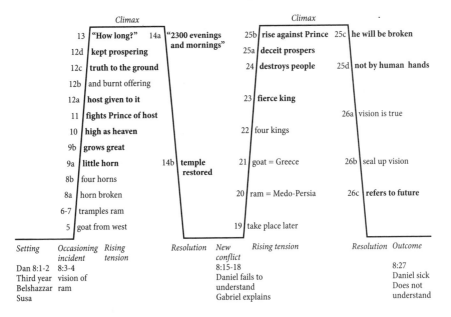

Setting	Occasioning incident	Rising tension	Resolution	New conflict	Rising tension	Resolution	Outcome
Dan 8:1-2	8:3-4			8:15-18			8:27
Third year	vision of			Daniel fails to			Daniel sick
Belshazzar	ram			understand			Does not
Susa				Gabriel explains			understand

The plot line shows that verses 13-14 and 25 are the major turning points in this vision, which will aid us in formulating the textual theme and in developing the sermon.

Character Description

Character description is also concentrated in "the little horn"/"king of bold countenance." The narrator describes him as coming out of one of the four horns, being "a little one" but growing "exceedingly great toward the south, toward the east, and toward the beautiful land"; and growing "as high as the host of heaven" (8:9-10a). The narrator further fills out the character of the little horn by relating its evil acts: throwing "down to the earth some of the host and some of the stars," trampling on them, acting arrogantly "even against the Prince of the host," taking "the regular burnt offering away from him" and overthrowing the place of his sanctuary, casting "truth to the ground," and "prospering in what it did" (8:10b-12).

In his interpretation, Gabriel describes this little horn as "a king of bold[7] countenance . . . , skilled in intrigue," or, as the NIV translates, "a fierce-

---

7. "There may be an intentional wordplay between 'bold,' 'brazen' (ʿōz) and 'goat' (ʿēz, vv. 5, 8)." Lucas, *Daniel*, 220.

looking king, a master of intrigue" (v. 23).[8] Gabriel further develops this terrifying character by noting that he "shall grow strong in power," "shall cause
fearful destruction," "shall succeed in what he does," "shall destroy the powerful and the people of the holy ones" (v. 24), and finally, "By his cunning he
shall make deceit prosper under his hand, and in his own mind he shall be
great. Without warning he shall destroy many and shall even rise up against
the Prince of princes. But he shall be broken, and not by human hands"
(v. 25).

Daniel describes the other figures much more briefly. The ram had two
horns, the second one being longer than the first; it was "charging westward
and northward and southward. . . . It did as it pleased and became strong" (3-4).
Daniel describes the goat as "a male goat" coming "from the west," with lightning speed ("coming across the face of the whole earth without touching the
ground"), and having a single "horn between its eyes." He further develops this
character with its actions: "It was enraged against . . . the ram," broke its two
horns, "threw the ram down to the ground and trampled upon it." Then "it
grew exceedingly great; but at the height of its power, the great horn was broken" (vv. 5-8).

Daniel describes the angel Gabriel as "having the appearance of a man"
(v. 15) and God's speaking as "a human voice" (v. 16). Daniel describes himself
as seeing himself in Susa (v. 1), trying to understand the vision (v. 15), becoming
frightened and falling prostrate (v. 17), falling into a trance (v. 18), and after the
interpretation of the vision being "overcome," lying "sick for some days," and
being "dismayed," not understanding the vision (v. 27).

Repetition

Similar to the dream-vision of Daniel 7, this vision is carried along by Daniel's,
"a vision appeared to me"/"I saw" (*rĕâh:* vv. 1 [2x], 2 [3x], 3, 4, 6, 7, 15, 20).
More important for detecting the theme is Goldingay's observation that the
word "become great" is repeated in verses 4, 8, 9, 10, 11, 25; "stand"/"arise"/
"place" is repeated in verses 3, 4, 7, 15, 17, 18 (2x), 22 (2x), 23, 25; "throw down"
in verses 7, 11, 12; "trample" in verses 7, 10, 13; "hand"/"power" in verses 4, 7, 25;
"strength" in verses 6, 7, 22, 24 (2x); and "might" in verses 8 and 24 (2x). "These
repetitions," writes Goldingay, "help to bind together the symbolic vision, the
angelic epiphany, and the interpretative vision. They have the cumulative effect [of] establishing the tone of what is being described as it repeats itself

---

8. "Used for evil ends, Antiochus's two characteristics are both key elements in the standard portrayal of a tyrant (Niditch, *Vision*, 230-31)." Goldingay, *Daniel*, 217.

through the story of the Medo-Persian empire, Alexander and his successors, and Antiochus."[9]

Lucas helpfully elaborates that these repetitions show that this vision "is about power and conflict. Added to this, a series of expressions describing movements heightens the sense of aggression."[10] The ram charges "westward and northward and southward" (v. 4). The goat comes from the west and covers the whole earth with lightning speed (v. 5). When its great horn is broken, it is replaced by four horns growing toward the four winds of heaven (v. 8). The small horn grows toward the south, the east, and "the beautiful land" (v. 9), and "as high as the host of heaven" (v. 10). Especially important for discerning the theme is the repetition of the verb "to become great" (*gādal*). The ram "became great/strong" (v. 4); the goat "grew exceedingly great" (v. 8); the little horn "grew exceedingly great" (v. 9); it "grew as great/high as the host of heaven" (v. 10); "Even against the prince of the host it acted arrogantly [grew great]" (v. 11). This repetition, Lucas suggests, provides a sense of movement which comes to a climax in the greatness of the little horn.[11]

Interpretation of Specific Images

In contrast to Daniel 7, Gabriel's identification of the ram as the Medo-Persian kingdom and the goat as the Greek kingdom (8:20, 21) simplifies our interpretation considerably. But there are still some other controversial images. We shall in turn discuss the identity of "the horn, a little one" (v. 9), "the host of heaven" (v. 10), "the Prince of the host" (v. 11), and the time of "two thousand three hundred evenings and mornings" (v. 14).

The Little Horn

There is virtually unanimous agreement that this little horn must be identified as the Seleucid king Antiochus IV, who severely persecuted the Jews and desecrated God's temple. This identification makes this little horn a different figure from the little horn in Daniel 7. The little horn in Daniel 7 came up from the remains of the *fourth* and last worldwide kingdom, among the *ten* horns, and replaced three of these horns/kings (7:24). That little horn will reveal its destructive power in the last days, just before the final judgment, and therefore can be

9. Goldingay, *Daniel*, 205.
10. Lucas, *Daniel*, 210.
11. Ibid.

identified with the person the New Testament calls "the Antichrist," and "the Man of Lawlessness."

By contrast, the little horn in Daniel 8 comes up from the remains of the *third* kingdom, which Gabriel identifies as Greece (8:21). Moreover, this horn comes from one of the *four* horns following the death of Alexander the Great. In addition, as Baldwin notes, "In chapter 7 the persecuted saints receive the kingdom [7:27], whereas in chapter 8, though the power of the little horn is broken, nothing is said about God's kingdom."[12] This little horn, then, "which grew exceedingly great toward the south, toward the east, and toward the beautiful land" (8:9), can be identified as Antiochus IV of the Seleucid kingdom but should be distinguished from the "little horn" of Daniel 7.

The Host of Heaven

Daniel says that the little horn "grew as high as the host of heaven. It threw down to the earth some of the host and some of the stars, and trampled on them" (8:10). Because the host of heaven is linked to the stars, some commentators interpret the host of heaven either as mythic[13] or literally as the starry hosts in the heavens.[14] But if the starry hosts were the right interpretation, it would surely be hyperbole,[15] for no human king, no matter how powerful, can attack the stars in the heavens.

Another interpretation is much more likely. Verses 11 and 12 continue, "Even against the prince of the *host* it acted arrogantly; it took the regular burnt offering away from him. . . . The *host* was given over to it together with the burnt offering." The immediate context, then, refers to this king's attack on

---

12. Baldwin, *Daniel*, 162, n. 1. For more detailed differences, see Young, *Prophecy of Daniel*, 276-79, and Steinmann, *Daniel*, 154.

13. "Given the traditional usage of 'host of heaven' and 'stars,' it is more likely that they too are mythic-realistic symbols." Collins, *Daniel*, 333. Buchanan, *Book of Daniel*, 246, counters, "The author of this narrative was not in heaven observing events there and consequently deducing what was happening on earth. He was on earth describing things that took place on the earth." Lucas, *Daniel*, 215, thinks that "the phrase ["host of heaven"] points to the transcendent dimension of the conflict between Antiochus and the Jews."

14. E.g., Baldwin, *Daniel*, 157, who acknowledges, however, that "stars could refer in a secondary sense to earthly monarchs (Isa 24:21); 'some of the host of the stars' are therefore rival kings who suffered a cruel fate at the march of this upstart."

15. "The author of Dan 8 applied the Isaianic text [14:12-15] to the Maccabean Rebellion just as hyperbolically as Isaiah had intended it originally. . . . Neither the author of Dan 8 nor the author of 2 Macc [9:8, 10] believed for one minute that Antiochus could . . . go up to heaven and join battle with the angels. They were describing their feelings about his arrogance rather than reporting actual fact. That is the intent of hyperbole." Buchanan, *Book of Daniel*, 243.

God's temple in Jerusalem and on God's people ("the host").[16] "The host of heaven" in verse 10, therefore, is best understood as "the host, the army, of heaven," that is, the people who worship and serve the God of heaven.[17] Elsewhere in the Old Testament, Israel is also called "the hosts (*ṣĕbā'ôt*) of the Lord" (Exod 12:41, NASB; the NRSV translates *ṣĕbā'ôt* as "companies"; see, e.g., Exod 6:26; 7:4; 12:17, 41, 51; Num 1:3; 2:3, 9, 10, etc.).

Daniel 8:10 says that the little horn "threw down to the earth some of the host and *some of the stars,* and trampled on them." In the Old Testament, the stars can also represent God's people on earth.[18] Balaam predicts, "A star shall come out of Jacob . . . ; it shall crush the borderlands of Moab" (Num 24:17). This refers to a future earthly leader. Daniel himself compares God's *people* with stars: "Those who lead many to righteousness [shall shine] like the stars forever and ever" (12:3). Therefore, when Daniel 8:10 predicts that the little horn will throw "down to the earth some of the host and some of the stars," it refers to the same group of people, namely, God's people whom Antiochus will slaughter.[19]

We conclude, therefore, that Daniel's "host of heaven" refers to the people who serve the "King of heaven" (4:37). This interpretation is also supported by Gabriel's interpretation, for he states that this king "shall grow strong in power. . . . He shall destroy the powerful and the *people* of the holy ones" (v. 24), that is, God's holy people.

16. The NIV translates Daniel 8:12, "Because of rebellion, the Lord's *people* and the daily sacrifice were given over to it." Cf. Goldingay, *Daniel,* 209, "References to the earthly sanctuary in vv. 11-12 could suggest that the heavenly army is the Jewish people, or the priesthood in particular, viewed as of heavenly significance because of their relationship with the God of heaven." Note, however, that Goldingay continues, "Yet the people attacked include 'some of the stars,' which rather points to the heavenly army being a supernatural body."

17. Cf. Daniel 4:26, "learn that Heaven [= God] is sovereign."

18. "As regards the stars which in Mesopotamia were identified with the gods, but which here designate the Saints." Lacocque, *Book of Daniel,* 162, referring to Daniel 12:3; Matthew 13:43; *1 Enoch* 46:7; 43:1-4. Cf. Montgomery, *Book of Daniel,* 333, "With few exceptions . . . the universal interpretation of 'the host of heaven' and its synonym 'the stars' is that they refer tropically to God's people." So also Young, *Prophecy of Daniel,* 171; Leupold, *Exposition of Daniel,* 346; and Steinmann, *Daniel,* 402.

19. "No real difference can be discerned between 'the host of heaven' and 'the stars,' as they seem to be used to refer to the same group. . . . In the context of verses 9-13 the best interpretation is that this verse [10] depicts attacks to be made by Antiochus IV upon the believing Jewish community who opposed his Hellenization of Jewish life and worship." Harman, *Study Commentary on Daniel,* 193. Cf. Leupold, *Exposition of Daniel,* 346, "The Hebrew phrase 'and of the stars' involves the epexegetical use of 'and' and should be translated '*namely* of the stars.'" Cf. Redditt, *Daniel,* 139, "'Host' and 'stars' are sometimes synonyms and might be used that way here."

The Prince of the Host

Daniel writes, "Even against the prince of the host it [the little horn] acted arrogantly" (8:11). Note that the NRSV prints "prince" with a lower case "p" (cf. 8:25, "Prince of princes"). Some commentators identify this figure as the high priest Onias III or as the angel Michael, who is called "your prince" in Daniel 10:21.[20] But the majority identify "the prince of the host" as God. Montgomery argues, "'The Prince of the host' (properly a military term, generalissimo, Gen 21:22 and often) is the same as 'the Prince of princes' . . . and can be none other than God, 'the God of Hosts,' as is accepted by almost all commentaries."[21] See further below under "Typology," pp. 267-68.

Two Thousand Three Hundred Evenings and Mornings

A final contentious issue we should discuss here is the length of the desolation and persecution. In response to the question "How long?" the answer is given, "For two thousand three hundred evenings and mornings; then the sanctuary shall be restored to its rightful state" (8:14). The text reads literally, "evening, morning, two thousand and three hundred." We have to decide between three possible interpretations. Do "evening, morning" refer to the evening and morning sacrifices, in which case the set time of 2,300 evening and morning sacrifices is 1,150 days? Or should "evening, morning" be taken as a Hebrew day (as in Gen 1, "there was evening and there was morning"), so that the set time is 2,300 days? Or should the number 2,300 be taken as a symbolic number?[22]

Many commentators[23] think that the 2,300 refers to the number of evening and morning sacrifices, so that the number indicates 1,150 days. Steinmann argues that this position explains "the unusual syntax of 'evening, morning' in

---

20. Lacocque, *Book of Daniel*, 162, mentions especially M. A. Beek, *Das Danielbuch* (Leiden, 1935), 80.

21. Montgomery, *Book of Daniel*, 335. Cf. Collins, *Daniel*, 333, "In view of the mention of the daily offering and 'his sanctuary,' there can be no doubt that the reference is to God." Cf. Lucas, *Daniel*, 216, "Most recent commentators see in the 'prince of the host' a reference to 'Yahweh of hosts.'" Cf. Baldwin, *Daniel*, 157, and Miller, *Daniel*, 226.

22. For a good overview of these positions, see Steinmann, *Daniel*, 404-6, and Miller, *Daniel*, 228-30. In the 1840s William Miller, a leader of the Millerites, defended a fourth position. He understood the 2,300 days as 2,300 years. This led him to conclude that Christ would return sometime between March 21, 1843, and March 21, 1844. Later the Seventh-Day Adventists split off from the Millerites.

23. E.g., Montgomery, *Book of Daniel*, 343; Porteous, *Daniel*, 126-27; Baldwin, *Daniel*, 158; Lacocque, *Book of Daniel*, 164; Collins, *Daniel*, 336; Archer, "Daniel," 103; Buchanan, *Book of Daniel*, 248; Hill, "Daniel," 150-51; and Steinmann, *Daniel*, 405-6.

8:14" — no conjunction. Further, he sees it "confirmed by 8:26, which calls this, literally, 'the vision of *the* evening and *the* morning.'" He finds further confirmation in the fact that "from the time that the temple altar was desecrated to its re-dedication was 1,106 days. . . . slightly short of 1,150 days. . . . However, we should keep in mind that OT prophecies concerning time periods are usually given in round numbers."[24]

But Keil rightly asserts that "a Hebrew reader could not possibly understand the period of time 2,300 evening-mornings as 2,300 half days or 1,150 whole days, because evening and morning at the creation constituted not the half but the whole day. . . . We must therefore take the words as they are, i.e., understand them as 2,300 whole days."[25] He further points out that "when the Hebrews wish to express separately day and night, . . . then the number of both is expressed. They say, e.g., forty days and forty nights" (Gen 7:4, 12; Exod 24:18; 1 Kings 19:8), and three days and three nights (Jonah 2:1; Matt 12:40)."[26] Since Daniel 8:14 uses the number 2,300 only once, 2,300 whole days are intended.[27]

A third option is to understand the 2,300 evenings and mornings as a symbol[28] — a well-known feature of apocalyptic literature. The number 2,300 is not an obvious symbolic number such as 4, 7, 10, 12, and their multiples, 40, 70, 1000, 144,000. But Goldingay observes, "The periods of time in chapters on either side (7:25; 9:24-27) have symbolic significance, . . . and it is appropriate to look for a significance for this one beyond the purely chronological."[29]

---

24. Steinmann, *Daniel,* 405-6.

25. Keil, *Book of Daniel,* 304. So also the Greek and Latin versions; Calvin, *Commentaries on Daniel,* II, 108; Young, *Prophecy of Daniel,* 174-75; Seow, *Daniel,* 125; Miller, *Daniel,* 229-30; and Feinberg, *Daniel,* 107.

26. Keil, *Book of Daniel,* 303.

27. This interpretation is further supported by Schwantes, "*'Ereb Bōqer* of Dan 8:14 Re-examined," *AUSS* 16 (1978) 375-85. He points out (pp. 376-77) that the adjective *tāmîd,* "continual/regular," is used as a noun, "the regular burnt offering," only in Daniel (8:11, 12, 13; 11:31; and 12:11). "It should be observed that *tāmîd* is a technical term in the language of the ritual to designate the double burnt offering of the morning and the evening which should be offered daily" (cf. Exod 29:38-42; Num 28:3-6). This would argue for 2,300 days. However, "one should observe that the word *tāmîd* itself is not found in Dan 8:14. It is simply assumed on account of the references to it in vv. 11-13" (pp. 380-81). But "the language of the ritual always designates the morning sacrifice before the one of the evening, without exception . . . [see, e.g.] Exod 29:39; Num 28:4; 2 Kings 16:15; 1 Chr 16:40; 23:30; 2 Chr 2:4; 13:11; 31:3; Ezra 3:3" (p. 381). "If the author borrowed the phrase *'ereb bōqer* [evening, morning] from Gen 1, as the evidence seems to substantiate, then its meaning points not to half days . . . but to full days" (p. 385).

28. See Keil, *Book of Daniel,* 306-7; Leupold, *Exposition of Daniel,* 355-57; Goldingay, *Daniel,* 213; Duguid, *Daniel,* 132; and Harman, *Study Commentary on Daniel,* 197.

29. Goldingay, *Daniel,* 213. So also Harman, *Study Commentary on Daniel,* 197, "In the previous chapter and the following one, numbers are also employed in a symbolic way, and this seems to be the best approach here."

In seeking to discern such symbolic significance, Keil notes that 2,300 "can stand in such a relation to the number seven as to receive a symbolic meaning." When we divide 2,300 days by 365 days, we arrive at 6 years and almost 4 months. Keil concludes, therefore, that "the oppression of the people by the little horn was to continue not fully a period of seven years. . . . The time of the oppression of Israel, and of the desolation of the sanctuary by Antiochus, . . . shall not reach the full duration of a period of divine judgment, shall not last so long as the severe oppression of Israel by the Midianites, ["seven years"] Judges 6:1, or as the famine which fell upon Israel in the time of Elisha ["seven years," 2 Kings 8:1]."[30] Leupold agrees that the 2,300 days fall short of a complete period of seven years, but he adds, "The fact that it is expressed in days reminds the troubled Israelites that the Lord will not let this period extend a day beyond what they can bear."[31]

For preaching this passage, I think we can use either option two or three, that is, we can understand the "2,300 evenings and mornings" as 2,300 literal days. If we choose option two, this time period happens to be roughly the time from 170 B.C. to 164 B.C. — from the time when Antiochus began persecuting the Jews and looting the temple until its reconsecration.[32] But because this is apocalyptic literature and the chapters before and after use symbolic numbers for periods of time (7:25, "a time, two times, and half a time"; and 9:24-27, "sev-

---

30. Keil, *Book of Daniel*, 306-7.

31. Leupold, *Exposition of Daniel*, 356-57. Cf. pp. 355, 356, "The very fact that neither the longer period of almost seven years nor the shorter of almost three-and-a-half can be made to tally with known historical facts should serve to cause interpreters to cease continuing along this line." "None of the numbers that occur in its [Daniel's] visions are in the nature of exact arithmetical calculations." Hence he opts for a symbolic interpretation. "From this point of view the number 2,300 can be interpreted in but one way" — symbolically. Goldingay, *Daniel*, 213, takes the symbolism one step further. He notes that *1 Enoch* 90:5 uses the numbers seventy and twenty-three, while Daniel 9:24-27 speaks of seventy weeks. "The first sixty-nine of the seventy weeks of years from the exile to Antiochus (Dan 9:24-27) might also be seen as three times twenty-three. The 2,300 days may, then, suggest a fixed 'significant' period, which might or might not denote a chronological period in the region of six or seven years."

32. Young, *Prophecy of Daniel*, 174, suggests that the 2,300 days cover roughly the period from 171 B.C., when Antiochus "began laying waste . . . the sanctuary," and 164 B.C., "the death of Antiochus." Cf. Keil, *Book of Daniel*, 306. Miller, *Daniel*, 229-30, notes that the text gives the termination of the 2,300 days as the reconsecration of the sanctuary, which took place in December of 164 B.C. Therefore, the beginning of the 2,300 days was in 170 B.C. In that year, "Onias III (a former high priest) was murdered at the urging of the wicked high priest Menelaus, whom Antiochus had appointed to that position for a bribe. From this point trouble between Antiochus's administration and the Jews began to brew (cf. 2 Macc 4:7-50). In 169 B.C. Antiochus looted the temple and murdered some of the Jewish people (cf. 1 Macc 1:20-28). The altar to Zeus was not set up until 167 B.C., but the persecution had been going on long before that event."

enty weeks," "seven weeks," "sixty-two weeks," "one week," and "half of the week"), I would choose option three, that is, understand the 2,300 days as a symbol: 2,300 days indicates a fixed, incomplete (less than 7-year) period of persecution.

Judging by the extensive argumentation among commentators for or against 1,150 or 2,300 days, one would think that the precise length of time is the issue. Hence preachers might be inclined to follow the commentaries and spend a significant amount of sermon time defending one side or the other. Personally, I would not make much of this issue in the sermon because these details detract from the main point of the vision. Baldwin makes the interesting observation that Gabriel does not even give an interpretation of the evenings and mornings "which formed the climax of the vision. The point of interest was not 'the future' as such, but the vindication of God's sovereignty by the restoration of His sanctuary."[33]

Theocentric Interpretation

Though this whole vision seems to focus on human power and kingdoms, that is not the case. Daniel 8:16 speaks of "a human voice," but it is clear that only God can order the angel Gabriel to explain the vision to Daniel. It is also clear that the "little horn" seeks to attack not only God's people but God himself: "Even against the Prince of the host it acted arrogantly" (v. 11); the "king of bold countenance" "shall even rise up against the Prince of princes" (v. 25).

Moreover, we must keep in mind again that Daniel frequently uses divine passives. When he writes in 8:1, "a vision appeared to me," it is *God* that gave Daniel this vision. When he writes in 8:8 that "at the height of its power, the great horn was broken," it means that God took down Alexander the Great. Similarly, when Daniel writes in 8:12, "Because of wickedness, the host was given over to it together with the regular burnt offering," he is really saying that because of Israel's wickedness, *God* gave his people over to the little horn (cf. 1:2). God is working behind the scenes. He is in control even when evil befalls his people. When an angel asks, "How long?" the response is that after a period of time set by Israel's sovereign God, "the sanctuary shall be restored to its rightful state" (v. 14) — another divine passive: God will restore his

---

33. Baldwin, *Daniel*, 160. Longman, *Daniel*, 207-8, also cautions, "The number is given not so much so that those who read Daniel's sixth-century prognostications in the second century could compute when the suffering would stop as much as to assure them that God had things under control. Furthermore, the number indicates with certainty that there would be a stopping point to the persecution, even if that number could not be computed into a definite date in the calendar as they knew it."

temple.[34] In addition, at the climax of the interpretation, Gabriel says that this "king of bold countenance" "shall be broken" (v. 25),[35] that is, *God* shall break him. Gabriel underscores this point by adding, "he shall be broken, *and not by human hands*" (v. 25; cf. Dan 2:34, 45, "a stone was cut out, not by human hands").

Textual Theme and Goal

Goldingay observes that "the symbolic vision builds up to verse 12, as the same elements recur in the portrait of ram, goat, and small horn: each appears, acts aggressively, enjoys success, but then falls."[36] Thus the theme could be about the rise and fall of human kingdoms. But we have seen that the vision's primary focus is on the little horn and its evil deeds (see above, "Structure," "The Plot Line," "Character Description," and "Repetition"). The textual theme should reflect this concentration on the evil king. We have also seen above that God is not only at work behind the scenes, allowing the evil king to do his worst, but God is also actively involved in breaking this king. Israel's God is sovereign.

God's sovereignty comes to the fore also in another way. Collins points out the importance of the question in verse 13, "How long?" "This question is highlighted by its position at the end of the vision, by the transition from vision to audition, and by the fact that it is expressed as a dialogue between angels. Most important is the assurance that the time is measured out and its duration determined."[37] Taking these ideas into account, we can formulate the textual theme as follows: *Although an evil king will attack God's temple and persecute God's people in the future, our sovereign God will limit the number of days of persecution by destroying the persecutor.*

Since this vision refers to a future persecution ("the vision is for the time of the end," v. 17, and "it refers to many days from now," v. 26), one of its goals is to forewarn Israel about this coming persecution. In addition, since God will limit the duration of this persecution and destroy the persecutor, another goal is to assure Israel that their God is sovereign and will set limits to the days of perse-

---

34. Cf. a similar passage in Zechariah 1:12-17 where an angel asks, "How long," and the response is, "Thus says the LORD, I have returned to Jerusalem with compassion; my house shall be built in it, says the LORD of hosts."

35. "'Broken' implies that God will make the object of his wrath appear as utterly shattered and impotent. . . . The verb involved is often used in the Old Testament with reference to the overthrow of kingdoms, armies, and individuals (cf. Jer 48:8; 2 Chron 14:12; Jer 17:18; Dan 11:26)." Leupold, *Exposition of Daniel,* 369.

36. Goldingay, *Daniel,* 204.

37. Collins, *Daniel* (1984), 88.

cution. Therefore, we can formulate the goal as a dual goal: *to forewarn Israel about a period of severe persecution in the future and to assure them that their sovereign God will limit the days of persecution and destroy the persecutor.*[38]

Ways to Preach Christ

In Daniel 8:13 we read, "Then I heard a holy one speaking." Because this holy one answers the question of "How long?" Calvin identifies him as Christ, "who is the chief of angels and far superior to them all." Also regarding "the appearance of a man" and "a human voice" (8:15-16), Calvin writes, "Christ therefore appeared as a man."[39] Young rightly objects that "such interpretations are not justifiable," and he himself identifies "the holy one" as an angel and the "human voice" as the voice of God.[40]

How, then, shall we move to Jesus Christ in the New Testament from the theme, "Although an evil king will attack God's temple and persecute God's people in the future, our sovereign God will limit the number of days of persecution by destroying the persecutor"? Since this chapter contains neither a promise of the coming Messiah nor a major contrast with the New Testament, we shall explore the remaining five ways to Christ. In order to avoid overlap, we shall combine redemptive-historical progression and longitudinal themes.

Redemptive-Historical Progression/Longitudinal Themes

This vision focuses on an evil king who will contend against God and persecute God's people, but God will limit the days of persecution and destroy this king. Such persecution began right at the start of redemptive history when Cain killed his brother Abel. But God called him to account: "Listen; your brother's blood is crying out to me from the ground! And now you are cursed from the ground" (Gen 4:8, 10-11). The persecution continued with God's people Israel even before they became a nation. God had told Abram, "Know this for certain, that your offspring shall be aliens in a land that is not theirs, and shall be slaves there, and they shall be *oppressed* for four hundred years; but I will bring *judgment* on the nation that they serve, and afterward they shall come out with

---

38. Cf. Steinmann, *Daniel*, 421. "For the original readers in the sixth century B.C. and for all those who lived before or during the persecution of Antiochus in the second century B.C., Daniel offered hope and comfort that God had already determined an end to the fierce persecution before it happened."

39. Calvin, *Commentaries on Daniel*, II, 106 and 112.

40. Young, *Prophecy of Daniel*, 173 and 175.

great possessions" (Gen 15:13-14). And, indeed, the Pharaoh "who did not know Joseph" commanded all Egyptians, "Every boy that is born to the Hebrews you shall throw into the Nile" (Exod 1:8, 22). But God judged the Egyptians with plagues and finally destroyed "the entire army of Pharaoh" (Exod 14:28).

Later, after God had led Israel into the Promised Land, they failed to live up to the Sinai covenant, and "the LORD gave them into the hand of Midian seven years" (Judg 6:1). But the Lord judged Midian, using Gideon to "strike down the Midianites, every one of them" (Judg 6:16). Centuries later, "the Lord let King Jehoiakim of Judah fall into his [Nebuchadnezzar's] power" (Dan 1:2), and Israel suffered in exile in Babylon. Again, the Lord judged Babylon, having its king, Belshazzar, killed and giving the kingdom to Medo-Persia (Dan 5:30-31).

While Israel suffered under the evil King Belshazzar, God gave Daniel a vision about an *end-time* persecutor of God's people, a little horn that appeared among the ten horns of the final beast. The angel explained, "He shall speak words against the Most High, shall wear out the holy ones of the Most High . . . ; and they shall be given into his power for a time, two times, and half a time" (Dan 7:25). This little horn will appear just before the final judgment and God's giving "the greatness of the kingdoms under the whole heaven" to his people as "an everlasting kingdom" (Dan 7:27; cf. 2:44). The New Testament identifies this final persecutor of God's people as the "Antichrist" who will come at "the last hour" (1 John 2:18), "the lawless one [who] will be revealed" at the end of time (2 Thess 2:8).[41] Again, God will judge this evil ruler and totally destroy him (Dan 7:26).

Meanwhile God's people can expect to be persecuted by evil kings that *prefigure*[42] this final persecutor. In Daniel 8 God gave Daniel a vision about an-

---

41. John also claims that "the spirit of the antichrist . . . is already in the world" (1 John 4:3). Paul states, similarly, that "the mystery of lawlessness is already at work" (2 Thess 2:7). The Old Testament reveals that throughout redemptive history various antigod figures have attacked God and his people — figures such as Pharaoh, Midian, Nebuchadnezzar, and Belshazzar. Such persecution continued in New Testament times: Roman emperors like Caligula, Nero, Titus, and Hadrian, and more recently Hitler, Stalin, Mao-Zedong, Idi Amin, and many others. Lederach, *Daniel*, 198, mentions "Caligula's decree in A.D. 39-40 (later rescinded) to convert Jewish places of worship into shrines for the imperial cult and erect a statue of the emperor as Zeus in the Jerusalem temple. . . . The destruction of the temple by Titus and the Romans in A.D. 70 . . . ; Hadrian's construction there of a temple honoring Jupiter around A.D. 130; and attempts to enforce emperor worship (Rev. 13:8, 12; 19:20)."

42. As there are types of Christ in the Old Testament that point forward to the antitype Jesus Christ, so there are types of the Antichrist in the Old Testament that point forward to the final Antichrist. Cf. Archer, "Daniel," 99, "We are to understand the relationship between the little horn of the Greek Empire and that of the latter-day fourth kingdom to be that of type and antitype similar to that between Joshua and Jesus (Heb 4:8) and Melchizedek and Christ (Heb 7)." See also ibid., 106. Because the little horn in Daniel 8 is a type of the final Antichrist, the two horns have many similarities. Both horns are called "little" (7:8; 8:9). Both attack God (7:25;

other "little horn" who would desecrate God's temple and persecute God's people (Dan 8:9-14, 23-25). This king is the Seleucid king Antiochus IV (175-164
B.C.) He is called a "little" horn because he acts like the Daniel 7 "little" horn,
the final Antichrist. But God judges Antiochus: "He shall be broken, and not by
human hands" (Dan 8:25).

In the New Testament, Jesus also links the evil King Antiochus with the final Antichrist. Jesus tells his followers, "So when you see *the desolating sacrifice*
standing in the holy place, as was spoken of by the prophet Daniel [e.g., 8:13][43]
(let the reader understand), then those in Judea must flee to the mountains. . . .
Immediately after the *suffering* of those days the sun will be darkened. . . . Then
the sign of the Son of Man will appear in heaven, and then all the tribes of the
earth will mourn, and they will see 'the Son of Man coming on the clouds of
heaven' with power and great glory" (Matt 24:15-16, 29-30). The final Antichrist
will persecute God's people relentlessly. But God will judge and destroy him.
Paul writes about the "lawless one" who is "destined for destruction. He opposes and exalts himself above every so-called god . . . , so that he takes his seat
in the temple of God, declaring himself to be God. . . . The mystery of lawlessness is already at work, but only until the one[44] who now restrains it is removed.
And then the lawless one will be revealed, whom the Lord Jesus will *destroy* with
the breath of his mouth, *annihilating* him by the manifestation of his coming"
(2 Thess 2:3-8) — the final judgment.

Typology

Earlier we identified "the Prince of the host" as God (see p. 260 above). Steinmann compares the phrases "the Prince of the army" (8:11; identified as "the
Prince of princes" in 8:25) with the longer phrase in Joshua 5:14, "the commander of the army of Yahweh," and identifies this Prince in Daniel 8 more precisely as "the preincarnate Christ, the Word not yet made flesh."[45] But, as we

---

8:25). Both persecute God's people (7:21; 8:12, 24). Both are limited in the amount of time God
allows them to persecute his people ("a time, times, and half a time," 7:25; "two thousand three
hundred evenings and mornings," 8:14). See Steinmann, *Daniel*, 151, 401, and Miller, *Daniel*, 232,
237-38.

43. Daniel 11:31, similarly, speaks of Antiochus setting up "the abomination that makes desolate" (cf. 9:27; 12:11).

44. "There have been many suggestions as to the identity of this restrainer: the Roman state
with its emperor, Paul's missionary work, the Jewish state, the principle of law and government
embodied in the state, the Holy Spirit or the restraining ministry of the Holy Spirit through the
church, and others." *NIV Study Bible*, 1829 (n. on 2 Thess 2:6). See also p. 283, n. 108 below.

45. Steinmann, *Daniel*, 402-3.

noted before, identifying an Old Testament figure with the preincarnate Christ does not make the sermon Christocentric in the sense of integrating "the message of the text with the climax of God's revelation in the person, work, and/or teaching of Jesus Christ as revealed in the New Testament."[46]

However, if one is convinced that "the Prince of the host" is indeed the preincarnate Christ, one can move to the New Testament by treating "the Prince of the host" as a *special type* of Christ and look for analogies (and escalations) between the Old Testament type and its New Testament antitype. The first major analogy is that both were attacked by evil people. "The Prince of the host" was attacked by the evil king (8:11, 25). Jesus was also attacked but much more severely. When Jesus was born, King Herod tried to kill him (Matt 2:13); the devil[47] tempted him three times (Matt 4:1-10); the people of his hometown of Nazareth tried to "hurl him off the cliff" (Luke 4:28); "The chief priests and the scribes were looking for a way to put Jesus to death" (Luke 22:2); Pilate had Jesus flogged and then "handed him over to be crucified" (Matt 27:26); the Roman soldiers mocked Jesus, "spat on him," struck him on the head with a reed, and crucified him (Matt 27:30-35). Surely, the spirit of the Antichrist was at work attacking the Christ even during Jesus' own lifetime.

The second major analogy is that the attacker will be destroyed. Daniel 8:25 declares that the evil king "shall even rise up against the Prince of princes. But he shall be *broken,* and *not* by human hands." The implication is that "the Prince of princes" will break the evil king. This prediction was fulfilled when King Antiochus was destroyed. But it will find final fulfillment at Jesus' Second Coming. Paul writes about the end of time: "Then the lawless one [the Antichrist] will be revealed, *whom the Lord Jesus will destroy* with the breath of his mouth, annihilating him by the manifestation of his coming" (2 Thess 2:8).[48]

Analogy

One can also draw an analogy from Daniel's goal to the goal Jesus had with his teaching: as Daniel sought to assure Israel that their sovereign God would limit

---

46. My definition. See *Preaching Christ from the Old Testament,* 10.

47. The devil here attacks Jesus directly; at other times he attacks through human intermediaries (e.g., "Satan entered into Judas" to betray Jesus; Luke 22:3). The Antichrist figures in history are all ultimately directed by Satan (cf. 2 Thess 2:9).

48. Jesus himself said, "Immediately after the suffering of those [last] days the sun will be darkened, and the moon will not give its light; the stars will fall from heaven, and the powers of heaven will be shaken. Then the sign of the Son of Man will appear in heaven, . . . and they will see 'the Son of Man coming on the clouds of heaven' with power and great glory. And he will send out his angels with a loud trumpet call, and they will gather his elect from the four winds, from one end of heaven to the other" (Matt 24:29-31).

the days of their future persecution, so Jesus assures his church that God will limit the days of their future persecution by the Antichrist. Jesus said, "If the Lord had not cut short those days, no one would be saved; but for the sake of the elect, whom he chose, he has cut short those days" (Mark 13:20).

New Testament References

The appendix to the Greek New Testament lists eight New Testament references or allusions to Daniel 8, six of them in Revelation, but none establish a way for preaching Christ from Daniel 8.[49]

Sermon Theme, Goal, and Need

We formulated the textual theme as, "Although an evil king will attack God's temple and persecute God's people in the future, our sovereign God will limit the number of days of persecution by destroying the persecutor." From our later perspective, we know that God did indeed limit the days of Antiochus's persecution. In the New Testament, Jesus applies Daniel's vision of the "desolating sacrilege" to the destruction of the temple, which would take place in A.D. 70 (Luke 21:20-24), and then to the end-time persecution (Luke 21:25-28). Jesus said, "At that time there will be great suffering, such as has not been from the beginning of the world until now, no, and *never will be. And if those days had not been cut short, no one would be saved; but for the sake of the elect those days will be cut short*" (Matt 24:21-22). Since the New Testament, like Daniel, looks for this persecutor in the future (Matt 24:21-22; 2 Thess 2:3-8; 1 John 1:18), we can basically make the textual theme the sermon theme. But we need to make two minor changes. Since the final Antichrist is not necessarily "a king," we will use the more general word "ruler," which will cover both King Antiochus and the Antichrist. And since the temple was destroyed in A.D. 70 and replaced by the church (John 4:21-23), we shall make "God's temple" "God's dwelling place," covering both the Old Testament temple and the New Testament church. The sermon theme, then, becomes, *Although an evil ruler will attack God's dwelling place and persecute God's people in the future, our sovereign God will limit the number of days of persecution by destroying the persecutor.*

We formulated Daniel's goal as, "to forewarn Israel about a period of severe persecution in the future and to assure them that their sovereign God will limit

---

49. Matthew 24:15, quoted on p. 267 above, is listed under Daniel 11:31. See p. 319, n. 92 below.

the days of persecution and destroy the persecutor." Since Jesus, Paul, and John also forewarn us about the persecution of God's people in the last days, the sermon goal can be similar to the textual goal: *to forewarn Christians about a period of severe persecution in the future and to assure them that their sovereign God will limit the days of persecution.*[50] This dual goal points to the needs this sermon ought to address: Some people are not prepared for the end-time persecution of the church and may give up hope as soon as it starts; others may wonder how long it will last.

Sermon Form

With this chapter we need to give some extra thought to the form of the sermon. An expository sermon usually follows the passage, reading and explaining verse by verse. But in this chapter the whole vision is related first, followed by Gabriel's explanation. For the sake of efficiency, several commentators combine sections of the vision with the appropriate section of Gabriel's interpretation. Anderson states, "It will greatly facilitate the treatment of this chapter if the interpretation (vv. 15-26) is applied immediately to the vision."[51] Ferguson, for example, combines Daniel 8:1-4 and 15-20; 8:5-8 and 21-22; and 8:9-14 and 23-27.[52]

Combining the vision and Gabriel's explanation is undoubtedly more efficient. The downside is that it forces preachers and their congregations to jump back and forth in this chapter. More importantly, it overrides the textual story line and eliminates any sense of suspense. The best option may be to use Gabriel's explanation in verses 20-22 to quickly identify the ram and the goat (vv. 3-8)[53] as well as to use verse 24, "the *people* of the holy ones," to quickly identify "the host" of verse 10, but to keep the story line and suspense by following the remainder of the preaching text verse by verse.

Another issue to consider with respect to sermon form is whether to include a formal sermon introduction preparing the congregation for the needs addressed in this sermon. If this sermon follows right after one on Daniel 7, I think we can best use the sermon introduction to give the congregation a quick

---

50. Cf. Longman, *Daniel*, 215, "The function of the highly symbolic numbers in Daniel and elsewhere. . . . Their purpose is not for date-setting but for comfort. They remind us that God knows what he is doing. God is sovereign and has set a limit on how long the present evil world will oppress us."

51. Anderson, *Signs and Wonders*, 92.

52. Ferguson, *Daniel*, 167-72.

53. See Leupold, *Exposition of Daniel*, 336-37, "Combining both halves at this place [v. 3 about the ram] will save us needless repetition as we go along. The ram is Persia or, according to verse 20, Medo-Persia." Cf. ibid., 358.

review of the broad vision of Daniel 7 and then move on to the more specific vision of Daniel 8.

Sermon Exposition

Last Sunday we explored the broad vision of world history in Daniel 7. Daniel saw four beasts coming up out of the sea: a lion, a bear, a leopard, and a monster. These beasts each represented an evil world empire. The lion is Babylonia. It will be replaced by the bear, which is Medo-Persia. Medo-Persia, in turn, will be replaced by the leopard, the kingdom of Greece. And Greece, finally, will be replaced by the monster, the Roman Empire. In its aftermath, a little horn will arise who will severely persecute God's people. But God will sit in judgment, destroy this little horn with fire, and give his everlasting kingdom to his people. In Daniel 7, then, God gives Daniel a grand vision of the sweep of human history from the time of Babylon to the destruction of the end-time Antichrist and the establishment of God's kingdom on earth.

Three years later, God gives Daniel another vision. This vision narrows the scope. In Daniel 8 the vision skips over Babylon and zooms in on the second and third beasts and especially on another little horn. We read in Daniel 8:1-2, "In the third year[54] of the reign of King Belshazzar a vision appeared to me, Daniel, after the one that had appeared to me at first. In the vision I was looking and saw myself in Susa the capital, in the province of Elam, and I was by the river Ulai." Susa was located in what today is southwest Iran. It was some 200 miles east of Babylon.[55] In Jewish thinking, it was "*the* seat of the Persian empire."[56] Thus in this vision Daniel was transported away from Babylon toward the next world empire, the Medo-Persian Empire. He sees himself by the river Ulai.[57]

---

54. Since Belshazzar probably began his co-regency in 550 B.C. his third year would be 548-547 B.C. Steinmann, *Daniel*, 390-91, notes that this was "around the time that Cyrus defeated the Lydian king Croesus. This was Cyrus' last major conquest before taking Babylon [in 539 B.C.].... [This] might explain why this vision begins with a ram that represents Medo-Persia."

55. "Susa . . . was located about 220 miles east of Babylon and 150 miles north of the Persian Gulf. At the time of Daniel's vision it was the capital of Elam and later became one of the Medo-Persian royal cities (cf. Neh 1:1 and 2:1; Esth 1:2). Susa was used as a winter residence by the Persian kings and was made the administrative capital of the empire by Darius I in 521 B.C." Miller, *Daniel*, 221.

56. Goldingay, *Daniel*, 208. Jeske, *Daniel*, 150, adds, "Since Daniel's vision predicted the downfall of the Persian Empire, the palace at Susa seems an appropriate background for the vision."

57. "According to Pliny, it flowed close by Susa. Apparently it was a large artificial canal (ca. 900 feet in breadth) which connected two other rivers, the Choaspes and the Coprates, and passed by Susa on the north east." Young, *Prophecy of Daniel*, 167.

In verse 3 Daniel reports, "I looked up and saw a ram standing beside the river. It had two horns. Both horns were long, but one was longer than the other, and the longer one came up second." This describes the Medo-Persian Empire. Persia came up after Media, but when it conquered Media it became the more important part of this empire.[58] This identification of the Medo-Persian Empire is confirmed in verse 20. The angel explains to Daniel, "As for the ram that you saw with the two horns, these are the kings of Media and Persia."

In verse 4 Daniel continues, "I saw the ram charging westward and northward and southward.[59] All beasts were powerless to withstand it, and no one could rescue from its power; it did as it pleased and became strong."[60] To the west, Medo-Persia conquered Babylonia, Syria, Asia Minor, and even made moves toward Europe by making raids on Greece. To the north it conquered Armenia and the area around the Caspian Sea. To the south it conquered Egypt and Ethiopia.[61] Medo-Persia did indeed become a mighty empire, doing as it pleased and becoming strong.[62] But it would not last forever.

Verse 5, "As I was watching, a male goat appeared from the west, coming across the face of the whole earth without touching the ground. The goat had a horn between its eyes." This goat comes from the west. It moves so fast that it sweeps across the face of the earth without touching the ground. It flies like lightning.

Verses 6-7, "It [the goat] came toward the ram with the two horns that I had seen standing beside the river, and it ran at it with savage force. I saw it approaching the ram. It was enraged against it and struck the ram, breaking its two horns. The ram did not have power to withstand it; it threw the ram down

---

58. "Before Cyrus came to power, Media already was a major force, while Persia was a small country holding less than fifty thousand square miles of territory. But Cyrus succeeded in gaining control of powerful Media to the north (ca. 550 B.C.) and then made Persia the more important of the two states. With these nations united, he established the vast Medo-Persian Empire." Miller, *Daniel*, 222.

59. Lederach, *Daniel*, 187, links the three directions with the three ribs of Daniel 7:5: "As the bear had three ribs, so the ram charged in three directions." Buchanan, *Book of Daniel*, 218, suggests, "There is no mention of Cyrus' eastward expansion, probably because the author, whose interest was Palestine, was not interested in any eastward expansion." Redditt, *Daniel*, 137, proposes that the author "perhaps . . . considered the territory east of Persia part of the Persian homeland."

60. "Became strong" is literally "became great." This word "can be used positively of Yahweh (Ps 126:2, 3) but often has a connotation of rebellion (Jer 48:26, 42)." Collins, *Daniel*, 330. Cf. Goldingay, *Daniel*, 209, and Steinmann, *Daniel*, 394.

61. See Young, *Prophecy of Daniel*, 168.

62. "The power of the Medo-Persian Empire was such that it was the unquestioned authority in the Near East for about two centuries (550-331 B.C.)." Steinmann, *Daniel*, 399.

to the ground and trampled upon it,[63] and there was no one who could rescue the ram from its power."

In verse 21 the angel explains to Daniel, "The male goat is the king of Greece, and the great horn between its eyes is the first king." The king of Greece is Alexander the Great, who conquered the Medo-Persian Empire with amazing speed. In 334 B.C. he launched his attack against Persia. "With only thirty-five thousand men, Alexander's forces plunged through the [Granicus] River attacking Darius's one hundred thousand footmen and ten thousand horsemen, reportedly killing twenty thousand at a loss of only one hundred Greek troops. Complete victory was assured at the battles of Issus the following year and at Guagamela in 331 B.C."[64] Within three years Alexander the Great conquered the whole of the Near East.[65]

Verse 8, "Then the male goat grew exceedingly great;[66] but at the height of its power, the great horn was broken, and in its place there came up four prominent horns toward the four winds of heaven." "At the height of its power, the great horn was broken." The implication of the passive voice is that *God* broke the great horn. God was still in charge. Alexander the Great became sick and died. He was only thirty-three years old. At his death his kingdom fell apart. "In its place there came up four prominent horns," that is, four kingdoms. Each of these four kingdoms was ruled by one of Alexander's generals.[67]

Verse 9 skips over some 150 years[68] of clashes between the Syrian Seleucids and the Egyptian Ptolemies until it comes to another horn: "Out of one of them came another horn, a little one, which grew exceedingly great toward the south, toward the east, and toward the beautiful land." Out of the Syrian Seleucid kingdom grew another horn, another king. This king started out as a little horn but "grew exceedingly great." We can identify this king as Antiochus IV, the eighth

---

63. "Trampling is a good term to describe what a large army does to the land through which it marches. It destroys the crops, loots the resources of the area, and leaves the land desolate. This is specially true if the army used elephants, as both the Persians and the Greeks did." Buchanan, *Book of Daniel*, 240.

64. Ferguson, *Daniel*, 170.

65. For details, see Towner, *Daniel*, 119; Miller, *Daniel*, 223, and Steinmann, *Daniel*, 400. Leupold, *Exposition of Daniel*, 342, writes, "Alexander's conquest was nothing less than as complete an overthrow of Persia as was thinkable. His conquests put a new complexion on the whole Asiatic world and set in motion ideas and principles that were to dominate the conquered areas for centuries to come."

66. "The ram 'became great' ["strong," v. 4] but the goat 'grew very great,' reflecting the greater extent of Alexander's conquests." Lucas, *Daniel*, 214.

67. "These are 1) Macedonia under Cassander, 2) Thrace and Asia Minor under Lysimachus, 3) Syria under Seleucus and 4) Egypt under Ptolemy." Young, *Prophecy of Daniel*, 169.

68. Alexander the Great died in 323 B.C., and Antiochus IV began his reign in 175 B.C.

ruler of the Seleucid kingdom in Syria (175-164 B.C.). He started out little because he was not heir to the throne — his nephew was. But through bribery, Antiochus became king and started his conquests. He "grew exceedingly great toward the south," where he invaded Egypt; "toward the east," where he conquered Persia, Parthia, and Armenia; "and toward the beautiful land," that is, the Promised Land.[69] It is because he would occupy "the beautiful land" of Canaan that this evil king becomes the climax of the vision. For God's covenant people lived in "the beautiful land."[70]

Verse 10, "It grew as high as the host of heaven. It threw down to the earth some of the host and some of the stars, and trampled on them." Having occupied "the beautiful land" where God's people lived, Antiochus "threw down to the earth some of the host and some of the stars, and trampled on them." In this context, "the host [or army] of heaven" and the stars refer to God's people, the people who worship the king of heaven.[71] In verse 24 the angel explains that this evil king shall destroy "the *people* of the holy ones," that is, God's holy people. So this evil king grows "as high as the host of heaven." He will dare to attack even God's holy people and trample on them. To trample on them indicates severe persecution.

A book about that persecution, the book of Maccabees, reports that Antiochus "ordered his soldiers to cut down without mercy everyone they encountered, and to butcher all who took refuge in their houses. It was a massacre of young and old, a slaughter of women and children, a butchery of virgins and infants. There were eighty thousand victims in the course of those three days, forty thousand dying by violence and as many again being sold into slavery" (2 Macc 5:12-14).[72]

Verse 11, "Even against the prince of the host it acted arrogantly; it took the regular burnt offering away from him and overthrew the place of his sanctuary." The Prince of the host is God himself. Antiochus acted arrogantly even against God. He did this by attacking the temple where God lived and was honored with daily sacrifices. He "took the regular burnt offering[73] away from him

69. "The land of God's promise could not but be most beautiful, especially to those exiled from it." Baldwin, *Daniel*, 157, with references to Daniel 11:41, Jeremiah 3:19, and Ezekiel 20:6, 15. Cf. Miller, *Daniel*, 225.

70. "Daniel's prophecy does not list Antiochus' military campaigns in chronological order. Instead, he names the attack on 'the beautiful [land]' last (Dan 8:9) so that he can continue by focusing on the king's atrocities toward the Jews in and around Jerusalem." Steinmann, *Daniel*, 402.

71. See "The Host of Heaven," pp. 258-59 above.

72. Quotations from the books of Maccabees are taken from *The Jerusalem Bible*, 1966.

73. "The regular burnt offering" was "the standard daily burnt offering ordained in Num 28:3, consisting of one lamb presented at sunrise and one presented at sunset, together with a quantity of flour and oil (Num 28:5). This offering presented the atonement of the believing nation." Archer, "Daniel," 100.

and overthrew[74] the place of his sanctuary." "In 167 B.C. Antiochus issued the order that the regular ceremonial observances to Yahweh were forbidden, and thus sacrifices ceased being offered to him (cf. 1 Macc 1:44-45)."[75] Moreover, the book of Maccabees reports that "the king erected the *abomination of desolation* above the altar" (1 Macc 1:54). This probably refers to setting up a pagan altar for the Greek god Zeus above the altar of burnt offerings.[76] This installation made it impossible for faithful priests to bring the morning and evening sacrifices to the God of Israel. Thus Antiochus "took the regular burnt offering away from" God. Moreover, since the temple area was now unfit for worshiping God, it became *desolate*, empty, unoccupied by God-worshipers. "The abomination of *desolation*."

But Antiochus insulted God even more. The book of Maccabees reports that "he had the audacity to enter the holiest Temple in the entire world . . . ; with his unclean hands he seized the sacred vessels" and took them away (2 Macc 5:15-16). And then he "defiled the altar with the first pagan sacrifices (1 Macc 1:59), which probably included [unclean] pigs (1 Macc 1:47; cf. 2 Macc 6:4)."[77] Thus Antiochus not only persecuted God's people but also directly attacked the God of Israel.

We wonder why God allowed Antiochus to attack God himself and to persecute his people. Verse 12 provides the answer, "Because of *wickedness*, the host

---

74. "The temple was not literally overthrown or destroyed in 167 B.C., in the manner of 587 B.C. and A.D. 70, though it was robbed of its valuables, emptied of its worshipers, and defiled by the accoutrements of an alien cult (1 Macc 1:20-24, 39-40; 3:45; cf. 4:43-48)." Goldingay, *Daniel*, 211. Cf. Lederach, *Daniel*, 190.

75. Miller, *Daniel*, 227.

76. "The suppression of the sacrifices was ensured by the installation of a pagan altar upon the altar of burnt offering in the temple [court] (1 Macc 1:59; cf. 2 Macc 6:5)." Collins, *Daniel*, 334. Commentators are not agreed on whether "the abomination of desolation" was a pagan altar or a statue of Zeus. This disagreement stems from ambiguity in Maccabees. In the words of Goldingay, *Daniel*, 212, "According to 1 Macc 1:54, the abomination was erected on the altar of sacrifice, and this has usually suggested it was an image of Zeus (and of Antiochus, according to Porphyry). 1 Macc 1:59, however, speaks of there being a (pagan) altar erected on the altar of sacrifice (cf. Josephus, *Ant.* 12.5.4 [12.253])." Steinmann, *Daniel*, 403, opts for a statue of Zeus: "Most likely this was an idol to Zeus (cf. 2 Macc 6:1-2) made to resemble Antiochus himself." So also Archer, "Daniel," 100. Miller, *Daniel*, 228, is more tentative: it "likely alludes to the Zeus statue (or altar) set up by Antiochus." Redditt, *Daniel*, 140; Russell, *Daniel*, 148; Lederach, *Daniel*, 191; and *The Jerusalem Bible*, 659, n. l, along with Collins (above), judge "the abomination" to be a pagan altar erected on the altar in front of the temple. I side with the latter because 1 Maccabees 1:59 clearly states that "sacrifice was offered on the altar erected over the altar of burnt offering," while the installation of a statue of Zeus is only an inference.

77. Steinmann, *Daniel*, 403. Cf. Archer, "Daniel," 104, "By . . . sacrificing swine on the altar, he committed the greatest possible sacrilege and affront to the Jewish people" and to Yahweh himself.

was given over to it together with the regular burnt offering." It was because of Israel's wickedness that "the host," that is, Israel, "was given over to it."[78] Again, we have the passive voice. What this verse is really saying is that because of Israel's wickedness, God[79] gave her over into the hands of Antiochus. Just as God earlier gave Israel over into the hands of King Nebuchadnezzar of Babylon (Dan 1:2), so here God gives his people over into the hands of this Seleucid king. In Deuteronomy God had warned Israel that disobedience would lead to serving "your enemies whom the LORD will send against you" (Deut 28:48; cf. Dan 9:11).

The second book of Maccabees also refers to Israel's wickedness. It reports the last words of one of Israel's martyrs: "We are suffering like this through our own fault, having sinned against our own God; the result has been terrible" (2 Macc 7:18). What was that wickedness? Maccabees relates that King Antiochus "issued a proclamation to his whole kingdom that all were to become a single people, each *renouncing* his particular customs. All the pagans conformed to the king's decree, and many Israelites chose to *accept his religion, sacrificing to idols and profaning the sabbath*" (1 Macc 1:41-43). This book further tells us that they "built a gymnasium in Jerusalem, such as the pagans have, disguised their circumcision, and *abandoned the holy covenant*, submitting to the heathen rule as willing slaves of impiety" (1 Macc 1:14-15). In short, many Israelites disobeyed God's law and broke his covenant.

The end of verse 12 tells us that this little horn "cast truth to the ground, and kept prospering in what it did." Casting "truth to the ground" means that Antiochus sought to destroy God's word, God's law (cf. Ps 119:142).[80] The first book of Maccabees (1:45-50) tells us that the king prohibited burnt offerings and sacrifices in the temple and ordered the Jews to *profane* "sabbaths and feasts," build altars and "shrines for *idols*," sacrifice "pigs and unclean beasts," and leave "their sons uncircumcised," "so that they should forget the Law and

---

78. This is a difficult verse to translate and interpret. Many commentators understand the "wickedness" to be that of Antiochus IV (see, e.g., Goldingay, *Daniel*, 211; Collins, *Daniel*, 335; Longman, *Daniel*, 204; and Steinmann, *Daniel*, 403). But many others understand the "wickedness" to be that of Israel (see, e.g., Calvin, *Commentaries on Daniel*, II, 102; Young, *Prophecy of Daniel*, 172; Feinberg, *Daniel*, 106; Miller, *Daniel*, 227; Duguid, *Daniel*, 131; and Hill, "Daniel," 150). In his prayer in the next chapter (Dan 9:4-19), Daniel acknowledges over and over that God sent Israel into the Babylonian exile because of their sin. Later the books of Maccabees make equally clear that Antiochus's persecution of Israel was God's punishment for their sin (see, e.g., 1 Macc 1:15-16, 41-43; 2 Macc 7:18).

79. "The passive verb 'given' or 'permitted' is a circumlocution for divine agency. The implication is that God is the one who gives or permits the results. Here, as elsewhere in the book, the actions of kings — even the most wicked tyrants — are subsumed under God's sovereignty." Seow, *Daniel*, 124.

80. "The 'truth' that is 'thrown to the ground' is no doubt the Jewish Torah." Lucas, *Daniel*, 217.

revoke all observance of it. Anyone not obeying the king's command was to be put to death." Further, "Any books of the Law that came to light were torn up and burned. Whenever anyone was discovered possessing a copy of the covenant or practicing the Law, the king's decree sentenced him to death" (1 Macc. 1:56-57). This evil king tried to destroy the very foundation of Israel's religion, yet we read that he "kept prospering in what he did." Would this persecution go on forever?

Suddenly Daniel hears an angel speaking. Verse 13, "Then I heard a holy one speaking, and another holy one said to the one that spoke, 'For how long is this vision concerning the regular burnt offering, the transgression that makes desolate, and the giving over of the sanctuary and host to be trampled?'"[81] The angel asks the very question that must have been on Daniel's mind and that of his readers: How long will this go on? It is an important question. It is the question often raised by God's people when they suffer. Many times the Psalmists cry out, "How long, O LORD? Will you forget me forever? How long will you hide your face from me? How long must I bear pain in my soul, and have sorrow in my heart all day long? How long shall my enemy be exalted over me?"[82]

The angel raises the same sorts of questions: How long will the regular burnt offering honoring God be extinguished? How long will "the transgression that makes desolate" remain in God's holy temple? He is referring to the altar for the Greek god Zeus set up on top of the altar of the Lord. That transgression made the temple desolate, empty of God-worshipers. How long will the giving over of the sanctuary to pagans continue? And how long will "the host," God's people, be trampled?

Verse 14, "And he answered him,[83] 'For two thousand three hundred evenings and mornings; then the sanctuary shall be restored to its rightful state.'" The Hebrews count days from evening to morning. For example, Genesis 1

---

81. Seow, *Daniel*, 125, suggests that the awkward Hebrew in this verse may reflect that "for the writer the problem of divine consent to allow the temple to be desecrated and its feasts suspended must have been so terrifying that even a member of the divine council could only stammer in response to the prospect. Hence, the question is posed with many ellipses, literally, 'Until when . . . the vision . . . the regular offering . . . and the transgression . . . devastating . . . delivering . . . and the sanctuary . . . an army . . . trampling.'"

82. Psalm 13:1-2. Cf. Psalm 79:5, "How long, O LORD? Will you be angry forever?" Psalm 80:4, "O LORD, God of hosts, how long will you be angry?" Cf. Psalms 6:3; 90:13; Isaiah 6:11; Jeremiah 12:4; Habakkuk 1:2; Zechariah 1:12. Even in Revelation 6:10, the martyrs in heaven cry out, "Sovereign Lord, holy and true, how long will it be before you judge and avenge our blood on the inhabitants of the earth?"

83. The NASB and NIV follow the Hebrew in translating, "He said to *me*." The NRSV follows the Septuagint and the Syriac translations, which "assume that the reply was given to the questioner ('to him,' making the alteration from *'ēli* to *'ēlayv*)." Harman, *Study Commentary on Daniel*, 196.

reads, "And there was evening and there was morning, the first day" (Gen 1:5). The persecution, therefore, will last 2,300 evenings and mornings, that is, 2,300 days.[84] Since this is apocalyptic literature, the number 2,300 is probably intended to be symbolic. 2,300 days is six years and almost four months. A complete period of God's judgment would be seven years.[85] So the 2,300 days means a fixed but foreshortened period of time. The comfort for Israel is that this persecution will last only a limited number of days. "The Lord will not let this period extend a day beyond what they can bear."[86]

Verse 14 concludes, "Then the sanctuary shall be restored to its rightful state." This did indeed come true. In 164 B.C. Judas Maccabaeus recaptured Jerusalem. He cleansed the temple and built a new altar. The dedication of this altar was called Hanukkah, which means "dedication."[87] To this day Jews celebrate the Feast of Hanukkah every December.

In verse 15 Daniel reports, "When I, Daniel, had seen the vision, I tried to understand it," but he couldn't. Small wonder Daniel did not understand the vision. Daniel is in exile in Babylon. In the vision he is transported to the later Medo-Persian Empire and receives a vision about a still later time. It has to do with God's temple in Jerusalem. But the last Daniel heard the temple had been destroyed in 587 B.C. by Nebuchadnezzar. Will God's people return to "the beautiful land"? Will they rebuild the temple? When will this persecution of God's people and the desecration of the temple take place? And how long will it last?

Verse 15 continues, "Then someone appeared standing before me, having the appearance of a man, and I heard a human voice by the Ulai, calling, 'Gabriel, help this man understand the vision.'" The person standing before Daniel is the angel Gabriel, who appears in human form.[88] Daniel hears a human voice above the river calling, "Gabriel, help this man understand the vision." Only God can command the archangel Gabriel to do something. So it is God speaking in a human voice.[89]

---

84. See the discussion above on pp. 260-63.

85. See, e.g., Judges 6:1 and 2 Kings 8:1.

86. Leupold, *Exposition of Daniel*, 357. Cf. Veldkamp, *Dreams and Dictators*, 186, "God will be counting the days. If he preserves the tears of the church in a jar, won't he also keep careful track of those 2,300 evenings and mornings?"

87. See John 10:22, "At that time the festival of the Dedication took place in Jerusalem. It was winter."

88. "The name itself, *Gabriel*, forms a play on the noun for 'a man,' *geber*, describing the angel's appearance in 8:15." Steinmann, *Daniel*, 413. Miller, *Daniel*, 231, takes this being "to be God himself. In the following verse it seems to be the 'voice' of this same person heard ordering Gabriel to explain the vision." This interpretation requires equating someone "standing before me," and the human voice "by the Ulai."

89. Cf. Daniel 4:31, "a voice came from heaven." Cf. Steinmann, *Daniel*, 412, "The human

Verse 17, "So he [Gabriel] came near where I stood; and when he came, I became frightened and fell prostrate.[90] But he said to me, 'Understand, O mortal, that the vision is for the time of the end.'" The vision is not for the exile but for "the time of the end." "The time of the end" does not mean the end of time when Christ will return on the clouds of heaven. "The time of the end" refers to the end of the future persecution Daniel has just seen.[91] In the vision an angel had asked, "How long?" And another responded, "two thousand three hundred evenings and mornings." Then Gabriel begins to explain to Daniel the time of the end of this terrible persecution.

Verses 18-19, "As he was speaking to me, I fell into a trance, face to the ground; then he touched me and set me on my feet. He said, 'Listen, and I will tell you what will take place later in the period of wrath; for it refers to the appointed time of the end.'" Gabriel will tell Daniel "what will take place *later* in the period of wrath." "The period of wrath" refers to God's wrath with his people,[92] that is, the period of the Babylonian exile, in which Daniel and his fellow Israelites find themselves, and onward.[93] Now Gabriel will tell Daniel what will

---

voice that Daniel heard came from 'between [the banks of] the Ulai . . . , on or above the water, where no mortal man could be standing' (cf. Matt 14:25-29 and the voice from heaven in Matt 3:17 when Jesus was being baptized in the Jordan)." Cf. Young, *Prophecy of Daniel*, 175.

90. "In Hebrew thinking, when a messenger of God is present, God is also fully present (Gen 16:7-13; Exod 23:20)." Lederach, *Daniel*, 192.

91. "'Time of the end' is the general prophetic expression for the time which, as the period of fulfilment, lies at the end of the existing prophetic horizon — in the present case the time of Antiochus." Keil, *Book of Daniel*, 310. Cf. Baldwin, *Daniel*, 159, and Lederach, *Daniel*, 192. See Goldingay, *Daniel*, 215, on the difference between "end" (*qēs*) and "closing part" (*'aḥărît*). Cf. Steinmann, *Daniel*, 409, 413. Young, *Prophecy of Daniel*, 176, writes, "This phrase is very difficult, but the key to its interpretation is to be found in the phrase 'in the latter part of the indignation' (v. 19). Thus it refers to the end of time when afflictions or indignation are to be permitted upon Israel."

92. "Except for Hos 7:16, the term 'wrath' . . . always designates the wrath of God." Lacocque, *Book of Daniel*, 170, with references to Isaiah 10:5, 25; 26:20; Jeremiah 10:10; 15:17; Lamentations 2:6; Ezekiel 21:36; 22:31; Nahum 1:6; Zephaniah 3:8; 1 Maccabees 1:64. Cf. Seow, *Daniel*, 128, "The term is often used of divine punishment of God's people at the hand of outsiders, such as the affliction of Judah by Assyria (Isa 10:5, 25)."

93. Commentators offer various opinions on the meaning of this verse. Most see "the period of wrath" as the period from the Babylonian captivity onward. Most also understand "*later* in the period of wrath" to refer to the time of Antiochus. The question is, Who is the object of God's wrath? On the one hand, Miller, *Daniel*, 233, states that "in this context the recipients of this [God's] wrath are Antiochus and the unfaithful Israelites of the Maccabean period." Steinmann, *Daniel*, 414, confines God's anger to Antiochus: "The indignant anger that God would have at Antiochus is not only a sign of his wrath against the king's sins but also the result of his zeal for defending and saving his people." Russell, *Daniel*, 158, on the other hand, claims that "here in Daniel it [the wrath of God] signifies that period during which God has been angry with his people and has subjected them to harassment at the hands of their enemies . . . (cf.

happen *later* in [literally, "at the end of"[94]] that period, in "the appointed time of the end." That is, Gabriel will tell Daniel especially about the final persecution Israel will suffer under the evil King Antiochus and the termination of that persecution.[95]

Gabriel begins at the beginning of the vision and quickly identifies the ram and the goat. Verses 20-23, "As for the ram that you saw with the two horns, these are the kings of Media and Persia. The male goat is the king of Greece, and the great horn between its eyes is the first king. As for the horn that was broken, in place of which four others arose, four kingdoms shall arise from his nation, but not with his power. At the end of their rule,[96] when the transgressions have reached their full measure, a king of bold countenance shall arise, skilled in intrigue."

"When the transgressions have reached their full measure" probably refers to the transgressions of the Israelites who broke God's covenant and introduced pagan customs in Israel.[97] For in verse 12 Daniel writes, "Because of *wickedness,* the host [Israel] was given over" to this little horn. "God in His mercy refrains from judgment until the measure of sin is such as to make it inevitable (Gen 15:16; 1 Thess 2:16)."[98] But "when the transgressions [of Israel] have reached their full measure," God will allow an evil king to punish his people for their wickedness. Gabriel describes the little horn as "a king of bold countenance," that is, "a fierce-looking king" (NIV), an "insolent" king (NASB).[99] Gabriel also

---

Isa 10:5, 25)." Lucas, *Daniel,* 220 agrees: "The 'last days of the time of wrath' refers to the Antiochene persecution, as v. 24 indicates." Young, *Prophecy of Daniel,* 177, takes a different tack: "When the abominations of Antiochus occur, it will be an evidence that the last time of the period of wrath has appeared. . . . This 'last time' is the appearance of Antiochus, after which the Messianic kingdom is to be established." Similarly, Keil, *Book of Daniel,* 312-13, and Leupold, *Exposition of Daniel,* 363-64.

94. Seow, *Daniel,* 128.

95. "The idea behind the phrase 'the end' (Heb. *qēṣ;* GK 7891) is a punctiliar moment in time, the end of the kingdom of Antiochus IV and hence his persecution of the Hebrews, and the reconstruction of the Jerusalem temple (v. 14)." Hill, "Daniel," 153.

96. "The text speaks of 'the end of their rule' (v. 23), the expression being an echo of the earlier expression, 'the end of the wrath' (v. 19). Hence one may now interpret 'the wrath' as the period under the rule of the kings of the [Babylonian,] Medo-Persian and Hellenistic empires." Seow, *Daniel,* 130.

97. Goldingay, *Daniel,* 217, argues that the rebels are likely Gentiles. But Young, *Prophecy of Daniel,* 179, is equally adamant that "the transgressors are not the heathen, but the apostate Jews who introduced heathen rites among Jews and built in Jerusalem a heathen gymnasium for their games." For the latter position, see also Miller, *Daniel,* 234, and Steinmann, *Daniel,* 415.

98. Baldwin, *Daniel,* 160. Cf. Matthew 23:32.

99. Steinmann, *Daniel,* 410, notes that the same word is used in Deuteronomy 28:50 for "a nation [literally] strong of face" which will show "no respect to the old or favor to the young." In its context (Deut 28:15-68) it "describes the merciless brutality by a nation God will use to pun-

describes him as "skilled in intrigue." This "seems to signify the crafty and deceptive nature of the king, who uses his intelligence for evil purposes (8:25)."[100]

In verse 24 Gabriel continues to describe the evil deeds of this king: "He shall grow strong in power,[101] shall cause fearful destruction, and shall succeed in what he does." The "fearful destruction" probably refers to Antiochus's looting of God's temple in Jerusalem (cf. 1 Macc 1:20-24).[102]

Gabriel continues in verse 24, "He shall destroy the powerful and the people of the holy ones." "The powerful" probably refers to the political enemies he will have to destroy in his climb to the top.[103] In contrast he will also destroy the *weak*, "the people of the holy ones," that is, God's people Israel. As mentioned earlier, according to 2 Maccabees (5:12-13), "He . . . ordered his soldiers to cut down without mercy everyone they encountered, and to butcher all who took refuge in their houses. It was a massacre of young and old, a slaughter of women and children, a butchery of virgins and infants."

Verse 25, "By his cunning he shall make deceit prosper under his hand, and in his own mind he shall be great." In verse 12 we read that the little horn "shall cast truth to the ground." Instead of truth, we read in verse 25 that "he shall make *deceit* prosper." "The king's mind is always busy hatching plots which he carries through to a great measure of success."[104] And "in his own mind he shall be great." He thought so much of himself that he took on the title "Antiochus Epiphanes," which means, "God made manifest." Antiochus actually thought that in him God was made visible.

Gabriel continues in verse 25, "Without warning he shall destroy many and

---

ish Israel and remove his people from the land when they prove unfaithful." Cf. Harman, *Study Commentary on Daniel*, 203, "The expression ['az-pānîm] denotes determination and ruthless carrying out of plans."

100. Steinmann, *Daniel*, 411. Cf. Russell, *Daniel*, 159, "He is skilled in political intrigue, a man given to double-talk." Cf. Porteous, *Daniel*, 129.

101. The NIV translates, "He will become very strong, but not by his own power." "The phrase 'not by his own power' is omitted from the LXX and other ancient versions and is treated by many commentators as a gloss (a later scribal insertion) in the MT." Hill, "Daniel," 156. If the pew Bible is the NIV, one can explain the phrase "not by his own power" as follows: he will become very strong "only by the permission of God." Lacocque, *Book of Daniel*, 165, 171. This is in harmony with Daniel's constant emphasis on the sovereignty of God. However, Miller, *Daniel*, 234, thinks it more likely that "the writer was saying that Antiochus's power (much of which he employed for evil purposes) would come from Satan, the prince of darkness."

102. "To 'destroy, corrupt, ruin' the divine service is the greatest act of violence against God and his people." Steinmann, *Daniel*, 410.

103. "The 'mighty men' (Heb. 'aṣûmîm) are probably other rivals to the Seleucid throne whom Antiochus 'liquidated' along the way on his rise to power." Hill, "Daniel," 155. So also Young, *Prophecy of Daniel*, 180; Leupold, *Exposition of Daniel*, 367; Russell, *Daniel*, 160; and Miller, *Daniel*, 235.

104. Porteous, *Daniel*, 129.

shall even rise up against the Prince of princes." We read about Antiochus's deceit and murder in 1 Maccabees (1:29-32). His tribute collector "came to Jerusalem with an impressive force, and, addressing them with peaceful words, he gained their confidence; then suddenly he fell on the city, dealing it a terrible blow and destroying many of the people of Israel. He pillaged the city and set it on fire, tore down its houses and encircling wall, took the women and children captive, and commandeered the cattle."

Gabriel says that this evil king "shall even rise up against the Prince of princes," that is, against God himself. "But he shall be broken, and not by human hands," that is, *God* will break him. Antiochus rose up against God by desecrating God's temple, killing God's people, and calling himself Antiochus Epiphanes, "God made manifest." But the king who rises up against God will be broken by God. Antiochus died an early, apparently gruesome, death in December of 164 B.C.[105] Our sovereign God is in control of human history. He controls even the most evil powers in this world and can annihilate them in an instant. As Job reminds us, "Shall one who hates justice govern? . . . In a moment they die; at midnight the people are shaken and pass away, and the mighty are taken away by no human hand" (Job 34:17, 20).

Having explained the vision, Gabriel continues in verse 26, "The vision of the evenings and the mornings that has been told is true. As for you, seal up the vision, for it refers to many days from now." Because the vision refers to events that will take place almost four hundred years after Daniel, Gabriel instructs Daniel to "seal up the vision." Daniel would have to roll up the scroll and seal it closed so as to preserve it for the future.

Daniel reports in verse 27, "So I, Daniel, was overcome and lay sick for some days; then I arose and went about the king's business. But I was dismayed by the vision and did not understand it." Daniel is "dismayed" by this vision of the terrible suffering God's people will undergo. And even after Gabriel's explanation, he still does not understand it. Why is this terrible suffering necessary? And when will it take place? He does not know.

Since we today live after the fulfillment of this vision, we can understand it better than Daniel did. We know that God punished his people Israel for their wickedness. But we also know that in his mercy God allowed this persecution by Antiochus for only a limited time — less than a complete seven years.

Jesus links Daniel's vision about Antiochus's persecution to the final perse-

---

105. Accounts of his death vary. According to 1 Maccabees 6:1-16 he died of "melancholy" after being defeated in Persia and hearing that his armies in Judah had been defeated. 2 Maccabees 9:5-7 says that "the all-seeing Lord, the God of Israel, struck him with an incurable and unseen complaint. . . . He was seized with an incurable pain in his bowels and with excruciating internal torture. . . . He suddenly hurtled from his chariot, and the violence of his headlong fall racked every bone in his body."

cution at the end of time. Jesus says, "So when you see the *desolating sacrilege* standing in the holy place, as was spoken of by the prophet Daniel (let the reader understand), then those in Judea must flee to the mountains. . . . At that time there will be *great suffering,* such as has not been from the beginning of the world until now, no, and never will be. And if those days had not been cut short, no one would be saved; but for the sake of the elect those days will be cut short" (Matt 24:15-22). Jesus tells us that the persecution Israel suffered under Antiochus will happen again at the end of time, but on a much larger scale. He predicts that there will be "great suffering, *such as has not been from the beginning of the world until now, no, and never will be.*" Jesus forewarns us about this final persecution of God's people so that we will not be taken by surprise and so that we will not give up on God. And Jesus also offers the comforting assurance that "for the sake of the elect those days *will be cut short.*" The final persecution of the church will not last forever.

We see, then, that the evil King Antiochus who persecuted the Jews foreshadows a ruler who will persecute God's people in the last days.[106] The New Testament calls this final evil ruler "the Antichrist." Although the Antichrist will persecute God's people especially at the end of time, even now he is active in this world. John writes to the early church, "Children, it is the *last* hour! As you have heard that antichrist is coming, so now many antichrists have come" (1 John 2:18).

One such Antichrist was King Herod. When Jesus was born in Bethlehem, this king sought to "destroy the child" (Matt 2:13). He even tried to kill the Messiah by killing "all the children in and around Bethlehem who were two years old or under" (Matt 2:16). Another figure foreshadowing the final Antichrist was the Roman emperor Nero, who persecuted the early Christians. Even in this modern period we see figures who resemble the final Antichrist: Hitler, Stalin, Mao-Zedong, Idi Amin, Kim Jong Il, and many others. But the end is not yet.

Paul calls the Antichrist, "the Man of Lawlessness." He writes, "[The Man of Lawlessness] opposes and exalts himself above every so-called god . . . , so that he takes his seat in the temple of God, declaring himself to be *God*" — much like Antiochus, who called himself "God made manifest." But in this present time the lawless one is being restrained. Paul writes in 2 Thessalonians (2:3-8), "The mystery[107] of lawlessness is already at work, but only until the one who now restrains it is removed.[108] And then the lawless one will be revealed,

---

106. See pp. 266-67, n. 42 above.

107. It is a "mystery" because it belongs "to the hidden counsel of God. . . . These secrets or mysteries are 'revealed' when by their realization at the time appointed they are manifested." Ridderbos, *Paul: An Outline of His Theology,* 509.

108. "This 'restraint' is in general to be defined as that which, in virtue of the council of God applying to it, checks the outbreak of satanic godlessness in the man of sin before the time

whom the Lord Jesus will destroy with the breath of his mouth, annihilating him by the manifestation of his coming." At his second coming the Lord Jesus will destroy this end-time Antichrist and usher in his perfect kingdom of peace.

Today God's people are persecuted in many countries around the world. Like Daniel, we may wonder why God permits this awful suffering of his people. We may begin to doubt God's promises. We may even begin to question whether our God is in control of this universe. But in this passage God reassures us that our sovereign God is indeed in control. Human kingdoms may seem ever so powerful, but God remains in control. Even when we suffer in the final days from the devastating persecution of the end-time Antichrist, God remains in control. He can and will limit the days of suffering. Jesus said about the final persecution by the Antichrist, "If the Lord had not cut short those days, no one would be saved; but for the sake of the elect, whom he chose, he has cut short those days" (Mark 13:20). Then Jesus will return on the clouds of heaven and destroy the Antichrist and all that is evil in this world (2 Thess 2:8). And he will usher in the perfect kingdom of God. This is the comforting vision that will sustain God's people in all times, places, and circumstances.

> Jesus, with your church abide;
> be our Savior, Lord, and Guide,
> while on earth our faith is tried:
> Lord, our Savior, hear us.
>
> May we holy triumphs win,
> overthrow the hosts of sin,
> gather all the nations in:
> Lord, our Savior, hear us.[109]

---

appointed for it by God. What is said in Revelation 20:2 about the shutting up and binding of Satan has not unjustly been called to mind (cf. Luke 8:31)." Ibid., 524-25. See pp. 524-26 for an elaboration of this proposal and pp. 521-24 for a discussion of other proposals. See also p. 267, n. 44 above and p. 247, n. 154.

109. Thomas Benson Pollock, "Jesus, with Your Church Abide," 1871, alt.

CHAPTER 9

Daniel's Prayer and God's Response of Seventy Weeks

Daniel 9:1-27

Seventy weeks are decreed for your people and your holy city: to finish the transgression, to put an end to sin, and to atone for iniquity, to bring in everlasting righteousness, to seal both vision and prophet, and to anoint a most holy.

Daniel 9:24

Daniel 9 offers Daniel's stirring prayer and God's hopeful response regarding the future. Although Daniel's prayer is easy to understand, God's response of the seventy weeks is another matter. Reading commentaries on the last four verses of Daniel 9 is akin to entering a bewildering maze: so many choices of ways to take, so many blind alleys and dead ends; which is the way out? In A.D. 400, the brilliant church father Jerome simply listed nine conflicting opinions of "the great teachers of the church" and left it "to the reader's judgment as to whose explanation ought to be followed."[1] That was long before rationalism, higher criticism, millenarianism, and dispensationalism added their various opinions. Today one is confronted with a mind-boggling variety of options and combinations of options.

Montgomery concludes, "The history of the exegesis of the 70 Weeks is the Dismal Swamp of Old Testament criticism."[2] Baldwin calls these four verses "the

---

1. *Jerome's Commentary on Daniel*, trans. Gleason Archer (Grand Rapids, Baker, 1958), 95, quoted by Duguid, *Daniel*, 162.

2. Montgomery, *Book of Daniel*, 400. Miller, *Daniel*, 252, echoes this thought: "These are the most controversial verses in the Bible." Cf. Young, *Prophecy of Daniel*, 191, "This passage . . . [vv. 24-27] is one of the most difficult in all the O.T., and the interpretations which have been offered are almost legion." Cf. Leupold, *Exposition of Daniel*, 403, "If there ever was an exegetical crux, this is it." Cf. Steinmann, *Daniel*, 451, "As can be seen from the quantity of textual notes on this passage, it is one of the most difficult and enigmatic portions of the O.T."

most difficult text in the book," and adds modestly, "Where others have failed it would be presumptuous to assume that one more commentator will succeed. All one can do is to continue to apply agreed criteria as consistently as possible, weigh carefully the conclusions of others, and make suggestions as to the most likely solution to a difficult problem."[3] Of course, we don't need to understand all the details of a passage before we can preach its basic message. Still, we desperately need the illumination of God's Spirit to rightly understand the message God first sent to Israel in exile and is still sending to his people today.

Text and Context

Determining the textual unit is again the easiest part of our task. Daniel 9:1 opens the unit with a chronological marker: "In the first year of Darius son of Ahasuerus. . . ." Since Daniel 10:1 has another chronological marker beginning the next unit, the textual unit here is Daniel 9:1-27.

Because the interpretation of the seventy weeks is so controversial, it is all the more important to take note of the context of this chapter in Daniel and in the whole of the Old Testament. (We will consider the New Testament later under "Ways to Preach Christ."). Daniel 2 records Nebuchadnezzar's dream of a huge statue that is brought down by a stone which "became a great mountain and filled the whole earth" (2:35). Daniel explains to the king that "the revealer of mysteries disclosed to you what is to be" (2:29). This revelation covers human history from the Babylonian kingdom to that of Medo-Persia, Greece, Rome and its aftermath, to the very end when the stone crushes human kingdoms and replaces them with the kingdom of God: "In the days of those kings the God of heaven will set up a kingdom that shall never be destroyed" (2:44). Chapter 7 records Daniel's first vision, the four beasts coming up out of the sea: again Babylon, Medo-Persia, Greece, and Rome and its aftermath. But now we receive more information about two prominent figures who will appear in the last days. From among Rome's ten horns a little horn appears: "He shall speak words against the Most High, shall wear out the holy ones of the Most High . . ." (7:25). It is the Antichrist who will appear in the last days to oppress God's people. The other figure is "one like a son of man coming with the clouds of heaven" (7:13). God will sit in judgment, destroy the Antichrist (7:11, 26), and give God's kingdom to the "one like a son of man," Jesus, and to God's people (7:14, 27).

Following these two all-encompassing pictures of history stretching from the Babylonian kingdom (605 B.C.) to the coming kingdom of God (eschaton), the vision of Daniel 8 zooms in on the second and third kingdoms, Medo-

3. Baldwin, *Daniel*, 163.

Persia and Greece and its aftermath. This vision focuses particularly on another little horn who *pre*figures the Antichrist: "Even against the Prince of the host it acted arrogantly; it took the regular burnt offering away from him and overthrew the place of his sanctuary" (8:11). Since Daniel did not understand the vision, the angel Gabriel explained that "it refers to many days from now" (8:26). In hindsight we know that this little horn coming out of the aftermath of Greece was the Seleucid king Antiochus Epiphanes, who persecuted God's people and desecrated God's temple (167-164 B.C.). "But he shall be broken, and not by human hands" (8:25).

Chapter 9 returns to the all-encompassing pictures of Daniel 2 and 7. The angel Gabriel again brings God's message: "Seventy weeks are decreed for your people and your holy city: to finish the transgression, to put an end to sin, and to atone for iniquity, to bring in everlasting righteousness, to seal both vision and prophet, and to anoint a most holy place" (9:24). This revelation focuses on the return from exile, the rebuilding of Jerusalem and the temple (9:25), "an anointed one" being "cut off" and the destruction of Jerusalem and the temple (9:26), and the destruction of the desolator (9:27). With the advantage of hindsight we see that this chapter covers the period from about a year before the return from exile (539 B.C.) to the destruction of Jerusalem by Rome in A.D. 70 to the destruction of "the desolator" on the last day.

Daniel's powerful prayer (9:4-19) fits with his earlier description: he not only prayed regularly (6:10) but made it a point to pray fervently in times of crisis (2:17-23). He acknowledges in his prayer that the exile was God's judgment upon Israel's sin (9:11-14), which was alluded to in 8:19, "the period of wrath." In fact, Daniel says that "the curse and the oath written in the law of Moses . . . have been poured out upon us" (9:11) — a reference to the covenant curses recorded in Leviticus 26:14-46 and Deuteronomy 28:15-68.

Daniel reports that he had been reading Jeremiah: "I, Daniel, perceived in the books the number of years that, according to the word of the LORD to the prophet Jeremiah, must be fulfilled for the devastation of Jerusalem, namely, seventy years" (9:2). Jeremiah 25:11-12 predicts that "these nations shall serve the king of Babylon seventy years. Then after the seventy years are completed, I will punish the king of Babylon and that nation . . . for their iniquity, says the LORD. . . ." Jeremiah 29:10 emphasizes that the exile will last a full seventy years: "Thus says the LORD: Only when Babylon's seventy years are completed will I visit you, and I will fulfill to you my promise and bring you back to this place." Since Daniel had now been in exile for about sixty-six years (from 605 B.C. until 539 B.C., "the first year of Darius"; 9:1), Daniel fervently prays for God to return his people to Jerusalem. His prayer is filled with allusions to the book of Jeremiah.[4] He also uses many of

---

4. E.g., "The acknowledgment that Israel has not listened to God's prophets echoes Jere-

the same words Solomon used in his prayer at the dedication of the temple (1 Kings 8:23-53).[5] In this prayer he also reminds God of redeeming his people from "the land of Egypt *with a mighty hand*" (9:15), which alludes to many passages in Exodus and Deuteronomy but also to Jeremiah 32:20-21.[6]

Literary Features

Although Daniel 9:20-27 can be classified as apocalyptic literature, the overall form of this chapter is different from the "symbolic visions" of Daniel 7 and 8. Collins calls the dominant form of Daniel 9, "angelic discourse." Since this covers only verses 22-27, he sees the other two forms, "the prayer" and "the epiphany of the angel," as "introductory material for the revelation."[7] Better is Lucas's proposal to call the overall forms of Daniel 9 and 10-12 "epiphany visions," which have similar structures:[8]

Circumstances [setting]	9:1-2	10:1
Supplication	9:3-19	10:2-3
Appearance of messenger	9:20-21	10:4-9
Word of assurance	9:22-23	10:10–11:1
Revelation	9:24-27	11:2–12:3
Charge to seer		12:4

---

miah's indictment of the people prior to the Babylonian exile (cf. Jer 25:4; 29:19, the very passages alluded to in v. 2). . . . The clause 'all the countries where you have scattered us' (v. 7b) repeats Jeremiah 16:15; 23:3; 32:37. . . ." Hill, "Daniel," 164. Also, Daniel says, "We have not listened to your *servants* the prophets" (9:6). "Jeremiah describes the prophets as God's 'servants' more often than any other OT book (Jer 7:25; 25:4; 26:5; 29:19; 35:15; 44:4). A further parallel is that Daniel notes how the prophets 'spoke in your name to our kings, princes, and fathers, and to all the people of the land' (9:6), and Jeremiah similarly characterizes the people of Judah as consisting of 'your fathers, your kings, your princes, and the people of the land' (Jer 44:21; cf. Jer 1:18). These parallels . . . demonstrate that Daniel had carefully read and studied Jeremiah's prophecies. He was not merely searching around in them for prophecies about the duration of the captivity. Instead, he had taken to heart Jeremiah's call for repentance and faith in the Lord." Steinmann, *Daniel*, 437. For further parallels between Daniel and Jeremiah, see ibid., 437-42.

5. E.g., Daniel speaks of God "keeping covenant and steadfast love" (9:4), the very words Solomon used in his prayer at the dedication of the temple (1 Kings 8:23). Daniel confesses, "we have sinned and done wrong, acted wickedly" (9:5), again the very words Solomon used in his prayer (1 Kings 8:47). Daniel urges the Lord, "listen and act" (9:19), the same words used by Solomon (1 Kings 8:32). For these and other examples, see Buchanan, *Book of Daniel*, 262-64.

6. Steinmann, *Daniel*, 440.

7. Collins, *Daniel* (1984), 91. On p. 92, he calls the prayer "a communal confession of sin and a petition for mercy." Towner, *Daniel*, 130, calls it a "prose prayer of penitence."

8. Lucas, *Daniel*, 35. Cf. p. 231. Miller, *Daniel*, 239, prefers "a prophetic revelation."

We shall analyze in some detail the scenic structure of this vision, its plot line, character description, and repetition.

Structure of the Vision

Hill observes, "The basic structure of chapter 9 is marked by the narrative framework: first in the date and occasion of the revelatory event (vv. 1-2); second, in the introduction to the prayer of confession (vv. 3-4a); and finally in the narrative introducing the occasion of the angel Gabriel's revelation to Daniel (vv. 20-20a)."[9] The literary unit consists of two scenes:

Scene 1. Daniel prays to the Lord his God (1-19)
    A. Setting and occasion (1-2)
        1. The first year of Darius (1)
        2. Daniel has read about the seventy years in Jeremiah (2)
    B. Daniel turns to God in prayer (3-19)
        1. Supplication with fasting, sackcloth, and ashes (3)
        2. Daniel's prayer (4-19)
            a. God's faithfulness and Israel's unfaithfulness (4-6)
            b. God's righteousness and Israel's shame (7-8)
            c. God's mercy and Israel's rebellion (9-10)
            d. God's just punishment for rebellion (11-14)
            e. God's saving his people from Egypt (15)
            f. Fourfold plea for God's mercy and action (16-19)
    Characters: Daniel and God
    (God responds by sending his messenger Gabriel)

Scene 2. The immediate appearance of Gabriel and his message (20-27)
    A. While I was praying Gabriel came in swift flight (20-21)
        1. "I have come to give you wisdom" (22)
        2. "A word went out . . . , for you are greatly beloved" (23)
    B. Gabriel's message about the remaining seventy weeks of history (24-27)
        1. The final result of the seventy weeks (24)
            a. To finish the transgression
            b. To put an end to sin
            c. To atone for iniquity
            d. To bring in everlasting righteousness
            e. To seal both vision and prophet
            f. To anoint a most holy place

9. Hill, "Daniel," 158.

2. The first seven weeks (25a)
3. The next sixty-two weeks (25b)
4. The seventieth week (26-27)

Characters: Daniel and Gabriel

The Plot Line

To understand this vision it will be helpful to sketch the plot line. Daniel 9:1 gives the setting, "In the first year of Darius. . . ." Daniel gives the occasioning incident in verse 2, "I, Daniel, perceived in the books the number of years that . . . must be fulfilled for the devastation of Jerusalem, namely, seventy years." Since the seventy years are almost up, this information moves Daniel to earnest prayer. He begins by fasting and putting on the signs of mourning: sackcloth and ashes (v. 3). Next he addresses God as "great and awesome, keeping covenant and steadfast love with those who love you and keep your commandments" (v. 4). The tension rises as he identifies with Israel and earnestly confesses their sins with a great variety of synonyms (vv. 5-10). He acknowledges that God rightly punished them by inflicting them with the covenant curse (vv. 11-14). But he reminds God that bringing Israel out of Egypt made his name renowned while now his city and his people are a disgrace (vv. 15-16). The tension rises further when Daniel urges God to "listen to the prayer of your servant," "let your face shine upon your desolated sanctuary," "incline your ear," "open your eyes" (vv. 17-18). The prayer reaches a climax in verse 19, "O Lord, hear; O Lord, forgive; O Lord, listen and act and do not delay! For your own sake, O my God, because your city and your people bear your name!" Will God answer Daniel's prayer?

The tension begins to resolve with the immediate arrival of the angel Gabriel (vv. 20-21). He assures Daniel that he will give him understanding: at the beginning of Daniel's prayer "a word went out, and I have come to declare it, for you are greatly beloved" (vv. 22-23). Then he delivers God's message: "Seventy weeks are decreed" to bring in the kingdom of God (v. 24). At the end of the first seven weeks an anointed prince will appear (v. 25a). For the next sixty-two weeks Jerusalem shall be built again "but in a troubled time" (v. 25b). This answers Daniel's prayer: Jerusalem will be rebuilt. But God has decreed even more of human history. *After* the sixty-two weeks, that is, in the final, the seventieth week, "an anointed one shall be cut off . . . , and the troops of the prince who is to come shall destroy the city and the sanctuary" (v. 26). The outcome is given in verse 27, "He shall make a strong covenant with many for one week, and for half of the week he shall make sacrifice and offering cease; and in their place shall be an abomination that desolates, until the decreed end is poured out upon the desolator."

We can sketch the plot line of Daniel 9 as that of a single plot:

Daniel 9:1-27

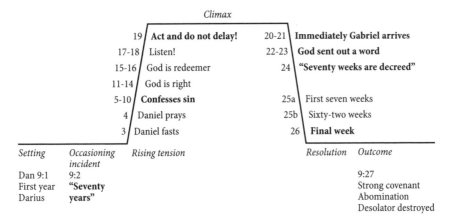

Climax

19	**Act and do not delay!**	20-21	**Immediately Gabriel arrives**
17-18	Listen!	22-23	**God sent out a word**
15-16	God is redeemer	24	**"Seventy weeks are decreed"**
11-14	God is right		
5-10	**Confesses sin**	25a	First seven weeks
4	Daniel prays	25b	Sixty-two weeks
3	Daniel fasts	26	**Final week**

Setting	*Occasioning incident*	*Rising tension*	*Resolution*	*Outcome*
Dan 9:1	9:2			9:27
First year	**"Seventy**			Strong covenant
Darius	**years"**			Abomination
				Desolator destroyed

Character Description

In his prayer Daniel characterizes God as "great and awesome," "keeping covenant and steadfast love" (v. 4). In line with this emphasis on God's covenant, Daniel here and only here uses God's covenant name, Yahweh, eight times (vv. 2, 3, 8, 10, 13, 14 [2x], and 20). He further speaks of God's "righteousness" (v. 7), his "mercy and forgiveness" (v. 9), his covenant "curse" (v. 11), bringing calamity on Israel (vv. 12, 14), the Lord's "favor" and "fidelity" (v. 13), and the Lord being "right in all that he has done" (v. 14). Daniel further describes God as delivering his people from Egypt "with a mighty hand," making his name "renowned" (v. 15). He speaks of God's "righteous acts" and pleads with God, negatively, to turn his "anger and wrath" *away* from Jerusalem (v. 16) and, positively, to let his "face shine *upon*" his desolated sanctuary (v. 17). Continuing with anthropomorphic language ("hand" and "face" above), he urges God to incline his "ear" and hear and to open his "eyes" and look (v. 18).

Daniel depicts the angel Gabriel as a "man" who comes "in swift flight" (v. 21) and who speaks in a human language (vv. 22-27). Gabriel describes Daniel as "greatly beloved" by God (v. 23). Daniel speaks of himself as having read the books of Moses and especially Jeremiah and turning to the Lord "with fasting and sackcloth and ashes" (vv. 2-3). His prayer marks him as very contrite, identifying with Israel ("*we* have sinned"; vv. 5-8, 11; cf. v. 20) and acknowledging that God is right in punishing his people (vv. 11-14). Yet he also counts on the Lord's "mercy and forgiveness" (vv. 9, 18) and is not afraid to remind the Lord that his redemption from Egypt made his name "renowned," but now Jerusalem and God's people "have become a disgrace" (vv. 15-16). Daniel concludes his prayer boldly: "O Lord, hear; O Lord, forgive; O Lord, listen and act and do not delay! For your own sake, O my God, because your city and your people bear your name!" (v. 19).

Repetition

Repetition of key words may again help us identify Daniel's emphases. We have already noted his emphasis on the covenant (*bĕrît*; 9:4), the repetition of God's covenant name, Yahweh (8x), God's covenant faithfulness and "steadfast love" as well as God's covenant curse for disobedience. Daniel further emphasizes God's covenant law with several synonyms: *miṣwâ* ("commandment"; vv. 4, 5), *mišpāṭ* ("ordinance"; v. 5), and *tôrâ* ("law"; v. 10). He highlights God's righteousness: "righteousness is on your side" (v. 7); "the LORD our God is right in all that he has done" (v. 14); and God's "righteous acts" (v. 16).

Daniel emphasizes Israel's disobedience with a variety of words: "We have sinned and done wrong, acted wickedly and rebelled, turning aside from your commandments and ordinances. We have not listened to your servants the prophets . . ." (vv. 5-6), "treachery" (v. 7), "we have sinned against you" (vv. 8, 11), "we have rebelled" (v. 9), "have not obeyed" (10), "all Israel has transgressed your law and turned aside, refusing to obey your voice" (v. 11), "our iniquities" (13), "we have disobeyed" (v. 14), "we have sinned, we have done wickedly" (v. 15), "our sins and the iniquities of our ancestors" (v. 16).

In addition, Daniel reveals his concern for Jerusalem by mentioning "Jerusalem" six times (vv. 2, 7, 12, 16 [2x], 25) and three times linking this city specifically to God: "your city" (vv. 16, 19), "the city that bears your name" (v. 18). Three times he also uses some form of desolation (vv. 18, 27 [2x]) and three times "to anoint," "anointed one" (vv. 24, 25, 26). The repetitions of "Jerusalem," "city," and "anointed one" have led to the proposal of a chiastic structure for verses 25-27:[10]

A   Construction of Jerusalem (9:25a)
   B   Coming of the Anointed One (9:25b)
      C   Construction of Jerusalem (9:25c)
         D   DEATH OF THE ANOINTED ONE (9:26a)
      C' Destruction of Jerusalem (9:26b)
   B' Activities of the Anointed One (9:27a)
A' Destruction of Jerusalem (9:27b)

Interpretation of Specific Images

Since Daniel 9:24-27 is the most controversial passage in Daniel, before proceeding to the textual theme and goal we will need to come to some clarity on

---

10. Stefanovic, *Daniel*, 368, with credit to Holbrook, *Symposium on Daniel*, 243.

the identity of the most controversial figures. We shall discuss in order the "seventy weeks" (v. 24a), the "anointed prince" (v. 25), the "anointed one" who shall be cut off (v. 26a), "the prince who is to come" (v. 26b), "he" who "shall make a strong covenant with many for one week" (v. 27a), the "desolator" (v. 27b), and finally "a most holy" (v. 24b).

Seventy Weeks

We begin with the "seventy weeks" because its interpretation is foundational for deciding on the identity of the other figures. Ironically, Daniel 9:24-27 has been called "the backbone of prophecy."[11] If it is a backbone, however, it is extremely flexible, for, as the many different interpretations show, it has been bent in many different directions.[12] A good rule of biblical hermeneutics is that difficult passages must be understood in the light of clear passages, not the other way around. Therefore we should understand the seventy weeks in the light of clearer passages in Daniel and elsewhere in Scripture.

When Gabriel says, "Seventy weeks are decreed" (v. 24), he places the noun "weeks" first "for the sake of emphasis."[13] Understood literally, seventy weeks is 490 days or 1 year and 125 days. Everyone realizes that this literal interpretation cannot be correct because it is not enough time for what God will accomplish in those seventy weeks: "to finish the transgression . . . , to bring in everlasting righteousness . . ." (v. 24). Therefore, appealing to the "seventy *years*" of Jeremiah (Dan 9:2; see Jer 25:11-12; 29:10) and/or to the Year of Jubilee ("You shall count off seven *weeks of years*, seven times seven years, so that the period of seven weeks of years gives forty-nine years"; Lev. 25:8),[14] most commentators understand the

---

11. Mentioned by Boice, *Daniel*, 104.

12. For reviews of many different interpretations, see Montgomery, *Book of Daniel*, 390-401; Young, *Prophecy of Daniel*, 191-95; Miller, *Daniel*, 252-57; Schwab, *Hope*, 134-47; and Steinmann, *Daniel*, 452-65.

13. Young, *Prophecy of Daniel*, 195. Hasel argues that "having the masculine plural ending, *šābû'îm* is to be rendered as 'weeks,' and nothing else. Such renderings as 'heptad,' 'hebdomad,' 'sevens' [NIV], or 'besevened' remove from this noun the specificity expressed by the sum total of 'weeks.'" Hasel, "The Hebrew Masculine Plural for 'Weeks' in the Expression 'Seventy Weeks' in Daniel 9:24," *AUSS* 31 (1993) 117.

14. 2 Chronicles 36:21 interprets Jeremiah's 70 years as 70 sabbatical years when the land would rest (cf. Lev. 26:34-35, 43). Some commentators go further and note that the first 7 weeks of Daniel 9 (49 years) constitute a year of jubilee when everyone would return to their property (Lev. 25:10) and the seventy weeks (490 years) are ten jubilees. E.g., Baldwin, *Daniel*, 170, notes that "a mind reared on the law of Moses, and told to understand 'seven sevens,'" would think of the year of jubilee "during which every man was to return to his inherited land and liberty proclaimed to prisoners." Lacocque, *Book of Daniel*, 178, argues that "Daniel announces the coming

"seventy weeks" as "seventy weeks of years,"[15] that is, 490 years. The RSV even translated Daniel 9:24 as, "Seventy weeks of years are decreed. . . ." These years are divided into three periods: "seven weeks," "sixty two weeks," and "one week." On a literal interpretation, then, one would have a 49-year period, one of 434 years, and a final 7-year period. We can visualize these years as follows:

7 weeks *from*	62 weeks		1 week *from*	
		troubled time		
word —→ *to* anointed	Jerusalem ———————————		anointed → *to* troops	
to restore prince	built with		cut off,	destroy city,
Jerusalem	streets and moat		"strong	desolator
			covenant,"	destroyed
			no sacrifices	

Now the important question becomes, What was the starting point of these weeks? Gabriel says, "from the time that the word went out to restore and rebuild Jerusalem until the time of an anointed prince, there shall be seven weeks" (v. 25). When did that "word" go out? The most natural understanding is that this "word" to rebuild Jerusalem refers to the decree of Cyrus authorizing the Jews to return to Jerusalem and rebuild the temple (2 Chron 36:22-23; Ezra 1:1-4; 6:3-5). This decree went out in 538 B.C. Understood literally, seventy weeks (490 years) after 538 B.C. would be 48 B.C.

But for scholars who hold to the Greek view[16] and who assume that the final week *must*[17] be that of the persecution by Antiochus Epiphanes (169-164 B.C.), 48 B.C. is much too late. Therefore they look for an earlier date than 538 B.C. when "the word went out." They move back to "the word that came to Jeremiah" (see Jer 25:1, 11). This still leaves them several options for the starting point of the seventy weeks.[18]

Montgomery opts for the starting point of the first 7 weeks in 586 B.C., the

---

of the ultimate Jubilee, the Eschaton." Cf. Redditt, *Daniel*, 160, "In the book of Jubilees a period of seven years was called a 'week of years'. . . . Also, 11 QMelchizedek 6-8 speaks of ten jubilees or 490 years until the final judgment."

15. Seow, *Daniel*, 147, backs this up further by noting that "in the Hebrew of the Dead Sea Scrolls, the word for 'weeks' refers to a cycle of seven years."

16. The Greek view assumes that the fourth kingdom is that of Greece: Alexander the Great and his successors, especially the Seleucids and the Ptolemies.

17. "The modern critical interpretation requires that the sixty-two weeks end shortly before the advent of Antiochus Epiphanes." Collins, *Daniel*, 356.

18. Some propose 586 B.C., the destruction of Jerusalem; others 597 B.C., when Jerusalem was first captured by Nebuchadnezzar; still others 604 B.C., the first year of Nebuchadnezzar. Those who opt for the latter subtract 7 weeks, 49 years, from 606 B.C. to arrive at ca. 558 B.C., the date of Cyrus's accession. "Cyrus would then be the 'Anointed Prince'" (v. 25). See Montgomery, *Book of Daniel*, 391.

destruction of Jerusalem, and has the 7 weeks "terminate at the Return" from exile. This (586 B.C. — circa 49 = 538 B.C.), he writes, leaves three candidates for the "anointed prince": "Cyrus, the 'Anointed' of Isaiah 45:1; Zerubbabel, the acclaimed Messiah of the Restoration; and his contemporary the high priest Joshua" — "the high priest Joshua is to be decisively preferred."[19] Although this works out nicely for the first seven weeks, Montgomery runs into trouble with the next period of 62 weeks. For when we subtract 62 weeks, 434 years, from 538 B.C. we end up at 104 B.C., which is more than 60 years *after* Antiochus Epiphanes. Montgomery frankly admits that the 62 weeks "take us down some 65 years too far." He resolves this problem as follows: "We can meet this objection only by surmising a chronological miscalculation on part of the writer."[20] But one has to wonder, Could it be that these scholars who hold to the Greek view have themselves made several "miscalculations"?

Some of the scholars who hold to the Roman view[21] face similar difficulties with the week-years. In contrast to the Greek view, they maintain that the final week must be Jesus' life on earth. If the starting point of the 70 weeks is Cyrus's edict in 538 B.C., the 69 weeks, 483 years, would take them to 55 B.C., which is much too early. Therefore they look for a starting point of the seventy weeks later than 538 B.C. Some begin the seventy weeks with Artaxerxes's commission to Ezra in 458 B.C. 483 years later (69 weeks) leads to the beginning of the final week in A.D. 25, near the beginning of Jesus' public ministry (there was no year 0 between 1 B.C. and A.D. 1). A problem with this starting point is not only that it ignores the date that best fits Daniel 9 (538 B.C.; see 9:1-2) but Ezra was not specifically mandated to rebuild Jerusalem (see Ezra 7). Others, therefore, begin the seventy weeks with Nehemiah, who received permission specifically to rebuild the walls of Jerusalem (see Neh 2:8). Unfortunately, this date, 445 B.C., leads to the final week occurring about eight years after Jesus' death and resurrection (445 B.C. — 483 [69 x 7] = A.D. 38).

Many scholars have proposed ingenious ways to make the years add up. For example, Miller seeks to make a case for understanding "the sevens . . . [as] literal seven-year periods totaling 490 years. The first seven sevens (forty-nine

19. Ibid., 379, 392.

20. Ibid., 393. Cf. p. 391, "Jewish historiography was affected by a remarkable oblivion as to chronology and sequence of events." Porteous, *Daniel*, 141, similarly, identifies the week-years as "587-539, 539-170, 170-164, 539 being the date of the fall of Babylon and 170 the date of the murder of the high-priest Onias III, while the terminal date is that of the rededication of the temple by Judas Maccabaeus." He also admits that "the middle division . . . (539-170 B.C.), was considerably shorter in actual fact than 62 week-years, i.e., 62 x 7 years," but he also attributes this to "the historical memory which the Jews retained of the period in question . . . [being] very dim as regards facts."

21. The Roman view assumes that the fourth kingdom is that of Rome and its aftermath.

years) commence with a command to rebuild Jerusalem (either the decree to Ezra in 458 B.C.[22] or the decree to Nehemiah in 445 B.C.) and terminate with the completion of the work of Ezra and Nehemiah about forty-nine years later (either ca. 409 B.C. or ca. 396 B.C.). The next sixty-two sevens (434 years) extend from the end of the first group of sevens to Christ's first coming (either his baptism in A.D. 26 or Christ's presentation of himself to the people as Messiah on Palm Sunday in A.D. 32/33)."[23]

Unfortunately, Miller runs into trouble with the last seven years. His solution is the dispensational "gap" or "parenthesis" theory. He writes, "After the coming of the Messiah, he was rejected by Israel; and the time of the Gentiles began, which is not counted in the 'seventy sevens.'. . . The last seven . . . immediately precede Christ's second advent."[24] But this interpretation is problematic. Verse 26 says, "*After* the sixty-two weeks, an anointed one shall be cut off." If this prediction speaks of Jesus' crucifixion, it took place in the final week. Therefore the final week cannot "immediately precede Christ's second advent."[25] Moreover, Hasel has pointed out that "the masculine plural form *šābû'îm* stands with the numeral 'seventy' for an entity of time in its totality, completeness, and unity — that is, it expresses the 'seventy weeks' as being a single unit of prophetic time. . . . It follows . . . that the unitary block of 'seventy weeks' cannot be split apart in such a way as to separate the final 'one week' (v. 27) from the remainder of the seventy-week period by means of any intervening time period, gap, or parenthesis. . . . All three of the sub-units of the 'seventy weeks' mentioned in verses 25-27 function *within* that 'seventy-week' time span; none can go beyond it in any manner."[26]

Others have gone to great length to make the "weeks" fit. A theoretical physicist proposed that "the 'sevens' can be any integer multiple of seven years. . . . Those in the first group are fourteen years long, while those in the second group are the usual seven years long." Thus, 7 x 14 = 98 years and 62 x 7 = 434 years adds up to a total of 532 years. Since Cyrus gave his decree in 538 B.C.,

22. This is the position of Archer, "Daniel," 26, as well as of Miller, *Daniel*, 263.

23. Miller, *Daniel*, 257. On p. 265 Miller acknowledges that "those who begin the sevens in 445 B.C. are faced with a dilemma; 483 years after 445 B.C. comes to A.D. 39, a date well after the time of Christ."

24. Miller, *Daniel*, 257. Cf. pp. 269-70. See also Harold W. Hoehner, "Chronological Aspects of the Life of Christ: Part 6, Daniel's Seventy Weeks and New Testament Chronology," *BSac* 132/525 (1975) 47-65, esp. p. 65, and Walter Kaiser, *Preaching and Teaching the Last Things*, 99-110.

25. Note that Miller, *Daniel*, 267, writes, "Apparently his [Christ's] coming would be immediately *at the end* of the sixty-nine sevens" (my emphasis).

26. Hasel, "The Hebrew Masculine Plural for 'Weeks,'" *AUSS* 31 (1993) 116-17. Cf. p. 113, "The masculine plural ending in the noun *šābû'îm* places stress on the totality and entirety of the 'seventy weeks' as a unitary whole, whereas the feminine ending -ôt, if it had been used, would have stressed the individual parts — i.e., the individual weeks — of the 'seventy weeks.'"

the seventieth week begins in 6 B.C., the birth of Christ.[27] The major problem with this proposal, of course, is that one needs to justify why it is that the first 7 weeks are each 14 years while the others are each 7 years.

Still others have argued that the "seventy weeks" are not 490 solar years but 490 "prophetic years." Since "prophetic years" have only 360 days, this allows them to place Jesus' death, which they date at A.D. 33, at the end of the 69th week.[28] Most scholars do not accept this "solution." Lucas responds, "The use of 'prophetic years' is unconvincing special pleading. Although, at various times and places in the ANE, calendars with twelve months of thirty days were used, it was always recognized that they ran out of step with the 'real world,' and various schemes of intercalary days or months were used to correct for this."[29]

One wonders why so many commentators use such literalistic interpretations and are at such pains to make the dates exactly fit the known history.[30] That's not the nature of prophecy, let alone the nature of apocalyptic literature. One of the characteristics of apocalyptic literature is that it frequently uses numbers as symbols.[31] The number 70 x 7 consists of standard symbolic num-

---

27. Lurie, "A New Interpretation of Daniel's 'Sevens' and the Chronology of the Seventy 'Sevens,'" *JETS* 33/3 (1990) 303-9. Leslie McFall, "Do the Sixty-Nine Weeks of Daniel Date the Messianic Mission of Nehemiah or Jesus?" *JETS* 52/4 (2009) 673-718, claims that "the seventy 'weeks' of Daniel 9:24 referred to the past 70 years of the Babylonian exile, not to the future, and . . . that the period of sixty-nine 'weeks' was intended to mark the coming of a messiah, and that messiah was Nehemiah, not Jesus" (p. 676). Admitting that "a different seventy 'weeks of years' (70 x 7) is nowhere mentioned in the Bible," he nevertheless uses these unmentioned 490 years to move from Nehemiah in 466 B.C. to Jesus in A.D. 25. This proposal raises more questions than it answers: How can the blessings of Daniel 9:24 refer to the past? And how does one justify using an unmentioned 490 years to move from Nehemiah to Jesus in A.D. 25?

28. This "solution" was first introduced by Robert Anderson, *The Coming Prince*, 10th ed. (London: Hodder & Stoughton, 1915), pp. 67-75. See Hoehner, "Chronological Aspects of the Life of Christ: Part 6, Daniel's Seventy Weeks and New Testament Chronology," *BSac* 132/525 (1975) 47-65, esp. pp. 62-65.

29. Lucas, *Daniel*, 246.

30. Of course, supporters of the Greek view who claim that Daniel's visions were written in the second century B.C., *after* these events took place, have reason to search for an exact fit between Daniel's description and history. But in doing so they ignore that Daniel's visions are apocalyptic literature. Some of the supporters of the Roman view are prone to making the same mistake because they claim that divine inspiration of prophecy must lead to an exact fit with later historical events. This is the first time in my life that I've had to use a calculator to check the claims of commentators. The fact that one needs a calculator to follow the arguments is a good reason to question whether this kind of "interpretation" is on the right track.

31. Keil, *Book of Daniel*, 339, observes that "satisfactory proof of such a meaning [year-weeks] has not been adduced." Cf. ibid., 376, "It cannot be year-weeks, or cycles of seven years, but only symbolically defined periods of measured duration." Poythress, "Hermeneutical Factors in Determining the Beginning of the Seventy Weeks (Daniel 9:25)," *TJ* 6 (1985) 143, notes, "If the writer had wanted to indicate years, he would normally have included the word 'year,' as

bers. The number 7 in the Old Testament is the number of completion, perfection.[32] The symbolic use of the number 7 goes back to God creating the cosmos in 7 days, "and indeed, it was very good" (Gen 1:31). Daniel has already used this symbolic number in 3:19 and 4:16. The number 10 is the number of fullness: think of the 10 plagues God showered on Egypt and the 10 commandments he gave Israel at Mount Sinai. Now 70 weeks is 7 x 10 x 7 days, which is a complete, full period of time. How long is this? Long enough, according to verse 24, "to finish the transgression . . . , to bring in everlasting righteousness. . . ." In other words, long enough to bring in the perfect kingdom of God.[33]

This interpretation of verse 24 is in harmony with Daniel 2 (Nebuchadnezzar's dream about the great statue) where God reveals the rise and fall of human kingdoms from the kingdom of Babylon until the coming of the kingdom of God (the stone becomes a great mountain that fills "the whole earth"; 2:35). It is also in harmony with Daniel's first vision (chapter 7), which covers the same history from Babylon until the coming of the Antichrist (7:8, 24-25), the Son of Man (7:13-14), judgment day (7:11, 26), and the kingdom of God (7:14, 27).

The seventy weeks are divided into three periods. The first period is 7 weeks, that is, 7 x 7, a relative short but complete period of time that runs "from the time that the word went out to restore and rebuild Jerusalem until the time of an anointed prince" (9:25a). The second period is 62 weeks, quite a long period of time, but a troubled time for Jerusalem (9:25b). "After sixty-two weeks," that is, in the final week, a short but complete period of time, "an anointed one shall be cut off," and Jerusalem and the temple destroyed (9:26).

When did the word go out to restore Jerusalem?[34] It seems forced to move this "word" back to the time of Jeremiah some 70 years before Daniel's prayer in

---

in Daniel 9:2." Baldwin, *Daniel*, 176, proposes "to keep to a symbolic interpretation of all the numbers." Cf. Young, *Messianic Prophecies*, 48, "Since these numbers represent periods of time, the length of which is not stated, and since they are thus symbolical, it is not warrantable to seek to discover the precise length of the sevens." Cf. Goldingay, *Daniel*, 257, "A fundamental objection to such attempts either to vindicate or to fault Daniel's figures is that both are mistaken in interpreting the 490 years as offering chronological information. It is not chronology but chronography: a stylized scheme of history used to interpret historical data rather than arising from them." Cf. Lucas, *Daniel*, 248, "Against this background it seems very likely that Daniel's seventy weeks uses numbers symbolically. . . . A span of seventy weeks represents a complete period, the one needed to bring in the perfect kingdom (Dan 9:24)."

32. See also Revelation's seven churches, seven spirits, seven lampstands, seven stars, seven seals, seven trumpets, seven thunders, seven plagues, and seven bowls.

33. Cf. Leupold, *Exposition of Daniel*, 410, "'Seventy heptads' is designed to describe all future time from the days of Daniel unto the end of time, the time fixed in God's councils for perfectly achieving His holy work as 7 x 7 x 10 suggests symbolically — God's program for all ages."

34. See Steinmann, *Daniel*, 468-71, for a discussion of six different proposals. Cf. Lucas, *Daniel*, 242-43.

539 B.C. (see pp. 294-95 above) or to move it forward to the time of Ezra or Nehemiah some 80 years after Daniel's prayer (see p. 295 above). Daniel makes clear that he read about Jeremiah's 70 years in 539 B.C. (9:1-2). In addition, he seems to have been well acquainted with God's promise in Leviticus 26 (the chapter of the covenant blessings and curses): "If they confess their iniquity and the iniquity of their ancestors . . . , then will I remember my covenant with Jacob" (Lev. 26:40-42). Accordingly, on behalf of "all Israel" (9:7) he confesses their sins, wickedness, rebellion, and disobedience (9:4-19). "While I was speaking" (two times; 9:20, 21), immediately Gabriel came "in swift flight" (9:21) to respond to his prayer for the Lord to let his face shine upon his "desolated sanctuary" (9:17) and to "listen and act and . . . not delay" (9:19). The Lord answered this prayer within the year: "The LORD stirred up the spirit of King Cyrus of Persia" to write an edict permitting the Israelites to return to Jerusalem "and rebuild the house of the LORD, the God of Israel" (Ezra 1:1-4; cf. 6:2-5).[35] "The word that went out to restore and rebuild Jerusalem" (9:25) went out in 538 B.C.

If it should be objected, as some have done, that Cyrus's "word" was an edict to rebuild the temple, not Jerusalem, the simple answer is that one cannot rebuild the temple without at the same time at least partially rebuilding the city.[36] Moreover, in Isaiah the Lord says, "I have aroused Cyrus in righteousness . . . ; he shall build my *city* and set my exiles free" (45:13; cf. 44:28). In fact, in the days of Artaxerxes I (465-424 B.C.) Israel's enemies lodged a complaint with the king: "Now may it be known to the king that the Jews who came up from you to us have gone to Jerusalem. They are rebuilding that rebellious and wicked *city;* they are finishing the walls and repairing the foundations" (Ezra 4:12; cf. 9:9). Thus there is little doubt that "the word that went out to restore and rebuild Jerusalem" (9:25) went out in 538 B.C.[37]

---

35. Although some hold that it should be a "word" that went out from God as in verse 23, Keil, *Book of Daniel*, 350-51, rightly points out that the "word" in verse 23 "is the divine revelation communicated in verses 24-27, which the angel brings to Daniel," while the "word" in verse 25 is, on the contrary, more fully determined by the words "to restore and to build, etc."

36. Leupold, *Exposition of Daniel*, 419, asks, "Would some 43,000 exiles have returned merely to build the Temple and have refrained from building . . . their homes in Jerusalem? Quite unthinkable." Poythress, "Hermeneutical Factors," *TJ* 6 (1985) 134, points out that Daniel 9:25 is not "the *complete* text of the decree. . . . Ezra 6:3-5 . . . contains some details not recorded in Ezra 1:2-4." See ibid., 134-40, for detailed argumentation that "Jerusalem was (partially) inhabited before Nehemiah's time" (p. 140). Josephus reports the contents of Cyrus's letter as follows, "To those among the Jews dwelling in my country, who so wished, I have given permission to return to their native land and to rebuild the city and build the temple . . ." (*Jewish Antiquities* 11.12 [11.1.3], Loeb edition).

37. Attempts to place this "word" some 70 years before or some 80 years after this prayer are clearly driven by extratextual motives, that is, attempts to make the textual givens fit precisely into the history as we know it.

If, then, "the word" went out in 538 B.C., when was that first period of 7 weeks completed?[38] The text seems to imply that it would be completed when Jerusalem was restored and rebuilt. Those who insist that Jerusalem was not completely rebuilt until its wall was finished, identify Nehemiah as the anointed prince, for in 445 B.C. he received permission from King Artaxerxes to rebuild Jerusalem, especially its wall (Neh 2:5-8; 6:15).[39] But I think it more likely that this "anointed prince" or "leader" is the priest/teacher/leader Ezra (see below), who arrived in Jerusalem in 458 B.C. when the rebuilding of the temple was long finished (516 B.C.) and during whose time the wall around Jerusalem was completed (445 B.C.). This is the answer to Daniel's prayer: Jerusalem and the temple restored.

But God's revelation of the future continues: the first complete period of 7 weeks will be followed by a much longer period of time: 62 weeks. During this time Jerusalem "shall be built again with streets and moat, but in a troubled time" (v. 25). This period runs from 445 B.C. to the time of occupation by the Roman Empire.[40] The troubled time reflects that Jerusalem will be occupied alternately by Greece, the Ptolemies, the Seleucids, especially the persecution under Antiochus IV (167-164 B.C.), and Rome (63 B.C.-A.D. 70). "After the sixty-two weeks," that is, in the final, seventieth week, "an anointed one shall be cut off" (v. 26). This week, the shortest, is also a complete period of time. In this week several major events will take place: "an anointed one" will be killed, Jerusalem and the temple will be destroyed (v. 26), the decreed end will be "poured

38. The NRSV places a semicolon after "seven weeks" in Daniel 9:25, reflecting the *athnach,* the break (disjunctive accent) the Masoretes placed there. The AV, NASB, and NIV follow ancient versions (e.g., Theodotion) that ignore the *athnach* and translate, "From the time the word goes out to restore and rebuild Jerusalem until the Anointed One, the ruler, comes, there will be seven 'sevens,' and sixty-two 'sevens'" (NIV). The unanswered question with the latter translation is, Why did the author split off "seven 'sevens'" from the "sixty-two 'sevens'"? Even though the Masoretic tradition is later than Theodotion, Walter Kaiser, *Preaching and Teaching the Last Things,* 107-8, convincingly argues for the *athnach* and thus for three parts: 7 weeks, 62 weeks, and 1 week.

39. Young, *Prophecy of Daniel,* 220, leaves the identity of the "anointed prince" open-ended: "the first period of sevens is evidently intended to include the time from the first year of Cyrus to the completion of the work of Ezra and Nehemiah." Cf. ibid., 205, "The 7 sevens apparently has reference to the time which should elapse between the issuance of the word and the completion of the city and temple; roughly to the end of the period of Ezra and Nehemiah." Steinmann, *Daniel,* 472, opts for a time frame of 538-445 B.C., arguing that "the perfect aspect of the Niphal verb" to build (v. 25) should be "translated by the English future perfect tense, 'will have been built.'" I was unable to find any Bible version that supports Steinmann's proposal. One can also put the emphasis in verse 25 as follows: "For sixty-two weeks it shall be built again with streets and *moat,*" that is, a water system.

40. Steinmann, *Daniel,* 472, marks it, "From Nehemiah to Jesus (445-2 BC)," but that may be a little too exact.

out upon the desolator" (v. 27), and the perfect kingdom of God will arrive (v. 24). This period covers what the prophets call "the last days." It runs from the life, death, and resurrection of Jesus to the last day.

If this seems like a long time for a single week, it should be remembered that the prophets often predict that the coming of the Messiah in "the last days" ushers in the perfect kingdom of God. Future events are "telescoped" together ("foreshortened"); the coming of the Messiah, judgment, and the restoration of the kingdom appear to come at once (see, e.g., Joel 2:1-11). Daniel 9 similarly portrays a short, complete, period of time: one final week for the coming of the Messiah, his death, the destruction of Jerusalem and the temple by the Romans in A.D. 70 (v. 26), the "abomination that desolates" and the destruction of the desolator (the Antichrist, v. 27), and the perfect kingdom of God (v. 24).

Once the Messiah arrives, however, we learn from the New Testament that the end is not yet. Jesus projected Daniel's prediction of war (v. 26) into the future: "You will hear of wars and rumors of wars; see that you are not alarmed; for this must take place, but the end is not yet" (Matt 24:6). On the evening of his death, Jesus taught his disciples about his *Second* Coming: "This is my blood of the (new) covenant, which is poured out for many for the forgiveness of sins [cf. Daniel 9:24, "to atone for iniquity"]. I tell you, I will never again drink of this fruit of the vine *until that day* when I drink it new with you in my Father's kingdom" (Matt 26:28-29). But at that time Jesus' disciples failed to understand that Jesus would have to come *again* (see Acts 1:6) to complete God's goal "to bring in everlasting righteousness" (Dan 9:24). Later they understood. Peter would write the early Christians: "The Lord is not slow about his promise . . . , but is patient with you, not wanting any to perish, but all to come to repentance" (2 Pet 3:9). It turns out that the final week God decreed extends from Jesus' First Coming to his Second Coming.

It may be helpful at this point to sketch an overview of Daniel's visions concerning the development of history (see p. 302).

An Anointed Prince (v. 25)

The diagram on page 302 will help us identify the various figures with some degree of certainty. Since the number of weeks is symbolic, we need not look for exactly 490-year, 49-year, 434-year, and 7-year periods of time. Nor is the message (theme) of Daniel 9 dependent on getting the identification of every one of these figures exactly right. Still, if we can identify the historical persons involved, it will make the sermon more explicit.

This is the only chapter in Daniel where he writes about "an anointed one" (*māšîaḥ*). Verse 25 reads, "Know therefore and understand: from the time that

Dan 2:	Gold	Silver	Bronze	Iron & clay	Stone	Mountain
	Babylon	Medo-Persia	Greece & aftermath	Rome & aftermath	Christ	Kingdom of God
Dan 7:	Lion	Bear	Leopard	Monster 10 horns little horn		Antichrist
					Son of Man	Kingdom of God
Dates:	605 B.C. –	539 –	331 –	63 B.C. –	present	Last Day

Dan 9:24   70 weeks decreed
538 B.C. ·· Kingdom of God
"end to sin,"
"everlasting
righteousness"

Dan 9:25a   7 weeks
word   anointed
went out   prince
538 ············ 445

Dan 9:25b   62 weeks
Jerusalem   troubled time
streets & conduits
445 ··· Rome

Dan 9:26   1 week
anointed   Jerusalem
cut off   destroyed
A.D. 30 ············ 70

Dan 9:27   same week   "strong covenant,"   "abomination,"
"sacrifices cease"   "desolator" destroyed

the word went out to restore and rebuild Jerusalem until the time of an *anointed prince,* there shall be seven weeks; and for sixty-two weeks it shall be built again with streets and moat, but in a troubled time." Who is the "anointed prince"?

We noted above that some commentators propose that the "word" went out earlier than 538 B.C.: some make it 586 B.C., the destruction of Jerusalem; others 597 B.C., when Jerusalem was first captured by Nebuchadnezzar; still others 604 B.C., the first year of Nebuchadnezzar. They then have three candidates for the "anointed prince: King Cyrus, Zerubbabel, and the high priest Joshua. Since we understand the "word" that went out as the edict of Cyrus in 538 B.C., we need to look for the "anointed one" later than these three candidates.

Unfortunately, the NIV translates Daniel 9:25, "Know and understand this: From the time the word goes out to restore and rebuild Jerusalem until the Anointed One, the ruler, comes, there will be seven 'sevens,' and sixty-two 'sevens.'" On this reading "the Anointed One" comes not after 7 weeks but after 7 plus 62 weeks, that is, after 69 weeks. He would then be the same person as the

"Anointed One" in verse 26 (NIV): "After the sixty-two 'sevens,' the Anointed One will be put to death." This Anointed One can be none other than Jesus Christ who was crucified. A problem with this translation is that it ignores the break between the 7 weeks and the 62 weeks indicated by the Masoretes (see p. 300, n. 38 above). Another problem is that it slights the significance of the complete period of 7 weeks before the 62 weeks since without the semicolon Daniel could just as well have written that the Anointed One will come after 69 weeks.

If, however, we accept the Masoretic clue and the NRSV translation, the "anointed prince" will come at the end of the first 7 weeks. This "prince" or "leader" or "priest"[41] cannot be Jesus Christ, for Jesus comes "*after* the sixty-two weeks" (v. 26).[42] Who, then, is this anointed leader? There are two candidates, Ezra and Nehemiah. Nehemiah was cupbearer to King Artaxerxes of Persia. He received permission to go and rebuild Jerusalem, specifically the city wall (Neh 2:4-20). In 445 B.C. he was appointed governor of Judah (Neh 5:14). After much opposition, the wall was completed in fifty-two days (Neh 6:15). Nehemiah certainly was a "leader," but he was not anointed.

The better candidate for the "anointed leader" is Ezra. Ezra's lineage is traced back to the chief priest Aaron (Ezra 7:1-5), Israel's first high priest. He is called "the priest Ezra" (Ezra 7:11, 12, 21), and priests were anointed (Exod 30:30; Lev. 4:3). He is also described as "a scribe skilled in the law of Moses" (Ezra 7:6). King Artaxerxes mandated him to "buy bulls, rams, and lambs, and their grain offerings and their drink offerings, and . . . [to] offer them on the altar of the house of your God in Jerusalem" (Ezra 7:17). Later Ezra denounced the mixed marriages, led Israel in repentance and purification, and appointed investigators (Ezra 9–10). Still later, after the wall was completed, Ezra taught Israel the law of Moses (Neh 8; a priestly function) and led them in a prayer of confession (Neh 9) and a renewal of the covenant (Neh 10). As an anointed priest and a leader of God's people[43] Ezra is a type of Jesus Christ, who would republish the

41. "While the term may, indeed, refer to an actual prince . . . , it may also be used of a priest (Lev. 4:3; 2 Macc 1:10; Neh 11:11; Jer 20:1)." Seow, *Daniel,* 148.

42. Note that Keil, *Book of Daniel,* 355, still identifies this anointed one as Jesus Christ. He does this by interpreting these 7 weeks as the period from the edict of Cyrus "till the appearance of an anointed one who at the same time is prince, i.e., till Christ." The 62 weeks then are the church age, and the final week is the Second Coming of Christ. Steinmann, *Daniel,* 472, also identifies this anointed one as Jesus Christ but for different reasons: He argues that the text does not say that "the Messiah will come immediately after the 'seven weeks.' Note that the 'Messiah' immediately precedes the seven weeks, and then 'Messiah' also immediately follows the description of the sixty-two weeks. This framing device indicates that there will be a seven-week period and also a sixty-two-week period before the coming of the Messiah."

43. John Bright, *A History of Israel* (London: SCM, 1960), 374, calls Ezra "a second Moses": "If Moses was Israel's founder, it was Ezra who reconstituted Israel and gave her faith a form in which it could survive through the centuries."

law of God (the Sermon on the Mount), renew the covenant (see below), and make the ultimate sacrifice that would end all sacrifices.

An Anointed One Cut Off (v. 26)

After Daniel has heard that God will answer his prayer for the restoration of Jerusalem and the temple, God's revelation continues to the next major event. Verse 26 reads, "After the sixty-two weeks, an anointed one shall be cut off and shall have nothing, and the troops of the prince who is to come shall destroy the city and the sanctuary. Its end shall come with a flood, and to the end there shall be war." "*After* the sixty-two weeks" means that we have now entered the final, seventieth week. Speaking for the Greek view, Collins writes, "Modern critics generally recognize here a reference to the murder of the high priest Onias III, recorded in 2 Macc 4:23-28, in about 171 B.C.E. (see also Dan 11:22)."[44] Being "cut off" does indeed refer to a violent death;[45] "the Niphal Hebrew verbal form is usually used in the sense of 'be cut off, be removed, be destroyed,' and intensively in the sense of 'exterminate.'"[46] But it is highly unlikely that this major event taking place after the 62 weeks should be a *former* high priest (he had been displaced by his brother).[47] A counter opinion is that this "is the Antichrist."[48] But it is equally unlikely that the Antichrist would be called "*messiah*," anointed one.

There can be little doubt that the prediction that "an anointed one shall be cut off" (v. 26) was fulfilled in the crucifixion of Jesus Messiah. He was literally "cut off." "This verb *(kārat)* is used of 'cutting a covenant,' a ritual that involved the death of the sacrificial victim (Gen 15:10, 18); it was also frequently used of death generally."[49] Isaiah uses a similar verb *(gāzar)* to describe the Suffering Servant: "He was cut off from the land of the living, stricken for the transgression of my people" (Isa 53:8). Jesus' death on the cross would bring about what verse 24 predicted for the seventieth week: "to finish the transgression . . . , and to atone for iniquity."

---

44. Collins, *Daniel*, 356. Cf. Redditt, *Daniel*, 160.

45. Cf. Genesis 9:11, "cut off by the waters of a flood"; Leviticus 7:20; Psalm 37:9; Proverbs 2:22; and Jeremiah 11:19.

46. Ouro, "Daniel 9:27a," *JATS* 12/1 (2001) 184.

47. Block, "Preaching Old Testament Apocalyptic," *CTJ* 41 (2006) 46, offers four reasons why "this interpretation is unlikely."

48. "This personage is neither of these [Onias III or Christ] but is the Antichrist," McComiskey, "The Seventy 'Weeks' of Daniel against the Background of Ancient Near Eastern Literature," *WTJ* 47/1 (1985) 30. So also Harman, *Study Commentary on Daniel*, 242-45.

49. Baldwin, *Daniel*, 171.

Verse 26 adds that this anointed one "shall have nothing." When Jesus hung on the cross between heaven and earth, he had "nothing": deserted by his disciples, rejected by his own people ("We have no king but the emperor"; John 19:15), crucified by the Roman world empire, and forsaken by God.

The Prince Who Is to Come (v. 26)

Verse 26 continues, "And the troops of the prince who is to come shall destroy the city and the sanctuary." Those committed to the Greek view identify this prince as Antiochus Epiphanes.[50] A major problem for this identification is that Antiochus never destroyed the city and the sanctuary. Montgomery admits this problem: "There was little destruction effected by the Greeks in the Holy City." His solution is to take "destroy" not in the physical sense but "in its moral sense, 'corrupt.'"[51] Others identify this "prince," "leader" (*nāgîd*) as either "Onias's successor Jason, who both corrupted and devastated . . . the people of Jerusalem,"[52] as the Antichrist,[53] or even as Christ.[54]

But why go so far afield when we know from history that the Romans physically destroyed Jerusalem and the temple? Jesus himself told his disciples, "When you see Jerusalem surrounded by armies, then know that its *desolation* has come near" (Luke 21:20). He also told them about the temple, "Truly I tell you, not one stone will be left here upon another; all will be thrown down" (Matt 24:2). Some forty years later, in A.D. 70, the Romans, under their general Titus, actually destroyed Jerusalem and the sanctuary. Young writes, "For our part, we believe that the people mentioned are the Romans and the prince is Titus Vespasianus, who came to Palestine and in the year 70 A.D. destroyed the city and the sanctuary. . . . This interpretation, and this alone, fills the requirements of the text. The Messiah has been cut off by death, and thereupon the city and the sanctuary will be destroyed. Historically, this prophecy was fulfilled in a most remarkable manner."[55]

---

50. "The 'ruler' in question is Antiochus." Collins, *Daniel*, 357.

51. Montgomery, *Book of Daniel*, 383.

52. Goldingay, *Daniel*, 262.

53. McComiskey, "The Seventy 'Weeks' of Daniel," *WTJ* 47/1 (1985) 32. So also Leupold, *Exposition of Daniel*, 428; Miller, *Daniel*, 268; and Feinberg, *Daniel*, 133.

54. "The most natural way to read the text is to understand 'Messiah, a Leader' in 9:25 to be the same 'Messiah' and 'Leader' in 9:26." Steinmann, *Daniel*, 458. Cf. ibid., 473-74. Cf. Kline, "The Covenant of the Seventieth Week," 463-64, n. 31.

55. Young, *Messianic Prophecies*, 64. Parry, "Desolation of the Temple and Messianic Enthronement in Daniel 11:36–12:3," *JETS* 54/3 (2011) 499, 510-19, argues that the "prince" is Vespasian, the father of Titus.

The One Who Makes a Strong Covenant (v. 27)

Verse 27 reads, "He shall make a strong covenant with many for one week, and for half of the week he shall make sacrifice and offering cease; and in their place shall be an abomination that desolates, until the decreed end is poured out upon the desolator." The question here is, Who is the "he" that shall make a strong covenant? Again, opinions vary. Collins and others claim that "he" is Antiochus;[56] Keil and others that "he" is the Antichrist;[57] and Young and others that "he" refers to Christ.[58]

The major issue is, What is the antecedent of "he." Usually this is the last-named person. In this case that would be "the prince who is to come" of verse 26b. Above we identified the "prince" as the Roman general Titus. This person, verse 27 says, shall do two things, "make a strong covenant with many," and "make sacrifice and offering cease." By destroying the temple, Titus did indeed make sacrifice cease, but he never made a strong covenant with many.[59] Moreover, "the prince who is to come," verse 26, is not the subject of the sentence — his troops are, and they cannot be the antecedent of the "he" in verse 27. Thus the antecedent of "he" cannot be the "prince."

Some identify the "he" as the Antichrist. In favor of this selection is the context of verse 27b with the "abomination that desolates." Also, it is possible that in the last days the Antichrist may make a strong covenant with many. However, the fact that verse 27a does not say that he will make a *different* covenant but that "he will *confirm* [*higbîr*] a covenant with many" (NIV) argues against identifying the "he" as the Antichrist. Kline asserts, "In this crucial statement the verb employed is not a verb for the initial making of a covenant. . . . The force of this verb *higbîr* excludes the notion that the covenant referred to in Daniel 9:27a is some arrangement imposed by a future Antichrist."[60] Moreover, the Antichrist cannot

---

56. Collins, *Daniel*, 357. So also Montgomery, *Book of Daniel*, 385-86, and Lacocque, *Book of Daniel*, 197-98.

57. Keil, *Book of Daniel*, 366-67. So also Baldwin, *Daniel*, 171-72; Leupold, *Exposition of Daniel*, 431-32; Harman, *Study Commentary on Daniel*, 144-45; Miller, *Daniel*, 271; and Feinberg, *Daniel*, 134.

58. Young, *Prophecy of Daniel*, 217. So also Kline, "The Covenant of the Seventieth Week," 462-69; Duguid, *Daniel*, 171, and Steinmann, *Daniel*, 27, 474-75.

59. Those who identify the "prince" as Antiochus suggest that the covenant "refers to the covenant between reformist Jews and Gentiles reported in 1 Macc 1:11." Goldingay, *Daniel*, 262. So also Collins, *Daniel*, 357, and Lucas, *Daniel*, 244.

60. Kline, "The Covenant of the Seventieth Week," 464-65. Cf. 463, "The whole context speaks against the supposition that an altogether different covenant from the divine covenant which is the central theme throughout Daniel 9 is abruptly introduced here at the climax of it all." Young, *Prophecy of Daniel*, 209, points out that this word "appears in only one other passage of the Old Testament, Psalm 12:4."

make sacrifices cease in the last days because they ceased when Titus destroyed the temple in A.D. 70.[61]

The next person in line as antecedent for the "he" is the "anointed one" who "shall be cut off" (v. 26a). Since this "anointed one" clearly refers to Jesus Christ, the question is, Did Jesus Christ "make a strong covenant," or "confirm a covenant with many for one week"? Interestingly, Isaiah used the same word *rab* ("many")[62] to describe those who benefit from the death of the Suffering Servant: "The righteous one, my servant, shall make *many* righteous, and he shall bear their iniquities" (Isa 53:11). Identifying himself as the Son of Man of Daniel 7, Jesus himself said, "The Son of Man came . . . to give his life a ransom for *many*" (Mark 10:45). Jesus also made "a strong covenant with *many*" in that final week. The night before he died, Jesus changed the Passover feast into the Lord's Supper, saying, "This cup that is poured out for you is the *new covenant* in my blood" (Luke 22:20).[63] According to Matthew, Jesus emphasized that this blood of the covenant "is poured out for *many* for the forgiveness of sins" (Matt 26:28).

The identification of Jesus as the one who makes "a strong covenant" fits the context of Daniel 9.[64] Daniel began his prayer, "Ah, Lord, great and awesome God, keeping *covenant* and steadfast love with those who love you" (9:4). His whole prayer for God's temple, God's city, and God's people, we have seen, is steeped in covenant language. God responds to that prayer: one complete period of 7 weeks will see the restoration of the people, the city, and the temple. Then a long period of 62 weeks with trouble will follow. Then comes the final week with the arrival of the Messiah. The night before Jesus died he made a new covenant in his blood, just as Jeremiah prophesied: "The days are surely coming, says the LORD, when I will make a new covenant with the house of Israel and the house of Judah. . . . I will put my law within them, and I will write it on their hearts; and I will be their God, and they shall be my people. . . . I will forgive their iniquity, and remember their sin no more" (Jer 31:31-34). Jesus initi-

---

61. Some dispensationalists believe that "the sacrificial system will be reinstituted in Israel." Miller, *Daniel*, 272, n. 116, mentions Whitcomb, *Daniel*, 134; Walvoord, *Daniel*, 235; and Wood, *Daniel*, 261. Miller himself allows for this possibility but also suggests that the ceasing of sacrifice "may only indicate that worship in general is forbidden." Ibid., 272.

62. "The partitive nature of the 'many' in Dan 9:27, the Messianic nature of the passage, the significance of the verb *higbir* ["make strong," "confirm," "prevail"], and the covenantal implications of the passage point to the meaning of 'the many' in Dan 9:27 as it is found in Isa 53:11." Ouro, "Daniel 9:27a," *JATS* 12/1 (2001) 187.

63. Cf. 1 Corinthians 11:25; Hebrews 7:22; 8:13; 9:15; 12:24.

64. It may also be confirmed by synonymous parallelism: "Verses 26-27 follow an A-B-A-B pattern in which the A-A lines describe the vicarious death of the Messiah and the confirmation of the new covenant, while the B-B lines describe the desecration of Jerusalem . . . and the resulting destruction of Jerusalem by the Romans in AD 67-70." Parry, "Desolation of the Temple and Messianic Enthronement in Daniel 11:36–12:3," *JETS* 54/3 (2011) 498.

ated this new covenant and offered his life so that God would remember our sin no more.

Verse 27 continues, "and for half of the week he shall make sacrifice and [grain] offering cease." Verse 26 indicated that two things would happen in this final week: "an anointed one shall be cut off" (Jesus' crucifixion in A.D. 30) and "the troops . . . shall destroy the city and the sanctuary" (the Romans in A.D. 70). If the final week began with the Messiah's birth, "half of the week," or "the middle" (NIV) of the week, would indicate the time of his being cut off. With his death, Jesus did indeed make the Old Testament sacrifices cease. We read in Matthew that when Jesus "breathed his last," "At that moment the curtain of the temple was torn in two, from top to bottom" (Matt 27:50-51). People no longer needed human priests as intermediaries to approach God; through Jesus' priestly sacrifice they had direct access to God. Since Jesus paid the penalty for the sins of the world (John 1:29), animal sacrifices were no longer required. The author of Hebrews writes, "When Christ had offered for all time a single sacrifice for sins, 'he sat down at the right hand of God.' . . . Where there is forgiveness of these [sins], there is no longer any offering for sin" (Heb 10:12, 18). Toward the end of that final week,[65] with the destruction of Jerusalem and the temple, animal sacrifices at the temple became impossible.[66]

The Desolator

Gabriel reveals that two more events will take place in that final week: the arrival of an "abomination that desolates," and the destruction of "the desolator." Verse 27 concludes, "And in their place [presumably "sacrifice and offering"][67] shall be an abomination that desolates, until the decreed end is poured out upon the desolator."[68] It is because of this conclusion that many hold that the one who makes a strong covenant is the Antichrist. But verse 27 speaks of two different persons: verse 27a refers to Christ making a strong covenant, and 27b

---

65. Young, *Prophecy of Daniel*, 220, raises the question, "What marks the termination of the 70 sevens? In answer it should be noted that the text does not say a word about the termination. . . . It would seem, therefore, that the *terminus ad quem* was not regarded as possessing particular importance or significance."

66. "After Christ's death the sacrifices continued for a time, until the destruction of the city by Titus. However, this actual cessation was in reality but the outward manifestation of that which had already been put into effect by our Lord's death." Ibid., 218.

67. The NRSV notes, "Meaning of Heb uncertain." The NIV follows the Septuagint and Theodotion to translate, "And at the temple."

68. Instead of translating *šōmēm* as "desolator," the NIV uses "him," with a note that it could also be "it," or "desolated city."

speaks of "the desolator." The "desolator" could not be Christ. Rather, the words "an abomination that desolates" and "the desolator" in verse 27 refer to the final sentence of verse 26, "*Desolations* are decreed."[69] Gabriel has just predicted in verse 26 that "an anointed one shall be cut off" (Jesus' crucifixion), "and the troops of the prince who is to come shall destroy the city and the sanctuary" (the Roman legions under Titus). Then follows, "Its end shall come with a flood, and to the end there shall be war. Desolations are decreed." These desolations must be the desolations brought about by the Roman legions. Verse 27b refers to these desolations. Literally the Hebrew reads, "on the wing of detested things (is) a desolator, until the decreed end is poured out on the desolator." Steinmann observes that "'wing' *(kānāp)* brings to mind (by synecdoche of a part for the whole) a swift raptor such as an eagle or falcon. 'Wing' is used several times in the Prophets in connection with swiftly attacking armies (Isa 8:8; Jer 48:40; 49:22; Ezek 17:3, 7). The 'desolator' (Dan 9:27) or 'detested thing of/causing desolation' (Mat 24:15; Mark 13:14) is the pagan Roman legions that conquered Jerusalem in A.D. 70 and again in A.D. 135."[70] Instead of identifying the Roman legions as the desolator, it may be more precise to identify as the desolator "the prince" (v. 26)[71] whose troops destroyed Jerusalem and the temple in A.D. 70, toward the end of the final week (see below). This "prince," the Roman general Titus Vespasianus, and his legions, in turn, prefigure the Antichrist and his legions. Inherent in this prediction "until the decreed end is poured out upon the desolator" (v. 27b), therefore, is the final destruction of the Antichrist.

To Anoint a Most Holy . . . (v. 24)

We need to make one final identification. Verse 24 states, "Seventy weeks are decreed for your people and your holy city: . . . to anoint a most holy place." Since the Hebrew does not have the word "place," the NRSV note explains that it can

---

69. This interpretation is also supported by the synonymous parallelism in vv. 26-27. See n. 64 above.

70. Steinmann, *Daniel*, 475. Similarly, Aalders, *Het Boek Daniel*, 207, except that he argues that in Matthew 24:15 and Mark 13:14, Jesus refers not to Daniel 9:27 but to 11:31 and 12:11. See Steinmann's defense quoted on p. 319, n. 92 below. Duguid, *Daniel*, 173, notes that "*kānāp* means 'wing,' but the same word can also indicate the extremity of a garment, or of the earth itself (see Isa 14:16)," so that he translates, "On account of the extremity of abominations that cause desolations." Cf. Calvin, *Commentaries on Daniel*, II, 228, "The preferable opinion is that which considers the word 'wing' to mean extremity or extension."

71. Although the "prince" is not the subject of the sentence, there must be a good reason why he is mentioned at all. Moreover, identifying the desolator with a person is in line with Daniel 8, where the little horn is a person (Antiochus IV).

also be "a most holy thing," or "a most holy one."[72] Again, opinions are divided. Collins and others claim that "the reference is to the rededication of the Jerusalem Temple, which was actually accomplished by Judas Maccabee late in 164 B.C.E. (1 Macc 4:36-59) but which was still awaited when this passage was written."[73] A problem with this interpretation is that a "rededication" is not an anointing. Steinmann comments, "No anointing is ever mentioned in connection with Solomon's temple. Neither is there any mention in the Old Testament of anointing for the second temple, rebuilt after the exile (Ezra). Moreover, 1 and 2 Maccabees say nothing about anointing the second temple when it was rededicated by Judas Maccabaeus (164 B.C.)."[74] Another problem with this interpretation is that even though the temple was rededicated by Judas Maccabee, he did not bring in the other decreed goals: "to finish the transgression, to put an end to sin, to atone for iniquity, [and] to bring in everlasting righteousness." One cannot select only one of the six goals ("to anoint a most holy place") and declare: Mission accomplished! Therefore we need to look for another place or person that accomplishes all six goals.

Some dispensationalists also understand this phrase as "to anoint a most holy *place*," but they see the reference to a future millennial temple.[75] Keil also thinks that the reference is to a place, but he explains it as "a new holy of holies which should be in the place of the holy of holies of the tabernacle and the temple of Solomon." He finds this new "holy of holies" in Revelation 21, "See, the *tabernacle* of God is among mortals. He will dwell with them as their God; they will be his people" (Rev. 21:3).[76] Another option is the traditional messianic interpretation.[77] This interpretation is supported by the context, which speaks of anointed *persons:* verse 25, "an anointed prince"; verse 26, "an anointed one shall be cut off." These anointed ones cannot be places. It also seems reasonable, therefore, to understand "to anoint a most holy" in verse 24 as a person: "to anoint a most holy *one*."[78] Since neither the Old Testament nor 1 and 2 Macca-

---

72. The NIV has "to anoint the Most Holy Place" in the text and "the most holy One" in a note.

73. Collins, *Daniel,* 354. So also Montgomery, *Daniel,* 375; Goldingay, *Daniel,* 260, and Lucas, *Daniel,* 242.

74. Steinmann, *Daniel,* 467.

75. "If a future temple is intended, which seems the best view, then it would be the edifice described in Ezek 40–48." Miller, *Daniel,* 262. So also Archer, "Daniel," 113, and Kaiser, *Preaching and Teaching the Last Things,* 111-21.

76. Keil, *Book of Daniel,* 348, 349. Cf. Leupold, *Exposition of Daniel,* 416.

77. Though Collins rejects a messianic interpretation, he does admit that "verse 24 presents a string of six infinitives, with God as the implied subject. Taken together they constitute an eschatological ideal." *Daniel,* 353.

78. Usually "a most holy" refers not to a person but to objects like the temple and the altar. Scholars have noted one possible exception: 1 Chronicles 23:13 (NASB), "And Aaron was set

bees speak about "anointing the second temple," Steinmann concludes that "the fulfillment of Daniel 9:24 must be the anointing of the Messiah, not any anointing of the second temple."[79]

Moreover, as Young points out, "In the Old Testament the anointing oil was a symbol of the Spirit of God (Zech 4)." For example, in anointing Saul, "Samuel took a vial of oil and poured it on his [Saul's] head . . . ; he said, 'The LORD has anointed you ruler over his people Israel. . . . Then the spirit of the LORD will possess you'" (1 Sam 10:1, 6). Also, in Isaiah 61:1 we read, "The spirit of the Lord GOD is upon me, because the LORD has anointed me." Young concludes, "The anointing of a Holy of Holies can only denote the communication of the Spirit to Christ, to which prominence is given in other prophecies of the Old Testament, as a distinguishing characteristic of the Messiah."[80]

This identification of "a most holy one" with Jesus Christ is confirmed by the New Testament. Peter says to Jesus, "We have come to believe and know that you are the Holy One of God" (John 6:69). Even an unclean spirit cries out to Jesus, "Have you come to destroy us? I know who you are, the Holy One of God" (Mark 1:24).[81] Thus this prediction that "seventy weeks are decreed . . . to anoint a most holy one" was fulfilled in Jesus' baptism when "he saw the heavens torn apart and the Spirit descending like a dove on him" (Mark 1:10). Jesus is the Anointed One, the Messiah / Christ, the Holy One of God.

Note that Gabriel compresses into the final week the time from the First Coming of Christ to his Second Coming: Jesus anointed by the Holy Spirit, the new covenant Jesus makes in his blood, his crucifixion, the end of animal sacrifices, the destruction of Jerusalem and the temple, "an abomination that desolates," and the destruction of "the desolator." In Daniel, all these events occur in the final week. It is only when the Messiah comes that we see another mountain peak behind this first one: in the last days there will be a final abomination by the Antichrist, a Second Coming of the Son of Man, a final judgment, the de-

---

apart to sanctify him as most holy." Lacocque, *Book of Daniel*, 193-95, argues for the translation, "to make a Holy of Holies Messiah."

79. Steinmann, *Daniel*, 467. He adds, "It is noteworthy that the temple is *not* called 'the Most Holy Place' . . . in Dan 9:26, but simply 'the holy place'. . . . While this could be seen as an abbreviation of the longer phrase, it more likely distinguishes the temple, which 'will be destroyed,' from the 'Most Holy One' in 9:24, who, though 'cut off' (9:26), will be raised and live forevermore." Ibid.

80. Young, *Prophecy of Daniel*, 201. The last sentence is a quotation from Ernst Wilhelm Hengstenberg, *Christology of the Old Testament*, III, trans. James Martin (Edinburgh: T&T Clark, 1856), no page.

81. Cf. Acts 2:27 and 13:35, alluding to Psalm 16:10, "You do not . . . let your faithful [holy] one see the Pit." See also Revelation 3:7.

struction of the Antichrist, the end of sin, "everlasting righteousness" (9:24), and the fullness of the Kingdom of God.

We can summarize our findings of these controversial figures in the following diagram.

Dates: 605 B.C. –	539 –	331 –	63 B.C. –		present	Last Day
Babylon	Medo-Persia	Greece & aftermath	Rome & aftermath	Christ		Kingdom of God

Dan 9:24	70 weeks decreed					
	538 B.C. ---					Kingdom of God
				"anoint a most holy" **Jesus**		"end to sin," "everlasting righteousness"
Dan 9:25a	7 weeks					
	word went out **Cyrus** 538 ------------	anointed prince Jerusalem wall **Ezra** 445				
Dan 9:25b	62 weeks					
		Jerusalem built streets & conduits 445 ------------------------------	troubled time Rome			
Dan 9:26	1 week			anointed cut off **Jesus** crucified A.D. 30 ------------	prince to come **Titus** A.D. 70	
Dan 9:27	same week			"strong covenant," "sacrifices cease" **Jesus**	"abomination desolates," "desolator" destroyed **Titus** prefigures the Antichrist	

Theocentric Interpretation

Daniel writes about "the word of the LORD to the prophet Jeremiah" (v. 2), turns to "the Lord God" (v. 3), and prays to "the LORD my God" (v. 4). His prayer is totally centered on Yahweh, the covenant God. He addresses God as "Lord, great and awesome God," and speaks of God's covenant keeping, steadfast love, and commandments (v. 4). He mentions God's "righteousness" (v. 7), his "mercy and forgiveness" (v. 9), his covenant "curse" (v. 11), his bringing calamity on Israel (vv. 12, 14), his "favor" and "fidelity" (v. 13), the Lord being "right in all that he has done" (v. 14), his "mighty hand" delivering Israel from Egypt (v. 15), his "righteous acts," and his "anger and wrath" (v. 16), and urges the Lord to let his "face shine" upon his desolated sanctuary (v. 17). He speaks of the city that bears God's name and of God's "great mercies" (18). He pleads with the Lord to hear, forgive, listen, and act (v. 19). After his prayer Daniel mentions that his supplication was "on behalf of the holy mountain of my God" (v. 20).

We should also note the veiled references to God in the divine passives. "In the first year of Darius . . . who was made ruler over the Babylonian kingdom" (v. 1, NIV) points to the sovereignty of God who made him king (cf. 2:21).[82] In his prayer Daniel declares, "All Israel has transgressed your law. . . . So the curse and the oath written in the law of Moses . . . have been poured out upon us" (v. 11), that is, God has poured the curse out upon us (see v. 12). Gabriel tells Daniel that "a word went out," that is, God sent out a word, which Gabriel will declare, "for you are greatly loved," that is, God loves you greatly (v. 23). "Seventy weeks are decreed" (v. 24), that is, "God . . . has decreed this period of time for the accomplishment of his redemptive purposes."[83] "Verse 24 presents a string of six infinitives, with God as the implied subject,"[84] that is, God will "finish the transgression," "put an end to sin," "atone for iniquity," "bring in everlasting righteousness," "seal both vision and prophet," and "anoint a most holy one." "From the time that the word went out," that is, from the time that God sent out the word (v. 25). "Desolations are decreed" (v. 26), that is, God decreed desolations. "Until the decreed end is poured out upon the desolator," that is, God will pour out upon the desolator his decreed end (v. 27). With these constant references to what God has done and will do, surely God will have to be the subject of the thematic statement.

Textual Theme and Goal

We can detect several themes in this chapter. Anderson suggests the general theme that the God of Israel is the Lord of history.[85] Kline focuses on the covenant: "The theme that pervades the entire chapter is Yahweh's covenant with Israel, particularly the actualization of the covenant sanctions through the faithfulness of God."[86] Steinmann states that "Daniel's prayer relies on another great theme that runs through this chapter: God always keeps his promises. . . . God's promise leads to the last great theme in this chapter: the messianic salva-

---

82. The NRSV apparently follows Montgomery's repointing of the Hebrew text to make it "became king." See Montgomery, *Book of Daniel*, 360-61.

83. Young, *Prophecy of Daniel*, 197.

84. Collins, *Daniel*, 353.

85. Anderson, *Signs and Wonders*, 118.

86. Kline, "The Covenant of the Seventieth Week," 455.

tion to be fulfilled when God puts an end to sin, atones for wickedness, and brings in everlasting righteousness (9:24)."[87]

Although these are all valid themes, for a unified sermon we need to formulate an overarching theme. The basic structure of this chapter is Daniel's prayer on behalf of all Israel for God's forgiveness and the restoration of Jerusalem and God's response that he has decreed seventy weeks in which not only to restore Jerusalem (v. 25) but also "to finish the transgression" and "to bring in everlasting righteousness" (v. 24). This structure indicates that there are two major themes, the one in Daniel's prayer, the other in God's response. The question now is, Which is dominant? Although Daniel's prayer is far longer, God's response to the prayer is the dominant theme. Therefore, in formulating the theme we can subordinate the theme of Daniel's prayer to that of God's response. This procedure leads to the following textual theme, *In response to Daniel's prayer for forgiveness and the restoration of Jerusalem, Israel's faithful covenant God promises in seventy weeks not only to restore Jerusalem but also to bring in his everlasting kingdom.*

The next question is, What was Daniel's goal in writing this message for Israel in exile? Hill proposes, "The immediate purpose of chapter 9 is to assure the persecuted Hebrews of the Babylonian Diaspora that the time of exile is almost over; the seventy years of Jeremiah's prophecy are about to be fulfilled (v. 2)."[88] Although this is a good suggestion, Daniel's goal is more than assuring Israel that their time of exile is almost over. We can give expression to this "more" by formulating Daniel's goal as follows: *to give Israel in exile hope by reassuring them that their time of exile is almost over because their faithful covenant God has decreed seventy weeks in which not only to restore Jerusalem but also to bring in his everlasting kingdom.*[89]

Ways to Preach Christ

Young makes an important point when he writes, "The passage is Messianic through and through. Well will it be for us, if we too, in our study of this supremely important prophecy, place our emphasis, not upon dates and mathematical calculations, but upon that central Figure who . . . by being cut off has made reconciliation for iniquity and brought in the only righteousness that is

---

87. Steinmann, *Daniel*, 426-27.

88. Hill, "Daniel," 158. Cf. Collins, *Daniel* (1984), 93, "The primary intention of Daniel 9 is to assure the persecuted Jews that the time of trial is coming to an end by locating it in an overview of history."

89. Cf. Goldingay, *Daniel*, 268: This passage "contains no exhortation to action. It is not concerned to urge people to obedience or resistance, but to offer them hope."

acceptable with God, even his own eternal righteousness."[90] Although "the passage is Messianic through and through," we still have to decide on the best way(s) to move from the stated theme to Jesus Christ in the New Testament. Therefore we shall again check the seven valid ways to move to Christ.

Redemptive-Historical Progression

In the beginning of Israel's history God had made a *covenant* with their forefathers Abraham, Isaac, and Jacob. Later, when Jacob's children were enslaved in Egypt, God had revealed himself as the covenant God Yahweh *(Lord)*,[91] "I am that I am," and, in keeping with his promise to Abram (Gen 15:14), had delivered them from slavery with *"a mighty hand"* (Exod 6:1-8). On the way to the Promised Land, at Mount Sinai, God had given them the ten words (Decalogue) of the covenant. Moses instructed Israel, "If you will only obey the Lord your God, by diligently observing all his *commandments* that I am commanding you today, the Lord your God will set you high above all the nations of the earth. . . . But if you will not obey the Lord your God . . . , then all these *curses* shall come upon you and overtake you" (Deut 28:1, 15). Israel disobeyed God time and again. Finally God punished them with the covenant curse: they were banished from the Promised Land. They lost the battle against Babylon; those who survived the battle were taken into exile, and Jerusalem and the temple of God were eventually destroyed. The prophet Jeremiah (25:11-12; 29:10) predicted that the exile would last *seventy years.* When the seventy years were almost over, Daniel fervently prayed God for forgiveness and for the restoration of Jerusalem. God responded that he had decreed seventy weeks in which Jerusalem would be restored and in which his *everlasting* kingdom would come.

God sent his servants Ezra and Nehemiah to the Promised Land. Under their leadership Jerusalem was indeed restored. Much later, in the fullness of time, God sent his only Son, Jesus, into the world. The angel told Joseph "to name him Jesus, for he will save his people from their *sins*" (Matt 1:21). Gabriel also told Mary to name him "Jesus," and added, "He will reign over the house of Jacob *forever,* and of his kingdom there will be no end" (Luke 1:31-32). Jesus began his public ministry by preaching, "The time is fulfilled, and *the kingdom of God* has come near; repent, and believe the good news" (Mark 1:15). Jesus demonstrated that the kingdom of God had come near by casting out demons, forgiving sins, restoring people to health, even raising them from the dead. But Jesus also realized that God's kingdom could not fully come until he had died to

---

90. Young, *Prophecy of Daniel,* 221.
91. I have italicized words used or concepts referred to in Daniel 9.

take away "the *sin of the world*" (John 1:29), been raised, and ascended to his Father's throne. The night before he died, Jesus celebrated the Passover with his disciples. He said, "I have eagerly desired to eat this Passover with you before I suffer; for I tell you, I will not eat it until it is fulfilled in the *kingdom of God.*" And then he changed the Passover into the Lords' Supper ("Do this in remembrance of me"), and the old covenant into the *new* covenant: "This cup that is poured out for you is the *new* covenant in my blood" (Luke 22:15, 19, 20).

The author of Hebrews explains the reason for the new covenant: "For this reason he is the mediator of a new covenant, so that those who are called may receive the promised *eternal* inheritance, because a death has occurred that redeems them from the transgressions under the first covenant" (Heb 9:15). After his resurrection, Jesus himself said to his disciples, "Thus it is written, that the Messiah is to suffer and to rise from the dead on the third day, and that repentance and forgiveness of *sins* is to be proclaimed in his name to all nations, beginning from Jerusalem" (Luke 24:46-47). When the good news of Jesus Christ has been proclaimed to all nations, Jesus will return on the clouds of heaven and establish God's perfect kingdom on earth (Matt 24:14). John writes that he saw "a new heaven and a new earth. . . . And I saw the holy city, *the new Jerusalem,* coming down out of heaven from God, prepared as a bride adorned for her husband. And I heard a loud voice from the throne saying, 'See the home [tabernacle] of God is among mortals'" (Rev. 21:1-3).

Promise-Fulfillment

The way of promise-fulfillment is the most direct way from this passage to Jesus Christ in the New Testament. The seventy weeks God decreed amount to God's promises for the future. Some of these promises are "to finish the transgression . . . , and to atone for iniquity" (v. 24a). These promises are fulfilled in the death of Christ on the cross. Gabriel foretells this all-important event: "After the sixty-two weeks, an anointed one [messiah] shall be cut off" (v. 26). Paul writes, "In him we have redemption through his blood, the *forgiveness of our trespasses,* according to the riches of his grace that he lavished on us" (Eph 1:7-8). And again, "Through him God was pleased to *reconcile* to himself all things, whether on earth or in heaven, by making peace through the blood of his cross" (Col 1:20). The author of Hebrews adds, "He had to become like his brothers and sisters in every respect, so that he might be a merciful and faithful high priest in the service of God, to make a sacrifice of *atonement for the sins* of the people" (Heb 2:17).

While God's promises of atonement and forgiveness have been fulfilled in the death and resurrection of Christ, other promises, such as "to put an end to sin" and "to bring in everlasting righteousness" (v. 24), await fulfillment at Jesus' Second Coming when Jesus brings in God's everlasting kingdom.

Typology

With promise-fulfillment being such a powerful bridge to Christ, it is not likely that one would add typology in the sermon. But if one were so inclined, the "anointed prince" who comes at the end of the first seven weeks, Ezra, can be seen as a type of Christ: in his person and work Ezra prefigures Christ, but Christ is much greater (analogies and escalations).

Ezra's lineage is traced back to Israel's first high priest, Aaron (Ezra 7:1-5). Ezra himself is called "the priest Ezra" (Ezra 7:11, 12, 21). Priests were anointed (e.g., Exod 28:41; 29:7; 30:30; Lev. 4:3-5; 6:22), that is, they were holy, set apart for serving God in a special capacity. Ezra was anointed with oil for his special task, but Jesus was anointed with the *Holy Spirit* (Mark 1:10) and was called the Messiah, the Anointed One (e.g., Luke 2:11; 9:20; Acts 10:38), the Holy One (Mark 1:24; John 6:69), our only High Priest. The author of Hebrews asserts, "The former priests were many in number, because they were prevented by death from continuing in office; but he holds his priesthood permanently, because he continues forever. Consequently he is able for all time to save those who approach God through him, since he always lives to make intercession for them" (Heb 7:23-25).

Ezra is further described as "a scribe skilled in the law of Moses" (Ezra 7:6) who taught Israel the law of their God and summoned them to new obedience (Neh 8). Jesus was a rabbi, skilled in the law, who taught people the depth dimension of God's law (e.g., Matt 5–7) and called them to radical obedience (e.g., Matt 5:48; 7:21). Ezra led Israel to covenant obedience to the law of Moses (Neh 9–10). Jesus made a "new covenant" in his "blood" (Luke 22:20) in which God's law was no longer external but internal: "I [God] will put my laws in their hearts, and I will write them on their minds" (Heb 10:16 citing Jer 31:33).

Ezra bought "bulls, rams, and lambs" to be offered as sacrifices on the altar of the rebuilt temple (Ezra 7:17). Jesus offered his own life, once for all: "When Christ had offered for all time a single sacrifice for sins, 'he sat down at the right hand of God.' . . . For by a single offering he has perfected for all time those who are sanctified" (Heb 10:12, 14).

Analogy

We can also use the way of analogy by drawing an analogy between Daniel's goal in sending this message to Israel in exile and Jesus' goal in proclaiming his good news in the New Testament: As Daniel offered hope to Israel by reassuring them that their faithful covenant God had decreed to bring in his everlasting kingdom, so Jesus offered hope to God's people by reassuring them that God's kingdom would surely come. Jesus began his public ministry by proclaiming, "The time is fulfilled, and the *kingdom of God* has come near" (Mark 1:15). Looking at his disciples, Jesus said, "Blessed are you who are poor, for yours *is* the kingdom of God" (Luke 6:20). After telling his disciples that he would soon be betrayed, Jesus said, "Do not let your hearts be troubled. . . . In my Father's house there are many dwelling places. . . . If I go and prepare a place for you, I will come again and will take you to myself, so that where I am there you may be also" (John 14:1-3). He further told them about the last day: "The powers of the heavens will be shaken. Then they will see 'the Son of Man coming in a cloud' with power and great glory. Now when these things begin to take place, stand up and raise your heads, because your redemption is drawing near" (Luke 21:26b-28). Jesus added that at that time, "The Son of man . . . will send out his angels with a loud trumpet call, and they will gather his elect from the four winds, from one end of heaven to the other" (Matt 24:30-31).

Longitudinal Themes

With several direct ways to Christ in the New Testament, it is not likely that one would use the way of longitudinal themes for this passage. But one could trace the theme of the covenant from the old covenant to the new covenant in Jesus' blood (close to redemptive-historical progression above). One could also trace the theme of God bringing in his perfect kingdom from God's "mother promise" in Genesis 3:15 to Jesus' First Coming to his Second Coming (see pp. 64-65 above, pp. 227-28, and pp. 229-30).

New Testament References

The Appendix of the Greek New Testament lists sixteen references to Daniel 9, many of them on details (such as "sackcloth and ashes" in Dan 9:3 and in Matt 11:21 and Luke 10:13). Those references that support the theme we have already used to support the above five ways to Christ in the New Testament. Cross-reference Bibles, concordances, commentaries, and *The Treasury of Scripture Knowledge* provide even more New Testament references that could possibly be used in the sermon. Some of these are the following:

Hebrews 9:11-12, "But when Christ came as a high priest of the good things that have come . . . , he entered once for all into the Holy Place, not with the blood of goats and calves, but with his own blood, thus obtaining *eternal redemption.*"

Matthew 24:1-2, "As Jesus came out of the temple and was going away, his disciples came to point out to him the buildings of the *temple.* Then he asked them, 'You see all these, do you not? Truly I tell you, not one stone will be left here upon another; all will be *thrown down.*'"

Mark 13:7-8, "When you hear of *wars* and rumors of wars, do not be alarmed; this must take place, but the end is still to come. For nation will rise against nation, and kingdom against kingdom; there will be earthquakes in various places; there will be famines. This is but the beginning of the birth pangs."

Matthew 24:15, "So when you see the *desolating sacrilege* standing in the holy place, as was spoken of by the prophet Daniel (let the reader understand), then those in Judea must flee to the mountains."[92]

Contrast

Except for the contrast between the old and the new covenant noted in redemptive-historical progression above, there is no contrast between the message of Daniel 9 and that of the New Testament.

Sermon Theme, Goal, and Need

We formulated the textual theme as follows: "In response to Daniel's prayer for forgiveness and the restoration of Jerusalem, Israel's faithful covenant God promises in seventy weeks not only to restore Jerusalem but also to bring in his everlasting kingdom." God did restore Jerusalem at the time of Ezra and Nehemiah, but God also foretold that Jerusalem and the temple would be destroyed again (Dan 9:26) — a destruction that took place in A.D. 70. The New Testament church today is not waiting for the earthly Jerusalem but for "the new Jerusalem, coming down out of heaven from God" (Rev. 21:2). Since "the restoration of Jerusalem" can refer to the earthly Jerusalem as well as "the new Jerusalem," the textual theme can function as the sermon theme: *In response to*

92. Cf. Mark 13:14-16. Steinmann, *Daniel,* 473, n. 94, observes, "Although the phrase Jesus uses in Matt 24:15 and Mark 13:14 is a fairly literal translation of the Hebrew phrases in Dan 11:31 and 12:11, those verses refer to the desolation accomplished under Antiochus IV Epiphanes (cf. also 8:13), whereas 9:27 refers to the desolation that would take place after Jesus' earthly ministry, so it is the most relevant for Matt 24:15 and Mark 13:14."

Daniel's prayer for forgiveness and the restoration of Jerusalem, Israel's faithful covenant God promises in seventy weeks not only to restore Jerusalem but also to bring in his everlasting kingdom.

Daniel's goal in sending this message to Israel was "to give Israel in exile hope by reassuring them that their time of exile is almost over because their faithful covenant God has decreed seventy weeks in which not only to restore Jerusalem but also to bring in his everlasting kingdom." Because of the progression in redemptive history — the earthly Jerusalem restored in the time of Ezra and destroyed again in A.D. 70 — the New Testament church is now looking forward to "the new Jerusalem, coming down out of heaven from God" (Rev. 21:2). The sermon goal, therefore, can be formulated as follows: *to give God's people today hope by reassuring them that our faithful covenant God has decreed seventy weeks in which to bring the new Jerusalem on earth as he brings in his everlasting kingdom.*

This goal suggests that the target for the sermon is the hopelessness of many people who have given up on God's coming kingdom. The wait seems too long. God's people still suffer from persecution and other calamities. Even more than in the first century A.D., people in the twenty-first century are asking themselves, "Where is the promise of his coming?" (2 Pet 3:4).

Scripture Reading

Since this is a fairly lengthy chapter, we should briefly consider our options with respect to Scripture reading. Some commentators recommend preparing two sermons on this chapter, the first on Daniel's prayer (vv. 1-19) and the second on God's answer (vv. 20-27).[93] But this is not a good solution. Since the author conveys his message in a literary unit, one should preach on complete literary units if at all possible (we may have to make an exception for Daniel 10–12). Moreover, Daniel's beautiful prayer is *not* a model for Christian prayer but a unique prayer for a specific time in redemptive history: Israel is in exile; Daniel realizes that the 70 years foretold by Jeremiah are almost up (9:2); he knows about the covenant "curse" (9:11) which brought about the "desolation" (*šāmēm;* 9:17, 18) — the word used in the very chapter on covenant blessings and curses (Lev. 26:22, 31, 32, 33, 34, 35, 43); he also knows that in that same chapter (in our Bibles) God promised, "If they confess their iniquity . . . , then I will remember my covenant with Jacob" (Lev. 26:41-42). Hence his specific prayer of confession and his supplication with God to restore his "desolated

93. Duguid suggests a sermon on Daniel 9:1-19, "Praying in the Darkness," followed by a sermon on Daniel 9:20-27, "Hope in the Darkness." See his *Daniel,* 148-75.

sanctuary" (9:17) and "city" without "delay" (9:19) and God's immediate response (9:20-21).[94] In preaching just on this unique prayer and seeking to apply it to Christians today, one can hardly help but fall into the traps of generalizing and moralizing.

A better option is to announce to the congregation that, because of the length of the text, its reading will be incorporated into the sermon — similar to what I will do in the "Sermon Exposition" below. Although this will save some time in the worship service, the downside is that the congregation will miss out on hearing the impact of the passage as a whole.

Another option is to assign two good readers, one for Daniel (vv. 1-22a), whose prayer should be read with passion, and one for Gabriel (vv. 22b-27). This way the congregation experiences the impact of the passage as a whole before the more piecemeal approach of the sermon.

Still another option is to incorporate the reading of Daniel's prayer earlier in the liturgy in the part of "confession of sin." For example, one can pray Daniel's prayer, followed by silence, and then offer a current prayer of confession.[95] Before the sermon one can then read Daniel 9:20-27.

This brings up another issue with respect to the sermon: the theme focuses on the last four verses, but they are preceded by sixteen verses of Daniel's prayer. If one were to give an exposition of the meaning of every verse in the prayer, one would throw the sermon out of balance. What's worse for the congregation listening, the sermon would stall and probably crash. Therefore it is advisable to organize the exposition of the prayer in a few key points (e.g., ACTS, as I do below), or comment on the meaning of only a few key verses (selected from the verses explained below[96]) in order to move rather quickly to the heart of this chapter, God's response in the last four verses.

Sermon Exposition

The sermon introduction can expose the need addressed by reminding the congregation of hardships recently suffered,[97] or a disaster that killed many Chris-

---

94. Daniel's prayer fits in the tradition of Old Testament *Todah*-prayers. See Kline, "The Covenant of the Seventieth Week," 456-58.

95. This creative solution was suggested by my brother and proofreader, Morris Greidanus.

96. One can order these selected verses by subject as I have done in the outline above (see p. 289, Scene 1, B. 2), or follow Daniel's confession of sins (vv. 4-6) with his appeals to God's mercy and forgiveness (vv. 9-10, 18), God's righteousness (vv. 7-8, 11-14), God's righteous acts (vv. 15-16), and God's own glory (vv. 17-19).

97. See the introductions of the sermons on pp. 415 and 421 below.

tians, or a recent instance of state-sponsored persecution of God's people.[98] Persecution of the church has spread so much that in the twentieth century an estimated 45 million Christians were martyred.[99] 45 million! Jesus promised to bring in the perfect kingdom of God. Meanwhile 45 million of his followers were slaughtered in the last century. No wonder many Christians today begin to lose hope.

Israel in exile was also losing hope. They were in exile in far-off Babylon. The Babylonian armies had defeated the army of Judah in 605 B.C. They had killed many Israelites, and carried the king and the brightest young men away to Babylon. Daniel was among this first group of exiles. Later (597 B.C.) the Babylonians had come back, captured Jerusalem, and taken more Israelites captive. Then they had come back a third time and destroyed the city of Jerusalem and God's beautiful temple (587 B.C.). The events described in Daniel 9 take place when the first captives had been in exile almost seventy years. A whole generation had died far from the Promised Land. No wonder the Israelites in exile felt hopeless and despondent.

Daniel 9:1-2, "In the first year[100] of Darius[101] son of Ahasuerus, by birth a Mede, who became[102] king over the realm of the Chaldeans — in the first year of his reign, I, Daniel, perceived in the books the number of years that, according to the word of the LORD to the prophet Jeremiah, must be fulfilled for the devastation of Jerusalem, namely, seventy years." The first year of Darius was the year 539 B.C. This was also the year the great Babylonian Empire collapsed. Daniel's "witness of the fall of Babylon may have caused him to turn to the Scriptures with new eyes."[103] Since he was captured in 605 B.C., he had been in exile for about sixty-six years.

98. As I write this, the news reports that Coptic Christians in Egypt are being persecuted. Marshall, *Their Blood Cries Out,* offers examples of persecution in many nations. Googling "persecution of Christians" will provide many current examples.

99. David Barrett and Todd M. Johnson, *World Christian Encyclopedia* (2d ed.; New York: Oxford University Press, 2001), I, 11.

100. "The data formula, 'the first year of Darius,' places the events of chapter 9 between 539 and 538 BC — some eleven or twelve years after the vision of chapter 8." Hill, "Daniel," 157.

101. In Daniel, Darius is probably another name for King Cyrus the Great. See p. 169, n. 79, above.

102. The NIV translation, "who was made ruler over," does justice to the passive. Since this is another divine passive, "the implication is that Darius has been made king by divine action. The Babylonian Empire is finished and history moves on by the will of God." Seow, *Daniel,* 138. Cf. Stefanovic, *Daniel,* 342, "The statement that Darius *was made ruler* is significant here because it reinforces the concept of God's providence and sovereignty: The same Lord who delivered Jerusalem and its king into Nebuchadnezzar's hand (Dan 1:2) was at work in bringing Darius (Cyrus) to power and making him ruler over the Babylonian kingdom (Dan 11:1)."

103. Longman, *Daniel,* 221. Cf. Young, *Prophecy of Daniel,* 183, "The mention of the date is

Then he read in Jeremiah the number of years "that must be fulfilled for the devastation of Jerusalem, namely, seventy years."[104] He likely read Jeremiah 25:11-12, "This whole land shall become a ruin and a waste, and these nations shall serve the king of Babylon *seventy years.* Then after seventy years are completed, I will punish the king of Babylon and that nation, the land of the Chaldeans, for their iniquity, says the LORD, making the land an everlasting waste."[105] Very recently God had punished the king of Babylon. Babylon had fallen. The seventy years must be almost up.[106]

But Daniel also knew that it would not be an automatic return to the Promised Land when the seventy years were up. In the very chapter in Leviticus where God spelled out his punishments for the disobedience of his covenant people, God also promised: "*If* they *confess* their iniquity and the iniquity of their ancestors . . . , [which caused me to bring] them into the land of their enemies . . . , then will I remember my covenant with Jacob" (Lev. 26:40-42; cf. Deut 30:1-5). Israel's return to the Promised Land was not automatic; they would first have to "confess their iniquity."[107]

We read Daniel's reaction in verse 3, "Then I turned[108] to the Lord[109] God, to seek an answer by prayer and supplication with fasting and sackcloth and ashes. I prayed to the LORD[110] my God and made *confession.* . . ." Daniel demon-

---

deliberate in order to call attention to the time. Babylon was now fallen and the liberating country was in the first year of its sovereignty. The time had come in which to expect the end of captivity."

104. Commentators who take "seventy years" literally cannot make it fit exactly with the historical givens. Therefore Miller, *Daniel,* 241, is satisfied to take it as "a round number." Goldingay, *Daniel,* 239, points out that "'seventy years' suggests a human lifetime (cf. Isa 23:15; Ps 91:10)." Cf. Collins, *Daniel,* 349. Lucas, *Daniel,* 235, calls it "a round number, indicating a lifetime." Still others observe that "seventy also suggests a symbolic number being seven multiplied by ten, two numbers of completeness." Longman, *Daniel,* 222. Baldwin, *Daniel,* 164, makes the valid point: "It is possible to be so preoccupied with numbers as to miss the essential truth which those numbers declare."

105. Jeremiah 29:10 also mentions the "seventy years" but does not speak of "the devastation of Jerusalem" which Daniel mentions in verse 2.

106. "His main concern . . . is not to know the precise meaning of the number seventy; it is to implore the Divine pardon for his and the people's sins." Young, *Prophecy of Daniel,* 184.

107. See Kline, "The Covenant of the Seventieth Week," 457-58, on the *Todah*-prayers.

108. Literally, "'gave his face' in prayer. . . . The idiom alludes to the practice of facing Jerusalem when a Hebrew prays." Hill, "Daniel," 162.

109. "His appeal was directed toward 'the Lord ['ădônāy] God.' The name 'ădônāy means 'owner, ruler, sovereign' . . . of the universe. Not only was he able to hear Daniel's prayer, but he had the power to direct affairs of world history in order to answer his prayer." Miller, *Daniel,* 242.

110. "LORD" printed in capital and small capital letters is the English way of indicating that the Hebrew here uses the special covenant name of God, Yahweh.

strates his penitence by fasting, wearing sackcloth, and sprinkling his head with ashes — "a sign of mourning and repentance in the Old Testament."[111]

Prayer basically consists of four parts. You can remember the four parts with the acronym ACTS: A for adoration, C for confession, T for thanksgiving, and S for supplication. This exquisite prayer of Daniel contains three of these parts: adoration, confession, and supplication. He begins with adoration. Verse 4b, "Ah, Lord, great and awesome God, keeping covenant and steadfast love with those who love you and keep your commandments." "Ah, Lord" — owner of the universe; "great and awesome God" — great and awesome beyond our imagining; "keeping covenant and steadfast love with those who love you and keep your commandments" — always faithful, always showing "steadfast love"[112] to your covenant partners "who love you and keep your commandments" (see Exod 20:6).[113]

Daniel follows his adoration of God with a lengthy confession of sin (vv. 5-14). This may seem strange to us because Daniel always sought to obey God's law. As far as we know, Daniel had always been faithful to God — faithful unto death. Only a short time ago Daniel had defied the law of King Darius that people should pray to no other god or human but to the king. Even though Daniel knew that the penalty for disobedience was death in the lions' den, he continued "to get down on his knees three times a day to pray to his God and praise him" (Dan 6:10). He was faithful to God unto death. Why then this lengthy confession of sin?

The reason is this: Daniel identifies with the people of Israel. He prays on behalf of the people of Israel. In his confession of sin in the next ten verses he will use the word "we" seven times and "us" eight times.

Verses 5-6, "*We* have sinned and done wrong, acted wickedly and rebelled, turning aside from your commandments and ordinances. *We* have not listened to your servants the prophets, who spoke in your name to our kings, our princes, and our ancestors, and to all the people of the land." In verse 5 Daniel piles up five different words for sin, thus seeking to cover all angles. "We have sinned" means, literally, we have missed the mark (cf. Judg 20:16). In other words, sins of omission: we have not done what we should have done. We "have done wrong" means, literally, we have turned "from the right way";[114] we have

---

111. Hill, "Daniel," 162, with references to Nehemiah 9:1, Esther 4:1-4; and Jonah 3:6. Cf. Steinmann, *Daniel*, 436, and Collins, *Daniel*, 349.

112. "The 'love' (*ḥesed*) is that loyal love of God by which he faithfully keeps his promises to his people, in this case, those of the covenant." Miller, *Daniel*, 244.

113. "The context makes clear that what is called for is not so much an emotional as a moral commitment (e.g., Deut 6:4-9; 10:12-13; 11:1). Yahweh's commands . . . express his will and he expects those who are committed to him to obey them." Lucas, *Daniel*, 237.

114. Leupold, *Exposition of Daniel*, 383.

made our "paths crooked."[115] We "acted wickedly" refers to "actions that put a person in the wrong in a legal . . . sense (e.g., Exod 22:9 [8]; Deut 25:1)."[116] In other words, sins of commission. Daniel's list of sins reaches a climax at the end of verse 5: We "have rebelled, turning aside from your commandments and ordinances" (see Exod 32:8). They had turned their backs on God's will, the ultimate insult.[117] Daniel adds in verse 6, "We have *not* listened to your servants the prophets, who spoke in your name to our kings, our princes, and our ancestors, and to all the people of the land." From royalty to commoners, from high to low,[118] "we have not listened to your servants the prophets." We are all guilty!

Daniel continues his confession in verses 7-8, "Righteousness is on your side, O Lord, but *open shame,* as at this day, falls on us, the people of Judah, the inhabitants of Jerusalem, and *all Israel,* those who are near and those who are far away, in all the lands to which you have driven them, because of the treachery that they have committed against you. *Open shame,* O LORD, falls on us, our kings, our officials, and our ancestors, because *we* have sinned against you." The open shame that has fallen on Israel is that of having its people captured and taken away into exile[119] and the destruction of the capital Jerusalem and God's temple.

What is the reason for this "open shame"? Daniel states it plainly at the end of verse 7, "because of the *treachery*[120] that they have committed against you." The NIV translates, "because of our *unfaithfulness* to you." And again at the end of verse 8: "because we have *sinned* against you." The captivity and the destruction of Jerusalem and the temple are God's just punishments of his covenant people. "Righteousness is on your side, O Lord, but open shame . . . falls on us" (v. 7).

In verse 9 Daniel brings in a new element. He has just confessed that "righteousness" is on God's side. God was just in punishing Israel for its sins. God was "right" in enforcing the punishment prescribed for covenant breakers. As a

---

115. "It appears to emphasize the fact that sin is 'something twisted or perverted' or that one who sins has veered from the straight and narrow road and 'made his paths crooked.'" Miller, *Daniel,* 245.

116. Lucas, *Daniel,* 237.

117. "Perhaps the verbs build up through verse 5 (and v. 6a): turning the back and closing the ears is the climactic rejection of Yahweh's word and the crowning insult." Goldingay, *Daniel,* 250.

118. Porteous, *Daniel,* 137, quoting A. Jeffery, *IB* (1956) 487, observes that this listing in verse 6 is a "'descending order of classes in the social scale,' i.e., 'royal house, princely houses, family houses, commoners.'"

119. "Probably no greater humiliation could come upon a nation than that of being conquered by a foreign power and having its citizens expelled." Miller, *Daniel,* 246.

120. Treachery is "a word that signifies violating an oath, such as the promise to keep the covenant. The covenant . . . contained commandments, laws and instructions (Dan 9:5, 10)." Lucas, *Daniel,* 252.

result, Israel has been suffering this "open shame" for almost seventy years. They are losing hope of ever returning to the Promised Land. But now Daniel adds in verse 9, "To the Lord our God belong *mercy and forgiveness.*" In the Hebrew these two qualities of God are both in the plural: "mercies" and "forgivenesses." The plural means either the intensity of God's mercy and forgiveness, or that God showed these qualities many times.[121] There is hope for Israel after all — their God is full of mercy and full of forgiveness.

Daniel repeats Israel's sins in verses 9-10, "for[122] we have rebelled against him, and have not obeyed the voice of the Lord our God by following his laws, which he set before us by his servants the prophets." Because of Israel's constant disobedience, they must appeal to God's mercy and forgiveness if there is to be any hope.

In verse 11 Daniel begins to explain further why righteousness is on God's side when he punishes his people. Daniel says, "*All Israel* has transgressed[123] your law and turned aside, refusing to obey your voice. So the *curse* and the oath written in the law of Moses, the servant of God, have been poured out upon us, because *we* have sinned against you." The "curse"[124] refers to the covenant curse, one of the penalties God would bring on covenant breakers (see Lev. 26:27-45; Deut 28:15-68). The most severe penalty was, "I will devastate the land, so that your enemies who come to settle in it shall be appalled at it. And you I will scatter among the nations . . . ;[125] your land shall be a *desolation,* and your cities a waste" (Lev. 26:32-33). That was the very curse that had been "poured out" upon Israel like a flood.

Daniel continues in verses 12-14, "He [God] has confirmed his words, which he spoke against us and against our rulers, by bringing upon us a *calamity so great* that what has been done against Jerusalem has never before been done under the whole heaven.[126] Just as it is written in the law of Moses, all this

---

121. Ibid., 238.

122. "The *kî* clauses that follow . . . do not, of course, involve a *kî* causal but a *kî* explicative and show more loosely, not why God is merciful, but why there is need for his manifesting mercy." Leupold, *Exposition of Daniel*, 386.

123. "All Israel" is "in the emphatic position in the sentence. Israel has 'transgressed' in the sense of having wilfully gone beyond, *'ābhar,* certain bounds that had been distinctly marked." Leupold, *Exposition of Daniel*, 387.

124. The curse (*'ālă*) "is singular and definite in the Hebrew, indicating that a particular curse was in view." Miller, *Daniel*, 247.

125. Cf. Deuteronomy 28:64, "The Lord will scatter you among all peoples, from one end of the earth to the other."

126. "Other nations had experienced defeat and deportation, but their gods were idols of lifeless wood, stone, and metal (cf. Ps 135:15-17; Isa 44:9ff.). Now the people of the true God were in exile, and his city and temple were in ruins. Truly nothing like this had ever happened in history." Miller, *Daniel*, 247.

calamity has come upon us. We did not entreat the favor of the LORD our God, turning from our iniquities and reflecting on his fidelity. So *the LORD kept watch over this calamity* until he brought it upon us. Indeed, the LORD our God is *right* in all that he has done; for we have disobeyed his voice." "The LORD kept watch over this calamity" means that God kept this calamity ready (he watched over it) "in case Israel did not repent."[127] Since Israel continued to break God's commandments, at the appropriate time the Lord brought this disaster upon them.[128] Again, Daniel concludes, "The LORD our God is *right* [just] in all that he has done."

After his brief adoration and his lengthy confession, Daniel is ready to conclude his prayer with a moving supplication. He begins with a reminder of God's redemption of his people Israel from Egypt. Verses 15-16, "And now, O Lord our God, who brought your people out of the land of Egypt with a mighty hand [cf. Exod 15:6] and made your name renowned even to this day — we have sinned, we have done wickedly. O Lord, *in view of all your righteous acts,* let your anger and wrath, we pray, turn away from your city Jerusalem, your holy mountain; because of our sins and the iniquities of our ancestors, Jerusalem and your people have become a disgrace among all our neighbors." Daniel pleads with God to turn his anger *away* from his city, Jerusalem, which has become a disgrace among the neighbors.

What is the basis for this plea? Daniel begins in verse 15 with a reminder of God's redemption from Egypt, and then continues in verse 16, "In view of all your righteous acts, let your anger and wrath . . . turn away." God's righteous acts are the basis for Daniel's plea. God is just. Well, justice had been served. "Israel had been punished for their sins, and now it would be right ('just') for God to restore the nation."[129]

Verse 17, "Now therefore, O our God, listen to the prayer of your servant and to his supplication, and *for your own sake,* Lord, let your face shine upon your desolated sanctuary." God's own renown, his own glory, is at stake. God's city and God's people are "a disgrace" among their neighbors (v. 16), and that reflects on God himself. The neighboring nations will think that Israel's God is weak. He cannot even protect his own temple and his own city. So for God's "own sake" Daniel pleads with God, "Let your face shine upon your desolated sanctuary." Daniel here uses the expression of the priestly benediction: "The

---

127. Ibid., 248. Cf. Lucas, *Daniel,* 239, "This verb *(šaqad)* is used in Jeremiah of Yahweh's watching over his word to perform it (1:12), and over his people 'for evil and not for good' (44:27)."

128. "The personal deliberateness of his [the LORD's] deed is underlined by speaking of him as watching over the trouble, keeping it ready; it comes as his carefully considered act (v. 14), the determined realization of a predetermined plan." Goldingay, *Daniel,* 252.

129. Miller, *Daniel,* 248, with references to Isaiah 40:2 and Leviticus 26:41.

LORD bless you and keep you; the LORD make his face to *shine* upon you . . ." (Num 6:24-25; cf. Ps 80). When God makes "his face to shine upon" people, he smiles on them. His anger is turned away, and he seeks to bless them and keep them. Now Daniel asks God to make his face *shine upon* his "desolated sanctuary." The temple is in ruins because of God's anger. Daniel is asking God to smile upon the temple so that it may be rebuilt and once again bring glory to God.

As Daniel continues his supplication in verse 18, he becomes more bold: "Incline your ear, O my God, and hear. Open your eyes and look at our desolation and the city that bears your name." He urges God not to be *deaf* to Israel's pain. He speaks to God in very human terms: "Bend your ear, O my God, and hear!" It's as if he asks God to cup his ear so he can hear better. And he urges God not to be *blind* to Israel's anguish: "Open your eyes and look at our desolation!" Daniel is bold — but also reverent. He continues in verse 18, "We do not present our supplication before you[130] on the ground of *our* righteousness, but on the ground of *your great mercies*." Israel is not righteous, not at all, but God is full of mercy. Israel's restoration is totally dependent on God's grace.

Verse 19 is the climax of Daniel's supplication, "O Lord, hear; O Lord, forgive; O Lord, listen and act and do not delay![131] *For your own sake*, O my God, because your city and your people bear your name!" For the second time (see v. 17), Daniel urges God to act for his *own* sake. God's own glory is at stake. God's city Jerusalem and his people Israel bear God's name. With Israel in exile and God's city in ruins, God's name is being dragged through the mud. So if not for God's mercy and forgiveness, if not for God's righteousness, God should at least "act and not delay" for his own sake.

It's a powerful prayer.[132] Daniel confesses Israel's sin time and again. Israel is

---

130. "Daniel uses a rare idiom, literally, 'we are causing our plea for grace to fall before you.' . . . The image is of casting a request on the ground before the king, showing abject humility and reliance entirely on his good will." Steinmann, *Daniel*, 441.

131. "This threefold petition has been called the *kyrie eleison* (= Lord, have mercy) of the Old Testament." Hammer, *Daniel*, 98. "In the MT it is brevity itself, seven words only, but in these seven words is the plea of a nation burdened by past sins, and stricken by a ruthless oppressor." Anderson, *Signs and Wonders*, 110. Regarding Daniel's words, "act and do not delay," Baldwin, *Daniel*, 167, notes, "Daniel asserts his expectation that his prayer will be heard, that God will cause both the city and temple at Jerusalem to be rebuilt, and that he will do so now without further delay."

132. Because of the length of this prayer, a brief summary of the highlights such as the following may be appropriate in a sermon: Daniel confesses Israel's sin time and again. Israel is not worthy of God's redemption. But, verse 9, "to the Lord our God belong *mercy and forgiveness*." It is true, verse 14, "The LORD our God is *right* in all that he has done," but, verse 16, "in view of all your righteous acts," it would be *just* to let your anger "turn away," for Israel has suffered long enough — as Isaiah puts it, "she has served her term" (Isa 40:2). Verses 16b-17, since Jerusalem

not worthy of God's redemption. And yet Daniel dares to bank on God's mercy and justice. Sometimes God's people have to wait months, years — even a lifetime — for God to answer their prayer. Not so Daniel. He reports in verses 20-21, "While I was speaking, and was praying and confessing my sin and the sin of my[133] people Israel, and presenting my supplication before the LORD my God on behalf of the holy mountain[134] of my God — *while I was speaking*[135] in prayer, the man Gabriel,[136] whom I had seen before in a vision, came to me *in swift flight* at the time of the evening sacrifice."[137] Even while Daniel was praying, the angel Gabriel came "in swift flight."[138] God's response was immediate.[139]

Verses 22-23, "He, [Gabriel] came and said to me, 'Daniel, I have now come out to give you wisdom and understanding. At the beginning of your supplica-

---

and Israel "have become a disgrace among all our neighbors . . . *for your own sake, Lord,* let your face shine upon your desolated sanctuary." Verse 18b, "We do not present our supplication before you on the ground of *our* righteousness, but on the ground of *your great mercies.*" Verse 19, "O Lord, hear; O Lord, forgive; O Lord, listen and act and do not delay!"

133. "Daniel takes the initiative in identifying himself with the people whom Yahweh has every ground for repudiating." Goldingay, *Daniel,* 247.

134. "This last phrase emphasizes that Daniel's concern for Jerusalem stems from the desire to reinstitute worship of God at the temple on Mount Zion. This concern is echoed in 9:21, where Daniel notes that Gabriel appeared 'about the time of the evening sacrifice,' about 3:00 pm." Steinmann, *Daniel,* 450.

135. The repetition of "while I was speaking" "emphasizes God's grace in the timing of his response to Daniel's supplication." Hill, "Daniel," 167.

136. Collins, *Daniel,* 351, comments, "Gabriel was explicitly identified in Dan 8:16, but the vision in chapter 8 was said to be 'after that which appeared to me in the beginning' (8:1). Gabriel is probably identified with the anonymous 'one of the attendants' in 7:16, who also has the function of interpreter." So also Lucas, *Daniel,* 240. If this identification is correct, and I think it is, it is another reason for interpreting Daniel 9 in the light of the broad vision of the coming kingdom of God in chapter 7 instead of restricting it to the reign of Antiochus IV as in chapter 8.

137. "Obviously no literal sacrifice was made in Babylon, but this was a time of day commonly used for prayer (cf. Ezra 9:5; Ps 141:2)." Miller, *Daniel,* 251.

138. "The phrase 'swift flight' here does not necessarily imply that Gabriel is a winged being. The point may simply be that the swiftness of his approach is like that of a fast-flying bird." Lucas, *Daniel,* 240. Hammer, *Daniel,* 98, adds, "In 1 Chron 21:16 the angel of the Lord is said to be 'standing between earth and heaven.' The reference to *flying* expressed a similar mediatorial role; he is the bearer of the divine message."

139. As God says in Isaiah, "Before they call I will answer, while they are yet speaking I will hear" (Isa 64:24). Jesus also said, "Your Father knows what you need before you ask him" (Matt 6:8). Goldingay, *Daniel,* 255-56, comments, "God is eager to respond to his servants when they come to him on behalf of his people in need. The picture of God 'responding' before Daniel actually prays perhaps also safeguards the sovereignty of God." Cf. Lucas, *Daniel,* 252, "A Jew who could recite Ps 139:4 ('Even before a word is on my tongue, lo, O LORD, you know it altogether') would have no difficulty with the idea that Yahweh does not have to sit back, let Daniel finish his prayer, think about it and then respond. The Hebrews were aware that time is not the same for God as it is for us (Ps 90:4)."

tions a word went out, and I have come to declare it, for you are greatly beloved. So consider the word and understand the vision." "The vision" is Gabriel's sudden appearance, and "the word" is his message.[140] Gabriel has come to give Daniel "wisdom and understanding" about God's plan for the future.[141] He says, "At the beginning of your supplications a *word* went out." That is how quickly God answers prayer. The word that "went out" from God is the word Gabriel will bring in the following verses.[142] "And," he continues, "I have come to declare it, for you are greatly beloved." God greatly loves Daniel, his faithful servant. Therefore God sent his messenger to declare God's plan for the future. "So," Gabriel says, "consider the word and understand the vision."

Then he proclaims the word of God: verse 24, "Seventy weeks are decreed for your people and your holy city:[143] to finish the transgression, to put an end to sin, and to atone for iniquity, to bring in everlasting righteousness, to seal both vision and prophet, and to anoint a most holy place." Because Daniel had read in Jeremiah about the "seventy *years*" (Dan 9:2), the "seventy weeks" are usually understood as seventy weeks of years, that is, 70 x 7 years, or four-hundred and ninety years (see above, pp. 293-94). We should keep in mind, however, that seventy in the Bible is a symbolic number (see above, pp. 297-98).

When Peter asked Jesus if he should forgive someone "as many as seven times," Jesus responded, "Not seven times, but, I tell you, seventy-seven times" (Matt 18:22). Jesus did not mean that you should forgive someone four hundred

---

140. "The word is the divine revelation itself, and the vision is the form in which this revelation came, namely, the appearance of the angel, and the manner in which he communicated the revelation." Young, *Prophecy of Daniel*, 190. Cf. Collins, *Daniel*, 352, "'Word' and 'vision' are apparently equivalent, both referring to a revelation that has both visual and auditory aspects."

141. "Within the implied sixth-century setting of chapter 9, the point was not that Daniel did not understand the *meaning* of Jeremiah's prophecy, but that it has a *reference* beyond its most obvious reference to the ending of the Babylonian exile. It is this future reference that Gabriel comes to reveal to Daniel." Lucas, *Daniel*, 241.

142. "This word *(dābār)* is a divine decree or oracle, entrusted to Daniel because he is 'greatly beloved.'" Baldwin, *Daniel*, 167. So also Young, *Prophecy of Daniel*, 190, and Leupold, *Exposition of Daniel*, 403. Cf. Collins, *Daniel*, 352, "The 'word' is the revelation that follows in vv. 24-27."

143. Because of the words "for your people and your holy city," many commentators restrict this prophecy to the Jewish nation. E.g., Goldingay, *Daniel*, 258, writes, "The concern of verse 24 is thus Israel and Jerusalem. It does not have a worldwide perspective; it is not speaking of the end of all history, or of the sin of the whole world." And Lucas, *Daniel*, 241, writes, "The prophecy is focused on Israel and Jerusalem. It is not about the wider history, unlike Dan 7–8 and 10–12." But it seems very strange that unlike Daniel 7–8 and 10–12 Daniel 9 should suddenly not be about "the wider history." Of course, the prophecy is about Israel and Jerusalem; that is what Daniel had prayed for. God's answer to him is that Israel shall return and Jerusalem shall be rebuilt (v. 25). But the prophecy goes far beyond that, as the goals of verse 24 plainly show: "to finish the transgression, to put an end to sin, and . . . to bring in everlasting righteousness."

and ninety times but that you should always be ready to forgive. So here, "seventy weeks" is a symbolic number. In apocalyptic literature such as Daniel and the book of Revelation, numbers are often symbols. "Seventy weeks" is 7 x 10 weeks. Seven is the number of completion and perfection: God created the cosmos in *seven* days, and "it was very good" (Gen 1:31).[144] Ten is the number of fullness: God gave the fullness of his law in *ten* commandments. Therefore, 7 x 10, seventy, is a complete, full period of time.[145] "Seventy *weeks*" is much longer; it is 7 x 10 x 7, that is, a complete, full, perfect period of time. "Seventy weeks" is a period of time that encompasses all of human history from Daniel's time to the coming of the perfect kingdom of God.

God has decreed these 70 weeks, this full period of time, to accomplish certain goals. Verse 24 says, "to finish the transgression, to put an end to sin, and to atone for iniquity, to bring in everlasting righteousness, to seal both vision and prophet, and to anoint a most holy place." These goals point to the end time when God brings in his perfect kingdom. We'll come back to these goals for the end time later.[146]

Gabriel divides the 70 weeks into three periods: 7 weeks, 62 weeks, and 1 week. Before going into details, it may be helpful again to present an overview of these three periods.[147]

7 weeks *from*	62 weeks		1 week *from*	
		troubled time		
word ⟶ *to* anointed	Jerusalem		anointed →	*to* troops
to restore prince	built with		cut off,	destroy city,
Jerusalem	streets and moat		"strong	desolator
			covenant,"	destroyed
			no sacrifices	

In verse 25 Gabriel explains what will happen in the first 7 weeks: "Know therefore and understand: from the time that the word went out to restore and rebuild Jerusalem until the time of an anointed prince, there shall be seven weeks." Daniel had prayed for the restoration of Jerusalem and the temple. Here

---

144. Cf. Leviticus 26:18, 21, 24, 28; Psalm 79:12; and Isaiah 30:26.

145. Cf. Exodus 1:5, "The total number of people born to Jacob was seventy." Cf. Genesis 46:27.

146. In expository preaching one usually explains the verses in the order provided by the author. Exceptions are possible, however, for a more chronological ordering or for a climactic arrangement in the sermon. Both of these reasons hold for this passage. Leaving verse 24 for last enables one to focus in order on the seven weeks, the sixty-two weeks, and the final week, before explaining the final goals of the seventy weeks. Also, instead of ending the sermon with the defeat of the Antichrist (v. 27b), one can end the sermon with the good news of God's coming kingdom (v. 24).

147. One can use PowerPoint or simply copy this chart on the church bulletin.

is God's answer, "from the time that the word went out to restore and rebuild Jerusalem until the time of an anointed prince, there shall be seven weeks." "Seven weeks" is a relatively short period of time. Still, it is a complete period of time to accomplish the rebuilding of Jerusalem and the temple.

The beginning of the seven weeks is "when the word went out to restore and rebuild Jerusalem." That "word" was the word of King Cyrus (see pp. 298-99 above). In 538 B.C. he permitted the captives to return to Jerusalem. Ezra (1:1-4) tells us that "the LORD stirred up the spirit of King Cyrus of Persia" to send a herald throughout his kingdom encouraging the Israelites to return to Jerusalem "and rebuild the house of the LORD, the God of Israel."[148]

The end of the seven weeks is "the time of an anointed prince." The "anointed prince" is probably the priest Ezra (see pp. 300, 301-3 above).[149] Ezra was an anointed priest, a descendant of Aaron, Israel's first high priest (Ezra 7:1-5). Ezra went to Jerusalem to revitalize worship at the rebuilt temple: he bought bulls, rams, and lambs, and offered them on the altar (Ezra 7:17). He also purified Israel by denouncing the mixed marriages the Israelites had entered into (Ezra 9–10). After the wall around Jerusalem was completed, Ezra taught Israel the law of Moses (Neh 8). He led them in a prayer of confession (Neh 9), which resulted in the people signing a new covenant agreement (Neh 10).[150] So in Ezra's time the word to restore and rebuild Jerusalem and the temple was fulfilled.

The first seven weeks, then, are "from the time that the word went out to restore and rebuild Jerusalem until the time of an anointed prince." It takes us from the time when King Cyrus gave permission to return to Jerusalem to the time of the priest Ezra when the temple was rebuilt and the wall around Jerusalem completed.

Verse 25b mentions the next complete period of time: "and for sixty-two weeks it shall be built again with streets and moat, but in a troubled time." For the next sixty-two weeks, a long period of time, Jerusalem "shall be built again with streets and moat." Since the Hebrew word *ḥārûṣ,* translated as "moat," oc-

---

148. Cf. Isaiah 45:13, where the LORD says, "I have aroused Cyrus in righteousness . . . ; he shall build my city and set my exiles free" (cf. Isa 44:28).

149. The NIV translates, "until the Anointed One, the ruler, comes, there will be seven 'sevens,' and sixty-two sevens." In other words, the Anointed One comes at the end of sixty-nine weeks. Then it would not be Ezra but Christ, the same as the Anointed One who "will be put to death" (v. 26). Where the pew Bibles are the NIV, preachers face the choice of either following the NIV or explaining to the congregation that the NRSV has the better translation in that it follows the Masoretic Text (see p. 300, n. 38 above). For the latter option, see the sermon on Daniel 9 in Appendix 4, p. 424.

150. "The rest of the people . . . join with their kin, their nobles, and enter into a curse and an oath to walk in God's law . . . , and to observe and do all the commandments of the LORD our Lord and his ordinances and his statutes" (Neh 10:28-29).

curs only here in the Old Testament, scholars were not sure of its meaning. It is not likely that dry, rocky Jerusalem would be surrounded by a water-filled moat.[151] The discovery of the Dead Sea Scrolls offered a solution. Scholars found this Hebrew word in the Copper Scroll with the meaning of "canal, conduit."[152] We know that Jerusalem had extensive water tunnels. These tunnels would transport water from a spring in one part of the city to another area, and, in one case, water from outside the city wall into the city (2 Sam 5:8).

So for a long, complete period of time "Jerusalem shall be built again with streets" and a water system. But, the text says, "in a troubled time." Looking back from our perspective, we can see that this really was a troubled time for Jerusalem. It was occupied first by Alexander the Great of Greece, then by the Ptolemies of Egypt, then by the Seleucids of Syria. At this time the Jews suffered terrible persecution under Antiochus IV (167-164 B.C.). And finally Jerusalem would be occupied by Romans (63 B.C.). A troubled time indeed.

Verse 26, "*After the sixty-two weeks,* an anointed one shall be cut off and shall have nothing, and the troops of the prince who is to come shall destroy the city and the sanctuary. Its end shall come with a flood, and to the end there shall be war." "*After* the sixty-two weeks" means that verse 26 describes what will happen in the seventieth week. This final week is a complete but, for Daniel, a relatively short period of time. Verse 26 mentions two major events that will take place in that week. First, "an anointed one shall be cut off and shall have nothing." There can be no doubt that Gabriel here predicts the crucifixion of Jesus (see pp. 304-5 above). Jesus was known as the Christ, that is, the Messiah, which means the Anointed One. When Jesus died on the cross, he was literally "cut off." Isaiah writes concerning the Suffering Servant: "He was cut off from the land of the living, stricken for the transgression of my people" (Isa 53:8).

Gabriel further predicts that this anointed one "shall have nothing."[153] When Jesus hung on the cross between heaven and earth, he had "nothing"; he had been stripped of everything. He had been deserted by his own disciples. Peter even denied him three times: "I do not know him" (Luke 22:54-62). He was rejected by his own people. When Pilate wished to release Jesus, the people cried out, "Away with him! Crucify him!" Pilate then asked them, "Shall I crucify your

---

151. "Although Babylon was encompassed by a moat, the idea of a moat surrounding Jerusalem in that dry area seems unlikely." Miller, *Daniel,* 266. The NIV translates, "It will be rebuilt with streets and a trench." This translation makes more sense: they could cut a trench in the rock outside the city wall in order to make the wall higher.

152. Porteous, *Daniel,* 142. Cf. Towner, *Daniel,* 143, and Redditt, *Daniel,* 162. See also the references in Poythress, "Hermeneutical Factors," *TJ* 6 (1985) 141.

153. "Will have nothing (*wĕ'ên lô* can mean either 'nothing' or 'no one'). This indicates that when the Messiah is cut off, he will be bereft of followers; all of them will flee from him at the time of his arrest, trial, and death." Archer, "Daniel," 113. Cf. Stefanovic, *Daniel,* 356.

King?" And the chief priests answered, "We have no king but the emperor" (John 19:15). Jesus was rejected by his own people. Then he was crucified by the world empire Rome. He hung between heaven and earth, cast out from the earth. And as he hung naked on the cross, he was forsaken even by his heavenly Father. Jesus cried out in anguish, "My God, my God, why have you forsaken me?" (Matt 27:46). "An anointed one shall be cut off and shall have *nothing.*"

Verse 26 mentions a second major event that will happen in that final week. "The troops of the prince who is to come shall destroy the city and the sanctuary." Jerusalem and the temple would be destroyed again. Jesus also foretold the destruction of the temple. One day as Jesus was leaving the temple, his disciples pointed out to him the massive buildings of the temple. Then Jesus said, "You see all these, do you not? Truly I tell you, not one stone will be left here upon another; all will be thrown down" (Matt 24:1-2). Some 40 years later, in A.D. 70, Jesus' prophecy was fulfilled. The Romans, under their general Titus, destroyed Jerusalem and the temple (see above, p. 305).

Gabriel adds concerning the destruction of the city, "Its[154] end shall come with a flood, and to the end there shall be war. Desolations are decreed." The mention of a flood reminds us of the great flood God used in the time of Noah to destroy a world that, contrary to his design, had turned wicked. The word "flood," then, emphasizes "the magnitude of the devastation."[155]

Verse 26 concludes, "And to the end there shall be war. Desolations are decreed."[156] To the end of the city there shall be war, for God has decreed *desolations:* the city will be laid waste and deserted. Jesus also foretold this time of suffering. He said, "When you see Jerusalem surrounded by armies, then know that its *desolation* has come near. Then those in Judea must flee to the mountains, and those inside the city must leave it, and those out in the country must not enter it; for these are days of vengeance, as a *fulfillment* of all that is written" (Luke 21:20-22).

"Desolations are decreed" means that *God* has decreed desolations. As God had permitted the Babylonians to destroy Jerusalem and his temple, so in the future God would allow the Romans to destroy Jerusalem and his temple. Only forty years after Jesus' death, Jerusalem was in ruins.

---

154. The NIV translates, "The end will come like a flood." "The word *qiṣṣô,* 'his/its end,' has a possessive suffix and should be rendered either 'its [the city's (and the sanctuary's?)] end' or 'his [the ruler's] end.'" Stefanovic, *Daniel,* 356. Cf. Hill, "Daniel," 172, "The logical antecedent is the city of Jerusalem and its temple." Cf. Miller, *Daniel,* 268, "In this context 'the end' alludes to the end of the city, that is, its destruction." Aalders, *Het Boek Daniel,* 204, suggests the end of Israel as a national entity.

155. Miller, *Daniel,* 268, with references to Isaiah 8:7-8; 28:2; and Daniel 11:10, 22, 26, 40.

156. Miller, ibid., 269, suggests the translation, "And until the end, war has been decreed with (or 'and') desolations."

Verse 27 mentions several more things that will take place during that final week: "He shall make a strong covenant with *many* for one week, and for half of the week he shall make sacrifice and offering cease." The pronoun "he" refers back to verse 26 to the "anointed one [who] shall be cut off," that is, to Jesus Christ (see pp. 306-8 above). Jesus made "a strong covenant" with many for a week. The night before he died, Jesus celebrated the Passover feast with his disciples. At this feast he turned the old covenant into a *new* covenant. This new covenant would be based on Jesus' sacrifice of his own life the next day. For that reason he turned the Passover Feast (in remembrance of God's deliverance from Egypt) into the Lord's Supper in remembrance of God's deliverance from sin through Jesus' sacrifice. Jesus said, "This is my blood of the [*new*][157] covenant, which is poured out for *many* for the forgiveness of sins" (Matt 26:28).[158] "Do this in remembrance of me" (Luke 22:19). In this way Jesus made the Lord's Supper one of the sacraments of his new covenant.

Verse 27 continues, "and for half of the week he shall make sacrifice and [grain] offering cease." If the final week began with the Messiah's birth, "half of the week," or "the middle" (NIV) of the week, would indicate the time of his death. Jesus did indeed make the Old Testament sacrifices cease with his death in the middle of that week. Matthew describes Jesus' death as follows: "Then Jesus . . . breathed his last. At that moment the curtain of the temple was torn in two, from top to bottom" (Matt 27:50-51). The sacred Holy of Holies was open to the world. People no longer needed human priests as intermediaries to approach God; through Jesus' sacrifice they had direct access to God. Since Jesus paid the penalty for the sins of the world (John 1:29), animal sacrifices were no longer required. The author of Hebrews writes, "When Christ had offered for all time a single sacrifice for sins, 'he sat down at the right hand of God.' . . . Where there is forgiveness of these [sins], there is no longer any offering for sin" (Heb 10:12, 18). By the end of that final week, with the destruction of Jerusalem and the temple, animal sacrifices at the temple became impossible.[159]

The last part of verse 27 reads, "and in their place[160] [presumably, in the

---

157. See NRSV footnote, "Other ancient authorities add *new.*" Luke 22:20 has, "This cup that is poured out for you is the new covenant in my blood." Cf. 1 Corinthians 11:25; Hebrews 7:22; 8:13; 9:15; 12:24.

158. Cf. Jeremiah 31:31-34: "The days are surely coming, says the Lord, when I will make a new covenant with the house of Israel and the house of Judah. . . . I will put my law within them, and I will write it on their hearts; and I will be their God, and they shall be my people. . . . I will forgive their iniquity, and remember their sin no more." Cf. Hebrews 9:11-15.

159. "After Christ's death the sacrifices continued for a time, until the destruction of the city by Titus. However, this actual cessation was in reality but the outward manifestation of that which had already been put into effect by our Lord's death." Young, *Prophecy of Daniel*, 218.

160. Literally, "on a wing of an abomination." Stefanovic, *Daniel*, 357. The NIV translates, "And at the temple he will set up an abomination that causes desolation," with a note at "tem-

place of the "sacrifice and offering" (v. 26)] shall be an abomination[161] that desolates, until the decreed end is poured out upon the desolator."[162] As mentioned, the "desolator" is Titus Vespasianus, "the prince" (v. 26) of the troops
that besieged and finally destroyed Jerusalem and the temple in A.D. 70. At the
end of this seventieth and final week this desolator prince will be destroyed. Titus Vespasianus died of a fever in A.D. 79. But this evil Roman prince prefigures
the end-time Antichrist. When we read, therefore, that "the decreed end is
poured out upon the desolator," we understand that this also speaks of the final
destruction of the Antichrist at the end of time.[163] "Poured out" graphically
"describes the flood of judgment that will overtake the Antichrist."[164]

With verse 27, which still speaks of the final week, we are hard-pressed to
keep the events within the week that runs from the Messiah's birth to the destruction of Jerusalem in A.D. 70. While Gabriel predicts that Christ will "make
a strong covenant with many for *one week*," the New Testament tells us that this
is an *eternal* covenant (Heb 9:15; 13:20). And when Gabriel predicts the decreed
end that will be "poured out upon the desolator," we know that the decreed end
of the Antichrist still lies in the *future*.

This stretching out beyond the final week is called "prophetic telescoping."[165] Think of a telescope, a tube perhaps a foot long. But when you step outside to look at the stars, you slide out the inner tubes and the telescope may now
be three feet long. Just so the prophets, from their perspective in the Old Testament, saw the arrival of the Messiah and the perfect kingdom of God as a single
event. But when you step into the New Testament, the Messiah comes and the

---

ple": "Septuagint and Theodotion; Hebrew *wing*." Archer, "Daniel," 118, comments, "Since there
is no word for 'temple,' it is more reasonable to understand 'wing' *(kĕnap)* as a figure for the
vulturelike role of the Antichrist as he swoops down on his beleaguered victims for the purposes
of oppression and despoliation." Cf. Gurney, *God in Control*, 125-26, "Surely it ["wing"] suggests
some great bird of prey coming from afar and swooping down on its victim and tearing it to
pieces. This is precisely what the Roman army did — moreover, its emblem was *the eagle!*"
Gurney cites Deuteronomy 28:49-66, the chapter to which Daniel alludes when he mentions
God's "curse" (Dan 9:11): "The LORD will bring a nation against you from afar, from the end of
the earth, as swift as the eagle flies. . . ."

161. "Throughout the Old Testament, the Hebrew word *siqqûṣ*, 'abomination,' is consistently associated with abominable idols." Stefanovic, *Daniel*, 358.

162. "The object is the destroyer who caused the desolation, most probably the ruler who
will come (v. 26). . . . The imagery also alludes to the story in chapter 5, where Belshazzar's end
was decreed and then came to pass." Ibid.

163. "'An end that is decreed' comes from Isaiah 10:23 and 28:22, where it is used in the context of God's final judgment." Ibid.

164. Miller, *Daniel*, 273, with references to Daniel 7:9-11, 26; 2 Thessalonians 2:8; and Revelation 19:19-21.

165. One finds "prophetic telescoping" or "foreshortening" also in the New Testament, e.g.,
Jesus' foretelling of coming events in Matthew 24.

telescope slides out: the full arrival of the kingdom of God still lies in the future. Prophetic telescoping has also been likened to climbing a mountain. While you are climbing the mountain, you think that you are climbing the highest mountain. But when you get to the top, you see an even higher mountain beyond.

Gabriel predicted that in the last week of human history the Messiah would be killed and that he would make a strong covenant with many "for one week." He also predicted the destruction of Jerusalem and the temple and the end of the desolator. It would all take place in that final week of human history. But when we get to the New Testament, we see that there is an even higher mountain behind this one. The final week expands beyond the destruction of Jerusalem, the temple, and the desolator. There will be another desolator at the end of time, the Antichrist. There will also be a *Second* Coming of Christ. Then, in Gabriel's words, "the decreed end is poured out upon the desolator." Paul writes that "the Lord Jesus will destroy [the Antichrist] with the breath of his mouth, annihilating him by the manifestation of his coming."[166] Then, finally, Christ can establish God's perfect kingdom on earth.

With this overview of the three periods of the seventy weeks, we are ready to understand God's goals for the seventy weeks. We read in verse 24, "Seventy weeks are decreed for your people and your holy city: to finish the transgression, to put an end to sin, and to atone for iniquity, to bring in everlasting righteousness, to seal both vision and prophet, and to anoint a most holy place."

The first three goals respond to the major problem Daniel struggled with in his prayer, Israel's sin. For example, in verse 5 Daniel piled up five different words for Israel's sin: "We have sinned and done wrong, acted wickedly and rebelled, turning aside from your commandments and ordinances." In verse 24 God responds with three different words for sin: "transgression," "sin," and "iniquity." These three words intend to include any and all kinds of sin.[167] Here is what God will accomplish in the seventy weeks: first, "to finish the transgression," that is, finish sin in all its forms.[168] Second, "to put an end to sin," literally "to seal up sin" so that it can no longer gush out and pollute the world. And third, "to atone for iniquity," literally "to cover iniquity," the way priests would

---

166. 2 Thessalonians 2:8, "Then the lawless one will be revealed, whom the Lord Jesus will destroy with the breath of his mouth, annihilating him by the manifestation of his coming."

167. "These three terms . . . together . . . represent the various aspects of that evil which has separated man from God. . . . Sin as such, in all its manifestations . . . , will be done away." Young, *Messianic Prophecies*, 49.

168. The Hebrew word translated as "transgression *(pešaʿ)* . . . , combining as it does the idea of rebellion and self-assertion, stands for sin in general and in its many forms." Baldwin, *Daniel*, 168. Cf. Colossians 2:13-14, God "forgave us all our trespasses, erasing the record that stood against us with its legal demands. He set this aside, nailing it to the cross." Cf. Hebrews 9:26.

cover the sins of Israel by sprinkling blood on the mercy seat in the Holy of Holies (cf. Lev. 16:15-16). "These three [phrases] assure Daniel that his sin and the sin of his people are forgiven through the coming Messiah."[169]

In the final week, we have seen in verse 26, "an anointed one shall be cut off and shall have nothing." On the cross Jesus paid for our sins[170] and the sins of the whole world (John 1:29). But the second goal, the *end* of sin, still lies in the future. The end of sin will come about only when Jesus returns to establish God's perfect kingdom on earth.[171]

The fourth goal God will accomplish in the seventy weeks also still lies in the future; it is "to bring in everlasting righteousness."[172] This can only refer to the "everlasting kingdom" God will give to the Son of Man and God's people (Dan 7:14, 18, 27).

God's fifth goal is "to seal both vision and prophet [prophecy]."[173] This is the same Hebrew word as is used for the second goal: "*to put an end to* sin." "To seal both vision and prophet" can also mean *to put an end* to both vision and prophet.[174] As Hebrews 1 says, "Long ago God spoke to our ancestors in many and various ways by the prophets, but in these last days he has spoken to us by a Son" (Heb 1:1-2). Jesus Christ is God's last word. When he comes again, no further visions and revelations are necessary.[175]

God's final goal is "to anoint a most holy." The Hebrew does not have the

---

169. Steinmann, *Daniel*, 465. Cf. Baldwin, *Daniel*, 169, "God has found a way of forgiving sin without being untrue to his own righteousness. This assurance was what the prayer had been feeling after."

170. See, e.g., 1 Corinthians 6:11; 2 Corinthians 5:18-21; Hebrews 9:26.

171. Those who seek to interpret the final week in terms of the iniquity of Antiochus IV (e.g., Collins, *Daniel*, 354; Goldingay, *Daniel*, 259; and Lucas, *Daniel*, 241-42) run into major problems with these verses. Steinmann, *Daniel*, 465, n. 65, rightly objects: "It is difficult to see how Daniel could call that act [of Antiochus IV] 'my sin,' or how the subsequent cleansing of the temple by Judas Maccabaeus could have been viewed as an atonement for Daniel's sin."

172. "The objective echoes references to the righteousness or justice of God in Daniel's prayer (vv. 7, 14, 16)." Hill, "Daniel," 169.

173. "The two nouns *ḥāzôn*, 'vision,' and *nābî*, 'prophet,' are used without the definite article; thus they may stand for biblical visions and prophecy in general." Stefanovic, *Daniel*, 355.

174. "A seal not only witnesses to the authenticity of the words on a scroll, but it also prevents further words from being written on it. Thus the sealing of 'vision and prophet' is an affirmation that no further prophecy will be needed once the seventy weeks are ended." Steinmann, *Daniel*, 466. Cf. Leupold, *Exposition of Daniel*, 414, "The same verb 'to seal up' is used here that was employed earlier in the verse, *ḥatam*. The objective is the same: to dispose summarily and finally of a thing that deserves to be relegated to the category of achieved things." Cf. Lacocque, *Book of Daniel*, "Daniel is conscious of ending prophecy in Israel once and for all."

175. "The 'sealing' of vision and prophecy denotes the cessation of prophetic activity in the ultimate kingdom of God." Harman, *Study Commentary on Daniel*, 236. Cf. Kaiser, *Preaching and Teaching the Last Things*, 106.

word "place," so we have to decide what fits the context better, "to anoint a most holy *place*"? or "to anoint a most holy *one*"? The context, we have seen, speaks of anointed *persons:* verse 25, "an anointed prince," verse 26, "an anointed one shall be cut off." These anointed ones cannot be places. It seems reasonable, therefore, to understand also the anointing of "a most holy" in verse 24 as a person: "to anoint a most holy *one*" (see pp. 309-11 above).[176] Who could be that "most holy one"?

When the angel Gabriel foretold the birth of Jesus to his mother Mary, he said, "The *Holy* Spirit will come upon you, and the power of the Most High will overshadow you; therefore the child to be born will be *holy*" (Luke 1:35). At his baptism Jesus was anointed with the *Holy* Spirit. We read in Mark that "he saw the heavens torn apart and the Spirit descending like a dove on him" (Mark 1:10; cf. Acts 4:27; 10:38; Heb 1:9). Later even an unclean spirit acknowledged, "I know who you are, *the Holy One of God*" (Mark 1:24). Still later Peter confessed, "We have come to believe and know that you are *the Holy One of God*" (John 6:69). Jesus Christ is the Messiah, the Anointed One, the Holy One of God. Therefore he is the one who fulfills the prediction of Gabriel that God's final goal is "to anoint a most holy one."[177]

Jesus Christ is the culmination of God's decrees. In him every one of these goals of verse 24 will be fulfilled. He will "finish the transgression" and "put an end to sin" when he comes again. Meanwhile he did "atone for iniquity" on the cross when he bore the sins of the whole world. At his Second Coming he will also "bring in everlasting righteousness" and "seal both vision and prophet" because they are no longer required in his perfect kingdom.

For that reason also, Jesus will not restore the earthly city of Jerusalem.

---

176. Preachers who wish to stick to the translation "to anoint a most holy place" will have to decide what that most holy place is. Dispensationalists argue for "a literal, future temple" (Miller, *Daniel*, 262; cf. Archer, "Daniel," 113; Feinberg, *Daniel*, 128; Kaiser, *Preaching and Teaching the Last Things*, 111-21). Others, e.g., Ferguson, *Daniel*, 201-2, argue that the temple is Jesus, who "tabernacled among us" (John 1:14) and sanctified himself (John 17:19) and compared his body to the temple (John 2:19-22; cf. Matt 12:6). Most persuasive, I think, is Keil, *Book of Daniel*, 348-49, who argues for "the new holy of holies," "the holy city," "the tabernacle of God among mortals" (Rev. 21:2-3): "The anointing is the act by which the place is consecrated to be a holy place of the gracious presence and revelation of God. . . . In this holy city there will be no temple, for the Lord, the Almighty God, and the Lamb, is its temple, and the glory of God will lighten it (vv. 22, 23). Into it nothing shall enter that defileth or worketh abomination (v. 27), for sin shall then be closed and sealed up; there shall righteousness dwell (2 Pet 3:13), and prophecy shall cease (1 Cor 13:8) by its fulfillment."

177. Those who are convinced that Gabriel implies "to anoint a most holy *place*" can still link this place, the Holy of Holies in the temple, to Christ, for the Holy of Holies represented God's presence with his people. As Emmanuel (Matt 1:23) Jesus represented God's presence with us; as the Word, Jesus tabernacled among us (John 1:14); and when Jesus comes again, the tabernacle of God will be among us, and God himself will be with us (Rev. 21:3).

John writes that he saw "a new heaven and a *new* earth. . . . And I saw the *holy* city, *the new* Jerusalem, coming down out of heaven from God, prepared as a bride adorned for her husband. And I heard a loud voice from the throne saying, 'See the home [tabernacle] of God is among mortals'" (Rev. 21:1-3). That is the awesome future that awaits God's people: heaven on earth.

When we see the continuing persecution of Christians in the world, however, we can lose hope. As happened in the early church, we, too, may wonder, Where is the promise of Jesus' coming again?[178] Daniel 9 encourages us to take heart. Our sovereign God is in control of his world. He decreed seventy weeks in which to bring an end to sin and evil and replace these with "everlasting righteousness." He promised Daniel that in seven weeks Jerusalem and the temple would be rebuilt. They were. He promised that for sixty-two weeks Jerusalem would continue to exist but in a time of trouble. It did. He promised that in the final week the Messiah would come, be killed, and Jerusalem destroyed. It all came about exactly as God decreed. Jesus came and with his death atoned "for iniquity." But he also rose again and ascended into heaven, promising to come again. With these events, human history has reached the last days. We are now traveling along the edge of human history, the boundary between time and eternity. Christ can return any day now "to put an end to sin [and] to bring in everlasting righteousness." Our God is the faithful covenant God. As he fulfilled his earlier promises, he will fulfill his promises for these last days. So take heart! Soon Jesus will come again to bring down to this earth "the holy city, the new Jerusalem" (Rev. 21:2), his church, and establish God's perfect kingdom on earth.

> The church's one foundation is Jesus Christ her Lord;
> she is his new creation by water and the Word.
> From heaven he came and sought her to be his holy bride;
> with his own blood he bought her, and for her life he died.
>
> 'Mid toil and tribulation and tumult of her war,
> she waits the consummation of peace forever more,
> till with the vision glorious her longing eyes are blest,
> and the great church victorious shall be the church at rest.[179]

---

178. 2 Peter 3:4.

179. Samuel J. Stone, "The Church's One Foundation," 1866. A sermon on Daniel 9 can be found in Appendix 4, pp. 421-28.

CHAPTER 10

Daniel's Final Vision of the Future

Daniel 10:1–12:4

Many of those who sleep in the dust of the earth shall awake,
 some to everlasting life,
 and some to shame and everlasting contempt.
Those who are wise shall shine
 like the brightness of the sky,
and those who lead many to righteousness,
 like the stars forever and ever.

Daniel 12:2-3

In this final vision, an angel not only gives Daniel more details on his second vision about the ram (Medo-Persia) and the goat (Greece), which Daniel did not understand (8:27), but also offers more details on events that will take place in the Middle East during the kingdoms of Persia, Greece, Syria, and Egypt. It also reveals the terrible suffering God's people will undergo in the future but ends with the comforting assurance of the resurrection of the dead and everlasting life.

The most obvious difficulty in preaching on this final vision is its length — three whole chapters. We will also have to decide how to handle chapter 11; we certainly cannot spend one hundred pages explaining this chapter, as Calvin did.[1] Further challenges are to get some clarity on the identity of several controversial characters: the "man clothed in linen" (10:5), "the prince of the kingdom of Persia" (10:13), "Michael" (10:13), "the prince of the covenant" (11:22), "the king" who "shall act as he pleases" (11:36), and "the king of the north" (11:40). With these challenges in mind, it is well to remember Block's advice,

---

1. Calvin used nine lectures to analyze chapter 11 and identify the various historical figures. See his *Commentaries on Daniel*, II, 268-369.

"Authoritative preaching of the message of apocalyptic literature demands that we major on the major themes, and be less concerned about the meaning and significance of fine details."[2]

Text and Context

After Daniel's vision of the seventy weeks, chapter 10:1 begins a new literary unit with the chronological marker, "In the third year of King Cyrus of Persia a word was revealed to Daniel." This unit ends in chapter 12:13 with the angel's promise to Daniel, "But you, go your way, and rest; you shall rise for your reward at the end of the days." Although one could select the entire unit as a preaching text, one can hardly do justice to all this material in a single sermon. We need to look, therefore, for a better alternative.

At first I considered breaking this unit up into three more manageable subunits, such as 10:1–11:1; 11:2-45; and 12:1-13. But this division creates more problems than it solves. For example, Feinberg has a sermon on each chapter: 10, "The Delayed Answer to Prayer"; 11, "The Wars of the Ptolemies and the Seleucidae, and Antichrist"; and 12, "The Time of the End."[3] As can be seen, preaching three sermons on this final vision results in three topical sermons instead of expository sermons.[4] Moreover, three separate sermons on this single vision disintegrate the full impact of this final vision. Is there a better way to divide this lengthy unit?

As we shall see below, the narrative of this final vision is a complex plot, a

---

2. Block, "Preaching Old Testament Apocalyptic," *CTJ* 41 (2006) 51.

3. Feinberg, *Daniel,* 137-87. Cf. Wallace, *The Lord Is King,* 171-200: chapter 10, "I Daniel"; chapter 11, "The History Inscribed in the Book"; chapter 12, "Waiting and Watching for the End." Cf. Ferguson, *Daniel,* 205-49: 10:1-11:1, "Vision of the Sufficiency of God" and "Conflict for the Kingdom of God"; 11:2-45, "The Wars of North and South" and "The Antichrist"; 12:1-13, "The Hope of Glory" and "Living with Unanswered Questions." Cf. Duguid, *Daniel,* 176-223: 10:1–11:1, "Prepared for Battle"; 11:2–12:3, "Wars and Rumors of Wars"; and 12:4-13, "How Long Will I Be Broken?" If one wishes to preach three sermons on this final vision, Boice, *Daniel,* 111-33, offers the best textual divisions and titles: chapter 10:1–11:1, "Spiritual Wickedness in High Places"; 11:2–12:4, "The Last Battle"; and 12:5-13, "Until the End Comes." Leupold suggests two topics in 10:1-11:1, "Human frailty in the face of divine disclosures about the future," and "angelic princes who exert controlling influence on the historical events in the life of great nations." Chapter 11, he writes, "might be treated in Bible classes. We do not see how it could be used for a sermon or for sermons." And chapter 12:1-3 constitutes "an excellent text on the consummation." But the section 12:5-13 "hardly constitutes a good text" because of the "strange and disturbing chiliastic interpretations [that] are put upon this passage. . . . It may become necessary to show how the passage may be construed according to the analogy of Scripture." *Exposition of Daniel,* respectively pp. 469, 525, and 549.

4. Topical sermons need not be unbiblical, of course, but they tend to ignore the intention of the specific biblical author.

main vision and a concluding vision, with a natural break occurring after 12:4, for 12:5 begins, "Then I, Daniel, looked, and two others appeared." Therefore we can select as our preaching text the main vision, Daniel 10:1–12:4, to be followed by a second sermon on the concluding vision, Daniel 12:5-13.

Daniel 10:1–12:4 echoes many ideas of the prior chapters.[5] The third-person introduction, "a word was revealed to Daniel" (10:1), is similar to the third-person introduction of the first vision (7:1). Lucas suggests that "this is probably a form of inclusio indicating that this vision ends the sequence that began with the vision of chapter 7."[6] The mention of Daniel's Babylonian name, Belteshazzar (10:1), connects with chapters 1:7; 2:26; 4:8, 9, 18, 19; and 5:12, where Daniel is called by this name. Daniel's mourning before receiving this final vision (10:3) is similar to his mourning before receiving the third vision (9:3). God's hearing his prayer "from the first day" (10:12) is also similar to the third vision, where God sent out a word "at the beginning of your supplications" (9:23). In both of these visions Daniel is also assured that he is "greatly beloved" (9:23; 10:19). Daniel's falling into a trance (10:9) is similar to his falling into a trance in the second vision (8:18), as is his being touched by an angel (cf. 10:10, 16 and 8:18).

In chapter 11:3, the rise of Alexander the Great repeats part of the first vision, the rise of the speedy leopard out of the sea (7:6), as well as the second vision, the male goat growing exceedingly great (8:8). The fall of Alexander and his kingdom being divided "toward the four winds of heaven" (11:4) repeats part of the second vision, the great horn being replaced by four horns "toward the four winds of heaven" (8:8, 22). Most of the remainder of chapter 11, dealing with the political intrigues and wars between kings north and south of Palestine (Seleucids in Syria and Ptolemies in Egypt) details the "troubled time" of the sixty-two weeks of the third vision (9:25).

"They shall abolish the regular burnt offering and set up the abomination that makes desolate" (11:31) harks back to the second vision (8:13). The king speaking "horrendous things against the God of gods" (11:36) is similar to the little horn of the first vision speaking "words against the Most High" (7:25). "He shall come to his end, with no one to help him" (11:45) is similar to the predictions in the three prior visions (7:26; 8:25; 9:27).

Although this final vision has connections with the third vision in Daniel 9, it expands especially on the second vision (Dan 8). To get a sense of how this final vision fits into the whole of Daniel, it may be helpful to incorporate its figures into the earlier (p. 216) diagram of Daniel 2, 7, and 8.

5. In contrast to Lacocque, *Book of Daniel*, 204, who claims that "it is chapter 9 which serves as the Author's rough draft," Goldingay, *Daniel*, 283, rightly states that "it is with chapter 8 that chapters 10–12 have most detailed points of contact. Reminiscences of almost every verse of chapter 8 reappear here."

6. Lucas, *Daniel*, 266.

Daniel 2	Daniel 7	Daniel 8	Daniel 10-12	Kingdom	Dates
Head of gold	Lion with eagles' wings			Babylon	605-539 B.C.
Chest and arms of silver	Bear with one side higher than the other	Ram with 2 horns, 1 longer	King Cyrus (10:1) Three kings (11:2a) Fourth king (11:2b)	Medo-Persia	539-331 B.C.
Belly and thighs of bronze	Leopard with 4 wings, 4 heads	Fast goat with 4 horns	Warrior king (11:3) Kingdom divided to four winds (11:4) Kings of south (11:5-20) Kings of north (11:6-20) Contemptible one (11:21-35)	Alexander (Greece) 4 generals Ptolemies Seleucids Anti-ochus IV	331-323 B.C. 323-63 B.C. 175-164 B.C.
Legs of iron Feet & toes of iron and clay	Monster with iron teeth, 10 horns			Rome and 10 kings	63 B.C.– A.D. 476 Present period
Stone smashes statue	God burns the monster	Little horn destroyed	The king (11:36-45) King destroyed (11:45) Time of anguish (12:1)	Antichrist	Final days
Mountain fills whole earth	Kingdom given to son of man and God's people		God's people delivered (12:1) Resurrection (12:2; 12:13) The wise exalted (12:3)	Kingdom of God	Ever-lasting

Daniel's final vision also echoes ideas in other Old Testament books, especially in Ezekiel. Daniel's description of "a man clothed in linen" (10:5-6) shows many similarities to Ezekiel's vision of God and his cherubim (Ezek 1).[7] Daniel 11:14-16, 31 uses identical words to those found in Ezekiel 7.[8] "There remains an end at the time appointed" (11:27) is similar to Habakkuk 2:3a, "For there is still a vision for the appointed time; it speaks of the end." The idea of

7. E.g., "a belt of gold around his waist" (10:5; Ezek 1:27); "his body was like beryl" (10:6; Ezek 1:27); "his face like lightning" (10:6; Ezek 1:13); "his eyes like flaming torches" (10:6; Ezek 1:4, 27); "his arms and legs like the gleam of burnished bronze" (10:6; Ezek 1:4, 27); "the sound of his words like the roar of a multitude" (10:6; Ezek 1:24). See Steinmann, *Daniel*, 499.

8. In Daniel 11:14-16 "the 'violent' (*prṣ*, Ezek 7:22) among the people will try to establish a 'vision' (*ḥzn*, Ezek 7:26) but will 'fail' (*kšl*, Ezek 7:19). A pagan king will come and stand in the 'beautiful' (*ṣĕbî*, Ezek 7:20) land." In Daniel 11:31 "the words 'desecrate' (*ḥll*), 'sanctuary' (*mqdš*) and 'fortress' (*'wz*) are all found in Ezek 7:24, and the word 'abomination' (*šqwṣ*) occurs in Ezek 7:20." Lucas, *Daniel*, 268.

angels battling for God's people is also found elsewhere in Scripture (e.g., Exod 32:34; 33:2; and Josh 5:14).

In the New Testament, Jesus speaks of "the desolating sacrilege standing in the holy place, as was spoken of by the prophet Daniel" (Matt 24:15; cf. Dan 11:31) and of "the suffering of those days" (Matt 24:9, 29; cf. Dan 12:1). Paul alludes to Daniel 11:36, "The king . . . shall exalt himself and consider himself greater than any god, and shall speak horrendous things against the God of gods," when he describes the "Man of Lawlessness": "He opposes and exalts himself above every so-called god or object of worship, so that he takes his seat in the temple of God, declaring himself to be God" (2 Thess 2:4).

The book of Revelation, of course, uses many images of Daniel's visions. The "man clothed in linen" (Dan 10:5-6) becomes "one like the Son of Man, clothed with a long robe and with a golden sash across his chest. . . . His eyes were like a flame of fire, his feet were like burnished bronze, refined as in a furnace, and his voice was like the sound of many waters. . . . His face was like the sun shining with full force" (Rev. 1:13-16). The angel Michael, who is first mentioned in Scripture in Daniel 10:13, 21, reappears in Revelation 12 as Michael with his angels fighting Satan and his angels (Rev. 12:7-9). Daniel 12:1-2 speaks of "a time of anguish, such as has never occurred," after which God's people who are "found written in the book" will be delivered. The dead "shall awake, some to everlasting life, and some to shame and everlasting contempt." Revelation 20:12-15 similarly speaks of a resurrection from the dead and of "the book of life": "Anyone whose name was not found written in the book of life was thrown into the lake of fire." But those whose names were found "in the Lamb's book of life" (Rev. 21:27) will inherit the new earth where God will dwell with his people and be their God (Rev. 21:1-3).

Literary Features

As with Daniel 7–9, the genre of chapters 10–12 is apocalyptic literature. But as we noted in Chapter 9, the overall form of Daniel 9 and 10–12 is different from the "symbolic visions" of Daniel 7 and 8. Collins calls this vision a "'historical' apocalypse in the form of an epiphany with an angelic discourse." He further identifies Daniel 12:1-3 as an "eschatological prophecy."[9] As we noted earlier, Lucas calls the overall forms of Daniel 9 and 10–12 "epiphany visions," which have similar structures:[10]

---

9. Collins, *Daniel* (1984), 99 and 101.
10. Lucas, *Daniel*, 35.

Circumstances [setting]	9:1-2	10:1
Supplication	9:3-19	10:2-3
Appearance of messenger	9:20-21	10:4-9
Word of assurance	9:22-23	10:10–11:1
Revelation	9:24-27	11:2–12:3
Charge to seer		12:4

Since this vision is apocalyptic literature, we should be prepared to interpret the various weapons (11:40), nations (11:40, 43), and numbers (12:7, 11, 12) symbolically rather than literally. Goldingay calls attention to the features of poetry in 12:1-3, rhythm, parallelism, metaphor, and simile, "which emphasize their significance at the high point of the main address."[11] Note the synonymous parallelism in 12:3,

> Those who are wise shall shine like the brightness of the sky,
>   and those who lead many to righteousness, like the stars forever. . . .

We shall look in greater detail at the structure of this vision, its plot line, character description, and repetition.

Structure

Daniel's fourth vision has four scenes, the last one being the preaching text for our second sermon on this vision.

Scene 1. Daniel's mourning, vision, and reaction (10:1-9)
   A. Date and summary of the message (10:1)
   B. Daniel's mourning for three weeks (10:2-3)
   C. Daniel's vision of a man clothed in linen (10:4-6)
   D. Daniel's reaction and trance (10:7-9)
   Characters: Daniel and the man clothed in linen

Scene 2. An angel touches Daniel and dialogues with him (10:10–11:1)
   A. The angel touches Daniel and gets him on his hands and knees (10:10)
   B. He will tell Daniel "what is to happen . . . at the end of days" (10:11-14)
   C. Daniel is speechless (10:15)
   D. The angel touches Daniel's lips; he can speak but is weak (10:16-17)
   E. The angel touches Daniel again and encourages him (10:18–11:1)
   Characters: Daniel and an angel

11. Goldingay, *Daniel*, 288.

Scene 3. The angel announces the truth about the future (11:2–12:4)
    A. Four Persian kings (11:2)
    B. A warrior king (11:3-4)
    C. Conflicts between southern and northern kings (11:5-9)
    D. The triumphs of a northern king and his fall (11:10-19)
    E. Another northern king (11:20)
    F. The career of a contemptible person (11:21-35)
        1. His rise and success (11:21-24)
        2. His invasion of the south and attack on the holy covenant (11:25-28)
        3. His failed invasion of the south and attack on the holy covenant (11:29-35)
    G. A king attacks God and his people (11:36-45)
        1. The king prospers (11:36-39)
        2. His final attack and fall (11:40-45)
    H. The deliverance of the faithful (12:1-4)
        1. A time of anguish followed by deliverance (12:1)
        2. A double resurrection of the dead (12:2)
        3. Exaltation of the wise (12:3)
        4. Conclusion: keep the book sealed (12:4)
    Characters: the angel and Daniel

Scene 4. Daniel's concluding vision and dialogue about the end (12:5-13)
    A. A vision of two angels (12:5)
    B. One angel asks, "How long until the end of these wonders?" (12:6)
    C. "The man" responds, "A time, two times, and half a time" (12:7)
    D. Daniel asks, "What shall be the outcome of these things?" (12:8)
    E. "The man" responds, "The words are to remain sealed until the time of the end" (12:9)
    F. "Many shall be purified . . . , but the wicked shall continue to act wickedly" (12:10)
    G. "One thousand two hundred ninety days" (12:11)
    H. "Persevere and attain the thousand three hundred thirty-five days" (12:12)
    I. Daniel shall rise at the end of the days (12:13)
    Characters: an angel and the man clothed in linen; when the angel leaves the stage, he is replaced by Daniel

The Plot Line

The setting of this apocalyptic narrative is given in Daniel 10:1, "the third year of King Cyrus." In his first year Cyrus had allowed the Jews to return to Jerusalem and rebuild the temple (Ezra 1:1-4). But things were not going well in Jerusalem. The Samaritans opposed the Jews, and soon the building project ground to a halt (Ezra 4). Daniel undoubtedly heard about the struggles of God's people in Jerusalem, for the angel says that Daniel had set his mind on gaining "understanding" (10:12).

A preliminary incident is Daniel's mourning for three weeks (10:2-3; cf. 9:3) in order to gain "understanding" (10:12). The occasioning incident is the vision he received of "a man clothed in linen" and Daniel falling into a trance (10:4-9). Will Daniel have the strength to hear God's message? The tension rises as the angel touches him and gets him up on his feet (10:10-14). But while the angel is speaking to him, Daniel turns his face toward the ground again and is speechless. The angel touches his lips, and Daniel complains of such pains that he has no strength and is breathless (10:15-17). But the angel touches him again and encourages him. Finally, Daniel is ready to hear the message (10:18-19). The angel underscores the importance of his message by telling Daniel that the demon prince of Persia held him up for twenty-one days before he could deliver his message to Daniel. "Now I will announce the truth to you" (10:20–11:2a). What will that message be?

God's message is a detailed account of what will happen in the future. The Persian kings will be succeeded by a Greek warrior king whose kingdom will split into four parts (11:2b-4). There will be wars between successive kings of the north (Syria) and kings of the south (Egypt), with Palestine caught in the middle (11:5-20). Then "a contemptible person" will usurp the northern kingdom, persecute God's people, and profane the temple (11:21-35). "The king shall act as he pleases, . . . speak horrendous things against the God of gods. . . . He shall prosper until the period of wrath is completed" (11:36-39). "The king of the north" will come into "the beautiful land," and tens of thousands shall fall victim" (11:40-45a). Where is God?

The narrative turns toward a resolution at 11:45b, "Yet he shall come to his end, with no one to help him." "At that time Michael, the great prince, the protector of your people, shall arise." There will be a time of terrible anguish, but in the end God's people will be delivered (12:1). Those who have died will be raised, "some to everlasting life" and "some to shame and everlasting contempt" (12:2). In the end, justice will prevail and the wise will be exalted (12:3). Daniel is told to keep the book sealed until the time of the end (12:4). The tension is fully resolved. But a new conflict develops (12:5), which will become the preaching text for our second sermon on this fourth vision.

We can sketch the plot line of Daniel 10–12 as that of a complex plot:

Climax

11:45b	**"He shall come to his end"**
11:40-45a	**king of north**
11:36-39	the king
11:21-35	contemptible king
11:5-20	many kings
11:3-4	Greek king
11:2b	Persian kings
11:2a	**"Announce truth"**
10:18-19	and again
10:15-17	again
10:10-14	angel touches Daniel

Rising tension

Climax

12:8	**"Outcome?"**
12:7	"time, times, half"
12:6	**"How long?"**

Rising tension

New conflict
12:5
Vision of
two angels

Resolution

12:1a	**Michael shall rise**
12:1b	terrible anguish
12:1c	**people delivered**
12:2	**resurrection**
12:3	**wise exalted**
12:4	book sealed

Resolution

12:9	words sealed
12:10	**wise understand**
12:12	**persevering blessed**

Outcome
12:13
**Daniel
will rise**

Setting	*Preliminary incidents*	*Occasioning incident*
Dan 10:1	10:2-3	10:4-9
Third year	Daniel	**Vision of "a man"**
Cyrus	mourning	Daniel in a trance

349

Character Description

Daniel describes especially four characters. He describes in great detail "a man clothed in linen, with a belt of gold from Uphaz around his waist. His body was like beryl, his face like lightning, his eyes like flaming torches, his arms and legs like the gleam of burnished bronze, and the sound of his words like the roar of a multitude" (10:5-6). In the concluding vision, Daniel further relates that the "man" was "above the waters of the river" (12:6, NIV) — a heavenly being — not "upstream" as the NRSV translates.[12]

Daniel describes himself as mourning for three weeks, fasting, and not anointing his body (10:2-3). He was standing on the bank of the river Tigris when he *"looked up"* and saw the "man" (10:4-5). The vision was so overpowering that his strength left him and he turned deathly pale (10:8): "The description is that of a person's being 'scared to death.'"[13] At the sound of the "man's" words he fell into a trance, face to the ground (10:8-9). A hand touched him and roused him to his hands and knees (10:10), and he stood up trembling (10:11). As the "man" spoke to him, Daniel turned his face to the ground and was speechless. After "one in human form" touched his lips, he could speak again and said that because of the vision such pains (birth pangs) came upon him that he had no strength. He was shaking and without breath (10:15-17). Again the "one in human form" touched him, strengthened him, called him "greatly beloved," and encouraged him not to fear and to "be strong and courageous." At that Daniel was strengthened and invited the messenger to bring his message (10:18-19).

Daniel further describes "a contemptible person" who will obtain the kingdom through intrigue (11:21). He will be extremely powerful, sweeping away whole armies as well as the prince of the covenant (11:22). He will act deceitfully, lavish plunder, spoil, and wealth on his friends, and devise plans to take strongholds (11:24). He will be bent on evil and lying (11:27). When confronted by Roman forces, he will lose heart, be enraged, and will take action against the holy covenant. His forces will "occupy and profane the temple and fortress. . . . abolish the regular burnt offering and set up the abomination that makes desolate." Then he will seduce with intrigue those who violate the covenant (11:30-32).

After this description, Daniel describes a "king" who will act as he pleases, exalt himself, consider himself greater than any god, and speak horrendous things against the God of gods (11:36). He will pay no respect to any god but instead honor the god of fortresses (11:37-38). He has many weapons at his dis-

---

12. "In chapter 12:6 he appears hovering over the waters of the river, the Tigris. This agrees also with the verse before us [10:5], according to which Daniel, while standing on the banks of the river, on lifting up his eyes beheld the vision." Keil, *Book of Daniel*, 410.

13. Redditt, *Daniel*, 171.

posal (11:40) and will slay tens of thousands in "the beautiful land" (11:41). He will become superrich (11:43), and "shall go out with great fury to bring ruin and complete destruction to many" (11:44). "Yet he shall come to his end, with no one to help him" (11:45).

Repetition

Repetition of keywords may also help us discern Daniel's message for Israel. Daniel begins by repeating three times the word "word" *(dābār)*: "a word was revealed to Daniel" (divine passive: God revealed a word to Daniel), "the word was true," and "he understood the word" (10:1). This repetition underscores the trustworthiness of the revealed "word" or "vision" (10:1).

Next, using various words, Daniel stresses his weakness in the face of the overpowering vision of "the man clothed in linen" (10:8-17). It takes three touches (*naga'a*, 10:10, 16, 18) before Daniel is strengthened and ready to hear the message. This lengthy introduction about Daniel's inability to receive the heavenly message underscores its weighty nature.

The angel's introduction to his message reveals the repetition of a chiastic structure:[14]

> A   "Do you know why I have come to you?" (10:20a)
>   B   "Now I must return to fight against the prince of Persia" (10:20b)
>   C   "But I am to tell you what is inscribed in the book of truth" (10:21a)
>   B′   "No one with me who contends against these princes except Michael" (10:21b–11:1)
> A′   "Now I will announce the truth to you" (11:2a)

This chiasm ties together the delivery of the earthly message and the reality of the spiritual conflicts. It also underscores the importance of the message since the messenger turned his attention away from these spiritual conflicts in order to deliver his message to Daniel.[15]

The angel's message highlights the pattern of the rise and fall of human kingdoms by the repetition of words like "arise," "stand," "raise" (*'md*, 16x); "come," "attack," "bring" (*bw'*, 12x); "turn," "return," "do again" (*šwb*, 12x); "make," "act," "do" (*'sh*, 10x). Goldingay comments, "These verbal phenomena contribute to the drawing of patterns in history such as . . . the ceaseless movement and warring between north and south, the unending rise and fall of rulers

---

14. See Lucas, *Daniel*, 267. Goldingay, *Daniel*, 292, speaks of "an a-b-a-b-a arrangement."
15. Goldingay, *Daniel*, 292.

and empires with their awesome power and authority yet their less acknowledged constraints and transience."[16]

While previously Daniel had used the word "covenant" *(běrît)* only twice (in the third vision, 9:4, 27), in this last vision he repeats the word "covenant" five times (11:22, 28, 30 [2x], and 32). This repetition indicates his concern for God's persecuted covenant people. But he also uses the word "the time appointed" *(mô'ēd)* three times (11:27, 29, 35), indicating that in spite of the suffering of God's people, God remains in control of the times. Finally, the phrase "time of the end" *('ēt qēṣ)*, which Daniel has used only once before (8:17; the second "vision is for the time of the end"), is repeated four times in this fourth vision (11:35, 40; 12:4, 9). This repetition underscores that Daniel's message ultimately concerns the last period before the end of time.[17]

The Identity of Controversial Figures

Since there is general agreement on the identity of the many kings mentioned in Daniel 11 (see the note below[18]), we need not spend time on them here. In

---

16. Ibid., 288.

17. "The phrase 'the time of the end' is carefully and consistently reserved for the last period preceding the End (see 11:35, 40; 12:4, 9)." Gooding, "The Literary Structure of the Book of Daniel and Its Implications," *TynBul* (1981) 75, n. 27. See also Steinmann, *Daniel,* 544, and Miller, *Daniel,* 309.

18. Data taken from the chart in Steinmann, *Daniel,* 521, Lederach, *Daniel,* 283, and other sources. See Introduction, p. 3, n. 8.

DANIEL 11			DATES (B.C.)
11:3	Alexander the Great		336-323
	EGYPT (Ptolemies)	**SYRIA (Seleucids)**	
11:4	Macedonian Empire divided among the four Diadochi		301
11:5	Ptolemy I Soter		323-285
11:5		Seleucus I Nicator	311-280
11:6	Ptolemy II		285-246
11:6		Antiochus II Theos	261-246
11:6	Berenice, daughter of Ptolemy II, married Antiochus II		252
11:7-9	Ptolemy III		246-221
11:7-9		Seleucus II Callinicus	246-226
11:10		Seleucus III Ceraunus	226-223
11:10-19		Antiochus III the Great	223-187

continued on p. 353

this section we shall seek to come to some clarity on the identity of several controversial figures. We shall deal in turn with the "man clothed in linen" (10:5-6; 12:6-7); the "hand" and the "one in human form" who touches Daniel (10:10, 16, 18), encourages him (10:11–11:1), and communicates God's message (11:2–12:4); "the prince of the kingdom of Persia" (10:13, 20); Michael (10:13, 21; 12:1); "the king" who "shall act as he pleases" (11:36); and "the king of the north" (11:40).

"A Man Clothed in Linen" (10:5-6; 12:6-7)

This "man" has been identified variously as the preincarnate Christ, God, the angel Gabriel, and an unidentified angel. Whatever identification we make does not, of course, alter the message Daniel has for Israel — it is a message that comes from God himself. But for the sake of clarity, it is well to try to establish the identity of this "man."

The "man" is clothed in linen. Linen vestments were associated with priests and holiness (Lev. 6:10; 16:4). But this "man" is much more than a priest. His awesome features identify him as a spiritual, heavenly being. With other commentators,[19] Steinmann identifies this "man" as "the preincarnate Christ, who appears in other Daniel passages. The parallels with Ezekiel and Revelation," he

DANIEL 11			DATES (B.C.)
11:11-12	Ptolemy IV		221-204
11:14-17	Ptolemy V		204-181
11:17	Ptolemy V married Cleopatra, daughter of Antiochus III		193
11:18-19		Death of Antiochus III	187
11:20		Seleucus IV Philopator	187-175
11:21-35		Antiochus IV Epiphanes	175-164
11:25-27	Ptolemy VI		181-146
11:25-28		Antiochus's first war against Egypt	169
11:29-35		Antiochus's second war against Egypt	168
11:30		Antiochus expelled from Egypt by ROMAN consul	168
11:31		Erection of pagan altar near Jerusalem temple	167
11:33-35		Persecution of the Jews	167-163

19. See, e.g., Keil, *Book of Daniel*, 410, "The *'îš* seen by Daniel was no common angel-prince, but a manifestation of Jehovah, i.e., the Logos"; Young, *Prophecy of Daniel*, 225, "The revelation . . . is a theophany, a preincarnate appearance of the eternal Son"; and Miller, *Daniel*, 282-83. By contrast, Goldingay, *Daniel*, 291, states, "There is no reason to link any of the figures here specifically with the humanlike figure of 7:13. Like chapter 7, the scene has the allusiveness that often characterizes vision reports."

writes, "clearly favor this identification."[20] But we should not read the picture of the exalted Christ in Revelation 1:13-16 back into Daniel, although in the sermon we can certainly move from Daniel to Revelation.

Other commentators identify the "man" as God. Arguments in favor of this identification are the parallels with Ezekiel, "the appearance of the likeness of the glory of the LORD" (1:26-28), Daniel's lengthy reaction to this figure (10:8-17),[21] and this "man's" superior knowledge, for an angel asks "the man clothed in linen," "How long?" (12:6). A strong argument against this identification, however, is that it is extremely unlikely that almighty God would be held up for twenty-one days by a demon (10:13), for the "man" does not show up before Daniel has been "mourning for three weeks" (10:2-5). Moreover, in answer to the question "How long?" "the man clothed in linen" swears "by the one who lives forever" (12:7), which probably indicates that he swears by one higher than himself.

If the "man clothed in linen" is not the preincarnate Christ nor God, he can be identified as an angel. Collins writes, "The angel in question is generally assumed to be Gabriel, as in chapters 8[:16] and 9[:21], but the identification is not explicit here."[22] In fact, in the second vision Gabriel's speaking also caused Daniel to fall into a trance and Gabriel touched him and set him on his feet (8:18; cf. 10:9-11). Although Daniel's weakness, trance, speechlessness, birth pangs, and breathlessness (10:8-17) far exceed his prior reactions to meeting Gabriel, this may be due to his three-week fast (10:2-3). Since the text does not identify the "man" specifically as Gabriel, however, we shall simply call him the angel.

"One in Human Form" Touching Daniel (10:10, 16, 18)

In order to be consistent, those who identify "the man clothed in linen" as God must also identify as God this person "in human form" who touches Daniel three times.[23] But this identification contradicts the person's claim that he has "been sent" (10:11). Almighty God has not been sent; he *does* the sending. Miller and other commentators[24] look for a way out of this dilemma by introducing a

---

20. Steinmann, *Daniel,* 498. The other Daniel passages he has in mind are 3:25; possibly 6:22; and from the visions, 7:13-14; 8:11, 25; and 9:24-27.

21. Cf. Daniel 7:28 and 8:17, 27.

22. Collins, *Daniel,* 373. Lacocque, *Book of Daniel,* 206-9, argues that the identification with Gabriel is "a mistake" and that this appearance is like the "son of man."

23. So Keil, *Book of Daniel,* 410-14, and Young, *Prophecy of Daniel,* 227, who are rightly faulted by Miller, *Daniel,* 282, n. 26.

24. Miller, *Daniel,* 282, n. 26, mentions G. C. Luck, *Daniel* (Chicago: Moody, 1958), 109, and J. F. Walvoord, *Daniel: The Key to Prophetic Revelation* (Chicago: Moody, 1991), 243 and 245.

second figure at 10:10 — an angel, probably Gabriel.[25] The problem is that the text does not introduce another angel at this point.[26]

Having identified "the man clothed in linen" as an angel, we have no problem identifying this individual "in human form" who touches Daniel three times and encourages him. This figure continues to be the unidentified angel of 10:5-6 who has been sent (10:11) and was delayed for twenty-one days (10:13).

Many commentators go further and identify this particular angel as Gabriel.[27] Miller, for example, gives two reasons for this identification: first, "Gabriel served as a communicator of God's messages on several occasions (cf. 8:15-16; 9:21; Luke 1:19, 26-27)." And second, "the interpreting angel evidently had great power (cf. 11:1), which would be true of a prominent being like Gabriel."[28] Collins adds a third reason, "The date [in 11:1, "in the first year of Darius the Mede"] serves to identify the speaker with Gabriel (cf. 9:1)."[29] Although these appear to be good reasons for identifying this figure with Gabriel, since he is not named "Gabriel" in this vision we shall continue to call him "the angel."

"The Prince of the Kingdom of Persia" (10:13, 20)

Calvin identified "the prince of the kingdom of Persia" as King Cambyses of Persia who "promulgated a cruel edict, preventing the Jews from building their temple, and manifesting complete hostility to its restoration."[30] Most commentators today, however, understand "the prince" as a spiritual being. In 10:13 "the prince of the kingdom of Persia" opposes the angel whom God has sent to respond to Daniel's mourning and holds him up for twenty-one days. It is unlikely that a human being could hold up an angelic messenger for even one day. Moreover, this "prince" is mentioned in the same breath as the angel Michael, "one of the

---

25. See Miller, ibid., 282. Miller correctly observes (n. 26) that "the language of vv. 10-14 is inappropriate as applied to deity. For example, no being could resist the power of God himself (certainly not the omnipotent, sovereign God described time and again in the Book of Daniel) for a moment much less for twenty-one days (cf. v. 13)."

26. Cf. Longman, *Daniel*, 250, "There is no clear textual signal that tells us that a second figure has come into play with verse 10."

27. See Montgomery, *Book of Daniel*, 420; Porteous, *Daniel*, 151; Collins, *Daniel*, 376; Redditt, *Daniel*, 171; Anderson, *Signs and Wonders*, 124-25; Miller, *Daniel*, 281-83; and Lucas, *Daniel*, 278. By contrast, Longman, *Daniel*, 250, notes, "We know so little of the details of the angelic world that such a naming [as Gabriel] is no more than an educated guess, an unnecessary one at that."

28. Miller, *Daniel*, 283.

29. Collins, *Daniel*, 376. Cf. Lucas, *Daniel*, 278, "11:1a has the function of identifying the angel who has been speaking as Gabriel (cf. 9:1)."

30. Calvin, *Commentaries on Daniel*, II, 252.

chief princes" (10:13), later called "the great prince, the protector of your people" (12:1). Hence we have to think of "the prince of the kingdom of Persia" as an evil angel, a demon, who influences the affairs in the kingdom of Persia in opposition to God's people.[31]

In Daniel 10:20 the angel (the one in human form) says, "Now I must return to fight against the prince of Persia, and when I am through with him, the prince of Greece will come." This verse amplifies the idea of spiritual warfare in the heavenly places. The thought seems to be that all human kingdoms are under the influence of demonic beings that are bent on hurting God's people.[32] God's angels, however, fight these demons in order to protect God's people. As Paul put it in Ephesians 6:12, "Our struggle is not against enemies of blood and flesh, but against the rulers, against the authorities, against the cosmic powers of this present darkness, against the spiritual forces of evil in the heavenly places."

Michael (10:13, 21; 12:1)

Michael has been variously identified as the angel of the Lord, that is, the preincarnate Christ,[33] and as an archangel. There is no biblical evidence for identifying Michael as the preincarnate Christ. The name Michael means, "Who is like God?" He is described as "one of the chief princes" (10:13), as "your [Daniel's] prince" (10:21), and as "the great prince, the protector of your [Daniel's] people" (12:1). Michael will be mentioned again in Jude 9, where he is called "the archangel" ("the first angel"), and in Revelation 12:7, "And war broke out in heaven; Michael and his angels fought against the dragon. The dragon and his angels fought back, but they were defeated." Michael is thus described as a powerful angel who fights to protect God's people. In Daniel 10:13 he came to the aid of the angel who was prevented from delivering God's message to Daniel. In 10:21 the angel describes Michael as the one "who contends against these princes," namely, the princes of Persia and of Greece — demons hostile to God's people. And in 12:1 the angel promises that at the end of time "Michael, the great prince, the protector of your people, shall arise."

---

31. Cf. Keil, *Book of Daniel,* 416, It "is a spirit-being; yet not the heathen national god of the Persians, but, according to the view of Scripture (1 Cor 10:20f.), the *daimonion* of the Persian kingdom, i.e., the supernatural spiritual power standing behind the national gods, which we may properly call the guardian spirit of this kingdom." Cf. Miller, *Daniel,* 285-88, and Redditt, *Daniel,* 172.

32. Cf. Deuteronomy 32:8-9, "When the Most High apportioned the nations, when he divided humankind, he fixed the boundaries of the peoples according to the number of the gods; the LORD's own portion was his people, Jacob his allotted share." Cf. Isaiah 24:21.

33. E.g., Gurney, *God in Control,* 158, and Anderson, *Unfolding Daniel's Prophecies,* 129.

"The King Shall Act as He Pleases" (11:36)

Although some of the above identifications make little or no difference in interpreting Daniel's message, *this* identification affects the interpretation directly. The issue is this: Does 11:36 continue to describe the activities of Antiochus IV from 11:21 on or does it switch gears to an even more powerful evil ruler, the Antichrist? Aside from some unique identifications,[34] in the history of interpretation three different identifications have found traction. They are, first, 11:36-39 continues to describe Antiochus IV; second, 11:36-39 continues to describe Antiochus, who is, however, a type of the Antichrist; and third, "the king" in 11:36 switches from the prior description of Antiochus to a description of the Antichrist.

Many modern scholars defend the position that "the king" in 11:36-39 is Antiochus IV. For example, Collins writes, "Verses 36-39 do not continue in chronological sequence but recapitulate the king's behavior during the persecution."[35] Collins acknowledges that there are discrepancies between the king's behavior described in these verses and the known behavior of Antiochus IV. He calls these discrepancies "probably deliberate polemical distortion" and "polemical exaggeration."[36] But one cannot get around these discrepancies so easily. Some of the descriptions are plainly contrary to the historical facts. Miller writes, "Antiochus did not exalt himself above every god (vv. 36-37), reject 'the gods of his fathers,' or worship 'a god unknown to his fathers' (v. 38); on the contrary, he worshiped the Greek pantheon, even building an altar and offering sacrifices to Zeus in the Jerusalem temple precincts."[37]

Second, some scholars defend the position that verses 36-39 exhibit some continuity with the earlier description of Antiochus but note that the so-called "exaggerations" portray him as the personification of evil — an evil king who foreshadows the end-time Antichrist mentioned in the New Testament. Keil argues, "That which is said regarding this king, verses 36-39, partly goes far beyond what Antiochus did, partly does not harmonize with what is known of Antiochus, and, finally, partly is referred in the New Testament expressly to the Antichrist (cf. v. 36 with 2 Thess 2:4, and 12:1 with Matt 24:21). These circumstances . . . show that in the prophetic contemplation there is comprehended in

---

34. E.g., Calvin, *Commentaries on Daniel*, II, 338-39, argues that "the king" in 11:36 refers to the Roman Empire.

35. Collins, *Daniel*, 386. Cf. Montgomery, *Book of Daniel*, 460-64; Porteous, *Daniel*, 169, and Anderson, *Signs and Wonders*, 140-42.

36. Collins, *Daniel*, 387, 388.

37. Miller, *Daniel*, 305. Cf. Archer, "Daniel," 144-46, and Keil, *Book of Daniel*, 463. Leupold, *Exposition of Daniel*, 513, notes, "Even in Athens he had a temple built in honor of this god [Zeus Olympius]."

the image of *one* king what has been historically fulfilled in its beginnings by Antiochus Epiphanes, but shall only meet its complete fulfillment by the Antichrist in the time of the end."[38]

This interpretation, which sees in 11:36-39 not only the historical Antiochus but also a type of the Antichrist, is reinforced by Daniel's second vision (chapter 8), where Antiochus, the "little horn," also functioned as a type of the Antichrist. Moreover, the description of Antiochus in chapter 8 has parallels in 10:36-39: The little horn "kept prospering in what he did" (8:12), and, "He shall prosper until the period of wrath is completed" (11:36); "In his own mind he shall be great" (8:25), and "He shall exalt himself and consider himself greater than any god" (11:36); He "shall even rise up against the Prince of princes" (8:25), and he "shall speak horrendous things against the God of gods" (11:36).

Although this interpretation of Antiochus IV as a type of the Antichrist is possible, it is rather complicated to communicate in a sermon because one has to shift from Antiochus (11:21-35) to Antiochus as a type of the Antichrist (11:36-39) to the Antichrist himself (11:40-45). A third option for Daniel 11:36-39 offers a more direct move to the Antichrist because it is of one piece with 11:40-45.

This third option is that "the king" mentioned in 11:36-39 is not Antiochus but the end-time Antichrist. This interpretation links up with Daniel's first vision (Dan 7) in which the Antichrist was portrayed as a little horn coming up among the ten horns of the Roman Empire: "He shall speak words against the Most High" (7:25; cf. 11:36, "He . . . shall speak horrendous things against the God of gods"). This interpretation is also supported by the fact that Daniel 7 and 10 each begin with a third-person introduction, suggesting an inclusio between the first and the fourth vision (see p. 343 at n. 6 above). Moreover, in 11:36-39 the word "God/god(s)" occurs an exceptional eight times, "thus emphasizing the profane character of the ruler."[39]

This third option does justice to the fact that the king's actions described in the text — such as, "consider himself greater than any god" (11:36), "pay no respect to the gods of his ancestors" (11:37) — are different from what is known historically about Antiochus IV. It also does justice to the literary context, which deals with the end-time "anguish" and the resurrection from the dead (12:1-2). The question is, Is there further support for this interpretation by some indication in the text that 11:36 moves beyond Antiochus IV to the Antichrist?

Steinmann observes that "there are two plain indications in the text that the king who is the focus in 11:36-45 is not the same as the king of the north in

---

38. Keil, *Book of Daniel*, 462-63. Cf. Baldwin, *Daniel*, 199-200; Wallace, *The Lord Is King*, 189, and Duguid, *Daniel*, 203-4.

39. Hill, "Daniel," 201. See also Kaiser, *Preaching and Teaching the Last Things*, 126-28.

11:21-35. First, 11:35 ends with the notice that the persecution of Antiochus will refine God's people 'until the time of the end.' . . . From that, it is reasonable to infer that the next part of the prophecy will begin a discussion about 'the time of the end.' . . . Second, 11:36 introduces the king in a unique way. He is simply referred to as *hamelek*, '*the* king.' No Hellenistic king prior to 11:36 is ever referred to simply as 'the king.' . . . Therefore, there are good indicators that there is a change of both timeframe and subject between 11:35 and 11:36. . . . This signals that this king is not a Hellenistic king, but an eschatological king who will arise at 'the time of the end' (11:35, 40; 12:4, 9)."[40]

"The King of the North" (11:40)

A final controversial figure is "the king of the north" in 11:40. Even the scholars who identify "the king" of 11:36-39 as Antiochus IV have to admit that 11:40-45 do not refer to the Antiochus we know from history. Towner writes, "The scenario described in 11:40-45 simply never transpired. None of the ancient sources tells of a new counterattack upon Antiochus by Ptolemy (v. 40), nor of a new appearance in 'the glorious land' of the former (v. 41), nor of his loot of Egypt and suzerainty over Libya and Ethiopia (v. 43), nor of his final demise on the Philistine plain (v. 45)."[41] These scholars account for these historical "errors" by claiming that verse 40 "marks the transition from *ex eventu* [from, after, the event] prophecy to real (and erroneous) prediction."[42] For example, Towner writes, "We know we are at the point at which the seer actually begins to look into the future because, historically speaking at least, he gets it all muddled. Once again, actual foretelling proves to be much more difficult than prophecy after the fact."[43] But why would an author who supposedly wrote thirty-eight verses of detailed history after the facts undercut his credibility by adding six verses about an unknown future? And why would he write that "Edom and *Moab* and the main part of the Ammonites shall escape from his

40. Steinmann, *Daniel*, 538-39. Cf. Harman, *Study Commentary on Daniel*, 264, "Verses 36 onwards describe a figure who far transcends any human king. He is one who will arise in 'a time of trouble' (12:1), which seems to be the same as 'the time of the end' (12:4). This figure appears to be not Antiochus Epiphanes but the true and ultimate Antichrist." Cf. p. 289, "The verses from 11:36 onwards lead into the depiction of end-time events (see especially 11:40, 45; 12:1, [2])." See also Leupold, *Exposition of Daniel*, 511.

41. Towner, *Daniel*, 164. Lucas, *Daniel*, 291, lists the four sources that relate the death of Antiochus in Persia. "Despite their disagreements and legendary elements, these accounts all agree that Antiochus embarked on a campaign in Persia, failed in an attempt to rob a temple, and met an untimely death, which three of them attribute to a sudden illness."

42. Collins, *Daniel*, 388.

43. Towner, *Daniel*, 164.

power" (11:41) when "Moab no longer existed as an independent nation"[44] in the time of Antiochus IV?

There is a much better option than identifying "the king of the north" as Antiochus IV. If Daniel 11:36-39 describes the Antichrist, 11:40-45 continue to describe the same person. Daniel 11:40 begins, "At the time of the end the king of the south shall attack him. But the king of the north shall rush upon him like a whirlwind. . . ." Steinmann comments, "'The time of the end' is an expression that occurs four times in this vision (11:35, 40; 12:4, 9). Just as it was used in 8:17 to signify the time when the period prophesied in that vision would end, so it is also used here to indicate the end of the period covered by the divine man's words. In the case of this vision, it is the end of the world at the return of Christ, since the timeframe of this vision ends with the resurrection (12:1-3). Therefore, 11:40-45 speaks of the end of the eschatological king immediately before the parousia of Christ, to be followed by the bodily resurrection (12:1-3)."[45]

Having described the wars between the kings of the south and the kings of the north, Daniel 11:40-45 describes a final, victorious, bloody war of a king of the north. "Yet he shall come to his end, with no one to help him" (11:45). This king of the north is the evil ruler the New Testament calls the Antichrist.

Theocentric Interpretation

Where is God in Daniel's final vision? Even though we came to the conclusion above that the "man clothed in linen" is not God but an angel, God is central in this vision. The passage begins, "In the third year of King Cyrus of Persia a word was revealed to Daniel" (10:1a, divine passive), that is, "God revealed a word to Daniel." "He understood the word, having received understanding in the vision" (10:1b, divine passive): "God gave him understanding in the vision." The angel says, "I have now been sent to you" (10:11): "God has sent me to you." The angel continues, "from the first day that you set your mind . . . to humble yourself before your God, your words have been heard" (10:12; cf. 2 Chron 7:14): "God has heard your words."

---

44. Harman, *Study Commentary on Daniel*, 290. See also references on p. 386, n. 132 below.

45. Steinmann, *Daniel*, 544. Cf. Miller, *Daniel*, 309, "The wars of Antichrist are described in vv. 40-45, and the time of this conflict is declared to be 'the time of the end' (v. 40). . . . These events have not yet transpired, and therefore the 'end' in view here must be the final days of the present age." Although Longman contends that "the explanation given for the transition from Antiochus IV to a future antichrist figure is not a particularly strong one" because "there are no clear textual signals that there is a change of referent as we move from verse 39 to verse 40," he does agree that since "the time of the end" of verse 40 "is followed in 12:1-3 by the resurrection of the dead, . . . we should take this as a clue that the end (in its ultimate sense) is the end of time." Longman, *Daniel*, 272 and 283. Cf. Lucas, *Daniel*, 301-2.

Seow notes perceptively that the following "history is bracketed by references to God's intervention brought about through the activities of God's celestial hosts (10:20–11:1; 12:1), and the history is a 'register of truth' [10:21], a record of God's reliability."[46] The angel's explanation of the coming wars also shows that God will be actively involved in the rise and fall of human kingdoms. "A warrior king shall arise. . . . And while still rising in power, his kingdom shall be broken and divided to the four winds of heaven" (11:4; divine passive): God shall break Alexander the Great's kingdom and divide it into four. God is also involved in the wars between the Ptolemies and Seleucids. "The forces of the south shall not stand, . . . for there shall be no strength to resist" (11:15). Baldwin observes, "Behind the passive verb lies God's active will, putting down one and setting up another (Ps 75:3-7 [cf. Dan 2:21])."[47] In the north, another king shall arise, "but within a few days he shall be broken" (11:20), that is, "God shall break him." "At the time appointed he shall return and come into the south" (11:29), that is, God has determined "the time appointed."[48] In these wars, "some of the wise shall fall, so that they may be refined, purified, and cleansed, until the time of the end" (11:35). It is God who does the refining, purifying, and cleansing.

"The king [the Antichrist] . . . shall speak horrendous things against the God of gods. He shall prosper until the period of wrath is completed, for what is determined shall be done" (11:36). The sovereign God also determined the boundaries of the end-time "period of wrath" when the Antichrist will inflict terrible persecution on God's people. In the end, God's people "shall be delivered, everyone who is written in the book of life" (12:1). God "wrote" (anthropomorphism) their names in the book of life, and God will deliver them. "Many of those who sleep in the dust of the earth shall awake" (12:2): only a sovereign God can awaken people from the dead and make them shine like stars in his kingdom (12:3).

Textual Theme and Goal

This lengthy passage gives several clues to its overarching theme. In 10:1 the "word revealed to Daniel" is described as "true, and it concerned a great *conflict*": a great war is coming. The angel tells Daniel that he has come "to help you understand what is to happen to your people at the *end of days*" (10:14), that is, in the last days, just before God will replace human kingdoms with his everlasting kingdom.

---

46. Seow, *Daniel,* 167.

47. Baldwin, *Daniel,* 188.

48. "The narrator implies again that history was being worked out in due time according to the sovereign will of God: 'at the time appointed' (168 B.C.E.), Antiochus again invaded Egypt." Seow, *Daniel,* 179.

Next, chapter 11 predicts a succession of three Persian kings, warfare between a fourth Persian king and Greece, the conquests of Alexander the Great and the four-way split of his kingdom, and warfare between the kings north and south of the Promised Land (11:2-20). This warfare reaches a critical point with Antiochus IV, who attacks God himself and persecutes God's people in Palestine (11:21-35). Daniel 11:36-45 switches to a "king of the north" much greater and more evil than Antiochus. This king, whom the New Testament calls the Antichrist, will appear in the final days to persecute God's people. But God will deliver his people, raising them from the dead and exalting them in his glorious kingdom (12:1-3).

Even though Daniel spends much time describing his reaction to the vision of the heavenly visitor (chapter 10) and the warfare between the kings of the north and the kings of the south (chapter 11), the climax of this last vision is that final period before the end. The detailed predictions of what happens in the Persian kingdom (Daniel's time) and the Greek kingdoms (north and south, persecution of the Jews) serve to highlight "the truth" (11:2; cf. 10:1, 21) that Israel's sovereign God controls even the details of human history, also what will happen to God's people "at the end of days" (10:14), "at the time of the end" (11:35, 40; 12:4, 9). Therefore we can formulate the textual theme as follows, *Our sovereign God, who controls even the details of human history, will deliver his people from the extreme persecution of the final days, even raising them from the dead and exalting them in his glorious kingdom.*

As to Daniel's goal in communicating this message, we must recall that Daniel wrote this vision first for Israel in exile and the Jewish remnant which had returned to Jerusalem to rebuild the temple two years earlier (10:1, "the third year of King Cyrus"). The latter experienced much opposition from the Samaritans, were discouraged, and stopped work on rebuilding the temple (see Ezra 4). "The euphoria that surrounded the initial return and the rededication of the altar was fading and the challenges of maintaining faithfulness over the long haul in the midst of great opposition would have been on Daniel's mind."[49] Daniel sought to "gain understanding" (10:12), and through this vision he received it (10:1). The vision shows that even though more persecution is to come, even "a time of anguish such as has never occurred since nations first came into existence" (12:1), God is in control of human history and will certainly deliver his persecuted people. "The disappointment associated with the beginning of Israel's restoration from exile is countered by a promise of final restoration (12:1-3)."[50] The goal, then, is *to encourage and comfort God's perse-*

---

49. Duguid, *Daniel*, 178.

50. Goldingay, *Daniel*, 290, with credit to O. Plöger, *Prophecy and Eschatology* (Oxford: Blackwell, 1968).

cuted people by giving them understanding of God's intent to deliver his people, even from death.[51]

Ways to Preach Christ

Preachers who identify the "man clothed in linen" as the preincarnate Christ may perhaps think that focusing on that figure is the way to preach Christ. But identifying a certain Old Testament figure, such as the Angel of the Lord or the Commander of the Lord's army, with the preincarnate Christ is not necessarily preaching Christ as the climax of God's self-revelation in the New Testament. To do the latter, we have to check the seven ways to Christ in the New Testament. Since there is no contrast between the message of our text and that of the New Testament, we shall explore the remaining six ways.

Redemptive-Historical Progression

When Israel suffered in exile and a remnant returned to Jerusalem only to face more harassment, Daniel brought God's people the message that, even though there would be more persecution to come, their sovereign God would deliver his people from the unheard-of anguish of the final days, even raising them from the dead and exalting them in his glorious kingdom. Those final days were foreshadowed in Antiochus's desecration of God's temple and his persecution of God's people. Those final days came closer with the first coming of Jesus. The evil King Herod tried to kill him. Evil people desecrated his body, the temple of God (John 2:21), by hanging him on a cross and piercing his side with a spear. But God raised him from the dead, "the first fruits of those who have died" (1 Cor 15:20), and exalted him to his right hand.

The risen Christ sent his Spirit to dwell in the church, which is now his body on earth, "God's temple" (1 Cor 3:16). From the beginning the church suffered persecution. Jesus himself predicted, "So when you see the desolating sacrilege standing in the holy place, as was spoken of by the prophet Daniel (let the reader understand), then those in Judea must flee to the mountains. . . . For at that time there will be great suffering, such as has not been from the beginning of the world until now, no, and never will be. And if those days had not been cut short, no one would be saved; but for the sake of the elect those days will be cut

---

51. Cf. Longman, *Daniel,* 245-46, "The prophecy . . . is more like a provocative glimpse at the future than anything a later reader can use to predict dates of specific events, but it is enough to serve its purpose: comfort and encouragement in spite of present suffering."

short" (Matt 24:15-16, 21-22).[52] Jesus' words were partly fulfilled when the Romans destroyed the temple in Jerusalem in A.D. 70, but they await further fulfillment "at the time of the end," when the Antichrist will seek to annihilate the church of Christ (2 Thess 2:4, 9-10).

On the island of Patmos, John received the following vision: "The beast was given a mouth uttering haughty and blasphemous words, and it was allowed to exercise authority for forty-two months. It opened its mouth to utter blasphemies against God, blaspheming his name and his dwelling, that is, those who dwell in heaven. Also it was allowed to *make war on the saints and to conquer them.* It was given authority over every tribe and people and language and nation, and all the inhabitants of the earth will worship it, everyone whose name has not been written from the foundation of the world in *the book of life* of the Lamb that was slaughtered" (Rev. 13:5-8). But God will deliver his people, even raising them from the dead. John describes the day of judgment: "Then I saw a great white throne and the one who sat on it. . . . And I saw the *dead,* great and small, standing before the throne, and books were opened. Also another book was opened, *the book of life.* And the dead were judged according to their works, as recorded in the books. . . . Anyone whose name was not found written in the book of life was thrown into the lake of fire. Then I saw a new heaven and a new earth. . . . Those who conquer will inherit these things, and I will be their God and they will be my children" (Rev. 20:11–21:1, 7).

Promise-Fulfillment

In this vision God promised his persecuted people that "at the time of the end" (11:40) he would raise them from the dead (12:2; cf. 12:13). Further, "those who are wise shall shine like the brightness of the sky" (12:3). These promises found their initial fulfillment in Jesus, whom God raised from the dead and seated at his right hand. They will receive their final fulfillment on the last day when the dead will be raised to life. Jesus himself said, "I am the resurrection and the life. Those who believe in me, even though they die, will live" (John 11:25). Paul wrote, "For since we believe that Jesus died and rose again, even so, through Jesus, God will bring with him those who have died" (1 Thess 4:14). Paul concluded his chapter on the resurrection of Christ and of all people with these words, "Thanks be to God, who gives us the victory through our Lord Jesus Christ" (1 Cor 15:57). John saw "the dead, great and small, standing before the

---

52. Jesus' words in Matthew 24:21 (Mark 13:19) allude to Daniel 12:1. For the similarities between the Old Greek of Daniel and the Greek of Mark 13:19, see Collins, *Daniel,* 110. Jesus' words about those days of suffering being "cut short" seem to reflect Daniel 12:7.

throne. . . . The sea gave up the dead that were in it, Death and Hades gave up the dead that were in them, and all were judged according to what they had done" (Rev. 20:12-13). "Then," Jesus said, "the righteous will shine like the sun in the kingdom of their Father" (Matt 13:43; cf. Phil 3:21).

Typology

Because it is difficult to communicate typology coherently and because it may not advance the theme, it is not likely that we will use the way of typology in the sermon. But for the sake of completeness we note that Daniel here is a type of Jesus Christ. We can see this because there are many analogies as well as escalations between Daniel and Jesus. As Daniel was "greatly beloved" by God (10:19), so was Jesus: "You are my Son, the Beloved" (Mark 1:11). As Daniel was a man of prayer, so was Jesus. As Daniel mourned over Jerusalem (10:2; cf. 9:19), so did Jesus: "Jerusalem, Jerusalem . . . ! How often have I desired to gather your children together . . . , and you would not" (Matt 23:37). Daniel predicted "a time of anguish, such as has never occurred" (12:1); Jesus predicted, "In those days there will be suffering, such as has not been from the beginning of the creation . . ." (Mark 13:19). Daniel spoke of a twofold resurrection from the dead — "some to everlasting life, and some to . . . everlasting contempt" (12:2); Jesus foretold, "The hour is coming when all who are in their graves will hear his voice and will come out — those who have done good, to the resurrection of life, and those who have done evil, to the resurrection of condemnation" (John 5:29; cf. Matt 25:46, "These will go away into eternal punishment, but the righteous into eternal life").

But Jesus is far greater than Daniel. Jesus not only spoke the Word of God but was the Word of God made flesh (John 1:1, 14). Moreover, Jesus was "the Lamb of God who [by his death] takes away the sin of the world" (John 1:29). God promised Daniel that he would raise him from the dead "at the end of the days" (12:13); God actually raised Jesus from the dead before "the end of the days." By his resurrection Jesus opened the door to eternal life for all who believe in him (John 11:25), thus becoming "the first fruits of those who have died" (1 Cor 15:20).

Analogy

In typology (above) we noted several analogies between Daniel and Jesus that could be used in the sermon as a bridge to Jesus in the New Testament. We can also use analogy at the level of Daniel's goal and Jesus' goal. Daniel's goal in writing down this vision was to encourage and comfort God's persecuted people by giving them understanding of God's intent to deliver his people, even from death. Jesus' goal with his preaching was also to encourage and comfort God's people facing persecution. Jesus said, "Truly I tell you, there is no one who has left house or brothers or sisters or mother or father or children or fields, for my sake and for the sake of the good news, who will not receive a hundredfold now in this age — houses, brothers and sisters, mothers and children, and fields *with persecutions* — and in the age to come eternal life" (Mark 10:29-30).

Jesus warned his disciples about the coming persecution: "Brother will betray brother to death, and a father his child, and children will rise against parents and have them put to death; and you will be hated by all because of my name." Jesus gave this warning in order to encourage his disciples, "But the one who endures to the end will be saved" (Matt 10:21-22). Later Jesus again raised the topic of persecution: "They will hand you over to be tortured and will put you to death, and you will be hated by all nations because of my name. . . . But the one who endures to the end will be saved" (Matt 24:9-13). Again, Jesus said, "In the world you face persecution. But take courage; I have overcome the world" (John 16:33).

Longitudinal Themes

We can trace through Scripture the theme of the persecution of God's people from the exile in Babylon to the rebuilding of the temple in Jerusalem, to the persecution by Antiochus IV, to the persecution of Jesus and the early church, to the end-time persecution by the Antichrist (see Chapter 8 above, "Redemptive-Historical Progression," pp. 265-67). We can also restrict our focus to the Antichrist in Daniel 11:36–12:1 and trace this figure through the Scriptures to the New Testament (see Chapter 7 above, "Longitudinal Themes," pp. 230-31).

It is also possible to trace the theme of spiritual warfare in the heavenly places and its impact on the kingdom of God breaking into this world. One can trace this theme from the angel being opposed by and fighting the demon prince of Persia (Dan 10:13) and the demon prince of Greece (10:20) to Jesus being tempted by Satan (Matt 4:1-11), to Satan entering Judas (John 13:27), to the cross where Christ "disarmed the rulers and authorities and made a public example of them, triumphing over them in it [the cross]" (Col 2:15), to Satan blocking Paul's way to visit the church in Thessalonica (1 Thess 2:18), to Paul urging Christians to "put on the whole armor of God so that you may be able to stand against the wiles of the devil. For our struggle is not against enemies of blood and flesh, but against the rulers, against the authorities, against the cosmic powers of this present darkness, against the spiritual forces of evil in the heavenly places" (Eph 6:11-12; cf. 1 Pet 5:8), to the final defeat of Satan and his demons at "the end, when he [Christ] hands over the kingdom to God the Father, after he has destroyed every ruler and every authority and power" (1 Cor 15:24). However, since this important topic is not the theme of this final vision, preachers could consider a separate topical sermon on this subject after concluding the series on Daniel's visions.[53]

New Testament References

The appendix to the Greek New Testament lists forty New Testament references or allusions to verses in Daniel 10:1–12:4 — many in Revelation, the apocalyptic book of the New Testament. Some of these references were used above to support the other five ways to Christ in the New Testament. Two other listed passages as well as others from Revelation may be considered for use in the sermon. The first is 2 Thessalonians 2:4-10, which reflects Daniel's (11:36) language:

> He [the Man of Lawlessness] opposes and exalts himself above every so-called god or object of worship, so that he takes his seat in the temple of God, declaring himself to be God. . . . And you know what is now restraining him, so that he may be revealed when his time comes. For the mystery of lawlessness is already at work, but only until the one who now restrains it is removed. And then the lawless one will be revealed, whom the Lord Jesus will destroy with the breath of his mouth, annihilating him by the manifestation of his coming. The coming of the lawless one is apparent in the working of Satan, who uses all power, signs, lying wonders, and every kind of wicked deception for those who are perishing, because they refused to love the truth and so be saved.

The second is Revelation 20:12: "I saw the dead, great and small, standing before the throne, and books were opened. Also another book was opened, the book of life."

Other references include Revelation 11:15-18 (quoted on pp. 390-91 below), and Revelation 12:12, after Michael and his angels defeated Satan and his angels in heaven and threw them down to the earth:

> Rejoice then, you heavens
>   and those who dwell in them!
> But woe to the earth and the sea,
>   for the devil has come down to you

---

53. For some helpful hints, see Lucas, *Daniel*, 298-300.

with great wrath,
    because he knows that his time is short!

Also Revelation 20:7-10:

> When the thousand years are ended, Satan will be released from his prison and will come out to deceive the nations at the four corners of the earth, Gog and Magog, in order to gather them for battle. . . . They marched up over the breadth of the earth and surrounded the camp of the saints and the beloved city. And fire came down from heaven and consumed them. And the devil who had deceived them was thrown into the lake of fire and sulfur, where the beast and the false prophet were, and they will be tormented day and night forever and forever.

Sermon Theme, Goal, and Need

We formulated the textual theme as, "Our sovereign God, who controls even the details of human history, will deliver his people from the extreme persecution of the final days, even raising them from the dead and exalting them in his glorious kingdom." Since the New Testament confirms this message, the textual theme could become the sermon theme. But since it is too complicated to be memorable, we shall shorten it for the sermon theme: *Our sovereign God will deliver his people from the extreme persecution of the final days, even raising them from the dead and exalting them in his glorious kingdom.*

Daniel's goal can also become the goal for this sermon: *to encourage and comfort God's persecuted people by giving them understanding of God's intent to deliver his people, even from death.* This goal shows that the need addressed directly is the discouragement and fatigue that sets in when people are severely persecuted. But it will also address people who are discouraged and fatigued by the hardships encountered living east of Eden.

Scripture Reading

We noted above that one of the problems in preaching on Daniel's final vision, even restricting it to Daniel 10:1–12:4, is its length. Reading this entire, complicated passage before the sermon would only lead to information overload. One option for Scripture reading would be to read only Daniel 10:1–11:2a before the sermon and informing the congregation that some of the remaining verses will be incorporated into the sermon itself. Another option is to read Daniel 10:1 for the setting, 10:20-21 for explaining the structure of these chapters, and finally 12:1-4 for the climax.[54]

The main issue is how to handle chapter 11 with all its historical details. Since one cannot explain all these details without stalling the sermon, one can either explain a few early verses and then skip to Antiochus IV (11:21) or skip to the Antichrist (11:36). For the sake of a complete exposition, the "Sermon Exposition" below will cover every verse of chapter 11 interspersed with brief comments, but for an actual sermon, one will have to *select a few* of the explanations that contribute most powerfully to the development of the theme. The main thing is not that the congregation knows *who* is who in chapter 11, but *why* Daniel provides all these details, namely, to show that Israel's sovereign God controls even the details of history. Once the reason for these details is communicated, one can illustrate it with a few examples from chapter 11 and then move on to the focal point, "the time of the end," chapters 11:36–12:4.

Sermon Exposition

In the sermon introduction one could highlight the need addressed by giving a current example of the discouragement God's people feel because they are suffering, transition to the discouragement of Israel in exile, and begin the exposition of this passage. But since time is of the essence, I would keep the sermon introduction very short in order to begin the exposition of the text as quickly as possible. The need addressed will become evident as soon as we get to Daniel's mourning in verse 2.

Daniel has been in exile in Babylon for nearly seventy years. God had given him three visions about the future. In this final vision God reveals especially what is to come at the end of time. Daniel 10:1, "In the third year of King Cyrus of Persia[55] a word was revealed to Daniel, who was named Belteshazzar. The word was true, and it concerned a great conflict. He understood the word, having received understanding in the vision."[56] "A word[57] was revealed to Daniel,"

---

54. In his sermon series on Daniel, my proofreader Ryan Faber read these verses, "moving through them with a short explanation of the chapters' structure."

55. "The use of the title 'king of Persia' here is probably a deliberate literary ploy, preparing the way for 10:13, 20; 11:2. The Persian period is the starting-point for the prophetic survey of history that is to follow." Lucas, *Daniel*, 274.

56. "The introductory summary here ["he understood the word"] anticipates the end of the revelatory process, not Daniel's initial reaction." Collins, *Daniel*, 372. Steinmann, *Daniel*, 496, observes that Daniel "now 'understood' the message which had been revealed to him progressively in four visions and that he acquired this understanding 'in the vision' itself, referring to this fourth vision."

57. "The message in chapters 10–12 is partly visionary (seen) and partly verbal (heard), so it

that is, *God* revealed a word to Daniel. And that word concerned "a great conflict."[58] God's final revelation to Daniel is about a great war that will take place.

Daniel received this fourth vision "in the *third* year of King Cyrus." In his *first* year King Cyrus had allowed the Jews to return to Jerusalem to rebuild the temple (Ezra 1:1-4). So the remnant that returned had been back in Jerusalem about two years.[59] But what a disappointment! They had come back with high hopes of returning to the Promised Land and rebuilding God's temple. But the Samaritans who lived there opposed their plans and did everything possible to make their lives miserable. We read in Ezra 4:4 that "the people of the land *discouraged* the people of Judah, and made them *afraid* to build." And the work ground to a halt.

Daniel must have heard about these setbacks and does not understand them (cf. 10:12). He seeks an answer from God. As he had fasted and mourned before receiving his third vision (9:3), so here we read in verses 2-3 that he went into a period of mourning: "At that time I, Daniel, had been mourning for three weeks. I had eaten no rich food, no meat or wine had entered my mouth, and I had not anointed myself at all, for the full three weeks." Today we might dress in dark clothes as a symbol of mourning; in those days people would forego items associated with feasting: rich food and wine and oil for moisturizing their body. For three full weeks Daniel was mourning about Jerusalem (cf. Dan 9:19; Neh 1:1-4).

Then, verses 4-6, "On the twenty-fourth day of the first month,[60] as I was standing on the bank of the great river (that is, the Tigris),[61] I looked up and saw a man clothed in linen, with a belt of gold from Uphaz[62] around his waist.

---

can be described both as an auditory 'word' here and as a 'vision' later in 10:1." Steinmann, *Daniel*, 488.

58. "The word translated "conflict" in the NRSV normally refers to warfare or an army. The word . . . indicates the basic thrust of the message itself: much warfare was on the way." Redditt, *Daniel*, 168.

59. If the question should be raised why Daniel did not return with the remnant, Jeske, *Daniel*, 185, offers two reasons: "Daniel was a senior citizen in his mid-eighties. . . . Too old for such a long trip, too old for the arduous work of rebuilding a war-torn country. . . . As one of three top officials in the Persian government, Daniel still had opportunity to help his people."

60. Since Daniel had been mourning for twenty-one days, he must have begun his fast on the fourth day of the first month. The Passover would be celebrated on the fourteenth day of that month, followed by the feast of unleavened bread for seven days. "The nearness of the festival days of the Passover, which were to commemorate Israel's deliverance, and the fact that under the present circumstances Israel was far from delivered — all this may have suggested to Daniel to choose this season for his 'mourning.'" Leupold, *Exposition of Daniel*, 447.

61. Since "the great river" was normally understood to be the Euphrates, Daniel here specifies that it was the Tigris. "The Tigris River originated several hundred miles to the north of Babylon and flowed through Babylonia to the Persian Gulf, passing within about twenty miles of the capital." Miller, *Daniel*, 280.

62. Gold from Uphaz "was the finest gold — 24 carat." Lederach, *Daniel*, 230.

His body was like beryl [a yellow gemstone],[63] his face like *lightning,* his eyes like *flaming torches,* his arms and legs like the *gleam* of burnished bronze [all is light about him], and the sound of his words like the roar of a multitude." Everything about this person points to his power and authority. It's the dazzling figure of an angel (see above, pp. 353-54). The angel is probably hovering above the river, where we see him again in a concluding vision in chapter 12.[64] He looked like a man "clothed in linen." White linen was worn by priests as they fulfilled their duties in the temple.[65] It was a sign of holiness. But this was not a priest. It was a heavenly visitor. This becomes clear in the rest of his description. Joyce Baldwin writes, "The translucent precious stone, the flash of lightning, the brilliance of flames and the gleam of polished metal — all convey impressions of the one who appears to Daniel but who is beyond description."[66]

Daniel continues in verse 7, "I, Daniel, alone saw the vision; the people who were with me did not see the vision, though a great trembling fell upon them, and they fled and hid themselves." Daniel alone was privileged to see the vision;[67] his companions did not see it but were aware that something awesome was happening. They fled and hid themselves.

Verse 8, "So I was left alone to see this *great* vision. My strength left me, and my complexion grew deathly pale, and I retained no strength." Daniel is "scared to death" by this vision.[68] Verse 9, "Then I heard the sound of his words; and when I heard the sound of his words, I fell into a trance, face to the ground." "The sound of his words [was] like the roar of a multitude" (10:6). "The sound of his words" bowls Daniel over. He falls, literally, "into a deep sleep," unconscious,[69] "face to the ground."

Verses 10-11, "But then a hand touched me and roused me to my hands and knees. He said to me, 'Daniel, greatly beloved, pay attention to the words that I am going to speak to you. Stand on your feet, for I have now been sent to you' [God had sent the angel to Daniel]. So while he was speaking this word to me, I stood up trembling." The angel touches Daniel and raises him to his

---

63. Miller, *Daniel,* 281.

64. The NIV translation of 12:6, "who was above the waters of the river," is better than the NRSV's "who was upstream." See Keil, *Book of Daniel,* 410, "In chapter 12:6 he appears hovering over the waters of the river, the Tigris. This agrees also with the verse before us [10:5], according to which Daniel, while standing on the banks of the river, on lifting up his eyes beheld the vision."

65. See Exodus 28:5, 39, 42 and Leviticus 16:4. For the linen being bleached white, see Baldwin, *Daniel,* 180.

66. Ibid.

67. "The fact that his companions did not see it [the vision] emphasizes the momentous character of Daniel's experience." Hammer, *Daniel,* 102. Cf. 2 Kings 6:15-17; John 12:29; and Acts 9:3-7.

68. Redditt, *Daniel,* 171.

69. Leupold, *Exposition of Daniel,* 452.

hands and knees. Daniel feels extremely weak; he cannot stand. But the angel orders him to stand on his feet, and slowly he rises to his feet, trembling. Daniel is terrified.

The angel says to him, verse 12, "Do not fear, Daniel, for from the first day that you set your mind to gain understanding and to humble yourself before your God, your words have been heard, and I have come because of your words." From the *first* day of his mourning, fasting, and prayers, God had heard his words and sent this angel with a message for Daniel. But that first day was twenty-one days ago. What happened?

The angel explains in verses 13-14, "But the prince of the kingdom of Persia opposed me twenty-one days. So Michael, one of the chief princes, came to help me, and I left him there with the prince of the kingdom of Persia, and have come to help you understand what is to happen to your people at the end of days. For there is a further vision for those days." The angel was held up for twenty-one days by the prince of the kingdom of Persia, that is, by an evil angel, a mighty demon who influenced the affairs of Persia against God's people (see above, pp. 355-56).

Remember, in his first vision Daniel had seen the human kingdoms as evil beasts coming up one after the other out of the chaotic sea. The first one he saw was a lion. That was Babylon, which took God's people into exile. The second beast looked like a bear. That is Persia. In Daniel's time frame Persia defeated Babylon three years ago. Now the angel says that he was held up for twenty-one days by the demon influencing affairs in Persia. Apparently there was a demon in Persia who opposed God's people. He held up God's messenger so that he could not deliver God's encouraging message for Daniel and for God's people.

We get a glimpse here of a mystery we cannot see with our eyes. We get a glimpse of what is going on behind the scenes of human history. It isn't just political intrigue, alliances, and one powerful kingdom replacing another. There is more going on than meets the eye. In chapter 2 we heard Daniel say that God "changes times and seasons, deposes kings and sets up kings" (2:21). God is involved in powerful human kingdoms' replacing one another. Now we learn more details of what is going on behind the scenes. A demon in Persia held up God's angel. Behind the events taking place in history there is spiritual warfare between demons and angels. This spiritual warfare affects human kingdoms and especially God's people on earth.[70]

70. "There are powerful forces of evil at work in and through the nations and their rulers to defeat and to overthrow the people of God. This may alarm and cause terror when one considers how powerful these demon potentates are. On the other hand, there are still more powerful agents of good at work who, by harmonious cooperation, will prevail over their wicked opponents. So the cause of the kingdom is in good hands, and its success is assured." Leupold, *Exposition of Daniel*, 459-60.

In the New Testament Paul writes to the church in Thessalonica, "We wanted to come to you — certainly I, Paul, wanted to again and again — but Satan blocked our way" (1 Thess 2:18). Satan blocked Paul's way for preaching the good news in Thessalonica. Consequently Paul writes to the church in Ephesus (Eph 6:12), "For our struggle is not against enemies of blood and flesh, but against the rulers, against the authorities, against the cosmic powers of this present darkness, against the *spiritual forces of evil in the heavenly places.*"

In Revelation 12 we read that "war broke out in heaven; *Michael* and his angels fought against the dragon. The dragon and his angels fought back, but they were defeated, and there was no longer any place for them in heaven. The great dragon was thrown down, that ancient serpent, who is called the Devil and *Satan,* the deceiver of the whole world — he was thrown down to the earth, and his angels were thrown down with him. . . . Then the dragon was angry with the woman [who had given birth to the male child], and went off to make war on the rest of her children, those who keep the commandments of God and hold the testimony of Jesus" (Rev. 12:7-9, 17). Ever since Satan was thrown out of heaven, he and his angels have been fighting God's people on earth.

The angel tells Daniel that a powerful demon of Persia had kept him from delivering God's message to Daniel right away. But the even more powerful angel Michael came to help the messenger angel so that he could deliver his message to Daniel.[71] It was an extremely important message for Daniel and God's people. The angel says in verse 14 that he has come "to help you understand what is to happen to your people *at the end of days.* For there is a further vision for those days."

"At the end of days" is, literally, "in the latter part of the days." Most often this phrase "refers to the future as it culminates in the advent of the Messiah and his kingdom."[72] God wants to reveal even more to Daniel about "the end

---

71. "Verse 13 shows that the angels of God have power to counteract and thwart the agents of the Devil. . . . As Hebrews 1:14 asks, 'Are not all angels ministering spirits sent to serve those who will inherit salvation?'" Archer, "Daniel," 125.

72. Steinmann, *Daniel,* 504, who refers to passages such as Numbers 24:14; Isaiah 2:2; Micah 4:1; and Hosea 3:5. He adds, "These OT verses often compress into this phrase the whole span of Christ's first advent, the church age, and his second advent." Cf. Miller, *Daniel,* 286-87; Leupold, *Exposition of Daniel,* 460-61; Young, *Prophecy of Daniel,* 70, 227. Collins, *Daniel,* 161, claims that this phrase "typically refers to some decisive change at a future time," but he also acknowledges that "in other passages the phrase has a more specifically eschatological meaning" while insisting that "an end of the world or of history is not envisaged." However, the context in this final vision with its double resurrection (12:2, 13) does envisage the end of human history and the fullness of the kingdom of God (12:3). See the same phrase (in Aramaic) in Daniel 2:28, the dream vision which also ends with God setting up "a kingdom that shall never be destroyed, nor shall this kingdom be left to another people. It shall crush all these kingdoms and *bring them to an end,* and it shall stand forever" (2:44).

of days" than he did in the three earlier visions. "There is a further vision for those days."[73]

Daniel is overwhelmed by the prospect of hearing this further revelation about "the end of days." He reports in verse 15, "While he was speaking these words to me, I turned my face toward the ground and was speechless." And for the second time the angel has to touch him, this time to give him back his speech. Verses 16-17, "Then one in human form touched my lips, and I opened my mouth to speak, and said to the one who stood before me, 'My lord, because of the vision such pains have come upon me that I retain no strength. How can my lord's servant talk with my lord? For I am shaking, no strength remains in me, and no breath is left in me.'" Daniel's pain is so severe that he uses a word for pain that is also used for birth pangs. He also complains of shaking, extreme weakness, and being unable to breathe. He is not at all ready to hear God's revelation about "the end of days."

But the angel does not give up. It is of vital importance that Daniel receive and record God's message. So for a third time the angel touches Daniel: verses 18-19, "Again one in human form touched me and strengthened me. He said, 'Do not fear, greatly beloved, you are safe.[74] Be strong and courageous!'" Daniel reports, "When he spoke to me, I was strengthened and said, 'Let my lord speak, for you have strengthened me.'" Finally Daniel is ready to hear God's message about "the end of days."[75]

In the next few verses the angel artfully weaves together the reason for his coming to Daniel and his battle against national demons.[76] He begins in verse 20 with a rhetorical question, "Do you know why I have come to you?[77] Now I must return to fight against the prince of Persia, and when I am through with him, the prince of Greece will come." Again we get a glimpse of what is going on behind the scenes. As soon as he has delivered his message, he must quickly return to fight the demon acting upon Persia. That battle will "continue for two centuries of Persian rule (539-331 B.C.). This struggle . . . [will involve] all of the

---

73. Cf. Habakkuk 2:3, "There is still a vision for the appointed time; it speaks of the end, and does not lie."

74. Literally, "Peace to you." "Generally the initial salutation in the O.T., e.g., in the address of letters [Dan] 3:31 [4:1], 6:26, etc. . . . The following verbs, 'Be strong and stout!' . . . are the usual form of farewell. . . . Thus the Alpha and Omega of friendly greetings are given in these phrases. . . . The seer forthwith is fully emboldened to receive the revelation." Montgomery, *Book of Daniel*, 414-15.

75. "The amount of detail given in connection with the repeated strengthening of the prophet serves the purpose of reminding all readers that the impending revelation must be of a most unusual and important character." Leupold, *Exposition of Daniel*, 464.

76. See the chiastic structure of verses 10:20–11:2a on p. 351 above.

77. "Because the angel has already stated the purpose of his coming in v. 14, the question here is rhetorical." Collins, *Daniel*, 376.

decisions and relationships pertaining to the Jews during the Persian period (e.g., the reconstruction of the temple, deliverance for the Jews during the time of Esther, permission for Ezra and Nehemiah to return, and their subsequent construction of the city)."[78] After Persia, another beast will come up out of the sea, the kingdom of Greece. That kingdom will also be influenced by a demon seeking to harm God's people. So the angel must next fight that demon to make sure God's people are not annihilated. The fact that the angel has momentarily left this critical battle underscores the importance of his message.

Verse 21, "But I am to tell you what is inscribed in the book of truth." "The book of truth," apparently, is God's register of what will happen in the future.[79] As we'll see in chapter 11, it's a very detailed account.[80] But before the angel relates this future, he comes back one more time to the battle being fought in the heavenly places. He says in chapters 10:21b and 11:1, "There is no one with me who contends against these princes except Michael, your prince. As for me, in the first year of Darius the Mede,[81] I stood up to support and strengthen him," that is, to strengthen Michael. Two years earlier Michael and this angel had worked together to protect God's people. At that time this angel had helped out Michael when God's people were oppressed by the evil Babylonian king Belshazzar. That king was killed, "and Darius the Mede received the kingdom" (5:31). "The heavenly war with the prince of Persia began at that time. As soon as God moved Darius/Cyrus to fulfill his gracious prom-

---

78. Miller, *Daniel*, 288. Cf. Keil, *Book of Daniel*, 419, "The plural ["kings of Persia" in 10:13b, Heb.] denotes that, by the subjugation of the demon of the Persian kingdom, his influence not merely over Cyrus, but over all the following kings of Persia, was brought to an end, so that the whole of the Persian kings became accessible to the influence of the spirit proceeding from God and advancing the welfare of Israel."

79. "As a prelude to the historical narrative in 11:2-39, the reference to the Book of Truth points to God's control of history. God is understood as having everything under his control. It is as if everything is written down in his record, both the past and the future. History must inevitably move in the direction of its divinely planned climax." Hammer, *Daniel*, 103. See, e.g., Psalm 139:16, "Your eyes beheld my unformed substance. In your book were written all the days that were formed for me, when none of them as yet existed."

80. The amount of detail bothers some theologians. Towner, *Daniel*, 154, calls this view "a theological liability" which somehow has to be "transcended." But Daniel has been stressing all along the sovereignty of God. Would a sovereign God not know the details of what will happen in the future? Longman, *Daniel*, 252-53, observes "that the people contemporary with this book and throughout most periods of history are the oppressed people of God, who see no human escape from oppression. The fact that God has scripted history and that the rescue of his people is the punch line is cause for great optimism and celebration."

81. "Dan 6:1 (ET 5:31) is the only other place in the book where the phrase 'Darius the Mede' occurs." Steinmann, *Daniel*, 506, n. 34. Interestingly, "The Septuagint has the name 'Cyrus the Persian' here [11:1] instead of 'Darius the Mede.'" Stefanovic, *Daniel*, 391. Cyrus and Darius are probably two names for the same king (see p. 169, n. 79 above).

ise to return his people to Jerusalem and rebuild the temple, the devil and his angels began a war to impede God's plan."[82] But now the angel informs Daniel that he will return to continue the fight against the demon of Persia (10:20), checking the power of evil that is "making life so miserable for the returned exiles."[83]

So Daniel now knows, and through him his readers know, that the future events the angel will reveal are influenced by this battle between God's angels and national demons.[84] The angel continues in chapter 11:2, "Now I will announce the truth to you.[85] Three more kings shall arise in Persia. The fourth shall be far richer than all of them, and when he has become strong through his riches, he shall stir up all against the kingdom of Greece." The angel begins with the Persian kingdom, the time in which Daniel is now living. The three kings after Cyrus are Cambyses, Smerdis, and Darius I.[86] The fourth king, then, is Xerxes I (486-465 B.C.), also known as Ahasuerus, the king who selected the Jewish orphan Esther as queen of Persia. He was superrich. He spent four years stirring up "all against the kingdom of Greece," attacking it with an army of, reportedly, a million men. Although he was defeated at the battle of Salamis (479 B.C.), his attack so angered the Greeks that more than a hundred years later (331 B.C.) they would invade Persia.[87]

---

82. Steinmann, *Daniel*, 506. Cf. Miller, *Daniel*, 290, "Cyrus released the Jews, but unknown to the Persian monarch angelic forces played a part in this decision." Cf. Harman, *Study Commentary on Daniel*, 261, "The dating suggests that the struggle had to do with the return of the Jews to Palestine, which was part of God's purpose in the historical development of his kingdom on earth." Cf. Leupold, *Exposition of Daniel*, 468.

83. Jeske, *Daniel*, 194.

84. "So the prophet is apprized of some of the undercover movements in history but also of the type of checking that God employs to keep them within proper bounds." Leupold, *Exposition of Daniel*, 466. Cf. Portier-Young, *Apocalypse against Empire*, 241, "The true word Daniel receives reframes his vision so that he sees the terrible battles to come within the context of a greater cosmic battle, waged in heaven, in which God's own armies fight on behalf of God's persecuted people. . . . When they learn that heaven's army fights on their behalf and that God has determined for them a favorable outcome, they will gain courage and strength in their own struggle to remain faithful."

85. Leupold, *Exposition of Daniel*, 476, comments, "We believe that the emphasis of this statement lies, not on the fact that it is truth and not a lie which he purposes to offer, but rather on this, that the things he foretells will truly come to pass. Therefore we have translated as Luther also does, 'I shall show thee what shall surely come to pass.'"

86. "It is a matter of historical record that the three kings who ruled between Cyrus and Xerxes I were Cambyses (530-522), Smerdis (pseudo-Serdis or Gaumata; 522), and Darius I Hystaspes (522-486)." Miller, *Daniel*, 291. See also Steinmann, *Daniel*, 518-19 and his list (n. 4) of commentators who identify the fourth king as Xerxes.

87. There were more Persian kings after Xerxes, but the angel moves straight to Greece. Goldingay, *Daniel*, 294-95, suggests that "three . . . and the fourth" recalls wisdom's 'graduated numerical saying' in, for example, Prov. 30 and Amos 1–2. . . . Thus the figure 'four' may need

The angel now moves on to that next empire, the kingdom of Greece. Verses 3-4, "Then a warrior king shall arise, who shall rule with great dominion and take action as he pleases. And while still rising in power, his kingdom shall be broken and divided toward the four winds of heaven, but not to his posterity, nor according to the dominion with which he ruled; for his kingdom shall be uprooted and go to others besides these." We meet again Alexander the Great (see Dan 7:6; 8:5-8, 21), whose star rose quickly so that he conquered the Persian Empire and ruled most of the then-known world. But he died at age thirty-two, his sons were murdered, and his kingdom was divided into four parts, each part ruled by one of his generals.

From here on the angel concentrates on the kings of the south, that is, Egypt, and the kings of the north, that is, Syria.[88] The Promised Land lay between these two powers, and God's people would be severely affected by their exploits. In Daniel 11:5-35 we read the detailed predictions of the political intrigue, the alliances, and the seesawing battles between the kings of the south and the kings of the north. The balance of power flows back and forth, and Judah and Jerusalem are caught in the middle. The point is that all these alliances and seesawing battles take place under the control of Israel's almighty God.[89] God controls even minute developments in human history. For example, in verse 6 we read, "After some years they shall make an alliance, and the daughter of the king of the south shall come to the king of the north to ratify the agreement." Historians tell us that this refers to the marriage of Berenice, daughter of Ptolemy II of Egypt, to Antiochus II of Syria. The point is that our sovereign God is in control not only of the broad sweep of history but also its details. As Jesus said, "Even the hairs of your head are all counted" (Matt 10:30).

*　　*　　*

(For the sake of complete exposition I will quote below every verse of Daniel 11:5-35 interspersed with brief explanations in brackets. In an actual sermon I would skip over most of this chapter because the congregation cannot absorb all this information orally.

---

not to be pressed, nor the kings specifically identified; the phrase may denote the Achemenids as a whole." Cf. Baldwin, *Daniel,* 185.

88. Commentators are in general agreement on the identity of the different kings mentioned. See the chart on p. 352, n. 18 above. Cf. Keil, *Book of Daniel,* 433-50; Montgomery, *Book of Daniel,* 427-45; Leupold, *Exposition of Daniel,* 480-93; Goldingay, *Daniel,* 295-99; Collins, *Daniel,* 378-82; Miller, *Daniel,* 292-97; Lucas, *Daniel,* 280-83, and Steinmann, *Daniel,* 520-25.

89. "One empire after another exercises dominion over God's people. Yet God is in control and responds to the prayers of the faithful, like Daniel. His people will survive. God knows what will happen, since the events are already written in the book of truth (10:21)." Lederach, *Daniel,* 234.

While the identities of all these kings are of little benefit to the hearers, it is important to communicate the point that God is in control even of the details of all these historical events.)

Daniel 11:5-6, "Then the king of the south shall grow strong, but one of his officers shall grow stronger than he and shall rule a realm greater than his own realm. [That officer was the first Seleucid king; he was forced to take refuge in Egypt, then returned to Syria and gained control of more territory than the king of Egypt controlled.][90] After some years they shall make an alliance, and the daughter of the king of the south shall come to the king of the north to ratify the agreement. But she shall not retain her power, and his offspring shall not endure. She shall be given up, she and her attendants and her child and the one who supported her. [This prediction was fulfilled in an alliance between the two kings which was sealed with the daughter of the king of Egypt marrying the king of Syria; their son would then become heir to the throne. The king, his new wife, and their son were all murdered.]"[91]

Verses 7-9, "In those times a branch from her roots [i.e., her brother in Egypt] shall rise up in his [father's] place. He shall come against the army and enter the fortress of the king of the north [the Seleucid capital Antioch], and he shall take action against them and prevail. Even their gods, with their idols and with their precious vessels of silver and gold, he shall carry off to Egypt as spoils of war.[92] For some years he shall refrain from attacking the king of the north; then the latter shall invade the realm of the king of the south, but will return to his own land."

Verses 10-13, "His sons [i.e., the sons of the king of Syria] shall wage war and assemble a multitude of great forces, which shall advance like a flood and pass through, and again shall carry the war as far as his fortress [probably Egypt;[93] at this time Palestine came under the control of the king of Syria]. Moved with rage, the king of the south shall go out and do battle against the king of the north, who shall muster a great multitude, which shall, however, be defeated by his enemy.[94] When the multitude has been carried off, his heart shall be exalted, and he shall overthrow tens of thousands, but he

---

90. This officer was Seleucis I Nicator. For details, see Miller, *Daniel*, 293, and Steinmann, *Daniel*, 523.

91. For details, see, e.g., Miller, *Daniel*, 293.

92. "This is the only verse in which 'Egypt' occurs for 'the south' in the Hebrew text. The Septuagint has it also in vv. 5, 6, 9, 11, 14, 15, 19, 40." Leupold, *Exposition of Daniel*, 484. Leupold also mentions here Jerome's report "that there was a sum of 40,000 talents of silver involved and 2,500 idol statues."

93. Collins, *Daniel*, 379, argues that "the referent is Egypt itself (compare the 'stronghold' of the king of the north in 11:7)." Steinmann, *Daniel*, 523, thinks that it probably means "that Antiochus [III] was 'stirred up as far as his [the king of Egypt's] fortress' (cf. 'the temple fortress' in 11:31)." In any event, during the reign of Antiochus III "Palestine fell under Seleucid control." Miller, *Daniel*, 294.

94. "According to Polybius [*Histories* 5.79], Ptolemy's [IV] forces consisted of 70,000 infantry, 5,000 cavalry, and 73 elephants; whereas Antiochus's [III] army had 62,000 infantry, 6,000 cavalry, and 102 elephants. When the battle ended [in 217 B.C.], Ptolemy had won a great victory over the Syrians at Raphia (located in Palestine)." Miller, *Daniel*, 295.

shall not prevail. For the king of the north shall again raise a multitude, larger than the former, and after some years he shall advance with a great army and abundant supplies."

Verses 14-19, "In those times many shall rise against the king of the south. The lawless among your own people [probably Jews siding with Syria] shall lift themselves up in order to fulfill the vision, but they shall fail.[95] Then the king of the north [Antiochus III] shall come and throw up siegeworks, and take a well-fortified city [probably Sidon, on the coast of the Mediterranean].[96] And the forces of the south shall not stand, not even his picked troops, for there shall be no strength to resist. [The siege resulted in a famine so that the troops had no strength.][97] But he [i.e., Antiochus III, the king of Syria] who comes against him shall take the actions he pleases, and no one shall withstand him. He shall take a position in the beautiful land [i.e., Palestine], and all of it shall be in his power.[98] He shall set his mind to come with the strength of his whole kingdom, and he shall bring terms of peace and perform them. In order to destroy the kingdom [of Egypt], he shall give him a woman [his own daughter] in marriage; but it shall not succeed or be to his advantage [because the daughter loved her husband, the king of Egypt, more than her father, the king of Syria].[99] Afterward he shall turn to the coastlands [the Greek islands and Thrace], and shall capture many. But a commander [the Roman commander Scipio] shall put an end to his insolence; indeed, he shall turn his insolence back upon him. [The king of Syria became a vassal to Rome.][100] Then he shall turn back toward the fortresses of his own land, but he shall stumble and fall, and shall not be found. [He was killed by a mob as he was robbing a temple for his tribute money for Rome.]"[101]

---

95. Commentators disagree on the identity of "the lawless ones" and "the vision." See Goldingay, *Daniel*, 297-98. Cf. Collins, *Daniel*, 379-80; Lucas, *Daniel*, 281-82; and Steinmann, *Daniel*, 524. Baldwin, *Daniel*, 187-88, comments, "For the first time reference is made to the reaction of Jews, in whose land much of this military activity must necessarily take place. Some among them will side with the invader against the Egyptians, under whose control they would have been living. They are 'the men of violence' (lit. 'sons of violence,' 'revolutionaries') with an ideology, 'vision' (*ḥāzôn*); whether or not this vision is inspired by a prophet of the Lord, their method of achieving it certainly is not, and their efforts will fail." Cf. Miller, *Daniel*, 295.

96. See Lucas, *Daniel*, 282. Cf. Montgomery, *Book of Daniel*, 439, who argues for Gaza.

97. "There shall be no strength to resist" "may refer to the famine caused by the siege; the famine forced Scopas to surrender." Steinmann, *Daniel*, 524.

98. Palestine would now "become a permanent possession of the Syrian Empire. This fact is extremely important because it sets the stage for the reign of terror to follow under the Syrian Greek ruler Antiochus IV Epiphanes." Miller, *Daniel*, 296.

99. See Miller, ibid., and Steinmann, *Daniel*, 524.

100. "Antiochus [III] turned to campaign in the west, taking islands in the Aegean and campaigning in Thrace in 196 BC, fulfilling 11:18. Rome warned him not to attack Greece itself, but Antiochus did not listen and did as he pleased, invading Greece in 192 BC. The Romans and their Greek allies defeated him at Thermopylae in 191. . . . In 188 BC, Antiochus was forced to accept the Treaty of Apamea, in which he became a Roman vassal." Steinmann, *Daniel*, 524-25. Cf. Collins, *Daniel*, 381.

101. "Antiochus [III] met an ignominious death at Elymais in 187 B.C.E., while attempting to sack the temple of Bel in order to get money to pay his tribute to Rome." Collins, *Daniel*, 381.

Verse 20, "Then shall arise in his place one who shall send an official [a tax collector] for the glory of the kingdom; but within a few days he shall be broken, though not in anger or in battle." [This king, Seleucis IV, was poisoned by his tax collector.[102] The intrigue, the political maneuvering, the battles for more and more power, the murders — it's not a pretty picture. But worse is still to come.

The next fifteen verses deal with a single king of Syria].[103] Verse 21, "In his place shall arise *a contemptible person* on whom royal majesty had not been conferred; he shall come in without warning and obtain the kingdom through intrigue. Verse 22 predicts, "Armies shall be utterly swept away and broken before him, and the prince of the covenant as well. [The "prince of the covenant" probably refers to the former high priest Onias III, who will be assassinated at Antiochus's court around 171 B.C.][104]"

Verses 23-24, "And after an alliance is made with him, he shall act deceitfully and become strong with a small party.[105] Without warning he shall come into the richest parts of the province [presumably to plunder their treasures][106] and do what none of his predecessors had ever done, lavishing plunder, spoil, and wealth on them [i.e., on his followers]. He shall devise plans against strongholds [such as Egypt], but only for a time [i.e., "the time decreed by God"[107]]."

Verses 25-28 go on to predict Antiochus's campaign against Egypt. "He shall stir up his power and determination against the king of the south with a great army, and the king of the south shall wage war with a much greater and stronger army. But he [the king of Egypt] shall not succeed, for plots shall be devised against him by those who eat

---

102. See Lucas, *Daniel*, 283.

103. Baldwin, *Daniel*, 192, suggests that so much space is devoted to Antiochus IV because "he attempts to unify his kingdom by imposing a particular ideology. Nebuchadnezzar had attempted this on one occasion (chapter 3); a ruler was coming who would make religion his main tool in imposing his will, and so would precipitate a conflict between commitment to the one God, revealed to his people, and the worldly-wise, unscrupulous way of life advocated by diplomacy. In the unequal struggle God's faithful servants would go through intense suffering. The era of the persecution of 'the church' had begun."

104. Calvin, *Commentaries on Daniel*, II, 307, thought it referred to Ptolemy Philometor. So also Miller, *Daniel*, 299. But Young, *Prophecy of Daniel*, 242, objects: "This does not seem adequately to describe the relations between Antiochus and Ptolemy. Furthermore, we should expect Ptolemy to be called the king of the South." Most modern scholars identify "the prince of the covenant" with the former high priest Onias III, who was removed from office around 175 B.C. and assassinated at Antiochus's court around 171 B.C. See Montgomery, *Book of Daniel*, 451. So also, e.g., Baldwin, *Daniel*, 192; Lacocque, *Book of Daniel*, 226; Lucas, *Daniel*, 284, and Longman, *Daniel*, 278. Collins, *Daniel*, 382, states that this identification "is universally accepted by modern scholars, although the reference anticipates a slightly later point in Antiochus's reign."

105. The "small party" refers to "those Jewish people in Jerusalem and Judea who apostatized from God and the true faith, and aided and abetted Antiochus." Steinmann, *Daniel*, 526. Cf. Redditt, *Daniel*, 181, "The recipients of the booty are the Judean Hellenizers who aligned themselves with Antiochus."

106. See Steinmann, *Daniel*, 527.

107. Young, *Prophecy of Daniel*, 242.

of the royal rations. [His Egyptian advisors would give him bad advice.][108] They shall break him, his army shall be swept away, and many shall fall slain. The two kings, their minds bent on evil, shall sit at one table and exchange lies.[109] But it shall not succeed, for there remains an end at the time appointed. [Their evil plan will not succeed because God has another plan.][110] He shall return to his land with great wealth [stolen from God's temple],[111] but his heart shall be set against the holy covenant [i.e., against the people who have a covenant relationship with God].[112] He shall work his will [kill people without mercy],[113] and return to his own land."

Verses 29-30 describe Antiochus's second campaign against Egypt: "At the time appointed [by God] he shall return and come into the south, but this time it shall not be as it was before. For ships of Kittim [Cyprus][114] shall come against him, and he shall lose heart and withdraw. [On these ships was a delegation from Rome which intercepted Antiochus near Alexandria and demanded that he leave Egypt. When he played for time, the Roman "envoy drew a circle around him in the sand and insisted that he give his answer before he left the circle."[115] Antiochus was thoroughly humiliated, but knowing the strength of Rome (he had been a prisoner there), he had no choice but to comply. He turned around and took out his anger on God's people in Palestine.]"

Verses 30b-31, "He shall be enraged and take action against the holy covenant [God's people]. He shall turn back and pay heed to those who forsake the holy covenant. [He will listen to the advice of apostate Jews who forsake their covenant with God and support Antiochus's idolatrous, Greek policies.] Forces sent by him shall occupy and profane the temple and fortress. They shall abolish the regular burnt offering and set up the abomination that makes desolate. [They will abolish the regular burnt offering honoring the God of Israel by setting up on the altar of the temple "the abomination," that is, an altar to Zeus (see p. 275, n. 76 above). This action will make the temple "desolate," that is, empty, deserted by God's people.]"

---

108. See Goldingay, *Daniel,* 301, and Steinmann, *Daniel,* 527.

109. Ptolemy VI and Antiochus IV plotted together to wrest control of Egypt from Ptolemy VII. See Miller, *Daniel,* 300.

110. "The repetition of *mô'ēd* ('set time' ['time appointed'], vv. 27, 29, 35; cf. 12:7) underlines the divine control and purpose at work even in the abominations and the suffering of the Antiochene period." Goldingay, *Daniel,* 294.

111. See Collins, *Daniel,* 383.

112. "Animosity against the Jews will break out again, but by using this phraseology 'holy covenant' more than that is implied, for it took two to make a covenant and God's initiation of it made any opponent anti-God." Baldwin, *Daniel,* 193.

113. "The Hebrew idiom has no object, but knowing the sort of character he was, the reader finds the silence ominous." Ibid.

114. "'Kittim' derives from the name of a city, Citium, on the south coast of Cyprus. According to Josephus (*Ant.* 1.6.1), the term came to be used 'for all islands and most maritime countries.'" Lucas, *Daniel,* 286. Cf. Redditt, *Daniel,* 183.

115. Collins, *Daniel,* 384. Cf. Steinmann, *Daniel,* 528-29, and Miller, *Daniel,* 300-301. Goldingay, *Daniel,* 301, calls this "a turning point in Roman history, a mark of the extent to which internationally the period from 200 to 150 is the story of the extension of Roman dominion in the Hellenistic empire."

Verses 32-35, "He shall seduce with intrigue those who violate the covenant [the apostate Jews]; but the people who are loyal to [who know] their God shall stand firm and take action. [They shall resist the imposed idolatrous policies.] The wise among the people [i.e., Israelites who know God's Word and ways][116] shall give understanding to many; for some days, however, they shall fall by sword and flame, and suffer captivity and plunder. [Thousands of faithful Jews will be killed and thousands of others carried away into slavery, but the persecution will last only a short time — "for some days."] When they fall victim, they shall receive a little help,[117] and many shall join them insincerely. Some of the wise shall fall, so that they may be refined, purified, and cleansed,[118] until the time of the end,[119] for there is still an interval until the time appointed [by God for the persecution to end]."

Russell observes that these detailed predictions in chapter 11 make "for dull reading, but for Daniel it declares with absolute certainty that, despite all indications to the contrary, God is in control of the affairs of men and will deliver his people from the hands of their oppressors."[120]

---

116. Lucas, *Daniel*, 287, "'The wise' are, no doubt, a group who are well versed in the Jewish Scriptures and who, on this basis, have an 'understanding' of God's ways in history and so of how to respond in the current situation of crisis." See ibid., 288-89. Cf. Baldwin, *Daniel*, 196, "The wise are the people who know their God (v. 32), who turn many to righteousness (12:3), who have understanding (12:10). It is the word 'skillful' in 1:4 and in 1:17, the God-given ability to apply learning." Cf. Portier-Young, *Apocalypse against Empire*, 235, "To 'know God' is to know what God will do, to know that God is sovereign, to know God's commitment to God's people, and to know what God requires of them in turn."

117. "'A little help' is a disparaging way to refer to the support that men will attempt to give." Baldwin, *Daniel*, 196. Cf. Collins, *Daniel*, 386, "The point of the verse is that the *maśkilîm* receive little real help." Keil, *Book of Daniel*, 459, argues that "the help is so named ["little"] in comparison with the great deliverance which shall come to the people of God in the time of the end by the complete destruction of the oppressor." Along with many other commentators, Lucas, *Daniel*, 287, writes that "a little help" may refer to "the activities of the Maccabees. The rest of the verse then may reflect the fact that the strong actions the Maccabees took against those who complied in any way with Antiochus' edict (1 Macc 2:44-47; 3:5-8) led some to join them out of fear rather than out of principle. Equally, this verse may simply mean that few will genuinely share the 'understanding' of 'the wise' and give them wholehearted support."

118. "The purpose of this fiery ordeal that fell upon Israel was to cleanse individuals and the nation as a whole of sinful practices and to strengthen their faith. It also separated the true believers from the unregenerate within the Jewish community." Miller, *Daniel*, 303.

119. Miller, ibid., writes, "In this context, the 'end' that has been 'appointed' by the Lord denotes the termination of Antiochus's persecutions," while Steinmann, *Daniel*, 518, linking it to "the time of the end" in 8:17; 11:40; and 12:4, 9 (see p. 409), argues that it refers "eschatologically to the period of time leading up to the return of Christ."

120. Russell, *Daniel*, 204. Cf. Leupold, *Exposition of Daniel*, 474, "Such prediction ["in minutest detail"] could well, in evil days, serve the purpose of reminding the people of God that all things great and small are under the guiding providence of God, for he both knows what will transpire and has all developments in hand as these things transpire. Such prediction offers no problem to the believer; it offers encouragement to faith."

*   *   *

These predictions of the kings of the north and kings of the south end with a detailed description of a king of the north who will severely persecute God's people. Verse 21 says that there "shall arise *a contemptible person* on whom royal majesty had not been conferred; he shall come in without warning and obtain the kingdom through intrigue." Here we meet Antiochus IV Epiphanes again, the little horn of the second vision who would take away "the regular burnt offering" and overthrow "the place of the sanctuary" (8:11; see 8:9-12, 23-25). The angel calls him "a contemptible person" because he will desecrate God's temple and persecute God's people. Verse 31 describes his contemptible deeds: "Forces sent by him shall occupy and profane the temple and fortress.[121] They shall abolish the regular burnt offering and set up the abomination that makes desolate." These forces will abolish the sacrifices brought to the God of Israel by setting up on top of God's altar "the abomination," that is, a pagan altar to Zeus. This action will make the temple "desolate," that is, empty, deserted by God's people.

The books of Maccabees describe the evil actions of Antiochus in detail:

He concluded that Judaea was in revolt. He therefore marched from Egypt, raging like a wild beast, and began by storming the city. He then ordered his soldiers to cut down without mercy everyone they encountered. . . . It was a massacre of young and old, a slaughter of women and children. . . . There were eighty thousand victims in the course of those three days, forty thousand dying by violence and as many again being sold into slavery. Not satisfied with this, he had the audacity to enter the holiest Temple in the entire world. (2 Macc 5:11-15)

Insolently breaking into the sanctuary, he removed the golden altar and the lampstand for the light with all its fittings, together with the table for the loaves of offering, the libation vessels, the cups, the golden censers, the veil, the crowns, and the golden decoration on the front of the Temple, which he stripped of everything. He made off with the silver and gold and precious vessels, he discovered the secret treasures and seized them, and removing all of these, he went back to his own country, leaving the place a shambles. (1 Macc 1:21-24)

---

121. Goldingay, *Daniel*, 302, suggests that Antiochus, "to strengthen his position in Palestine," developed a fortress near the Temple Mount "from which his forces and members of the Hellenistic city-state could oversee temple and city. . . . The fortress would be a base from which gentile as well as Jewish 'citizens' could enter the shrine of 'their' city, which is effectively taken away from Jews who do not belong to the Hellenistic community (cf. 2 Macc 11:24-25)."

Antiochus's persecution of faithful Jews foreshadows the terrible persecution that will be inflicted on God's people in the end time by an even more evil ruler. Jesus uses Daniel's words in verse 31 about "the abomination that makes desolate" to point to this future persecution of God's people. Jesus says, "So when you see the *desolating sacrilege* standing in the holy place, as was spoken of by the prophet Daniel (let the reader understand), then those in Judea must flee to the mountains. . . . For at that time there will be great suffering, such as has not been from the beginning of the world until now, no, and never will be. And if those days had not been cut short, no one would be saved; but for the sake of the elect those days will be cut short" (Matt 24:15-16, 21-22).[122]

In chapter 11:36 Daniel shifts from the persecutor Antiochus and begins to describe the actions of this end-time Antichrist (see above, pp. 357-60). "The king shall act as he pleases. He shall *exalt himself* and consider himself *greater than any god,* and shall *speak horrendous things against the God of gods.*"[123] In the New Testament Paul uses this verse to describe the Antichrist — he calls him "the Man of Lawlessness." He writes in 2 Thessalonians, "He *opposes and exalts himself above every so-called god* or object of worship, so that he takes his seat in the temple of God, *declaring himself to be God*" (2 Thess 2:4).

The angel predicts in verse 36 that this evil ruler of the final days "shall prosper until the period of wrath is completed, for what is determined shall be done." *God* has determined what shall be done. He will allow the Antichrist to "prosper until the period of wrath is completed." "The period of wrath" is the period of God's wrath on the sinful world.[124] The good news is that the persecution will not go on forever. God has set a limit to the period of wrath. In the New Testament, Jesus also says that "for the sake of the elect those days will be cut short" (Matt 24:22).

Verses 37-38 continue to describe this future Antichrist figure: "He shall pay no respect to the gods of his ancestors, or to the one beloved by women;[125]

---

122. Jesus' words about the "great suffering" (Matt 24:21) allude to Daniel 12:1. Jesus' words about those days of suffering being "cut short" (Matt 24:22) seem to reflect Daniel 12:7, "a time, two times, and half a time."

123. Antiochus did not consider himself greater than any god. In fact, he worshiped the Greek gods and promoted the worship of Zeus in Jerusalem. He even built an altar to Zeus at the Jerusalem temple.

124. "The phrase 'the time of wrath' is a translation of one Hebrew word, *zā'am,* a term that usually denotes the wrath of God (cf. Isa 10:25; 26:20; 30:27; Mal 1:4), and that is the meaning here." Miller, *Daniel,* 307.

125. Those commentators who think this verse still describes Antiochus argue that he paid no respect to the gods of his ancestors or to the god beloved by women, Tammuz-Adonis, which had many female devotees. But there is no historical evidence for his rejection of these gods. See, e.g., Keil, *Book of Daniel,* 463-64. Goldingay, *Daniel,* 304, translates, "the god [sing.] of his fathers" and argues that this refers to Antiochus replacing "Apollo by Zeus as *the* god of the

he shall pay no respect to any other god, for he shall consider himself *greater than all*. He shall honor the god of fortresses instead of these; a god whom his ancestors did not know he shall honor with gold and silver, with precious stones and costly gifts." Instead of the other gods which he has rejected, he shall honor "the god of fortresses." Keil explains, "He will regard no other god, but only war; the taking of fortresses he will make his god; and he will worship this god above all as the means of his gaining world-power."[126] He will honor war "with gold and silver, with precious stones and costly gifts." He will give everything he has to this god. His ancestors did not know this god "because no other king had made war his religion."[127]

Verse 39, "He shall deal with the strongest fortresses by the help of a foreign god [i.e., the god his ancestors did not know: war as religion].[128] Those who acknowledge him he shall make more wealthy, and shall appoint them as rulers over many, and shall distribute the land for a price."[129] To those who acknowledge him as the king of kings he will give land and make them "rulers over many." Thus with warfare and political favors for his supporters, the Antichrist will rapidly gain control of the world.

Verse 40, "At the time of the end [i.e., the last period before the end of time][130] the king of the south shall attack him. But the king of the north shall

---

Seleucid dynasty.... 'The one women love' is then plausibly taken as a god especially favored in Egypt, Adonis or Dionysus, who was slighted by Antiochus through his various encroachments on the southern kingdom." However, Steinmann, *Daniel*, 541, notes that the phrase "'the God of his [or: our, your, their] fathers' occurs forty-five times in the OT and is always a description of Yahweh." He acknowledges that "'the gods of his fathers' ... is grammatically possible, but is unsupported by the rest of the OT, where it always means 'the God of his fathers.'" Ibid., 542, n. 23. Miller, *Daniel*, 307, adds that "the god beloved by women" could be translated as "the one desired by women," which would refer to the Messiah, since Jewish women desired to become the mother of the Messiah. So also Feinberg, *Daniel*, 175. On this reading, the coming Antichrist will pay no respect to God nor to Jesus Christ.

126. Keil, *Book of Daniel*, 466. Cf. Kaiser, *Preaching and Teaching the Last Things*, 128.

127. Ibid. On p. 465, Keil argues that the words "a god whom his ancestors did not know" "in no respect agree with Antiochus, and do not permit us to think on any definite heathen deity," such as Zeus or Jupiter, because his ancestors knew these gods. Cf. Young, *Prophecy of Daniel*, 249, "For religion he will substitute war, and war he will support with all that he has.... This verse does not apply to Antiochus.... The words best apply to the activities of the Antichrist."

128. E.g., Leupold, *Exposition of Daniel*, 518, and Miller, *Daniel*, 308.

129. "The NIV translation interprets the Hebrew as meaning that the distribution of land will involve payment to Antichrist.... It is worth noting that the verb for 'divide,' or 'distribute' (*ḥālaq*, Pi.), is used of God's action in distributing the land of Canaan to Israel (see Josh 13:7; 18:10; 19:51; cf. Ezek 47:21). Antichrist, the great deceiver, will attempt to imitate God." Harman, *Study Commentary on Daniel*, 294-95.

130. "The phrase 'the time of the end' is carefully and consistently reserved for the last period preceding the End (see 11:35, 40; 12:4, 9)." Gooding, "The Literary Structure of the Book of

rush upon him like a whirlwind, with chariots and horsemen, and with many ships. He shall advance against countries and pass through like a flood." It sounds like this will be another battle between the north and the south, just like the many we read about earlier in this chapter. But this is "the time of the end," and the stakes are raised. The king of the north and the king of the south now are symbols of the combatants in the final war that will be waged on earth. The king of the north is the Antichrist. The king of the south probably represents a nation that seeks to protect God's people. The Antichrist will "rush upon him like a whirlwind, with chariots and horsemen, and with many ships." The battle is pictured as being fought with weapons of that time.[131] From our contemporary perspective we understand that the Antichrist will probably have weapons of mass destruction at his disposal.

Verse 41, "He shall come into the beautiful land, and tens of thousands shall fall victim, but Edom and Moab and the main part of the Ammonites shall escape from his power." Here the battle is pictured in terms of ancient geography. Because this will take place in "the time of the end," that is, our future, we need to update these symbols as well. Literally "the beautiful land" is Palestine, the place where God's people lived. After the coming of Christ, God's kingdom is no longer geographically bound. God's people now come from every tribe and nation and are gathered together in his church. So the Antichrist shall attack the church, "and tens of thousands shall fall victim." But, verse 41 predicts, "Edom and Moab and the main part of the Ammonites shall escape from his power." Edom, Moab, and Ammon were the ancient enemies of Israel. Updating these symbols, the Antichrist will not attack the enemies of the church; these nations are his allies.[132]

Verses 42-43, "He shall stretch out his hand against the countries, and the land of Egypt[133] shall not escape. He shall become ruler of the treasures of gold and of silver, and all the riches of Egypt; and the Libyans and the Ethiopians shall follow in his train." Almost nothing can stop the Antichrist. He will con-

---

Daniel and Its Implications," *TynBul* (1981) 75, n. 27. Cf. Steinmann, *Daniel,* 544, and Stefanovic, *Daniel,* 438.

131. "Prophetic visions view the future in terms of the contemporary. The understanding of them requires the recognition of symbolism." Ferguson, *Daniel,* 238.

132. "It should be noted that, at the time of Antiochus, Moab no longer existed as a nation. These three nations were ancient enemies of God's people, the Israelites. They are mentioned here as symbolical representatives of nations which are enemies of God's people and who will escape the wrath of the king of the north." Young, *Prophecy of Daniel,* 252. Cf. Keil, *Book of Daniel,* 471; Leupold, *Daniel,* 521; and Steinmann, *Daniel,* 545.

133. Leupold, *Exposition of Daniel,* 522, states "that Egypt symbolized a major world power." Cf. Young, *Prophecy of Daniel,* 252, "Egypt probably stands as a representative of the powers which will resist the Antichrist."

quer even a major world power such as Egypt was in the past. He will strip it of all its wealth and become superrich. Libya and Ethiopia were located west and south of Egypt. "The idea is that the complete territory of the king of the south comes under the control of the king of the north."[134]

But just as quickly as the Antichrist achieves great power, so quickly will he come to his end. Verse 44, "But reports from the east and the north shall alarm him, and he shall go out with great fury to bring ruin and complete destruction to many." He will seek "to destroy and annihilate many" (NIV).[135] Verse 45, "He shall pitch his palatial tents between the *sea and the beautiful holy mountain*." Literally, this is between the Mediterranean and Mount Zion. Like the other places mentioned such as Egypt and Lybia, we should also understand "between the sea and the beautiful holy mountain" symbolically.[136] "The beautiful holy mountain" is the mountain where God dwells.[137] Today we would say, the church, God's people — that's where God is present in a special way. So the angel here describes the Antichrist's "last desperate assault upon the church."[138]

But just when it looks like the Antichrist will annihilate the church, the end of verse 45 predicts, "Yet he shall come to his end, with no one to help him." "He shall come to his end!" Suddenly! Unexpectedly! But certainly![139] And no one can help him.[140] For it is judgment day. It's the same as the picture God gave in Daniel 7 about the Antichrist: at the end of time "the court shall sit in judgment, and his dominion shall be taken away, to be consumed and totally destroyed" (7:26). In the New Testament, Paul echoes this thought when he writes about "the Man of Lawlessness": "Then the lawless one will be revealed, whom the Lord Jesus will destroy with the breath of his mouth, annihilating him by the manifestation of his coming" (2 Thess 2:8).

Chapter 12:1, "At that time [i.e., "at the time of the end" (11:40) when the Antichrist will seek to annihilate God's people] Michael, the great prince, the

---

134. Stefanovic, *Daniel*, 414.

135. "The word 'annihilate' translates a Hebrew verb *(ḥāram)* used in relation to what happened to the Canaanites when Israel invaded. They were given over irrevocably to destruction.... Antichrist seeks to mimic God's actions and appropriate them to himself, in an attempt to stand in his place." Harman, *Study Commentary on Daniel*, 297-98.

136. "Inasmuch as such names as Egypt, Moab, Edom, Ammon, etc., are employed in these verses in a symbolical sense, so also is this present description employed." Young, *Prophecy of Daniel*, 253.

137. See, e.g., Isaiah 56:7; and Psalms 2:6; 15:1.

138. Leupold, *Exposition of Daniel*, 523.

139. "The verb *bā'*, 'to come,' is used here in the perfect tense, describing an accomplished action that points to the certain fulfillment of the prediction. God's word is as good as done." Stefanovic, *Daniel*, 415.

140. "Since that end is the judgment of God, there 'shall be none to help him.' God's judgments cannot be resisted." Leupold, *Exposition of Daniel*, 524.

protector of your people, shall arise. There shall be a time of anguish, such as has never occurred since nations first came into existence. But at that time your people shall be delivered, everyone who is found written in the book." This verse continues to speak of the end time and the persecution that awaits God's people. "There shall be a time of *anguish*, such as has never occurred since nations first came into existence." This world has seen many wars and disasters, and much anguish. But this final time of anguish the world has never seen. It will be unparalleled. Jesus alludes to these words when he predicts, "At that time there will be great suffering, such as has not been from the beginning of the world until now, no, and never will be" (Matt 24:21).

At that time the archangel Michael, the protector of God's people, shall arise. He will not prevent God's people from undergoing persecution, but he *will* sustain them during the suffering and "deliver them in the midst of it."[141] For verse 1 continues, "But at that time[142] your people shall be delivered, everyone who is found written in the book."[143] These are the people John saw in his vision on the island of Patmos: "These are they who have come out of the great *ordeal*; they have washed their robes and made them white in the blood of the Lamb" (Rev. 7:14).

Even those who died shall be delivered. Verse 2, "Many[144] of those who sleep

141. Baldwin, *Daniel*, 203. Cf. Veldkamp, *Dreams and Dictators*, 241, "The power of God's angels will animate the holy ones in those last days and give them superhuman spiritual power. Just as an angel strengthened Jesus in Gethsemane, his followers will be given strength to drink the cup of suffering when they are being dragged down the road to the cross."

142. "Three times in all the reader is made to hear the sound of a phrase that resounded ominously in the ears of those who lived in desperate days. The very real possibility that these words have a deliberate evocative purpose must not be discounted. For they immediately call to mind the language of Joel 3:1, 18 (RSV); Isa 26:1; 27:1, 2, 12, 13, as well as the frequently occurring 'on that day' in Zechariah 12–14." Anderson, *Signs and Wonders*, 145.

143. "The book in question is undoubtedly the book of life, as distinct from, though related to, the 'books' of judgment in Dan 7:10 and the 'book of truth' of 10:21. The notion of a 'book of life' is well attested in the Hebrew Bible, where it seems to refer to membership of the covenant community." Collins, *Daniel*, 391. Cf. Archer, "Daniel," 150, "This is apparently 'the Book of Life' first referred to in Exodus 32:33 as the roster of professing believers who stand in covenant relationship with God, though apostates among them may have their name removed from this list." Goldingay, *Daniel*, 306, speaks of "a list of those who belong to God's people, the citizen list of the true Jerusalem." See further Psalms 69:28; 87:6; Malachi 3:16; Luke 10:20; Revelation 3:5; 20:12, 15; 21:27.

144. Although Steinmann, *Daniel*, 560, claims that "'many' here simply . . . [signifies] a large number, with no upper limit on how large that number is" (so also Keil, *Book of Daniel*, 481, and Young, *Prophecy of Daniel*, 256), Baldwin, *Daniel*, 204, makes a good case for understanding this word as "all": "Hebrew *rabbîm*, 'many,' tends to mean 'all,' as in Deut 7:1; Isa 2:2, where 'all nations' becomes 'many peoples' in the parallel verse 3; and in Isa 52:14, 15; 53:11, 12, where this key-word occurs no less than five times, with an inclusive significance." Cf. Calvin, *Commentaries on Daniel*, II, 374, "The word 'many' seems here clearly put for all."

in the dust of the earth shall awake, some to everlasting life, and some to shame and everlasting contempt." "Sleeping in the dust of the earth" is a good metaphor for death. It reminds us, first of all, that death is God's punishment for sin ("You are dust, and to dust you shall return"; Gen 3:19). But, second, it reminds us that death is not permanent; we shall awake from this sleep: God's people to "everlasting life" and those who opposed God to "everlasting contempt." This is the clearest verse in the Old Testament teaching the resurrection of the body.[145] Jesus probably had this verse in mind when he said, "The hour is coming when all who are in their graves will hear his [the Son of Man's] voice and will come out — those who have done good, to the resurrection of life, and those who have done evil, to the resurrection of condemnation" (John 5:28-29).[146]

But there is even more good news for God's people. They will not only be raised to everlasting life. Verse 3 states, "Those who are wise shall shine like the brightness of the sky, and those who lead many to righteousness, like the stars forever and ever." "Those who are wise" are the same people as "those who lead many to righteousness."[147] "Those who lead others to righteousness . . . are those who demonstrate their faith and encourage others to faith, and this the humblest believer can do."[148] After their resurrection, they "shall shine like the brightness of the sky"; even more, they shall shine "like the stars forever and ever."[149] Jesus promises a similar outcome for God's people. At "the end of the age," he says, "the righteous will shine like the sun in the kingdom of their Father" (Matt 13:39, 43). The righteous will be exalted in the glorious kingdom of God.

God's people may suffer much in this world. Even today, millions are persecuted for their faith. In the final days, God's people will face the worst persecution ever. But the good news is that even if they are martyred, God will raise them from the dead to everlasting life. Then they shall shine "like the stars forever and ever."

---

145. "This is the first and only unambiguous reference to resurrection from the dead in the OT, although the concept is not entirely foreign to Hebrew thought." Hill, "Daniel," 205. Cf. Collins, *Daniel*, 391-92, "There is virtually unanimous agreement among modern scholars that Daniel is referring to the actual resurrection of individuals from the dead, because of the explicit language of everlasting life." For other Old Testament passages implying a resurrection from the dead, see, e.g., Job 14:12; 19:25-27; Psalms 16:10; 17:15; and Isaiah 25:7; 26:19.

146. Cf. Matthew 25:46, "These will go away into eternal punishment, but the righteous into eternal life."

147. Synonymous parallelism.

148. Baldwin, *Daniel*, 206.

149. "The statement in this verse presents 'a dramatic reversal of destiny' from what is said in Daniel 8:10, where the little horn ascends as high as *the host of heaven*, casts some of the starry host down to earth, and tramples on them. In this way, the ambitious enemy who attempts to reach the stars (Dan 8:10; 11:36, 37) is brought low, whereas those who have fallen (8:10; 11:33-35) are in the end exalted." Stefanovic, *Daniel*, 441.

The angel concludes his message in verse 4, "But you, Daniel, keep the words secret and the book sealed until the time of the end. Many shall be running back and forth, and evil shall increase." The NIV has a better translation here: "But you, Daniel, *roll up* and seal the words of the scroll until the time of the end." Miller explains the process of sealing a scroll: "In the ancient Near East the custom was to 'seal' an important document by impressing upon it the identifying marks of the parties involved and the recording scribe. A sealed text was not to be tampered with or changed. Then the original document was duplicated and placed ('closed up') in a safe place where it could be preserved."[150] The angel, therefore, instructs Daniel not to keep his message secret but to preserve it, especially for those who will need this encouragement and good news at "the time of the end."[151] "It must be on record for God's people so that the events of the end will not take them by surprise."[152]

Verse 4 ends with the prediction, "Many shall be running back and forth, and evil shall increase." This statement seems to be an allusion to Amos 8:12, "They shall run to and fro, seeking the word of the LORD, but they shall not find it."[153] Seeking to find the word of the Lord with their own wisdom and strength, they shall not find it. Instead "evil shall increase"[154] — the evil which will culminate in the Antichrist, who will seek to annihilate God's people. But, as we have seen, God has the last word. When his people's anguish is greatest, he will deliver them by raising them even from death. Then they will "shine like the brightness of the sky . . . , like the stars forever" in God's glorious kingdom.

The last book of the Bible also speaks about this time:

Then the seventh angel blew his trumpet, and there were loud voices in heaven, saying,

---

150. Miller, *Daniel*, 320, who illustrates this process with Jeremiah 32:9-12. Cf. Archer, "Daniel," 153-54. See also Chapter 11, below, n. 16.

151. Note the contrast with Revelation 22:10, where John is told, "Do not seal up the words of the prophecy of this book, for *the time is near.*"

152. Ferguson, *Daniel*, 245.

153. See Young, *Prophecy of Daniel*, 258. So also Collins, *Daniel*, 399.

154. The NIV follows the MT, "Many will go here and there to increase *knowledge.*" The RSV also has "knowledge." The NRSV follows the LXX, with a note, Hebrew *knowledge.* Collins, *Daniel*, 399, observes that the emendation "involves a very common corruption (*r* to *d* [Hebrew *resh* to *daleth*]) and makes better sense of the OG." I would just follow the pew Bible and not make an issue of this detail in the sermon. For those who use the NIV, Miller, *Daniel*, 321, observes, "An 'intense' searching seems indicated by the verb form. The purpose of this search will be 'to increase knowledge.'" Seow, *Daniel*, 190, adds, "The resurrection is an expression of hope that the power of God manifested in the resurrection would enable many to roam about the earth so that 'the knowledge' — surely meaning here the knowledge of God — might increase."

"The kingdom of the *world* has become
    the kingdom of *our Lord and of his Messiah,*
and he will reign *forever and ever.*"
Then the twenty-four elders who sit on their thrones before God fell on
their faces and worshiped God, singing,
    "We give you thanks, Lord God Almighty,
        who are and who were,
    for you have taken your *great power*
        and begun to *reign.*
    The nations raged,
        but *your wrath* has come,
        and the time for judging the dead,
    for *rewarding your servants,*
        the prophets and saints and all who fear your name,
        both small and great,
and for destroying those who destroy the earth." (Rev. 11:15-18)

Be encouraged, then, people of God, to remain faithful to God, even in the fiercest persecution. Our sovereign God is in control of human history to its smallest details. Jesus predicted, "You will be hated by all because of my name. But not a hair of your head will perish. By your endurance you will gain your souls" (Luke 21:17-19). Remain faithful to God! When our need is greatest, God's deliverance is near. Jesus himself encouraged us, "Now when you see these things begin to take place [the signs of the end: "signs in the sun, the moon, and the stars, and on the earth distress among nations confused by the roaring of the sea"], stand up and raise your heads, because *your redemption is drawing near*" (Luke 21:25, 28). Remain faithful to God, and Jesus will remain faithful to you.[155]

---

155. "If you conquer, you will be clothed like them in white robes, and I will not blot your name out of the book of life; I will confess your name before my Father and before his angels" (Rev. 3:5).

CHAPTER 11

Daniel's Concluding Vision
of "the Time of the End"

Daniel 12:5-13

"But you [Daniel], go your way, and rest;
you shall rise for your reward at the end of the days."

Daniel 12:13

This subunit not only concludes the final vision but also the book of Daniel as a whole. This brief passage, therefore, makes an ideal preaching text for wrapping up a sermon series on Daniel. Since it deals with "the time of the end," it also provides the opportunity in the sermon to link up with New Testament eschatological passages.

One challenge in preaching this passage is to come to terms with the three different time frames: "a time, two times, and half a time" (12:7), "one thousand two hundred ninety days" (12:11), and "the thousand three hundred thirty-five days" (12:12). These different numbers have led to much debate and speculation. It is well, however, to take to heart Luther's advice: "Daniel concludes the record of his terrifying visions and dreams on a note of joy, namely with the coming of Christ's eternal reign of glory. . . . Whoever wants to study them profitably dare not focus his attention on the details of the visions and dreams, but will find comfort in the Savior Jesus Christ whom they portray and in the deliverance he brings from sin and its misery."[1]

---

1. Martin Luther, *Sämmtliche Schriften* (St. Louis: Concordia, 1880), quoted by Jeske, *Daniel*, 228.

Text and Context

Because of the length of Daniel's fourth vision, we broke it into its two natural parts as determined by its complex plot. The first part begins in chapter 10:1 and ends at 12:4 with the first conflict about the future of God's people resolved. A new conflict breaks out with Daniel's concluding vision of two more angels (12:5) and one of them asking (12:6), "How long shall it be until the end of these wonders?" In addition, Daniel himself asks (12:8), "My lord, what shall be the outcome of these things?" These issues are resolved when the "man clothed in linen" responds with "a time, two times, and half a time" (12:7) and "Happy [blessed] are those who persevere and attain the thousand three hundred thirty-five days" (12:12). Finally, Daniel is told to "rest; you shall rise for your reward at the end of the days" (12:13). The preaching text is, therefore, Daniel 12:5-13.

The obvious literary context of this passage is Daniel's fourth vision, which began in chapter 10:1 with the chronological marker, "In the third year of King Cyrus of Persia a word was revealed to Daniel." The setting of "the bank of the great river" (10:4) is the same as the setting given in 12:5, the "bank of the stream." The command to Daniel to keep "the book sealed until the time of the end" (12:4) is repeated in 12:9: "the words are to remain . . . sealed until the time of the end." The prediction that "some of the wise shall fall, so that they may be refined, purified, and cleansed" (11:35) is restated in 12:10: "Many shall be purified, cleansed, and refined."

Daniel 12:5-13 also has links with Daniel's prior visions. Daniel by a river overhearing the dialogue between angels about "how long?" (12:5-7) is similar to his overhearing such dialogue about "how long?" by the river Ulai in his second vision (8:13-14). Daniel 12:7 speaks of "the shattering of the power of the holy people" for "a time, two times, and half a time." This prediction harks back to the first vision where the "horn made war with the holy ones and was prevailing over them," and "they shall be given into his power for a time, two times, and half a time" (7:21, 25).

This passage also has several connections with the book of Revelation. The designation "a time, two times, and half a time" (Dan 12:7) is used also in Revelation 12:14, where the woman (the church) is given wings to flee into the desert where she will be "nourished for a time, and times, and half a time." The statement that "many shall be purified, cleansed, and refined, but the wicked shall continue to act wickedly" (Dan 12:10) is similar to Revelation 22:11, "Let the evildoer still do evil, and the filthy still be filthy, and the righteous still do right, and the holy still be holy." Finally, in 12:9 Daniel is told that the words are to remain "sealed until the time of the end." In contrast, John is told, "Do not seal up the words of the prophecy of this book, for the time is near" (Rev. 22:10).

Literary Features

The genre of Daniel 12:5-13 continues to be apocalyptic literature. Collins identifies the forms in this passage as "revelatory dialogue, including a very brief description of the epiphany of the angelic figures."[2] We shall again analyze the structure of this passage, its plot line, character description, and repetition.

Structure

Daniel 12:5-13 is the fourth and concluding scene of the fourth vision:

Scene 4. A concluding vision and dialogue about the end (12:5-13)
  A. A vision of two angels (12:5)
  B. One angel asks, "How long until the end of these wonders?" (12:6)
  C. "The man" responds, "A time, two times, and half a time" (12:7)
  D. Daniel asks, "What shall be the outcome of these things?" (12:8)
  E. Response, "The words are to remain sealed until the time of the end" (12:9)
  F. "Many shall be purified; the wise shall understand" (12:10)
  G. "One thousand two hundred ninety days" (12:11)
  H. "Persevere and attain the thousand three hundred thirty-five days" (12:12)
  I. Daniel shall rise at the end of the days (12:13)
  Characters: an angel and the man clothed in linen; when the angel leaves the stage, he is replaced by Daniel

The Plot Line

Daniel 12:5-13 is the second subplot of the final vision's complex plot. Daniel receives a concluding vision of two angels with "the man clothed in linen." The conflict begins when one of the angels asks the "man," "How long shall it be until the end of these wonders?" (12:6). The "man" swears "by the one who lives forever" that it will be "a time, two times, and half a time," and "when the shattering of the power of the holy people comes to an end" (12:7). Daniel does not understand, and the story reaches a new climax with his question, "What shall be the outcome?" (12:8). Will he get an answer?

The conflict turns to a resolution when Daniel is told to "go your way, for

2. Collins, *Daniel* (1984), 101.

the words are to remain . . . sealed until the time of the end" (12:9). But this does not answer Daniel's question about the outcome. He receives an answer in the following verses, "Many shall be purified . . . , but the wicked shall continue to act wickedly. . . . Those who are wise shall understand. . . . Happy [blessed] are those who persevere" to the end (12:10-12). The tension is resolved. The plot outcome is God's promise to Daniel, "You shall rise for your reward at the end of the days" (12:13).

We can sketch the plot line of Daniel 12:5-13 as follows:

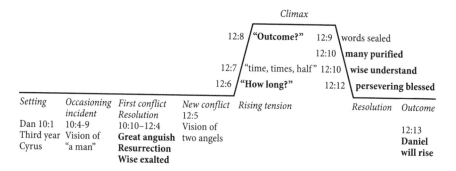

Character Description

Daniel mentions twice that "the man clothed in linen" hovered "above the waters of the river" (12:6, 7; NIV; cf. 10:5).[3] He further describes the "man" as swearing an oath "by the one who lives forever" and raising "his right hand and his left hand toward heaven" (12:7). Daniel describes himself as not understanding and asking the further question about "the outcome" (12:8). Finally, he describes the wise as being "purified, cleansed, and refined," understanding (12:10), and "blessed" (12:12), while the wicked "continue to act wickedly" and shall not understand (12:10).

Repetition

We noted above that Daniel mentions twice that the "man" hovered "above the waters of the river" (12:6, 7), thus emphasizing that this really was not a man but a heavenly being. Daniel is also told twice to "go your way" (12:9, 13), an inclusio that provides unity for the angel's response to Daniel's question (12:9-13). The

---

3. "In chapter 12:6 he appears hovering over the waters of the river, the Tigris. This agrees also with the verse before us [10:5], according to which Daniel, while standing on the banks of the river, on *lifting up his eyes* beheld the vision." Keil, *Book of Daniel*, 410. My emphasis.

phrase "time of the end" (*'et qēṣ*), which was used in 8:17 (the second "vision is for the time of the end") and three times in the first part of this final vision (11:35, 40; 12:4), is used one more time in this passage (12:9). God's promise that "many of those who sleep in the dust of the earth shall awake, some to everlasting life" (12:2), is repeated for Daniel personally, "You shall *rise* for your reward at the end of the days" (12:13). Finally, repetition is used for inverted parallelism in Daniel 12:10[4] with antithetic parallelism between A and B, and between B′ and A′.

A   *Many* shall be purified . . . ,
   B   But the *wicked* shall continue to act wickedly.
   B′ None of the *wicked* shall understand,
A′ But those who are *wise* shall understand.

Theocentric Interpretation

When one of the two angels asks, "How long shall it be until the end of these wonders?" "the man clothed in linen" swears "by the one who lives forever" (12:7), that is, God (cf. Dan 4:34; 6:26; Deut 32:40). The "man" then presents God's answer to this question: "it would be for a time, two times, and half a time . . . when the shattering of the power of the holy people comes to an end, all these things would be accomplished" (12:7). In 12:10 the angel predicts, "Many shall be purified, cleansed, and refined." If these are indeed passives,[5] they can be understood as divine passives, that is, God will purify, cleanse, and refine many (cf. Dan 11:35; Mal 3:2-3). Finally, the angel assures Daniel, "You shall rise for your reward at the end of the days" (12:13). Only God can raise people from the dead.

Textual Theme and Goal

The message of this passage centers on the answers to the two questions, "How long?" (12:6) and "What shall be the outcome?" (12:8). The answer to the first question is, "a time, two times, and half a time," that is, the "time of anguish" (12:1) will last not a perfect time (12:7) but a limited amount of time. The answer to the question "What shall be the outcome?" is that "many shall be purified, cleansed, and refined" (12:10), and "Happy [NIV, "Blessed"] are those who persevere" to the end (12:12). Then the angel assures Daniel, who had perse-

---

4. Stefanovic, *Daniel*, 447, calls this a "chiastic structure," but it is more precise to call it inverted parallelism since it lacks the "climactic centrality." See my *Modern Preacher*, 249.

5. "Despite the Hithp. stem of the first two, all are to be treated like the third (Nif.) as passives (so AV) rather than reflexives (RVV JV)." Montgomery, *Book of Daniel*, 477.

vered throughout his life, "You shall rise for your reward [NIV, "inheritance"] at the end of the days" (12:13).

We could formulate the theme of this passage as, "God promises that his people who persevere during the limited time of the final anguish will be blessed." However, the word "blessed" is too general for the theme. We can make "blessed" more concrete with the words of verse 13, "will rise for their reward at the end of days." But the word "reward" is also too general. What specifically is the "reward," the "inheritance"? It is "everlasting life" (12:2). Therefore we can formulate a succinct theme as follows, *God promises everlasting life to his persecuted people who persevere to the end.*

The goal of this passage is quite obvious. God has just revealed to Daniel that at the end of time God's people will undergo severe persecution for a limited period of time (esp. 11:40–12:1). The goal of this message, therefore, is *to encourage God's persecuted people to persevere to the end, for "at the end of the days" God will give them everlasting life.*

Ways to Preach Christ

Since there is no type of Christ in this passage,[6] we shall explore the remaining six ways to Christ in the New Testament.

Redemptive-Historical Progression

God promises everlasting life to those who persevere to the end. But God's penalty for sin is death: "You are dust, and to dust you shall return" (Gen 3:19). How can those doomed to die receive eternal life? It can come about only because in the fullness of time God would send his Son, Jesus. With his death on the cross Jesus would pay the penalty for sin. With his resurrection three days later Jesus would conquer death for all who believe in him. Jesus said, "This is indeed the will of my Father, that all who see the Son and believe in him may have eternal life" (John 6:40).

Promise-Fulfillment

God promises everlasting life "at the end of the days" to those who persevere to the end. This promise can be fulfilled only through Jesus Christ, who paid the

---

6. Those who identify the "man clothed in linen" as the preincarnate Christ (see pp. 353-54 above) could use a special typology to move to Christ in the New Testament.

penalty for sin and defeated death. Jesus said, "I am the resurrection and the life. Those who believe in me, even though they die, will live" (John 11:25). Paul called Jesus "the first fruits of those who have died. . . . For as all die in Adam, so all will be made alive in Christ. But each in his own order: Christ the first fruits, then at his coming those who belong to Christ" (1 Cor 15:20-23). Paul also wrote, "For since we believe that Jesus died and rose again, even so, through Jesus, God will bring with him those who have died" (1 Thess 4:14).

Analogy

The way of analogy offers another option for preaching Christ from this passage. As Daniel's goal was "to encourage God's persecuted people to persevere to the end," so Jesus also encouraged his followers to persevere to the end. Jesus warned them that they would be "hated by all because of my name. But the one who *endures to the end* will be saved" (Matt 10:22). Later Jesus again raised the topic of persecution: "They will hand you over to be tortured and will put you to death, and you will be hated by all nations because of my name. . . . But the one who *endures to the end* will be saved" (Matt 24:9, 13). From heaven the risen Lord still encouraged his persecuted people: "If you conquer, . . . I will not blot your name out of the book of life; I will confess your name before my Father and before his angels. . . . To the one who conquers I will give a place with me on my throne, just as I myself conquered and sat down with my Father on his throne" (Rev. 3:5, 21).

Longitudinal Themes

We can trace through Scripture the longitudinal theme of the resurrection of the body. In the Old Testament there are several hints of a bodily resurrection. For example, Psalm 17:15 declares, "As for me, I shall behold your face in righteousness; when I awake I shall be satisfied, beholding your face." Job states, "After my skin has been thus destroyed, then in my flesh I shall see God" (19:26). And Isaiah 26:19 asserts, "Your dead shall live, their corpses shall rise. O dwellers in the dust, awake and sing for joy" In Daniel 12:13 God promises Daniel, "You shall rise for your reward at the end of the days." This promise, along with the prediction of a two-fold resurrection in Daniel 12:2, is the clearest teaching in the Old Testament of a bodily resurrection "at the end of the days."

The New Testament confirms the teaching of a bodily resurrection many times.[7] But it adds more good news: although God's people have to wait until

---

7. E.g., Matthew 22:30-32; John 5:25-29; 6:39-40, 44, 54; 11:24-25; 1 Corinthians 15:12-57; 1 Thessalonians 4:14-16; and Revelation 20:12-13.

"the end of the days" for their bodily resurrection, upon dying they will immediately be "with the Lord." Jesus said to the criminal on the cross, "Truly I tell you, today you will be with me in Paradise" (Luke 23:43). And Paul wrote to the Philippians, "My desire is to depart and be with Christ, for that is far better" (1:21). Paul added in his letter to the Corinthians, "For we know that if the earthly tent we live in is destroyed, we have a building from God, a house not made with hands, eternal in the heavens. . . . We would rather be away from the body and at home with the Lord" (2 Cor 5:1, 8; cf. 1 Thess 5:10; Rev. 14:13).

We can also trace from the Old Testament to the New the theme of God blessing his people who persevere. God gave his people his law, promising that they would be richly blessed if they persevered in keeping his commandments. Moses said, "I have set before you life and death, blessings and curses. Choose life so that you and your descendants may live, loving the LORD your God, obeying him, and holding fast to him; for that means life to you and length of days" (Deut 30:19-20; cf. 32:47). Isaiah wrote, "For the LORD is a God of justice; blessed are all those who wait for him" (Isa 30:18). In Daniel 12:12 God proclaims, "Blessed are those who persevere."

In the New Testament Jesus said, "Blessed are those who are persecuted for righteousness' sake, for theirs is the kingdom of heaven. Blessed are you when people revile you and persecute you . . . on my account. Rejoice and be glad, for your reward is great in heaven" (Matt 5:10-12). Jesus promised several times that "the one who endures to the end will be saved" (Matt 10:22; 24:13). Paul also encouraged God's people, "Let us not grow weary in doing what is right, for we will reap at harvest-time, if we do not give up" (Gal 6:9). James wrote, "Blessed is anyone who endures temptation. Such a one has stood the test and will receive the crown of life that the Lord has promised to those who love him" (Jas 1:12). The risen Lord promised many times that those who conquer will inherit the kingdom of God: "To everyone who conquers, I will give permission to eat from the tree of life that is in the paradise of God" (Rev. 2:7; cf. 2:11, 17, 26; 3:5, 12, 21); "Those who conquer will inherit these things, and I will be their God and they will be my children" (Rev. 21:7).

New Testament References

The appendix to the Greek New Testament lists eleven New Testament references or allusions to verses in Daniel 12:5-13 — six of these in the book of Revelation. Some of these references we have used above to support the other ways to Christ in the New Testament. Two other passages come to mind concerning the question, "How long?" (12:6). Jesus' disciples raised a similar question: "Tell us, when will this be, and what will be the sign of your coming and of the end of the age?" Jesus responded, "This good news of the kingdom will be proclaimed throughout the world, as a testimony to all the nations, and then the end will come" (Matt 24:3, 14). The second passage is Revelation 6:9-11, "When he opened the fifth seal, I saw under the altar the souls of those who had been slaughtered for the word of God and for the testimony they had given; they cried out with a loud voice, 'Sovereign Lord, holy and true, *how long* will it be before you judge and avenge our blood on the inhabitants of the earth?' They were each given a white robe and told to rest a little longer, until the number would be complete both of their fellow servants and of their brothers and sisters, who were soon to be killed as they themselves had been killed."

Contrast

Daniel was told that "the words are to remain . . . sealed until the time of the end" (12:9). John, by contrast, was explicitly told, "Do *not* seal up the words of the prophecy of this book, for the time is near" (Rev. 22:10). The reason for this contrast between Daniel and John is that by John's time Jesus had come and inaugurated the "last days."

Sermon Theme, Goal, and Need

Since the New Testament confirms the message of this passage, the textual theme can become the sermon theme: *God promises everlasting life to his persecuted people who persevere to the end.*

Daniel's goal in writing this passage was "to encourage God's persecuted people to persevere to the end, for 'at the end of the days' God will give them everlasting life." Under "longitudinal themes" above, we noted that the New Testament confirms this teaching of the resurrection of the body "at the end of the days." It adds, however, that immediately upon death God's people will be "with the Lord." In the light of this New Testament teaching, we will have to explain in the sermon that we don't have to wait to "the end of the days," Jesus' Second Coming, to receive part of our "inheritance." But since the focus of this text is on the *resurrection of the body,* our goal in preaching this sermon can be similar to the author's goal: *to encourage God's persecuted people to persevere to the end, for at the end of time God will give them everlasting life.* This goal shows that the need addressed in this sermon is that God's people tend to become discouraged and fail to persevere during times of persecution.

Sermon Exposition

In the sermon introduction one can highlight the need addressed by giving a specific example of the fatigue that sets in when God's people suffer east of Eden or undergo severe persecution. Concerning "the end of the age" Jesus himself predicted, "because of the increase of lawlessness, the love of many will grow cold" (Matt 24:3, 12). Transition to the suffering exiles, and begin the exposition of this passage. But since this is the second sermon on Daniel's final vision, one can also briefly review the first part of that vision.

Last Sunday we saw that Daniel receives this final vision by the river Tigris. Suddenly he sees above the river the dazzling figure of a "man clothed in linen." It is an angel sent by God to reveal what will take place in the future. The angel predicts in great detail the wars that will be fought between the kings of the north (Syria) and the kings of the south (Egypt). God's people in Palestine will be caught in the middle and suffer greatly. The angel calls the last king of the north "a contemptible person" (11:21), for he will desecrate God's temple and severely persecute God's people. It is the evil King Antiochus IV of Syria.

But in chapter 11:36, and especially in verse 40, the angel shifts from Antiochus to "the time of the end." "The time of the end" means "the time prior to the second coming of Christ."[8] The angel begins to describe a final war that will take place in human history. The leader in this war is a powerful, evil person. The New Testament calls him the Antichrist. At "the time of the end" the Antichrist will make war on God's people. He will seek to annihilate the church. The persecution will be worldwide — wherever the church is found. It will be a terrible time of suffering for God's people.

Chapter 12:1 says, "There shall be a time of *anguish*, such as has never occurred since nations first came into existence." But just when the need is greatest, God will come to the rescue of his people. For verse 1 continues, "But *at that time* your people shall be delivered, everyone who is found written in the book. Many of those who sleep in the dust of the earth shall awake, some to *everlasting life*, and some to shame and *everlasting contempt*. Those who are wise *shall shine* like the brightness of the sky, and those who lead many to righteousness, like the stars forever and ever." It's a picture of the last day: resurrection day and the glory of God's kingdom on earth.

Before Daniel can close his book, however, God has still further revelations for him. Verses 5-6, "Then I, Daniel, looked, and two others appeared, one standing on this bank of the stream and one on the other. One of them said to

---

8. Stefanovic, *Daniel*, 313. Cf. Gooding, "The Literary Structure of the Book of Daniel and Its Implications," *TynBul* (1981) 75, n. 27, "The phrase 'the time of the end' is carefully and consistently reserved for the last period preceding the End (see 11:35, 40; 12:4, 9)."

the man clothed in linen, who was upstream [or "above the waters of the river"],[9] 'How long shall it be until the end of these wonders?'" The word "wonders" refers to God's mighty acts of judgment and salvation.[10] In this case it refers to the "anguish," the persecution of God's people, the amazing resurrection from the dead, and the arrival of God's glorious kingdom on earth. The angel wants to know how long the persecution will last and how long till God's perfect kingdom arrives on earth. How long?[11]

Verse 7, "The man clothed in linen, who was upstream, raised his right hand and his left hand toward heaven." Normally in swearing an oath a person would raise only one hand (see, e.g., Deut 32:40), but the angel raises both hands. "Lifting both hands is especially emphatic."[12] It's a solemn oath. The answer will be reliable. "And I heard him swear by the one who lives forever [i.e., God] that it would be for a time, two times, and half a time, and that when the shattering of the power of the holy people comes to an end, all these things would be accomplished."

We have heard the figure "a time, two times, and half a time" before. In Daniel 7:25 we were told that the Antichrist "shall wear out the holy ones of the Most High . . . ; and they shall be given into his power for a time, two times, and half a time." These symbolic numbers add up to three and a half times. In the Bible, seven denotes a full, complete period of time — God created the world in seven days. Three and a half times is half of the complete, perfect number "seven." Therefore it denotes a relatively short period of time, a short period of persecution.[13]

9. NIV. See p. 395, n. 3 above.

10. "In the Bible, the word *happelāôt*, 'wonders,' describes both God's mighty acts of salvation on behalf of his people (Exod 15:11; Ps 77:11, 15; Isa 25:1) and his judgments on the wicked (Isa 29:14)." Stefanovic, *Daniel*, 443. Cf. Seow, *Daniel*, 193.

11. "Behind that question lie two alternatives that apparently give rise to the questions: 'Will these events that have been foretold follow in quick succession upon one another and so be concluded in a comparatively short time; or will it be a case of a development that is long drawn out and extends over long ages to come?'" Leupold, *Exposition of Daniel*, 538.

12. Collins, *Daniel*, 399.

13. "As half of the perfect number, seven, it denotes a short period of evil." Lucas, *Daniel*, 194. Cf. Lederach, *Daniel*, 167. Leupold, *Exposition of Daniel*, 540, suggests that it may indicate that the Antichrist will have only modest success for a time, be very successful for two times, and then, "half a time" — "its power shall . . . suddenly be much reduced, and with that it shall be at an end." Cf. Calvin, *Commentaries on Daniel*, II, 383, "'Time' signifies a long period; 'times,' double this period. . . . With respect to the 'half of a time,' this is added for the comfort of the pious . . . to prevent them from despairing through excessive weariness." Steinmann, *Daniel*, 570, interprets the "three and a half times" as "the NT era, or the church age, from the first advent of Christ until his return." He overlooks at this point that the question in verse 6 has to do with the "wonders" of the final persecution, the resurrection, and the coming of the kingdom of God (11:40–12:3), which is the final period of world history.

As Daniel 7:25 stated that the Antichrist "shall wear out the holy ones of the Most High," so here in verse 7 the angel says that "when the shattering of the power of the holy people comes *to an end,* all these things [will] be accomplished." The good news is that the shattering of the power of God's people will come to an end. But it will not come to an end until the attacks of the Antichrist will *shatter* the power of God's people. We tend to think that when the church is strong, the kingdom of God will fully come on earth. But the angel tells us just the opposite. When the Antichrist breaks the power of God's people,[14] then all these things, the wonders of the resurrection and God's glorious kingdom on earth, will be accomplished.

In the New Testament Jesus also says, "At that time there will be great suffering, such as has not been from the beginning of the world until now, no, and never will be. And if those days had not been cut short for the sake of the elect, *no one* would be saved; but for the sake of the elect those days will be cut short" (Matt 24:21-22). The arrival of God's kingdom on earth is not accomplished by the church; before the perfection of God's kingdom comes, the power of the church will be *shattered.* Thus it will be evident that only *God* can bring his eternal kingdom on earth, and that he alone deserves all the honor and glory.

In verse 8 Daniel says, "I heard but could not understand." Small wonder! How could he understand "a time, two times, and half a time" and "the shattering of the power of the holy people"? "So I said, 'My lord, what shall be the outcome of these things?'" Daniel wants to know about "the outcome of these things," the result, especially the result of the shattering of God's people.[15] Will they be annihilated?[16]

The angel does not seem to give Daniel an answer to his question, for he says in verse 9, "Go your way, Daniel, for the words are to remain secret and sealed until the time of the end." The NIV offers a better translation, "Go your way, Daniel, because the words are *closed up*[17] and sealed until the time of the

---

14. "The Antichrist will practically have destroyed God's people, when Antichrist himself will be destroyed. In the time of deepest need, God works on behalf of his elect. The word translated 'breaking' . . . means rather 'to shatter, to beat in pieces,' as, e.g., 'thou shalt dash them in pieces like a potter's vessel' (Ps 2:9b)." Young, *Prophecy of Daniel,* 260. Cf. Leupold, *Exposition of Daniel,* 540, "This part of the answer conveys the solemn news that the holy people must pass through the sad experience of having their power shattered. 'Shatter,' *nappēṣ,* or 'break in pieces' (A.R.V.) involved complete demolition of power."

15. "These things" could be all the things mentioned in 11:40–12:3, but the answer of verse 10 focuses particularly on the persecution.

16. Cf. Leupold, *Exposition of Daniel,* 543, "Who shall win in this great struggle? What shall the permanent achievements of it all be? How shall all the participants fare?"

17. "To shut up (i.e., guard, preserve, protect, as in 8:26)." Young, *Prophecy of Daniel,* 257. Cf. Miller, *Daniel,* 320, "'Close up [*sĕtôm*] and seal [*ḥôtām*] the words of the scroll' (cf. 12:9) is

end." The "go your way, Daniel" is a firm way of telling Daniel that he does not have to understand everything.[18] For these words pertain to the distant future, "the time of the end," that is, the time of the final persecution by the Antichrist.[19] At that time especially God's people will need to hear these words in order to persevere. The persecution they will undergo is not outside the control of the sovereign God. He controls even the details of history, as we saw in Daniel 11. He has also set a limit to this final anguish: "a time, times, and half a time."

Still, the angel does give Daniel an answer about the outcome of the persecution. He says in verse 10, "Many shall be purified, cleansed, and refined, but the wicked shall continue to act wickedly." There is a positive outcome to the persecution: "Many shall be purified, cleansed, and refined." As gold is refined by fire, so God's people will be refined by the firestorm of persecution; they will be purified and cleansed.[20] The "suffering will prepare a people for the immediate presence of their Lord (cf. Mal 3:2, 3)."[21]

Even as "many shall be purified, cleansed, and refined," verse 10 continues, "the wicked shall continue to act wickedly. None of the wicked shall understand, but those who are wise shall understand." The wicked will join the

---

made up of two synonymous clauses, 'close up the words' and 'seal the scroll.' As in 8:26, this admonition concerned the preservation of the document, not its being kept 'secret' (NRSV)." Cf. Harman, *Study Commentary on Daniel*, 307-8, "What Daniel is told is that these things are going to be kept hidden until the end time of human history arrives. Hence he is dismissed with the word of command, 'Go!' The implication is that neither Daniel nor anyone else should try to uncover the things that have been sealed in this way (cf. the teaching in Deut 29:29 regarding the secret things that belong to God)."

18. See Young, *Prophecy of Daniel*, 260, "Go! — i.e., inquire no further, leave this matter alone." Cf. Leupold, *Exposition of Daniel*, 543, "The spirit of this answer is: 'There is no use trying to get any farther in the understanding of these matters; they simply will not be fully understood until these things come to pass.'" Cf. Calvin, *Commentaries on Daniel*, II, 386, "Although Daniel was not induced by any foolish curiosity to inquire of the angel the issue of these wonderful events, yet he did not obtain his request. God wished some of his predictions to be partially understood, and the rest to remain concealed until the full period of the complete revelation should arrive. This is the reason why the angel did not reply to Daniel."

19. See p. 401, n. 8 above.

20. According to Young, *Prophecy of Daniel*, 261, "This verse [10] presents a general description of the future. It is not a characterization merely of the time of the end (Driver)." Longman, *Daniel*, 286, also takes verse 10 "as words that describe the period from Daniel's time to the end." Cf. Steinmann, *Daniel*, 571-72, "purification of Christians throughout the church age." But the context here is the "time of the end" (11:35, 40; 12:4, 9; cf. 12:11, 12). This is not to deny that persecution at any time tends to refine God's people, but I see no valid textual reason for isolating verse 10 from its context of the end time and applying it to the whole church age. Cf. Miller, *Daniel*, 324, "The time when 'many will be purified, made spotless and refined' is the tribulation period of the last days."

21. Baldwin, *Daniel*, 209.

Antichrist in persecuting God's people. Paul writes, "Indeed, all who want to live a godly life in Christ Jesus will be persecuted. But wicked people will go from bad to worse, deceiving others and being deceived" (2 Tim 3:12-13). The wicked will be blind to the signs of the times; blind to the fact that judgment day is just around the corner. Ever since the first coming of Christ, we have entered "the last days." In these last days we are traveling along the edge of time; it's like walking a trail winding along the edge of a cliff.[22] "Those who are wise shall understand." The end can be upon us any time. The wise will understand this and be prepared.[23]

Verse 11 offers further details about "the time of the end": "From the time that the regular burnt offering is taken away and the abomination[24] that desolates is set up, there shall be one thousand two hundred ninety days." We are reminded of the time when Antiochus IV took away the regular burnt offering in the temple and set up the abomination that desolates. He took away the burnt offering honoring Israel's God and instead set up on top of the altar of God an altar for the Greek god Zeus. This led to the desolation, the emptiness, of the temple; God's people could no longer worship in that desecrated place. At the end of time, an even more powerful and evil ruler will emerge. The Antichrist will make regular, public worship of God impossible. Worldwide, churches will be shut down and be desolate of God's people.[25] Another god will be promoted: perhaps the god of military might, or the god of scientism, materialism, capitalism, secularism, communism, or a combination of these. The Antichrist will not tolerate the public worship of the true God and severely persecute God's people.

22. I first heard this helpful illustration in a 1965 lecture by Prof. G. C. Berkouwer of the Free University, Amsterdam. Recently I found it again in Helge Kvanvig, "The Relevance of the Biblical Visions of the End of Time," *HBT* 11/1 (1989) 47-48: In apocalyptic literature "history does not only move toward the end, it also moves along the end. History moves on the border of chaos like a track is winding along a cliff. . . . History is close to the end. . . . At one particular time . . . history will turn over the edge. Then the real end time tribulations will break loose. . . . This means that all believers who through periods of tribulations have seen the signs of the end were not mistaken. The signs of the end were present. The mistake was done if they thought that they could, through these signs, calculate the time when the real end time battle would take place. Then they were wrong, for this is only up to God to decide."

23. "The context of Daniel's visions confirms the fact that the wise are those people who have understanding of prophetic revelations. The book of Daniel repeatedly and emphatically states that only God gives this type of understanding." Stefanovic, *Daniel*, 444.

24. "Throughout the Old Testament, the Hebrew word *šiqqûṣ*, 'abomination,' is consistently associated with abominable idols." Ibid., 358.

25. Luther comments, "It may yet come to pass that the world becomes so entirely Epicurean that throughout the entire world there may be no pulpit left from which the gospel is still publicly preached . . . but it will be preserved only in the home through the father of the house." *Sämmtliche Schriften* (St. Louis: Concordia, 1880), VI, p. 938, quoted by Leupold, *Exposition of Daniel*, 546.

In verse 7 we heard that the persecution would last "a time, two times, and half a time," that is, three and a half years. In verse 11 the length of the persecution is given in days, "one thousand two hundred ninety *days*."[26] The number of days makes the length of the persecution very precise and relatively short.[27] The God who knows the details of Israel's future history (chapter 11) also knows the details of the end-time persecution. And he will not allow it to go on one day longer than he has prescribed.[28]

Verse 12, "Happy [blessed] are those who persevere and attain the thousand three hundred thirty-five days."[29] God's people need to persevere even beyond the 1,290 days of persecution. Here they are told to "persevere and attain 1,335 days." We may be puzzled by the different numbers,[30] but the point is that

---

26. "The Babylonians used a lunar calendar that produced a year of 354 days, the Essenes a solar calendar of 364 days, the Hellenistic regimes a luni-solar one of 360 days; in each case the calendar was corrected to the true length of the solar year — just over 365 days — by intercalating months. . . . When allowance is made for intercalation, 1290 days can represent 3.5 lunar years . . . or 3.5 solar years . . . ; 1335 days can also be reckoned to comprise 3.5 solar years." Goldingay, *Daniel*, 309-10, with references to articles in German journals.

27. "By the naming of 'days' instead of 'times' the idea of immeasurable duration of the tribulation is set aside, and the time of it is limited to a period of moderate duration which is exactly measured out by God." Keil, *Book of Daniel*, 502.

28. "It is not just a vague period of judgment but one that is predetermined by God down to the very day it will end." Duguid, *Daniel*, 215.

29. "The two sets of numbers given by the angel here [1,290 and 1,335] do not correspond with the number of days given in 8:13-14 for the vindication of the sanctuary from the violations perpetrated by Antiochus [2,300 evenings and mornings]. This shows, then, that 12:11-12 does not refer to the desolation of the sanctuary by Antiochus during the third great movement, but to another such desolation in the fourth great movement, the time of the end." Gooding, "The Literary Structure of the Book of Daniel and Its Implications," *TynBul* (1981) 75, n. 27.

30. Scholars have tried to account for the different numbers in various ways. Critical scholars generally follow Gunkel's suggestion (*Schöpfung und Chaos*, 269), cited with approval by Montgomery, *Book of Daniel*, 477: "The two verses are successive glosses intended to prolong the term of 1,150 days announced at 8:14; that term was not fulfilled and these glosses, which must be very early, successively extend the time to 1,290 and 1,335 days." Aside from the late dating of Daniel, one wonders why a later editor would not replace an incorrect number instead of just adding two more to it. For other attempts at explaining the numbers, see n. 26 above and Redditt, *Daniel*, 194-97. Dispensationalists generally argue that "the extra forty-five days are needed to set up the millennial government" (Miller, *Daniel*, 326; cf. Archer, "Daniel," 156), but this hypothesis lacks biblical support. Steinmann, *Daniel*, 575-76, contends that the "time, times, and half" of 12:7 is the time from Jesus' birth to his parousia; the 1,290 days of 12:11 is the time from 167 B.C. (Antiochus desecrating the temple) to Jesus' parousia; and the 1,335 days of 12:12 is the time from Daniel's final vision in 536 B.C. to Jesus' parousia. This urge for exact historical verification seems to have lost sight of the fact that this is apocalyptic literature. "The main emphasis is not so much on trying to unravel the secret of the 1,290 or 1,335 days, but on endurance to the end." Harman, *Study Commentary on Daniel*, 309.

God's people should persevere to the very end.[31] "Blessed are those who persevere" to the very end of days.[32]

Jesus also spoke of this time of persecution and encouraged his followers to persevere to the end. He said, "Then they will hand you over to be tortured and will put you to death. . . . Then many will fall away. . . . And because of the increase of lawlessness, the love of many will grow cold. But the one who endures *to the end* will be saved" (Matt 24:9-13).

Jesus also told a parable about a master who went on a journey and left his household to his slaves until his return. Unfortunately, he was delayed on his return trip. Jesus said, "*Blessed* is that slave whom his master will find at work when he arrives" (Matt 24:46). Even when Jesus' Second Coming seems to take longer than we expect, we are to keep working for him until the very end. "Blessed are those who persevere and attain the thousand three hundred thirty-five days."

Daniel's picture of the end-time persecution of the church is similar to the picture we find in the New Testament. Paul writes that "the day of the Lord" will not come before the "Man of Lawlessness" (the Antichrist) is revealed. Right now he is being restrained, but when that restraint is removed, "the lawless one will be revealed, whom the Lord Jesus will destroy with the breath of his mouth, annihilating him by the manifestation of his coming" (2 Thess 2:8). In the book of Revelation, John writes similarly that he saw an angel come down from heaven who bound Satan "for a thousand years" — that is, Satan is bound for the full period of time from Jesus' First Coming to just before his Second Coming. He is like a lion on a chain who now can inflict only limited damage. But "when the thousand years are ended, Satan will be released from his prison and will come out to *deceive* the nations at the four corners of the earth . . . in order to gather them for *battle* [against the church]. . . . They marched up over the breadth of the earth and surrounded the camp of the saints and the beloved city [the church]. And fire came down from heaven and consumed them. And the devil who had deceived them was thrown into the lake of fire. . . . Then I saw a great white throne. . . . And I saw the dead, great and small, standing before the throne, and books were opened [judgment day]. . . . Then I saw a new heaven and a new earth. . . . And I heard a loud voice from the throne saying, 'See, the home of God is among mortals. He will dwell

---

31. "The inclusion of this number [1,335] seems designed to heighten the sense of mystery that surrounds the Lord's timing and the need for faithful perseverance on the part of the saints, even when according to human wisdom God's arrival seems to be overdue." Duguid, *Daniel*, 215-16. Cf. Longman, *Daniel*, 287.

32. "The oppression of the church will not be a matter of centuries or generations but only of days. The suffering believers will simply have to take courage and wait patiently on the Lord. There will certainly be some very difficult days, but they will only be days. One by one we can mark them off on the calendar." Veldkamp, *Dreams and Dictators*, 249-50.

with them as their God; they will be his peoples. . . . Death will be no more; mourning and crying and pain will be no more, for the first things have passed away'" (Rev. 20:2, 7-12; 21:1-4).

The angel's final word to Daniel is a personal one. Verse 13, "But you, go your way, and rest." Daniel is again told to "go your way"[33] and not ask any more questions. Daniel does not have to know exactly *when* the day of resurrection will be. Jesus said, "About that day and hour no one knows, neither the angels of heaven, nor the Son, but only the Father" (Matt 24:36). God has given Daniel, and through him God's people, sufficient information about the future. Knowing about God's ultimate victory over evil, the resurrection, and the coming of God's perfect kingdom, they will be motivated to persevere to the end.

Daniel is now a very old man. He has run his race and remained faithful to God. His whole life he had labored for the welfare of God's people. Now the angel tells him, "Go your way, and rest," that is, die peacefully and rest in the grave[34] to "the end of the days." Leave the future to your sovereign God.

The angel closes with God's wonderful promise for Daniel personally, "You shall rise for your reward [the NIV has "your allotted inheritance"[35]] at the end of the days." Earlier the angel told Daniel that "many of those who sleep in the dust of the earth shall awake, some to everlasting life" (12:2). Now the angel assures Daniel that he will be among those who awake to everlasting life. Earlier the angel also told Daniel that "those who are *wise* shall shine like the brightness of the sky" in the kingdom of God (12:3). Now the angel assures Daniel that "at the end of the days" he will receive his inheritance in the kingdom of God.

God's promise of resurrection to everlasting life holds for all of God's people. This resurrection can take place because in the fullness of time God sent his Son, Jesus. With his death on the cross, Jesus paid God's penalty for sin. With his resurrection on Easter morning, Jesus conquered death for all. Jesus said, "This is indeed the will of my Father, that all who see the Son and believe in him may have eternal life; and I will raise them up on the last day" (John 6:40; cf. 5:28-29). Again, Jesus said, "I am the resurrection and the life. Those who be-

---

33. See Daniel 12:9. The NRSV follows the Greek translations. The NIV follows the Hebrew, "go your way till the end."

34. "'Thou shalt rest — i.e., in the grave.'" Young, *Exposition of Daniel*, 264. Cf. Lucas, *Daniel*, 298, "The language of rest and arising from it picks up on the imagery of death and resurrection as sleep and awakening used in 12:2." Cf. Steinmann, *Daniel*, 577, "A synonym for the sleep of death (12:2)." Cf. Job 3:13, 17.

35. "'Inheritance' (Hebrew, *gôrāl*) is the word used for casting 'a lot,' as, for example, in the distribution of the land of Palestine to the various tribes (see Josh 14–18). . . . Because the word was also used to denote the piece of land so allocated, it became virtually synonymous with words like 'inheritance' . . . and 'possession' . . . and then came to denote the idea of a person's allotted destiny (. . . see Ps 16:5; Isa 17:14; 34:17; Jer 13:25)." Harman, *Study Commentary on Daniel*, 309-10.

lieve in me, even though they die, will *live*" (John 11:25). Because Jesus rose from the dead, Paul called Jesus' resurrection "the *first* fruits of those who have died" (1 Cor 15:20); we will follow Jesus by rising from the dead "at the end of the days." Paul explained, "Since we believe that Jesus died and rose again, even so, through Jesus, God will bring with him those who have died" (1 Thess 4:14).

God's people may become discouraged under constant persecution. It may look like they are on the losing side. But through this vision God seeks to encourage his persecuted people to persevere to the end, for they will receive their inheritance[36] "at the end of the days." They will be raised to "everlasting life."

The New Testament has even more good news. We don't have to wait till "the end of the days" to get a taste of everlasting life. When Jesus hung on the cross, one of the criminals crucified with him said to him, "Jesus, remember me when you come into your kingdom." And Jesus replied, "Truly I tell you, today you will be with me in Paradise" (Luke 23:42-43). *Today!* Not just "at the end of the days" but *today!* Jesus is in heaven today, and when his followers die, he will welcome them in heaven. Paul writes, "We know that if the earthly tent we live in is destroyed, we have a building from God, a house not made with hands, eternal in the heavens" (2 Cor 5:1). So we need not fear death. When we die, we will immediately be with the Lord in heaven. And "at the end of the days" he will raise our bodies from "the dust of the earth" (12:2). Paul says, "Listen, I will tell you a mystery! We will not all die, but we will all be changed, in a moment, in the twinkling of an eye, at the last trumpet. For the trumpet will sound, and the dead will be raised imperishable, and we will be changed" (1 Cor 15:51-52).

So no matter how fierce the persecution, we ought to persevere in working for the Lord. Then one day we will hear Jesus say to us, "Well done, good and trustworthy servant; you have been trustworthy in a few things . . . ; enter into the joy of your master" (Matt 25:21).[37]

---

36. Cf. 1 Peter 1:3-4, "Blessed be the God and Father of our Lord Jesus Christ! By his great mercy he has given us a new birth into a living hope through the resurrection of Jesus Christ from the dead, and into an *inheritance* that is imperishable, undefiled, and unfading, kept in heaven for you. . . ."

37. For the prayer following the sermon, one could consider using the prayer with which John Calvin closed his lectures on Daniel. See *Commentaries on Daniel*, II, 393 (I have updated the language):

> Grant, Almighty God, since you propose for us no other end than that of constant warfare during our whole life, and you subject us to many cares until we arrive at the goal of this temporary racecourse: Grant, I pray, that we may never grow fatigued. May we ever be armed and equipped for battle, and whatever the trials by which you prove us, may we never be found deficient. May we always aspire towards heaven with upright souls, and strive with all our endeavors to attain that blessed rest which is laid up for us in heaven, in Jesus Christ our Lord. Amen.

Ten Steps from Text to Sermon

1. Select the preaching text.
Select the preaching text with an eye to congregational needs. The text must be a literary unit and contain a vital theme.

2. Read the text in its literary context.
Read and reread the text in its context and jot down initial questions.

3. Outline the structure of the text.
In the Hebrew/Aramaic or Greek text, note the major affirmations, clausal flow, plot line, scenes, or other literary structures. Mark major units with headings and verse references.

4. Interpret the text in its own historical setting.
  a. Literary interpretation;
  b. Historical interpretation;[1]
  c. Theocentric interpretation.
Review your results with the help of some good commentaries.

5. Formulate the text's theme, goal, and need addressed.
  a. State the textual theme in a brief sentence that summarizes the *message* of the text for its original hearers: subject and predicate. What is the text saying?
  b. State the goal of the author for his original hearers. What is the text doing? Does the author aim to persuade, to motivate, to urge, to warn, to comfort? Be specific.
  c. State the need the author addressed — the question behind the text.

---

1. In order to avoid repetition, in the chapters above I combine historical interpretation with determining the author's goal in Step 5b.

6. Understand the message in the contexts of canon and redemptive history.

a. Canonical interpretation: interpret the message in the context of the whole canon;

b. Redemptive-historical interpretation: understand the message in the context of God's redemptive history from creation to new creation;

c. Christocentric interpretation: explore the ways of (1) redemptive-historical progression, (2) promise-fulfillment, (3) typology, (4) analogy, (5) longitudinal themes, (6) New Testament references, and (7) contrast.

7. Formulate the sermon theme, goal, and need addressed.

a. Ideally, your sermon theme will be the same as your textual theme (Step 5a). If Step 6 forces a change, stay as close as possible to the textual theme. Your theme will guide especially the development of the body of the sermon.

b. Your goal must be in harmony with the author's goal (Step 5b) and match the sermon theme. Your goal will guide the style of the sermon as well as the content of its conclusion.

c. State the need you are addressing. This need should be similar to the need addressed by the author. The need will inform the content of your introduction.

8. Select a suitable sermon form.

Select a sermon form that respects the form of the text (didactic or narrative, deductive or inductive) and that achieves the goal of the sermon.

9. Prepare the sermon outline.

If possible, follow the flow of the text (Step 3) in the body of the sermon. Main points, derived from the text, support the theme. The introduction should expose the need. The conclusion should clinch your goal.

10. Write the sermon in oral style.

Say it out loud as you write it. Write in oral style, using short sentences, vivid words, strong nouns and verbs, active voice, present tense, images, and illustrations.

An Expository Sermon Model

A. **Introduction** (usually no more than 10 percent of the sermon)
   1. Normally, begin with an illustration of the **need** addressed (Step 7c).
   2. Connect this illustration to the need of the present hearers.
   3. **Transition:** Show that this need or a similar issue was also the question behind the biblical text.
   4. State the **theme** of the text/sermon (Step 7a). For the sake of maintaining suspense, you may postpone disclosing the theme at the beginning (inductive development), but by statement and restatement, you must make sure that the hearers catch the point of the sermon.

B. **The Sermon Body**
   1. Expose the **structure of the text**. The main points, affirmations, moves, and scenes of the text (Step 3) normally become your main points in the sermon.
   2. The **main points** should usually support the theme and be of the same rank.
   3. Follow the **textual sequence** of the points unless there is good reason to change it, such as climactic arrangement (Step 9).
   4. Use simple, **clear transitions** that enable the hearers to sense the structure of and movement in the sermon.
      E.g., "Not only . . . but also. . . ."
      Or, "Let's first see. . . . Now we see secondly. . . ."
      Or, "Let's look at verse 8." "Now please look with me at verse 12."
   5. Use **verse references** before quoting the text so that the hearers can read along. Visual learning is nine times more effective than aural.
   6. Use some personal observations to **illustrate** difficult concepts or to make the point. Personal illustrations are more natural and powerful

than canned illustrations about Bishop Whately. Personal experiences may also be used but be careful not to preach yourself but Christ.

C. Conclusion

1. Be brief.
2. Don't introduce new material. Narrow the focus; don't expand it.
3. Clinch **the goal** (Step 7b).
4. Be concrete. Can you offer some concrete suggestions of what the hearers can do in response to the Word preached?

"Resolved"

A Sermon on Daniel 1[1]

RYAN FABER[2]

While proofreading the chapters of this book, my former seminary stu-dent, the Reverend Ryan Faber, preached two series of sermons on Daniel, six on the narratives and five on the visions. We decided to include two of these sermons in these appendices, one from the narratives and one from the visions.

The sermon on Daniel 1 demonstrates how one can preach a relevant biblical sermon without resorting to moralizing. It also beautifully illus-trates how one can apply to a contemporary American church a message originally addressed to Israel suffering in exile. Although the sermon ap-plication would be most direct when preaching Daniel to a church suffer-ing overt persecution, Ryan preached this sermon to a church in Pella, Iowa, which is not suffering state-sponsored persecution. He managed to set the stage for the contemporary application of all of Daniel's messages by explaining that we today are still in exile, suffering the consequences of our ancestors having been driven out of Paradise and now spending our earthly lives "east of Eden" where we struggle with thorns and thistles, tornadoes and earthquakes, and endure the enmity of Satan, broken rela-tions, pain, death, and murder (Gen 3–4).

The sermon on Daniel 9 shows how one can preach a well-focused sermon on a passage that contains not only Daniel's lengthy prayer but also his controversial and complicated vision. Note how Ryan explains only key verses in the prayer so that he can move rather quickly to the mes-

---

1. This sermon was preached on May 2, 2010, at Faith Christian Reformed Church, Pella, Iowa. Unless otherwise noted, Scripture quotations are from the New International Version (1984), which is the church's pew Bible.

2. Ryan Faber is Pastor of Worship and Administration at Faith Christian Reformed Church, Pella, Iowa.

sage of the vision of the seventy weeks. He then explains the rather abstract "seven weeks" (7 × 7 = 49) with the vivid Old Testament image of the Year of Jubilee when Israelites who had lost their inheritance would return to their land as well as the "seventy weeks" (10 × 7 × 7 = 490) as the Year of Jubilee, the "new heaven and new earth" of which Revelation 21 speaks. This sermon also illustrates how one can gently correct the NIV pew Bibles not with one's own translation but with another respected version, in this case the NRSV. Most impressive, perhaps, is that Ryan managed to turn some fifty-five pages of research into a powerful seven-page sermon.

Yesterday, for the second time in as many weeks, a funeral was held here at Faith Church. Two weeks ago, we mourned the death of Deb Veenstra, killed by cancer well before her time. Yesterday, we mourned the death of Jan Nikkel, also killed by cancer well before her time.

As we mourned, we affirmed a core conviction of the Christian faith: This is wrong. Cancer is wrong. Death is wrong. It is not the way it's supposed to be, not the way God wants his world to work. God does not delight in disease, depression, darkness, or death. Such things are a powerful, poignant, painful reminder of the place we now live — east of Eden.

Our world is sin-sick, broken, and scarred. And all too often, it leaves us feeling battered and bruised. Here, in our exile from Paradise, east of Eden, our lives are marked by pain. With great pain we bring forth our children. Through painful toil we eat the fruit of the earth. Until the day we return to it — for dust we are, to dust we will return (Gen 3:16-19).

How do we remain faithful to God? How do we hold on to hope in this world?

It is not only *our* question tonight. It was also the question of the ancient Israelites to whom the book of Daniel was first written. Like us, they too were in exile. Removed from the place of God's presence, the land long-promised their ancestors.

First, the Babylonians took the most promising young men — members of "the royal family and the nobility, young men without any physical defect, handsome, showing aptitude for every kind of learning, well informed, quick to understand, and qualified to serve in the king's palace" (Dan 1:3-4).

Then, eight years later, the Babylonians returned and removed "all the officers, all Israel's fighting men, and all the craftsmen and artisans. Only the poorest people of the land were left" (2 Kings 24:14). And then, ten years later, the Babylonians again returned. This time they set fire to the temple of the Lord, the royal palace, and all the houses of Jerusalem. Every important building was burned down. The city walls were broken down. And all those who remained in the city were carried into exile, except for a few of the poorest, who were left to work the vineyards and fields (2 Kings 25:9-12).

There, by the rivers of Babylon, the people sat and wept when they remembered Zion. They said, "The LORD has forsaken me; the Lord has forgotten me" (Isa 49:14). Their captors asked them for songs, but how, they wondered, how can we sing the songs of the Lord in a foreign land, far from the place of God's presence (Ps 137:1-4)? How do we hold on to hope, even in exile, east of Eden? In this sin-scarred world that so often leaves us weary and wounded?

The book of Daniel was written to comfort and encourage God's people in exile with this good news: Our God reigns. However things around us appear, whatever our circumstances, our God reigns. And he is working out his purposes.

It began, verse 1 says, "in the third year of the reign of Jehoiakim king of Judah. Nebuchadnezzar king of Babylon came to Jerusalem and besieged it. The Lord delivered Jehoiakim king of Judah into his hand, along with some of the articles from the temple of God. These he carried off to the temple of his god in Babylonia and put in the treasure house of his god" (Dan 1:1-2).

At first glance, it appears that Israel's God has been defeated. The Babylonian king ransacked God's temple and plundered its treasury. It was a sign, one student of Scripture says, a sign that Nebuchadnezzar and his gods were victorious over Israel and its God.[3] Another Babylonian king would later use some of the plunder, gold goblets from the temple of the Lord, to praise his gods of gold and silver, of bronze, iron, wood, and stone (Dan 5:3-4). No doubt Nebuchadnezzar thought he was greater than God. And, at least at first glance, it seems so.

"A modern historian would say that Judah fell because it was overpowered by the most powerful nation on earth. A Babylonian priest would have said that the powerful gods of Babylon simply overpowered the God of Israel."[4] But notice what the biblical author says in verse 2: "*The Lord* delivered Jehoiakim king of Judah into his hand."

Even Israel's exile into Babylon was within God's control, under his power, part of his providential plan for the world. The king of Babylon had no authority, no power over God's people except that which was given him from above (John 19:11). Even when the wrong seems great and strong; when we are exiled in Babylon; when we experience the brunt of another's bitterness; when we are devastated by betrayal, disaster, disease, depression; when we experience abuse or abandonment — even when "the wrong is great and strong, God is the ruler yet."[5]

---

3. Goldingay, *Daniel*, 15.

4. Greidanus, p. 45 above.

5. Maltbie Babcock, 1901, "This Is My Father's World," st. 2, rev. by Mary Babcock Crawford, 1972.

Verse 2 tells us that "*The Lord* delivered Jehoiakim king of Judah into Nebuchadnezzar's hand, along with some of the articles from the temple of God. These Nebuchadnezzar carried off to the temple of his god in Babylonia." Literally, in Hebrew, the place is called Shinar. That's an important word choice for the ancient writer. For the ancient Israelites in exile, Shinar is a word of hope — a reminder that though Babylon is a dark and dangerous place, a place opposed to God, it stands under God's judgment.

Perhaps you remember the story. It was after the great flood, when the whole world had one language and a common speech, that the peoples of the earth moved eastward. "They found a plain in Shinar and settled there." And there the people built themselves a city with a tower that had its head in the heavens, so that their name would be great and that they would not be scattered over the whole earth. But God came down, confused their languages, and scattered them over the face of the whole earth (Gen 11:1-9).

For the ancient Israelites in exile, Shinar is a word of hope. Many commentators place the story of Daniel within what theologians call "the antithesis."[6] The Bible calls it "enmity." The enmity God promised between the woman and the serpent, between her seed and his. The reference to Shinar reminds the ancient Israelites of God's great promise: the serpent might strike your heal, but you will crush his head (Gen 3:15). The reference to Shinar reminds the people concerning Babylon: "lo! his doom is sure!"[7] God has brought her low before; he can, he will, do it again.

By the rivers of Babylon, the people sat and wept (Ps 137:1). They wondered if God had forgotten them; if he had forsaken them (Isa 49:14). And some of them were no doubt tempted to forsake him. To forget him. Especially when life left them battered and bruised.

It was precisely what Nebuchadnezzar wanted. In verse 3 he "ordered Ashpenaz, chief of his court officials, to bring in some of the Israelites from the royal family and the nobility." Ashpenaz "was to teach them the language and literature of the Babylonians." The young men "were to be trained for three years, and after that they were to enter the king's service."

"Among those who were brought in were Daniel, Hananiah, Mishael and Azariah. The chief officials gave them new names: to Daniel, the name Belteshazzar; to Hananiah, Shadrach; to Mishael, Meshach; and to Azariah, Abednego" (Dan 1:3-7).

Those brought in were members of the royal family. They were children of the king — the King of kings and Lord of lords. But Nebuchadnezzar wants to train them, not for God's service, but for his own. The Israelite youth are to be

---

6. See Gordon Spykman, *Reformational Dogmatics* (Grand Rapids: Eerdmans, 1992), 65-66.
7. Martin Luther, 1529, "A Mighty Fortress Is Our God," trans. Frederick H. Hedge, 1852.

reeducated. "Reprogrammed," one person said.[8] They must learn the language and literature of the Babylonians. No longer loyal to the God of Abraham, Isaac, and Jacob, they must become "totally Babylonian in their outlook and conduct." And so, his court official changes their names.[9] Their new names are meant to reflect their new allegiance, their new loyalty — to the gods of Babylon.

Daniel, whose name means "God is my judge," becomes Belteshazzar, which means "may Bel, (the chief Babylonian god) protect his life." Hananiah, whose Hebrew name means "the Lord has been gracious," becomes Shadrach, which means "the command of Aku," the Babylonians' moon god. Mishael, whose Hebrew name means "Who is like God?" becomes Meshach, which means "Who is like Aku?" And Azariah, whose Hebrew name means "the Lord is my helper," becomes Abednego, which means "servant of Nebo," the Babylonian god of wisdom and agriculture.[10]

The chief of the king's court officials gave new names to Daniel and his friends. The new names were meant to reflect their new allegiance to the gods of Babylon. But Daniel remains faithful to the Lord his God. In response to the new name set on him, verse 8 tells us that Daniel set his heart "not to defile himself with the royal food and wine." Daniel remains Daniel — a child of the king, the King of kings and Lord of lords. Nebuchadnezzar may have changed their names, one preacher said, but he could not change their hearts. "They remained faithful to the true God of Israel."[11] And so "Daniel resolved not to defile himself with the royal food and wine" (Dan 1:8).

It isn't entirely clear why the royal food and wine would have defiled Daniel. Perhaps some of the royal food came from animals that were not kosher, animals God had told his ancient people they must not eat. And perhaps, probably, the royal food and wine had been sacrificed to idols, to the Babylonian gods.

To eat that food, to drink that wine, would have been to worship those gods, as Paul told the Corinthians: "The sacrifices of pagans are offered to demons, not to God. And we ought not participate with demons. We cannot drink the cup of the Lord and the cup of demons too. Nor can we have a part both in the Lord's table and the table of demons. To do so would rouse the Lord to anger," Paul said (1 Cor 10:20-22).

But Daniel won't defile himself. Even if it rouses the king's anger. The chief official was afraid it might. In verse 10 he tells Daniel, "I'm afraid of my lord the king." And for good reason. In the next chapter, the king becomes "so angry and

---

8. Greidanus, p. 46 above.
9. Herman Veldkamp, *Dreams and Dictators,* 8.
10. James Montgomery Boice, *Daniel,* 22; see also Greidanus, p. 47 above.
11. Ibid.

furious that he orders the execution of all the wise men in Babylon" (Dan 2:12). "I am afraid of my lord the king," the chief official says, "Why should he see you looking worse than the other young men your age. He'll have my head because of you" (Dan 1:10). But Daniel was determined. Resolute. He would not defile himself with the royal food and wine.

By God's grace, verse 9 tells us, "God had caused the official to show favor and sympathy to Daniel." And by God's grace, the guard the chief official had appointed agreed to a test. He would give Daniel and his friends "nothing but vegetables to eat and water to drink" for ten days (Dan 1:12). At the end of the ten-day trial, verse 15 says, Daniel and his three friends "looked healthier and better nourished than any of the young men who ate the royal food. So the guard took away their choice food and wine they were given to drink and gave them vegetables instead."

Verse 17 continues, "To these four young men God gave knowledge and understanding of all kinds of literature and learning. And Daniel could understand visions and dreams of all kinds." It sort of sounds like someone else, doesn't it? Another young man who wound up far from the place of God's presence, the land long-promised his ancestors. Joseph. Like Joseph, Daniel was a "handsome" young man (Gen 39:6; Dan 1:4). And like Joseph, Daniel "found favor" in the eyes of his master, as Joseph found favor in the eyes of Potiphar his master (Gen 39:4; Dan 1:9). And like Joseph, Daniel "could understand visions and dreams of all kinds" (Gen 40–41; Dan 1:17).

The allusions are intentional. Daniel is another Joseph. Brought to Babylon "for such a time as this" (Esth 4:14). It is, for the ancient Israelites in exile, another word of hope. Perhaps God will accomplish through Daniel what he did through Joseph — the saving of many lives (Gen 50:20). As the story ends, we find Daniel in the same place Joseph ended up, in the king's service.

Verse 18, "At the end of the time set by the king to bring them in, the chief official presented Daniel and his three friends to Nebuchadnezzar. The king talked to them, and he found none equal to Daniel, Hananiah, Mishael and Azariah." Notice that the writer continues to use their Hebrew names. And "they entered the king's service" (Dan 1:18-19). But they did so as servants of the great king — the King of kings and Lord of lords, the God who reigns, whose purposes are being worked out.

As the story ends, we rightly expect great things from Daniel. That's the way the writer wants it. He encourages the Israelites to remain faithful and hopeful, even in exile. To look to God and also to Daniel — the one God guided into exile, the one on whom his favor rests, the one he gave knowledge and understanding.

In the same way, we are encouraged today, in our exile, in this broken and battered world, east of Eden, to remain faithful and hopeful. To look to God.

And to the one he sent into exile — even the God-forsaken exile of the cross, for us and our salvation. There is no good reason to have hope in the world but this: Our God reigns. He is working out his purposes.

In the end, he will set things right. He will bring us home, home from exile. To the renewed creation described by Peter as "the home of righteousness" (2 Pet 3:13). In the end, God "will end our wars, heal our hurts, and make the crooked straight."[12] In the end, the sin-sick way of our world will pass away. And God will make all things new. There will be no more death, no more mourning, no more crying, no more pain. God himself will wipe the tears from our eyes (Rev. 21:4-5).

He has given proof of this, the Bible says, not simply by guiding Daniel to a position of power in exile. "He has given proof of this," the Bible says, "by raising Jesus from the dead" (Acts 17:31). And "exalting him to the highest place, and giving him the name that is above every name, that at the name of Jesus every knee should bow, in heaven and on earth and under the earth, and every tongue confess that Jesus Christ is Lord, to the glory of God the Father" (Phil. 2:9-11). Amen.

---

12. "Our World Belongs to God" (Grand Rapids: Christian Reformed Church in North America, 1986), para. 58.

"Seventy 'Sevens' Are Decreed"

A Sermon on Daniel 9[1]

Ryan Faber[2]

My mother e-mailed the other day. Uncle Len Gerbrandt was working at their church's fall clean-up day. He was trimming a tree when he fell off the ladder, landing on a concrete curb. The blunt force trauma knocked him out. He has not yet regained consciousness. The latest word was that he likely will not. His body remains very much alive, but humanly speaking there is no hope of recovery.

It's not the way our world was meant to be. Children are not supposed to be born crippled or diseased. Young people — even those only in their early sixties — are not supposed to die before their time. Spouses aren't supposed to betray us. Parents aren't supposed to abandon us. As Simon, a character in *Grand Canyon,* says, "Everything's supposed to be different than what it is."[3]

Everything once was different than it is now — in that garden God had planted in the east, in Eden (Gen 2:8), Paradise, the place God came to walk with us in the cool of the day (Gen 3:8). But we no longer live there. We have been exiled, banished (Gen 3:23). Now the ground produces thorns and thistles for us. Life is hard. Painful. Completely out of whack.[4] Nothing is as it's supposed to be.

That's what ancient Israel thought too, as they sat in exile. They were supposed to be living in the land long-promised their ancestors. They were sup-

---

1. This sermon was preached on October 24, 2010, at Faith Christian Reformed Church, Pella, Iowa. Unless otherwise noted, Scripture quotations are from the New International Version (1984), which is the church's pew Bible.

2. Ryan Faber is Pastor of Worship and Administration at Faith Christian Reformed Church, Pella, Iowa.

3. Cornelius Plantinga Jr., *Not the Way It's Supposed to Be* (Grand Rapids: Eerdmans, 1995), 7.

4. Barbara Brown Taylor, *Speaking of Sin* (Cambridge: Cowley, 2000), 44.

posed to meet God in his temple, the place he had chosen as his special dwelling place on earth (Deut 12:5, etc.). But they couldn't. The temple had been destroyed. The Holy City reduced to ruin. And they had been carried off into exile in Babylon (2 Kings 25:8-11). Nothing was as it was meant to be.

Yet there were glimmers of hope. Verse 1 reminds us that "Darius son of Xerxes (a Mede by descent) had been made ruler over Babylon." The dream God gave Nebuchadnezzar that the head of gold would be replaced by the chest and arms of silver (Dan 2) was coming true. The vision Daniel had that the lion nation would be replaced by a bear (Dan 7) was coming true. Verse 2, Daniel "understood from Scripture, according to the word of the LORD given to Jeremiah the prophet, that the desolation of Jerusalem would last seventy years."

The prophet had said: "This whole country [Israel] will become a desolate wasteland, and these nations will serve the king of Babylon seventy years. But when the seventy years are fulfilled, I will punish the king of Babylon and his nation, the land of the Babylonians, for their guilt" (Jer 25:11-12).

And God had. The writing was on the wall: "Mene, mene, tekel, parsin." "That very night Belshazzar, king of the Babylonians, was slain, and Darius the Mede took over the kingdom" (Dan 5:30-31).

Daniel knew that Israel's time of exile was nearly over. The seventy years were almost up. But he also knew that restoration was not automatic. Moses had long before predicted exile, should the people break covenant with their God. And Moses had long before promised restoration, should the people "confess their sins and the sins of the fathers, their treachery against God and their hostility toward him." Then God would remember his covenant with them. Then God would restore them (Lev 26:40-45).

Daniel knew that Israel's time of exile was nearly over. But he also knew that restoration was not automatic. So, in verse 3, Daniel "turned to Lord God and pleaded with him in prayer and petition, in fasting, and in sackcloth and ashes." He identified himself with the people, confessing their sin. Verse 4, "O Lord, the great and awesome God, who keeps his covenant of love with all who love him and obey his commands, we have sinned and done wrong. We have been wicked and have rebelled; we have turned away from your commands and laws" (Dan 9:4-5).

The exile was not God's fault: he keeps his covenant of love (Dan 9:4). The exile was Israel's fault. They were covered with shame because they had sinned, because they had not obeyed the Lord their God nor kept the laws he gave them through his servants the prophets (Dan 9:7-10). God had been exceedingly gracious and profoundly patient. He sent them prophet after prophet after prophet to call them back to himself. But the people did not listen to his servants the prophets (Dan 9:6). And so they were sent into exile.

Not because God broke covenant with them, but because they broke covenant with him.

In fact, Daniel understands, according to the word of the Lord given to Moses — Daniel understands that even exile is a sign of God's covenant faithfulness. The exile itself is understood in verse 14 as a sign that God is indeed "righteous in all he does." The people should have known that this would happen. Verse 11 describes it as "the curses and the sworn judgments written in the Law of Moses." In delivering "Jehoiakim king of Judah into the hands of the Babylonians" (Dan 1:2) God was simply fulfilling his word (Dan 9:12). In verse 13, Daniel acknowledges that all the disaster that came upon Israel was "just as it has been written in the Law of Moses."

"If you do not listen to me but remain hostile toward me, then in my anger, I will be hostile toward you," God said, "and I myself will punish you for your sins seven times over. . . . I will turn your cities into ruins and lay waste your sanctuaries. I will lay waste your land. . . . I will scatter you among the nations" (Lev. 26:27-33). And so it was!

God kept his word. He did not hesitate to bring disaster because he is righteous in all he does. Strange as it may sound, it was how God kept his covenant of love with his people. "The Lord disciplines those he loves" (Heb 12:6 [Prov. 3:12]). But even then, when his people are "in the land of their enemies," God promised "not to reject them or abhor them so as to destroy them completely" (Lev. 26:44). "Even when we are faithless, he remains faithful" (2 Tim 2:13). He keeps his covenant of love.

That is the only basis for hope. If God fulfilled his word by sending Israel into exile, how much more would he keep his word to restore them. And so, Daniel prays in verse 16, "O Lord, in keeping with all your righteous acts" — he remembers how God kept his promise to Abraham that after his descendants had been slaves in Egypt for 450 years, he would bring them out with a mighty hand and an outstretched arm (see Gen 15:13-14) — "O Lord, in keeping with all your righteous acts, turn away your anger and your wrath from Jerusalem, your city, your holy hill." Verse 19, "Listen! Forgive! Hear and act!"

While Daniel "was speaking and praying," "Gabriel came to him in swift flight" and told Daniel in verse 23, "As soon as you began to pray, an answer was given, which I have come to tell you": "Seventy 'sevens' are decreed for your people and your holy city to finish transgression, to put an end to sin, to atone for wickedness, to bring in everlasting righteousness, to seal up vision and prophecy and to anoint the most holy" (Dan 9:24).

"Seventy 'sevens' are decreed" (Dan 9:24). That is when the people will be restored. That is when salvation will be fully known. That is when God will finally and forever "put an end to sin" and "bring in everlasting righteousness" — in "seventy 'sevens.'" But what does that mean?

No one is quite sure. The vision Gabriel gives Daniel has been called "a dismal swamp" in biblical interpretation,[5] "the most controversial passage in the Bible."[6]

It is helpful to remember what sort of literature we are reading. This is an apocalyptic vision. And apocalyptic literature tends to employ vivid imagery and symbolic numbers. It tends not to lend itself to literal interpretations. That might well be the case here.

The NIV calls them "seventy 'sevens.'" Other translations refer to them as "seventy weeks," (NRSV) or "seventy weeks of years" (RSV). Each "seven" is probably a unit of seven years. These "seventy 'sevens'" are divided into three stages:[7] seven 'sevens' "from the issuing of the decree until the Anointed One, the ruler, comes"; sixty-two 'sevens' described by Gabriel as "a time of trouble"; and then a final 'seven' when the Anointed One is cut off and the city is destroyed.

Unfortunately, the NIV fudges the translation. The NRSV is better.[8] It translates verse 25, "Know therefore and understand: from the time that the word went out to restore and rebuild Jerusalem until the time of an anointed prince, there shall be seven weeks; and for sixty-two weeks it shall be rebuilt again with streets and a moat, but in a troubled time" (Dan 9:25, NRSV).

There will be seven "sevens" from "the time that the word went out"[9] — presumably this word of Cyrus: "The LORD, the God of heaven, has given me all the kingdoms of the earth and he has appointed me to build a temple in Jerusalem in Judah. Anyone of his people among you — may the LORD his God be with him, and let him go up" (2 Chron 36:23).

---

5. Montgomery, *Book of Daniel*, 400.
6. Miller, *Daniel*, 252.
7. To help hearers follow the three stages, the following was projected on a screen.

The Seventy "Sevens"
Phase 1 — Seven "sevens"
"from the issuing of the decree
until the Anointed One comes" (v. 25a)

Phase 2 — Sixty-two "sevens"
"a time of trouble" (v. 25b)

Phase 3 — The final "seven"
"when the Anointed One is cut off" (v. 26)

8. Again, to help hearers follow, the NRSV text was projected on a screen.
9. As the first phase was described, the following was projected on a screen.

The Seventy "Sevens"
Phase 1 — Seven "sevens"
"from the issuing of the decree
until an anointed one comes" (v. 25a)

Verse 25 says that "from the issuing of the decree until an anointed one comes will be seven 'sevens.'" In the Old Testament, each "seven" years the land was given rest. The seventh year was a sabbath year (Lev. 25:1-7). And every seven "sevens" was a year of Jubilee (Lev. 25:8ff.).

Israel's return from exile, the rebuilding of Jerusalem, the arrival of "an anointed one" — it will be a year of Jubilee, a "year of the LORD's favor." But it will not yet be "*the* year of the LORD's favor" (Isa 61:2). It will not yet usher in "everlasting righteousness."

The Jubilee that will be Israel's restoration is only a shadow of things to come, things that will come after "seventy 'sevens,'" or ten sets of seven "sevens." Because "ten" is the biblical number for completion, fullness, perfection, the end of the seventy "sevens" probably marks the final Jubilee, described by the writer to the Hebrews as "the eternal rest for the people of God" (Heb 4:1-11).

There is another problem with the NIV's translation of verse 25. It capitalizes "Anointed One," suggesting that the "Anointed One" who appears after seven "sevens" is Jesus. But it probably isn't. Just as the Jubilee that Israel's restoration would be a foreshadowing of the "eternal rest for the people of God," so too this anointed one, this ruler, is a shadow of things to come, a shadow of the One to come. The "anointed one, the ruler" who comes at the end of the seven "sevens" is not Jesus, but more likely Ezra the priest.

Israel's return from exile anticipates the ultimate return of creation from its exile east of Eden to the "glorious freedom of the children of God" (Rom 8:21), "a new heaven and new earth, the home of righteousness" (2 Pet 3:13), "everlasting righteousness" (Dan 9:24). So, too, this anointed one, Ezra the priest, anticipates the Anointed One, the long-awaited Savior, the Messiah. He comes, not after the first set of "seven 'sevens'" but after the "sixty-two 'sevens'" that follow.

In verse 25, Gabriel describes those "sevens," the "sixty-two 'sevens,'" as a "troubled time"[10] (Dan 9:25, NRSV). It was. First the people were occupied by the Greeks under Alexander the Great, then the Ptolemies of Egypt, until the Seleucids of Syria conquered. That brought Antiochus Epiphanes to power. Under Antiochus, the Jews suffered incredible persecution. There was a brief reprise after the Maccabean revolt, but it was short-lived. In 63 B.C. the Roman reign began.

Then, "after the sixty-two 'sevens'" — that is, in the seventieth "seven" —

---

10. Here the following was projected on a screen.

The Seventy "Sevens"
Phase 2 — Sixty-two "sevens"
"a time of trouble" (v. 25b)

verse 26 describes two things that happen:[11] the "Anointed One is cut off" and "the people of the ruler who will come will destroy the city and the sanctuary." Most likely these refer to Jesus' crucifixion — he is the Anointed One who is cut off — and to the destruction of Jerusalem and its temple in A.D. 70 under the Roman general Titus.

Other things also happen during the seventieth "seven."[12] Again, unfortunately, the NIV's translation is not what it should be. The NIV suggests that the same "he" does all the things listed in verse 27: "confirm a covenant with many," "put an end to sacrifices," and "set up an abomination of desolation." But the "he," whoever that might be, does not do all of these things — as the NRSV's translation makes clear.[13]

"He shall make a strong covenant with many for one week, and for half of the week he shall make sacrifice and offering cease; and in their place shall be an abomination that desolates, until the decreed end is poured out upon the desolator" (Dan 9:27, NRSV).

"He makes a strong covenant" and "makes sacrifice and offering cease." He does not "set up an abomination of desolation." The "desolator" does that. They are two different persons. The desolator is most likely Titus, the Roman general who destroyed the temple in A.D. 70, while the "he" who "makes a strong covenant with many" and "makes sacrifices and offering cease" must be Jesus.

The grammar makes that clear.[14] "The ruler who will come" is not the subject of the prior sentence. His people are. They cannot be the grammatical antecedent of the pronoun "he." "The Anointed One" is. These are things Jesus does. He "confirms a covenant with many" (Dan 9:27).

On the night he was betrayed, the Lord Jesus took bread, and when he had

---

11. Here the following was projected on a screen.

The Seventy "Sevens"
Phase 3 — The final "seven"
(or "after the sixty-two 'sevens'")
"the Anointed One will be cut off"
"they will destroy the city and the sanctuary" (v. 26)

12. Here the following was projected on a screen.

The Seventy "Sevens"
Phase 3 — The final "seven"
"He will confirm a covenant with many. . . .
he will put an end to sacrifice. . . .
he will set up an abomination" (v. 27)

13. Here Daniel 9:27, NRSV, was projected on a screen.
14. Here Daniel 9:26-27, NIV, was projected on a screen.

given thanks, he broke it and offered it to his disciples: "Take, eat; this is my body." In the same way, after supper, he took the cup, saying: "This cup is the new covenant in my blood, which is poured out for many for the forgiveness of sins" (1 Cor 11:23-25; Matt 26:26-28), "to atone for wickedness" (Dan 9:24).

Verse 27 says that Jesus "confirms a covenant with many" and "in the middle of the 'seven' he puts an end to sacrifice and offering" (Dan 9:27). If, at least in Gabriel's mind, this final "seven" begins with Jesus' birth and ends with the destruction of Jerusalem in A.D. 70, then it really was "in the middle of it" that Jesus "put an end to sacrifice and offering."

The Old Testament priests offered the same sacrifices again and again, ones that could never take away sins (Heb 10:26), because "it is impossible for the blood of bulls and goats to take away sins" (Heb 10:4). But Jesus "sacrificed for our sins once and for all when he offered himself" (Heb 7:27), "unblemished to God" (Heb 9:14). Then, "when he had offered for all time this one sacrifice for sins, he sat down at the right hand of God." No other sacrifice is ever needed (Heb 10:13, 18).

In verse 24, Gabriel says, "Seventy 'sevens' are decreed, for your people and your holy city to finish transgression, to put an end to sin, to atone for wickedness, to bring in everlasting righteousness, to seal up vision and prophecy and to anoint the holy one." Like many of the Old Testament prophets, Gabriel envisioned all these things happening when in the final "seven" "the Anointed One is cut off." Some of them did. Jesus finished the transgression. He atoned for our sin. But he has not yet put an end to it. Nor has he brought everlasting righteousness.

It becomes clearer in the New Testament that what the Old Testament foresaw as a single event is actually two — the Messiah comes. And he comes again. And when he does, he will finally and forever put an end to sin. When he does, "every challenge to God's rule will finally and forever be crushed."[15] "The decreed end will be poured on the desolator" (Dan 9:27). When he comes, he will bring "everlasting righteousness," a new heaven and a new earth where "there will be no more death or crying or mourning or pain," for the old, sin-sick order of things has passed away (Rev. 21:4).

Like Daniel, we understand from Scripture, that our exile from Eden will not last forever. "Seventy 'sevens' have been decreed." God, "the great and awesome God, who keeps his covenant of love," has spoken (Dan 9:4). He is "righteous in everything he does" (Dan 9:14). He kept his word to Abraham. He fulfilled his words given to Moses and Jeremiah. He will keep his word through Daniel and usher in everlasting righteousness. "Seventy 'sevens' have been de-

---

15. "Our World Belongs to God" (Grand Rapids: Christian Reformed Church in North America, 2008), para. 55.

creed" (Dan 9:24). And because of that — because our God is faithful and his word is sure and certain — because of that we can be "sure of what we hope for and certain of what do not see" (Heb 11:1).

Maranatha — come, Lord Jesus! Amen.

Select Bibliography

Aalders, Gerhard Charles. *Het Boek Daniel.* Kampen: Kok, 1951.

Anderson, Robert A. *Signs and Wonders: A Commentary on the Book of Daniel.* Grand Rapids: Eerdmans, 1984.

Anderson, Roy Allan. *Unfolding Daniel's Prophecies.* Mountain View, CA: Pacific, 1975.

Archer, Gleason Leonard, Jr. "Daniel." In *The Expositor's Bible Commentary.* Vol. 7: *Daniel-Minor Prophets.* Grand Rapids: Zondervan, 1985, pp. 3-157.

Armerding, Carl Edwin, and W. Ward Gasque. *Dreams, Visions and Oracles: The Layman's Guide to Biblical Prophecy.* Grand Rapids: Baker, 1977.

Armistead, David. "The Images of Daniel 2 and 7: A Literary Approach." *Stulos Theological Journal* 6/1 (1998) 63-66.

Arnold, Bill T. "Wordplay and Narrative Techniques in Daniel 5 and 6." *JBL* 112/3 (1993) 479-85.

Arthurs, Jeffrey D. *Preaching with Variety: How to Re-create the Dynamics of Biblical Genres.* Grand Rapids: Kregel, 2007.

Avalos, Hector I. "The Comedic Function of the Enumerations of Officials and Instruments in Daniel 3." *CBQ* 53 (1991) 580-88.

Baker, David W. "Further Examples of the *Waw Explicativum.*" *VT* 30 (1980) 129-36.

Baldwin, Joyce G. *Daniel: An Introduction and Commentary.* Madison, WI: InterVarsity Press, 1978.

Beale, Gregory K. "The Origin of the Title 'King of Kings and Lord of Lords' in Revelation 17:4." *NTS* 31/4 (1985) 618-20.

Block, Daniel I. "Preaching Old Testament Apocalyptic to a New Testament Church." *CTJ* 41/1 (2006) 17-52.

———. "When Nightmares Cease: A Message of Hope from Daniel 7." *CTJ* 41/1 (2006) 108-14.

Boice, James Montgomery. *Daniel: An Expositional Commentary.* Grand Rapids: Zondervan, 1989.

Boogaart, T. A. "Daniel 6: A Tale of Two Empires." *RR* 39/2 (1986) 106-12.

Bruce, Les P. "Discourse Theme and the Narratives of Daniel." *BSac* 160 (2003) 174-86.

Buchanan, George Wesley. *The Book of Daniel* (The Mellen Biblical Commentary, Vol. 25). Lewiston, NY: Edwin Mellen, 1999.

Bulman, James M. "The Identification of Darius the Mede," *WTJ* 35 (1972-73) 247-67.

Calvin, John. *Commentaries on the Book of the Prophet Daniel.* Vols. I and II. Trans. Thomas Myers. Grand Rapids: Eerdmans, 1948.

Clifford, Richard J. "History and Myth in Daniel 10–12." *Bulletin of the American Schools of Oriental Research* 220 (1975) 23-26.

Colless, Brian E. "Cyrus the Persian as Darius the Mede in the Book of Daniel," *JSOT* 56 (1992) 113-26.

Collins, Adela Yarbro. "Introduction: Early Christian Apocalypticism." In *Semeia,* Vol. 36: *Early Christian Apocalypticism: Genre and Social Setting.* Ed. Adela Collins. Decatur, GA: Scholars Press, 1986, pp. 1-11.

———. "The Influence of Daniel on the New Testament." In John J. Collins, *Daniel: A Commentary on the Book of Daniel.* Ed. Frank Moore Cross. Minneapolis: Fortress, 1993, pp. 90-123.

Collins, John Joseph. *The Apocalyptic Vision of the Book of Daniel.* Missoula, MT: Scholars Press, 1977.

———. *Daniel: With an Introduction to Apocalyptic Literature.* Grand Rapids: Eerdmans, 1984.

———. *Daniel: A Commentary on the Book of Daniel.* Ed. Frank Moore Cross. Minneapolis: Fortress, 1993.

Coxon, Peter W. "Daniel III 17: A Linguistic and Theological Problem." *VT* 26 (1976) 400-409.

———. "The 'List' Genre and Narrative Style in the Court Tales of Daniel." *JSOT* 35 (1986) 95-121.

Dorsey, David A. *The Literary Structure of the Old Testament: A Commentary on Genesis-Malachi.* Grand Rapids: Baker, 1999.

Duguid, Iain M. *Daniel.* Phillipsburg, NJ: P&R, 2008.

Dunn, James D. G. "The Danielic Son of Man in the New Testament." In *Book of Daniel: Composition and Reception,* Vol. 2. Eds. John Joseph Collins and Peter Flint. Boston: Brill, 2001, pp. 528-49.

Evans, Craig A. "Daniel in the New Testament: Visions of God's Kingdom." In *Book of Daniel: Composition and Reception.* Vol. 2. Ed. John Joseph Collins and Peter Flint. Boston: Brill, 2001, pp. 490-527.

———. "Defeating Satan and Liberating Israel: Jesus and Daniel's Visions." *JSHJ* 1/2 (2003) 161-70.

Feinberg, Charles Lee. *Daniel, the Kingdom of the Lord.* Winona Lake, IN: BMH, 1984.

Feinberg, Paul David. "An Exegetical and Theological Study of Daniel 9:24-27." In *Tradition and Testament.* Eds. John S. Feinberg and Paul D. Feinberg. Chicago: Moody Press, 1981, pp. 189-220.

Ferguson, Sinclair B. *Daniel.* Waco: Word Books, 1988.

Gammie, John G. *Daniel* (Knox Preaching Guides). Atlanta: John Knox, 1983.

———. "A Journey through Danielic Spaces: The Book of Daniel in the Theology and Piety of the Christian Community." *Int* 39/2 (1985) 144-56.

Gardner, A. E. "Decoding Daniel: The Case of Dan 7:5." *Bib* 88/2 (2007) 222-33.

Goldingay, John E. "The Stories in Daniel: A Narrative Politics." *JSOT* 37 (1987) 99-116.

—————. *Daniel* (Word Biblical Commentary, Vol. 30). Dallas: Word Books, 1989.

Gooding, David W. "The Literary Structure of the Book of Daniel and Its Implications." *TynBul* 32 (1981) 43-79.

Greidanus, Sidney. *The Modern Preacher and the Ancient Text: Interpreting and Preaching Biblical Literature*. Grand Rapids: Eerdmans, 1988.

—————. *Preaching Christ from the Old Testament: A Contemporary Hermeneutical Method*. Grand Rapids: Eerdmans, 1999.

Gurney, Robert J. M. *God in Control: An Exposition of the Prophecies of Daniel*. West Sussex: H. E. Walter, 1980.

Hammer, Raymond. *Daniel* (The Cambridge Bible Commentary). Cambridge: Cambridge University Press, 1976.

Harman, Allan M. *A Study Commentary on Daniel*. Darlington, IL: Evangelical Press, 2007.

Hasel, Gerhard F. "The Identity of 'The Saints of the Most High' in Daniel 7." *Bib* 56 (1975) 173-92.

—————. "The Book of Daniel: Evidences Relating to Persons and Chronology." *AUSS* 19/1 (1981) 37-49.

—————. "The Book of Daniel and Matters of Language: Evidence Relating to Names, Words, and the Aramaic Language." *AUSS* 19/3 (1981) 211-25.

—————. "The Hebrew Masculine Plural for 'Weeks' in the Expression 'Seventy Weeks' in Daniel 9:24." *AUSS* 31/2 (1993) 105-18.

Hill, Andrew E. "Daniel." In *Daniel-Malachi* (The Expositor's Bible Commentary, Rev. Ed. Vol. 8). Grand Rapids: Zondervan, 2008, pp. 19-212.

Hilton, Michael. "Babel Reversed-Daniel Chapter 5." *JSOT* 66 (1995) 99-112.

Hoehner, Harold W. "Chronological Aspects of the Life of Christ," Part 6 of "Daniel's Seventy Weeks and New Testament Chronology." *BSac* 132/525 (1975) 47-65.

Hoekema, Anthony. *The Bible and the Future*. Grand Rapids: Eerdmans, 1982.

Jeske, John C. *Daniel*. Milwaukee: Northwestern, 1978.

Jones, Larry Paul, and Jerry L. Summey. *Preaching Apocalyptic Texts*. Saint Louis: Chalice, 1999.

Kaiser, Walter C., Jr. *Preaching and Teaching the Last Things: Old Testament Eschatology for the Life of the Church*. Grand Rapids: Baker, 2011.

Kalafian, Michael. *The Prophecy of the Seventy Weeks of the Book of Daniel: A Critical Review of the Prophecy as Viewed by Three Major Theological Interpretations and the Impact of the Book of Daniel on Christology*. Lanham, MD: University Press of America, 1991.

Keil, C. F. *Biblical Commentary on the Book of Daniel*. Trans. M. G. Easton. Grand Rapids: Eerdmans, 1959.

Kline, Meredith G. "The Covenant of the Seventieth Week." In *The Law and the Prophets: Old Testament Studies in Honor of Oswald T. Allis*. Ed. J. H. Skilton. Nutley, NJ: P&R, 1974, pp. 452-69.

Kvanzig, Helge S. "The Relevance of the Biblical Visions of the End Time." *HBT* 11/1 (1989) 35-58.

Lacocque, André. *The Book of Daniel*. Trans. David Pellauer. Atlanta: John Knox, 1979.

Lederach, Paul M. *Daniel* (Believer's Church Bible Commentary). Scottdale, PA: Herald, 1994.

Leupold, Herbert Carl. *Exposition of Daniel*. Columbus, OH: Wartburg, 1949.

Linderberger, James M. "Daniel 12:1-4." *Int* 39/2 (1985) 181-86.

Long, Thomas G. "Preaching Apocalyptic Literature." *RevExp* 90/3 (1993) 371-81.

Longman, Tremper, III. *Daniel* (The NIV Application Commentary). Grand Rapids: Zondervan, 1999.

Lucas, Ernest C. "The Origin of Daniel's Four Empires Scheme Re-Examined." *TynBul* 40/2 (1989) 185-202.

———. *Daniel* (Apollos Old Testament Commentary, Vol. 20). Downers Grove: InterVarsity Press, 2002.

———. "Daniel." In *Theological Interpretation of the Old Testament: A Book-by-Book Survey.* Ed. Kevin J. Vanhoozer. Grand Rapids: Baker, 2008, pp. 236-42.

Lurie, David H. "A New Interpretation of Daniel's 'Sevens' and the Chronology of the Seventy 'Sevens.'" *JETS* 33/3 (1990) 303-9.

McComiskey, Thomas E. "The Seventy 'Weeks' of Daniel against the Background of Ancient Near Eastern Literature," *WTJ* 47/1 (1985) 18-45.

Marshall, Paul, with Lela Gilbert. *Their Blood Cries Out: The Worldwide Tragedy of Modern Christians Who Are Dying for Their Faith.* Dallas: Word Books, 1997.

Mason, Rex A. "The Treatment of Earlier Biblical Themes in the Book of Daniel." *PRSt* 15/4 (1988) 81-100.

Millard, Alan. "Daniel 1–6 and History." *EvQ* 49/2 (1977) 67-73.

———. "Daniel and Belshazzar in History." *BAR* 11/3 (1985) 73-78.

Miller, Stephen R. *Daniel* (The New American Commentary, Vol. 18). Nashville: Broadman & Holman, 1994.

Montgomery, James Alan. *A Critical and Exegetical Commentary on the Book of Daniel.* Edinburgh: T&T Clark, 1950.

Morris, Leon. *Apocalyptic.* Grand Rapids: Eerdmans, 1972.

Murphy, Frederick J. "Introduction to Apocalyptic Literature." In *The New Interpreter's Bible Old Testament Survey.* Nashville: Abingdon, 2005, pp. 355-70.

Nel, M. "A Literary-Historical Analysis of Daniel 2: Two Powers in Opposition." *Acta Theologica* 22/1 (2002) 77-97.

Orchard, Bernard. "St Paul and the Book of Daniel." *Bib* 20/2 (1939) 172-79.

Ouro, Roberto. "Daniel 9:27a: A Key for Understanding the Law's End in the New Testament." *JATS* 12/2 (2001) 180-98.

Parry, Jason Thomas. "Desolation of the Temple and Messianic Enthronement in Daniel 11:36–12:3." *JETS* 54/3 (2011) 485-526.

Payne, J. Barton. "The Goal of Daniel's Seventy Weeks." *JETS* 21/2 (1978) 97-115.

———. "The Goal of Daniel's Seventy Weeks: Interpretation by Context." *Presb* 4/1 (1978) 33-38.

Polaski, Donald C. "Mene, Mene, Tekel, Parsin: Writing and Resistance in Daniel 5 and 6." *JBL* 123/4 (2004) 649-69.

Porteous, Norman W. *Daniel: A Commentary.* Philadelphia: Westminster, 1965.

Portier-Young, Anathea E. *Apocalypse against Empire: Theologies of Resistance in Early Judaism.* Grand Rapids: Eerdmans, 2011.

Poythress, Vern S. "The Holy Ones of the Most High in Daniel VII." *VT* 26/2 (1976) 208-13.

———. "Hermeneutical Factors in Determining the Beginning of the Seventy Weeks (Daniel 9:25)." *TJ* 6 (1985) 131-49.

Prinsloo, G. T. M. "Daniel 3: Intratextual Perspectives and Intertextual Tradition." *Acta Patristica et Byzantina* 16 (2005) 70-90.

Rad von, Gerhard. *Old Testament Theology.* Vol. 2: *The Theology of Israel's Prophetic Traditions.* Trans. D. M. G. Stalker. New York: Harper & Row, 1965.

Redditt, Paul L. *Daniel* (New Century Bible Commentary). Sheffield: Sheffield Academic, 1999.

————. "Daniel 9: Its Structure and Meaning." *CBQ* 62/2 (2000) 236-49.

Ridderbos, Herman. *Paul: An Outline of His Theology.* Trans. John R. De Witt. Grand Rapids: Eerdmans, 1975.

Ringgren, Helmer. *"yam." TDOT,* Vol. VI. Eds. G. J. Botterweck and H. Ringgren; trans. David E. Green. Grand Rapids: Eerdmans, 1990, pp. 87-98.

Rowley, Harold Henry. "The Meaning of Daniel for Today: A Study of Leading Themes." *Int* 15/4 (1961) 387-97.

————. "The Unity of the Book Daniel." In his *The Servant of the Lord and Other Essays on the Old Testament.* 2nd Ed. Rev. Oxford: Blackwell, 1965, pp. 249-80.

Russell, David Syme. *Daniel.* Philadelphia: Westminster, 1981.

Sandy, D. Brent, and Martin G. Abegg. "Apocalyptic." In *Cracking Old Testament Codes: A Guide to Interpreting the Literary Genres of the Old Testament.* Eds. D. Brent Sandy and Ronald L. Giese Jr. Nashville: Broadman and Holman, 1995, pp. 177-96.

Schwab, George M. *Hope in the Midst of a Hostile World: The Gospel according to Daniel.* Phillipsburg, NJ: P&R, 2006.

Schwantes, S. J. *"'Ereb Bōqer* of Dan 8:14 Re-Examined." *AUSS* 16 (1978) 375-85.

Segal, Michael. "From Joseph to Daniel: The Literary Developments of the Narrative in Daniel 2." *VT* 59/1 (2009) 123-49.

Seow, Choon-Leong. *Daniel.* Louisville: Westminster John Knox, 2003.

Shea, William H. "Further Literary Structures in Daniel 2–7: An Analysis of Daniel 4." *AUSS* 23/2 (1985) 193-202.

————. "Further Literary Structures in Daniel 2–7: An Analysis of Daniel 5 and the Broader Relationships within Chapters 2–7." *AUSS* 23/3 (1985) 277-96.

Shepherd, Michael B. "Daniel 7:13 and the New Testament Son of Man." *WTJ* 68/1 (2006) 99-111.

Sims, James H. "Daniel." In *A Complete Literary Guide to the Bible.* Eds. Leland Ryken and Tremper Longman III. Grand Rapids: Zondervan, 1993, pp. 324-36.

Smith-Christopher, Daniel L. "The Book of Daniel." In *The New Interpreter's Bible,* Vol. 7. Ed. Michael E. Lawrence. Nashville: Abingdon, 1996, pp. 37-152.

Stander, H. F. "Chrysostom's Interpretation of the Narrative of the Three Confessors in the Fiery Furnace." *Acta Patristica et Byzantina* 16 (2005) 91-105.

Stefanovic, Zdravko. *Daniel: Wisdom to the Wise.* Nampa, ID: Pacific, 2007.

Steinmann, Andrew E. *Daniel* (Concordia Commentary). Saint Louis: Concordia, 2008.

Tanner, J. Paul. "The Literary Structure of the Book of Daniel." *BSac* 160 (2003) 269-82.

Towner, W. Sibley. *Daniel* (Interpretation Commentary). Atlanta: John Knox, 1984.

Valeta, David M. "The Book of Daniel in Recent Research (Part 1)." *CBR* 6/3 (2008) 330-54.

Van Deventer, H. J. M. "Struktuur en Boodskap(pe) in die Boek Daniel." *HervTS* 59/1 (2003) 191-223.

Van Niejenhuis, Cecil. "Daniel in the Lions' Den: The Real Story." *The Banner,* April 8, 2002, 22-24.

Veldkamp, Herman. *Dreams and Dictators: On the Book of Daniel.* Trans. Theodore Plantinga. St. Catherines, ON: Paideia, 1978.

Venter, P. M. "The Function of Poetic Speech in the Narrative in Daniel 2." *HervTS* 49/4 (1993) 1009-20.

Wallace, Ronald S. *The Lord Is King: The Message of Daniel.* Downers Grove, IL: InterVarsity Press, 1979.

Waltke, Bruce K. "The Date of the Book of Daniel." *BSac* 133 (1976) 319-29.

Walton, John H. "The Four Kingdoms of Daniel." *JETS* 29/1 (1986) 25-36.

———. "The Decree of Darius the Mede in Daniel 6." *JETS* 31/3 (1988) 279-86.

Wenham, David. "The Kingdom of God and Daniel." *ExpTim* 98/51 (1987) 132-34.

Wesselius, Jan-Wim. "The Literary Nature of the Book of Daniel and the Linguistic Character of Its Aramaic." *AS* 3/2 (2005) 241-83.

Wolters, Al. "The Riddle of the Scales in Daniel 5." *HUCA* 62 (1991) 155-77.

———. "Untying the King's Knots: Physiology and Wordplay in Daniel 5." *JBL* 110/1 (1991) 117-22.

Woodard, Branson L. "Literary Strategies and Authorship in the Book of Daniel." *JETS* 37/1 (1994) 39-53.

Young, Edward Joseph. *The Prophecy of Daniel: A Commentary.* Grand Rapids: Eerdmans, 1953.

———. *The Messianic Prophecies of Daniel.* Delft: van Keulen, 1954.

Subject Index

"Abomination of desolation," 9, 251, 267, 269, 275n.76, 277, 283, 290, 301, 306, 308-9, 311, 336, 343, 345, 350, 363, 381, 383, 405n.24

Angel of the LORD, 94, 95, 185, 265, 267-68, 353-54, 363

Anthropomorphism, 152, 209, 291, 328, 361

Antichrist, 218-19, 230-32, 245-48, 257-58, 266-68, 283, 306, 337, 357-62, 366, 384-87, 401, 403, 405-6
  types of, 266n.42, 283, 287, 309, 336

Apocalyptic literature, 18-19, 202, 205-7, 252, 297, 346, 424

Application, xi, 25-26, 52-53, 82-83, 109-12, 143-44, 171-72, 198-200, 246-49, 283-84, 340, 390-91, 408-9

Aramaic, 14, 16, 57, 205, 251-52

Chiasm. See Rhetorical structures: chiasm

Christ. See Ways of preaching Christ

Daniel
  allusions to Joseph, 32, 49, 56-57, 86, 117, 147, 176, 419
  as historical person, 14n.44, 32-33, 47, 50-51
  author of, 14
  date of, 5-14

difficulties for preaching, 1-2, 54n.1, 173-74, 201-3, 250, 285-86, 341, 392

genres of, 16-19, 118

goal of, 22-23

original audiences of, 14-15

overall message of, 21-22

three friends of, 33, 47, 50, 99, 103-11

unity of, 19-21

Daniel/friends faithful to God, 39, 53, 94, 110-11, 174, 184-85, 199

Darius is Cyrus, 12-13, 169n.79, 197n.73, 375n.81

Divine passives, 26, 59n.15, 74, 124, 155n.27, 224-25, 237n.110, 263-64, 276n.79, 313, 334, 360, 369-70, 396

Exiles from Eden, 25-26, 40, 99, 109, 200, 368, 415, 421, 425, 427

Goal. See Preaching text: goal; Sermon: goal

God's blessing, 38, 50-51, 299, 328, 397, 399

God's covenant, 22, 91, 106, 110, 276, 280, 288, 290-92, 301, 303, 306-8, 312-20, 323-24, 335-37, 340, 352, 422-23

God's curse, 45, 287, 290, 295, 299, 312-13, 315, 320, 326, 399

God's grace/mercy, 37n.16, 280, 282, 312-13, 325-26, 329

God's judgment, 21-22, 45, 137-41, 166-69,

435

Select Scripture Index

To avoid needless duplication of texts and to avoid overloading this index, I have included only primary references and have excluded the numerous references in the "Ways to Preach Christ" sections.